INFORMATION SYSTEMS
MANAGEMENT
IN PRACTICE

Fifth
Edition

INFORMATION SYSTEMS
MANAGEMENT
IN PRACTICE

Barbara C. McNurlin
Writer—Information Systems

Ralph H. Sprague, Jr.
University of Hawaii

Prentice
Hall

UPPER SADDLE RIVER, NJ 07458

Library of Congress Cataloging-in-Publication Data

Information systems management in practice / Barbara C. McNurlin, Ralph H.
  Sprague, Jr.— 5th ed.
      p. cm.
    Includes bibliographical references and index.
    ISBN 0-13-034073-1
    1. Management information systems.   2. Information resources management.
  I. McNurlin, Barbara C. (Barbara Canning)   II. Sprague, Ralph H.
  T58.64 .I54 2001
  658.4'038—dc21   2001018560

Executive Editor: Robert Horan
Publisher: Natalie Anderson
Associate Editor: Lori Cerreto
Editorial Assistant: Erika Rusnak
Media Project Manager: Joan Waxman
Senior Marketing Manager: Sharon Turkovich
Marketing Assistant: Jason Smith
Production Manager: Gail Steier de Acevedo
Production Coordinator: Kelly Warsak
Permissions Coordinator: Suzanne Grappi
Associate Director, Manufacturing: Vincent Scelta
Manufacturing Buyer: Natacha St. Hill Moore
Cover Designer: Jayne Conte
Composition: BookMasters, Inc.
Full-Service Project Management: BookMasters, Inc.
Printer/Binder: The Maple Press Company
Cover Printer: Phoenix Color Corporation

10 9 8 7 6 5 4
ISBN 0-13-034073-1

This book is dedicated to our parents

Dick and Peggy Canning
and
Ralph and Virginia Sprague

for all their inspiration, guidance, and support.

Brief Contents

Contents

Preface

This book deals with the management of information technology (IT) as it is being practiced in organizations today. Successfully managing IT has become crucial for several reasons:

- IT is now a strategic asset that is being used to mold competitive strategies and change organizational processes.
- The situations in which organizations are applying IT have increased in complexity, including more interorganizational environments.
- The capabilities of IT and the complexities of using the technologies are also growing at an accelerating rate.
- As IT and its uses become more complex, developing strategies and systems to deliver the technology has become more difficult.

The net result is a growing need for guidance on the issues, strategies, and tactics for managing the use of information technology. To partially satisfy this need, universities and colleges have developed courses that focus on the management of IT. Textual material for these courses has been sparse for two particularly troublesome reasons.

First, IT is changing so rapidly that textbook authors, practitioners, researchers, and academics have a difficult time staying current. For example, in the past couple of years, two major developments stand out. One has been the surprisingly fast uptake of business uses of the World Wide Web. This dramatic shift appears to be a precursor of a coming revolution—wireless handheld computing—which is touted to change how we all work, live, and play. So while information systems (IS) departments are busily creating an Internet-based platform for their enterprises to become e-corporations, they must also be experimenting with yet another anticipated computing platform: small wireless devices.

The second major development, which is much more subtle but equally profound, is the movement toward knowledge management—which is a far different task from data management or information management. The concern these days is for managing intellectual assets because they provide true competitive advantage. Enterprises are delving for ways to leverage the knowledge in people's heads by fostering fast and efficient sharing, globally. As a result of these and other changes, courses have often had to rely on periodicals to stay up-to-date.

Another reason for the paucity of IT textual material for these courses is that the principles and strategies of effective management are evolving out of the experiences of practicing managers. Merely collecting reports from the current literature fails to provide the interaction needed to decipher principles from the lessons learned in practice. Current developments and experiences need interpretation and coalescence to provide the guidance that new and practicing managers need to further develop their knowledge and managerial skills.

CONTRIBUTION OF THIS BOOK

We believe this book makes a major contribution to both of these problems. The primary resource for this book is work we recently performed for several organizations—Gartner Executive Programs, The Sourcing Interests Group, and Hawaii International Conference on System Sciences (HICSS), in particular. Our work for these organizations does not merely report current developments and practices, it includes thoughtful interpretation to provide guidance, principles, and strategies for IS executives.

Our objective in this book is to capture the material of most current importance to IS executives, and to organize it around a framework that provides guidance for the IS department. A key element of our writing continues to be examples of actual work in companies. This book includes over 84 company case examples.

USE OF THIS BOOK BY PRACTICING MANAGERS AND CONSULTANTS

In the management of information technology, this book is useful to several levels of managers:

1. To senior executives who want an overview of the issues and strategies in managing IT, with examples of what other companies are doing
2. To chief information officers who must implement IT as a strategic resource, to help their organizations attain their overall goals and objectives
3. To IS managers who are responsible for major technical areas, such as system development, technology planning, and operations
4. To managers of functional units who (a) want to better understand the issues and processes of providing IT support for their areas of responsibility, or (b) are now responsible for overseeing the management of IT in their function

We believe that practicing managers of all types will find this book valuable. By focusing on issues and strategies, while explaining technical concepts, this book provides an overview of IS management for corporate executives and managers. By combining the experiences of successful executives in "the real world," this book provides a unique perspective for all IS managers.

Consultants to executives and managers will also find this book a useful reference for staying up-to-date on important issues in the field.

USE OF THIS BOOK AS A TEXT

Future IS managers who are graduate or undergraduate students will find that this book presents a view of what "the real world" has in store. As a text, it has been intended for students who have had at least one IS course.

At the graduate level, it has been used since its first edition in 1986 for the second course, beyond the required IS course. It is especially well suited for the final course in a graduate curriculum on IS management. In addition, as MBA students have become more computer literate in recent years, the book has been increasingly used as the text in the MBA IS-core course. In both uses, the book gives students conceptual and practical guidelines for dealing with the management of today's IS function.

At the undergraduate level, the book can serve as the text for a course dealing specifically with the management of IT, or in the capstone course that summarizes the practice of IT for students about to begin their careers. Most undergraduate majors in IT take entry-level positions in the IS department, and then proceed into management. In the short term, they work with IS managers who are facing the problems and using the principles dealt with in this book.

Although this book has not been aimed at students majoring in other areas, non-information systems majors are taking IS courses in increasing numbers to better understand how to deal with systems professionals. Most chapters in this book are pertinent to them, because the theory is illustrated by real-life case studies, which are easily understood by students in all business disciplines.

At the end of each chapter are three types of questions and exercises to reinforce the material in the text.

- *Review questions* are based directly on the material in the chapter, allowing the reader to assess comprehension of the chapter's key principles, topics, and ideas.
- *Discussion questions* are based on a few topics in the chapter for which there is a legitimate basis for a difference of opinion. These questions focus discussion on these issues when the book is used in a seminar or classroom setting.
- *Exercises* provide an opportunity for the reader to put some of the concepts and ideas into practice on a small scale. In particular, one exercise in each chapter requires a student, or a team of students, to visit a local company and discover how the ideas in the chapter are being implemented in that company.

THE INSTRUCTOR'S GUIDE

We accompany this fifth edition with an Instructor's Guide, originally prepared by Jerry McBride of Marist College in Poughkeepsie, New York. Again, Jerry supplied the all-important critical questions in the guide. The purposes of the guide are (1) to help instructors prepare a strategy and outline for conducting an advanced systems course using this text, and (2) to provide support materials and techniques to enhance the course.

We believe there are five approaches for using this text. The five course modes are:

- A lecture-based course
- A seminar-based course
- A directed study course
- An independent study course
- An action research course

In the Instructor's Guide, Jerry suggests some interesting resources to use in these different course approaches. For example, he explains how he has used a computer-based simulation game to help his students understand the consequences of their actions, as they try to introduce technology innovation into an organization.

The Instructor's Guide includes:

1. Outlines for the five course approaches
2. An overview for each chapter
3. Answers to the review questions in the text
4. Transparency masters for all the figures in the text
5. Suggestions on how to conduct site visit exercises
6. Several sample syllabi
7. An approach to using simulation software
8. Critical questions for each chapter, and how to create them

These critical questions deserve a short explanation. Like the discussion questions in the text, critical questions are designed to stimulate critical thinking and discussion among students. In the Instructor's Guide, we present critical questions for each chapter, as well as an explanation of how Jerry has helped his students create them, thereby stimulating their critical thinking.

A course in IS management can be exciting—to teach and to take. We have provided the Instructor's Guide to make this one of those exciting courses.

FORMAT AND CONTENTS

This book is divided into five major parts, each dealing with a major portion of the field of IT. Chapter 1 precedes Part I because it serves as the framework around which the rest of the book is built. It traces the growing importance of IS management and presents a conceptual model to show the key areas, how they fit together, and the principal issues for executives in each area. It also presents a very interesting longitudinal case example of how these ideas have been implemented in a company over the lifetime of this book—since 1986. In a nutshell, it presents a 15-year historical view of the evolution of IS management.

Part I deals with *leadership issues*, including the top IS job, the strategic area of electronic commerce, and approaches to systems planning. Part II treats the all-important issues in *managing the essential information technologies*, distributed systems, telecommunications, information resources, and operations. Part III deals with *managing system development*; its evolution continues to present management with important, yet risky, challenges. Part IV explores *systems for supporting knowledge work* and includes the expanding universe of computing, supporting group work, executive IS, and document management. Part V concludes the book and discusses *moving into the new economy*.

Throughout the book, our objectives have been to keep the material practical, to give examples, and to derive guidance for today's and tomorrow's IS executives based on the experiences of others. To that end, chapters are sprinkled with company examples. These are not so much case studies that require "solutions" or recommendations; rather, they are case examples that show how companies have put some of the ideas in a chapter into practice.

ACKNOWLEDGMENTS

We wish to acknowledge the contribution of Richard G. Canning, Barbara's father. His insight and foresight originally made this book possible in 1986. In the early 1960s, he recognized the data processing executive's need for case studies, practical research findings, and thoughtful analysis. Through publishing and editing *EDP Analyzer* (now *I/S Analyzer Case Studies*) from 1963 until his retirement in 1986, Dick Canning devoted a major portion of his professional career to that purpose. His legacy continues in this book.

Special thanks go to William Chismar of the University of Hawaii, who took the responsibility for Chapters 3 and 9. His material on the strategic value of E-Business makes a particularly important contribution to this edition.

We also wish to thank the organizations that have allowed us to draw on work we performed for them—Gartner Executive Programs, The Sourcing Interests Group, and HICSS in particular.

Reviewers for this edition included Jacquelin Dunn of the University of South Dakota, William Nance of San Jose State University, Sasan Rahmatian of California State University at Fresno, and Reza Torkzadeh of the University of Texas at El Paso.

Finally, we thank Jerry McBride and Tracia McNurlin Barbieri. Jerry was again instrumental in creating the all-important Instructor's Guide—and without Tracia's assistance, the Instructor's Guide would not have been completed so quickly.

Barbara Canning McNurlin
Ralph H. Sprague, Jr.
April 2001

CHAPTER

1

THE IMPORTANCE OF INFORMATION SYSTEMS MANAGEMENT

INTRODUCTION

Finally, information technology (IT)—computers and telecommunications—is having the kind of revolutionary, restructuring impact that has been expected and promised for years. The rapid advances in the speed and capacity of computing devices, coupled with the pervasiveness of the Internet, digital storage, wireless and portable devices, and multimedia content, is making major changes in the way we live and work.

Although information technologies affect nearly all aspects of human endeavor, this book emphasizes their use in managing and operating organizations, including business enterprises, government organizations, and social and charitable organizations. Any time people work together to jointly pursue objectives, information technology is changing the way they work.

Managing and operating information technology for these purposes has been a "field of practice" for some 40 years. First known as business data processing and later as management information systems, the field is now called information systems (IS). The operative word is *systems,* because it combines the technologies, people, processes, and organizational mechanisms for improving organizational performance.

Themes of This Book

Due to the growth and pervasiveness of IT, organizations are operating in a different environment from just a few years ago. The nature of this environment is explored in several "themes" in this edition of the book. Each theme is discussed in some detail in one chapter but is also woven throughout the book as part of the backdrop or environment for topics in the other chapters. The themes we emphasize are the following:

- *The "New Economy."* Although doing business electronically has been a fundamental use of computers since the 1950s, we are now at the emergence of an electronic economy, where the Internet is the hub of conducting business. New terms describing this new economy are continually popping up. The term *e-business* has the broad connotation of doing business of any kind electronically. E-business has much to do with building relationships with consumers and other enterprises, not just performing transactions. E-commerce, on the other hand, is being used in the more limited sense of buying and selling electronically, as in handling commerce transactions.

  Far from being just "the next computer fad," the new economy will dominate the development of commerce and business for the foreseeable future. Chapter 3 explores the new economy in some detail, both e-business and e-commerce, but the concepts and implications permeate every chapter.

- *The Internet.* As just noted, the technical infrastructure that is enabling the e-economy is the Internet. The foundations of the Internet began in the late 1960s with research on packet switching sponsored by the U.S. government. Various technologies have been developed over the years by university researchers, industrial research laboratories, and technology vendors. In the 1990s, these developments converged and congealed into what we now call the Internet—a global network of networks.

  Recent developments lead to the vision of full interconnectivity among everyone on earth, with the ability to communicate electronically, transfer multimedia files, and access information around the world at the touch of a button in the blink of an eye. Details on the Internet as the technical infrastructure are presented in Chapters 5 and 6, but the ramifications are everywhere in this edition of the book.

- *Knowledge Management and Knowledge Sharing.* The third major theme in this edition is how to deal with "all the world's knowledge." Knowledge management and knowledge sharing have become major limiting factors in business success. One aspect of the issue is transferring knowledge between people (sharing) because the most important asset in enterprises is the people and the knowledge they possess. The other aspect is transferring the knowledge from people's heads into lasting things, such as processes, products, practices, databases, directories, software, and such. People walk out the door each night (or leave the company); these other artifacts do not, but they do grow stale and outdated. This second area is "knowledge management." Both aspects have a lot to do with managing people and the knowledge they possess—a major underpinning of the e-economy.

Later in this chapter, we discuss two kinds of knowledge work: procedure based and goal based. Emphasis on knowledge work is shifting from the former to the latter. At the same time, a major shift is taking place from information access to "content management," which includes searching, filtering, synthesizing, assimilating, and sharing knowledge resources. The importance of content management is reinforced by the fact that knowledge-based intellectual assets are considered, by many, to be the only source of sustainable competitive advantage for organizations in the future. We devote an entire section of four chapters to technologies to support knowledge work.

Management of IS

Management has become the prime user of information technology. Although communication and computer technologies are used in space exploration, weapon systems, medicine, entertainment, and most other aspects of human activity, the majority of information technologies are used to manage organizations.

The process of managing technology in organizations is getting more complex as it becomes more important. To illustrate why, here are just three of the major trends that impact IT management:

- The initiative and responsibility for managing IT is shifting from IS executives toward a collaborative effort, requiring a rich partnership among all senior executives.
- The role of the IS department is shifting from application delivery to system integration and infrastructure development.
- Outsourcing is becoming a way of life for IS departments, to the extent that a major responsibility is developing and managing the contracts and relationships with outsourcing vendors.

The purpose of this book is to provide guidance to present and future executives who manage the application of IT to improve organizational performance, which no longer means just IS executives. Historically, managing IT has been the job of technical managers, but it is increasingly becoming an important part of the responsibilities of top executives, line managers, and employees at all levels of an organization. Thus, this book is increasingly appropriate for present and future chief executive officers (CEOs), chief operations officers (COOs), business unit executives, and other managers who now have the responsibility, in partnership with the chief information officer (CIO), for using technology to improve the performance of the organization.

This responsibility does not stop with managing the technology. *Technology* is configured into *systems* that help manage *information* to improve *organizational performance.*

In this chapter, we first review the recent history of the growth of information systems and their management in organizations. Then we identify several technical and organizational trends that are having a major impact on IT management and organizational performance. Finally, we develop a framework for thinking about how information systems are used and managed in organizations. This framework serves as the roadmap for the rest of the book.

A LITTLE HISTORY

As we begin to consider the management of IT in organizations, a little history provides some perspective. Most people are surprised to find that the United States passed from the industrial era to the information era as early as 1957. In that year, the number of U.S. employees whose jobs were primarily to handle information (information workers) surpassed the number of industrial workers. Figure 1-1 shows Marc Porat's well-known division of the economy.

In the late 1950s and early 1960s, however, "information technology" to support information work hardly existed. Only the telephone was widespread, and even it did not reach every desk. Computers were just beginning to be used in data processing applications, replacing the older electric accounting machines. Even where computers were in use, their impact was modest.

Most other information work was done in general offices without much support from technology. Xerographic office copiers existed but were only beginning to catch on. Electric typewriters were commonplace, but the first word processor would not arrive until 1964. Facsimile was used only in specialized applications and would not begin

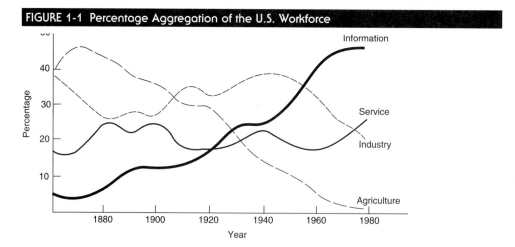

FIGURE 1-1 Percentage Aggregation of the U.S. Workforce

Source: Marc U. Porat, *The Information Economy,* Office of Telecommunications Policy, U.S. Department of Commerce (Washington DC, 1977).

general office use until the 1970s. However, the future of technology support for information workers was extremely bright. Many of the foundations of IT today had been invented, and costs were starting their steady long-term fall.

Another milestone was reached in about 1980 when the number of information workers surpassed the number of workers in all other sectors combined. In other words, information workers exceeded 50 percent of the U.S. workforce. However, the technology to support these information workers remained slow, expensive, and segmented into special purpose categories.

During the past 20 years, we have been in the midst of the "information age" regardless of how it is defined, but the growth and power of the technology to manage and work in this information-rich environment has changed radically. IT was used to perform existing information work more quickly and more efficiently. Then it was applied to additional activities that extended the traditional tasks. Now we are well into the third stage of technology assimilation in which IT makes pervasive changes in the structure and the operation of work, business practices, organizations, industries, and the global economy.

The next two sections explore the changes in the work environment, both internal and external to the organization, and the emerging technical environment.

THE ORGANIZATIONAL ENVIRONMENT

The way information technology is used depends on the environment surrounding the organization that uses it. This environment includes the economic conditions, the characteristics of principal resources (especially labor), management philosophies, the social mores of the society, and other factors. This environment has been changing constantly. Simultaneously, technological advances affect the way technology can be used. An ongoing debate centers around whether technology drives change in organizations or merely supports it. This "chicken or egg" debate is giving way to the realization that IT and its use evolve together. While academics discuss "technology assimilation models," management practices and the technologies to implement them evolve simultaneously.

In this section, we explore two aspects of the organizational environment: the external forces that are causing executives to reexamine how their firms compete successfully, and the internal structural forces that affect the way organizations operate or are managed. We then will consider how these environmental trends have led to a new set of goals for thriving in the new work environment.

The External Business Environment

The changes taking place in the worldwide business scene have been widely discussed in both the public and technical press. Today, our turbulent business world includes dot-com companies rising and falling faster than we can keep track of them, deregulation of regulated industries, and mega-mergers in industry after industry. IT contributes to this turbulence because it allows information to move faster, thus increasing the speed at which events can take place and the pace at which individuals and organizations can respond to events. Following are the main changes we see taking place in the marketplace.

The New Digital Economy. Far and away the largest external driver is the new economic world being formed around the Internet. This new economy began with business-to-consumer (B2C) retailing, commonly called e-tailing, which means selling over the World Wide Web (Web). The leader was Amazon.com. The action then moved to business-to-business (B2B), with buyers and sellers using marketplaces on the Internet to find and consummate business deals. This new economy has new rules, which are in the process of being discovered, so success is not garnered in the same way as in the brick-and-mortar "Old Economy." The main point is that the New Economy will encompass both old and new, and IT is the underpinning of this e-economy.

Globalization. The entire world has become the marketplace. To succeed, large companies believe they need to be global, meaning huge and everywhere. Merger mania is occurring across industries as companies aim for this goal. The mergers even cross country boundaries. It is not unusual for a British food company to own U.S., French, and other food and beverage companies, or a Swiss pharmaceutical company to buy out American and Japanese counterparts.

In addition, the Internet allows companies to work globally—with three main operating arenas, Asia/Pacific, the Americas, and Europe—and work around the clock by passing work from one to the next following the sun.

Globalization has become a two-way street. Firmly entrenched companies suddenly find unexpected competitors from halfway around the world bidding on work via the Internet—an unlikely occurrence just a few years ago. Parts and subassemblies are being manufactured in many countries, then shipped to other countries for final assembly, to cut overall labor costs.

The Internet also allows small firms to have a global reach. Norwegians can order extra hot chili sauce from Texas. Europeans can order books over the Internet from U.S. companies before those books are available in their country's bookstores. And so on. The business environment is now global, but local tastes still matter.

Ecosystems. A new term is creeping into the business lexicon: *ecosystem.* An ecosystem is a web of relationships surrounding one or a few companies. For example, Microsoft and Intel are the center of the Wintel ecosystem that has dominated the PC world. Yet, although they dominate the PC ecosystem, they are far less dominant in other ecosystems, such as the Internet ecosystem and the wireless communications ecosystem. The point about ecosystems is that they appear to follow biological "rules" rather than industrial-age machine-like rules. They require flexibility because relationships change more frequently; they are more organic. Relationships and co-evolution and such thinking require a different corporate mindset from the command-and-control mindset of the past.

Idea Economy. Whereas tangible items, such as capital, equipment, buildings, and such, were the tenets of power in the industrial age, in the New Economy, intangible items such as ideas, intellectual capital, and knowledge have become the scarce, desirable items. For this reason, managing talent has become more important to corporate success than managing finances. Without talent, ideas dwindle, the new-product pipeline shrivels up, and the company is less competitive. More and more talk focuses on managing intellectual capital (the knowledge in people's heads), and this talk will only increase.

Deregulation.   The deregulation of major industries—banking, telecommunications, transportation, utilities, and others—has made it easier for new companies to enter these industries. In the United States, for example, regional airlines have literally driven major carriers out of some short haul, but lucrative, markets. The U.S. banking industry has been fighting hard to get the U.S. Congress to limit the ability of nonbanking firms to enter the banking field. Although it is true that deregulation in the United States is more widespread than elsewhere in the world, this trend is underway in many countries. The fierce global competition in the telecom industry worldwide, especially in the wireless area, has resulted from deregulation.

Deregulation has prompted companies to cross industry boundaries, such as major brokerage firms offering bank-like services with their cash management accounts (loans, credit cards, etc.). Insurance companies are essentially in the securities business, with their single payment life insurance policies in which owners can direct the investment of the policy cash values. Major brands are entering the entertainment business, not only sponsoring sporting and other major events but broadcasting them via their Web sites. GM, for example, webcast the Detroit Auto Show with commentary and other features on its Web site—creating a spike in hits on its site that lasted long after the webcast. Most of these boundary-crossing examples are led by IT-enabled products or services.

Faster Business Cycles.   The tempo of business has accelerated appreciably, so companies do not have as much time to develop new products or services and move them into the marketplace. Once on the market, the useful lives of goods and services tend to be shorter as well, so speed has become of the essence. Efforts to accelerate "time to market" or reduce "cycle time" often depend on innovative uses of IT. Even "Internet time" seems to be getting shorter. It used to be that four Internet years equaled one calendar year. We recently heard it is now seven. No wonder twenty-something millionaires "retired" in their thirties. They probably reached Internet retirement age.

The Internal Organizational Environment

The work environment is also changing, so the art of managing people is undergoing significant shifts. These changes are profound enough to change the structure of organizations. Here are some of the changes that impact how people work and how organizations operate.

Talent Wars.   In the early 1990s, companies were laying off people right and left. In the late 1990s, all of a sudden, companies could not find enough people to go around. The Information Technology Association of America[1] estimated 850,000 IT jobs were left unfilled at the end of 2000 in the United States alone! What happened? An explosion of innovation in business was fueled by the Internet and the e-economy. It led to severe labor shortages in certain areas and "talent wars" where companies compete for all manner of talent. At long last people have actually become "our most important asset," as companies touted for years, but did not truly practice. The shortage is causing companies to locate near talent, often in faraway places. It is causing cities, states, and countries to rethink their educational system, infrastructure, and mindsets, and it is leading to employees who expect much different treatment from their employer than in the past.

Demand-Pull. The 1990s saw an increase in systems that let consumers access corporate computer systems. Bank automated teller machines (ATMs) were an early example. Customers could check account balances, determine whether certain checks had cleared, and establish automatic bill-paying processes. The Internet has accelerated such consumer computing beyond anyone's forecasts; wireless Internet access will blow even the wildest forecasts. We can safely say that most companies have, or are planning, B2C systems that allow consumers to purchase products, inquire about the state of an order, and in general, do business with the firm online through the World Wide Web. FedEx was one of the first companies to leverage the Web by allowing customers to directly access its package tracking system via its home page. Today, companies that ship products via FedEx have links to the same home page, providing that service to their customers.

This access is causing a shift in kind from supply-push to demand-pull. In the industrial age, companies did their best to figure out what customers wanted. They were organized to build a supply of products or services and then "push" them out to the end customer, on store shelves, in catalogs, and such. The Internet, which allows much closer and one-to-one contact between customer and seller, is moving the business model to demand-pull. Companies offer customers the components of a service or product, and the consumers create their own personalized versions, creating the demand that pulls the product or service through the supply chain, or rather, now, the demand chain.

Companies thus need to essentially reverse their business processes to be customer-facing to move to this consumer-pull mass customization business model. In fact, this model can lead to suppliers and customers cocreating products and services. For example, book buyers who put their critiques of books on Amazon.com's Web site are in a sense cocreating part of Amazon's service to other book buyers. Demand-pull is just one of the ways the e-economy operates differently from the past economy.

Team-Based Working. The trend now is toward people working together on projects. Rather than depend on chains of command and the authority of the boss, many organizations are emphasizing teams to accomplish major tasks and projects. Peter Drucker's classic article in the *Harvard Business Review*[2] uses the analogy of a symphony, where each member of the team has a unique contribution to make to the overall result. Task-oriented teams form and work together long enough to accomplish the task, then disband, perhaps to form another project team. This project-based working, where people are simultaneously working on several projects with different teams across different organizations, is generating major interest in information systems called groupware, which support meetings, promote collaborative work, and enrich communications among far-flung team members.

Anytime, Anyplace Information Work. Information workers are increasingly mobile so the need for computers is not just for accessing information but for communicating with others. One of the hallmarks of the new economy is that the communications capabilities of computers are more important than the computing capabilities. Communication technology has developed to the point where information work can be done anywhere with a laptop computer, cellular telephone, and modem. Electronic mail, facsimile, and voice-mail systems cross time zones to allow work anytime, anywhere. People are sporadically working at home, rather than commuting daily, and they are working in their preferred geographical location, even if it is remote from the main office. The advances in wireless technology enable many people to work in their car, on the beach, while walking, and so on.

Outsourcing and Strategic Alliances. To become more competitive, organizations are examining which work they should perform internally and which can be done by others. Outsourcing may be a simple contract for services or a long-term strategic alliance. Between these two extremes are a variety of relationships that are redefining the way organizations work together. Strategic alliances built around an organization's core competencies is becoming known as the "extended enterprise." IT is providing the information and communication flows necessary to manage complex sets of relationships.

The Demise of the Hierarchy. The traditional hierarchical structure groups several people performing the same type of work, overseen by a supervisor. The supervisor allocates the work, handles problems, enforces discipline, issues rewards, provides training, and so on. Management principles such as division of labor, unity of command, and chain of control define this traditional work environment.

But it is no longer the most appropriate in factories or offices. Self-managed groups, whether working on an assembly line or in an insurance company, provide much of their own management, have lower absenteeism, yield higher productivity, produce higher quality work, and are more motivated than workers in traditional settings.

A major reason for the demise of the hierarchy is that the more turbulent business environment—represented by the changes just noted—challenges the premises of a hierarchical structure, because it cannot cope with rapid change. Hierarchies require a vertical chain of command where lines of responsibility do not cross and approval to proceed on major initiatives is granted from above. This communication up and down the chain of command takes too much time for today's environment. IT enables team-based organizational structures by facilitating rapid and far-flung communication.

Goals of the New Work Environment

As a result of these changes in the internal and external organizational environment, companies around the world are in the throes of redefining their work environment—a tumultuous proposition, at best—without any true guidance. Their goal is to either simply survive in the new business climate or to thrive in it. We see the following overarching goals for thriving in the new work environment:

- Leverage knowledge globally
- Organize for complexity
- Work electronically
- Handle continuous and discontinuous change

Leverage Knowledge Globally. The newly recognized asset, the new form of capital, in companies is knowledge. Not "knowledge" in an expert system or a Lotus Notes database, but knowledge in people's head. Knowledge they "know" but cannot really explain to others is called tacit knowledge, as opposed to explicit explainable knowledge. Companies that are able to leverage it globally will be successful—provided, of course, its use is directed by a sound strategy.

Brook Manville and Nathaniel Foote of McKinsey & Company[3] point out that knowledge-based strategies begin with strategy, not knowledge. Intellectual capital is meaningless unless companies have the corporate fundamentals in place, such as knowing what kind of value they want to provide and to whom.

They also point out that executing a knowledge-based strategy is not about managing knowledge but about nurturing people who have the knowledge, tapping into the knowledge that is locked in their experience. Although companies have numerous systems in place to share explicit knowledge, the key to unlocking tacit knowledge is a work environment in which people want to share.

A manufacturer that tried to foster greater "knowledge transfer" while downsizing discovered that the combination was impossible. Why would employees share what they know when the bosses were looking for ways to consolidate expertise?

The means to tap tacit knowledge is to foster sharing in the work environment and support the sharing with technology. E-mail and groupware can provide the interconnection, but the driving force is the culture. When people want to share, they form "worknets"—informal groups whose collective knowledge is used to accomplish a specific task. So sharing and leveraging knowledge happens through organizational "pull"—people needing help from others to solve a problem—rather than organizational "push," which overloads people with information. Therefore, leveraging knowledge is all about raising the aspirations of each individual, say Mansville and Foote.

Organize for Complexity.   A second overarching goal of companies, whether they recognize it or not, is to be able to handle complexity. Why? One reason is because the world has become so interconnected that simple solutions no longer solve a problem. Corporate decisions can have an environmental impact, human resources impact, economic impact, and even ethical impact. The issues are systemic. Furthermore, capturing market share today oftentimes requires allying with others who have complementary knowledge. Alliances increase complexity; so does specialization. Have you bought shampoo, crackers, or tires lately? Those used to be fairly straightforward decisions. Today, the choices are so numerous that consumers can spend an inordinate amount of time making a selection. To thrive in this new age, companies need to be organized to be able to handle complexity.

Work Electronically.   Just as the marketplace is moving to the marketspace, the workplace is moving to the workspace. Taking advantage of the Internet, and networks in general, is a third major goal of enterprises these days. But just as the move from horse and buggy to train to automobile to jet plane each was not simply a change in speed but a change in kind, so too is the move to working in a "space" rather than a "place" a change in kind. It requires different organizing principles, compensation schemes, office structures, and more. It also changes how organizations interact with others, such as their customers.

George Gilder,[4] columnist and author, noted that business eras are defined by the plummeting price of the key factor of production. During the industrial era, this key factor was horsepower, as defined in kilowatt hours, which dropped from many dollars to 7.5 cents. For the past 35 years, the driving force of economic growth has been transistors, translated into million instructions per second (MIPS) and bits of semiconductor memory. The latter has fallen 68 percent a year, from $7 per bit to a millionth of a cent. We are now approaching yet another "historic cliff of cost" in a new factor of production: bandwidth. "If you thought the price of computing dropped rapidly in the last decade, just wait until you see what happens with communications bandwidth," said Gilder, referencing a remark by Andy Grove, CEO of Intel.

Up to this point, we have used MIPS and bits to compensate for the limited availability of bandwidth. However, as we move into an era of bandwidth abundance, the economy will change. The microchip moved power within companies, allowing people to vastly increase their ability to master bodies of specialized learning. Microchips both flattened corporations and launched new corporations. Bandwidth, on the other hand, moves power all the way to the consumer. That's the big revolution of the Internet, Gilder said, and the reason behind the move to "relationship marketing" with consumers.

This revolution creates a different world. For example, TV is based on a top-down hierarchical model, with a few broadcast stations (transmitters) and millions of passive broadcast receivers (televisions). The result is "lowest common denominator" entertainment, like what we get from Hollywood. The Internet, on the other hand, is a "first-choice" culture, much like a bookstore, where you walk in and you can get your first-choice book. First-choice culture is vastly different from lowest common denominator culture, says Gilder. As the Internet spreads, the culture will move from "what we have in common" to one in which our aspirations, hobbies, and interests are manifested.

Handle Continuous and Discontinuous Change. Finally, to keep up, companies will need to innovate continually—something most have generally not been organized to do. Continual innovation, however, does not mean continuously steady innovation. It goes in fits and starts. Change takes one of two forms: continuous change (the kind espoused by total quality management techniques) or discontinuous change (the kind espoused by reengineering). When a product or process is just fine, but needs some tuning, continuous change is needed to improve efficiency. However, when it is not fine, discontinuous change is needed to move to an entirely new way of working. The two often form a cycle. Companies need to be able to handle both for their products and processes.

These four major goals, then, are what we believe underlie the new work environment. With the organizational environment as a backdrop, we now explore the emerging technology environment.

THE TECHNOLOGY ENVIRONMENT

The technology environment enables advances in organizational performance. The two have a symbiotic relationship; IT and organizational improvements evolve jointly. The IT evolution is now described in the four traditional areas of hardware, software, data, and communication.

Hardware Trends

In the 1950s and '60s, the main hardware concerns of data processing managers were machine efficiency and tracking new technological developments. Batch processing was predominant, with online systems emerging later. At that time, hardware was centralized, often in large "showcase" data centers behind glass walls.

In the mid-1970s processing power began to move out of the central site, but only slowly. Often, it was at the insistence of users who bought their own departmental minicomputers and word processors. In the 1980s, mainly due to the advent of personal computers (PCs), this trend accelerated far beyond the expectations of most people, especially IS managers.

Now this trend is well established. Desktop and portable laptop computers are faster and contain more memory than the centralized mainframes of just a few years ago. Client-server computing involves computers working together via networks with the "client" machine on the desktop or laptop providing the user interface and the "server" on the network holding the data and applications. This same client-server model will be used for personal communication systems (PCSs) interacting with the Web.

This major development in hardware toward mobile and handheld devices is led by two factions: telecom companies (and the cell phone manufacturers that serve them) and handheld computer manufacturers, such as Palm. The hardware is getting smaller and more powerful. Use of wireless hardware is becoming the norm for a growing segment of the anytime, anyplace workforce.

These hardware trends are further distributing processing beyond organizational boundaries, to suppliers and customers. The result is the movement of enterprisewide hardware and processing power out of the control—although perhaps still under the guidance—of the IS department

Software Trends

The early dominant issue in software and programming was how to improve the productivity of in-house programmers, those who created mainly transaction processing systems. Occasionally, IS management discussed using outside services, such as timesharing services, application packages, and contract programming from independent software houses. The software industry was still underdeveloped, however, so application development remained the purview of IS managers.

Later, programming issues centered first around modular and structured programming techniques. Then the topic expanded to life cycle development methodologies and software engineering, with the goals of introducing more rigorous project management techniques and getting users more involved in the early stages of development. Eventually, prototyping (quick development of a mock-up) became popular.

Then two other software trends appeared. One, purchased software became a viable alternative to in-house development for many traditional, well-defined systems. Two, IS managers began to pay attention to applications other than transaction processing. Software to support decision support systems (DSS), report generation, and database inquiry shifted some programming from professional programmers to end users. Today, many end users develop their own systems on their PCs using such languages as Visual Basic.

During the 1990s a push for open systems was driven primarily by software purchasers who were tired of being "locked in" to proprietary software (or hardware). The open systems movement continues to demand that different products work together, that is, "interoperate." Vendors initially accommodated this demand with hardware and software black boxes that performed the necessary interface conversions, but the cost of this approach is lower efficiency.

Another major trend in the 1990s was toward enterprise resource planning (ERP), spurred by management's desire for cross-enterprise financial figures and manufacturing tracking, and by concerns that their existing systems were not Y2K compliant. Implementing ERP involves integrating components, which is called systems integration rather than application development. Companies replace legacy systems with a suite of tightly integrated ERP applications. ERP has proven to be expensive and troublesome, especially for those companies wanting to modify the software to fit their unique processes.

Like hardware, software is migrating to be network centric. Rather than replace legacy systems, many companies are outfitting them with Web front-ends to broaden access and "empower" employees, customers, and suppliers. Furthermore, companies are turning toward buying software off the Web on a per-use basis. One example is what is called a "corporate portal," where employees log into their company intranet (which is maintained by a third party) and utilize software housed on that site. This approach moves the software from being decentralized (on PCs) to being centralized (on a server somewhere). It also reduces the capital outlay for software; the software is rented (or more properly, leased) rather than bought.

Data Trends

The evolution of the third core information technology area—data—has been particularly interesting. At first, discussions centered around file management and organizational techniques for files that served individual applications. Then generalized file management systems emerged, for managing corporate data files. This more generalized approach led to the concept of corporate databases to serve several applications, followed a few years later by the concept of establishing a data administration function to manage these databases.

In the 1970s, the interest in data turned to technical solutions—database management systems. As work progressed, it became evident that a key element of these products was their data dictionary/directory. The early function of these dictionaries was merely specification and format, but that function has expanded significantly. Dictionaries store more than data definitions, they store information about relationships between systems, sources and uses of data, time cycle requirements, and so on.

So for the first 20 years of information processing, discussions on data were about techniques to manage data in a centralized environment. It was not until the advent of fourth-generation languages and PCs that interest in letting employees directly access corporate data began to develop. Then users began to demand it.

In addition to distributing data, the major trend in the early 1990s was expanding the focus from data resources to information resources, both internal and external to the firm. Data management organizes internal facts into data record format. Information management, on the other hand, focuses on concepts (such as ideas found in documents, especially digital documents such as Web pages), from both internal and external sources. Thus "information resources" contain a richer universe of digitized media, including voice, video, graphics, animation, and photographs.

Managing this expanded array of information resources requires new technologies. Data warehousing has arisen to store huge amounts of historical data from such systems as retailers' point-of-sale systems. Data mining uses advanced statistical techniques to explore data warehouses looking for previously unknown relationships in the data, such as which clusters of customers are the most profitable. Similarly, the massive amount of document-based information is organized into document repositories and analyzed with document mining techniques. And as noted earlier, businesses now emphasize managing the intellectual capital of the organization. Some believe knowledge can reside in machines, others believe it only resides in people's heads. Either way, knowledge management is of major importance in the new economy because the intangibles hold the competitive value.

Communications Trends

The final core information technology is telecommunications. This area has experienced enormous change, and has now taken center stage. Early use of data communications dealt with online and time-sharing systems. Then interest in both public and private (intra-company) data networks blossomed.

Telecom opened up new uses of information systems so it became an integral component of IS management. Communications-based information systems were used to link organizations to their suppliers and customers. In the early 1980s, a groundswell of interest surrounded interorganizational systems, because some provided strategic advantage.

Communication technology is a crucial enabler for distributing computing. Local area networks connected to wide area networks (WANs) allow computer connectivity to be at a level akin to that of voice connectivity provided by the worldwide telephone system. The growth of these network infrastructures within companies further shifted mainframe-centered computing to network-centric computing. The slogan "the network is the computer" has become the dominant view of information systems.

The Internet, and its dramatic growth in business, primarily through electronic mail and the World Wide Web, has completed this shift. Development of the telecom infrastructure that interconnects organizations and individuals around the world has launched electronic commerce, communications, education, and entertainment on a global scale.

Networking of computer-based equipment is also blurring the boundaries between industries, and between private and working life. Cable TV provides Internet access, consumer electronic firms make hybrid PC/TVs, and telephone companies make smart phones, combining the functionality of PCs, cellular telephones, pagers, and a fax in small, portable products. The development of these and other "information appliances" is leading to the vision of an ever-present, ubiquitous "information window" through which people network.

Add to these options the explosion of wireless communication, and we can see that people use wireless networks to do their jobs anytime, anyplace. The interweaving of the business and IT revolutions make now an exciting time to live, perhaps too exciting for some.

THE MISSION OF INFORMATION SYSTEMS

With the organizational and IT environments as backdrops, we now turn to the mission of information systems. In the early days of transaction processing, systems acted as "paperwork factories" to get employees paid, customers billed, products shipped, and so on. During that era, the objectives of information systems were defined by productivity measures, such as percentage of up-time for the computer, throughput (number of transactions processed per day), and lines of program code written per week.

Later, during the management information systems era, the focus of IS departments shifted to producing reports for "management by exception" or summary reports for all levels of management. This era gave us the classic information system objective to "get the right information to the right person at the right time."

For today's environment, we suggest a broader focus. We see the mission for information systems organizations to be:

> To improve the performance of people in organizations through the use of information technology.

The ultimate *objective* is performance improvement—a goal based on outcomes and results rather than a go-through-the-steps process goal. The *focus* is the people who make up the organization. Improving organizational performance is accomplished by the people and groups that comprise the organization.

Finally, the *resource* for this improvement is IT. Many intertwining factors contribute to performance improvement but this book focuses on resources available from the development and use of IT: computers, software, information, and communication technologies.

A SIMPLE MODEL

We propose a simple model to help define a structure for the IS function in organizations. Figure 1-2 represents the process of applying IT to accomplish useful work. On the left is the technology, and on the right are the users who put it to work. The arrow represents the process of translating user's needs into implemented systems that apply the technology. In the early days of information systems, this translation was performed almost entirely by systems analysts.

Figure 1-3 is a simple representation of what has happened during the past 40 years. Technology has become increasingly complex and powerful; uses have become increasingly sophisticated. Information systems are now viewed as system "products" and users have become "customers." The increased distance between the two boxes represents the increasingly complex process of specifying, developing, and delivering these system products. It is no longer feasible for one system analyst to understand the fine points of the technologies needed in an application as well as the nuances of the application. More specialization is required of systems professionals to bridge this wider gap.

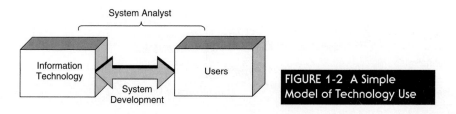

FIGURE 1-2 A Simple Model of Technology Use

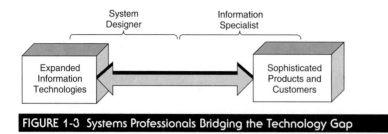

FIGURE 1-3 Systems Professionals Bridging the Technology Gap

Systems professionals are not the only ones who can help bridge this gap between the technology and its users. Technology has become sophisticated enough to be used by many employees and consumers. At the same time, they are becoming increasingly computer-literate; many employees even develop their own applications. Figure 1-4 depicts this trend. Today, some of the technology is truly user-friendly, and some applications, such as Web page development, database mining, and spreadsheet manipulation, are handled by employees. Transaction systems, however, are still developed by professional developers, either inside or outside the firm.

The main point of this discussion is that the technology is getting more complex, the applications are becoming more sophisticated, and users are participating more heavily in the development of applications. The net result is that management of the process is getting more complex and difficult as it is becoming more important to do well.

A BETTER MODEL

Expanding the simple model gives us more guidance into managerial principles and tasks. We suggest a model with four principal elements:

1. A *set of technologies* that represent the technology infrastructure installed and managed by the IS department
2. A *set of users* who need to use the technology to improve job performance

FIGURE 1-4 Users Bridging the Technology Gap

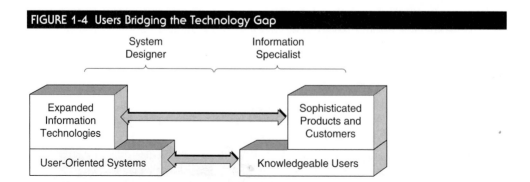

3. A *delivery mechanism* for developing, delivering, and installing applications and functions that serve the users
4. *Executive leadership* to manage the entire process of applying the technology to achieve organizational objectives and goals.

Let us look more carefully at each of these elements.

The Technologies

Several forces contribute to the increased importance and complexity of IT. One, of course, is the inexorable growth in computing and communications capacity accompanied by significant reductions in cost and size of computers and telecom components. Another is the merging of the previously separate technologies of computers, telephones/telecom/cable TV, office equipment, and consumer electronics. Still a third is the ability to store and handle voice, image, and graphical data, and to integrate them. Here is a brief list of some rapidly growing technology areas:

- Handheld wireless devices
- The Internet
- Wireless and fiber-based networks
- Multimedia, integrating voice, image, text, graphics, and more
- Integration of consumer electronics and IT

These technologies form systems products that are useful to employees, customers, suppliers, and consumers. No longer relegated primarily to automating transactions, information systems now fill major roles in management reporting, problem solving and analysis, distributed office support, customer service, and communication. In fact, most activities of information workers are supported in some way by IT; the same is becoming true of suppliers, customers, and consumers.

The Users

As IT becomes pervasive, the old categories of users are no longer appropriate. The users of electronic data processing and management information systems were relatively easy to identify, and the function of a system was defined to meet a set of their needs. Now, however, employees need systems to do their daily work, making new taxonomies necessary.

One helpful dichotomy to describe activities of information workers defines procedure-based activities and knowledge-based (or goal-based) activities. The value of this model is that it focuses on the important characteristics of information workers—their job procedures and knowledge—rather than on the type of data (for example, numbers versus text) or the business function (production versus sales), or even job title (managerial versus professional).

Procedure-based activities are large-volume transactions, where each transaction has a relatively low cost or value. The activities are well defined, so the principal performance measure is efficiency (units processed per unit of resource spent). For a procedure-based task, the information worker is told what to accomplish and the steps to follow. Procedure-based activities mainly handle data.

Procedure Based	*Knowledge Based*
• High volume of transactions	• Low volume of transactions
• Low cost (value) per transaction	• High value (cost) per transaction
• Well-structured procedures	• Ill-structured procedures
• Output measures defined	• Output measures less defined
• Focus on process	• Focus on problems and goals
• Focus on efficiency	• Focus on effectiveness
• Handling of "data"	• Handling of concepts
• Predominantly clerical workers	• Managers and professionals
• Examples	• Examples
"Back office"	Loan department
Mortgage servicing	Asset/liability management
Payroll processing	Planning department
Check processing	Corporate banking

FIGURE 1-5 A Dichotomy of Information Work

Knowledge-based activities, on the other hand, handle fewer transactions, and each one has higher value. These activities, which can be accomplished in various ways, must therefore be measured by results, i.e. attainment of the objectives or goals. Therefore, the information worker must understand the goals because part of the job is figuring out how to attain them. Knowledge-based activities are based on handling concepts, not data. Figure 1-5 summarizes these two kinds of information-based work, giving several examples from banking.

Some authors use the words "clerical" and "managerial" to refer to these two types of activities. Looking at the attributes, however, it is clear that managers often do procedure-based work, and many former procedure-based jobs now have knowledge-based components. Furthermore, the distinction between manager and worker is blurring.

The most important benefit of this dichotomy is that it reveals how much of a firm's information processing efforts have been devoted to procedure-based activities, which is understandable because computers are process engines that naturally support process-driven activities. As important as they are, however, it is clear that procedure-based activities are the "wave of the past." The wave of the future is applying information technology to knowledge-based activities, where the objective is more important than the process. For the task "pay employees" or "bill customers," the systems analyst can identify the best sequence of steps. On the other hand, the task "improve sales of the Asian market" has no best process. Decision makers need a variety of support systems to leverage their judgment.

System Development

In our model, system development and delivery bridges the gap between technology and users, but systems for procedure-based activities differ from systems for knowledge-based information work.

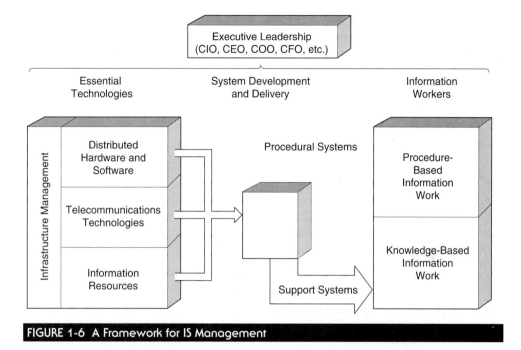

FIGURE 1-6 A Framework for IS Management

Figure 1-6 shows, on the left side, the set of technologies that form the IT infrastructure. Organizations build systems on these technology resources to support both procedure-based and knowledge-based activities. The three main categories, called "essential technologies," are computer hardware and software, communication networks, and information resources. We call management of them "infrastructure management."

On the right are the two major kinds of information work, procedure-based and knowledge-based work. These two categories are not distinct or separate, of course, but it is helpful to keep their major differences in mind because they lead to different approaches, and frequently different teams, in the bridging function of systems development and delivery. Figure 1-6 separates the delivery of services to procedure-based users and knowledge-based users.

Information Systems Management

The fourth component of this book's model may be the most important of all—executive leadership of the process of applying IT to accomplish organizational goals. Changes required to support emerging organizational structures require a significant amount of well-coordinated business *and* IT executive leadership. The IT leadership comes from a "chief information officer" (CIO) who must be high enough in an organization to influence organizational goals, and have enough credibility to lead the harnessing of the technology to pursue those goals. The business executive leadership includes all the Cs—CEO, COO, CFO—plus the lead executives of the functional areas. The technology is becoming so fundamental and enabling, that this executive team must work together closely to manage and utilize it fully.

To summarize, this model of the IS function has four major components:

1. The technology, which provides the electronic and information infrastructure for the enterprise
2. Information workers in organizations, who use IT to accomplish their work goals
3. The system development and delivery function, to bring the technology and users together
4. The management of the IS function, with the overall responsibility to harness IT to improve the performance of the people and the organization.

ORGANIZATION OF THIS BOOK

This book is designed to meet the needs of information systems managers—current ones and students who will become managers in the future. The organization of the book corresponds to the major parts of Figure 1-6.

- Part I (Chapters 2 through 4) deals with the strategic issues that are the responsibility of the top systems executive—the CIO—and the executive committee. Chapter 2 deals with the leadership components of the CIO job; Chapter 3 looks at the strategic imperative of electronic commerce; Chapter 4 treats the subject of IS planning.
- Part II (Chapters 5 through 8) deals with the management of the essential information technologies (on the left side in Figure 1-6). Respective chapters discuss the distributed systems architecture that now dominates computing, building and managing the telecom system, managing corporate information resources, and managing day-to-day operations.
- Part III contains two chapters on the system development process used primarily to build procedure-based systems. Chapter 9 describes the evolution of system development, the tools and approaches used, the trend toward system integration, and the growth of Web-based development. Chapter 10 discusses important issues in managing system development.
- Part IV consists of four chapters on technology support for knowledge work. Chapter 11 describes the exploding universe of information technologies— including mobile technologies, multimedia, and the Internet—along with IS management's responsibilities for supporting this expanding universe. Many of these computing possibilities will be used for knowledge-based computing.

    The three other chapters describe knowledge-based systems that support information workers. Included are systems to support decision making by executives and nonexecutives, systems to support collaborative work, and systems to leverage the expanding world of information resources.
- Part V, and the final chapter of the book, looks to the future.

To illustrate how one IS department has evolved over the years, as the technologies and its users have changed, consider the case of Mead Corporation. Mead's story has appeared since the first edition of this book in 1985. Notice how this case example puts a number of the ideas discussed in this chapter into a real-life setting.

CASE EXAMPLE

MEAD CORPORATION

Mead Corporation, with headquarters in Dayton, Ohio, is a $3.8 billion forest products company with more than 100 mills, plants, and distribution centers throughout the United States and Canada. It produces 1.8 million tons of paper per year and 1.8 million tons of paperboard. The company is highly decentralized, with 10 operating divisions, including paper, packaging, paperboard, consumer, distribution, and electronic publishing.

THE 1960S AND 1970S: DECENTRALIZE SOME FUNCTIONS

In the 1960s, Mead's corporate information services (CIS) department provided all divisions with data processing services. By 1967, the department's budget had grown so large that management decided to spin off some of the functions to the divisions. Divisions could establish their own data processing and process engineering groups, if they so desired. Or they could continue to purchase data processing services from CIS. Many of the divisions did establish their own IS departments, but all continued to use the corporate data center for their corporate applications.

In the late 1970s, the corporate information services department had six groups, as illustrated in Figure 1-7. The director reported to the vice president of

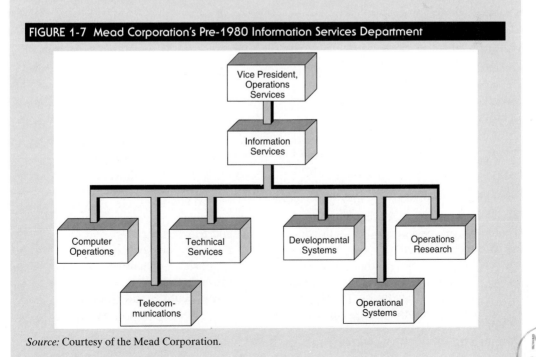

FIGURE 1-7 Mead Corporation's Pre-1980 Information Services Department

Source: Courtesy of the Mead Corporation.

(Case Continued)

operations services. The six groups under the director were:

- Computer operations to manage the corporate data center
- Telecommunications to design the telecom network and establish standards
- Technical services to provide and maintain systems software
- Developmental systems to handle traditional system development
- Operational systems to maintain systems after they become operational
- Operations research to perform management science analysis

THE 1980S: FOCUS ON END USER COMPUTING

In 1980, management realized that its CIS organizational structure would not serve the needs of the rapidly growing end user community. Furthermore, to become an "electronic-based" organization, Mead needed a corporatewide network. Therefore, the department reorganized as shown in Figure 1-8 so that the director of corporate information resources (CIR) reported directly to the company president. This change signaled the increased importance of information resources to Mead.

CIR was responsible for creating hardware, software, and communication standards for the entire corporation; it ran the corporate data center; and it operated the network. All the divisions used the network and corporate data center, and they followed the corporate standards; some operated their own small, distributed systems as well, which linked into the corporate network. The three departments within the new group were as follows:

Decision Support Applications (DSA) provided all end user computing support for the company. At the time of the reorganization, DSA had no users, no products, no common applications among multiple locations, and only five staff members in operations research and two in office systems support. By 1985, they were serving 1,500 users in some 30 Mead locations with 10 staff members. DSA offered 14 products and eight corporatewide applications.

- *Interactive help center* provided hotline support and evaluated new end user computing products.
- *Office systems* supported the dedicated word processing systems and IBM's Professional Office System (PROFS), which Mead used as the "gateway" to end user computing. Divisions were free to select any office system, but most followed the recommendations of this group, to ensure corporatewide interconnection.
- *Decision analysis* built a number of companywide decision support systems, such as a corporate budgeting model and a graphics software system. It also used operations research tools to develop linear programming models and simulations for users needing such sophisticated analysis tools.
- *Financial modeling coordination and EIS* was in charge of Mead's integrated financial system. It also supported executive computing, through IBM PCs used by corporate executives and an executive information system (EIS) accessed through PROFS.

(Case Continued)

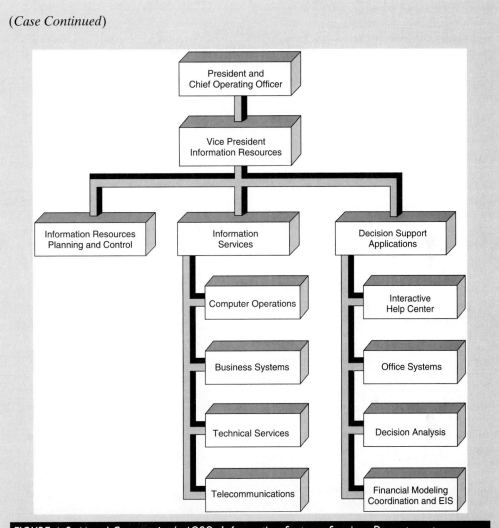

FIGURE 1-8 Mead Corporation's 1980s Information Systems Services Department

Source: Courtesy of the Mead Corporation.

Information Services was responsible for most of the traditional information systems functions from the old information services department—companywide telecom support, data center operations, development of corporatewide systems, database administration, system software support, and technical support for end user computing.

Most divisions developed their own applications, following the guidelines created by this department. The EDP steering committee—composed of the president and group vice presidents—established a policy that applications should be transportable among the various computing centers and accessible from any Mead terminal. The company's telecom network established the guidelines for making this interconnection possible.

(Case Continued)

Information Resources Planning and Control was responsible for planning future information systems and technology. This department grew out of the company's strong planning culture, and decentralization in the 1970s highlighted the need for a coordinating IT body. Although it was small, it had two important roles. First, it took the corporate perspective for IT planning to ensure that Mead's IT plans meshed with business plans. Second, it acted as planning coordinator, helping various groups and divisions coordinate their plans with corporate and CIR plans.

LATE 1980S: ADJUST THE STRUCTURE

The 1980 reorganization separated the more people-oriented activities under DSA from the more technical activities under the information services department. The technology was better managed, and relations with users improved. However, this split caused two problems. One, traditional programmers and system analysts felt that DSA received all the new and exciting development work. The second problem was coordinating the two departments. A matrix arrangement evolved to handle both problems, with both information services and DSA people staffing most projects.

The departmental structure implemented in 1980 remained essentially intact throughout the 1980s, with only two major changes. In early 1988, the vice president of information resources began reporting to Mead's chairman and CEO. Second, the DSA group was reorganized, as shown in Figure 1-9.

As users became more sophisticated and less generic, the department created

small groups with expertise in specific areas. By the end of the 1980s they were supporting more than 5,000 users corporatewide in three ways: service center help, application development consulting, and local area experts.

- The *service center* continued to introduce new users to technology and provide telephone hotline assistance to experienced users.
- The *application development consultants* helped users develop more sophisticated applications and guided maintenance of user-written applications, which had become a noticeable problem. They also up-dated traditional applications to permit end user systems to access the data.
- The *local area experts* worked in the functional departments supporting users in their area. They reported directly to their area manager and indirectly to the information resources department. Due to the growing number of user-written applications, they too helped users keep their applications up-to-date.

So, during the 1980s, Mead found its end user computing focus shifting from introducing new technology to making more effective use of the technology in place. By the end of the decade, they were concentrating on harvesting their investment in IT by using it as a lever to change the way they were doing business.

1990: LEVERAGE THE IT INFRASTRUCTURE

In 1990, CIR underwent another reorganization to bring it in line with a new strategy. We first discuss the reorganization, then the strategy.

(Case Continued)

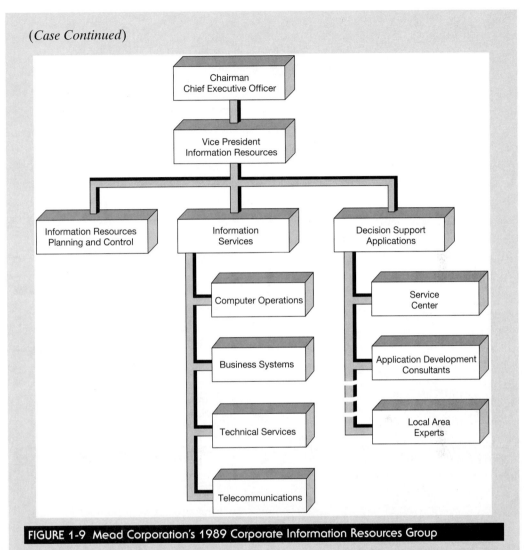

FIGURE 1-9 Mead Corporation's 1989 Corporate Information Resources Group

Source: Courtesy of the Mead Corporation.

Management realized the end user systems and large-scale business systems needed to cross-pollinate each other. Users needed one place to go for help; therefore, application development was placed in one group, which was renamed "Information Services," as shown in Figure 1-10.

The emphasis turned to strengthening the mainframe-based electronic infrastructure of the company, of which the corporatewide network had become paramount. Although the network had been created in 1983, its value in connecting Mead to vendors and customers had not been recognized until the late 1980s. Therefore, in 1990, CIR created a new group—network services—to handle computer operations, technical services, and telecom. The 1990 reorganization also consolidated administrative functions (such as chargeback) into the technology planning and control group.

(Case Continued)

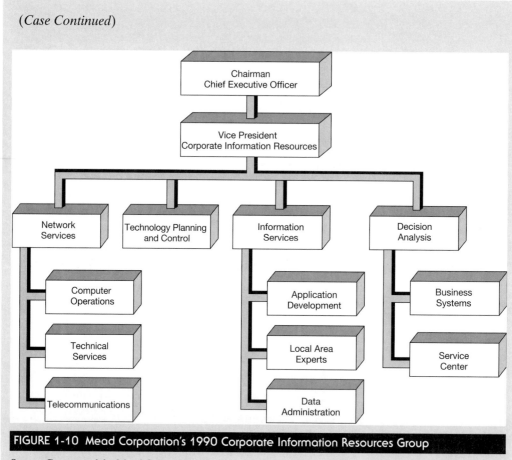

FIGURE 1-10 Mead Corporation's 1990 Corporate Information Resources Group

Source: Courtesy of the Mead Corporation.

So while the 1990 reorganization did not add new functions, it shifted emphasis from end user computing to building an infrastructure and integrating development of all sizes of applications.

1990 Strategy

In the early 1980s, Mead installed its first information resources business plan, which emphasized networking and end user computing. By the late 1980s, the objectives had been accomplished. In hindsight, management realized the 1980 plan had been a technology plan, not a business plan, be-

cause its goal had been to get control of IT. Having accomplished this goal, Mead decided to create a true business plan, one that addressed employing its IT resources.

Using the two-by-two matrix shown in Figure 1-11, management realized that Mead had only been building systems that fit into the lower right quadrant—systems to support traditional products and internal business processes. Rather than focus on company operations, management decided to shift emphasis in two directions: (1) toward reengineering company operations, and (2) toward using

(Case Continued)

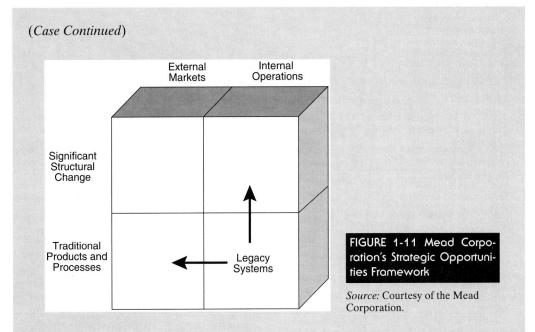

FIGURE 1-11 Mead Corporation's Strategic Opportunities Framework

Source: Courtesy of the Mead Corporation.

IT to work better with suppliers and customers.

Business process reengineering— that is, significantly restructuring the internal operations in a business—became a major strategic direction, with the companywide network playing a key role. Because IT removes many time and distance barriers associated with business processes, Mead decided to use IT to build new processes rather than simply accelerate existing ones.

In rethinking all the major Mead processes, one of the major processes carved out to be recentralized and reengineered was purchasing. The reengineering group discovered, for example, that 240 people handled accounts payable, mainly reconciling mismatches between goods received and purchase orders. By reengineering purchasing, they eliminated the need to do such reconciliations. So they outsourced the function while they developed the new purchasing system.

Putting in the corporate purchasing system was Mead's first big venture into reengineering. The company learned a lot from that experience. It also accomplished something few others have yet to achieve: create standard part number for all 800,000 MRO (maintenance, repair, and operations) parts. This excruciating data cleansing exercise was done so that Mead could automatically consolidate parts orders from all 10 divisions and reap larger discounts due to the higher volumes. The result was large savings.

The second emphasis involved doing business electronically by extending current business processes and products to suppliers and customers. The motto was: "It is easy to do business with us," using any means customers wanted— through electronic data interchange (EDI) for application-to-application transactions across company boundaries, through terminals at customer sites linked to Mead's computers, or even using the telephone

(Case Continued)

using voice response. In essence, Mead installed various front-ends on its mainframe applications. For the purchasing system, Mead went to major parts suppliers and required them to use EDI as a condition of selling to Mead. The system was fully automatic. If a part was in stock, it was supplied; if not, an order was generated.

So, the basic strategy set forth in 1980 remained in force in 1990—to retain central control of the IT infrastructure and distribute responsibility for building and maintaining applications in the operating divisions. As the uses of IT changed, CIR reorganized to focus on those new uses: end user computing in the 1980s, business reengineering and customer-oriented systems in 1990.

THE 1990S: IMPLEMENT VISION 2000

In 1993, CIR management recognized that client-server computing was a paradigm shift in computing, so Mead's mainframe-based structure would (at long last) need to be changed, and changed significantly. So CIR launched Vision 2000 to develop a vision of what Mead computing and communications would look like in the Year 2000.

Vision 2000 foresaw computing in three-tiers: mainframe, midrange servers, and desktops. Workstations were to be users' "window to the world" of information access, analysis, and communication. Interfaces, data, and applications would be at the appropriate level. Applications would be of three types: enterprisewide, division, and local; and they would use a global network that reached out beyond Mead.

CIR continued to focus on shared services (providing the infrastructure and supporting enterprise applications), while divisions would tailor systems to their customers and business. Users would not need to worry about where processing occurred, where data was housed, or how the "mechanics" of information processing were handled; CIR would handle all these details. Data was to be viewed as a resource and managed accordingly, balancing access with integrity and security. And users would have greater geographic independence than in the past.

This vision is based on a "demanding partnership" in which the divisions "buy into" the infrastructure and its standards while CIR provides a flexible and responsive infrastructure.

CIR made the following five major assumptions when developing Vision 2000 in 1993:

1. The mainframe would continue to be the best platform for large-volume transaction systems or systems requiring massive computing power. In addition, it could become an enterprise server. This role was consistent with the adoption of an enterprise-wide client-server architecture.
2. Integration of voice, image, video, and so on would occur at desktops, servers, and portable devices; therefore, higher-capacity networks would be needed to transmit and route these massive amounts of data.
3. Although unit costs of technology would continue to decline, overall IT usage at Mead would increase.

(Case Continued)

4. PCs presented a hidden cost that was at least as large as the visible IT costs.
5. Technology advancements would increase; therefore, the challenge was to balance the need for standards while keeping up with the pace of change.

New Organizational Structure

To implement Vision 2000, Mead had two organizational options. One was to set up a skunk works to create the new infrastructure and systems. The other was to embed the new client-server paradigm into CIR's organizational structure. CIR chose the latter, so the entire corporate information resources group was reorganized to match the client-server model, as shown in Figure 1-12.

The core is the *Vision 2000 Project*, managed by a high-level CIR executive. Around this core is the technology layer of the CIR organization—the four core technologies that provide the IT infrastructure on which Mead operates. *Data Services* provides data and information. *Server Technology Services* handles all servers on the network, from mainframes on down. *Client Services* handles all devices that customers touch, which include desktop workstations, fax machines, and telephones. CIR defines their customers as Mead employees as well others who interface with Mead. *Network Services* handles everything that ties these other pieces together, both voice and data communications as well as the Internet, intranet, gateways, firewalls, and working with their Internet service provider.

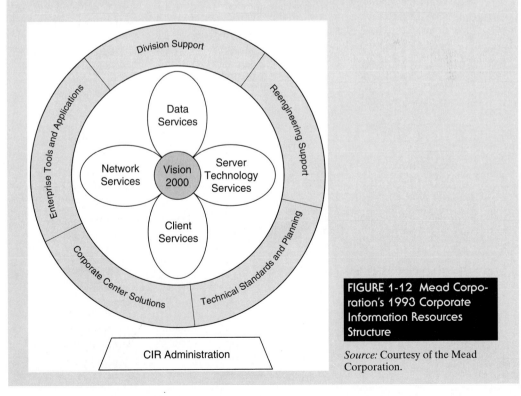

FIGURE 1-12 Mead Corporation's 1993 Corporate Information Resources Structure

Source: Courtesy of the Mead Corporation.

(Case Continued)

All four groups report to the vice president of CIR, John Langenbahn, who, by the way, has led Mead's IS department through all editions of this textbook (since 1985). All four groups had two jobs: (1) to run current operations, and (2) to build Vision 2000. Langenbahn notes that the move from mainframe to client-server shifted CIR from managing hundreds of components to managing thousands of them—an order-of-magnitude change.

On the outside layer of the organization chart, closer to the customer, are the application groups. To serve their constituencies, they draw on Vision 2000 and the IT infrastructure provided by the inner layers. *Division Support* supports the applications developed by Mead's 10 operating divisions. *Reengineering Support* is concerned with a few companywide business processes that have been recentralized and reengineered to improve efficiency and lower costs. These processes include Mead's financial systems and purchasing system, all of which do not touch customers. *Enterprise Tools and Applications* provides a common desktop toolkit to all Mead staff, which consists of hardware and a suite of software products such as spreadsheet, e-mail, word processing, graphics, browser, EDI, and knowledge tools (such as Notes). *Corporate Center Solutions* handles application development and maintenance of corporate applications. *Technical Standards and Planning* is a one-person think tank devoted to determining the standards that underlie Vision 2000, while everyone else works on the day-to-day issues. And finally, as shown below the circle, is *CIR Adminis-*

tration, which handles contracting and financials.

Like other companies, Mead encountered the typical staff problems of getting the mainframe staff to move into the client-server environment and getting new client-server talent to follow the discipline needed to develop enterprisewide systems.

Progress To Date

The Internet has had a large impact on Vision 2000 in that more and more of the vision is being served by it. For example, the vision foresaw storing lots of data on servers, so that CIR, not users, could handle backup. But, with so much information on the Internet, CIR has not needed to acquire so much public information, install it, or maintain it in-house. For instance, CIR had planned to install the U.S. telephone directory on a CD-ROM server. After it became available on the Net, CIR simply added an icon to the standard desktop for quick access to the directory.

Mead learned that client-server computing was not cheaper than mainframe computing, as was touted in the early 1990s. In 1993, Mead placed the cost of a PC at $9,024 a year ($2,517 hard costs, $6,507 soft costs). With the Vision 2000 standards, Mead believes the soft costs have been cut to $3,005 a year.

The vision was conceived in 1993, implementation began at the end of 1994, and by 2000, right on schedule, the company had rolled out 8,000 workstations. During that time, only one change was made to the organization structure: adding Vision Support Services to handle operations (Figure 1-13).

(Case Continued)

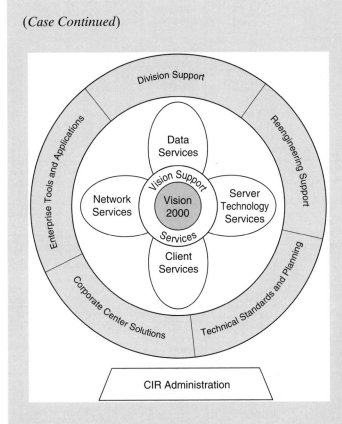

CIR Administration

FIGURE 1-13 Mead Corporation's Current Corporate Information Resources Structure

Source: Courtesy of the Mead Corporation.

INTO THE 2000S: LEVERAGE CENTRALIZATION

The "leverage the infrastructure" viewpoint begun in 1990 has persisted through the 1990s and is expected to yield significant business results in 2003 when Mead will have installed SAP in all eight divisions. At that time, they will use one image of SAP to run the entire company. This accomplishment has been the goal of enterprise resource planning (ERP) since its inception in the early 1990s, but it is a vision that few companies have actually attained. By 2003, Mead will have spent $124 million dollars on the endeavor. The first division went live in late 1999, the second in 2000, and so on. Thus, from the 1960s to 2000, Mead's Information Resources division will have moved

from significant decentralization to significant centralization of systems.

Implementing ERP

In the early 1990s, Mead looked at SAP, the leading ERP system, but decided the software was not appropriate for the forest products industry. In 1995, they looked at it again, and although the software was better, management felt the company did not have the necessary companywide standards, so it declined to move forward on ERP again.

In 1997, however, management forced the issue. They had increasingly been running the company via a "shared services" vision, where they took functions out of divisions and centralized them, making them best-of-breed. Logistics, purchasing,

(Case Continued)

finance, and IR were provided via shared services. This collaboration left the divisions with the customer-facing work. But management saw a "train wreck" coming once the first division wanted to install an ERP system. The company would then have to decide, "Do we want to be good at satisfying customers or have good shared services?" Management decided, "We have to do both." To do so, they had to put in the same ERP system company-wide to both leverage their back-end shared services and be number one in customer satisfaction.

They spent 1998 determining the design of the enterprisewide system and began implementation in the first division in 1999. From the early 1990s reengineering work on the purchasing system, Mead learned that significant company change requires business leadership, so the SAP effort has been led by a business executive and 70 of the 100 team members also come from the business; only 30 come from IR. In addition, some 80 IBM consultants have been involved. Mead chose IBM as its SAP implementation partner because IBM had helped Monsanto implement SAP and had created the IBM/Monsanto Solution Center. Mead was able to draw on that center and Monsanto's experience, and even reuse 80 percent of Monsanto's business design, down to the general ledger, giving them a running start. ERP implementations are huge, expensive, and many have failed. Mead has been able to avoid those pitfalls by learning from others.

Mead is using the entire suite of SAP modules except human resources, which is handled by PeopleSoft; it was installed in the mid 1990s and has worked well. Mead is one of the first to install a recent module, Advanced Optimization Planning (AOP), which handles all planning and scheduling. SAP was originally designed to support "build to inventory" manufacturing, which is 60 percent of Mead's business. AOP is for the other 40 percent: "build to order."

Lotus Notes, a sophisticated database system from IBM, and part of Vision 2000, has been invaluable in providing the building blocks for defining the new ways of working under SAP. SAP required Mead to define 800 roles and describe the work flows and security flows among these roles. This task is not handled by SAP, so Mead used Lotus Notes for it and other SAP support work.

SAP is unifying the company, but it is a large and complex system. And it requires strict adherence to its rules, which is its downside. A division can no longer tailor its own systems to meet its market's changing needs; in some instances, changes can be accommodated easily, but for major changes it must get concurrence from the other seven to change SAP. It *could* make Mead less nimble; it remains to be seen.

As SAP is turned on, old systems are turned off. In fact, SAP is replacing the last generation of systems Mead built itself. Today, all software work is integrating packages, or system integration. Nothing is coded from scratch. Once SAP is implemented, the development work done by the divisions will go away through natural attrition. However, each division will probably still have an executive information officer, who will be a mentor to the division and a coach on how to use IT. They will focus on reengineering to leverage SAP. They will be business people with IT exposure and IT people with business exposure.

(Case Continued)

Electronic Commerce

The Internet has, of course, changed everything. So far, the greatest effect has been internal. Mead's intranet is becoming how the company conducts its business processes. The homepage is employees' gateway to most of what they need to do at Mead. Soon, SAP will be browser based.

Mead would have preferred to implement e-commerce on SAP because e-commerce exposes all a company's legacy system inefficiencies. But the company could not wait until 2003, and because its legacy systems are still functional, it has put browser-based front-ends on its legacy systems. Once SAP is in place, only the system interfaces need to change.

In some sense, Mead sees business-to-business e-commerce as old wine in new bottles. In 1986, Mead built a cluster terminal system for its paper business. The system was proprietary; it ran on Mead's network and Mead gave proprietary terminals to customers to order paper. Even though the terminals were only character-based, with no graphics, customers could see Mead's stock levels, delivery times, and prices. One-third of its business came through this system. Today, the system is essentially the same, but it is Internet based. All a customer now needs is a browser to log into Mead's extranet to place orders.

However, Mead has discovered that although it has broken down its own internal silos in installing SAP, it is encountering silos in customers' operations. So true end-to-end electronic commerce will not occur until these partners improve their internal operations.

What Lies Ahead?

Mead's industry, like most others, is undergoing unprecedented global competition. To survive, companies need to become larger or be a niche player. Mead expects to be one of the survivors, and they see SAP aiding in achieving that goal. If, for example, they acquire another company, they will be able to merge it into operations within 90 days because of SAP. That capability makes SAP a valuable acquisition tool.

In conclusion, the CIO job has definitely changed since 1985, says Langenbahn. "In the 1990s, we always talked about IT being strategic, but it was really a wish. Today, it is reality. The role of the CIO has become more strategic and the role has grown, but at the end of the day, information technology is inherently valueless. Value is created by business change and true business change cannot be led by the IT side; it must spring from the business side. The major role of the CIO is to bridge the gap between the business and technology, and to have the enabling technology in place to deliver what the business requires, although the business might not as yet realize what it requires." ■

QUESTIONS AND EXERCISES

Review Questions

Review questions are based directly on the material in the chapter, allowing the reader to assess comprehension of the chapter's key principles, topics, and ideas.

1. We define the information era in terms of information work and information workers. How has this sector of the U.S. workforce changed during the past 100 years? What is the current status?
2. What changes are taking place in the external business environment?
3. What changes are occurring in the internal organizational environment?
4. What are the goals of the new work environment?
5. Give two or three characteristics of the technology trends in hardware, software, data, and communications.
6. What is the mission for information systems recommended by the authors? How does it differ from earlier perceptions of the purpose and objectives of information systems?
7. In the simple model of information technology and its uses (Figure 1-3), why are the two boxes moving apart? Why are end user systems not joining them completely? (Figure 1-4)
8. Summarize the four main components of the model of the IS function (Figure 1-6).
9. List several attributes of procedure-based and knowledge-based information activities. Which do you think are most important? Why?
10. How did Mead focus on end user computing in the 1980s?
11. What was Mead's 1990 strategy?
12. Describe the new organizational structure for Vision 2000.
13. Why did Mead choose to implement ERP?
14. What is the job of the CIOs in each division once SAP is implemented in a division?
15. How has Langenbahn's job changed since 1985?

Discussion Questions

Discussion questions are based on a few topics in the chapter that offer a legitimate basis for a difference of opinion. These questions focus discussion on these issues when the book is used in a seminar or classroom setting.

1. Even though the PC dispersed control of processing power out of the IS department, the Internet will return control to the department. Agree or disagree? Discuss.
2. Do we really need a major change in the way the information systems function is structured? Are the necessary changes just minor modifications to accommodate normal growth in computer uses?
3. The procedure-knowledge dichotomy does not add much beyond the clerical-managerial distinction. Do you agree or disagree? Give reasons for your opinion.
4. The e-economy is going to end up just like the old economy with the huge conglomerates controlling everything. Agree or disagree? Is this situation desirable or not?

Exercises

Exercises provide an opportunity for the reader to put some of the concepts and ideas into practice on a small scale. In particular, one exercise in each chapter requires a student, or a team of students, to visit a local company and discover how the ideas in the chapter are being implemented in that company.

1. Show how Mead's new organizational structure compares to the model in Figure 1-6 by entering Mead's functions on the figure.
2. Contact a company in your community and prepare a diagram and narrative to describe the organization of its information systems function. Compare it to Figure 1-6 and to Mead's current structure.
3. Find an article about the e-economy that contains a description of how it differs from the past. Present those ideas to the class.

REFERENCES

1. *Bridging the Gap: Information Technology Skills for the New Millennium,* Information Technology Association of America, 1616 N. Ft. Myer Dr., Suite 1300, Arlington, VA 22209, www.itaa.org, April 2000.
2. Drucker, Peter F. "The Coming of the New Organization," *Harvard Business Review,* January/February 1988.
3. Manville, Brook and Nathaniel Foote, "Strategy As If Knowledge Mattered," *Fast Company,* www.fastcompany.com, 1996.
4. Gilder, George, speech at the Aspen Institute, July 18, 1996.

PART

I

LEADERSHIP ISSUES

Part I of this book consists of three chapters that address the leadership issues of managing information, information systems, and information technology. To establish the context, Part I deals with the shaded portion of the following figures—executive leadership—based on Figure 1-6 in Chapter 1, the conceptual framework for this entire book.

Leadership of the information systems function is no longer limited to IS managers and professionals, or even to the chief information officer. Increasingly, this leadership role is shared with the chief executive officer and other CXOs. Thus the need for the management and nurturing of this shared relationship is one of the underlying themes of this book.

Chapter 2 discusses where the IS department might be headed and presents major responsibility areas of the CIO. Chapter 3 presents today's strategic imperative for companies and IS departments: e-business. Chapter 4 completes the leadership section by discussing the changing world of IS planning and a number of planning approaches and techniques.

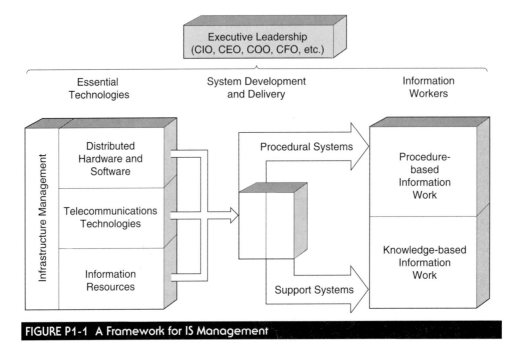

FIGURE P1-1 A Framework for IS Management

CHAPTER

2 | THE TOP IS JOB

INTRODUCTION

The management of information technology in organizations has changed drastically in the past 30 years. In the early years, the big job was to manage the technology—get it to work, keep it running, and thus reduce the cost of doing business. Later, the main thrust was to manage the information resources of the organization, particularly to support management decision making by delivering information when and where it was needed.

Today, IT is pervasive in organizations, and is becoming a mandatory link between organizations. Hence, it affects every aspect of organizational performance and is leading to an "electronic ecosystem" in which organizations operate. Today, proper deployment of IT can determine an organization's growth, direction, structure, and viability.

The responsibilities of the head of the IS function therefore now go far beyond operating highly efficient "production programming shops." These executives must understand the goals of the enterprise and work in partnership with business unit peers to utilize IT to attain the organizational goals. These partnerships also require a much heavier involvement in IS leadership from the CEO, CFO, other CXOs, and other members of top management. Yet, the CIO is the focal point for IT deployment.

In this chapter, we look at two dimensions of the top IS job. First, we ask the question, "Where is the IS department headed?" Second, we look at the responsibilities of the chief information officer in what appears to be the emerging role of the IS department.

WHERE IS THE IS DEPARTMENT HEADED?

The role and responsibilities of the IS department have been evolving since the first electronic data processing departments were formed in companies in the 1950s. We create the context for this discussion of the evolution by looking at the escalating benefits of IT, which in turn change the way executives view IT's role in the business.

The Escalating Benefits of Information Technology

Kenneth Primozic, Edward Primozic, and Joe Leben, authors of *Strategic Choices*,[1] present one view of the evolution of IT and the escalating benefits it provides organizations. They introduce the notion of "waves of innovation," which they define as how IT is used by industries and by enterprises. They identify five waves of innovation, as shown in Figure 2-1, with "time" on the horizontal axis and "benefit" on the vertical access. The waves are

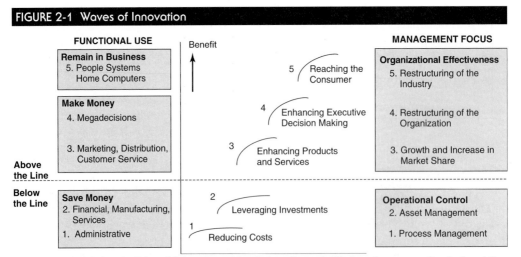

FIGURE 2-1 Waves of Innovation

Source: Kenneth Primozic, Edward Primozic, and Joe Leben, *Strategic Choices: Supremacy, Survival, and Sayonara* (New York: McGraw-Hill, 1991).

- Wave 1: Reducing costs.
- Wave 2: Leveraging investments.
- Wave 3: Enhancing products and services.
- Wave 4: Enhancing executive decision making.
- Wave 5: Reaching the consumer.

Wave 1: Reducing costs.   This wave began in the 1960s when use of IT focused on increasing the productivity of individuals and business areas. The goal was to achieve clerical and administrative savings by automating manual processes

Wave 2: Leveraging investments.   This wave began in the 1970s and concentrated on making more effective use of corporate assets, to increase profitability. Systems were justified on return on investment and increasing cash flow.

As shown in Figure 2-1, both Wave 1 and Wave 2 are "below the line," which means both focused on saving money, not making money, through better management of processing and assets. Systems were developed mainly for administration, finance, and manufacturing.

Wave 3: Enhancing products and services.   This wave began in the 1980s and was the first time that attention shifted to using IT to produce revenue by gaining strategic advantage or by creating entirely new businesses. In conjunction with the new goals of using IT to grow the business or increase market share, IT was used to improve outward-looking functions, such as marketing, distribution, and customer service.

Wave 4: Enhancing executive decision making.   This wave began later in the 1980s and focused on changing the fundamental structure of the organization as well as creating real-time business management systems.

The authors point out that Waves 1 and 2 could be implemented at any time, because of their internal focus, but Waves 3 and 4 must be implemented once an industry leader has set the precedent. Companies that do not follow suit cease to be competitive.

Wave 5: Reaching the consumer.   This wave began in the 1990s, say the authors. It uses IT to communicate directly with consumers, leading to new marketing, distribution, and service strategies. It changes the rules of competition, which has been precisely the focus of leading edge firms—to restructure their industry by focusing on creating new businesses using the Internet, Web technology, and electronic commerce.

Waves 3, 4, and 5 are "above the line" because they concentrate on making money and staying in business. Due to the worldwide ubiquity of the Internet and the standard browser interface to the Web, most organizations have jumped to Wave 5 in the past few years.

Once companies cross "the line," top management must be involved in guiding IT use, say the authors, because they must steer the company in the new business environment. The risks of inappropriately using IT for competitive purposes are too great for the senior executives to abrogate leadership to the technicians. So joint planning by top management and IS management must take place.

To illustrate how one company has maneuvered through these five waves, consider the example of the American Airlines SABRE system.

CASE EXAMPLE

THE SABRE SYSTEM

The American Airlines' computer reservation system—SABRE—represents a prime example of a system that has progressed through the five waves of innovation.

Waves 1 and 2

SABRE was initially built to reduce the costs of making airline seat reservations and to leverage the reservation-making assets of the airline. The system moved American from a manual-based reservation operation to a computer-based one.

Wave 3

American then expanded the system so that it could be used by travel agents, giving them a means of making reservations directly through online terminals. American also enhanced the offering by adding functions of importance to travel agents, such as preparing trip itineraries. SABRE was a win-win proposition—the travel agents liked the direct access and American increased the barriers to agents switching to other another carrier's reservation system.

Wave 4

American later expanded their reservation service to include hotels and rental cars, through alliances with these suppliers. In so doing, American was transforming themselves, and perhaps the entire industry, from an airline company to a travel company. At about the same time, American also added a yield management component to SABRE, which allowed them to more dynamically reprice seats, to maximize revenue.

Wave 5

American extended their reach to the consumer in three major moves. First, they introduced EAASY SABRE, the computer reservation system that consumers could access directly from their PCs.

Second, American introduced their frequent flyer program, AAdvantage, thereby stimulating frequent business flyers to fly American and gain points for free trips. Furthermore, the airline began allying the program with credit card and long distance telephone companies, giving their AAdvantage members free miles by using the credit cards and telephone companies.

Third, American enhanced their Wave 5 connections to consumers via the Web. As reported by Patricia Seybold in her book *Customers.com*,[2] American was the first major airline to develop a Web site, so that passengers could not only plan their trip via the Internet but also buy tickets online and obtain real-time flight information, such as arrival and departure information. Even the name of the movie(s) being shown on flights could be accessed. Before the Web site, some 85 percent of telephone calls to the SABRE call center were not booking related. After the Web site, this percentage dropped significantly.

Importantly, writes Seybold, American targeted their site at the most prof-

(Case Continued)

itable customers—the 32 million AAdvantage members—practically all of whom had access to a computer. The goal was to give them better control of their own travel planning and rescheduling. Thus, on the site, AAdvantage members can see their accumulated frequent flyer points, make reservations, book electronic tickets (so they do not have to worry about paper tickets), and so on. American promoted use of the site by offering extra frequent flyer miles; bookings spiked every time a promotion was run, notes Seybold. And American has continued to enhance the functionality of the site, helping flyers find hotels and restaurants.

In addition, American has used the site to experiment with different offerings to flyers in general. One of these experiments has proven to be a real winner. In essence, it integrates the three themes in this text: knowledge management, the Internet, and e-commerce.

John Samuel, a marketing manager at AMR, American's parent company, asked, "How can we market to fill seats?" He and his team decided to offer to send an e-mail message every Wednesday listing "the specials of the week"—empty seats on flights the upcoming weekend—to anyone who signed up for the NetSAAver service. Not knowing what to expect, they were overwhelmed with the response—20,000 subscribers within 30

days, 100,000 in 60 days, and 775,000 in one year, notes Seybold.

This marketing strategy not only lets American remind subscribers of their service each week, at the subscribers' own request, it also allows American to sell "distressed inventory" (the unsold seats). This revenue has significantly improved the airline's bottom line.

Both uses of the Internet, the AAdvantage Web site and the NetSAAver e-mail service, have required American to appropriately manage knowledge about these flyers, use the Internet to interact with them, and create an e-commerce engine to support the financial interactions with them. In the knowledge management arena, for example, the airline learned that keeping Web sites pertinent requires operating like a newspaper publisher, with strict deadlines, publishing guidelines, dispersed accountability, and so forth, notes Seybold.

This example makes it clear that management had to be involved as soon as SABRE moved into the money-making Wave 3, when they began offering the system to their customers, the travel agents. That was a heart-of-the-business move, and it had to be led by the business executives, not the information system executives. The same has been true of their use of the Web. ■

This SABRE example illustrates that as the benefits of IT increase, the importance of executive guidance also increases. It also raises the question, "What's the job of the IS department?" We will illustrate IS's involvement in designing SABRE's Web site architecture toward the end of the chapter. First, we discuss where the IS department could be headed.

Traditional Functions Are Being Nibbled Away

IT has become an essential piece of business strategy, as SABRE demonstrates; therefore, the speed of IT deployment affects when and how companies can carry out their strategy. Not keeping up in IT may even mean going out of business. The role of the IT department is thus expanding and moving to center stage; in so doing, the job has become too large for one group. Thus, we see two phenomena occurring simultaneously: While the growing importance of IT is causing the IS department's work to expand into new areas of responsibility, management is realizing that the traditional and more operational portions of the job do not all need to be performed by the IS department. They can be performed by others. The traditional set of responsibilities for IS has included:

- Managing operations of data centers, remotes systems, and networks
- Managing corporate data
- Performing system analysis and design, and constructing new systems
- Planning systems
- Identifying opportunities for new systems.

While all these functions still need to be performed, the following trends are moving their performance out of the IS department into other parts of the organization or to other enterprises:

- *Distributed systems* have led to software applications migrating to user areas, operated under the control of the users, and generally purchased with their funds. Sometimes these applications are acquired following guidelines (or even standards) promulgated by the IS department; sometimes they are not.
- *Ever more knowledgeable users* have taken on increased IS responsibilities. They often identify high-leverage applications and lead the multifunctional teams (which include IS staff members) that acquire these systems.
- *Better application packages* have resulted in less need for armies of programmers and analysts to develop systems in-house from scratch. The job of IS has changed to integrating purchased applications so they function together as a system, or "system integration." A case in point is enterprise resource planning (ERP) systems. Implementing these purchased systems has involved system integration rather than system development.
- *Outsourcing* has spread widely, perhaps more than most people expected, because companies see the value in drawing on the expertise of another company by turning IT functions over to them. Outsourcing may be the most effective strategy, based on fiscal and managerial considerations, for handling data center operations, application maintenance, network management, and PC support.

Thus, as shown in Figure 2-2, the work of the IS department is being "nibbled away." On the other hand, the IS job is also expanding.

New Roles Are Emerging

Gartner Executive Programs (EXP), part of the well-known Gartner IT analysis firm, presents complementary analyses of the situation and provides useful insights into the structure of IS organizations and where they are likely to be headed. In one report,

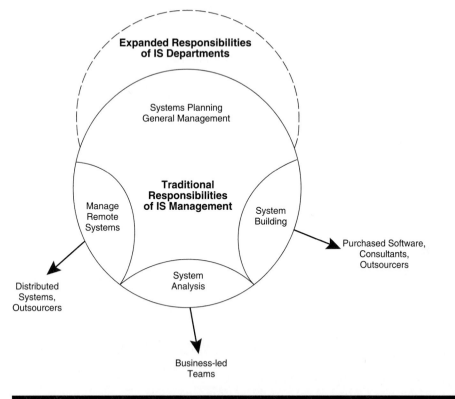

FIGURE 2-2 Traditional Responsibilities Being "Nibbled Away" from IS Departments

George Cox[3] states that IS is not a single monolithic organization, but rather a cluster of four functions:

- *Run operations*: Running the computers and networks
- *Develop systems:* Developing and maintaining systems, designing new systems, and updating existing ones
- *Develop architecture*: Setting a strategy and maintaining an architecture for both IT and information, providing a framework or standard for systems operations
- *Identify business requirements*: Helping articulate what the business needs from information technology.

Each of these functions requires a different set of skills and a different management strategy. A function that aims for cost efficiency and requires technical skills (such as running operations) needs to be managed differently from one that aims to add business value and requires business expertise (such as identifying business requirements).

Figure 2-3 shows the four functions on a matrix with two dimensions: the kind of impact an activity has on the organization (from cost efficiency to value added), and the type of expertise needed by the activity (from technical to business expertise).

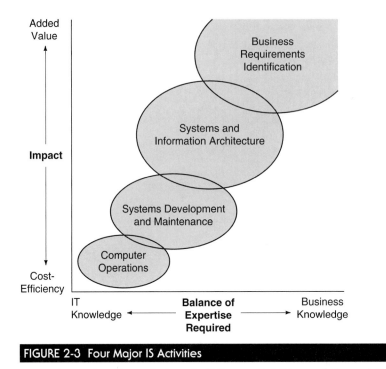

FIGURE 2-3 Four Major IS Activities

Source: George Cox, *Time to Reshape the IS Department?,* Wentworth Research Program (now part of Gartner Executive Programs), Egham, England, June 1994.

Two technical activities that focus on cost efficiency—operations and system development and maintenance—are of less importance to the business, hence they are smaller bubbles. Meanwhile, the business-oriented activities that seek to add value to the enterprise are of far greater importance to the enterprise, hence the larger bubbles.

Companies that have failed to recognize the differences among these four areas—the relative importance of each and how to manage each properly—have, in some cases, misplaced their resources or underdeveloped their expertise. For example, most IS organizations have historically invested heavily in computer operations and system development/maintenance, while neglecting the other two (developing architectures and identifying business requirements). Unfortunately, operations and systems development can be purchased because they are commodity-like; architecture development and business requirements identification cannot because they are unique to each organization.

Most IS departments have had to reskill their staff to move to these more value-added kinds of work. As they do, they are seeing a "squeeze" similar to the "nibbling" discussed earlier. As shown in Figure 2-4, external services in the form of outsourcing are competing well in the lower left of the matrix, the technical arena. Meanwhile, increasingly knowledgeable users are assuming more of the responsibility and initiative in the upper right area of the matrix, the business-centric arena.

Will these trends continue? Will the IS organization be squeezed into oblivion, outsourced on one end and absorbed into business units on the other? Cox thinks not! Two roles will emerge as dominant for the IS function.

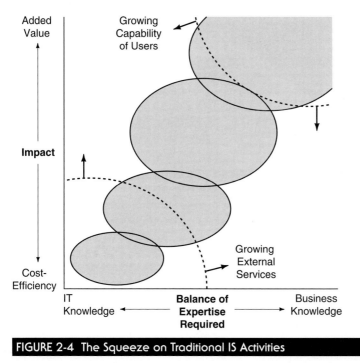

FIGURE 2-4 The Squeeze on Traditional IS Activities

Source: George Cox, *Time to Reshape the IS Department?,* Wentworth Research Program (now part of Gartner Executive Programs), Egham, England, June 1994.

First, it is not reasonable to expect an outsourcing service provider to understand and satisfy all the needs of the organization without active management and counsel. They sell commodities. The IS organization therefore is needed to develop and manage these contract relationships with a variety of external suppliers. So the department will become a broker between technical service providers and business units, which is indeed happening.

Second, a crucial role for IS organizations is development and management of the IT architecture for the enterprise, providing the framework for information technology to support the business. It is the biggest challenge, especially given IS departments' systems development and operations heritage. As Cox notes, "The precious baby of a coherent framework for systems should be differentiated from the bath water of system delivery and operation." Figure 2-5 shows these two new roles and how they overlap the past roles.

In short, Cox describes the metamorphosis of IS departments as follows:

- *In computer and network operations,* IS started out being the sole provider, then moved to being the preferred provider, next was seen as a competing supplier, and finally is becoming the broker and contract manager for outsourcing this work.
- *In system development and maintenance,* in-house programmers initially wrote the code, then they became software product specialists, next systems integrators, and finally brokers and contract managers for acquiring software. Most

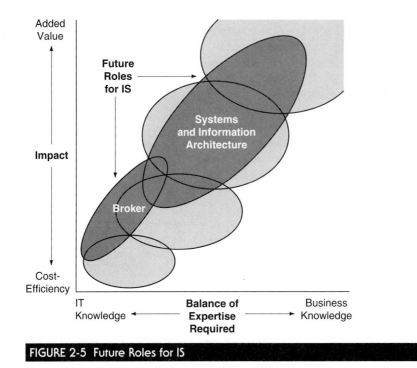

Added Value

Future Roles for IS

Systems and Information Architecture

Impact

Broker

Cost-Efficiency

IT Knowledge ← **Balance of Expertise Required** → Business Knowledge

FIGURE 2-5 Future Roles for IS

Source: George Cox, *Time to Reshape the IS Department?*, Wentworth Research Program (now part of Gartner Executive Programs), Egham, England, June 1994.

recently, for example, they contract with application service providers (ASPs) who rent software on a transaction basis.

- *In systems and information architecture,* IS began as the technology guru and standards setter, then evolved into being the custodian of technical standards, later became the specialist in IT trends, and most recently morphed into information systems strategist.
- *In business requirements identification,* IS initially defined the specifics of computer programs, then focused on analyzing information flows and business systems, later moved to contributing to multidisciplinary analysis teams, and finally has been partnering with the business in looking at business processes.

In short, IS departments have moved in Figure 2-3 from lower left to upper right in their role in the business, from efficiency to value added and from technical to business expertise.

Toward IS Lite

More recently, Roger Woolfe[4] has furthered the thinking at Gartner Executive Programs about the role of IS departments by studying how they have responded to this evolution. He notes that whereas IS may have started as a single centralized organization, it has evolved into a federal model, where some activities (such as standards setting and operations) are handled centrally because they can be leveraged across the enterprise, while other activities (such as application development) have been dispersed to business units so they can best meet local needs. Unfortunately, making this split has been far from easy, and has produced continual swings between centralizing and decentralizing specific activities to try to best fit the current business environment.

As an example, where should Web sites be developed? Initially, most of them were built by enterprising business people in marketing and other functions, without standards or guidance. When the importance of these sites was recognized, and the diversity began to impinge on "creating a single, powerful corporate image on the Web," Web site development was often pulled into a newly created electronic commerce group. Yet the job is too large for one group, so those with responsibility for the content (in marketing, operations, and other functions) have added Web content management to their job.

But the split continues to change as Web sites take on new uses and greater importance. In fact, some companies outsource Web site development to firms that specialize in this work, they outsource their Web operations to others that specialize in handling spikes in demand, and they perhaps outsource the hosting of "events" on the site to others who specialize in that activity. In short, the federal model can become quite complex, and it has.

To make the federal model work better, companies are shifting attention from roles to processes. In this view, the IS department can be viewed as managing three overall processes:

- Driving innovation
- Managing change
- Supporting infrastructure

Applying the federal model to these processes sharpens the distinction between IT activities performed centrally and those performed in business units. Woolfe sees the division coming from distinguishing supply-side activities and demand-side ones. "Supporting infrastructure" and aspects of "managing change" (such as delivering applications) are supply side. They involve providing the networks, databases, and processing; they are best centralized because they gain from economies of scale.

Most of "managing change" and all of "driving innovation," on the other hand, are demand side. They create the demand for IT services; they are best localized in business units, which can tailor services to their needs.

In conjunction, some IS departments are creating centers of excellence to pool expertise and leverage it across the enterprise. Such centers now exist for such areas as electronic commerce, supply chain management, policies and standards, help desk support, and systems integration.

The result is that much of the supply and demand sides of IS's work is being given up, as noted previously, to outsourcers and knowledgeable users. The result is that IS departments are moving to "IS Lite" as shown in Figure 2-6.

The remaining processes are driving innovation, which includes information and systems architecture, and managing supplier and user relationships, which includes brokering.

A company that is moving in this direction is LifeScan. Here is what their information management (IM) department is doing, as described in the paper submitted to the Society for Information Management's annual paper competition.[5]

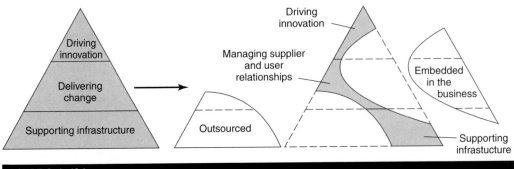

FIGURE 2-6 IS Lite

Source: Reprinted with permission from Roger Woolfe, *IS Lite,* Gartner Executive Programs, 56 Top Gallant, Stamford, CT 06904, July 2000.

CASE EXAMPLE

LIFESCAN

LifeScan, a wholly owned subsidiary of Johnson & Johnson, is the world leader in blood glucose monitoring for diabetes management. Located in Silicon Valley, the company offers an array of consumer and hospital products. In 1981, LifeScan pioneered the modern era of blood glucose monitoring by eliminating wiping and timing procedures. This breakthrough took blood glucose testing out of the laboratory and into the hands of patients. LifeScan's mission is to improve the quality of life for people with diabetes.

In 1986, Johnson & Johnson acquired LifeScan and in 1996 J&J began promoting greater use of IT in business strategy. The company created the board-level position of chief information officer and it encouraged all 188 affiliates (including LifeScan) to do the same. At the time, LifeScan Information Management (IM) was led by a director—two levels below the president.

In 1998, LifeScan appointed its first CIO, Hugo Yepez, who brought with him

an agenda to align a department with the business. This agenda is leading the IM department to an IS Lite type of structure.

The Alignment Roadmap

Yepez has drawn on a three-stage maturation of IM departments as his roadmap to moving his department from supporting the business to partnering with the business. His framework defines maturity by the value the IM department delivers at each stage:

- "Stage One" IM organizations are "backroom" in nature. Their purpose is to keep the business running. Their value is defined through the internal IM measures of faster/better/cheaper.
- "Stage Two" IM organizations work closely with business units. Hence, their value is measured from the business units' viewpoint, in terms of delivery and execution. In measuring their success, some use the

(Case Continued)

Balanced Scorecard because it measures performance on four dimensions—financial, internal performance, customer satisfaction, and health and growth.

- "Stage Three" IM organizations partner with business units and have direct influence on business strategy. Their value is therefore gauged through the business's own performance measures. The two are integrated; there are no separate measures for IM.

Yepez believed the LifeScan IM department was at Stage One when he arrived, but he believed they could move into Stage Two in a couple of years, and into Stage Three in several more years.

To progress toward Stage Two, Yepez focused on execution and measurement to gain credibility with the business units. Execution meant bringing in IM projects on time and within budget. Focusing on project execution would help move the department to a Stage Two mindset because IM staff would view their performance from the results they deliver to the business.

To deliver on their promises in implementing new systems, IM staff learned they had to have strong project management and not allow "scope creep" (users asking for additional functions in applications as development proceeded). To deliver on promises in maintenance, IM began outsourcing the work on several major systems. They use Tata Computing Systems in Calcutta, India, which has impressive software quality processes and high-quality software maintenance programmers.

LifeScan also outsourced maintenance of its desktop machines, drawing on the corporate outsourcing agreement negotiated by Johnson & Johnson's IM department. Furthermore, LifeScan has turned over its computer operations to J&J's corporate operations department, National Computing Service.

Outsourcing these supply-based IM areas has freed IM staff from doing the work to overseeing the work—performing the brokering and relationship management role in the IS Lite model.

IM also began measuring new projects, to make execution visible, by giving LifeScan employees an IM scorecard on the company intranet to show which milestones were being hit or not. The scorecard is expanded, as appropriate, to include Stage Two and Stage Three measures—such as the business impact of new systems on such areas as customer service, operations, and so on. The goal is for the board of LifeScan to be able to link IM measures and LifeScan's corporate measures, to see where IM is best supporting the business.

In the areas of driving innovation and managing change, Yepez has undertaken several initiatives to involve business units in IM work. For example, he brought in an alignment process that assists business unit executives both to determine the priority of LifeScan's business drivers and then to rank IM projects in their support of those drivers.

Being a manufacturer, LifeScan has instituted quality processes. IM is aligning itself with that quality-driven culture so that the entire company speaks the same language. In one initiative IM is working with three other departments that develop software (for products, services, and quality assurance) to implement a company-wide quality-based software development life cycle.

(Case Continued)

In addition, all IM projects are business led, which moves the ownership of systems to the businesspeople.

Finally, IM staff members who have the skills needed in a Stage Three IM organization—those with strong project management, business process, change management, and interpersonal skills—are being promoted and given opportunities to partner with business peers. In so doing, these employees present a leadership model, one that emphasizes relationship management and brokering skills, as noted in the IS Lite model. ∎

Death of IS?

We cannot leave this subject of where the IS department is going without presenting the provocative view of Forrester Research[6] in their report "Death of IT." Their premise is that IS departments as we know them today will not be able to keep up with the pace of change required by e-business models. Hence, IS departments will disappear; business process teams will take over the job of managing IT.

The key aspect of e-businesses is processes, especially processes that interconnect enterprises into "e-business networks," says Forrester. These networks will be dynamic, in that companies will plug into the one that best fits the situation at hand, and then unplug when it is no longer needed. They will collaborate with a continually changing mix of partners, using a variety of processes.

The enabler is information technology, but to keep pace, the technology needs to be managed at the process level, so that companies can plug and unplug from different processes quickly. Thus, the technology will be managed by business process owners who decide which process to use for a given situation.

These process owners, and their teams, will merge technology and business management within the processes they manage, such as supply chain management and customer service. In essence, they will manage the applications that automate their process. Furthermore, they are likely to draw on the technology services offered by external service providers, perhaps renting applications from application service providers (ASPs) or reconfiguring automated processes leased from others.

Applications will be run by external service providers, who, in turn, may rely on other service providers for the electronic infrastructure and intervendor system connections that form the e-business networks.

Whether Forrester's view of the future of the IS department comes true remains to be seen. Forecasts of the death of IS departments have been circulating for years. They have been based on the assertion that IT has become a commodity. While computing power and network connections may look like commodities, applications and processes are not. They provide the source of competitive advantage, especially in the emerging e-economy. For this reason, the death knell for the IT department is premature.

Given these descriptions of where the IS department might be headed, we now look at the responsibilities of CIOs.

THE CIO'S RESPONSIBILITIES

In line with the evolution of IS departments, the emphasis of the top IS job has changed through the five editions of this textbook as follows.

In 1986, when the first edition of this book was published, the leading IS executives were talking about their new role as architects of the enterprisewide information systems infrastructure. Much of the talk centered around the strategic use of information systems.

In 1989, attention shifted to helping formulate corporate policy, with an emphasis on creating a vision of the role of information systems in the future. In other words, from 1986 to 1989, the focus of the top information systems job had swung significantly toward addressing business issues.

In 1992, the challenge for IS executives was to use IT as a catalyst for revamping the way enterprises worked. To accomplish this task, they needed to be in a high enough position to influence the use of IT as a major underpinning of the enterprise of the future. Reflecting this higher level of responsibility, the title "Vice President of MIS" or "Information Systems Director" evolved to "Chief Information Officer (CIO)," a position often occupied by someone with general management expertise, rather than a traditional technology manager.

In 1998, the need to revamp business operations using information technology continued with the Internet expanding the CIO's horizon beyond company boundaries out to potential customers. IT began playing a more "front office" role, especially in the rapidly changing Internet marketspace.

Today, the CIO is the technical member of top management. The job is to make sure the electronic infrastructure for e-commerce and e-business is in place, to ensure that IS staff are working as partners with business units on value-adding initiatives, and to rapidly deploy new IT uses. We see IS executives in this role having the following six primary responsibilities:

1. *Understand the business* and the markets in which the firm sells its products and services.
2. *Establish credibility of the IS department*, thereby increasing the confidence of executive management in ideas presented by IS management.
3. *Develop a competent IS staff and IT-savvy users*, so the enterprise can leverage IT.
4. *Create a vision of the future and sell it*, by working to set a goal for the use of IT within the enterprise and convincing others to embrace this vision.
5. *Implement an information system architecture* that will support the vision and the company in the future.
6. *Foster relationships* with senior management, line executives, suppliers, alliance partners, and customers, both external and internal.

Some of these responsibilities may be new to some IS executives, as part of the expanding responsibilities described earlier. Some have been in the job description for years, but are taking on new dimensions. Item 6, for example, has always included getting top management involvement, but today's shared leadership requires much closer relationships. Most IS executives will not need to start from scratch in all six areas, but many may find that they must work to move ahead in several of them.

Understand the Business

If IS executives are to play an important role in reshaping a business's use of IT—to leverage the Internet with supply chain partners and customers, they must understand the business. In the past, studying a business generally meant learning how part of it was run. However, studying internal operations is not enough nowadays. Today, it is also important to understand the environment in which the business operates, because the rules of competition have changed with electronic commerce and are likely to change even further as more ways of working move onto the Web. Here are seven approaches CIOs are using to understand the business and its environment.

- Encourage project teams to study the marketplace.
- Concentrate on lines of business.
- Sponsor weekly briefings.
- Attend industry meetings with line executives.
- Read industry publications.
- Hold informal listening sessions.
- Become a "partner" with a line executive.

Encourage Project Teams to Study the Marketplace. To learn about the business, broaden the kinds of information that project teams seek in their study of the business, then have them describe their findings to IS management. For example, the project study might begin with a broad overview of the company, gathering the following information about the company and its industry:

- Current industry environment
- Business goals and objectives
- Major practices of competitors
- Pertinent government regulations
- The inputs, outputs, and resources of the firm

Such an overview study can be conducted for a business unit or a product in a few weeks. The study is apt to uncover some surprises, revealing things about the industry and company that even line people might not know, especially if, for example, a dot-com (an Internet start-up) has moved aggressively into the company's marketspace. IS management can be briefed on the findings, thus educating them about the markets in which their firm participates.

Concentrate on Lines of Business. Robert Benson and Marilyn Parker[7] have long studied how to manage information on an enterprisewide basis. They began thinking that they should develop data modeling tools. However, their thinking has broadened significantly. To help a company be successful, they found, IS needs to serve individual lines of business rather than the entire company. Planning for an entire enterprise without considering "lines of business" overlooks both competitive and performance matters. A line of business is where business and technology planning can be linked, they believe.

A line of business is an organizational unit that conducts business activities with common customers, products, and market characteristics, says Benson. For example, certain schools in a university have one line of business—undergraduate education. Others have two—undergraduate and graduate education. The customers, products, and market characteristics for the two are different, thus they are different lines of business.

Information technology can serve lines of business in two ways. One is by supporting current operations, which Benson and Parker call "alignment." The second is by using systems to influence future ways of working. They recommend asking the following questions about each line of business, to decide what each one needs.

1. Are we organized to serve that line of business?
2. Do we have an account manager in IS who has responsibility for that line of business?
3. Do we have someone within that line of business who oversees IT activity and talks the business language?
4. Do we have a sponsor in the line of business?
5. Do we have the attention of their management?
6. Does the line of business offer an opportunity to use systems in new ways?

By becoming familiar with lines of business, IS executives can better help them use IT to support current operations and influence the future, say Benson and Parker.

Sponsor Weekly Briefings.   Another way to learn about the business is to sponsor short briefings each week for IS management and staff, presented by *line* management or staff. We have attended such meetings and found them most informative. They were about one-half hour long, with one speaker describing a part of the business. Managers and staff from different departments were invited to talk to a small group of IS managers and staff about their business and its marketplace: the products and services they offered versus what the competitors offered, the strengths and weaknesses of the firm and competitors, growth projections, possible changes in the market, and so on.

For example, in the aircraft industry an engineer could give the basics of the commercial aircraft business: sizes of planes, passenger capacity, distance capability, expected competition, changes in the industry, 5-year market projections, and so on. In the financial services industry, a manager could describe various types of customers and how each is using the Internet, products now offered by the firm and competitors, the impact of globalization and the Internet on financial markets, and so on. At such briefings, it is helpful if the presenter provides a written summary of the ideas presented, so attendees can take something away with them. A brief question and answer period is also useful.

To understand the business, one needs to understand the marketplace. Few employees are given exposure to this breadth of knowledge. By sponsoring short presentations by the people closest to a business, IS management can help fix that problem without cutting into working time too greatly.

Attend Industry Meetings with Line Executives.   Another way to learn about the business is to accompany a line executive to an industry conference—not a computer conference. We have found that attending a conference is one of the quickest ways to uncover issues currently facing an industry. These conferences contain the jargon used in the industry and the approaches others have used to market products, handle regulations, respond to competition, and so on. Attending with a line executive can be even more enlightening, because he or she can explain what the company is or is not doing in areas discussed by the speakers. Such joint attendance is also likely to foster a new friendship.

Read Industry Publications. One of the best ways to stay abreast of an industry is to read its publications, perhaps online. Getting a well-rounded view of an industry may require reading several publications a month. For example, news publications can provide information on new products, current issues, company changes, and so on. Newsletters, reports, and research journals generally provide better analyses of industry trends, discussions of ongoing research, and projections about the future.

One information systems executive we know spreads this job around in his department. Every systems person is responsible for reading certain periodicals and routing interesting articles and Web addresses to others.

Hold Informal Listening Sessions. In his book, *Thriving on Chaos,*[8] consultant Tom Peters presents hundreds of suggestions on how managers can learn to not just cope with a chaotic business environment but thrive on it. In numerous places in the book, Peters urges people to simply listen and learn. His ideas are appropriate for IS management in their dealings with their customers, both internal to the firm and external.

Yogi Berra, the famous baseball player, once said, "You can see a lot by observing." Similarly, Peters urges employees to learn a lot by listening to others' needs. Because product life cycles are shrinking, companies need to spot new trends earlier. Becoming a listening-intensive organization can help.

Peters recounts several instances where people have created informal "meetings" to break down barriers among people who usually do not talk with one another. These get-togethers are held in a setting that is not charged with tension, participation is voluntary, and their purpose is to "just chat." For instance, one hospital administrator set aside one early morning each week to having coffee and rolls available in her office, with an open invitation for doctors and administrators to drop by and chat. She had some lonely breakfasts at first, she told Peters, but the chats eventually evolved into the "real staff meeting" of the week. Another hospital administrator held an informal staff meeting at lunchtime every two weeks at a local pub and invited some doctors. The doctors felt honored to be invited and their attendance helped break down stereotypes on both sides and improve communications.

Become a "Partner" with a Line Manager. The Society for Information Management presents a Partners in Leadership Award each year to honor an IS business executive team who, through their alliance, have achieved significant business results. This award has been well received and is highly sought. It reinforces the partnering needed to successfully guide and deploy IT these days. We discuss partnering in more depth later in this chapter.

Summary. Through these approaches, then, CIOs and their staff can learn the businesses of the organization. With this knowledge, CIOs are in a better position to foster a vision of IT's use in their firm. Unless these or similar specific steps or mechanisms are implemented and become commonplace, the job of learning the business will be displaced by urgent, but less important, day-to-day work.

Establish Systems Department Credibility

The second major responsibility of the CIO is to establish and then maintain the credibility of the IS organization. Before an IS executive and the department can be viewed as an important strategic voice, they must be viewed as successful and reliable today.

Management consultant Joseph Izzo[9] suggests that IS departments have two missions: maintain today's systems and work on tomorrow's systems.

These two missions have distinctly different goals and therefore need to be managed separately and specifically. The "today" operation should concentrate on providing service, says Izzo, while the "tomorrow" operation needs to focus on helping the business operate better. The first job of IS management is to get the "today" operation in shape. Until that task is accomplished, CIOs will have little credibility with top management.

Managing the "Today" Organization Better.   The "today" organization includes computer operations, technical support (including telecom network support), and maintaining and enhancing existing applications. Because its main mission is service, the service levels of these various operations need to be measured.

To run the "today" operation, Izzo suggests hiring managers for each of these functions who are like supervisors—that is, they are delivery oriented and demand a high level of service from their people.

Today, an increasing number of CIOs outsource these support functions to companies that specialize in this work. This outsourcing releases in-house staff to higher value work, generally reduces costs, and should result in gradually increasing levels of service. But reaping these benefits requires negotiating good contracts and managing the suppliers.

Once the "today" organization is in shape, then IS management has the credibility to propose its new ideas for the future. In Chapter 8, we further discuss running today's operations.

Develop a Competent IS Staff and IT-Savvy Users

Managing IS operations once took an inordinate amount of management attention. Now that this supply-side activity is being outsourced, staffing the IS department has become the activity that commands a larger-than-expected amount of management attention. And just like operations, if IS does not have the right staff, the entire enterprise suffers because the enterprise's needs cannot be met fast enough. Not only does just about every IS department have some vacant positions, but staff turnover has skyrocketed in many companies, as staff members are lured to companies with more exciting New Economy plans.

Staffing quandaries can be relieved to some extent by outsourcing, which is one reason that option is growing. But suppliers in "hot technology" areas face the same dearth of talent. And because we are at the beginning of this Internet-based New Economy, where each new service or product opens up even more opportunities, this situation is likely to last for quite some time. We discuss staffing in Chapter 10.

Besides staffing the IS department, CIOs also need to nurture an IT-knowledgeable workforce in business units, and then keep pace with those who have become IT-savvy. Thus, IS departments need to help line executives become comfortable *managing* the use of IT, enable employees to become comfortable *using* IT, and encourage everyone to be comfortable *exploring* innovative new uses of IT, especially on the Web with personal digital assistants (PDAs) and handheld communicators, and in creating consumer connections to the firm. IT-savvy organizations are the ones most likely to excel in this Internet-based economy.

In some cases, raising IT comfort levels means providing computers to those who do not have them, so they can explore the Web on their own. But with younger employees, who have been brought up with computers, IS departments face the opposite challenge—providing the access speed and computer power they expect.

Few corporate executives need assistance these days keeping abreast of the IT field because the publications they read now continually report on new developments. In fact, many IS executives now face "airline magazine syndrome," where the CEO or other top executive sends an e-mail to the CIO that says, "What are we doing on this?" and references an article from an airline magazine or a Web site about a "hot new technology" or a competitor's new use of the Internet.

As the rate of change in the IT field has increased, we have heard IS executives say they need to encourage IT experimentation, especially by people in the operating units. Here are the ideas of two researchers and one user company on how to do that—by supporting information technology "champions."

Encourage Championing of IT Projects. A champion is someone with a vision who gets it implemented by obtaining the funding, pushing the project over hurdles, putting his or her reputation on the line, and taking on the risk of the project, state Professors Cynthia Beath and Blake Ives.[10]

The first step in encouraging champions is to be able to recognize these people. They are likely to be people you already know about, and they may be doing things that make you uncomfortable, say Beath and Ives. For instance, they are probably already circumventing established project approval processes, they are creating isolated information systems, and they may be using nonstandard equipment. They may already be pursuing a vision of how IT can help their business, whether systems people help them or not.

These people are opinion leaders, and they have a reputation for creative ideas or being involved with innovations. They also have developed strong ties to others in their organization, and they command respect within the firm. They have the organizational power to get strategic innovations implemented.

Information systems champions need three things from information systems management, say the authors: information, resources, and support.

They need information. "Championing" an IT innovation is an information-intensive activity, note Beath and Ives. Therefore, champions need information, facts and expertise for persuading others that the technology will work. Information systems people can help champions gather and assess information about a technology's capabilities, its costs, risks of operation, and how it might be used in an experiment. Information systems staff also can help by sharing their expertise and by putting champions in contact with other experts, such as vendors or users of a new technology.

Information systems staff can assist champions in understanding current applications and data relevant to their project. Finally, they can help champions understand how the company manages change, because systems people are continually involved in implementing system changes throughout the enterprise.

They need resources. The authors cite Rosabeth Kanter, author of *ChangeMasters*,[11] who says champions most need staff time. Giving champions "free" staff time is especially helpful during the evaluation and persuasion portions of a project. But systems management can go even further, by assigning, say, information center consultants to help champions.

In addition to staff time, champions are likely to need material resources, such as hardware and software. These resources can be loaned to them free of charge or provided in some other way.

They need support.   Finally, champions need supporters, people who approve of what they are doing and give legitimacy to their project. It is important that IS management corroborate statements made about the technology by the champion. The champion does not need to know how the technology works, only how it might be used. The systems department should handle the technical aspects. Beath and Ives urge demonstrating the champion's claims about the technology, and promoting the technology to build enthusiasm for it and to win support from others.

Finally, IS management can help a champion win endorsement of upper management by helping to create the plans for introducing the new technology. The IT department can assist by contacting vendors and in choosing an appropriate implementation approach. All these supportive actions will improve the quality of the proposal and strengthen it in the eyes of management.

So, Beath and Ives encourage information systems management to make it easier for IT champions to arise and succeed. One company that supported champions is Aetna Life and Casualty.

CASE EXAMPLE

AETNA LIFE AND CASUALTY

Aetna Life and Casualty, a financial services company with headquarters in Hartford, Connecticut, sells employee benefit and pension programs to large companies; commercial insurance; and personal insurance, including health, life, automobile, and home.

Much of the IT work has been decentralized; therefore, the corporate administration department focuses on three functions, which they call "plan, build, and run." The operations group runs data center and telecommunication operations. The corporate technology services group assists divisions in selecting, building, and implementing computer systems.

The people and technology group also helps divisions build and implement successful systems; they emphasize the human perspective.

The "plan" function is the responsibility of the corporate technology planning group, which is meant to be a catalyst for introducing new technology. Its charter is to help Aetna understand and use breakthrough technologies throughout the company. By "breakthrough" they mean technologies that will increase performance by at least 100 percent. "We constantly seek to make the future credible by encouraging innovation, experimentation, and evaluation," a member of

(Case Continued)

this group told us. They see their job as encouraging end users to talk about new technologies and test them out in "real life" situations. The corporate technology planning group fosters discussions and experimentation in three ways.

They Seek Out Business Champions

The group tests technologies by cosponsoring end user projects, acting as a "magnet," to attract people who wanted to experiment with a technology. They hold workshops on specific technologies, publish one-page issue papers describing certain technologies, and talk to people in a wide number of functions.

Their goal is to find business "champions" who think a technology might solve their business problem. These people also needed to be willing to share the funding and direction of a pilot project using that technology. The users agree to let the planning group study their use and write about it. So, for a project to be funded, it must have a business champion and be aimed at solving a business problem.

In several cases, the group has found champions who recognize the need to test several technologies, some with expected results and others that might change future work life dramatically. These are "smart champions" because they see the value of investing in a portfolio of new technologies.

They Study Pilot Projects

In one pilot project of a 500-user communication system, the planning group did systematic research during this pilot, using before-and-after questionnaires to measure how attitudes changed. They looked to see whether "telephone tag" increased or decreased. They held focus group discussions. And they had some users keep daily diaries of their activities.

Based on this research, they concluded that the system would benefit a majority of employees. To then promote its use, they created a brochure and videotapes, which they handed off to the corporate operations group for the marketing and management of the system.

They Establish Steering Committees

Steering committees can be surrogate champions to guide and build support for a new technology. When the corporate technology group sees a technology that appears interesting, they may hold a one-day "magnet" session to find champions. Sometimes they find steering committees rather than individual champions, when a topic is really "hot." In one case, 200 people volunteered to do pilot projects. Because it made too large a group, a smaller steering committee was formed. It put on four seminars, got end users thinking about how they might use the technology, and oversaw some projects.

Challenges They Have Encountered

The technology planning group has encountered the following three challenges.

One is simply getting people's attention. When a technology is not immediately available, people do not want to take any action. But many technologies require a learning curve. Even when a technology is not readily available, people should be experimenting with it, so that the company has in-house knowledge when products do begin to appear. So, making a future technology credible to people today is one hurdle.

(Case Continued)

Keeping people in an experimental mode is another challenge. Once people are funded for a pilot, they want to do it right. They do not want to create a quick-and-dirty system, they want to create a production-quality system. It is hard to get people to create only quick, experimental systems.

The third challenge is making sure that use will really pay off. The planning group does not want small productivity improvements, they want orders-of-magnitude improvements—at least two-to-one to three-to-one payoffs. So they must constantly ask users: How do you know you will get this payback?

The group's goals are education and action. They want end users to be comfortable using future technologies and achieve a good payback at the same time. For more ideas on how to stimulate innovation, see *Managing Organizational Innovation.*[12]

How does such an approach make a company more IT savvy? By putting them in a position to more likely spot new opportunities, experiment with them, and put them into widespread use before their competitors. In a fast-changing world, nimbleness as a sign of being open to accepting emerging technologies is needed. ■

Create a Vision of the Future and Sell It

IS executives are no longer reactive, providing only support. They manage some of the most important tools for influencing the firm's future; therefore, they are becoming more "proactive" by helping to create a vision of the firm's future and its use of IT, and then selling those ideas to others.

What Is a Vision? It is a statement of how someone wants the future to be or believes it will be. It is used to set direction for an organization. One of the most often-cited examples is the compelling statement U.S. President John Kennedy made in 1961: "We will put a man on the moon, and return him safely to earth, by the end of the decade." And it did come to pass. On July 21, 1969, the United States landed a man on the moon. His vision provided a direction for the U.S. space program for a decade.

Beath and Ives[10] present several corporate visions:

- Otis Elevator: Any salesperson can completely order an elevator in a day.
- USAA, an insurance company for current and retired military officers: Policy holders can accomplish their objective in a single phone call or Web site visit.
- Rittenhouse Homes: Customers can get a house designed and built from a retail store.
- Fidelity Investments: Mutual funds can be repriced on an hourly, rather than daily, basis.

Why Develop a Vision? The word *vision* is seen everywhere because in turbulent times such as we face today, people are looking for some stability. A vision of a desirable future can provide stability when it sets direction for an organization. In the past, long-term strategies were created. They told how companies were going to get somewhere. Such multiyear plans are fine as long as the future is relatively predictable. But in today's environment, people cannot predict some of the most important future events because those events are likely to appear random, not linear or rational. In such times, direction setting and short-term explorations within that space are most appropriate. Today, most corporate visions have an IT underpinning—leveraging the Internet for business purposes. That vision sets their direction.

Who Should Create the Vision? Some CEOs are relying on their IS executive to create the corporate vision for using IT, because innovative uses of computers provide ways to significantly change the way companies do business. However, in a growing number of cases, it is the management team, including the CIO, that creates the vision, together. How can they come up with such inspirations? Listen to all ideas, no matter how crazy they sound, recommends Joel Barker,[13] a futurist.

Barker asks: What types of people are most likely to find new ways to solve problems? His answer: people who anticipate dramatic shifts that might occur in the future. These types of people are generally outsiders, he says, because they see things in different ways. They have faith in themselves but they are unpracticed in the field under question. So they bring a fresh viewpoint to problems in that field. They do not know what cannot be done, so they try many new things. These visionaries are generally young people just entering a field or older people who are changing careers—they both love to tinker.

Insiders have an investment in maintaining the status quo, because they understand the way a field operates. Outsiders do not have this investment, so they are more likely to come up with new solutions, says Barker.

Getting a Vision. We found two ways to create visions. One is to explore the present. Think about how it might be improved. For example, study the problems your company faces today and think of ways use of the Internet or handheld devices might solve those problems. A second approach to create a vision is to "scout" the future. Look at trends that appear likely to continue as well as changes that might disrupt current trends. The Internet has disrupted every field through e-mail and the Web. Handheld devices will do the same, as will broadband service to the home. What other disruptions lie ahead? People who uncover such shifts and take advantage of them early can give their firm a competitive edge.

Exploring the present. Peters[8] suggests four approaches. One is to ask: What bothers you most about the organization? When people are (or are not) working well with one another, what seems to be going on? Based on answers to these and similar questions, fix things that are wrong. Second, try participation by involving people inside and outside the firm to uncover their top 10 irritants and their 10 best experiences. Their ideas might inspire a vision. Third, clarify the vision, perhaps by meeting with subordinates to study the data and stories in detail, to refine shared views and values. And fourth, listen. Visions are seldom original, notes Peters. A visionary may simply be the person who focuses attention on an idea at a point in time, but that visionary is likely to have heard the idea from someone else.

Scouting the future.   The Institute for the Future[14] studies trends and publishes a 10-year forecast. The Institute helps organizations plan their long-term futures by discussing near-term and long-term outlooks in numerous areas such as the United States economy, demographics of the United States, U.S. labor force, technology, U.S. government, and international situations. They present issues that they see arising from the trends.

Another way to scout the future is to look for discontinuities, or shifts in trends. The people at the Institute for the Future call them "wild cards," Joel Barker calls them "paradigm shifts." By whatever name, they create major changes in the way people think about the world. The cell telephone is such a shift, concern for privacy is another, and computer-based sensors could be another.

Barker encourages people to "scout" the future looking for discontinuities by listening to screwy ideas and new ways to solve existing problems. The more people a company has scouting the future, the better off they are, says Barker, because the future is more likely to be revolutionary than evolutionary. By spotting a revolutionary event early, a company has an advantage over competitors that are not thinking about the future.

At a conference held by the Dooley Group,[15] attendees offered the following ideas on possible shifts that could change the way we live:

- Decline in the growth of cities
- Holograms to replace travel
- Small is better than big
- Personalized products (a market of one)
- Portable and personal two-way communications
- Small but powerful batteries
- Manufacturing in outer space
- A power shift from a manufacturing base to a knowledge base
- Deterring the aging process

Selling a Vision.   Once you have a vision about how your think the business should operate in the future, you need to sell that idea to others. Here are some recommendations.

Selling an idea requires understanding the marketplace, meaning, what potential customers *want* rather than what they *should have*. To find out what they want, listen. Listening is actually a potent form of selling. By understanding and fulfilling someone's needs, you help them be successful. And, by making the buyer successful, the seller becomes successful.

Often, personal relationships are the key to successfully selling an idea because people like to do business with people they know and trust. But if you believe you will not be effective, bring in a spokesperson.

Finally, to be a successful salesperson, keep your customers informed. If you can do nothing else to ease a bad situation, at least keep the other party informed. Customer care is important in selling products or ideas.

The following case example illustrates how one company developed and used a vision of IT to enhance its business performance.

CASE EXAMPLE

THE BOEING COMPANY

The Boeing Company, a major U.S. aerospace company with headquarters in Seattle, Washington, is the largest manufacturer of airplanes in the world. Over time, Boeing has developed three visions. The third is meant to carry them into the year 2010.

Vision 1: The Right Part in the Right Place at the Right Time

In the late 1960s, business was good at Boeing, but the company had a severe parts shortage that was hindering production. If a part was unavailable when needed, a tag—called a "traveler"—was affixed to the aircraft in place of the missing part. At that time, the company had 2,500–5,000 travelers per month attached to planes under construction.

To correct this situation, they created this vision: *the right part in the right place at the right time.* Over a number of years, Boeing installed 15 major information systems as well as dozens of smaller ones to implement this vision. The parts shortage problem used to be greatest when a new aircraft was being introduced. For example, when the 737 was rolled out, the number of travelers jumped to more than 8,000 a month, but later leveled out at fewer than 100 a month. By the time the 757 and 767 models were introduced, Boeing experienced barely noticeable increases in parts shortages.

Information systems helped them solve the parts shortage problem and implemented their vision. In doing so, however, Boeing created islands of auto-

mation; systems had trouble passing information back and forth to one another. Meanwhile the company's marketplaces changed, so they needed a new vision.

Addressing the Changing Marketplace

Deregulation led the commercial airlines to expand their hub-and-spoke operations, making shorter flights and smaller planes more the norm. Fluctuating fuel prices made fuel economy a major concern in aircraft design. Boeing also faced more intense competition from foreign as well as domestic aircraft companies. They believed their competitiveness in the commercial airplane market depended on their use of information systems in three ways:

1. *To increase their responsiveness to the market.* Systems would help them "design to cost"—meaning that planes would be designed with the aircraft purchaser's operational costs in mind. Information systems would also help Boeing keep aircraft delivery schedules flexible, so they could deliver products earlier than competitors. They also believed information systems would help them tailor an existing aircraft for a customer without having to completely redesign it.

2. *To make after-sale support more efficient.* With IT, they would be able to create airplane documentation based on original design data. They would be better able to manage

(Case Continued)

spare parts inventories worldwide. And they could use artificial intelligence in embedded diagnostics systems to do troubleshooting during maintenance.

3. *To help them streamline their design-and-build process.* Their vision was based on this third use of IT.

Vision 2: An Enhanced Information Stream

Boeing's vision was to create an *enhanced information stream,* because building and supporting an aircraft is really an information process. An enhanced information stream means that every step in designing and building an aircraft uses, adds to, and enhances a continuing stream of information.

First, a product is defined using a computer-aided design/computer-aided manufacturing (CAD/CAM) system. Then, each succeeding step in the design, build, and support process uses that digital information, adds to it, and enhances it. The various "islands of automation" feed into one "seamless information pipeline." Even after-sale support information is based on this enhanced digital description of a product.

This vision required a number of significant changes in the company. One was organizational. Boeing had to break down traditional organization barriers because the islands of automation were based on organizational structure. If information was to be used better, it had to cross organizational lines. One way Boeing restructured itself was to establish design/build teams composed of people from engineering and manufacturing as well as other disciplines.

Boeing also streamlined its design and manufacturing processes *before* they were automated, rather than automate the traditional ways of doing business. Finally, the company uses computers for as many jobs as possible, such as tracking engineering changes.

Vision 3: A Strategic Business Process Architecture

To develop a vision for both the company's business processes and information systems to the year 2010, Boeing reassessed their position and undertook a long-range study. The team found that the Boeing had often put the cart before the horse, in that IS plans drove business plans. The company had a clear vision for IT but none for business processes. The study therefore defines the world-class production processes the commercial airplane group and the defense and space group needed to succeed in 2010, as well as the computing infrastructure to support those processes.

The study began with Boeing defining their existing business process architecture, to understand how they conduct business and compare it to how they want to conduct business in 2010. The 2010 "strategic business process architecture" provides the basis for their IT architecture, as shown in Figure 2-7. To define this business vision, Boeing asked the following fundamental questions:

- What business processes should we use?
- What information do we need to accomplish these processes?
- How are the processes and information related?
- How is the data managed?
- Which hardware, software, and networks are required?

(Case Continued)

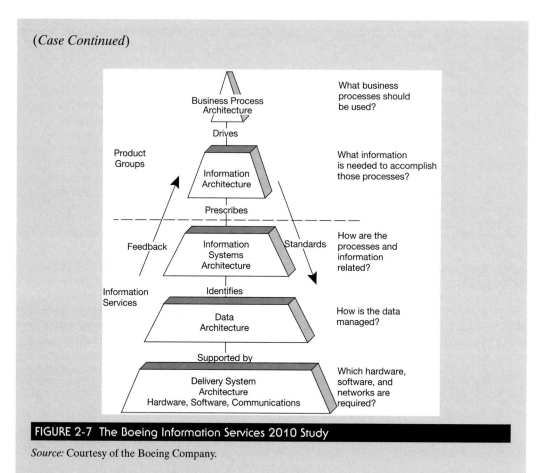

FIGURE 2-7 The Boeing Information Services 2010 Study

Source: Courtesy of the Boeing Company.

Once the future business processes were defined, Boeing developed them with the same intensity they used to design and develop a new airplane. This process required changing their legacy systems. "Owners" of business processes developed the migration plans, for the business processes and the computing infrastructure. ■

Implement an Information System Architecture

An architecture is a blueprint. It shows how the overall system, house, vehicle, or other product will look and how the parts interrelate. Designing a system architecture used to be considered strictly a technical issue; however, more and more it occurs when a company rethinks how it works, what it does, with whom it works, and so on, because the architecture needs to support new ways of operating. In e-commerce, it is a crucial component of the business planning. Let's return to SABRE's move onto the Web.

CASE EXAMPLE

THE SABRE SYSTEM

The system architecture underlying American Airline's Web site is modular. The existing SABRE computer reservation system serves as "the reservation service" module. Other modules perform the functions related to the Web. They included an input-output module for turning browser-entered data into data that can be processed by SABRE, and vice versa; an authentication module to verify users' identity; a session management module to manage each Web user's interaction with the system; and so on.

Due to this component-based architecture, it was fairly easy to add new functions, states Seybold.[2] Electronic ticketing, for example, was housed in its own module using appropriate components.

But, as so often happens, when American looked at the underlying databases, they found customer profiles in one database, AAdvantage member profiles in another, and NetSAAver subscriber profiles in a third. In a huge redesign, they consolidated and linked these databases to have just one profile for each flyer.

Another challenge was figuring out how to present a personalized Web site to each flyer. It required creating a data architecture, which, in turn, required tagging all the content shown on the Web site so that different pieces could be presented to different groups of flyers for different purposes. The decision was made to create an object database that would contain the tagged pieces of information. Tagging took much longer than anyone projected. To use this database to present personalized Web sites, American used Broadvision's One-on-One software and worked with two system integrators and design firms, says Seybold.

Finally, to do electronic booking, which required a more flexible database than the existing fares database, American created a separate fares database that contains tags such as "skiing" and "golf" attached to appropriate destinations. This database is accessed by "business rules" created by the system based on the choices customers make in their profiles. With this database, the system can make appropriate recommendations of places to travel based on the preferences stored in the profiles.

In all, American's Web site architecture has numerous pieces, including links between systems, components, modules, databases, data elements, and business rules. ■

The Emerging Role of Chief Technology Officer (CTO). Due to the increased importance of information systems architectures caused by the rise of e-commerce and e-business, the new job title of chief technology officer has appeared in IS departments during the past couple of years. Due to its newness, the role does not have one description, it has several. In most cases, the CTO is in charge of the technology and its architecture, whereas the CIO is in charge of the use of information technology. Therefore, the CTO is the chief IT architect and generally reports to the CIO, although there are cases where the CTO reports to the CEO.

In a few cases, CIOs have changed their title to CTO to emphasize their role as the technical head within their firm. This has been fairly rare.

In the dot-com world, the title CTO has been more prevalent than CIO. These CTOs have viewed the CIO as the one who runs a traditional IT department, including operations and maintenance. These CTOs preferred the title CTO to reflect their seemingly more strategic role as chief architect of the company's Web presence. Some even have taken on the title chief engineering officer, rather than CIO or CTO, to stress their job of "engineering" their firm's Web presence. Most dot-coms began life outsourcing all or most of the operational aspects of their IT department, so the CTO title might have appeared more appropriate than CIO. However, some dot-coms that have prospered have decided to bring their outsourced work in-house to gain more control of their own destiny. The role of these CTOs is morphing into that of CIO, as they broaden beyond the architectural aspects of IT to all the aspects discussed in this text. Yet, they may retain their CTO title, so the breadth of this new job title is likely to change as the field changes.

Nurture Relationships

An increasingly important role for CIOs is to develop and nurture relationships. Leadership in the development and use of IT now requires a "partnering," as exemplified in the IS Lite model. Three sets of partnerships are of particular importance:

- Relationships with senior management: CEO, CFO, COO, division presidents, and other members of the top management team
- Relationships with customers: both internal and external
- Relationships with suppliers and other external partners

Relationships with Senior Management. The relationship between CIOs and other senior executives, especially CEOs, is diversifying, says Chuck Gibson,[16] who has presented executive education seminars for years and is co-author of an article on the Stages of Growth theory described in Chapter 4.

At one end of the relationships spectrum is the traditional relationship between CEOs and CIOs. The CIO is expected to implement technology to support business plans in a boss-subordinate, and somewhat distant, relationship. Behind this is the view and practice of business and IT services as separable, and IT in a support role.

The emergence of the dot-coms has demonstrated a much closer relationship between the technologists and CEOs, Gibson points out. This closeness represents the other end of the spectrum. In dot-coms, the business is inseparable from IT. Acting as a team to respond to change, and build the infrastructure and applications quickly, CEOs know a lot more about IT and dot-com CIOs know a lot more about running the business because they see the two as inseparable. In fact, the CEO may be the CIO, or the operations vice president might be the CIO.

One of the reasons for the breadth of this relationship spectrum is our current place in history, says Gibson. We are at the technological discontinuity on the Stages of Growth diagram (Figure 4-7 on page 121) where the Micro Era is ending and the Network Era is beginning. Today, both eras coexist, but the relationships, issues, and discussions of Micro Era executives are different from those of Network Era executives.

While Micro Era executives are talking about implementing and extending their ERP system (inside-out view), Network Era executives are talking about how to achieve customer-led product design (outside-in view).

Of course these approaches fall along a spectrum, but the point is that not all CEO-CIO teams today talk about the same issues as they did, say, five years ago before the dot-coms merged IT and business. Moreover, there is a greater diversity of issues, roles for IT, and relationships required between CEOs and CIOs across businesses. As a result, it is far less appropriate to generalize about CEO-CIO discussions; the context now sets the agenda and the agendas now vary widely. Gibson speculates that as established companies integrate their business operations with their Internet operations, the relationship between CEO and CIO will become closer and the discussion points may coalesce as the requirements of the Network Era come into clearer focus and apply more generally to all businesses.

Relationships with Customers. A major set of partnerships revolves around internal and external customers of the IS function. Line managers and other users are the internal customers. Increasingly, the organizations' customers, who buy services and products, are becoming customers of the IS function also.

The first job, as noted earlier, is to build credibility with business peers, at all levels. This move toward credibility is happening most often in companies that use multifunctional teams to run systems projects. Peer-to-peer working can break down stereotypes, improve relationships, and hopefully lead to a "partnering" mentality, which seems to be the goal of most IS departments these days. It sets the stage for moving work to business-led teams where IT staff are participants but not the leaders.

As an example of getting in closer contact with internal customers, consider Federal-Mogul.

CASE EXAMPLE

FEDERAL-MOGUL

Federal-Mogul makes engine bearings, oil seals, ball bearings, fuel systems, electronics, and other parts for cars, light trucks, and heavy trucks. About one-half their parts are sold to original equipment companies such as Ford, General Motors, and Chrysler. The other half goes to the "after market," that is, to repair businesses. Most of the effort at the corporate IS department goes toward supporting the aftermarket portion of the business.

To reorient the IS department from cost reduction to customer service, IS management realized the staff would have to know as much about each line of business as the people in those business units. They therefore decided to model their department after an independent sales organization, even though they would not actually be an independent unit. It meant getting IS managers to know the line executives and their teams So, a new position was created—account executive.

Account Executives

The departments of sales and marketing, logistics, corporate staff, and world trade each have one account executive; manufacturing has two. They report directly to their respective line executive and indirectly to the CIO. They supervise members of the IS staff that specialize in building systems for that function. In effect, the line executives have their own IS manager and IS staff. The line executives are also in charge of their own IS budget for that group. Thus, each month, the functional executives see what they are spending on IS support, and they can reallocate resources as they choose.

Besides managing their functional IS staff, the account executives are also responsible for keeping their function's IT plans coordinated with corporate direction. Decisions concerning which requests to implement are frequently based on how well the requested work matches the firm's strategic direction. IS staff formerly filled all user requests and were measured on user satisfaction. That measure was appropriate because users were mid-level managers. Now, however, the users are top management, so the focus is strategic impact.

Benefits

Federal-Mogul is deriving several benefits from this organizational structure. One, users accept systems changes more readily because they sense the desire of the IS department to be of better service. Two, line executives more clearly understand their IT responsibilities. Because they now are in charge of their own IT budget, they are more involved in systems planning. Three, the change signaled a change in culture to IS professionals "partnering" with business unit staff. And four, IS executives have spurred line management to plan further ahead to provide longer lead times to install the supporting systems.

Challenges

One challenge in this structure is encouraging the account executives to think beyond the function they serve. It is being accomplished by their reporting indirectly to the CIO, who expects them to include companywide considerations in their own systems planning. They get together to discuss cross-functional implications of future plans.

Other challenges in this new arrangement are career paths and training. With only two levels of IS professionals in each functional area, little career growth occurs in that area, except to move back into corporate IS management or into the line group.

One key to making this approach work is getting the support of the business executives. The CIO initially had to push for this closer working relationship by telling them the IS staff would better support their business. Interestingly, one account executive who sought the priorities in the business unit found the priorities of the top executive differed from those of his middle managers. This discrepancy encouraged the group to reexamine their priorities, and led to a meeting with the company president, who in turn explained his priorities.

A second key to success is placing the most senior people in the account executive positions. Federal-Mogul has people who have had 15 to 20 years of IT experience, understand the business, have credibility with the users, and have bought into the philosophy of the job. In all, the vice president of information services is optimistic this step toward partnering will pay off in even better use of IT resources. ■

Relationships with Suppliers and Alliance Partners.   Due to the fast-moving changes in many industries driven by the move to e-commerce and the huge investments needed to react to these changes, IS departments are establishing cooperative external relationships with all sorts of suppliers to put in needed systems quickly. In such relationships, both supplier and customer know more about each other's future plans, they work more closely on projects, and they may even undertake some joint ventures. Because it has not been the traditional mode of working between IS departments and vendors, some new forms of partnering mechanisms need to be developed.

Another trend that has required IS has been supplier rationalization by businesses. IS must work more closely with the suppliers' executives to forge closer working relationships with suppliers that remain after their enterprise reduces suppliers from thousands to tens. Internally within IS departments, the same reduction is occurring. IS departments not only outsource their help desks, PC acquisition-maintenance-disposal, data center, network management, and other functions, they also establish "deeper" relationships with these suppliers. They tell them of future plans, do joint planning, perhaps work together on projects, and so forth. They treat these suppliers more as partners than as suppliers. This trend has opened up the need for vendor relationship management techniques, training, job holders, and role models. As the IS Lite model and Forrester Research propose, managing suppliers will be a major job in the new IS department. In Chapter 8 we explain what Eastman Kodak has done to develop working procedures with its main outsourcers.

Summary of Responsibilities

These then are the six responsibilities of CIOs. Understanding the business, and requiring the staff to do the same, are preambles for becoming part of the business. Establishing credibility of the department, while it focuses mainly on the supply-side job of keeping legacy systems up and running, can also foster the strategic role of bringing in new systems on time and on budget. It may mean outsourcing a major portion of the work, such as e-commerce links via the Net. Creating capable staff and fostering IT-savvy business people both portend closer IS-business ties. Visioning, too, is a joint IS-business affair because it revolves around e-commerce. Implementing an architecture moves IS into a strategic role, as does nurturing relationships.

The role of IT is growing. The role of the IS department has gone through several stages of evolution, and will continue to evolve. It is possible that business teams will one day handle IT just as they now need to handle other resources—people and money.

CONCLUSION

The transformation IS departments are grappling with these days, says Dick Dooley,[15] is learning how to create organizations where IT decision making is shared. The main responsibility for managing the *use* of IT needs to pass to the line, while the management of the IT infrastructure is retained by the IS group. This transformation is reflected in the following saying attributed to du Pont, says Dooley:

- "We used to do it *to* them"—meaning, IS required end users to obey strict rules for getting changes made to systems, submitting job requests, and so on.
- "Next, we did it *for* them"—meaning, IS moved to taking a service orientation.
- "Now, we do it *with* them," which reflects "partnering."
- "We are moving toward teaching them *how to do it themselves.*"

To achieve this transformation, CIOs must play a leadership role in their enterprise and develop partnerships with senior management, internal and external customers, and suppliers.

QUESTIONS AND EXERCISES

Review Questions

1. Describe the five waves of innovation from Primozic and colleagues.
2. Describe the three ways American Airlines is reaching the consumer.
3. What four trends are nibbling away at traditional IS functions?
4. According to Cox what are the four areas that make up the overall responsibility of the IS function?
5. What are the two major roles IS departments are likely to play in the future?
6. What is IS Lite?
7. What are the three stages in the LifeScan alignment roadmap?
8. According to Forrester, who will manage IT in the future?
9. Briefly summarize the CIO's six areas of responsibility.
10. The text suggests seven ways to "Understand the Business". Briefly summarize these seven ways.
11. Describe the needs of champions.
12. Describe Boeing's three visions.
13. What three kinds of partnerships must be developed by the IS executive?
14. Describe the job of an account executive at Federal-Mogul.

Discussion Questions

1. A vision is not the responsibility of the CIO. It is the responsibility of the CEO or the top management team. Agree or disagree? Why?
2. Present both sides of the argument that business process owners will/will not take over management of IT.
3. What is going to happen to organizations whose senior executives do not appreciate the value of data processing, let alone information or knowledge processing?

Exercises

1. There is considerable discussion of the evolving role of the chief information officer. At one time, the term "CIO" was defined as "career is over." Find at least two articles on the role of CIOs that make conflicting arguments; summarize the differences.
2. There is also much discussion about partnering between IS and line organizations. Find at least two articles that discuss such partnering and summarize the factors they mention that contribute to successful partnering.
3. Contact the CIO in an organization. What is his or her title? How does he or she perceive the leadership role of the job? How do these characteristics relate to those in the text? How is he or she encouraging partnering with line departments?
4. Some CIOs in dot-coms would rather be known as chief technology officers rather than chief information officers. They see their job as providing the e-commerce infrastructure, so they see themselves as engineers, technologists. Do you see this interpretation as a step forward for CIOs or a step backward? Discuss your thinking.

REFERENCES

1. Primozic, Kenneth, Edward Primozic, and Joe Leben, *Strategic Choices: Supremacy, Survival, or Sayonara*, McGraw-Hill, New York, 1991.

2. Seybold, Patricia with Ronni Marshak, *Customers.com*, Times Books, New York, 1998.

3. Cox, George, *Time to Reshape the IS Department?* Wentworth Research Program (now part of Gartner Executive Programs), Egham, England, June 1994.

4. Woolfe, Roger, *IS Lite*, Gartner Executive Programs, 56 Top Gallant, Stamford CT 06904, July 2000.

5. Yepez, Hugo, Dorothy Cooney, and Barbara McNurlin, "Aligning the Information Management Department with the Business at LifeScan, a Johnson & Johnson Company," Third Place Winner in 1999 paper competition, Society for Information Management, 401 N. Michigan Ave., Chicago, IL 60601, www.simnet.org.

6. Cameron, Bobby, Ron Shevlin, and Aaron Hardisty, *Death of IT*, Forrester Research, January 2000, *www.Forrester.com*.

7. Parker, Marilyn, Robert Benson with Ed Trainor, *Information Economics: Linking Information Technology and Business Performance*, Prentice Hall, 1988, European edition 1989; Japanese edition, 1990.

8. Peters, Tom. *Thriving on Chaos: Handbook for a Management Revolution*, Alfred A. Knopf Inc., New York, 1987, 561 pages.

9. Joseph Izzo, The Teton Group, 13428 Maxella Ave, #414, Marina del Rey, CA 90292, personal interview.

10. Beath, Cynthia and Blake Ives, "The information technology champion: Aiding and abetting, care and feeding," *Proceedings of the Twenty-First Annual Hawaii International Conference on System Sciences*, Vol. IV, pp. 115–123. Available from the IEEE Computer Society, Los Alamitos, CA.

11. Kanter, Rosabeth, *ChangeMasters*, Simon & Schuster, NY, 1983, 432 pages.

12. Johnson, Bonnie and Ron Rice, *Managing Organizational Innovation*, Columbia University Press, 136 S. Broadway, Irvington-on-Hudson, NY 10533, June 1987.

13. Barker, Joel, *Discovering the Future: The Business of Paradigms*, Infinity Limited, 831 Windbreak Trail, Lake Elmo, MN 55042, 1985.

14. The Institute for the Future, 2740 Sand Hill Road, Menlo Park, CA 9405.

15. The Dooley Group, 1380 Kenilwood Lane, Riverwoods, IL 60015.

16. Chuck Gibson, MIT Sloan School's Center for Information Systems Research (CISR), personal interview.

CHAPTER

3

TODAY'S STRATEGIC IMPERATIVE: E-BUSINESS

INTRODUCTION

In the 1990s, the commercialization of the Internet set off a revolution in the use of information technology for conducting business. Old assumptions about the cost structure and geographic limits of networked systems became irrelevant; it became possible to build systems with worldwide reach quickly and inexpensively. Business people responded by creating entirely new types of businesses and fundamentally altering existing businesses. The once limited "strategic use" of IT became widespread. New terms were created to label this revolution: electronic commerce (more commonly called e-commerce) and electronic business (e-business).

We define "strategic use" of IT as "having a significant, long-term impact on a firm's growth rate, industry, and revenue." Historically, the strategic use of IT has followed an evolution from improving internal processes and structure of a firm, to improving the firm's products, services, and relationships with its customers, to improving its processes and relationships with its business partners. We characterize these stages of evolution into three roles:

1. Looking inward: To improve processes and structure
2. Looking outward: Incorporated in products and services
3. Looking across: Linking to other organizations

As Figure 3-1 illustrates, these three roles take an internal-external view of the business world. Internally, IT has been used to improve business processes and change organizational structure. Examples of inward-looking strategic uses of IT include business process reengineering and enterprise resource planning (ERP) systems. Outward-looking systems connect the firm more closely to customers or create new products or services. Examples of outward applications are package tracking systems for delivery companies and reservation systems used by airlines, hotels, and rental car companies. Systems that look across have links to business partners to improve transactional efficiency or create new business opportunities. Such systems, known as interorganizational systems, include electronic data interchange (EDI) systems and cross-industry reservation systems.

Each of these strategic roles of IT shares a common characteristic: Stated simply, the strategic value of IT comes from communication, which allows companies to reorganize and integrate business processes within and across boundaries. With the rapid growth of the Internet, a public network with low communication costs, many of the traditional strategic systems are being replaced with Internet-based, e-business applications.

FIGURE 3-1 Strategic Uses of Information Systems

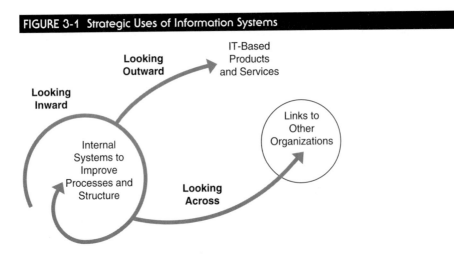

What Is E-Business?

We define e-business as the use of telecommunication networks, particularly the Internet, to conduct business transactions. E-business can be divided into three categories (see Figure 3-2), which map directly into the three strategic roles of IT—inward, outward, and across:

- Business-to-employee: Intranet-based applications internal to a firm
- Business-to-consumer: Internet-based applications for a firm's customers
- Business-to-business: Extranet-based applications for a firm's business partners

The terms *e-commerce* and *e-business* have led to some confusion. E-commerce was coined originally to refer to all three categories. However, as the consumer-oriented e-commerce—the buying and selling of goods over the Internet—began to receive considerable attention both in the IT industry and in the popular press, e-commerce began to refer only to the business-to-consumer applications. With this more limited interpretation of e-commerce, the term *e-business* took on the more inclusive meaning. Even though we recognize the ongoing debate over meanings, we use the term *e-business* to encompass all three arenas.

E-Business Drivers

At first, the rapid growth of e-business seems astounding, but a closer look reveals some clear reasons for the growth. Use of Internet technologies has provided several key components that have accelerated the acceptance of e-business:

- Wide access to a public network
- Standard communication protocol
- Standard user interface

Earlier systems that linked firms with their customers or business partners required private networks with proprietary applications. Indeed, the private, proprietary

FIGURE 3-2 Types of E-Business

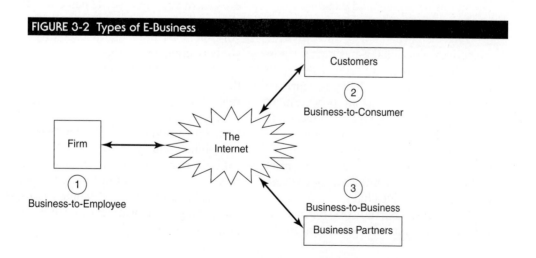

nature of the systems was key to their strategic value. The high cost of implementation, training, and use of these systems provided a means of locking in customers and created barriers to competitors building similar systems. But the high cost also limited access to the systems, thus restricting their widespread use; only large firms could afford to build such systems. For example, pre-Internet data estimated that 95 percent of the *Fortune* 500 companies in the United States used EDI, while only 2 percent of all U.S. companies used EDI.

Because e-business applications run over a public network, the Internet, access and communications costs are drastically reduced. Further, with standardized communication protocols and user interfaces, implementation and training costs are far lower. As a result, a much broader set of users and firms has access to the systems, allowing rapid growth. Indeed, in just a few years, use of the Internet for e-mail and company Web sites has become standard business practice.

RESEARCH REPORT

THE E-BUSINESS VALUE CHAIN

The research firm Economist Intelligence Unit (EIU) and the consulting firm KPMG surveyed 331 industry executives and held personal interviews with 42 senior executives throughout North America, Europe, and Asia. The resulting report, entitled *The E-Business Value Chain: Winning Strategies in Seven Global Industries,*[1] assessed cross-industry trends and examined winning strategies in seven industries.

Fifty-seven percent of the surveyed executives stated that e-business is transforming their company's role within their industry. E-business is changing nearly all that companies do, from procurement of supplies to delivery of products and services. Furthermore, new industry e-entrants, value-added services, and delivery channels are shifting the boundaries within and between industries, greatly altering existing value chains.

The greatest barriers to e-business lie within the corporation, according to the report. The three most formidable barriers to implementing an e-business strategy are the need to redesign business processes, the dearth of e-business skills, and the lack of integration between front-end and back-end systems. Significant involvement by senior management was also found to be crucial to the success of e-business strategies, yet 42 percent of the companies experienced inadequate involvement by their senior executives in strategy implementation.

The respondents were evenly split on the question of whether to form a separate e-business unit. Fifty-two percent believed that the e-business operation had to be integrated into the lines of business for online and physical operations to truly support each other. Others argued that e-business operations must be independent and flexible to compete successfully; integration with existing business bogs them down.

(Case Continued)

More than a third (37 percent) of the survey respondents noted that a reluctance to cut out intermediaries is a major obstacle to their e-business plans. However, the Internet is improving both internal and external collaboration *between* business partners. Seventy-four percent considered this ease of collaboration to be a highly important objective, and most expect improved knowledge management to play an important role in achieving this goal.

Nearly half of the respondents believed that within 18 months online business-to-business exchanges (where companies buy and sell goods and services from each other) will be important to their own supply chains.

But, to play a crucial role, these online marketplaces will have to evolve from being mere auctions for commodities to full-service markets that allow companies to buy customized goods.

According to the study, the top e-business goal is to provide value-added products and services—to both meet the escalating demands of customers and keep their goods and services from becoming commodities. Another top goal is reaching new customers, particularly overseas. For some companies, e-business is not just an opportunity to tap a larger pool of customers, but a way to target specific groups and meet their particular needs. ■

LOOKING INWARD: BUSINESS-TO-EMPLOYEE

The primary e-business way to reach employees is via "intranets." Intranets are private company networks that use Internet technologies and protocols, and possibly the Internet itself. Applications use the Web interface and are accessed through browsers; communications use several protocols, including hypertext transfer protocol (HTTP) for addressing Web sites, hypertext markup language (HTML) for Web content structuring, and transmission control protocol/Internet protocol (TCP/IP) for network routing. The result is open systems using nonproprietary technologies.

The benefits from intranets have been significant: wider access to company information, more efficient and less expensive system development, and decreased training. By using an intranet's open-system architecture, companies can significantly decrease the cost of providing companywide information and connectivity. One of the most important attributes of intranets is that they support any make or brand of user device—from high-end workstation to PC, to laptop, to handheld device—as well as existing databases and software applications. Such interconnectivity has been the promise of open systems for many years. The Internet provides the connecting standard protocols to make the open-system promise a reality.

Furthermore, investments in a companywide electronic infrastructure are significantly less than building a proprietary network. Companies only need the servers, browsers, and a TCP/IP network to build an intranet. If, in addition, the company wishes to use the infrastructure of the Internet to geographically extend its intranet, the only additional components needed are firewalls to keep the public from accessing the intranet and local access to the Internet. Figure 3-3 shows the basic architecture of an

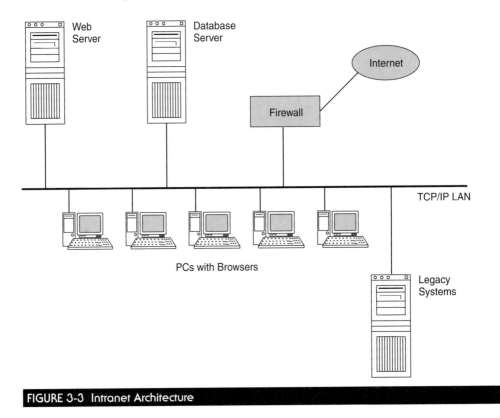

FIGURE 3-3 Intranet Architecture

intranet. The link to the Internet allows the company to expand its intranet worldwide easily and inexpensively—a significant benefit that was unthinkable before the Internet.

Finally, because an intranet uses the browser interface, users do not need extensive training on different products. And, due to the HTML standard and the availability of easy-to-use Web page authoring tools, employees can easily create their own Web pages for whatever purpose they need. As a result, all employees are potential site creators, reducing the IS department's programming bottleneck, while adhering to companywide standards. And companies only need to record information in one place, where it can be kept up-to-date for access by all employees no matter where in the world they are located. In the following case, Microsoft[2] shows how it effectively implemented an intranet for human resource management.

CASE EXAMPLE

MICROSOFT

Like many successful companies, Microsoft Corporation views its employees as its greatest asset. The company has always prided itself on hiring smart, highly productive people who are focused on developing innovative products, programs, and services. To help ensure ongoing employee satisfaction and enthusiasm, Microsoft provides a robust human resources (HR) benefits package, including such perks as stock option grants, an employee discount stock-purchasing program, comprehensive health care, and a matching 401K retirement savings program.

In the past decade, Microsoft has grown from fewer than 10,000 employees to more than 30,000, contributing to a significant increase in the resources needed to manage the company benefits programs. Early on, all HR materials, including benefits information, enrollment forms, and time cards, resided on several file servers and in stacks of paper forms, making it difficult for employees to easily and efficiently locate needed HR information. Responding to the need to streamline HR processes, access to information, and completion of transactions, the HR department decided to design a "one-stop shopping" intranet portal to better service Microsoft employees. To that end, HR Web was developed in 1995 to be the foundation of a growing number of specialized employee benefits and HR applications.

HR Web is a secure intranet site that provides Microsoft employees with pro-tected access to various benefit enrollment forms, investment programs, retirement savings planning, and health care programs. Being Web-based, the system makes it convenient for employees to electronically submit timecards, report absences, view pay stubs, and access human resources news and information as well as view campus maps, commuting options, and community volunteer opportunities. HR Web is integrated with SAP R/3, Microsoft's enterprise resource planning system. This integration has increased HR productivity and decreased the time spent by all other employees providing information to the HR staff. With thousands of employees worldwide accessing this HR portal each month, HR Web has eliminated the reuse of more than 200 paper forms and associated processing costs, and saved Microsoft well over 1 million dollars each year.

The direct benefits of HR Web include:

- Streamlined processes, information, and transactions for Microsoft's human resources department.
- Reduced postal and material costs by 75–90 percent.
- Saved Microsoft over $1 million a year and has eliminated more than 200 paper forms.
- Reduced the time employees spend searching for HR information and forms.
- Streamlined workflow by directly interacting with SAP R/3.

(Case Continued)

The initial HR Web intranet site took two people only four weeks to develop. Since then, HR Web has been modified to incorporate new capabilities, to take advantage of new technologies, and to integrate with other corporate systems. Employee information, such as name, social security number, manager, hire date, and employment status, is gathered directly from the HR module of SAP R/3. Every 24 hours this data is automatically replicated to an SQL Server 2000-based database used by HR Web to reduce redundant manual data input and ensure that employee information is current.

In addition to direct access to benefits enrollment and management via a benefits feature of HR Web, other features within HR Web simplify the process for reporting vacation and sick time. These features are designed to automatically determine the status of an employee, such as exempt or nonexempt, and display the appropriate absence-reporting forms or time cards, in addition to calculating remaining vacation and sick time hours. The replacement of a paper-based time-card system and e-mail-based absence-report systems with HR Web has resulted in a 50 percent reduction in processing time, over the legacy absence reporting methods.

The secure payroll area of HR Web includes several electronic features, including an online direct-deposit feature that allows employees to determine how they want their paychecks allocated. A second payroll feature provides each employee with a comprehensive view of individual pay stubs, including earning statements for the entire fiscal year, month, or pay period in addition to W-4 tax resources for U.S. employees. Mov-

ing to this paperless payroll system virtually eliminated the need for manual processing and significantly reduced the need to print and mail checks, which led to Microsoft saving more than $600,000 a year.

The employee investment programs feature in HR Web supports some of Microsoft's most valued employee benefits, including the matching 401K retirement savings plan, the employee stock purchase program (ESPP), and Microsoft stock options. Using HR Web's employee investment programs feature, employees have secure access to view-only pages that provide confidential records of their stock-purchase and stock option grant exercise history. In addition to providing these services, ESPP maintains a real-time Microsoft stock ticker, the history of Microsoft's stock splits, and information to help employees navigate tax-related issues. Employees can also use the ESPP application to enroll or withdraw in the program, receiving a full refund on their contribution at any time. By managing the employee stock purchase program via the intranet, HR Web has helped to dramatically reduce costs associated with administering stock options and stock purchases. For example, the stock-option application provides an individualized account of an employee's stock-option history, including how many options an employee has, how many options the employee has vested, as well as what options have been exercised. The HR department relies on this application to distribute stock-option grants for new hires after a review period, and to confirm when an employee exercises options. Finally, by maintaining all stock options

(Case Continued)

records online, HR Web has helped reduce the time required to distribute option exercise confirmations—from 15 hours to 5 hours.

Collectively Microsoft employees access HR Web more than 100,000 times each month. HR Web continues to evolve by taking advantage of the latest technology, resulting in continual improvement and greater value to employees. ∎

Managing Intranets

Although intranets offer many advantages to companies, they create a number of managerial concerns as well. Two key issues are figuring out how to integrate legacy systems into the intranet and deciding how much control of the systems should be decentralized. A large amount of the information a company wants to make available to its employees resides in legacy systems, but the proprietary interfaces on those legacy systems make it difficult to integrate them into an intranet. Enterprises have two basic options, either leave the legacy systems untouched and replicate the data for the intranet, as Microsoft did in its HR Web system, or modify the legacy systems to allow direct access to their data through a browser. With a history of failures in IT projects, many companies resist modifying working legacy systems for fear that the systems may stop functioning properly.

Due to the ease with which Web sites can be created, many employees have built their own, leading to a proliferation of sites with company information. As employees build more and more Web sites, employees' desktops become cluttered with confusing icons and links, many of which are obsolete or incorrect. In addition, potentially valuable company information is stored on independent sites—sites most likely not under central control. The result is problems of data redundancy, integrity, and security. Managers face the old trade-off between central control, which provides greater data management, and decentralized control, which provides more timely and relevant data.

One proposed solution to this control conundrum is to create a corporate portal to act as the gateway to the firm's internal resources, information, and Internet services. This solution brings access to company data and applications together in a single site. Employees simply need a browser. At the same time, the portal provides IS management with a way to monitor and control the growth of internal Web sites, and the portal provides a link to Internet resources external to the company, such as sites for industry news, customers, and business partners.

Although the concept of corporate portals seems straightforward, many firms are reluctant to implement them because portals require changing existing systems and processes. These same reasons are why firms have had so many problems implementing enterprisewide ERP applications. One approach to manage the inherent problems and risks involves developing separate departmental or divisional portals, such as sales, HR, operations, and finance portals. These portals can then be linked to form a corporate portal.

CASE EXAMPLE

KPMG

The accounting and consulting firm, KPMG, has more than 20,000 employees accessing its intranet and more than 100 content managers responsible for developing and maintaining it. Recognizing the true potential value of an intranet, KPMG wanted to move its intranet beyond simply an electronic source of notices and forms; it wanted a truly interactive site that would provide information that employees act upon. The goal was an intranet that was used as a strategic business tool.

KPMG thus began negotiating with outside firms to provide content and functionality to its intranet. In the United Kingdom, KPMG added a service to its intranet called FT Discovery, sourced from the *Financial Times* newspaper. FT Discovery provides immediate access to critical business intelligence from more than 4,000 information sources. The company also settled on Corporate Navigator from Story Street Partners, a Cambridge-based company. The system shares the look and feel of KPMG's intranet but provides in-depth advice on where to go for information on issues and companies important to KPMG. The information is prefiltered, presorted, and presearched by Story Street Partners.

So to make its site more "actionable," KPMG added content provided by third parties. It has become "the" way to keep content fresh and global. ■

LOOKING OUTWARD: BUSINESS-TO-CONSUMER

Business-to-consumer e-business is the most widely reported form of e-business. It entails linking a company to its customers over the Internet, providing a means of selling products or services, and managing customer relations. Nearly every type of product can now be purchased online, from books, CDs, and flowers, to automobiles, legal services, and wine. But, success is not easily achieved. Arguably the most visible e-retailer, Amazon.com, continues to have its business viability questioned. Levi Strauss, a leader in the use of IT for strategic purposes, was ahead of its target for online sales, yet, in January 2000, it quit selling jeans over the Internet. Senior managers stated that selling over the Internet was a complex proposition and management had better uses for company funds.

The advantages of selling online are numerous and seem obvious. Figure 3-4 lists some of the many advantages. Indeed, it is not difficult to find success stories, such as Dell Computer, eTrade, and Cheap Tickets. However, the potential problems are also numerous but not so obvious. Figure 3-5 lists some of the potential problems faced in creating a successful business-to-consumer system.

FIGURE 3-4   Advantages of B2C E-Business

Global accessibility: The Internet eliminates geographic boundaries.

Reduced order processing: Automated order processing improves efficiency.

Greater availability: The company is available online 24 hours a day, 7 days a week.

Closer customer relationships: With a direct link to customers, the company can quickly address concerns and customize responses.

Increased customer loyalty: With improved customer service and personalized attention comes greater customer loyalty.

New products and services: With direct links to customers, the company can provide information-based products and services.

Direct marketing: Manufacturers can bypass retailers and distributors, selling directly to customers.

FIGURE 3-5   Potential B2C Problems

Technical: The information systems are not always reliable or may be poorly designed.

Logistics: Getting products to customers around the world in a timely manner brings "physical" barriers to the virtual business.

Personnel: Few people have expertise in dealing with the new environment, both in technical and business arenas.

Legal: Doing business across geographic boundaries means dealing with multiple legal systems.

Competitive response: The ease of creating a Web presence brings low barriers to entry for competitors.

Transparent prices: Customers can easily compare prices across Web sites, reducing profit margins.

Greater competition: The elimination of geographic boundaries means a firm must compete with competitors from around the world.

CASE EXAMPLE

STOP & SHOP SUPERMARKET

The online grocery business has had a turbulent beginning with well-publicized startup companies like HomeGrocer, Webvan Group, and HomeRuns.com all losing money. Yet Accenture expects online grocery shopping to thrive, reaching $60 billion to $85 billion by 2007. *Business Week*[3] reported on the strategy of one competi-

tor, Stop & Shop Supermarket. As an 85-year-old New England grocer, Stop & Shop has something the others don't: retail bricks with the clicks.

In order to rapidly gain a foothold in cyberspace, Stop & Shop's parent company, Royal Ahold, bought a 51 percent controlling interest in Peapod, the Illinois

(Case Continued)

delivery service that has been selling groceries online since 1990. This move, criticized by some because Peapod's operation was losing money, allowed Stop & Shop to combine its expertise in the physical marketplace with Peapod's expertise in the e-commerce world. Stop & Shop's strategy was to compete by combining online and physical shopping. Stop & Shop's biggest rivals are Webvan and HomeGrocer, which merged in mid-2000. The combined company, Webvan Group, is pursuing a pure online-only sales strategy.

Stop & Shop believes its customers will want to stroll down both physical and virtual aisles; they will not use one or the other method of shopping exclusively. They will shop online primarily for speed and convenience. They could shop the virtual aisle in half the time of the physical aisle. In addition, the online site provides services not available in the physical store. For example, health-conscious consumers can sort products by nutritional value—keeping track of saturated fat or carbohydrates.

Customers are required to open an online account with a credit card. After completing their shopping and while checking out, they are asked to choose a 2-hour delivery window, no sooner than the next day. When the driver arrives at their doorstep, buyers can either leave the bill on their credit card or pay by check or debit card. Stop & Shop and other companies are also testing new types of "mail boxes": climate-controlled boxes at the customer's door into which groceries can be left, thus eliminating the need for someone to be at home to accept delivery.

On the downside, Stop & Shop's online shoppers will not find many bargains. The retailer's newspaper circulars often beat its online prices, and some customers must pay for delivery. Boston residents who buy less than $60 worth of goods pay $7.50—otherwise, delivery is free. Connecticut residents must order at least $50, although delivery is always free. As with other e-business retailers, Stop & Shop must find out how much consumers are willing to pay for convenience and new services.

On the operations side, Stop and Shop is finding that it must make adjustments. Originally, it filled online orders by having employees pull groceries off the shelves in its more than 200 stores on the East Coast. Other online competitors were filling orders from large, centralized distribution facilities. Acknowledging that the centralized facilities were more cost-efficient, Stop & Shop is now building distribution centers adjacent to its larger stores. These centers will be used to fill online orders.

Even though the future of the online grocery business is far from certain, Stop & Shop is aggressively pursuing its e-commerce strategy. Current activities include accelerating the online purchase process and providing in-store Internet access so that consumers can review previous purchases. In addition, by 2002, the grocer plans to offer special wireless Internet content for mobile computer users who want to shop but not stop. ∎

The E-Business Model

Successful selling over the Internet entails much more than setting up a Web site and taking orders. It involves organizing the entire value chain around the Internet. As shown in Figure 3-6, the retail value chain crosses several organizations. Success in e-business requires retailers to rethink their value chain from end to end, determining where they can exploit technology to add value. E-business affords new opportunities to redefine value to customers and add value by redesigning relationships with business partners.

Redefining Customer Value. Information technology has changed what consumers value. They now expect service to be fast; the key term is "demanding on-demand." E-business allows firms to respond by drastically reducing the time it takes to respond to customer requests for company, product, and price information, to process an order, and to get products to customers.

Consumers also expect convenience. They want more than one-stop shopping, they want a single point of contact in the company. E-business allows gathering and managing customer information so that whoever interacts with the customer has all the relevant customer information at hand.

Consumers further expect personalization of service. E-business allows direct, ongoing communication with customers, so that preferences and buying patterns can be tracked and analyzed to provide individual service. By reducing the time to process orders, e-business allows firms to customize products to individual customers. Thus, products from music CDs to automobiles can be made to order.

E-business forces companies to rethink their pricing of products and services. Consumers now have access to a wide range of competitive prices and sellers for products, driving down profit margins and the price of products. Some observers have speculated that e-business will drive profit margins to miniscule levels. Although some initial studies have confirmed the lower prices for goods purchased online, the highest volume sellers do not always have the lowest price. Prices are offset by branding, awareness, and customer trust. Indeed, most successful online retailers spend a significant amount of money on marketing and customer acquisition through traditional media, such as TV and magazine advertisements, to build brand awareness and customer trust.

Redesigning Relationships with Business Partners. Many retail value chains include intermediary firms between the manufacturer and customers. The intermediaries can be distributors or sellers of the products, such as travel agents, automobile dealerships, department stores, and real estate brokers. E-business allows for "disintermediation,"

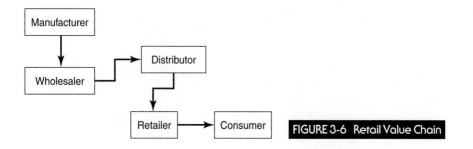

FIGURE 3-6 Retail Value Chain

which means bypassing intermediaries by directly linking customers to the manufacturer. For example, airlines now sell tickets to consumers over the Internet, saving commissions to travel agents.

E-business also allows the development of "virtual organizations." In a virtual organization, a firm does not own parts of the value chain but rather controls the coordination of other firms to appear as a single firm. The following case illustrates how one company, Garden.com,[4] created a virtual organization.

CASE EXAMPLE

GARDEN.COM

Many e-business models and strategies are being employed today, some revisions of old models, some entirely new. Garden.com is cultivating a whole new business model—a *virtual warehouse.*

Started in September 1995, Garden.com offers a wide range of plants, gardening products, gifts, and services. Its founders looked at the large, highly fragmented gardening industry—at $46.8 billion, it was more than twice the size of the book industry that Amazon.com took online—and figured it was ripe with opportunity. The difficulties of warehousing live plants had prevented any single player from capturing more than 1 percent of the market. The question was how to capitalize on the capabilities of the Internet in order to capture a large portion of the market.

The standard e-business strategy for retailers—replacing paper catalogs with electronic ones and using large, centralized warehouses to minimize inventory and order processing costs—would not work with live plants, which could not be consolidated into a central warehouse. Instead, Garden.com decided to use the Internet to build a network of business partners. The partners would grow and handle all the live plants; Garden.com would handle all the customer relationships, from providing product information and taking orders to supporting customers, thus creating a virtual warehouse.

Garden.com located the best gardening suppliers and signed them to two-way, mutually exclusive online agreements. Garden.com would take the orders and the suppliers would ship the orders to customers in their geographic regions. To offset the expense of multiple shipments for orders filled by different growers, Garden.com saves money by having its suppliers carry nearly all of its inventory. Only gift items—some 15 percent of the product line—are warehoused and shipped from Garden.com's Austin headquarters. The company also ships exclusively through FedEx.

Garden.com serves as the front end of the supply chain (planning, merchandising, and marketing to link customers and suppliers online) as well as the back end (billing customers and paying suppliers). The company also picks up shipping costs and handles returns and complaints. And specialists in its call center field questions from gardeners.

(Case Continued)

The Internet allows Garden.com to build a supply chain of many small businesses throughout the country yet have them appear to the customer as a single company. By creating a virtual warehouse, Garden.com has not only turned the L.L. Bean model on its head, but the Amazon.com model as well. ■

LOOKING ACROSS: BUSINESS-TO-BUSINESS

Businesses have long used IT to reduce the cost and time of interorganizational transactions; interorganizational systems (IOS) have become standard business tools. For airlines, hotels, and rental car companies, a computer reservation system that links major business partners is essential. In banking and financial services, electronic funds transfer systems have been in use for decades. In manufacturing, electronic data interchange systems (EDI) were developed in the 1960s and are now almost universally used. Business-to-business e-business represents the next stage in the evolution of IOS.

Electronic Data Interchange

Simply stated, EDI is the transmission, in standard syntax, of data for business transactions between computers of independent organizations. As soon as businesses began using computers, the amount of paper they generated began to expand. Soon most of the paper generated by one computer was used as input into another—not an efficient way to run a business. For example, purchasing supplies might involve generating and transferring purchase orders, invoices, shipping notices, and payment verification notices.

Traditional EDI.   The initial goal of EDI was to replace the paper documents involved in business transactions. This goal only required automating existing business processes; it did not involve redesigning processes. Although it sounds like a modest undertaking today, two barriers to successful EDI systems proved extremely challenging: technology and standards. The first barrier was the available technology. To link two computers, firms needed a telecommunications interface between them, which meant leasing a data line between the companies, sending data over standard phone lines using modems, or contracting with a third party to handle the data transmission. Each of these three options had various advantages and disadvantages, but they all entailed costly, inflexible systems.

The second barrier to EDI, standards, or more precisely, the lack of standards, includes both technical and business standards. To exchange data, the two computers needed compatible communication protocols, and the messages or documents needed to be in a standard format. In an EDI transaction, a company-specific form needs to be translated into a generic form and transmitted to the business partner, who then translates the generic form into its own company-specific form. For EDI to be successful, firms needed to agree on these generic-form standards.

Competing "universal" standards were developed, such as X12 from the American National Standards Institute (ANSI) and EDIFACT from the United Nations Economic Commission for Europe. In addition, industry-specific standards were developed for document formats. The development of standards became, and still is, a major task in facilitating EDI.

An entire industry has emerged to facilitate the use of EDI: value-added network providers, or VANs. A VAN is a third party company that provides communication links and EDI services to other companies. The services include translations between communication protocols and business standards, and message store-and-forward services. In eliminating the need for companies to work out all the details of implementing EDI systems, VANs provided valuable services and proved to be successful businesses.

Because EDI provides an efficient and safe method of sending purchase orders, invoices, product information, shipping data, and other business documents, many large companies have adopted and continue to use EDI. However, the barriers to EDI have proven too expensive and difficult for most small and medium-sized companies. E-business is changing that.

Internet-Based EDI. The Internet adds several important dimensions to IOS (see Figure 3-7). First it overcomes many of the technical barriers to EDI. Being an inexpensive public network that is widely available, it eliminates the need for expensive telecommunication networks. This wide access also provides for more flexible systems; trading partners can join the EDI system without high start-up costs, allowing small-volume partners to participate. Next, the Internet provides a standard communication protocol. Finally, it provides the means to send multimedia documents, rather than simple streams of text. EDI systems can include visual product information and more easily integrate with other e-business systems.

Supply Chain Integration

The supply chain covers all the processes involved in creating products and delivering them to customers. These activities include logistics, procurement, production, and distribution. Management and redesign of the supply chain has become a major strategic issue. Over the last dozen years, firms such as Dell Computer and Procter & Gamble (P&G) have gained significant competitive advantage by streamlining their supply chains, reducing operational costs but, more importantly, allowing them to offer new and faster services to their customers. The use of e-business to integrate the supply chain has proven to be the e-business application with the highest payoff.

Traditional	Internet
• Private networks	• Public networks
• High setup cost	• Low setup cost
• Specific groups	• Large group
• Secure networks	• Less secure network
• Value-added services	• Limited services

FIGURE 3-7 Traditional Versus Internet-Based EDI

Integrating the supply chain requires coordinating many activities across organizations and maintaining close communication with customers. As orders for products are placed, the company needs to know immediately whether the products are available for shipment, and if not, how long it will take to manufacture and deliver the products. The manufacturing plant needs to know what raw materials are on hand, which suppliers can supply the materials, and how long it will take to get the materials. The delivery department needs to track the status of all deliveries.

Support for the activities of the supply chain has long been in individual information systems, for example, scheduling, inventory, procurement, production planning, and demand forecasting systems. Business-to-business e-business aims to facilitate the integration of all these systems within a company and across business partners. Once integrated, the firms reap the cost reduction benefits of more efficient operations. They can then consider more strategic options.

The strategic options include shifting from mass production and selling from inventory to a build-to-order mode of operation. In the automotive industry, we expect to see consumers being able to custom-design their car over the Internet and have it manufactured and delivered in a matter of days.

Another strategic option is to eliminate intermediaries in the supply chain. For example, in the computer industry, manufacturers like Dell Computer have been successful selling directly to customers.

A third strategic option is redesigning the procurement process by using electronic markets or auctions. General Electric (GE) uses an Internet-based system, Trading Process Network, to do more than $1 billion in business per year with about 1,500 suppliers. Using the system, GE purchasers specify their requirements and suppliers submit bids. The bids might contain a variety of information, including product drawings. The software also helps manage the processing of bids.

Movement in a number of industries is fueling the creation of common e-business procurement systems. One of the most notable is in the automotive industry.[5]

CASE EXAMPLE

COVISINT

In September 2000, the U.S. Federal Trade Commission gave its approval to a global Internet auto supply marketplace developed by the Big Three automakers. In February 2000, General Motors Corp., Ford Motor Co., and DaimlerChrysler AG announced the formation of Covisint, a B2B exchange that will offer services to assist in product design, supply chain management, and procurement by auto manufacturers and their direct and indirect suppliers. It is expected to be the largest B2B exchange in the world and was the first to be reviewed by the FTC for antitrust implications.

Regulators have been concerned that the auto giants could flex their combined muscles in such a business combination

(Case Continued)

and dictate prices and purchasing practices to suppliers. Together the three account for about one-half of total worldwide auto production. The automakers said the exchange is open to other car manufacturers, and the FTC expects the collaboration to cut prices. However, the FTC retained the right to monitor the venture and take action if needed as the electronic marketplace takes shape.

Shortly after its formation, the Big Three automakers were joined by Renault SA of France, Nissan Motor Co. Ltd. of Japan, and two information technology firms, CommerceOne and Oracle. Covisint is to operate as an independent company. ■

Integration with Back-End Systems

Most, if not all, business-to-business systems must integrate with existing back-end systems, which has proven to be particularly challenging. Back-end systems cover a wide range of applications, including accounting, finance, sales, marketing, manufacturing, planning, and logistics. Most of these systems have been around for years, operate on a variety of platforms, and were not designed to integrate with other systems. Modifying these systems entails many risks, particularly when the integration must cross organizations. Luckily, most organizations have a head start on interorganizational integration because they have been working for a number of years on internally integrating their systems.

Understanding the need for internal integration, many companies replaced, or are currently replacing, their old back-end systems with newer ones using database management systems (DBMS) and ERP systems. The benefits of DBMS and ERP systems have always stemmed from their ability to provide integration. Recognizing the importance of e-business, DBMS and ERP vendors have modified their products to integrate with Internet-based applications. In doing so, the vendors provide platforms for building business-to-business systems.

Another approach to establishing B2B integration is to create an extranet. An extranet is a private network that uses Internet protocols and the public telecommunication system to securely share part of a business's information or operations with suppliers, vendors, partners, customers, or other businesses. An extranet is created by extending the company's intranet to users outside the company. The same benefits that Internet technologies have brought to corporate intranets have accelerated business between businesses.

Whatever the approach, the goal is to extend the company's back-end systems to reengineer business processes external to the company. Example activities include sharing product catalogs, exchanging news with trading partners, collaborating with other companies on joint development efforts, jointly developing and using training programs, and sharing software applications between companies. Initially, the benefits come in the form of greater cost and time efficiencies. Ultimately, the systems will change the structure of industries.

CASE EXAMPLE

WORLDCATCH.COM

On July 31, 2000, WorldCatch.com and Fishmonger.com, two of the seafood industry's leading online marketplaces, announced a merger; they would operate as WorldCatch.com.[6] The goal was to create the seafood industry's most comprehensive global business destination on the Internet. WorldCatch provided extensive industry experience and Fishmonger provided the industry's most advanced online business.

The $352 billion-a-year seafood industry has consisted of disparate buyers and sellers. Their main concerns have been shipping, purchase and sale prices, government regulations, product quality, and time to market. Thus, they are always looking for ways to use technology, new forms of payment, and innovations in logistics. WorldCatch aims to leverage IT to deliver faster, fresher seafood at the best price.

It provides three kinds of services: an online seafood auction, a real-time industry information resource, and a virtual seafood industry community center. The company's online auction, developed by Fishmonger.com, allows seafood buyers and sellers to more quickly and cost-effectively transact business. Developed in two months using database and e-business software from IBM, the auction quickly became popular. After just three weeks of operation, the auction was handling $400,000 worth of seafood trading.

The information resource service of Worldcatch.com provides real-time information about prices, the environment, and weather. In addition, a library contains information from research to recipes. The virtual community features industry association activities, discussions of legislative and regulatory issues, including direct e-mail links to political representatives and industry decision makers, a newsletter, and weekly polls. ■

TECHNICAL CONSIDERATIONS

As with any new technological development, especially one as profound as the Internet, a new economy is created. That new economy brings challenges with it. In the world of the Internet, two of the technical challenges are concerns about the future of the Internet and what to do about security.

Evolution of the Internet

As use of the Internet continues to grow, concerns have been raised about its ability to handle the traffic generated by e-business. Chief among these concerns are quality of service, availability, and security. In network engineering, "quality of service" refers to the ability of a network to provide a range of assured levels of performance.

Performance is characterized by many metrics including bandwidth, latency (the time required to transmit data across the network), and packet loss rate (the percentage of data packets that do not reach their destination).

The current version of the Internet was not designed to provide guaranteed quality of service levels. The TCP/IP protocols were designed using a philosophy of best effort in the delivery of packets. Delivery is not guaranteed nor is the sender notified in the event of nondelivery. Even in the face of rapid expansion of fiber links, bandwidth on the Internet has had trouble keeping up with the growing demand, and that produces bottlenecks, causing problems with latency and availability. As a relatively inexpensive public data network, the Internet remains the network of choice for e-business. Companies continue to upgrade components on the Internet, but how long can it continue to provide a minimum level of quality of service?

Two major cooperative efforts are underway to develop a replacement network that will provide higher levels of quality of service, availability, and security. The first is the U.S. government's Next Generation Internet (NGI) project; the second consists of two projects sponsored by a private sector organization, the University Consortium for Advanced Internet Development (UCAID).

The NGI initiative began in October 1997 and involves a number of federal agencies, including the Defense Advanced Research Projects Agency (DARPA), the National Science Foundation (NSF), and the National Aeronautics and Space Agency (NASA). NGI has three components: research and development on advanced network technologies, the deployment of high-speed testbed networks, and the development and demonstration of revolutionary applications that demand high-speed networks not currently possible on today's Internet.

UCAID, incorporated in 1998, sponsors two related projects: the Internet 2 and Abilene projects. The Internet 2 project will link more than 100 member universities with an advanced academic network. It will also support research, which requires applications that cannot be run over the current Internet. Abilene is seen as a second Internet 2 backbone. Spearheading this project are Qwest, Cisco Systems, Nortel, and Indiana University. Abilene will build a network to support the demands of the advanced research applications of UCAID members and a testbed for new networking technologies.

Security

Security ranks as one of the top management and consumer concerns about e-business. Managers are concerned about protecting company assets and information, and ensuring the integrity of e-business transactions. Consumers are concerned about protecting their privacy and financial transactions. We divide the security concerns into the three categories:

1. Sniffing
2. Spoofing
3. Hacking

Sniffing is the interception and reading of electronic messages as they travel over the communication networks. Spoofing is the assumption of a false identity and the execution of fraudulent transactions. Hacking is the unauthorized access to a host computer. This access may be a direct intrusion or via a computer virus or Trojan horse.

To protect against hacking, a firm must install a firewall. A firewall is a device placed between the company's network and the Internet that monitors and controls all data traffic entering and leaving the company's network. Firewalls can take many forms, from routers, which screen packets, to hardened host computers, to software applications. Hardened firewall hosts are stripped down computers especially designed for security; they provide the highest level of security. Routers and software provide less security, but have a much lower price.

To protect against sniffing, messages must be encrypted before being sent over the Internet. The two classes of encryption methods in use today are the secret key encryption and the public key encryption. The most common secret key method is the Data Encryption Standard (DES) developed by IBM, the National Security Agency, and the National Bureau of Standards. Using this method, the sender and receiver of the message use the same key to code and decode a message. The level of security is a function of the size of the key. DES is widely used and available in many software applications.

The most common public key encryption method is RSA, named for the three developers: Rivest, Shamir, and Adleman. To send an encrypted message using RSA, two keys are necessary: a public and a private key. As its name implies, the public key is known to many people and is not kept secret. However, the private key must be kept secret. The two keys are used to code and decode messages; a message coded with one can only be decoded with the other.

Figure 3-8 shows how an encrypted message is sent. First the message is encrypted using the receiver's public key. The message is now secure—it can only be decoded using the receiver's private key, which is only known to the receiver. Note that the sender uses the receiver's public key, not a key belonging to the sender. If a secure message is to be sent back to the original sender, then the public key of the original sender would be used. Thus, for two-way secure communications, both parties must have a set of keys.

The RSA method is secure and widely used. It is incorporated into all major Web browsers and serves as the basis for the Secure Socket Layer (SSL) in Internet communications. However, full two-way secure communications requires all parties to have a public and private key. Because most individuals do not have such keys, most business-to-consumer applications requiring encryption, such as the transmission of credit card numbers, are only secure transmissions from the consumer to the merchant, not from the merchant to the consumer.

Finally, to protect against spoofing, firms need a way to authenticate the identity of an individual. This verification requires a form of digital ID. The most common form of

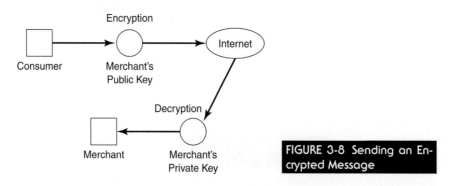

FIGURE 3-8 Sending an Encrypted Message

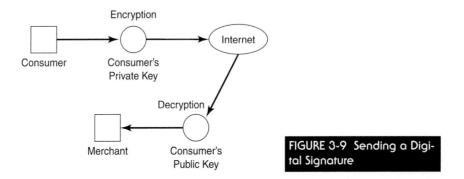

FIGURE 3-9 Sending a Digital Signature

digital signature uses the RSA encryption method. Because the private key is known only to one person and a message encrypted with that key can only be decoded with the matching public key, the private key provides a way of verifying that the message came from a certain individual. Figure 3-9 shows the basic process.

For digital signatures to work, a trusted third party must issue the keys to individuals and firms. These parties are called "certification agencies" and can be government agencies or trusted private companies. The agency issues a digital certificate containing the user's name, the user's public key, and the digital signature of the certification agency. See Figure 3-10. The digital certificate can then be attached to a message to verify the identity of the sender of the message.

LEGAL AND ETHICAL CONSIDERATIONS

As with any other business activity, e-business must adhere to legal and ethical codes. However, e-business entails some new legal and ethical issues of which managers must be aware, including the following:

- Privacy
- Intellectual property rights
- Legal jurisdiction
- Content regulation

Privacy

Privacy includes freedom from intrusion, the right to be left alone, the right to control information about oneself, and freedom from surveillance. It is a major issue in e-business because of the widespread availability of personal data and the ease of tracking a person's activities on the Internet.

User's name
User's public key
Digital signature of certificate issuer

FIGURE 3-10 A Digital Certificate

The United States and many other countries have enacted laws to control certain types of personal information, such as medical, credit, and other financial information. These laws carry over to the e-business environment. However, in the United States no laws protect the privacy of consumer purchasing data. As companies build large databases on their e-business customers, the value of this data makes the selling of the data an attractive business option.

Internet technologies, cookies in particular, make tracking the browsing activities of individuals possible. Consumer concerns about this perceived invasion of privacy is requiring companies to post and adhere to privacy statements on their Web sites. The following hypothetical scenario found on zeroknowledge.com dramatizes these concerns:

Bob's father has just been diagnosed with cancer. In an effort to learn more about it, Bob visits cancer Web sites and posts several inquiries to a discussion group. A month later, Bob's insurance company informs him that he is no longer eligible for a certain rate given his "condition."

Some companies use third party cookies (that is, cookies set by a firm other than the owner of the site being visited) to do "online profiling." It is also known as profile-based advertising, and it is a technique that marketers use to collect information about online behavior of Internet users and to facilitate targeted advertising. Profile-based advertising could easily be considered a form of online surveillance. What's worse, some third party cookies are often placed on Web browsers' computers without their knowledge when banner advertisements appear. It is not necessary to click on the banner ad to generate a cookie.

RESEARCH REPORT

SURFER BEWARE

In a report on its third annual review of the privacy practices of the 100 most popular shopping Web sites on the Internet, the Electronic Privacy Information Center (EPIC)[7] concluded, as it did in its earlier studies, that the current practices of the online industry provide little meaningful privacy protection for consumers. EPIC's study focused on shopping sites because many consumers are now buying online, and EPIC wanted to assess whether online merchants are adequately protecting consumer privacy. For all 100 sites, EPIC looked for compliance with "Fair Information Practices"—a set of principles that provides basic privacy protection. The study looked at several elements of the Fair Information Practices, including the ability to find the privacy policy of an e-commerce site, whether personal information is collected and used with the consent of the consumer, whether the consumer is able to access and correct such information, whether the information is limited to those uses for which the information was given, and whether the uses of the information are specified.

The study also looked at whether commercial sites utilized profile-based advertising, and employed cookies in their

(Case Continued)

Web site operations. Both of these controversial techniques have been the subject of recent investigations.

EPIC found that 18 of the top shopping sites did not display a privacy policy, 35 of the sites had profile-based advertisers operating on their pages, and 86 of the e-commerce operations used cookies. Not one of the companies adequately addressed all the elements of Fair Information Practices. The study also found that the privacy policies available at many Web sites are typically confusing, incomplete, and inconsistent.

EPIC did find that more sites are posting privacy policies than in 1997, when it conducted its first formal review of Web site policies. Unfortunately, the presence of a privacy policy does not always ensure privacy protection. Today, marketers are using new and more sophisticated techniques to track consumers on the Internet.

On balance, EPIC believes that consumers are more at risk today than they were in 1997. Profiling is more extensive and marketing techniques are more intrusive. Anonymity, which remains crucial to privacy on the Internet, is being squeezed out by the rise of electronic commerce. EPIC believes that industry-backed self-regulation has done little to protect online privacy and that legally enforceable standards are necessary to ensure compliance with Fair Information Practices. ■

Intellectual Property Rights

The protection of intellectual property is critical to e-business because many products and services contain intellectual property, copies are easy to make, and the copy is as good as the original. Examples of e-business activities in which intellectual property rights are critical include electronic publishing, software distribution, virtual art galleries, music distribution over the Internet, and online education.

We look at four types of legal protection of intellectual property: copyrights, patents, trademarks, and trade secrets.

Copyrights. Copyright law aims to protect an author's or artist's expression once it is in a tangible form. The work must be expressive rather than functional; a copyright protects the expression, not the idea. For example, a cartoon duck is an idea and cannot be copyrighted, but Donald Duck and Daffy Duck are expressions of that idea and are copyrighted. Registering a copyright is not a requirement; putting the expression into tangible form is sufficient. A copyright is valid for the life of the author plus 50 years.

Just about all original content on a Web site can be copyrighted by the creator of the site, from buttons to video, from text to site layouts. If a company hires someone to develop a site, by default, the copyright belongs to the developer, not the company. The developer can then demand royalties from the company if it uses the Web site; therefore, it behooves companies to clearly define the ownership of the copyright in the contract.

The Internet raises many interesting issues for copyright law, which was developed for physical media. Placing copyrighted material, such as a photograph, on a Web site without permission of the copyright holder is a clear violation of the law. Less obvious is whether inserting a link to someone else's copyrighted material is a violation of the law. If, for example, the site contains a direct link to the content of another site, say a photograph, is it a violation of copyright law? In this case, the answer is probably yes. However, if one includes a link to the homepage of the site rather than a direct link to the content, then probably no violation has occurred. Internet copyright issues are now being worked out in the courts and legislatures.

Patents.   Patent law aims to protect inventions—things or processes for producing things—that is, "anything under the sun made by man" but not "abstract ideas" or natural laws, according to U.S. copyright law. Valid for 20 years, the protection is quite strong. In the United States, patents are granted by the U.S. Patent and Trademark Office after stringent thresholds on inventiveness have been met.

The United States recognizes patents for business processes. Although software, in general, cannot be patented—it must be copyrighted—certain business practices implemented in software can be patented. In the e-business area, Amazon.com has received a patent for "one click purchasing." The company has enforced its patent rights against its main competitor, Barnes and Noble. Barnes and Noble cannot use one click purchasing on its Web site. British Telecom has claimed to have invented the hyperlink. To obtain the patent, the company will have to show that no prior use of hyperlinks occurred before its use. Any prior use would invalidate the patent.

Trademarks.   Trademarks protect names, symbols, and other icons used to identify a company or product. Trademarks can be registered with the U.S. Patent and Trademark Office. A trademark is valid indefinitely, as long as it is used and does not become a generic name for the goods or services. The aim of trademark law is to prevent confusion among consumers in a market with similar identifying names or symbols. The standard for trademark infringement is whether the marks are "confusingly similar."

The biggest area of trademark conflicts in e-business has to do with domain name registration. For a while, "cybersquatters" were registering domain names that clearly referred to known companies, realizing those companies would eventually want the domain name and would be willing to pay for it. Although this tactic worked for a while, anticybersquatting laws were passed and the practice is now illegal. To avoid potential problems, firms should obtain and register a trademark for its domain name. Note that most online services that register domain names do not check for trademark infringements. Firms are advised to do a search for possible trademark infringements before using a domain name to avoid future litigation.

Trade Secrets.   Trade secrets, as the name implies, protect company secrets, which can cover a wide range of processes, formulas, and techniques. A trade secret is not registered and is valid indefinitely, as long as it remains a secret. Although laws protect against the theft of trade secrets, it is not illegal to discover a trade secret through reverse engineering. Trade secrets are the area of intellectual property rights least applicable to e-business.

Legal Jurisdiction

Laws are written for particular jurisdictions with clear geographic boundaries, so how do those laws apply in cyberspace, which has no geographic boundaries? Take for example the case of trademark rights, which are limited to geographic areas. In the physical world, a sign over "Lee's Computer Services" in Singapore would not have a significant impact on "Lee's Computer Services" in Honolulu—neither in customers nor competition. However, in cyberspace the Web pages of the two companies would clearly overlap and, if the companies were to take advantage of the global reach of the Internet, significant competitive overlap could be an issue. The companies have little legal recourse for resolving the identical trademarks.

Gambling provides another interesting example. Do Hawaiian laws against gambling apply to a Nevada company with a gambling site on its Web server located in Las Vegas? The Attorney General of Minnesota has asserted the right to regulate gambling that occurs on a foreign Web page that is accessed and "brought into" his state by a local resident.

Similar cases have involved sites dealing with pornography and securities trading. Alabama successfully prosecuted a California couple for bringing pornography into Alabama; their server was in California. Note that U.S. pornography laws are based on "community standards"; Los Angeles standards are clearly different from those of Mobile. The state of New Jersey is attempting to regulate securities trading over the Internet, if anyone in the state has access to it, and many states are revising their tax codes to gain revenues from e-commerce.

We see a trend that, at best, is disturbing and, at worst, could greatly disrupt e-business: Faced with the inability to control the flow of electrons across physical boundaries, some authorities strive to impose their boundaries on cyberspace. When technological mechanisms, such as filters, fail, the authorities assert the right to regulate online trade if their local citizens may be affected. In essence, under this approach, all Internet-based commerce would be subject simultaneously to the laws of all territorial governments. Imagine a Hawaiian company setting up a Web site for retailing over the Internet needing to consider the laws of Hawaii, California, New York, and the other forty-seven states, plus Singapore, Peru, Syria, and any other place you might name. This situation would clearly cripple e-business.

The concepts of "distinct physical location" or "place where an activity occurred" fall apart in cyberspace; no clear answer is available to the question: Where did this event take place? Of relevance are the locations of the business's offices, warehouses, and servers containing the Web sites. Some of the uncertainty can be resolved by placing online contracts on the site specifying the legal jurisdiction that will be used for disputes. Users who agree to the contract designate so by clicking a button that says "I agree." In most cases, the contract will hold.

In the United States, states have adopted the Uniform Commercial Code (UCC), a wide-ranging codification of significant areas of U.S. commercial laws. The National Conference of Commissioners of Uniform State Law and the American Law Institute, who sponsor the UCC, are working to adapt the UCC to cyberspace.

Internationally, the United Nations Commission on International Trade Law has developed a model law that supports the commercial use of international contracts in electronic commerce. This model law establishes rules and norms that validate and recognize contracts formed through electronic means, sets standards governing electronic contract performance, defines what constitutes a valid electronic writing and original document, provides for the acceptability of electronic signatures for legal and commercial purposes, and supports the admission of computer evidence in courts and arbitration proceedings.

Online Contracting

A contract is a voluntary exchange between two parties. Contract law looks for evidence that the parties have *mutually assented* to the terms of a particular set of obligations before it will impose those obligations on them. Before the law will recognize the existence of a binding contract, there must be

1. A definite *offer* by one party, called the "offeror"
2. A timely *acceptance* by the "offeree"
3. Some *consideration* must pass between the offeree and the offeror

A widespread misconception holds that contracts must be in writing and signed before they are enforceable in court. The general rule is that offerees can show their acceptance of a contract offer by any means that are "reasonable under the circumstances." Reasonable acceptance includes oral agreements. Some exceptions do apply, however. For example, sales of real property require signed writings and, in the United States under the Uniform Commercial Code, any contract for the sale of goods for a price greater than $500 requires a signed writing.

In e-business, evidence of acceptance of a contract can be a simple click on a button saying "I Accept" or "I Agree." The case becomes more complex when the transaction involves payment greater than $500. The relevant questions are: Is our purely electronic communication "in writing" and have we "signed" the agreement? The answers are as yet unresolved. No cases have been presented regarding whether a file that exists in a computer's memory is "written" for purposes of contract law. Most commentators think the answer is probably "yes" but the final answer will have to wait until courts have reviewed the issue more closely.

In June 2000 President Clinton signed the Electronic Signatures in Global and National Commerce Act (E-Sign). Basically, E-Sign grants electronic signatures and documents equivalent legal status with traditional handwritten signatures. It is technology-neutral so that the parties entering into electronic contracts can choose the system they want to use to validate an online agreement. Many browsers contain minimal authentication features and companies are developing pen-based and other types of technologies to facilitate online contracting. In addition, a number of companies already provide digital signature products using public key encryption methods.

The full impact of E-Sign may not be as revolutionary as some would hope. The act specifies that no one is obligated to use or accept electronic records or signatures—all parties must consent to using the method. The act does not apply to a wide range of situations, such as the creation and execution of wills, adoptions, divorces, any notice of cancellation or termination of utility services, or foreclosure or eviction under a credit agreement. In addition, the marketplace has to sort out some serious problems with varying electronic signature standards. For example, a number of companies issue digital certificates, but none of them can operate with the others. It would require parties interested in adopting electronic signatures for their business to provide several technologies, or risk losing access to some customers.

CASE EXAMPLE

CLICKWRAP AGREEMENTS

On its Web site, the Cyberspace Law Institute[8] offers an interesting case. You subscribe to an electronic newsletter on a Web site with the following text:

> You may obtain a one-year subscription to our newsletter XYZ News for the special low price of $5.00 for each monthly issue, simply by filling in your name and e-mail address on the form below and then clicking the SUBSCRIBE button. By subscribing, you agree to the terms and conditions set forth in our Subscriber's Contract; to read the Subscriber's Contract, click on CONTRACT TERMS below.

Suppose you fill in your name and e-mail address and click SUBSCRIBE but, like most folks, you don't actually take the time to look at, let alone read, the Subscriber's Contract. Do you have a contract with XYZ?

Absolutely. You received an offer (to deliver the weekly newsletter to you); you took a specific action that the offeror deems to constitute acceptance of the offer (clicking on the SUBSCRIBE button); and you agreed to pay consideration for the contract (the offeror will deliver the newsletter to you for $5.00 per issue).

This "clickwrap contract" is an example of what the law calls a "contract of adhesion"—a contract you did not really bargain over in any way, but which was presented as more of a take-it-or-leave-it offer. Generally speaking, adhesion contracts are legally enforceable.

The use of the term *clickwrap contract* is an extension to the "shrinkwrap licenses" used in purchased software. Mass-marketed software comes with the terms of the contract—the license agreement—packaged under clear wrapping, with the notice that by opening the package you are agreeing to the terms of that license. Clickwrap is the same idea: by clicking here, you similarly agree to the contract's terms. ■

CONCLUSION

Over the years, a few innovative companies have used information technology for strategic advantage. The firms served as models of what could be done, but most companies did not have the resources or skills to follow the examples. With the growth of the Internet and the development of e-business, information technology has become a strategic tool in every industry. Companies are changing their business models and new companies are creating entirely new business models—many of which fail, but some succeed.

Long-established companies need to rethink their relationships with their customers and business partners. Business-to-consumer e-business allows a company to build a more personal relationship with its customers and to easily expand into new markets. It also provides consumers with greater choice, pressuring companies to offer higher levels of customer service. Companies must rethink the value they provide customers. Similarly, business-to-business e-business is forcing companies to restructure the entire supply chain.

Unencumbered by existing structures, new companies are able to quickly capitalize on the opportunities e-business brings. However, the large number of failures, mergers, and acquisitions shows the high level of uncertainty and risk in e-business. Just as the technology continues to evolve, so do the business models. It is not clear what the future holds for e-business, but it is clear that e-business has made a permanent change in the nature of business.

QUESTIONS AND EXERCISES

Review Questions

1. What are the three basic types of e-business and how do their strategic roles differ?
2. Why has e-business grown so quickly?
3. What are the major barriers to e-business?
4. What are the basic features of Microsoft's HR Web intranet?
5. What is a corporate portal, and how does it help solve some of the problems with managing an intranet?
6. How has the Internet changed consumer expectations?
7. In what way did Garden.com develop a virtual organization?
8. Describe what is meant by "supply chain integration."
9. How is WorldCatch.com changing the seafood industry?
10. Give two examples of how the current Internet may not be capable of handling the growth of e-business.
11. What are the three categories of e-business security concerns and how do they differ?
12. Describe the public key encryption method.
13. What are the four methods of legal protection of intellectual property?

Discussion Questions

1. With the failure of many high-profile e-retailers, and with many, such as Amazon.com, failing to make a profit, some have argued that selling over the Internet will be limited to a few products. Do you agree? Support your opinion.
2. As companies, often competitors, join together to form electronic markets and other business-to-business applications, they may violate antitrust laws. Discuss the relative merits of these cooperative ventures and antitrust laws.
3. Companies are using e-business applications to build profiles of customers. Privacy advocates consider this practice to be dangerous. Do you agree? Discuss.

Exercises

1. Research the history of two Internet retailers in the same industry. Compare their business strategy and performance. Describe how they differ and which you think will be more successful in the long run.
2. Visit a local company and talk to a manager about the firm's e-business strategy. What sorts of functions do they currently have on their Web site, and what do they plan for the future?
3. Compare and contrast the privacy policies of three Internet sites. Do any of them seem particularly favorable or unfavorable to site visitors? Explain.
4. Find two recent articles on legal issues in e-business. What concerns are being discussed, and what measures are being considered to address the concerns?

REFERENCES

1. *The E-Business Value Chain: Winning Strategies in Seven Global Industries,* Economist Intelligence Unit, http://www.eiu.com, October 2000.

2. Microsoft Corporation, http://www.microsoft.com/technet/showcase, October 2000.

3. Ferguson, Kevin, "Stop & Shop: An Earthbound Grocer Stocks Its Virtual

Aisles," *Business Week,* September 26, 2000.

4. Cummings, Elaine and Terris Haas, "Seeing Green," *Darwin Magazine,* CXO Media, http://www.darwinmag.com, June 1, 2000.

5. Mosquera, Mary, "Feds OK Big Three Auto-makers' B-To-B Market," *TechWeb News,* September 11, 2000.

6. "Worldcatch and Fishmonger to Merge," Worldcatch company press release, www.worldcatch.com/corporate.php, July 31, 2000.

7. "Surfer Beware III: Privacy Policies Without Privacy Protection," Electronic Privacy Information Center, http://www.epic.org/reports/surfer-beware3.html, December 1999.

8. Lessig, Larry, David Post, and Eugene Volokh, "Lesson 68—Contract Law in Cyberspace," The Cyberspace Law Institute, Social Science Electronic Publishing, http://www.cli.org, 1999.

4

INFORMATION SYSTEMS PLANNING

INTRODUCTION

We noted in Chapter 1 that IS management is becoming more difficult and more important at the same time, especially in strategic systems planning. On the one hand, the technology is changing so fast that it is tempting to say, "Why bother?" On the other hand, most organizations' survival is dependant on technology, and planning its effective use is a matter of organizational life and death.

How can this apparent paradox be resolved? The good news is that a variety of approaches, tools, and mechanisms have been developed to assist in systems planning. The bad news is that no "best" way to go about it has been devised. The result is that most organizations use more than one approach or tool to assist in this important information systems management function.

It is important to establish the appropriate mindset for planning. Although some managers believe planning means "determining what decisions to make in the future," this view is untenable today because the business environment is so turbulent, making the future unpredictable. A better view is that *planning* means

developing a view of the future that guides decision making today.

This seemingly subtle difference significantly changes how managers approach and execute the planning process. In such turbulent times, some executives now think in terms of "strategy-making" rather than planning. Our definition of *strategy* is

stating the direction you want to go and how you intend to get there.

The result of strategy-making is a plan.

In this chapter we first describe the traditional view of planning, then we turn to a current version of strategic systems planning, that is, strategy-making, which is intended to synchronize with the Internet-paced world. Finally we describe some approaches that are used in strategic systems planning.

Types of Planning

Planning is usually defined in three forms, which correspond to three planning horizons. Figure 4-1 summarizes these three planning types and some of their characteristics. Our emphasis in this chapter is strategic planning—the top row. In Chapter 3 we defined *strategic* as "having a significant, long-term impact on the growth rate, industry, and revenue" of an organization. Strategic systems planning deals with planning for the use of information systems and technology for strategic purposes.

Strategic planning has traditionally been thought to have a longer planning horizon than operational or tactical planning, as shown in Figure 4-1. In today's Internet age, however, some strategic planning is now short term indeed. Nevertheless, strategic planning attempts to form a view of the future 3–5 years out, in order to help determine what should be done now.

FIGURE 4-1   Three Types of Planning

Horizon	Focus	Issues	Primary Responsibility
3–5 years	Strategic	Vision architecture, business goals	Senior management CIO
1–2 Years	Tactical	Resource allocation, project selection	Middle managers IS line partners Steering committee
6 Months–1 Year	Operational	Project management, meeting time and budget targets	IS professionals Line managers Partners

Although systems planning efforts are usually called strategic, the emphasis on strategy has undergone a definite shift over the past several years. Figure 4-2 illustrates some of these shifts. The basic trend is to move from a tactical midrange focus to a truly strategic effort.

Why Planning Is So Difficult

Some fundamental reasons explain why systems planning is so difficult. Here are a few of them.

Business Goals and Systems Plans Need to Align.   Strategic systems plans need to align with business goals and support those objectives. Unfortunately, if top management believes the firm's strategic business goals are extremely sensitive, and the CIO is not a member of the top management team, the IS department can be left out of the inner circle that develops these plans. Fortunately, more and more CIOs are being made part of senior management. In addition, a strong trend is moving systems planning into a responsibility shared among the CIO, CTO, and other members of senior management. With the emergence of e-commerce, CEOs are realizing they need to be directly involved in systems planning.

Technologies Are Rapidly Changing.   How can you plan when information technologies are changing so rapidly? One answer is continuous planning. Gone are the days of an annual planning cycle that is done in the last few months of the year and then put aside until the following year. Rather, the planning process first needs to form a best-available vision of the future on which to base current decisions. Then the technology is monitored to see whether that future vision needs alteration. When it does, adjustments in current decisions are made. Some organizations have an "advanced technology group" charged with the responsibility for watching and evaluating new technologies.

Companies Need Portfolios Rather Than Projects.   Another planning issue is the shift in emphasis from project selection to portfolio development. This move requires a more sophisticated form of planning because projects must be evaluated on more than their individual merits. How they fit into other projects and how they balance the portfolio of projects become more important measures. The Internet Value Matrix described later is an example of this approach.

Infrastructure Development Is Difficult to Fund.   Everyone knows intuitively that the development of infrastructure is crucial. It is extremely difficult, however, to get funding *just* to develop or improve infrastructure. Often it must be done under the auspices of a large application development project. The challenge then is to develop im-

FIGURE 4-2 Shifts in Systems Planning Emphasis	
Then	***Now***
Tactical	Strategic
Project selection	Project integration
Building infrastructure as a project	Building infrastructure as a process
Steering committees	CIO/Senior executive partnership

proved applications over time so that the infrastructure improves over time. Most recently, companies have had to undertake a rapid succession of infrastructure investments, first converting from a mainframe to a client-server architecture that divvies up processing, then implementing an enterprise resource planning (ERP) system that cleans and synchronizes data, and finally shifting to Internet telecom protocols for communications. Boards of directors have finally realized they have to "bite the bullet" and fund these huge multiyear projects, just to remain competitive. Making these large-stakes bets increases the difficulty of the systems planning process.

Responsibility Needs to Be Joint. It is often easier to do something yourself than to gather a coalition to do it. But systems planning initiated by and driven by the CIO has not proven as effective as systems planning done by a full partnership among the CXOs (CEO, CFO, CIO, COO) and other top executives. Systems planning has become business planning; it is no longer just a technology issue.

Other Planning Issues. Several other characteristics of planning in general make strategic systems planning difficult. Because a tension is always present between top-down and bottom-up approaches, the planning must strike a balance between radical change and continuous improvement. Most organizations have developed a planning "culture" with which systems planning must be compatible. Taken together, this sampling of issues clearly illustrates why systems planning is a difficult but crucial task.

THE CHANGING WORLD OF PLANNING

"The Internet changes everything" has become a familiar phrase in many areas. Planning is one of those areas. The Internet has turned many traditional planning assumptions on their heads. For example, the speed it has introduced into the business environment has transformed how people think about time and how much time they have to plan and react to competitors' moves. In turn, time factors have changed how companies view planning and strategy-making. In this section we discuss these changes.

Traditional Strategy-Making

As Gartner Executive Programs (EXP) notes in its report, *Tactical Strategy,*[1a] traditional strategy-making followed the fairly linear progression shown in Figure 4-3:

1. Business executives created a strategic business plan that described where the business wanted to go.
2. From that plan, IS executives created an IS strategic plan to describe how IT would support that business plan.
3. An IT implementation plan was created to describe exactly how the IS strategic plan would be implemented.

Companies felt comfortable spending quite a bit of time, often a full year, creating a single strategic plan that they would implement over, say, the coming 5 years. That plan was created by top management. If the CIO was part of that group, then IS was involved in the planning; otherwise, IT considerations may or may not have been taken into account.

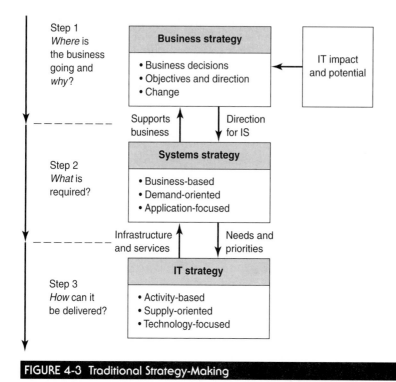

Step 1
Where is
the business
going and
why?

Business strategy

• Business decisions
• Objectives and direction
• Change

IT impact
and potential

Supports ↑   Direction
business   for IS ↓

Systems strategy

Step 2
What is
required?

• Business-based
• Demand-oriented
• Application-focused

Infrastructure ↑   Needs and
and services   priorities ↓

IT strategy

Step 3
How can it
be delivered?

• Activity-based
• Supply-oriented
• Technology-focused

FIGURE 4-3 Traditional Strategy-Making

Source: Reprinted with permission from Roger Woolfe, Barbara McNurlin, and Phil Taylor, *Tactical Strategy,* Wentworth Research Program (now part of Gartner Executive Programs, 56 Top Gallant, Stamford, CT 06904), November 1999.

From the corporate strategy, IS staff developed the systems strategy, which described what was required to support the business plan. Finally, from that systems strategy, the IS staff developed the technology-based IT strategy, which described how the company could deliver the needed capabilities.

This traditional planning stance was based on the following assumptions:

• The future can be predicted.
• Time is available to progress through this three-part sequence.
• IS supports and follows the business.
• Top management knows best because they have the broadest view of the firm.
• The company can be viewed as an army: Leaders issue the orders and the troops follow.

Today, due to the Internet, these assumptions no longer hold true.

The Future Cannot Be Predicted.   The Internet has caused "discontinuous change," that is, change now occurs in unexpected ways. Industry leaders may not be able to use the same strategies they used in the past to maintain their superior market position. Unexpected and powerful competitors can emerge out of nowhere. For example, in the mid-1990s, how many booksellers predicted Amazon.com's business model of selling only on the Web, or the success it would have? Not very many. Likewise, how many top executives seriously considered eBay's online auction model as one that could transform the way they would buy and sell? Not very many. And the surprises—even newer Internet-based business models—are still coming. Industry after industry is encountering discontinuous changes to the way they have traditionally operated.

Time Is Not Available for the Sequence. Due to the Internet, time is now of the essence. Companies no longer have the luxury of taking a year to plan and several years to implement. Worse yet, the most time-consuming phase of the sequence—IT implementation—is at the end, which means the IS department is "late" in supporting the business' strategic plan from the outset. So the sequence of planning events no longer supports Internet-based time. To move quickly, IT implementation planning actually needs to be out ahead of business strategizing. Furthermore, it needs to be fast, to keep up with the pace of dot-com implementation.

IS Does Not Just Support the Business Anymore. Information technology has become the platform of business; it makes e-business possible. Bob Benson and Marilyn Parker[2] have pointed out that IT can serve lines of business in two ways. As shown in Figure 4-4, one is by supporting current or planned operations, which they call "alignment." The second is by using systems to influence future ways of working, which they call "impact." To fulfill this second role, IS needs to get ahead of the business, to demonstrate IT-based e-business possibilities. At the very least, IS and the business need to strategize together, not follow the old model of business first, IS second.

Top Management May Not Know Best. Due to the rapid pace of change, and due to management's distance from the "front lines" of the business (interacting with customers, partners, and suppliers), having strategy formulated by top management limits

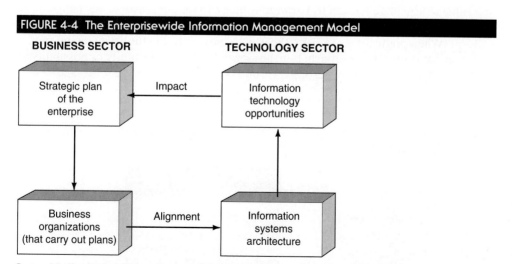

FIGURE 4-4 The Enterprisewide Information Management Model

Source: Marilyn Parker, Robert Benson, with Ed Trainor, *Information Economics: Linking Information Technology and Business Performance,* Prentice Hall, 1988. European edition, 1989. Japanese edition, 1990.

it to what these few members of the firm can distill. Today, the trend is toward customizing products and services to smaller and smaller niche markets, even to markets of one. This goal requires diversity in strategy-making, and may be best performed by those closest to customers—if not customers themselves—because they know the local environment. Hence, the former "inside out" approach to strategy-making needs to be shifted to be "outside in," as illustrated in Figure 4-5.

An Organization Is Not Like An Army.   Industrial-era planning has implicitly viewed companies as an army: Top management edicts will ripple down through the organization, layer by layer, finally being implemented by the troops on the front line who deal with customers. This metaphor is not holding true. Take, for example, the business process reengineering fiascos of the early 1990s. Executives learned that their mandates to institute major changes in business processes, imposed from the top, often ended in disaster. Not only did the projects fail but they also ate up resources, burned out employees, created animosity, and even destroyed valuable company knowledge assets because experienced employees left.

A new and controversial view is to see organizations as living entities that evolve. Thus, they cannot be commanded; they can only be nurtured or tended, like a garden. This new approach, if believed, obviously requires a different form of leadership.

Today's Sense-and-Respond Approach

If yesterday's assumptions no longer hold true, thus making yesterday's approach to strategy-making less effective, what is appearing to take its place? The answer is a kind of sense-and-respond strategy-making, as reported in Gartner's *Tactical Strategy* report.[1b]

Rather Than Plan the Strategy, Let It Unfold.   In the past, top management took the time to articulate one enterprisewide strategy. In times of fast-paced change, such as we are now experiencing, this approach is risky. If a bet proves wrong, it could be disastrous.

When predictions are risky, the way to move into the future is step by step, using a sense-and-respond approach. It means sensing a new opportunity or possibility and immediately responding by testing it via an experiment. Hence, the sense-and-respond ap-

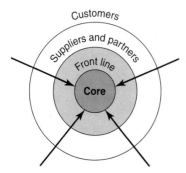

FIGURE 4-5 Outside-In Strategy Development

Source: Reprinted with permission from Roger Woolfe, Barbara McNurlin, and Phil Taylor, *Tactical Strategy*, Wentworth Research Program (now part of Gartner Executive Programs, 56 Top Gallant, Stamford, CT 06904). November 1999.

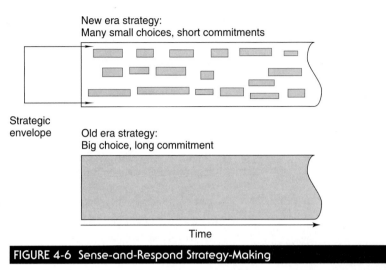

New era strategy:
Many small choices, short commitments

Strategic
envelope

Old era strategy:
Big choice, long commitment

Time

FIGURE 4-6 Sense-and-Respond Strategy-Making

Source: Reprinted with permission from Roger Woolfe, Barbara McNurlin, and Phil Taylor, *Tactical Strategy*, Wentworth Research Program (now part of Gartner Executive Programs, 56 Top Gallant, Stamford, CT 06904), November 1999.

proach has a myriad of small experiments going on in parallel, each testing its own hypothesis of the future, as illustrated in Figure 4-6.

A company that illustrates this "semi-coherent" sense-and-respond approach to developing strategy in the Internet space is Microsoft, say Shona Brown and Kathy Eisenhardt in their book *Competing on the Edge: Strategy as Structured Chaos.*[3]

CASE EXAMPLE

MICROSOFT

Microsoft, the software giant in Redmond, Washington, has taken a sense-and-respond approach to creating its Internet strategy. The company began by building a proprietary version of a network, Microsoft Network, as an alternative to AOL's proprietary network and the Internet. But they gave up this stance, even though it had cost a lot of money, when it did not capture enough customers.

They moved on to buying Internet companies as well as aligning with Sun to promote Java (and create a proprietary version of Java), and even forging an alliance with AOL.

Over time, they moved into a variety of technologies:

- Web-only magazine, *Slate*
- Web news site, with NBC
- Cable news channel, with NBC
- Digital movie production, via Dreamworks
- Cable modems

(Case Continued)

- Operating system for handhelds, WindowsCE
- Video servers
- Online music standard to compete with MP3
- Online multiplayer gaming

Microsoft has taken no single defining move, except perhaps Bill Gates's announcements focusing the company on the Internet. Each announcement fostered even more explorations. Its family of strategies did not all come from top manage-

ment either. The company's first server came from a rebel working on an unofficial project. In addition, management mistakenly passed up some "cheap" acquisitions that later cost them much more via licensing agreements. Some of these moves could have been predicted, but others are surprising. In short, Microsoft has been sensing and responding to the moves of the industry, getting its fingers into every pie that might become important. ■

Formulate Strategy Closest to the Action. The major change allowed by the Internet is faster communication, not only within organizations but, more importantly, with others—customers, suppliers, and partners. Aligning corporate strategy with the marketplace in these fast-paced times requires staying in close contact with that marketplace. Hence, strategy development needs to take place at these "edges" of the organization, with the people who are closest to the action, those employees who interact daily with customers, suppliers, and partners.

Furthermore, employees who are closest to the future should become prime strategizers as well. In the Internet age, that means including younger employees because they have grown up in this era, they take it for granted, they "wear it like clothing." One company that is taking this premise of "downside-up" strategizing to heart is Skandia AFS, described in the Wentworth report.[1a] Note that this example (coupled with the Skandia case presented later in the chapter) intertwines all three major themes in this edition of the text: e-business, knowledge management, and the Internet.

CASE EXAMPLE

SKANDIA FUTURE CENTERS

Skandia Future Centers, located in Stockholm, Sweden, is an incubator for testing ideas on IT, social relationships, and networking for Skandia, the large Swedish insurance company. The center acts as an inspirer and advisor to those who do the strategy-making within Skandia.

(Case Continued)

The center was created in 1996 by Leif Edvinsson to give Skandia a laboratory to break out of its current ways of thinking and to provide a place where different generations can collaborate on on-the-edge projects.

3G Teams

One of the first concepts used at the center was 3G teams, getting three generations (25+, 35+, 45+) to work together. The teams were part-time and cross-cultural from Venezuela, Germany, Sweden, and the United States. The participants were chosen by peers as well as nominated from different parts of the company.

To get the generations to actually talk to each other, their mandate was to focus on questions rather than answers. "When you ask for answers, you get a debate. When you focus on questions, you get a dialog," says Edvinsson. The five initial teams were to develop strategic questions on five subjects, the insurance industry in Europe, technology, world economics, demographics, and leadership and organization.

Based on their questions, they arrived at a number of interesting contexts for the questions, such as the evolution of the financial community around the world and the evolution of IT. These contexts were presented to 150 Skandia senior managers not through a report, but through scenarios of these five future environments performed by professional actors in a theater play.

Knowledge Café

The play led to the first knowledge café among the 150 executives. The café was created by one of the 3G teams and a few of the executives. At it, the 150 gathered for one hour around stand-up tables at different Skandia sites. Each table had coffee and a laptop loaded with groupware from Ventana Software. In all, 20 laptops were interconnected forming a virtual community of the 150 executives. During the hour, they discussed the questions presented in the play through anonymous entries. The discussion was spiked by the drama they had seen, then nourished and cultivated through the exchange. The result was a collective intelligence of the 150.

The entire project was videotaped and sent to a larger community, along with the questions and a video of the play and the café. The goal of this project was to show the power of collective intelligence. The knowledge café accelerated innovation at Skandia, transforming them into an innovation company. The effect has been demonstrated by their growth, the shift in their organizational design, and the shift in their office design.

Nurturing the Project Portfolio

Edvinsson thinks of the center as a garden, where some of the projects are growing and some are not. He tends them by looking at the level of interest surrounding each one and at the progress each made, which he equates with gardening.

To peer into the future of information technology, Edvinsson believed the center needed ideas from four generations—the current generation of leaders (50+), the second generation of leaders (40+), the third (30+), and the fourth (20+). So he formed groups that include young people between the ages of 15 and 25 because they have a much different relationship with information technology than older people. These young people integrate themselves with the technology. They walk into it and do something with it.

(Case Continued)

In building the multigenerational teams, the center has learned that 35- to-45-year-olds have the lowest risk propensity or drive for change. Innovative behavior is among young people and seniors. In fact, the more senior, the more risk-prepared they have become because they see themselves as bulletproof. Combining senior wisdom with young people's entrepreneurship leads to a real powerhouse. ■

Guide Strategy-Making with a "Strategic Envelope". Having a myriad of potential corporate strategies being tested in parallel could lead to anarchy without a central guiding mechanism. That mechanism is "a strategic envelope." Creating and maintaining this envelope is the job of top management. Rather than devise strategy, they define its context by setting the parameters for the experiments (the strategic envelope), and then continually managing that context. Thus, they need to meet often to discuss the shifts in the marketplace, how well each of the experiments is proceeding, whether one is gaining followership or is showing waning interest.

They may perform this work by defining a territory, as Microsoft did. Or they may hold "strategic conversations," as espoused by Brown and Eisenhardt.[3] A strategic conversation is a regular, frequent meeting at which the executives share the workload of monitoring the business environment and responding to it. Perhaps the vice president of operations might be charged with reporting on "today," such as the size of the company's mobile workforce. The emerging technologies director might be charged with reporting on "tomorrow," such as recent announcements of new technologies. The HR vice president might be the team's eyes and ears to "people" issues. The purposes of each meeting are to stay in tempo with the marketplace (which may mean setting new priorities), spotting trends in their infancy, launching new projects, adding resources to promising ones, cutting funding for others, and so forth.

Another way to create a strategic envelope is to meet regularly with the experimenters, as in the case of Shell Oil, described by Richard Pascale in an issue of *Sloan Management Review* entitled "In Search of Strategy".[4]

CASE EXAMPLE

SHELL OIL

Steve Miller, incoming general manager of oil products at Royal Dutch/Shell, believed change would only occur if he went directly to his front lines—employees at

(Case Continued)

Shell gas stations around the world. He felt he had to reach around the middle of the company to tap the ingenuity of employees at the gas stations, encouraging them to devise strategies best for their local market.

He set aside 50 percent of his own time for this work, and required his direct reports to do the same. His goal was *not* to drive strategy from corporate, as had been tried and failed, but to interact directly with the grass roots and support their new initiatives, thus overwhelming the old order in the middle of the company.

Action Labs

His technique was to use action labs. He invited six teams of 6 to 8 people from gas stations from various countries to a week-long "retailing boot camp" at which they learned how to identify local opportunities and capitalize on them. They were then sent home for 60 days to develop a proposal of how to double their net income or triple their market share.

The following week, a fresh set of six teams came to headquarters.

After 60 days, the first six teams returned for a "peer challenge" at which time they critiqued each other's plans. They then returned home for another 60 days to hone their plan for the third action lab: approval or disapproval.

At this third lab, each team took turns sitting in "the hot seat" facing Miller and his direct reports, who grilled them for three hours on their plan. The teams, in turn, described what they needed from Miller as the other teams watched. The plans were approved, denied, or modified. If funded, the promised results were factored into an operating company's goals. The teams then had 60 days to implement their plan, and return for a fourth session with Miller and his reports.

The Results

These action labs had a powerful effect. They caused stress on Shell's way of doing business, in effect, unfreezing the status quo. The corporate middle, which had not formerly seen good results from corporate efforts, saw solid plans and energized subordinates. In turn, they became energized. In addition, the labs led to much more informal communication up, down, and across the company. The action lab teams, for instance, felt comfortable calling up Miller and his staff—a significant departure from the past.

They also affected the way Miller and his staff made decisions. In the labs, these executives had to make on-the-spot decisions in front of the front-line teams rather than behind closed doors. They found they had to be consistent and straight with the teams. It was a difficult and trying experience for all, but humanizing for the teams.

In the various countries, "guerilla leaders" emerged and initiated innovative experiments. One, for example, was "the soft drink challenge." Whenever a customer was not offered the full gamut of services at a Malaysian gas station, they received a free soft drink. The results: a 15 percent increase in business.

The projects spawned many more projects and Miller learned that small local projects can have large effects. The focus was on tapping the intelligence at the nodes, with controls and rewards supporting that goal

Formerly, top management had the illusion of being in control via their directives. Through the action labs, they

(Case Continued)

learned with their staff, they received much more feedback, and they knew far more about their customers and the marketplace. Guidance and nurturing came from the top, so there was not complete chaos. In fact, Miller believes the key is to get the right tension between chaos (at the team level) and order (at the managing director level). He sees it as treating the company as if it were a living system. ■

Be at the Table. As noted earlier, IS executives have not always been involved in business strategizing. This situation is untenable in today's Internet-driven world. But to have a rightful place in the strategizing process, the IS function needs to be strategy oriented. Many have been tactical and operational, reacting to strategies formulated by the business. To become strategy oriented, CIOs must first make their departments credible, as noted in Chapter 2, and second, outsource more and more operational work, thus releasing IS staff for new roles in assisting their business partners with strategizing and experimenting.

Test the Future. To get a running start, as well as contribute ideas about the future, IS departments need to test potential futures before the business is ready for them. IS needs to take on a new role of thinking ahead of the business. One mechanism for testing the future is to provide funding for experiments. Another is to work with research organizations. Yet another is to have an emerging technologies group. Again, Skandia Future Centers provides an example of testing the future, in this case an IT-based infrastructure project.[1a]

CASE EXAMPLE

SKANDIA FUTURE CENTERS

The charter for Skandia Future Centers is organizational prototyping. One project, the knowledge exchange, has addressed the question of putting a value on intangibles, such as knowledge.

Today, some 70 percent of investments in the United States are for intangibles; in Sweden it is 90 percent. However, no mechanism for establishing their value nor trading that value is yet available. A knowledge exchange increases the accessibility of hidden knowledge, and will act as a multiplier for wealth creators, both people and organizations.

(Case Continued)

Skandia's knowledge exchange began as a network for exchanging knowledge using software akin to Lotus Notes. Over time, it has evolved into a Web-based trading arena where people can buy and sell knowledge assets. It is now based on Nonet, a Notes-like product from Metaphor, a Spanish company.

It has two test sites called ICuniverse.com (IC stands for intellectual capital) and futurizing.com. On ICuniverse.com, for example, before responding to an e-mail message, the recipient and the sender first agree on a price to be paid to the responder, perhaps via an auction. Thus people are paid for the knowledge they provide. Ideas and writings can be housed on ICuniverse.com and resold, which gives high yield to currently unvalued intellectual assets.

The two sites run on an infrastructure (IQport) owned by NatWest in the United Kingdom and built over the past four years. It includes software and a financial clearing mechanism so that information that is generally thrown away can be wrapped into a package and given a price tag. The sites are linked to two accounts at NatWest; one is in financial currency (traditional money), the other is in digital currency, which can be used to purchase other knowledge. Skandia is testing this concept because it could become a new global currency. It is part of the new digital economy.

The knowledge exchange project has been self-organizing from the start. The center simply provides the arena for "knowledge entrepreneurs" or "knowledge nomads"—people who go from arena to arena working on their latest ideas. Thus, the center supports an untraditional working model.

To illustrate its migration, the project began with IT people from the United Kingdom, who were then joined by IT people from Sweden and the United States. Later, students and the professor from Venezuela who developed Nonet in Venezuela for oil companies were the mainstay. The students collaborated with the professor at the center and with Metaphor, the Spanish company that bought Nonet. Today, the knowledge exchange team has people from Sweden and Denmark.

The question the Future Center is now asking itself is: How can we reward knowledge nomads? They do not want a career, they want a journey and freedom. Their lifestyle does not fit into traditional organizational models, yet working with them helps speed up accounting and organizational remodeling because they act like bees, moving among research centers pollinating companies with ideas. ∎

Put the Infrastructure in Place. Moving quickly in Internet commerce means having the right IT infrastructure in place. Hence, the most critical IT decisions are infrastructure decisions. Woolfe and his colleagues[1a] therefore recommend that IT experiments include those that test painful infrastructure issues, such as how to: create and maintain common, consistent data definitions, create and instill mobile commerce standards among handheld devices, implement e-commerce security and privacy measures, and determine operational platforms, such as ERP and supply chain management.

Experimentation is the new sense-and-respond approach to IS strategy-making. It differs markedly from the traditional planning described at the outset of this chapter. In fact, it represents a revolution in planning. Now we move to describing some tools and approaches that can be used to both focus and broaden thinking during planning and strategy-making.

SIX PLANNING APPROACHES AND TECHNIQUES

Due to the importance and the difficulty of systems planning, it is valuable to have a framework or methodology to use in the process. Over the years, a number of approaches have been proposed to help IS executives do a better job of planning. The six approaches presented here take different views of information systems planning, including looking at the assimilation of IT in organizations, defining information needs, understanding the competitive market, categorizing applications into a portfolio, and mapping relationships. The six planning approaches and techniques discussed are:

- Stages of Growth
- Critical Success Factors
- Competitive Forces Model
- Value Chain Analysis
- Internet Value Matrix
- Linkage Analysis Planning

Stages of Growth

Richard Nolan and Chuck Gibson published a landmark paper in 1974 entitled "Managing the Four Stages of EDP Growth."[5] In it they observed that many organizations go through four stages in the introduction and assimilation of new technology.

- *Stage One: Early Successes.* The first stage is the beginning use of a new technology. Although some stumbling generally occurs, early successes lead to increased interest and experimentation.
- *Stage Two: Contagion.* Based on the early successes, interest grows rapidly as new products and/or services based on the technology come to the marketplace. They are tried out in a variety of applications; growth is uncontrolled and therefore rises rapidly. This proliferation stage is the learning period for the field, both for uses and for new products and services.
- *Stage Three: Control.* Eventually it becomes apparent that the proliferation must be controlled. Management begins to believe the costs of using the new technology are too high and the variety of approaches generates waste. The integration of systems is attempted but proves difficult, and suppliers begin efforts toward standardization.
- *Stage Four: Integration.* At this stage, the use of the particular new technology might be considered mature. The "dominant design" of the technology has been mastered, setting the stage for newer technologies, wherein the pattern is repeated. An organization can be in several stages simultaneously for different technologies.

Nolan has since used the Stages of Growth theory to describe three eras, as shown in Figure 4-7.[6] Underlying the three organizational learning curves pictured are the

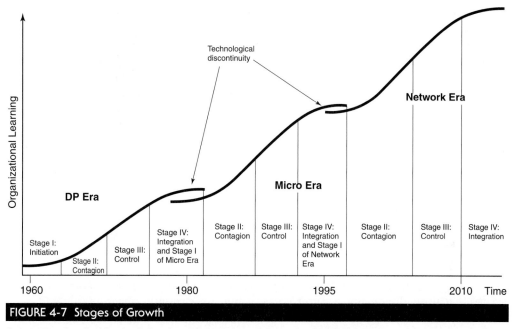

FIGURE 4-7 Stages of Growth

Source: Reprinted with permission from R. L. Nolan, "Information Technology Management from 1960–2000," *A Nation Transformed by Information,* Alfred D. Chandler and James W. Cortad (Eds), Oxford Press, 2000.

dominant designs of each era. The DP (Data Processing) Era's dominant design was the mainframe, the Micro Era's design was the PC, and the Network Era's is the Internet. The eras overlap each other slightly at points of "technological discontinuity," states Nolan, which occur when proponents of the proven old dominant design struggle with the proponents of alternative new and unproven designs. Inevitably, the new wins out.

The importance of the theory to IS management is understanding where a technology or a company currently resides on the organizational learning curve. If, for example, use of wireless access to the Internet is in the trial-and-error Stage Two, where experimentation and learning are taking place, then exerting too much control too soon can kill off important new uses of the technology. Management needs to tolerate, even encourage, experimentation.

Because the management principles differ from one stage to another, and because different technologies are in different stages at any point in time, the stage model continues to be an important aid to the systems planning process.

Critical Success Factors

In 1977, Jack Rockart[7] and his colleagues at the Center for Information Systems Research (CISR), Sloan School of Management, at the Massachusetts Institute of Technology, began developing a method for defining executive information needs. The result of their work is the Critical Success Factors (CSF) method. It focuses on individual managers and their current information needs, whether factual or opinion information. The CSF method has become a popular planning approach and can be used to help companies identify information systems they need to develop.

For each executive, critical success factors are the few key areas of the job where things must go right for the organization to flourish. Executives usually have fewer than 10 of these factors that they each should monitor. Furthermore, CSFs are both time-sensitive and time-dependent, so they should be reexamined as often as necessary to keep abreast of the current business climate. These key areas should receive constant attention from executives, yet CISR research found that most managers had not explicitly identified these crucial factors.

Rockart finds four sources for these factors. One source is the *industry* that the business is in. Each industry has CSFs relevant to any company in it. A second source is the *company itself* and its situation within the industry. Actions by a few large, dominant companies in an industry most likely provide one or more CSFs for small companies in that industry. Furthermore, several companies may have the same CSFs but, at the same time, have different priorities for those factors.

A third source of CSFs is the *environment,* such as consumer trends, the economy, and political factors of the country (or countries) in which the company operates. A prime example is that prior to, say 1999, few chief executives would have listed "leveraging the Internet" as a CSF. Today, they monitor this factor intently.

The fourth source is *temporal* organizational factors, or areas of company activity that normally do not warrant concern but are currently unacceptable and need attention. A case of far too much or far too little inventory might qualify as a CSF for a short time.

In addition to these four sources, Rockart has found two types of CSFs. One he calls *monitoring,* or keeping abreast of ongoing operations. The second he calls *building,* which involves tracking the progress of "programs for change" initiated by the executive. The higher an executive is in the organization, the more "building" CSFs are usually on his or her list. Rockart sees CSFs varying from organization to organization, from time period to time period, and from executive to executive.

One way to use the CSF method is to list the current corporate objectives and goals, then use them to determine which factors are critical for accomplishing the objectives, along with two or three prime measures for each factor. Discovering the measures is the most time-consuming portion, says Rockart. Some measures use hard, factual data; they are the ones most quickly identified. Others use "softer" measures, such as opinions, perceptions, and hunches; these measures take more analysis to uncover their appropriate sources. IS plans can then be developed based on these critical success factors.

Competitive Forces Model

The most widely quoted framework for thinking about the strategic use of IT is the competitive forces model proposed by Michael Porter[8] of the Harvard Business School in his book *Competitive Strategy.* Porter believes companies must contend with five competitive forces, as shown in Figure 4-8.

One force is the *threat of new entrants* into one's industry. For instance, the Internet has opened up a new channel of marketing and distribution that has allowed all kinds of unexpected new entrants into numerous markets. Travel Web sites, for example, are threats to travel agencies.

The second force is the *bargaining power of customers and buyers.* Buyers seek lower prices and bargain for higher quality. Web-based market exchanges, auction sites,

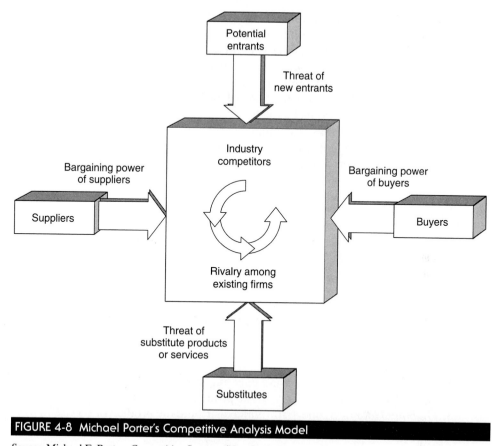

FIGURE 4-8 Michael Porter's Competitive Analysis Model

Source: Michael E. Porter, *Competitive Strategy* (New York: The Free Press, 1980).

shopping robots, and intelligent agents are all giving buyers much more information about potential suppliers and thus increasing their bargaining power. In fact, much of the power of the Internet has to do with this force.

A third force is the *bargaining power of suppliers.* For example, the net again is permitting small companies to compete against large companies in uncovering requests for bids and bidding on them—leveling the playing field.

The fourth force is *substitute products or services.* The Internet provides a myriad of examples here. E-mail is a substitute for paper mail. Music downloads are substitutes for CDs. Book and music Web sites are substitutes for book and music stores.

The fifth force is *the intensity of rivalry among competitors.* IT-based alliances can change rivalries by, for instance, extending them into value-chain-versus-value-chain competition rather than just company-versus-company competition.

Porter goes on to present three strategies for dealing with these competitive forces. His first is to *differentiate products and services.* By making them different—that is, "better" in the eyes of customers—firms may be able to charge higher prices or perhaps deter customers from moving to another product, lower the bargaining power of buyers, and so on. It is probably the most popular of his three strategies.

Porter's second strategy is to *be the lowest-cost producer.* He warns that simply being one of the low-cost producers is not enough. Not being the lowest causes a company to be stuck in the middle, with no real competitive advantage.

His third strategy is to *find a niche,* such as focusing on a segment of a product line or a geographical market. Companies that use this strategy can often serve their target market effectively and efficiently, at times being both the low-cost producer and having a highly differentiated product as well.

This framework guides IS planning because all five forces and three strategies are either enabled by, or implemented by, technology. Once management analyzes the forces and determines company strategy, the necessary information systems can be included in the plan.

Value Chain Analysis

A few years after proposing the five forces model just described, Porter presented the value chain in *Competitive Advantage;*[8] it too became a popular strategic planning tool. As shown in Figure 4-9, a value chain for a product or service consists of the major activities that add value during its creation, development, sale, and after-sales service. According to Porter, primary activities and support activities take place in every value chain.

The five primary activities deal with the creation of the product or service, getting it to the buyer, and servicing it afterward. These activities form the sequence of the value chain:

1. *Inbound logistics:* receiving and handling inputs
2. *Operations:* converting inputs to the product or service
3. *Outbound logistics:* collect, store, and distribute the product or service to buyers
4. *Marketing and sales:* the means/incentives for buyers to buy the product or service
5. *Service:* enhancements or maintenance of the value of the product or service

The four supporting activities underlie the entire value chain:

1. Organizational infrastructure
2. Human resources management
3. Technology development
4. Procurement

By studying how a firm performs the primary and support activities for each product or service, a firm can explore how it might add more value at every activity. Alternatively, it could determine where another company adds more value and team up with that firm, outsourcing that activity to that partner.

Virtual Value Chains. Jeff Rayport and John Sviokla[9] distinguish between market*places,* where physical products and physical location are important, and market*spaces,* where information substitutes for physical products and physical location. In the world of Internet commerce, they ask "How can companies create value in marketspace?" or "How can they create value in marketspace and marketplace concurrently, leveraging off each other?" They draw on Porter's value chain in their answer.

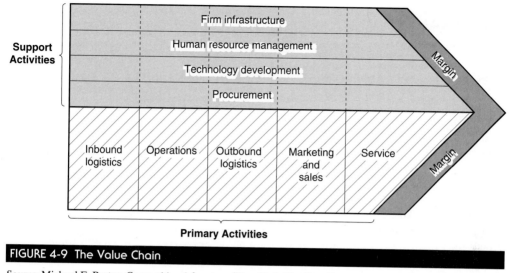

FIGURE 4-9 The Value Chain

Source: Michael E. Porter, *Competitive Advantage* (New York: The Free Press, 1985).

In the traditional value chain, note Rayport and Sviokla, companies treat information as a support element, not as a source of value itself. To compete in marketspace, however, companies need to use information to create new value for the customer (such as FedEx did in opening up its tracking system to consumers via its Web site). Creating value in marketspace also involves a value chain, but it is a virtual value chain, they say, because the steps are performed with information and through information. At every step in the chain, value via information can be added in five ways: gather it, organize it, select it, synthesize it, or distribute it. The IS organization should therefore be playing a major role in marketspace.

Rayport and Sviokla have observed that companies seem to follow an evolution in using information to add value: first by making operations visible, then by putting in place mirroring capabilities, and finally by creating space-based customer relationships.

Making operations visible.   Companies first create ways to see their physical operations through information. That is, they foster visibility of operations, generally through their production systems, allowing employees to coordinate activities across the physical value chain, sometimes in ways that lead to competitive advantage. Frito-Lay's field employees input information on store-by-store sales as well as information about competitors' promotions and new competitive products. With all this field data, managers can better schedule production to match demand, route trucks most efficiently, and tailor promotions to suit local buying patterns. Frito-Lay can more quickly react to marketplace changes. This sort of visibility, say Rayport and Sviokla, lays the foundation for a virtual value chain.

Mirroring capabilities.   Second, companies begin to substitute virtual activities for physical ones. Here's a case in point from a report by Roger Woolfe.[1b]

CASE EXAMPLE

AN AUTOMOBILE MANUFACTURER

This auto manufacturer has dealerships around the United States, many of which have a satellite dish, as does headquarters. In addition to other uses, these dishes are used by the firm's rental car subsidiary to auction used vehicles to dealers. These vehicles, which have fewer than 10,000 miles, are made available to the company's dealers so that they have good, clean used cars to sell.

For 30 minutes at a specified time, an auctioneer is able to sell 60 vehicles online. As a car comes up for bid, the dealers view it on the monitors at their premises. They can see it from several directions, read its ratings (on cleanliness and condition), and use a mouse to bid against the other dealers online. Headquarters staff monitor the progress of the auction and advise the auctioneer on, say, lowering minimum bids to ensure that every vehicle is sold. The auctions are held once or twice a month.

The dealers have been extremely satisfied with the system because it saves them from having to travel to auctions, and they can get good-quality used cars without much effort. And the manufacturer guarantees satisfaction. If, after taking delivery of a vehicle, the dealer decides he does not want it, he can send it back. ■

Another example is virtual worldwide teams, such as design teams in the United States, Europe, and Asia who work on designs and prototypes in a virtual information space. Time and space no longer become limitations. The teams can be located anywhere, work can be performed 24 hours a day, and many more virtual designs can be created and tested in a shorter time and for less cost than in the physical world. This mirroring of capabilities, say Rayport and Sviokla, marks the beginning of creating a parallel virtual value chain.

Space-based customer relationships. Third, companies draw on their flow of information to deliver value to customers in new ways. In essence, they create new space-based customer relationships. USAA, the insurance company for military officers, exemplifies this third step, note Rayport and Sviokla. For many years, USAA collected information about customers and made it available companywide so that employees could provide advice and answer questions anytime a customer called (visibility). The company then discovered it could create customer risk profiles and customize policies. From that point, it created new product lines, such as insurance for boat owners (mirroring capabilities). From there, USAA expanded to new areas, such as offering financing to boat purchasers. In fact, it even offers to replace stolen items in a theft claim, rather than send the insured a check—a service many seem to prefer. USAA is managing its information to create new value for customers.

When searching for strategic uses of information, Rayport and Sviokla point out that many of the "rules" differ from those of the physical marketplace. Digital assets are not used up in consumption; therefore, information can be reused in many forms at a low cost. New economies of scale are present, so small companies can effectively compete against large companies, due to lower overhead, while still covering large geographic areas. And new economies of scope allow insurance companies to offer financing and even discount buying programs to policyholders, as USAA is doing, for example. Finally, transaction costs are lower in marketspace; thus companies can capture information that was not possible to capture in the past, as Frito-Lay is doing.

To take advantage of these four changes, however, a significant mindshift is required from supply-side thinking to demand-side thinking, say Rayport and Sviokla. That is, companies need to "sense and respond" rather than "make and sell" products and services. That appears to be a significant strategic opportunity for companies, and IS should play a role in identifying and helping their company take advantage of it.

E-Business Value Matrix

At a Networld+Interop conference, Peter Alexander of Cisco Systems[10] described a portfolio planning technique used at Cisco to ensure they are developing a well-rounded portfolio of IT projects. The approach is further described in *Net Ready*.[11] These days, that portfolio revolves around the Internet, e-commerce, and e-business.

It can be difficult for executives to prioritize projects, said Alexander, because of the wealth of opportunities. A portfolio management approach is therefore of great value to senior and functional executives to ensure that they are working on a broad front that will lead to success in the Internet economy.

The portfolio management approach Cisco uses is called the e-business value matrix, and every IT project is meant to be placed in one of four categories to assess its value to the company. As shown in Figure 4-10, the value of each project is assessed as high or low in two categories: criticality to the business and newness of the idea—newness not just to the company but to the world. The result is four categories of projects: new fundamentals, operational excellence, rational experimentation, and breakthrough strategy.

New Fundamentals. These projects provide a fundamentally new way of working in overhead areas, not business-critical areas. They are low risk and focus on increasing productivity. They can provide significant cost savings by measurably improving

FIGURE 4-10 E-Business Value Matrix

	Criticality to Business	*Newness of Idea*
New fundamentals	Low	Low
Operational excellence	High	Low
Rational experimentation	Low	High
Breakthrough strategy	High	High

Source: Adapted from a speech by Peter Alexander and *Net Ready: Strategies for Success in the E-conomy* by Amir Hartman, John Sifonis, and John Kador (New York: McGraw-Hill, 2000).

operations. An example is Web-based expense reporting, described in the following Cisco case example.

These projects should be managed as quick hits: Implement a project to increase productivity in finance within three to six months, said Alexander, then move on to another area. Often, such projects can be implemented by IT with little user involvement during development. However, an important point to remember is that these systems aim at the grass roots of the company. Thus, they can lead to a cultural shift, such as shifting the company to an Internet culture, that is, working via the Internet or intranet.

Operational Excellence.   These projects are of medium risk because they may involve reengineering work processes. They do not aim for immediate returns but rather intend to increase such areas as customer satisfaction and corporate agility. In essence, they revolve around providing faster access to information. These projects can be important in improving IT credibility because of their high visibility. An example is an executive information system for quickly viewing operational metrics. Such a system is highly visible to executives.

These projects have about a 12-month horizon. They should involve cross-functional teams (to ensure that the reengineering does indeed take place), and they should use tested technology.

Rational Experimentation.   These projects test new technologies and new ideas. Hence, they are risky. But every company needs some of these projects to hope to move ahead of competitors. When described as experiments, they set the realistic expectation that they may fail. The goal is to prove the concept in, say, several months' time or less. One example could be streaming media, another could be desktop video conferencing. When treated as experiments, these projects will not hurt the company if they fail. If they do pan out, however, they could prove a new business or IT model and thus become one of the other three types.

These incubator-type projects should be managed as experiments, with short time frames and incremental funding. The team may be full-time, but they do not need to move out of IT. And participants should not be penalized if one of these projects fails.

Breakthrough Strategy.   These projects potentially have a huge impact on the company, and perhaps even on the industry, if they succeed. These projects capture the imagination; but they are high risk. The typical response, once someone sees the potential is, "If this works, it would change. . . ." An example of a breakthrough strategy is eBay. Its auction business model altered people's thinking about global buying and selling. Another example is partner extranets; if these succeed, they could move to the operational excellence cell.

Breakthrough strategy projects require strong functional buy-in. One way to get this commitment is to brainstorm with functional partners on the possibilities. And because they are generally bet-the-farm types of projects, they need to be managed like a start-up. They need venture-capital-like funding, not month-to-month milestones. So, for example, the request may be for $10 million, with the possibility of failure, but also with the possibility of huge upside returns.

These IT-based projects need dedicated staff from numerous functions. To attract top talent and foster the intense communication and collaboration needed among the team members, they probably need to be housed in a dot-com-like setting. So they are set apart organizationally and report to the CEO or CFO, who protects them from corporate politics and from the "but this is the way we've always done it" mindset. Finally, the skunk works team needs to be given financial incentives if the project succeeds.

In conclusion, Alexander stated that IT departments can get functional buy-in if they create such a portfolio of IT projects and then manage that portfolio properly. A key to success is leadership. All the CXOs (CEO, CFO, COO, CIO) need to evangelize and empower others to make these projects happen. They need to encourage risk and accept failure of the right kind. Because CXO involvement is key, they may need to be educated on their role.

To illustrate this portfolio approach, here are examples of Cisco IT projects.

CASE EXAMPLE

CISCO SYSTEMS

Cisco Systems manufactures computers that provide the infrastructure for the Internet. Cisco makes use of the e-business value matrix described by Alexander[10] as the means for managing its portfolio of IT projects, to place a value on each project based on the newness of the idea it employs and the criticality of the system to the company.

Here are examples of systems in each of the four cells in the matrix, new fundamentals, operational excellence, rational experimentation, and breakthrough strategies:

New Fundamentals

Cisco's expense reporting system, Metro, is a fundamentally new way of performing this function. It aims to reduce costs in this overhead area.

To submit an expense report, an employee now goes to a Web page to build the report online. As the report is filled in, the system checks to see whether the employee has adhered to company policy.

When submitted, the system routes the report to the employee's manager and explains the purpose of the expense report, the total expenses, and whether any policies were violated. If the manager does nothing, the employee's credit card account and personal account are credited in two days' time.

This system quickly delivered major cost savings to the firm because Cisco now only needs three people to manage expense reports for all 31,000 employees. Although abuse is possible, the cost of potential losses from questionable charges is a fraction of the cost of having a larger administrative staff.

Operational Excellence

Cisco's "executive dashboards" for each functional area are seen as operationally differentiating the company from its competitors. In fact, Cisco executives

(Case Continued)

have said, "I cannot live without this system because . . . it allows me to model sales programs, . . . it allows me to manage the supply chain, . . . it allows me to do trend analysis on component availability, and so on."

Each dashboard is a Web front end to the company's data warehouse. In essence, it is an executive information system that allows executives to drill down into the data to pull up a snapshot of, say, the company's revenues, bookings, or margins (the fundamentals of the company) at a point in time by business unit, region, entire enterprise, product line, and so on. Thus, executives can see, for example, how well a division is progressing on meeting its forecasts.

Furthermore, the system allows the CFO to close the company's books within one day of the end of each quarter, and the company expects to reduce this lag to just two to three hours.

Such a system is not excellence in product, it is excellence in IT and it is operational excellence, said Alexander.

Rational Experimentation

Cisco has a continual stream of such experiments going on in IT. One has been streaming video. They have put in the capability to handle multicast streaming media and are watching to see the business value of this new technology to the various functional areas. For example, they have made all-company meetings available online to employees through IP TV. If this technology proves useful, it could be used for new product training.

Breakthrough Strategy

Cisco views its development of a virtual supply chain as a breakthrough strategy. Of the 26 factories that build Cisco products, only five are owned by Cisco. Thus, the company's ability to scale and respond is not tied to capital assets. It is a function of their building an effective supply chain. Although not easy, they believe it is critical to their business. If their gamble on virtual manufacturing goes awry, it would present an enormous problem. However, they see it as worth the effort because the returns will be extremely high if they succeed.

Cisco takes its portfolio of IT projects and Internet initiatives so seriously that CEO John Chambers holds a review of leading Internet capabilities each quarter. At these reviews, each functional area describes how they are implementing Internet capabilities that are ahead of their peers in the industry. Most company CEOs do not make this effort, said Alexander. If they did, they would see spectacular returns, he believes. ∎

Linkage Analysis Planning

Linkage analysis planning examines the links organizations have with one another with the goal of creating a strategy for utilizing electronic channels. This approach to strategic systems planning is espoused by Kenneth Primozic, Edward Primozic, and Joe Leben in their book *Strategic Choices.*[12] The methodology includes the following steps:

1. Define power relationships among the various players and stakeholders.
2. Map out your extended enterprise to include suppliers, buyers, and strategic partners.
3. Plan your electronic channels to deliver the information component of products and services.

Define Power Relationships. To create a strategy for building electronic links among enterprises, Primozic's team believes that management must first understand the power relationships that currently exist among these various players. For this analysis, they begin with Michael Porter's classic model of competitive forces, which includes competitors, buyers, substitutes, suppliers, and potential entrants. To this model they add technology, demographics, global competition, government regulations, and "whatever is important in your environment." The goals of this step follow:

1. Identify who has the power.
2. Determine future threats and opportunities for the company.

The analysis begins by identifying *linkages,* which are relationships the organization has with other entities. Figure 4-12 on page 134 is a good illustration. The links are represented by lines between organizations (shown in boxes). Once identified, management needs to determine who is managing each link. Oftentimes, no one is, which should be of concern. From here, the team picks the most important link and decides how the firm can control that link. The authors believe that winning organizations in the 1990s will be those that control the electronic channels, or the electronic linkages among enterprises.

The discussion of how to gain power within one's world of linkages brings up a host of questions. Two important ones are: How might alliances with other firms across industries or even with competitors help us? How do we need to restructure ourselves to seize an opportunity or ward off a threat?

Map Out Your Extended Enterprise. These questions lead to the second step in their approach to planning—the extended enterprise. An extended enterprise includes all of one's own organization plus those organizations with which one interacts, such as suppliers, buyers, government agencies, and so forth (see Figure 4-11).

The purpose of this step is to get management to recognize the existence of this extended enterprise and then begin to manage the relationships that exist in it. Primozic and colleagues believe successful managers will focus on extended enterprises. They see two fundamental principles to managing these relationships:

1. The enterprise's success depends on the relationships among everyone involved, which includes employees, managers, suppliers, alliances, distribution channels, and so forth.
2. Some 70 percent of the final cost of goods and services is in their information content; therefore, managing information as a strategic tool is crucial.

An extended enterprise diagram might deal only with external players, such as the government, stockholders, traditional competitors, the financial community, and so forth. Such a chart includes everyone whose decisions affect the organization or who are affected by its decisions. The analysis then moves on to discussing how the links might change, and who and how each link should be managed.

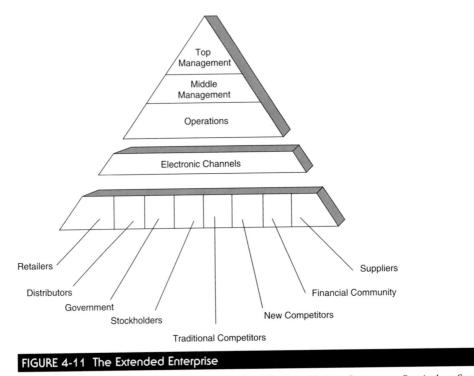

Top Management

Middle Management

Operations

Electronic Channels

Retailers

Distributors

Government

Stockholders

Traditional Competitors

New Competitors

Financial Community

Suppliers

FIGURE 4-11 The Extended Enterprise

Source: K. I. Primozic, E. A. Primozic, and J. F. Leben, *Strategic Choices: Supremacy, Survival, or Sayonara* (New York: McGraw-Hill, 1991).

In the extended enterprise, each relationship will prosper only when it is "win-win," say the authors. For example, in return for maintaining a buyer's parts inventory and providing just-in-time delivery, a supplier may be paid electronically upon delivery of goods. Such an arrangement profits both parties.

Competitive advantage will depend increasingly on being able to exploit the collective resources of one's extended enterprise, say Primozic and colleagues. Such enterprises often require electronic channels to execute business transactions, which leads to the third step in their planning approach—planning the electronic channels.

Plan Your Electronic Channels. An electronic channel is an electronic link used to create, distribute, and present information and knowledge as part of a product or service or as an ancillary good. These channels focus on the information component of products, which is mainly in marketing, administration, distribution, and customer service. The authors believe that those who control the electronic channels will be the winners because they will be able to address new niche markets as they arise. Furthermore, as use of IT leads to a smaller, faster-paced world, organizations with the longest electronic reach into their extended organization will have an advantage.

The authors use linkage analysis charts to help executives conceptualize the key issues they face in an extended enterprise, and focus on the factors that are critical to their future success. This methodology has been used by the Electric Power Research Institute, whose story we tell next.

CASE EXAMPLE

ELECTRIC POWER RESEARCH INSTITUTE

The Electric Power Research Institute (EPRI), with headquarters in Palo Alto, California, is a large private research firm serving more than 700 electric member utilities. Their 350 staff scientists and engineers manage some 1,600 R&D projects at any one time. The projects, which study such subjects as power generation, superconductivity, electronic and magnetic fields, and acid rain, are conducted by more than 400 utility, university, commercial, government, and other R&D contractors, on behalf of the members.

Their Challenge

EPRI's mission is to deliver the information and knowledge from their research projects to the 400,000 employees in the 768 member utilities to help them be more competitive. Management realized EPRI had to compress the "information float," the elapsed time from the availability of research findings to the use of those results in industry.

The institute was suffering from "infosclerosis," the hardening and clogging of their information arteries. Due to the volume of research findings—gigabytes of information—moving information in and out of EPRI was extremely difficult. In addition, because of the documentation and publishing process, the results often were *unavailable* for up to 24 months, so the reports were not as timely as they could be. Nor were the results accessible, because they were in massive reports. Solving this information delivery challenge was critical to EPRI's survival.

Their Vision

Their vision was to assist their members in exploiting EPRI's product—knowledge—as a strategic business resource, whenever and from wherever they choose. To accomplish this vision, EPRI built an electronic information and communication services.

As described by Maria Mann and her colleagues,[13] their delivery vehicle is EPRINET, an electronic "channel" that includes

- A natural-language front end for accessing online information
- Expert system-based products that contain the knowledge of their energy experts
- Electronic mail facilities for person-to-person communications
- Video conferencing to foster small-group communication.

Using Linkage Analysis Planning

To focus the EPRINET effort, and to identify the services and products that would offer strategic business advantages to their members, EPRI used the linkage analysis planning methodology in a three-day workshop led by Kenneth Primozic. The workshop began with management stating that (1) EPRI was both an R&D organization and a knowledge provider, and (2) the goal was to leverage knowledge as a strategic asset.

From this starting point, Primozic asked, "Who is linked to EPRI in creating and distributing knowledge?" The

(Case Continued)

participants identified the co-creators as contractors, research firms, universities, the government, and technology. They identified the recipients as the utility industry, universities, research labs, government policies, and knowledge as capital—as shown in Figure 4-12. Each represented a link to EPRI, so the group then studied the present and future power relationships in each buyer-seller link. During these discussions, they saw how some current customers, such as universities or research labs, could become future competitors and change the power relationship in a link.

Management's goal was to leverage knowledge, so the group listed all the ways it could be achieved. Then they focused on the most important way, which turned out to be treating knowledge as capital. During this analysis, management defined the following critical success factors for giving EPRINET a sustainable competitive advantage:

- Establish the "right" mix of product offerings, a mix that allows people to pick, choose, and combine at the lowest possible cost.
- Keep all customers in mind, which includes utility executives, research engineers, and operations people.
- Use IT—specifically expert systems and natural language—to make the system easy to use and access.
- Create a range of "knowledge packages" targeted to specific audiences.
- Establish a timely, reliable, secure global distribution channel.

Once EPRINET was made available, a marketing campaign began soon thereafter. The number of users has climbed steadily since. Frequent users report that the system is indeed broadening the number of people they can stay in contact with and allowing them to uncover EPRI research findings that they would not have found otherwise. ■

FIGURE 4-12 EPRI'S Linkage Analysis

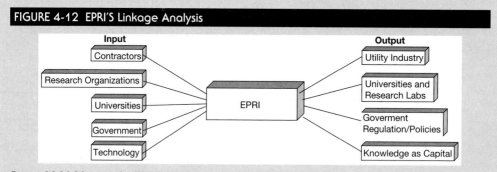

Source: M. M. Mann et al., "EPRINET: Leveraging Knowledge in the Electric Utility Industry," *MIS Quarterly,* September 1991, 403–421.

CONCLUSION

Based on the successes and failures of past information systems planning efforts, we see two necessary ingredients to a good strategic planning effort. One is that the plans must look toward the future. This point may seem obvious, but in these turbulent times, the future is not likely to be an extrapolation of the past. So a successful planning effort needs to support "peering into the future"—most likely in a sense-and-respond fashion.

A second necessary ingredient is that information system planning must be intrinsic to business planning. This point may also seem obvious, but, again, unless the planning process specifically requires joint development, the systems plans may not be relevant because they do not align with corporate strategy. A misalignment is not so likely with the advent of Internet commerce, but it is also not yet "natural" in many companies.

In this chapter, we have described a new approach to strategic systems planning and a number of the most popular techniques. No single technique is best and no single one is the most widely used in business. In fact, many companies use a combination because they deal with different aspects of planning. The main goal these days is to meld speed with flexibility. That goal can best be achieved by creating an overall strategic envelope and conducting short experiments within that envelope—then move quickly to implement an experiment that proves successful. Sense-and-respond is the new strategy-making mode.

QUESTIONS AND EXERCISES

Review Questions

1. What are the primary differences between operational planning, tactical planning, and strategic planning?
2. Identify and describe several reasons why strategic systems planning is so difficult.
3. What assumptions in traditional strategy-making no longer hold true?
4. What is a sense-and-respond approach to planning?
5. Describe Skandia Future Centers' 3G teams.
6. What is a strategic envelope?
7. Describe Shell Oil's action labs.
8. What are the most important IT experiments, according to Gartner EXP?
9. What is the main contribution of the stages of growth theory to information systems planning?
10. What are critical success factors? How do they contribute to the systems planning process?
11. Describe Porter's five competitive forces.
12. Describe the components of Porter's value chain.
13. What is the evolution of ways companies use information to add value, according to Rayport and Sviokla?
14. Describe the four types of applications in the e-business value matrix.
15. Briefly describe the goal of linkage analysis planning and the three steps in it.

Discussion Questions

1. Which of the frameworks for systems planning seems most useful to you? Why?
2. If you were in charge of system planning for a small firm, what questions would you ask the company officers to determine which planning approach(es) would be most appropriate?
3. In Chapter 2, we stated that strategies are out, visioning is in, because no one can plan in turbulent times. In this chapter we say that planning is crucial. How would you reconcile these two viewpoints?

Exercises

1. Survey the current literature on the subject of systems planning. What other approaches or frameworks are not mentioned in this text? What automated products are available on the market to assist information systems executives in the planning process?
2. Visit the chief information officer of a local organization. What planning process does it use? What is the planning horizon? To what degree do the systems plans and the business plans relate to each other?
3. Create a simple information linkage analysis chart of your current personal relationships. Put yourself in the middle box and each relationship in its own box around you, with a line from you to each of them. Who has the "power" in each link? How might that power shift in the future? Which is the most important relationship to you? How could you make it more "win-win"?
4. Ask the CIO of a nearby company what electronic channels his or her firm has in place. Ask about the benefits both parties receive in each link.

REFERENCES

1. Wentworth Research Program (now part of Gartner Executive Programs, 56 Top Gallant, Stamford, CT 06904):
   a. Woolfe, Roger, Barbara McNurlin, and Phil Taylor, *Tactical Strategy,* November 1999.
   b. Woolfe, Roger, *Supporting Inter-Business Collaboration,* September 1995.

2. Parker, Marilyn, Robert Benson, with Ed Trainor, *Information Economics: Linking Information Technology and Business Performance,* Prentice Hall, 1988. European edition 1989. Japanese edition, 1990.

3. Brown, Shona and Kathleen Eisenhardt, *Competing on the Edge: Strategy as Structured Chaos,* Harvard Business School Press, Cambridge, MA, 1998.

4. Pascale, Richard, "Surfing the Edge of Chaos," *Sloan Management Review,* Spring 1999, pp. 83–94.

5. Nolan, R. L., and C. F. Gibson, "Managing the Four Stages of EDP Growth," *Harvard Business Review,* January/February 1974, p. 76ff.

6. Nolan, R. L. "Information Technology Management from 1960–2000," chapter 7 in *A Nation Transformed by Information,* Alfred D. Chandler and James W. Cortad (Eds), Oxford Press, Cambridge, England, 2000.

7. Rockart, John, "Chief Executives Define Their Own Data Needs," *Harvard Business Review,* March/April 1979, pp. 81–92.

8. Porter, Michael E., *Competitive Strategy,* The Free Press, New York, 1980; *Competitive Advantage,* The Free Press, 1985.

9. Rayport, Jeffrey and John Sviokla, "Managing in the Marketspace," *Harvard Business Review,* November/December 1994, pp. 141–150, and "Exploiting the Virtual Value Chain," November/December 1995, pp. 75–85.

10. Alexander, Peter, "Aligning the IT Organization with Business Goals," presentation at Networld+Interop 2000, May 8, 2000.

11. Hartman, Amir, John Sifonis, with John Kador, *Net Ready: Strategies for Success in the E-conomy,* McGraw-Hill, New York, 2000.

12. Primozic, K. I., E. A. Primozic, and J. Leben, *Strategic Choices: Supremacy, Survival, or Sayanara,* McGraw-Hill, New York, 1991.

13. Mann, M. M., R. L. Ludman, T. A. Jenckes, and B. C. McNurlin, "EPRINET: Leveraging Knowledge In the Electric Utility Industry," *MIS Quarterly,* September 1991, pp. 403–421.

PART

II

MANAGING THE ESSENTIAL TECHNOLOGIES

Part II—Chapters 5 through 8—focuses on infrastructure management, as shown in the following figure. The purpose of this part is to present the technological underpinnings of a corporate IT operation, and point out the major issues that must be addressed for it to be well managed.

Chapter 5 looks at various kinds of distributed systems architectures and discusses the important concepts of IT architecture and infrastructure.

Chapter 6 discusses telecom—the new infrastructure being built, how the telecom industry is transforming itself, the underpinnings of today's networks, the Internet, and the new frontier of wireless Internet access.

While Chapters 5 and 6 deal with the "structure" of distributed systems, Chapter 7 deals with the "content," or the information resources. These resources have been referred to as data. But increasingly, this content has context (making it information) and intelligence and "actionability" (making it knowledge). All three aspects are discussed in Chapter 7.

Finally, Chapter 8 explores operations, the day-to-day concerns of keeping elaborate, far-flung corporate distributed systems up and running. Back in the old mainframe days, operations were pretty much taken for granted and housed in "the glass room." Today, even Internet users have operational concerns, such as security and having access to Web sites during spikes in demand.

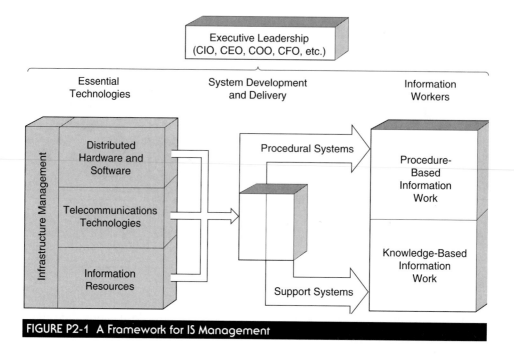

FIGURE P2-1 A Framework for IS Management

CHAPTER

5

DISTRIBUTED SYSTEMS: THE OVERALL ARCHITECTURE

INTRODUCTION

Way back in 1964, Paul Baran at the Rand Corporation wrote a paper about distributed systems. At the time, computing meant mainframes and hardwired terminals; distributed systems were just theory. Today, distributed systems are the architecture of choice. Thus, we begin this part—Part II, which deals with the essential technologies of computing—with a discussion of this important computing framework.

Definitions.   To start, we need to point out that the two terms *architecture* and *infrastructure* are often used interchangeably, which can make discussions of distributed systems confusing. In this book, we make the following distinction:

> An IT *architecture* is a blueprint. A blueprint shows how a system, house, vehicle, or product will look and how the parts interrelate. The more complex an item, the more important its architecture, so that the interrelationships among the components are well defined.
>   An IT *infrastructure,* on the other hand, is the implementation of an architecture. In a city, the infrastructure includes its streets and street lighting, hospitals and schools, utilities, police and fire departments, and so on. In a corporation, the IT infrastructure includes the processors, software, databases, electronic links, and data centers as well as the standards that ensure the components work together, the skills for managing the operation, and even some of the electronic processes themselves.

An interesting use of the term *infrastructure* has occurred recently. Rather than talk about hardware, software, data, and communications as the components of computing, some people now refer only to applications and infrastructure. The infrastructure provides the electronic highways, processing, and storage sites, while the applications use these facilities to produce value for the organization. Suffice it to say, when you hear "infrastructure," think of city streets or electronic highways. At the end of this chapter, we delve into both architecture and infrastructure in a bit more depth, after looking at various kinds of distributed systems.

The Evolution of Distributed Systems.   In the first IT architecture—mainframes doing batch processing—some input came from "dumb" terminals and some output went to dumb terminals. These user devices had no processing capabilities of their own. All the processing was on the mainframe and most of it was for corporate needs, such as payroll and billing. With the advent of minicomputers, computers moved into departments, but the master-slave computing model persisted. Processing was centralized; although gradually distribution or sharing of processing among mainframes and minis began to occur.

With the microcomputer, however, the model changed significantly because processing power moved first onto desktops, then into briefcases, and now into pockets, game consoles, MP3 players, and so on. This distribution of processing led, in the 1990s, to processing being thought of as being split between a "client" that requests services and a "server" that provides those services. This model continues today.

However, an interesting twist has developed. We are seeing a move back toward a type of centralized processing, with an interconnected network of servers, rather than a mainframe, as the central source. Information appliances and diskless computers make requests to the Internet, where all the processing is handled via the servers.

Throughout this evolution, stand-alone processors (or processors with dedicated terminals) appeared first and then were gradually linked to other computers. As that happened, the notion of a distributed architecture developed. Today we have the Internet, an example of a global distributed system. Devices and computers of all sizes, from any vendor that uses the appropriate standards, use the Internet to send files to each other, perform processing for each other, house data for each other, and send messages to one another. The Internet has become the center of a worldwide, distributed system. It is because of this global electronic infrastructure that the e-business revolution we now see is taking place at all. But, as we discuss later in this chapter, the Internet is not the end-all and be-all of distributed systems.

To get a grounding in this important notion in computing, we now delve into distributed system thinking.

Four Attributes of Distributed Systems

The degree to which a system is distributed can be determined by answering four questions.

1. Where is the processing done?
2. How are the processors and other devices interconnected?
3. Where is the information stored?
4. What rules or standards are used?

Distributed processing is the ability for more than one interconnected processor to be operating at the same time, typically for processing an application on more than one computer. The goal in distributed processing is to move the appropriate processing as close to the user as possible, and to let other machines handle the work they do best (such as house and manage video databases or process airline reservations).

An advanced form of distributed processing permits interoperability, which is the capability for different machines using different operating systems on different networks to work together on tasks. They exchange information in standard ways without requiring changes in command languages or functionality and without physical intervention.

Charlie Bachman, a pioneer in the database and distributed system fields, pointed out that only two forms of interoperability are possible. One is the transparent communication between *systems* using system protocols. In this form, the systems decide when to interoperate. Companies implementing the International Standards Organization Open System Interconnection (OSI) reference model have developed protocols for standard file and job transfers to permit this form of interoperability, says Bachman. The Internet fits into this category. (We discuss OSI in Chapter 6.)

The second form of interoperability is the interactive or two-way flow of messages between *user applications*. In this form, user applications can be activated by receiving messages; this activity, of course, is supported on the Internet and on intranets. Both kinds of interoperability are important, says Bachman.

Connectivity among processors means that each processor in a distributed system can send data and messages to any other processor through electronic communication links. A desirable structure for reliable distributed systems has at least two independent paths between any two nodes, enabling an automatic alternate routing in case one node is down. Planned redundancy of this type is critical for reliable operation. Such redundancy has not been implemented in most LANs, which is one reason they have been so fragile. It is, however, a major feature of the Internet as well as most corporate wide area networks (WANs).

Distributed databases are being defined in at least two ways. One divides a database and distributes its portions throughout a system, without duplicating the data. Any portion is accessible from any node, subject to access authorization. Users do not need to know where a piece of data is located to access it because the system knows where all data is stored.

The second type of distributed database stores the same data at several locations, with one site containing the master file. Synchronization of data is a significant problem in this approach, which is why it has not been the preferred way to distribute data.

An interesting development in this area is "edge servers" on the Web. An edge server is defined as being on the edge of the Internet, which means close to a set of users (such as a city); it holds a copy of an organization's Web site. Many edge servers, located strategically around the world, hold the same information. Edge servers arose to accelerate downloads to Web site visitors, so they would not leave the site because they had to wait too long to see it appear on their screen. Edge servers—essentially distributed databases—have become an integral part of the Internet.

Systemwide rules mean that an operating discipline for the distributed system has been developed and is enforced at all times. These rules govern communication between nodes, security, data accessibility, program and file transfers, and common operating procedures. Since the 1990s, these systemwide rules have been increasingly based on the "open system" concept. Products utilizing "open standards" can operate together in one or more distributed systems, such as the Internet. Users' goal is to avoid being locked into the proprietary products of one vendor. Interestingly, the meaning of "open systems" has expanded over time as open systems have become a reality.

In the 1980s, open systems referred mainly to telecom and meant that a company intended to implement products that followed the OSI reference model whenever they became available. At that time, OSI implementation was not a reality, just a target.

About 1990, the definition expanded to include operating systems, specifically UNIX, because it runs on many more platforms than any other operating system and is not owned by any one company. At that time, UNIX was tentatively seen as appropriate for mainline business computing. Today, it is an important operating systems for servers on the Internet. In business computing, it has gained a foothold but has not displaced proprietary operating systems, such as Microsoft's Windows.

At the same time, in the data world, "open" meant structured query language (SQL), the standard intermediary language for accessing relational databases.

In the early 1990s, the definition shifted to the interfaces between applications. "Open" meant standardized interfaces that would allow products to interoperate across multivendor networks, operating systems, and databases. Application program interfaces (APIs) came into being. They define the way data is presented to another component of a system—a machine, a database, even an electronic mail system. APIs allow individual products to be innovative, yet connectable, and they make writing distributed systems far easier. Their importance continues today.

Today, the term *open* includes the already mentioned definitions and stresses interconnectivity. In this realm, the OSI reference model remains the definition of "open." Most people, however, are only familiar with its widest implementation: the network protocol used in the Internet, Telecommunication Protocol/Internet Protocol (TCP/IP). Corporate networks, both LANs and WANs, are increasingly migrating to TCP/IP to allow easier interconnection to the Internet.

An interesting twist on the term *open* hit critical mass not long ago. When the Internet first arrived, it allowed programmers to offer software free (or for a small donation), which many did. This freeware has come to be called *open source,* which means the source code can be downloadable by anyone and can thus be modified. (Companies that sell application packages do not ship the precious source code.) The open source movement led to developers taking some freeware, improving it, and re-posting it to the Net. In the 1990s, Linus Torvald offered his operating system, Linux, as open source; he has since gained a huge following. Developers around the world have contributed to it, improved and expanded it. And because it is free, it is being used in many of the Internet's servers. Some contend that the open source mindset is an integral part of the way the e-world should work.

So the term *open systems* keeps expanding because it truly is the crux of distributed systems, allowing products from multiple vendors to work together.

Although some people see the main reason for distributing systems as improving the use of computer resources, that is just a technical reason. The organizational impetus behind distributed systems is to move responsibility for computing resources to those who use them. With this in mind, we now briefly address the business reasons for distributing applications and the responsibilities that go with them.

When to Distribute Computing Responsibilities

Information systems management needs a corporate policy for deciding when the development, operation, and maintenance of an application should be distributed. Individual end users and departments should not be left on their own to make these decisions, especially where enterprise connectivity, and even ecosystem connectivity, is important. Although technical considerations are critical, they should not be the determining factors behind a system architecture. Rather, the major reason for choosing a particular distributed system architecture hinges on: *Who should make the key management operating decisions?*

Decision-making responsibilities are being pushed down and out in organizations, with local sites and teams given more autonomy and responsibility for the resources they use. One such resource is IT. People who make the decisions about how their portion of the business operates also should be making the decisions about how they use IT. Teamwork between IS management and business management is important in designing a distributed processing architecture that supports the business's goals.

Francis Wagner, a computing pioneer, once said he believes people perform best when they are responsible for their own mistakes. If they have no one to blame but themselves, then the quality of their performance increases. The result is a more effective use of corporate resources.

Therefore, a driving force behind distributed processing is the desire to give more people more control over their work. This autonomy can happen at any of six levels: company, division, site, department, team, or individual.

Professor James Wetherbe[1] suggested asking the following three *business questions* before distributing information systems functions and the responsibilities that go with them. Systems responsibilities can be distributed *unless* the following are true.

Are the Operations Interdependent?   When it is important for one operation to know what another is doing, those operations are interdependent; therefore, their planning, software development, machine resources, and operations need to be centrally coordinated to synchronize their operation. Two industries in which interdependency is important are manufacturing and airlines, which is why they have continued to have large centralized systems even in this era of distributed systems.

Are the Businesses Really Homogeneous?   If the operations do not need to know what each other is doing, then many systems functions can be decentralized, *unless* the operations truly have a lot in common.

For example, in the fast food business, each franchise has the same information processing needs which makes them homogeneous. But they do not need to know what each other is doing, so they are not interdependent. Under these circumstances, processing may be distributed, but planning, software development, and hardware selection should be centralized, to keep processing costs down and to more easily migrate to new systems.

Deciding whether the information processing in two parts of a business is truly homogeneous is not always obvious, says Wetherbe. For instance, not all retail chains are the same. One major retailer found that they needed to create two information systems for handling credit charges—one for their upscale stores and one for their discount stores. The needs of the two types of stores were so different that a single system would not suffice. But, their corporate IS department does control planning, which gives them the ability to seize marketing opportunities quickly when they can reuse systems built by either operation. So, centralized planning is important, whether processing is distributed or not, he says.

Does the Corporate Culture Support Decentralization?   Even if the business units do quite different things and do not need to know what each other is doing, corporate culture might dictate that some functions be centralized.

Wetherbe cites the example of a large company with 60 widely diverse business units. Although it might appear logical for this company to distribute all functions, they chose to centralize finance, human resources, and systems planning. They want to offer corporatewide career opportunities, with as little retraining as possible. With the central staff doing systems planning and coordination, the company can more easily move people and reuse systems.

If none of these three criteria—interdependency, homogeneity, or corporate culture—forces centralization, each business unit can direct its own information systems activity, with the central organization coordinating the plans.

Two Guiding Frameworks

Now that we have briefly addressed why to distribute systems, we look at how, via two guiding frameworks: one from an organizational perspective and the other from a technical perspective.

An Organizational Framework.   One possible distributed system structure is to serve six organizational levels. Figure 5-1 illustrates the six levels.

1. Enterprise
2. Region or country
3. Site (plants, warehouses, branch offices)
4. Department or process
5. Work group or team
6. Individuals

These levels exist within a single organization, and increasingly, they link to other organizations. For example, the current "hot" level is level four where companies are changing from a functional orientation to a process orientation. In the area of supply chain management, for example, companies want to electronically share information about customer orders and the status of internal operations with suppliers so those suppliers can have the specific parts on hand when needed. Process thinking requires linking disparate systems in different organizations. This linkage can be made one-to-one with suppliers or through intermediaries, such as electronic marketplaces, which act as matchmakers over the Internet. The Internet is playing an important role in creating electronic links for processes.

Work groups and teams have also become tremendously important as companies change how they work. We see two types at this level five. One type of work group is a group of people who do essentially the same work. Anyone in the group can substitute for any other, if necessary. Such groups are found in the customer service centers of small Internet service providers (ISPs), where the reps need to answer questions on every facet of linking to the Internet. In large ISPs, reps often specialize in answering questions on specific operating systems. Both groups need systems to support their work with customers.

The second type of group or team is *self-managed work teams.* They contain all the people who serve a particular set of customers or offer a particular product. These people represent all the necessary functions, such as manufacturing, marketing, customer service, and so forth. The intent is to give them more autonomy and decision-making power to serve their customers better. By allowing them to manage themselves, it is hoped they will provide more personalized and faster service. They need their own systems. But these systems will be far different from the ones needed by the ISP reps.

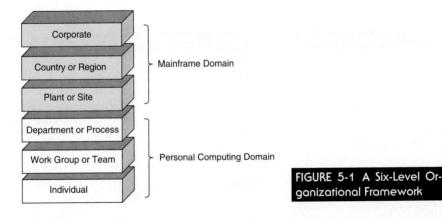

FIGURE 5-1 A Six-Level Organizational Framework

In all, systems are needed for each of the six organizational levels. Interorganizational links can occur at all six levels as well.

A Technical Framework. Way back in 1982, Einar Stefferud, David Farber, and Ralph Dement developed a conceptual framework for distributed systems.[2] It uses the acronym SUMURU, meaning "single user, multiple user, remote utility." Surprisingly, SUMURU is as appropriate today as it was in 1982, perhaps even more so because distributed systems are today's architecture. Their framework includes four components: processors, networks, services, and standards. Figure 5-2 summarizes the SUMURU components, and Figure 5-3 illustrates the architecture.

Processors. The authors see three levels of processors, usually with associated information storage. The name of their architecture, SUMURU, comes from these three levels of processors. *Single-user systems* (SUs) can operate in a stand-alone mode but also will be connected to local networks (LNs). Today, SUs are the "clients" in distributed systems. *Multiple-user systems* (MUs) serve local groups of users. Today, they are work group servers in corporate local area networks. These MUs also provide (1) backup facilities for other MUs, (2) heavier-duty processing for SUs, (3) program libraries for themselves and SUs, and (4) database management for central files.

Ideally, say the authors, the SUs will be scaled-down versions of the MUs, able to run the same software (to reduce software development and maintenance) but without all the features needed for shared operation on an MU.

Remote utility systems (RU) provide heavy-duty computing, corporate database management, remote processing, and backup for the MUs. For most organizations, RUs are the corporate hosts, although they are increasingly becoming external service providers (ESPs) that take over the running of corporate data centers or corporate applications. They may house and operate a company's Web site operation, its extranet, and even its intranet. Or they may handle the human resources function for a firm. In addition, Web sites on the Internet can be considered RUs, especially if they provide subscription services to firms.

Networks. The authors see a network architecture consisting of two levels. *Local networks* (LNs) will provide high-speed information transfer as well as close coupling between several SUs and a local MU. Today these are LANs. MUs may provide personal

---

FIGURE 5-2   Components of the Sumuru Distributed System Architecture

Processors	**Services**
Single-user systems (SU)	Terminal access
Multiple-user systems (MU)	File transfer
Remote utility systems (RU)	Computer mail
Networks	**Standards**
Local network (LN)	Operating systems
Remote networks (RN)	Communications protocols
	Database systems

Source: E. Stefferud, D. Farber, and R. Dement, "SUMURU: A Network Configuration for the Future," *Mini-Micro Systems,* May 1982, 311–312.

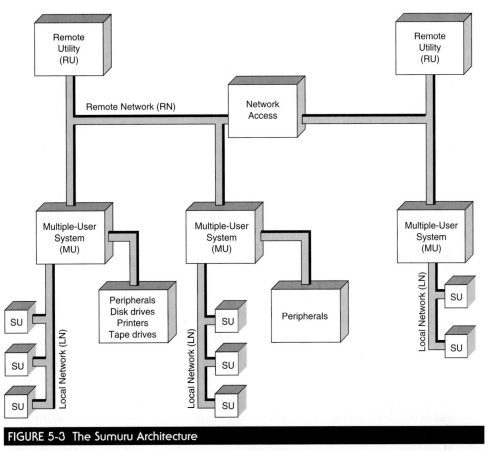

FIGURE 5-3 The Sumuru Architecture

Source: E. Stefferud, D. Farber, and R. Dement, "SUMURU: A Network Configuration for the Future," *Mini-Micro Systems,* May 1982, 311–312.

files, shared files, and program libraries for the SUs, and they can be the gateway between the LNs and remote networks.

Remote networks (RNs) provide connections among MUs and connection to both in-house and commercial RUs. RNs—which today include metropolitan area networks (MANs), wide area networks (WANs), cell phone and satellite networks, and the Internet—generally have lower transfer speeds than the LNs, but they still should have enough bandwidth to provide downloads within reasonable time limits.

Services.   The authors see three main types of services in this network architecture. One service is *access* to any SU, MU, or RU, subject only to management constraints, not technical barriers. Users must also have *file transfer* capabilities, to send and receive files. It means that a user must have both read and write privileges at both ends of the transfer. Finally, the system must provide an *electronic mail* service. Note that all three are available to PCs via the Internet. The challenge today is providing the same capabilities for handheld devices and wireless computing, which many believe are the second generation of the Internet.

Standards. Standards are needed in three areas: operating systems, communication protocols, and database management systems (DBMSs). Operating system standards are designed to minimize barriers to transferring and using programs and data. Ideally, the selected operating systems should run on more than one vendor's equipment. Standard communication protocols are needed for access, file transfers, and e-mail. In the communication area, TCP/IP (which is used in the Internet) has become the defacto standard. In the database arena, no distributed database management system has become a standard, although SQL has become the language of choice for accessing different databases.

As mentioned, we believe this distributed system framework has stood the test of time; it is still an appropriate design guide for distributed system architects. And although we have not seen it used these days, it provides a clear conceptual framework for understanding the various components of a distributed system.

Now we turn to some specifics: six system structures that have been called *distributed.*

SIX TYPES OF DISTRIBUTED SYSTEMS

As we noted earlier, the distributed system field has been continually evolving. The six forms of distributed systems basically developed as follows.

Host-Based Hierarchy

A hierarchy of processors was the first *data processing* distributed system structure. It was favored by mainframe vendors because the large host computer at the top of the hierarchy controlled the terminals at the lowest level. It is a master-slave relationship. More than one level of processors can be part of this hierarchy, as shown in Figure 5-4, with the total workload shared among them. The important characteristic of this structure is that the host computer is the central and controlling component. The other important characteristic is that the processing is done on the computers; the terminals are simply access devices; they have no processor or hard disk.

It is not always clear just where to store the data in such a system. One view is to store all data at the top. Another is to have the master records at the top but selected subsets at intermediate levels; the master records are then updated periodically and revised records are sent to the intermediate files. Still another view is to store master records where they are most used, and periodically provide updated records to the top for backup purposes. In any of these views, however, it is assumed that any processor in the hierarchy can access any data record within the system, as long as it is authorized to do so.

Network computers (NCs), which are diskless computers meant to obtain their applications from a server (perhaps on the Internet), are an intriguing flashback to this form of distributed computing. They, however, have two important distinctions from the terminals of old. First, NCs initiate requests; terminals of old did not. Second, NCs can do processing; terminals could not. So it is not the same master-slave relationship as with mainframes and terminals.

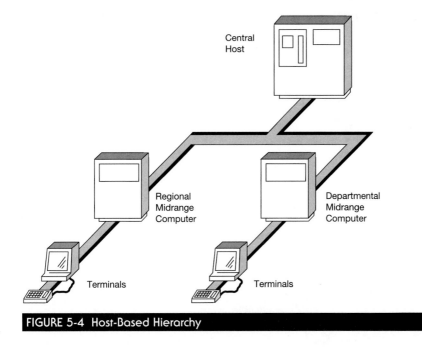

Central
Host

Regional
Midrange
Computer

Departmental
Midrange
Computer

Terminals

Terminals

FIGURE 5-4 Host-Based Hierarchy

The network computer concept is spreading and is often referred to as a "thin client," which means not much processing power is needed at the client. This architecture is favored for devices requesting tasks over the Internet.

Decentralized Stand-Alone Systems

Decentralized stand-alone systems do not really form a distributed system at all. They are basically a holdover from the 1960s, when departments put in their own minicomputers with no intention of connecting them to the corporate host or to other departmental systems. Hence, they are decentralized, not distributed (see Figure 5-5). Over the years, many such "islands of computing" have appeared and still exist. They have been connected to allow a little data to flow, but this flow has been mostly upward to the corporate host.

A major goal in the introduction of ERP systems has been the replacement of such disparate systems—in finance, manufacturing, administration—with a single platform with interconnectable modules that serve these various functions.

Peer-to-Peer LAN-Based Systems

Local area networks (LANs) have become the basis for distributed systems of desktop machines. This approach began in the office system arena with LANs providing the links between PCs, print servers, and gateways to other networks. As shown in Figure 5-6, this structure has no hierarchy. No computer is more superior than another. Communications among the components are "peer to peer" rather than through a hierarchy using a central hub. It is the key characteristic of this structure.

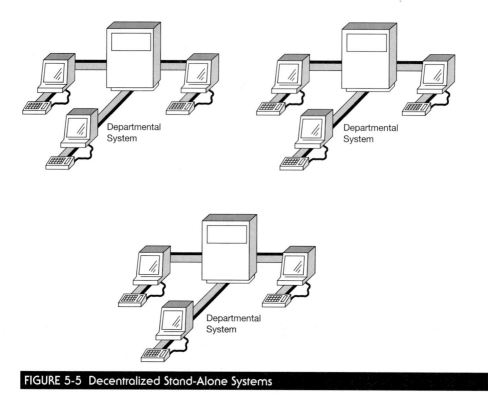

FIGURE 5-5 Decentralized Stand-Alone Systems

Hybrid Enterprisewide Systems

The current structure of distributed systems draws on these three forms of distributed systems linking them via three kinds of networks: metropolitan area networks (MANs), wide area networks (WANs), and the Internet. This system is illustrated in Figure 5-7. Today's distributed systems mix and match hierarchical host-based processing favored

FIGURE 5-6 Peer-to-Peer LAN-Based System

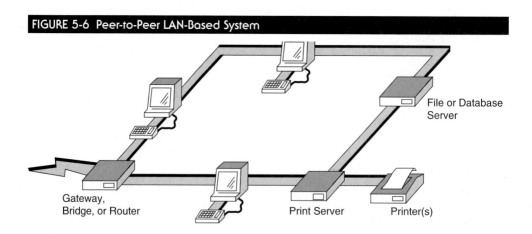

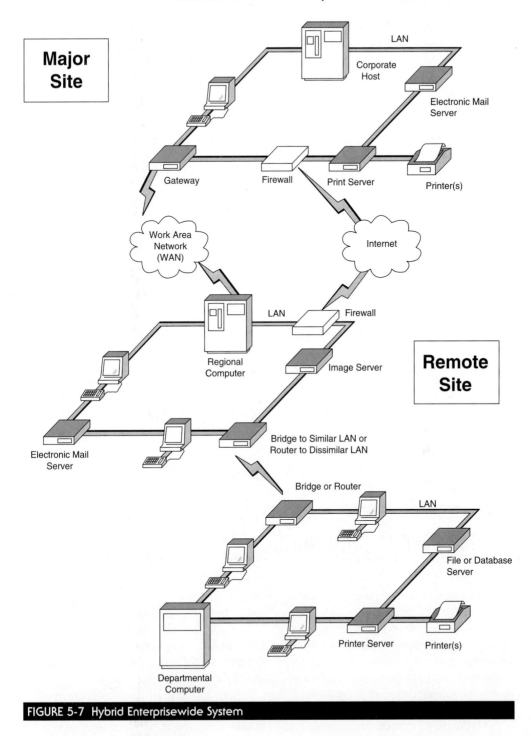

FIGURE 5-7 Hybrid Enterprisewide System

for corporate and Web site computing, with departmental processing favored by departments such as manufacturing and engineering, and the LAN-based systems used in offices. This hybrid structure is likely to be the structure of choice for many years as companies link their various islands of automation and increasingly link to systems in other organizations.

One important point is that this hybrid approach does not necessarily put all the machines under the aegis of a host mainframe computer. In fact, a number of companies have gotten rid of their mainframe(s) altogether, dispersing applications to departmental machines and servers. A host computer is shown in this diagram, but it is not the central control. For some applications, it could be the host, for others, it could be merely just another server, perhaps a "compute server."

A second important point is that this structure allows companies to automate business processes that span several functions within the organization, or work cooperatively with systems in other enterprises. It is the tenet of e-business and e-commerce. For example, to obtain sporting event tickets, once you enter your order on a ticketing Web site, the system needs to verify that the seats are available (probably on another system), it needs to verify that your credit is good (on another system), and if both are satisfied, it processes the order. Currently, tickets are mailed to you, but if your printer had an IP address (as is likely to happen soon), your tickets could be electronically sent to a ticket broker (yet another system) who then sends them to your printer where they are printed out.

Such cooperating processes allow companies to take advantage of specialized computer programs, while at the same time extending the usefulness of some legacy systems. The process of pulling together such individual applications or components is called *system integration*. Following is an example of a mainstream application that uses these distributed processing principles and was built via system integration.

CASE EXAMPLE

NORTHWEST AIRLINES

When Northwest Airlines, with headquarters in St. Paul, Minnesota, merged with Republic Airlines, they doubled their business and became a major national carrier. To compete as a world-class carrier, they realized they had to revamp a number of their core systems. One of these systems calculates revenue from passengers.

At the time, Northwest sampled a small percentage of their passenger tick-

ets to estimate revenue, but this approach did not yield accurate passenger or revenue data. To improve accuracy, they needed to audit all their redeemed tickets—something few major airlines did at the time.

With the help of Andersen Consulting (now Accenture), they built a system that integrates products from eleven vendors and just about as many different

(Case Continued)

technologies, including expert systems, imaging, relational databases, high-resolution workstations, servers, and LANs.

Management's Goals

Management established the following six major goals for the passenger revenue accounting (PRA) system:

- Enforce their pricing and commission rules to ensure their services are properly priced and that travel agencies sell them at the correct fares.
- Calculate earned income for the corporation as well as track and reconcile air transport liability accounting.
- Cope with the volume explosion and the rapid pace of change caused by airline deregulation.
- Unhook volume growth from staff increases, so the department could handle more work without equivalent increases in staff. The department had grown 700 percent to 600 people. At that projected growth rate, the department would soon need its own building, unless it changed the way it worked.
- Gather, organize, and disseminate marketing information for making decisions on pricing, flight scheduling, and response to competitors' moves.
- Provide the flexibility to audit and report on special deals with travel agents and corporate purchasers.

The Distributed Architecture

Data communication is an integral part of this distributed system, which uses both LANs and a metropolitan area network among three buildings. The host

IBM 3090 is linked to the backbone Ethernet LAN via an SNA-TCP/IP gateway.

The Ethernet backbone acts as a metropolitan area network, linking numerous Ethernet subnetworks. Ten of the subnetworks connect a Sun application server to about 40 diskless Sun workstations, which run UNIX. Northwest has minimized traffic across the backbone by designing the network to keep most client-to-server traffic on each subnet. In addition to the application servers, Northwest also has an image server for storing images of redeemed ticket coupons. Several specialized servers perform the ticket auditing each night using expert system technology.

The workstations provide the PRA auditors with windows to the data stored on the various systems: the mainframe that stores the ticket database, external computer reservation systems, the application servers that store tickets with discrepancies, and the image database. The system accommodates large file transfers between these workstations and the mainframe because part of the processing is done on the IBM host and part is done on the workstations. For these file transfers, Northwest created a standard way for the COBOL applications (on the mainframe) to talk to the C applications (on the workstations). The workstations also draw on the host applications via 3270-terminal emulation on the Suns.

Image processing is also a key element. Each day, Northwest receives some 50,000 auditor coupons from travel agents and 100,000 lift coupons (redeemed ticket stubs) from passengers. Formerly, Northwest employed 20 to 40 people full-time just to retrieve these coupons from their huge storage basement. Now, Northwest

(Case Continued)

scans both types of coupons, creating a photograph-like image and an index for each one. The images are stored on optical disks in jukeboxes.

The Revenue Accounting Process

Each day, Northwest receives data from three sources: (1) magnetic tapes of ticket sales taken from computer reservation systems and consolidated by regional clearinghouses, (2) "audit coupons" from travel agents, and (3) "lift coupons" redeemed from passengers as they board a plane.

The sales data is stored in a DB2 relational database and processed on the IBM mainframe. If all the information is not provided, the sales data is queued to an auditor, who adds the missing information by viewing the appropriate auditor coupon image that has been scanned into the system. Then, the sales data for performing the nighttime audits is downloaded to Sun servers, and a C program retrieves all the travel agency rules that apply to each of these tickets.

At night, this sales data is run through expert systems, which apply the appropriate rules to recalculate the lowest fare, commission, and taxes. If the recalculation does not match the travel agency's auditor coupon data, the recalculation and corresponding coupon image are made available to an auditor for review.

The next morning, Northwest auditors view the various pieces of data in different windows on their workstations, and decide how to handle the discrepancies. Because all the coupon images are available electronically, handling one box of coupons takes two to three hours, rather than the former two to three days.

When passengers' redeemed flight coupons are received by the department,

the verified sales data is credited as earned income. Monthly books now close on the seventh of the month, which is one-half the time previously required. Thus, earned revenue can be recognized 50 percent faster.

Lessons Learned

Northwest learned the following four major lessons about developing complex distributed systems such as PRA.

1. *Benchmark and prototype new technologies to verify vendors' claims.* Do not let vendors run the benchmarks by themselves. In image processing, for instance, have the vendors scan most of the kinds of documents in the application, especially if different kinds of paper and different colors of ink are common.

2. *An open architecture works on mission-critical applications.* The passenger revenue accounting system had to integrate a variety of technologies. By using an open architecture, Northwest reduced the risk in building such a system. Risk was further controlled by creating an interface to these systems that shielded the developers from the technicalities of the new technologies. Finally, integration was demonstrated early, through a small test project.

3. *Large distributed system projects need a vendor coordinator.* Due to the complexity of PRA, a clean design for creating a stable set of specifications for the vendors was unlikely, so a big challenge was keeping the right people on the Northwest, Andersen, and vendor

(Case Continued)

teams informed of current status. To fill this role, a full-time coordinator made sure all the various project teams stayed in close contact with each other. Otherwise, the end results would not have worked together.

4. ***Use of a computer-based development methodology was mandatory.*** Management believes that Northwest could not have done a project of this size without the tools and approaches of a computer-based methodology. For one thing, it allowed developers to work on different components of the system in parallel. Without it, they could not have supported the team of up to

170 developers. Furthermore, it allowed users to play a larger role in development; even to the point of using the design tool to document user procedures, design reports, and supply the text in the help system. Finally, it will allow them to use the data definitions from PRA in future systems, which will substantially shorten development time and improve system quality.

The huge system, which took 65,000 workdays to complete, has become a model for airline revenue accounting systems. Managers from more than a dozen airlines around the world have visited Northwest to study it. ∎

Client-Server Systems

The 1990s version of distributed systems was client-server systems. It arose to take advantage of the processing capabilities of both host machines and PCs in the same system. Even though the host could handle huge databases and order processing, the PCs, laptops, and smaller devices could handle graphics, sound, even video, which were important in some applications.

Client-server computing splits the computing workload between a "client," which is a computer that makes a request, and a "server," which answers the request. A request might be to print a document (handled by the print server on the LAN), or it could be the gate number of one's soon-to-leave flight—a request sent by a WAP-enabled cell phone from a taxi to the Internet and handled by the airline's Web site.

The most famous depiction of client-server computing comes from Gartner,[3] a research firm. It shows the possibilities for splitting work between clients and servers, as illustrated in Figure 5-8.

As shown, the network presents the dividing line between what is housed on a client and what is housed on a server. The three components being split are the presentation software (what the user sees on the screen), the application software itself, and the data management software. Briefly, from left to right, the spectrum is as follows:

- ***Distributed presentation*** puts all the data, all the application software, and some of the presentation software on a server. Only part of the presentation is on the client. This approach is one way to leave a mainframe-based legacy system in place while updating user screens, making it graphical rather than

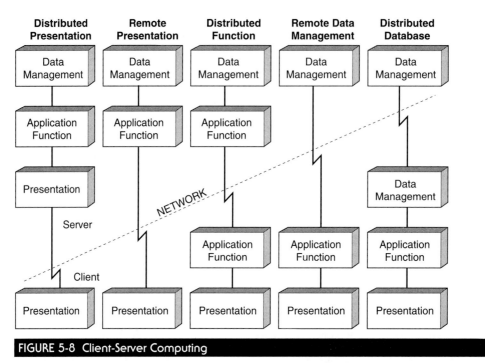

FIGURE 5-8 Client-Server Computing

Source: Roger Woolfe, *Managing the Move to Client-Server,* Wentworth Research Program (now part of Gartner Executive Programs, 56 Top Gallant, Stamford, CT 06904), January 1995.

character-based, for example. This approach is also likely for wireless Web-based computing.

- ***Remote presentation*** pulls all the presentation software onto the client machine, but leaves all the applications and data on the remote server. This approach also is a way to preserve a legacy system, and simply update the face it shows users. It has been used to put transaction processing behind Web sites.

- ***Distributed application function*** places all the presentation software on the client, all the data on the server, and splits the application software between the client and server. This option is quite complex, because splitting application processing between two machines requires coordination. However, it might be the most appropriate option for applications that run packaged software, such as spreadsheets or word processing, on a client in combination with corporate applications on a mainframe. It can also be appropriate for wireless computers used to front-end major applications, such as order entry, inventory inquiry, and so on. E-mail systems use this alternative: part of the processing on the client, part on the servers.

- ***Remote data management*** places all presentation and application software on the client, leaving only data and data management software on the server. This option is popular, because it keeps all the application software in one place (on a "fat" client), and takes advantage of the huge processing capacity of today's PCs. Although this solution is less complex, it has the disadvantage of requiring all the machines to be updated at the same time with a new release of the software. This level of coordination can be difficult unless all the machines are under a rigorous systems management system that routinely updates them when they connect to the corporate network.

- ***Distributed database*** places all the presentation and application software as well as some of the data on the client. The remaining data is on the server. It is a complex solution, especially if the numerous databases are intended to remain in sync. Even so, it is an important option used in mobile computing, where each salesperson needs some data locally (probably the less dynamic data). Up-to-the-second data can be stored on the master database and accessed only when needed. This option also leads to "fat" client machines.

Another way to look at client-server systems is to view their architecture. The preferred architecture has been three-tiered, notes Roger Woolfe, now of Gartner Executive Programs.[3a] As Figure 5-9 shows, Tier 3 is the superserver, perhaps a mainframe, perhaps a cluster of Web site servers. It can be connected directly to an in-house client-server network, or it may be routed through Tier 2 servers to the network. Companies have chosen this latter option to extend the life of their still-good-but-old legacy applications. Short-lived and fast-changing data, as well as corresponding integrity rules, are also stored at this superserver level so the data can be shared.

Tier 2 is specialized servers. Data specific to departments or workgroups is stored here, as is data that does not change often, yet needs rapid access. Tier 2 also houses "middleware," or software that eases connection between client and server. Middleware became an important concept in client-server systems and continues to be important in Internet-based systems because it performs translations between disparate systems. With middleware, a major application written for UNIX can later be used to support

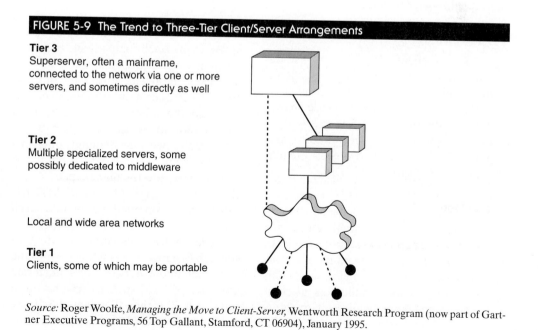

FIGURE 5-9 The Trend to Three-Tier Client/Server Arrangements

Tier 3
Superserver, often a mainframe, connected to the network via one or more servers, and sometimes directly as well

Tier 2
Multiple specialized servers, some possibly dedicated to middleware

Local and wide area networks

Tier 1
Clients, some of which may be portable

Source: Roger Woolfe, *Managing the Move to Client-Server,* Wentworth Research Program (now part of Gartner Executive Programs, 56 Top Gallant, Stamford, CT 06904), January 1995.

Windows and Linux as well without needing to be rewritten. Without middleware, companies would be hard pressed to serve the proliferation of new kinds of computing devices with their existing systems.

Tier 1 is the clients, either desktop or portable, connected via some sort of network.

The alternative architecture is two-tier, consisting of only clients and servers or clients and a mainframe. The three-tiered architecture reduces client complexity by decreasing the number of interfaces that need to be accommodated by the client machines. The drawback is that clients are more complex and access to Tier 3 data is slower than to Tier 2. Woolfe presents a case of a company that uses two of Gartner's client-server approaches in a three-tier architecture. Here is that story.

CASE EXAMPLE

AN AEROSPACE COMPANY

A corporate enterprise systems group develops systems for use across the company. The group's goal is to never again build monolithic applications. Instead, they intend to build systems—even million-dollar systems—from off-the-shelf hardware and software components.

The Software

All the client-server systems use the same structure, with application code on the clients, data on the servers, and communication middleware software shared between the two. The software is written using object-oriented technology, and most of it comes from a object-oriented component library.

The Data

The heart of the architecture is a repository, which allows reuse of objects. The repository holds "meta data": information about the data being used. This repository lets them build sets of common data under the auspices of an enter-

prise master database, so data has common definitions. When in use, data is split between operational data in production systems and data warehouses, which are updated daily via replication software.

The Network

The network is an integral part of this architecture. Each company site has three components: desktop machines, servers, and one or more site hubs. Each of these components uses standard, plug-in equipment, so the architecture can be used anywhere in the world. To cope with the increased networking demands of client-server systems, the company is migrating from Ethernet to the higher-speed Asynchronous Transfer Mode (ATM) network. The conversion takes place at each site hub.

The applications communicate to a site hub (a gateway), which plugs into the public telephone network, forming a ring structure of ATM switches. The speed of the ring is 600 mbps. (See Figure 5-10.)

(Case Continued)

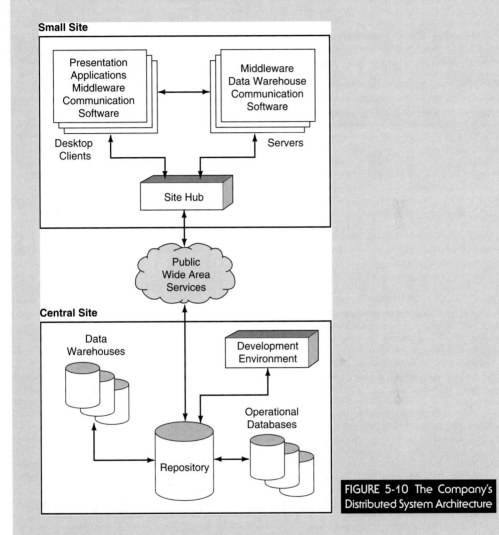

Small Site

Presentation
Applications
Middleware
Communication
Software

Middleware
Data Warehouse
Communication
Software

Desktop
Clients

Servers

Site Hub

Public
Wide Area
Services

Central Site

Data
Warehouses

Development
Environment

Operational
Databases

Repository

FIGURE 5-10 The Company's
Distributed System Architecture

The Architecture

The client-server architecture is "remote data management," to use the Gartner terminology. Data resides on servers, and applications reside on clients. The company chose this approach because it discovered that only 5–6 percent of the average PC is utilized. The company plans to use the remaining 94–95 percent spare desktop capacity for application code.

The company also uses the "distributed function" approach, but only on a few complex systems, because this approach requires more effort than remote data management.

The "distributed presentation" and "remote presentation" approaches do not take full advantage of the spare PC capacity, so they are not used. The company also does not plan to use the

(Case Continued)

"distributed database" approach, where databases are housed on client machines, because it is just too complex. The client machines must be polled to get the data, which is impractical except for highly structured workflow applications or conversation-oriented applications, such as Lotus Notes.

In short, the company uses the distributed function and remote data management configurations because they minimize total costs. The company's migration strategy has been first to build the architecture then to build applications using as many reusable components as possible. ∎

Benefits of Client-Server Computing. Client-server computing promised numerous benefits in the early 1990s. The following have held true. The primary benefit of client-server computing was to give people access to data or information when they needed it. This capability was especially pertinent to salespeople, who, for example, wanted to download information about customer orders from a central database using a PC while at the customer's site.

Retail chains have also used client-server systems to look into their stores to see what is selling, what is in inventory, and what is on order. Greater precision lets them keep less stock on hand and replenish inventory more on a just-in-time basis. It also lets them more closely watch the market and react to changes faster. So it has shifted the focus of computing from keeping track of the business to using information to fulfill its strategic objectives.

Client-server computing also blended the autonomy of PCs with the systemwide rules and connectivity of traditional systems. This combination turned traditional computing on its head, reversing the role of the host and the desktop. Whereas the host was previously the focus of attention, in client-server computing, the desktop is. This change shifts the focus of computing to end users, empowering employees, especially those who directly serve customers.

Client-server systems have also been used to streamline workflows by encouraging people to work together via networks, giving them powerful local processing power as well as access to other people and access to internal and external information.

Most powerfully of all, client-server computing supports new organizational structures via its connectivity. By providing a platform that supports individuals and groups who are geographically dispersed, it allows companies to experiment with new ways of working. In fact, experience with these technologies and their infrastructure enabled companies to more easily take advantage of the Internet. It is like a big client-server system.

However, client-server systems have not been lower in cost than mainframe systems (as first touted) because they entail so much coordination. What initially looked like simple connections between clients and servers has turned into large, often fragile, complex systems. So although client-server systems are easier for end users to use, they are far more complex for the systems department to manage, making some IT professionals wish for the good old all-in-one-box mainframe days. Day-to-day management of the complex infrastructure, where servers can be in hundreds of locations, is the most costly part of client-server systems.

On the human side, the systems led to organizational turmoil as people dealt with cross-boundary data flow, empowered employees, and cultural differences between people using the same data. The biggest changes were thus often organizational and cultural.

Internet-Centric Computing

In the late 1990s, the client-server computing trend was interrupted by the Internet, because the Internet provided a ubiquitous communication platform, which was sorely needed by companies wanting to work electronically with the outside world. Since then, the model of a distributed system includes the Internet. In fact, the Internet has become the heart of most distributed systems. The tenets of client-server computing remain in that processing is split between various kinds of machines.

The advent of business use of the Internet prompted a new form of distributed computing known as network-centric computing. It can be depicted as simply a computer and a network cloud (Figure 5-11).

Initially, it was expected that network computers—with no hard disk, just a browser, memory, keyboard, and a modem—would access the Internet. When they needed to perform a function, they would call into the Internet, and use the program from the Net. Sometimes the software might be downloaded, sometimes it might not.

Network computers have not taken off, at least not for desktop machines, but the concept of utilizing programs off the Internet has. The field distinguishes between "fat clients" (typical PCs loaded with all the programs) and "thin clients" (PCs or devices that utilize remote programs). The thin client concept often applies to retrieving small programs (applets) off the Web that are written in Java, a programming language created specifically for the Internet.

To illustrate the versatility of Java-based computing, IBM and Sun Microsystems (among others) present interesting case studies on their Web sites. Following are three examples from their sites. Both Sun and IBM have whole-heartedly embraced integrating the Internet into business computing, and are using the Java language to do so. The first and last examples come from IBM's site,[4] the middle one is from Sun's.[5]

FIGURE 5-11 Network-Centric System

CASE EXAMPLE

CHUBB & SON INSURANCE COMPANY

Chubb is a multinational property and casualty insurance company. Management has decided to compete in the dot-com world by converting legacy systems to Java-based systems. For example, they converted their cargo certificate issuance system to being an extranet application. It is used to insure ocean shipments and has proven especially important for customers outside the United States. Furthermore, importers, exporters, freight forwarders, and banks can draw on this application to round out the services they offer shippers.

Likewise, Chubb has put its builder's risk application on an extranet. It is used to provide insurance policies to builders of small inland marinas. The application is like "an underwriter in a box" so that agents can rate, quote, and book a policy immediately, making Chubb easy to do business with.

Similarly, Chubb launched a self-service accident benefit life application on the Internet so that consumers can obtain travel insurance at various travel sites at the same time they purchase tickets online.

All three applications feed into Chubb's mainframe but have a Java-based Web front end so that client machines only need access to the Web to perform the application. Users do not need special application software on their machine.

Chubb has used a number of IBM technologies to convert these applications, including VisualAge for Java and WebSphere Application Server. Chubb's goal is not only to make the applications Web-centric but also to deliver them in record time. They believe that by moving to thin-client delivery, where Java applets are delivered to client machines on demand, they can reduce their total cost of ownership by 30 to 40 percent.

Previously, Chubb developed applications in the client-server world using IBM's VisualAge Smalltalk, which is an object-oriented language. When VisualAge for Java became available, they decided to try it out, to move applications from client-server to being Web-based. Much to their pleasure, they discovered they could reuse some 15 percent of their code (even some of the most difficult-to-write portions), so the migration to Web-centricity was not as difficult as they had anticipated. ∎

CASE EXAMPLE

BULL SECURITIES

Bull Securities (a pseudonym) is a global broker-dealer that serves its high-net-worth clients in 40 countries from its offices in New York City, London, and Tokyo. To improve its service to these clients, Bull has installed an extranet using Sun servers and firewalls, and given these clients access to special "javatized" Web pages. These clients have also received a handheld device with a Web browser to access that page from anywhere in the world.

To reach the page, they simply turn on the device and it automatically dials the page and brings up the screen. The client can then click on, for example, "North American Market Update," which might download an audio applet with a recent update by Bull's chief economist. (Such audio updates are recorded on the Web site by Bull personnel using telephones anywhere in the world.) The client might then choose to see an updated summary of their portfolio, with current prices and performance statistics, a graph of asset allocation, historical charts, and a money market balance. The summary is downloaded in spreadsheet form along with a spreadsheet applet with which they can manipulate the data to test out different investment strategies. By double clicking on a stock's code, they can also automatically receive recent news about that stock along with historical charts. In addition, the client can ask to see pertinent research updates, which are downloaded along with an e-mail applet and perhaps some notes from their Bull financial advisor.

In essence, Bull has created an extranet to make information available to these high-net-worth customers continuously, rather than periodically, and with less (costly) human intervention. Furthermore, by offloading work to this extranet, the staff can concentrate on the 20 percent of these clients (and prospects) who appear most likely to generate the highest returns for the firm. ∎

CASE EXAMPLE

THE SABRE GROUP

IBM has been working with the SABRE Group (the airline reservation company) and Nokia (the handheld phone manufacturer) to create a real-time, interactive service delivered via mobile phone.

The service allows business travelers to not only receive updates from airlines (anytime, any place) but even initiate changes. For example, if a traveler's meeting runs significantly overtime and she realizes she is going to miss her flight, she can request flight details using her WAP-enabled Nokia phone and then make new travel arrangements. She can also make or change her hotel reservation, rental car reservation, and so forth. Likewise, if a flight is delayed or cancelled, the service notifies the traveler so she can adjust her itinerary.

The service draws on SABRE's online corporate travel purchasing system and Nokia's WAP server, which transmits the travel information to a wireless network and to its WAP phones. The service also utilizes several new technologies. One is wireless application protocol (WAP), a standard for wireless access to WAP-enabled Web sites. A second is extensible markup language (XML), a language that allows objects to be identified by type, which is important for constructing a user's Web site screen on-the-fly, custom-tailored to that user. A third technology is Java, a language for writing small applets used to deliver applications over the Internet. In this case, SABRE is using Java to translate its travel information into XML. And the fourth technology is wireless markup language (WML), a language for presenting XML information to WAP-enabled devices. ∎

Server-Based Computing. The concept of housing programs on the Net is growing and it not only applies to small Java applets but also to, for example, providing in-house applications to mobile employees. The following example illustrates this concept, which is called server-based computing.

CASE EXAMPLE

3i

3i, which stands for Investors In Industry, is a U.K.-based venture capital firm with investments in more than 3,000 start-ups and other companies. To expand beyond England to Southeast Asia and the United States, the company needed to give its investment professionals anytime-anywhere access to its systems. Then they could conduct business and complete a deal on the spot with just a laptop and a modem. To permit such "location-independent" remote and mobile working, with up-to-date information in their laptop, 3i turned to server-based computing.

3i called on Specialist Computer Centre in England to create new data centers in the United Kingdom and elsewhere. These centers consist of Citrix application server software installed on Hewlett-Packard servers.

Remote employees dial in to one of the centers through a secure modem service, which uses both authentication to verify their identify and encryption to jumble the messages. Using Microsoft Windows terminal server software and Citrix software, in essence, they create a virtual office for themselves. They have secure access to 120 in-house applications, all of which are housed on a variety of devices. The sessions are managed by the Citrix software.

From the IS department's point of view, the applications are much easier to manage because the software is housed in one place. Thus, updates are made once and remote employees always use the latest version. If employees had the software on their machines, all laptops would need to be updated at once, a difficult task.

The arrangement has allowed 3i to expand globally and let their employees work wherever they happen to be. ∎

A great debate centers around where server-based computing will take hold. It seems logical for handheld devices; the Internet houses the data and processing and the handheld handles mainly the presentation work. It also appears to make sense for consumer applications. It may also prove to be the norm for corporate computing. Employees would use the browser on their computer to access programs stored on the corporate portal, like a corporate intranet. They might or might not download the program to use it. Such a scenario eases the huge headache now faced by IS departments, as just noted, in managing the desktop. When a new version of a widely used package is released, IS departments would like to upgrade their software once and know that every employee is using that latest release. However, when the package is located on every machine, this simultaneous upgrading is difficult. IS departments have installed automated procedures for downloading latest releases, but a much easier solution would be to have only one copy of the software, which may or may not happen.

Peer-to-Peer Computing.   We cannot leave this subject of Internet-based computing without mentioning a recent development called peer-to-peer computing. It means distributing a task over a wide number of computers (peers) connected to the Internet. It is a grassroots movement, much like the open source movement, but some corporations are now taking it seriously.

The most infamous example of peer to peer is Napster, a central directory of music, and the PCs on which the music is located. Using Napster software, people can find music titles at the Napster site and then download that music from the listed PCs. Everyone swaps with everyone. Napster is infamous because the music industry contends it infringes on copyright laws by encouraging music piracy.

Author Jeremy Rifkin[6] says the dispute goes to the heart of two economies: the old economy that is made up of buyers and sellers and the e-economy that has clients and servers. He believes the Napster model will win out because it allows worldwide distribution of intangibles (even an entire music collection) faster than ringing up the sale of a single CD. Furthermore, Web distribution reduces traditional production costs— including distribution, packaging, inventory, and merchandising. At the same time that sales of hard goods aim to maximize production, distribution via Web sites aims to pool risks and share savings.

The issue has been how to make money in the peer-to-peer environment. Rifkin believes subscriptions will replace sales. People will pay for access rather than for ownership. Why buy one CD when you can have unlimited access to a continually growing gigantic music collection for a month? he asks. In physical markets, physical property is purchased. In networks, access to experiences is purchased. When hyperspeed and continuous change are the norm, as they are today, it makes less sense to own and more sense to subscribe. Furthermore, continual connection provides other benefits, such as a steady stream of new music or other intangibles. Thus, says Rifkin, Napster is just the tip of the iceberg.

These six, then, are the different types of distributed systems that have emerged. To conclude this chapter, we come back around to beginning of the chapter and discuss the subjects of architecture and infrastructure.

DESCRIBING THE OVERALL ARCHITECTURE

For more than 20 years, John Zachman,[7] an independent consultant, has been preaching the value of enterprise architecture and modeling data, processes, and networks. He has the most comprehensive view of this subject we have seen, so we briefly describe it here.

An Enterprise Architecture Framework

The real world (an airplane, an enterprise, or a skyscraper) is so complicated that we cannot get our brain around it at one time, says Zachman, so we abstract out single variables. To completely describe an IS architecture, we need to look at the roles people play and the components they deal with. Together, these create the rows and columns of a framework.

The Rows: Planner, Owner, Designer, Builder, Subcontractor, and Consumer or User.
No single architectural representation is available for an information system, says Zachman, because of the six roles involved in building complex products: planner, owner, de-

signer, builder, subcontractor, and consumer. Six perspectives, six models. For instance, an airframe manufacturer needs a statement of the objectives for the planner, an architect's drawings for the owner, an architect's plans for the designer, a contractor's plans for the builder, and detailed representations for the subcontractors. The completed airplane is the consumer's view. The same is true in IS. IS needs a scope statement, a model of the enterprise, a model of the information system, a technology model, and a description of the components to produce the finished functioning system. These components make up the rows in Zachman's enterprise architecture framework, Figure 5-12.

Each role has its own constraints. For instance, the owner is constrained by the use of the end product. The designer is constrained by physical laws. And the builder is constrained by the state-of-the-art and the technology available. For these reasons, six models, rather than one, are needed and they need to be maintained in sync through configuration management.

The Columns: Data, Function, Network.   Another significant factor is the lack of a single graphical representation for the components of a complex system or for an

---

FIGURE 5-12 An Architectural Framework

	Data (What)	Function (How)	Network (Where)
Scope *Planner*			
Enterprise Model *Owner*			
Information System Model *Designer*			
Technology Model *Builder*			
Components *Subcontractor*			
Functioning System *Consumer or User*			

Source: Adapted from John Zachman, Zachman International, 2222 Foothill Blvd., Suite 337, LaCanada, CA 91011.

information system. As in engineering, IS needs three components to worry about: data models (*What* is it made of?), functional models (*How* does it work?), and network models (*Where* are the components located?). These represent the physical manifestations of the system.

In addition, we need three more, he says, who (people), when (time), and why (motivation). These elements represent the soft side of systems. Together, the six are all we need to know to build a complex system. So, the good news is that defining an enterprise architecture is not an infinite problem. The bad news is, no one has done it yet. But, a few are making progress. The entire enterprise architecture is shown in Figure 5-13.

Use of the Framework.   The framework is populated with a set of diagrammatic models that can be used to describe any complex thing—an enterprise, an airplane, even a bicycle. All these models exist, the question is whether an enterprise spends the time to make them explicit.

For instance, your organization has a data model, whether it is defined or not. And it is intended to work as your enterprise works. A problem occurs, however, when IS or users bring in a package that follows a different data model. If the rules in that model are inconsistent with the rules in your company, you will spend a lot fixing the package, says Zachman. It is one reason models are important: They allow you to properly evaluate packages. They also help builders align with what owners want. And they can help companies realize what changes need to be made when they move to a new model, such as deciding to reorganize around customer sets rather than products.

To be an enterprise and not disintegrate as changes are made, you need to understand its architecture, says Zachman. It is the most important reason to make architecture explicit.

THE IT INFRASTRUCTURE

In the arena of IT infrastructure, the best work to date has been performed by Peter Weill and Marianne Broadbent.[8] They distinguish between different types of IT infrastructures and describe different ways companies justify infrastructure investments. Such investments are a vital part of corporate information systems portfolios, yet they are the most difficult to cost-justify beforehand and to measure benefits afterwards.

Four Types of IT Investments

Weill and Broadbent categorize IT investments into four types, as shown in Figure 5-14. Each has different purposes and different measures of benefits.

Strategic investments aim to change the way a firm competes, the products or services it offers, or how it intends to increase revenues. These investments can be longer term, so they may need a longer lead time before producing returns. Their income stream is difficult to estimate; therefore, meaningful return on investment (ROI) calculations are not always possible. These investments are depicted at the top of the pyramid because they rely on and are supported by those underneath.

Informational investments provide the information employees need to manage and control the enterprise. These systems include executive information systems, support planning, accounting, management control, and communications. They have a

FIGURE 5-13 Enterprise Architecture—A Framework

	Data *What*	Function *How*	Network *Where*	People *Who*	Time *When*	Motivation *Why*
Objectives/ Scope (Contextual)	List of things important to the business Entity = Class of business thing	List of processes the business performs Function = Class of business process	List of locations in which the business operates Node = Major business location	List of Organizations/agents important to the business Agent = Class of agent	List of events significant to the business Time = Major business event	List of business goals/ strategies Ends/Means = Major bus goal/ critical success factor
Planner	e.g., Semantic model	e.g., Business process model	e.g., Logistics network	e.g., Organization chart	e.g., Master schedule	e.g., Business plan
Enterprise Model (Conceptual)	Ent = Business entity Reln = Business relationship	Proc = Business process I/O = Business resources	Node = Business location Link = Business linkage	Agent = Organization unit Work = Work product	Time = Business event Cycle = Business cycle	End = Business objective Means = Business strategy
Owner	e.g., Data model	e.g., "Application architecture"	e.g., Distributed system Architecture	e.g., Human interface architecture	e.g., Processing structure	e.g., Knowledge architecture
System Model (Logical)	Ent = Data entity Reln = Data relationship	Proc = Application function I/O = User views	Node = I/S function (processor, storage, etc.) Link = Line characteristics	Agent = Role Work = Deliverable	Time = System event Cycle = Processing cycle	Ends = Criterion Means = Business rules
Designer	e.g., Data design	e.g., System Design	e.g., System architecture	e.g., Human/technology Interface	e.g., Control structure	e.g., Knowledge design
Technology Model (Physical)	Ent = Segment/Row/etc Reln = Pointer/Key/etc	Proc = Computer function I/O =Screen/Device formats	Node = Hardware/System software Link = Line specifications	Agent = User Work = Job	Time = Execute Cycle = Component cycle	Ends = Condition Means = Action
Builder	e.g., Data definition	e.g., Program	e.g., Network architecture	e.g., Security architecture	e.g., Timing definition	e.g., Knowledge definition
Detailed Representations (out-of-context)	Ent = Field Reln = Address	Proc = Language stmt I/O = Control block	Node = Addresses Link = Protocols	Agent = Identity Work = "Transaction"	Time = Interrupt Cycle = Machine cycle	End = Subcondition Means = Step
Sub-Contractor						
Functioning System	e.g., Data	e.g., Function	e.g., Network	e.g., Organization	e.g., Schedule	e.g., Strategy

Source: Adapted from John Zachman, Zachman International, 2222 Foothill Blvd., Suite 337, LaCanada, CA 91011.

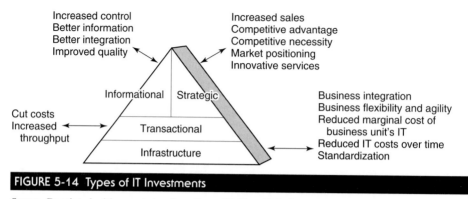

FIGURE 5-14 Types of IT Investments

Source: Reprinted with permission from Peter Weill and Marianne Broadbent, *Leveraging the New Infrastructure* (Boston: Harvard Business School Press, 1998).

medium-term horizon, and like strategic investments, depend on the firm's transactional and infrastructure investments. In fact, usually, the two lower levels must be in place before informational and strategic systems are feasible.

Transactional investments support operational management. They are intended to cut operating costs by substituting capital for labor so that higher volumes can be handled without requisite increases in people. They process repetitive transactions and support such operational activities as inventory control, order processing, receivables, payables, and so on. They generally have a short-term ROI. These systems feed summary data up the pyramid to the informational systems, and they are supported by the firm's infrastructure.

Infrastructure investments provide the base foundation of IT capability in a firm. The other three levels contain the applications for running specific business functions or processes. The infrastructure does not run applications, it simply supports them.

What Is an IT Infrastructure?

Weill and Broadbent define an IT infrastructure as the foundation of an enterprise's IT portfolio. It provides the capability for reliable services and sharing, and it includes both the technical and managerial expertise required to provide these services. In turn, the infrastructure is linked to external industry infrastructures, such as banking payment systems and airline reservation systems.

The shared characteristic differentiates an infrastructure from IT investments used by just one function. Elements in an IT infrastructure can include company-wide networks, data warehouses, large-scale computing facilities, electronic data interchange capabilities, and even R&D aimed at identifying emerging technologies. On top of this infrastructure sit applications that perform the business's processes. As such, infrastructure does not provide direct business performance benefits. Rather it enables other systems that do yield business benefits, which is what makes infrastructure so difficult to cost-justify.

Similar to Public Infrastructure. IT infrastructure is strikingly similar to public infrastructure, such as roads, hospitals, sewers, and schools, note Weill and Broadbent.

1. Both are provided by a central agency and funded by some form of taxation.
2. Both are long term and require large investments.
3. A central agency provides an essential service that users are not motivated or able to provide.
4. Both enable business activity by users that would otherwise not be economically feasible.
5. Flexibility is valued in both because they must be in place before the precise business activity is known.
6. Both are difficult to cost-justify in advance as well as to show benefits in hindsight.
7. Both require a delicate investment balance: Too little investment leads to duplication, incompatibility, and suboptimal use, whereas too much discourages user investment and involvement and may result in unused capacity.

Three Views of Infrastructure

The benefits a firm actually realizes from its infrastructure investments depend on its objectives for the infrastructure. Weill and Broadbent point out three possibilities, which they call maxims (expectations from IT investments). A firm might invest in infrastructure to provide the following:

1. Economies of scale (utility)
2. Support for business programs (dependent)
3. Flexibility to meet changes in the marketplace (enabling)

Utility.   Companies that view their infrastructure as a utility see it as a necessary and unavoidable service that must be provided by IS. Expected benefits are cost savings achieved through economies of scale. Normally, firms with this perspective treat infrastructure cost as an administrative expense, and they act to minimize this expense. They offer the fewest infrastructure services. For instance, they might promote use of networks for messaging but not as part of inter- or intraorganizational business processes. This objective requires the lowest investment but it also only results in lowering costs (not in reengineering the business). Outsourcing may be viewed favorably, because the IT infrastructure is not seen as strategic.

Dependent.   A business that ties its infrastructure investments to specific, known business programs, takes the dependent view. Because investments are tied to business plans, the infrastructure is treated as a business expense and its value is measured by short-term business benefits. Firms with this view include infrastructure planning in current business planning. They also see the network as critical. Furthermore, this view of infrastructure appears to smooth the way for simplifying business processes. In fact, Weill and Broadbent surmise that this view is a minimum requirement for successfully implementing business process reengineering.

Enabling.   A firm that develops and continually modifies its infrastructure in "co-alignment" with its business strategy—where infrastructure influences strategy, and vice versa—takes the enabling view of infrastructure. The primary benefit is long-term flexibility, so the firm does not limit infrastructure investments to current strategy. The infrastructure is intended to provide the foundation for changing direction in the future, if need be. Thus, infrastructure costs are seen as business investments. So, for example, the firm might use networks extensively in businesses processes, both within the firm and with their customers and suppliers.

Needless to say, the appropriate viewpoint is not a technical decision, it is a top management decision. It is IS management's job to make this clear to senior management, and show them the options. Again, as we pointed out in Chapter 2, teamwork among the various levels of management is absolutely necessary to align technical investments with business strategy.

No view is superior, however; different views are appropriate for different strategies. Moving from utility to dependent to enabling views increases up-front investments and the number of IT infrastructure services provided.

To see how one organization has approached investing in infrastructure, consider the City of Sunnyvale.[3b]

CASE EXAMPLE

CITY OF SUNNYVALE, CALIFORNIA

The City of Sunnyvale, California, in the heart of Silicon Valley, is rated as one of the best-run cities in the United States. Its performance-based budgeting system, which has been honed over the past 25 years, has fostered citywide fiscal soundness and day-to-day accountability by city administrators. This budgeting process, along with the city's 20-year planning horizon, is aiding the IT department in creating and financing the city's information infrastructure.

Sunnyvale's director of information technology was hired to move the city into the future. He has thus concentrated on building the city's information infrastructure because the city sees infrastructure as its foundation for the future. Says the director,

"If the city of Sunnyvale is to succeed in leveraging technological resources to deal with increasing customer demands, as well as improve efficiency and customer service, the IT Department must first take responsibility for capturing accurate information and delivering that information in a timely manner."

This statement is the driving force behind the city's IT department. The driver for investing in infrastructure is quality of service. To provide high-quality service to customers, the infrastructure users (city departments) must have timely and accurate information to do their jobs. For it to happen, the IT department must have the right pieces of information at the right place at the right time. The IT director believes the city needs to develop an expandable infrastructure to leverage technology and capitalize on opportunities.

(Case Continued)

The infrastructure provides connectivity between the city's traditional mainframes with attached terminals/PCs, numerous stand-alone LANs, and the outside world. It is based on a fiber optic backbone, Internet-based computing, and relational database technology. A three-level distributed architecture is used, with enterprise servers, mid-tier servers, and desktop clients. The architecture encompasses more than traditional computing equipment, however. For example, the 40+ copiers throughout the city will someday be replaced by laser printers, so that employees can send a request for 50 copies of a report from their desktop rather than request a secretary or clerk to make the copies.

The information infrastructure is like the foundation for a home, says the director. It needs to withstand all the weight, all the noise, and all the things you want to plug into it. Because information technology is changing so rapidly, the city must think long term about its infrastructure, to ensure that it can be easily expanded and upgraded. Unfortunately, traditional fiber optic vendors have not been able to support upgradability. As a result, the city laid a new type of fiber optic conduit. From the end, it looks like a honeycomb with 19 cells, only two of which were used initially. New fiber bundles can easily be blown through the spare cells in the future using a special gas, thus making it easy to upgrade the fiber backbone to accommodate new services like video teleconferencing or heavy-duty video conferencing or combined voice and data transmission.

Infrastructure investments are paid through chargeback. When the IT department places equipment on someone's desk, installs a software package on a computer, or hooks up a PC to a LAN, that equipment, software or communication link immediately begins generating its own replacement funds. Sunnyvale charges back everything on rental rates, because it knows everything will eventually need to be replaced.

"Super" rules guide technology investments. One such rule is that the city will standardize on products to make effective use of resources. Another, unwritten super rule is that a person using a computer at, say, the Senior Center will have the same access and response time as someone working next to the mainframe. Another IT super rule is: All projects are subject to review by an executive body that represents all city departments. Thus, continuous buy-in, support, and fine-tuning of demands form an improvement cycle. An outcome of this super rule is a more participative executive body—one that understands departmental priority and guides the city's IT goals as a high-performance team. A joint environment is established for a consistent framework from which all departments can benefit. ■

CONCLUSION

Distributed systems dominate the computing landscape these days, with the Internet now at the heart. Distributing the processing, databases, and communications allows companies to move more quickly because they can essentially "snap in" products and services from others. This possibility has fueled the rapid growth and continual changes in the e-economy.

Although the concepts behind distributed systems were conceived more than 30 years ago, the use of distributed systems moved into a new era with the advent of the Internet. Prior, the bulk of distributed systems were in-house, linking systems within an enterprise. The Internet turned attention outward because it provides the infrastructure for global distributed systems. It is an underlying message throughout this edition of the book: IS management needs to turn its attention outward toward customers and suppliers. With IT providing the foundation for the New Economy, CIOs also need to work closely with top management in ensuring that the firm's IT infrastructure not only meshes with corporate strategy but is flexible enough to support changes in strategy. This infrastructure is the challenge facing CIOs and CTOs. Many of them got caught flat-footed with the Internet. It crept up behind them. They now realize how important infrastructure is to corporate success. And even though they might outsource the operation of their infrastructure, they and their top management peers must do the strategic thinking behind selecting infrastructure elements.

With the overall technical framework for systems provided, we now turn to the essential technologies used in distributed systems.

QUESTIONS AND EXERCISES

Review Questions

1. What is the difference between an architecture and an infrastructure?
2. What are the four attributes of a distributed system?
3. What does "open source" mean?
4. List and briefly explain the questions that can be asked in deciding whether to distribute computing responsibilities.
5. Give six examples of system structures that can be called distributed.
6. What are the components of the guiding framework for distributed systems by Stefferud, Farber, and Dement?
7. What four lessons did Northwest learn about building their PRA systems?
8. What are Gartner's five types of client-server systems? Which two did the aerospace company choose and why?
9. What are server-based computing and peer-to-peer computing?
10. According to Rifkin, what is the Naptser dispute really about?
11. What are the six rows and six columns in Zachman's framework? Describe each briefly.
12. Describe four kinds of IT investments that companies make, according to Weill and Broadbent.
13. In what three ways can companies view an IT infrastructure?

Discussion Questions

1. Some people want all their programs and data stored locally, on a PC. Others would be willing to get everything from a corporate portal. Which would you prefer? Why?
2. Is Internet-centric computing taking us back to the architecture of mainframes and dumb terminals? Are we coming full circle? Why or why not?

Exercises

1. Find an article in the current literature that describes a distributed system.
   a. Describe it using the four attributes given in this chapter.
   b. Does it relate to the SUMURU architecture? How?
   c. What benefits are claimed for the system?
   d. Describe its infrastructure.
2. Identify a company in your local community that is using what it calls a distributed system. What was top management's or business unit management's involvement in justifying the system? How do the system's characteristics compare with those given in this chapter? What challenges has the IS department encountered building the system, and how has it dealt with these challenges?
3. Identify a company in your local community that has an information system infrastructure. Does management see it as utility, dependent, or enabling? Explain their rationale.
4. Find a description of a Internet-based application. Why was this approach taken? What benefits are expected?

REFERENCES

1. Wetherbe, J. C., "IS: To Centralize or to Decentralize," *SIM Network,* Society for Information Management, Chicago, IL, January 1987.

2. Stefferud, E., D. Farber, and R. Dement, "SUMURU: A Network Configuration for the Future," *Mini-Micro Systems*, May 1982, pp. 311–312.

3. *Wentworth Research Program,* now part of Gartner Executive Programs, 56 Top Gallant Road, Stamford, CT 06904.
   a. Woolfe, Roger, "Managing the Move to Client-Server," January 1995.
   b. Varney, Cornelia, "Justifying Infrastructure Investments," May 1995.

4. "IBM Java Success Stories," IBM Corporation, Armonk, NY, www.ibm.com.

5. "Sun Technology Applications for Financial Services," Sun Microsystems, Mountain View, CA, www.sun.com.

6. Rifkin, Jeremy, "Where Napster Has Gone, Others Will Follow," *Los Angeles Times,* August 21, 2000, p A13.

7. Zachman, John, Zachman International, 2222 Foothill Blvd., Suite 337, La Canada, CA 91011.

8. Weill, Peter and Marianne Broadbent, *Leveraging the New Infrastructure: How Market Leaders Capitalize on Information Technology,* Harvard Business School Press, Boston, MA, 1998.

CHAPTER

6

MANAGING TELECOMMUNICATIONS

INTRODUCTION

It is interesting to note that with each edition of this book a new area is "the hot area." For this edition, that hot area is telecommunications—and the Internet is really just the tip of the iceberg. "Telecom is due to explode" is one of the most oft-heard phrases these days. In this chapter we describe what that prediction means.

    We treat telecommunications in the broad sense: electronically sending information in any form from one place to another. In this view, the telecommunications system is an "electronic highway system" for the flow of information among individuals, work groups, departments, customer sites, regional offices, between enterprises, and with the outside world. Generally, IS departments have been responsible for designing, building, and maintaining that information highway in the same way that governments are responsible for building and maintaining streets, roads, and freeways.

Once built, the network, with its nodes and links, provides the infrastructure for the flow of information and messages. That flow is managed not by IS professionals but by users, just as users manage the flow of vehicles on physical highways. Government agencies provide standards and laws for the flow of highway traffic, enforced by the police and highway patrol. In the same way, IS departments select and enforce telecom standards for information traffic while governments divvy up spectrum for different wireless uses. This analogy could be pursued in more detail, but the point is clear: Telecom is the basis for the New Economy—the e-business economy. It provides the infrastructure for moving information and messages, just as a transportation system, including the shipping lanes, railroad right of ways, and the airspace, provides the infrastructure for the movement of people and goods.

This analogy presents telecommunications as a technical linking mechanism, which it is. However, the Internet has also opened up a whole new way to view telecom: that of providing a "cyberspace," a place where people can "exist" in a virtual world, where organizations can conduct business, and in fact, a place where organizational processes exist. It is the "e-world" being created these days. It is sort of like a cybercity. This view too is providing the foundation for the New Economy.

But even more is happening. Just about everything about telecom is shifting, from the industry itself to the protocols (the "languages" networks use to communicate with each other).

THE EVOLVING TELECOMMUNICATIONS SCENE

Telecom has become an exciting place, perhaps too exciting for some people. The changes are coming fast and furiously, and the rate of change is coming faster and faster. To give an inkling of what is happening, here are some major changes that are taking place.

A New Telecommunications Infrastructure Is Being Built

The telecom "infrastructure of old" is the telephone network, commonly called the public switched telephone network (PSTN), or affectionately called POTS (plain old telephone service). This global network was built on twisted-pair copper wires and was intended for voice communications. It uses analog technology (signals sent as sine waves) and circuit switching, which means a virtual (temporary) circuit is created between caller and receiver and that circuit is theirs alone to use; no other parties can share it during the duration of their telephone call. Although appropriate for delivering high-quality voice, circuit-switching is inefficient because of all the unused space in the circuits when no sound is being transmitted.

The overhead of establishing a circuit was tolerable for voice calls because they lasted several minutes, says PricewaterhouseCoopers,[1] the large consulting firm, but data traffic is sent in bursts that last less than a second. Opening and closing circuits at this rate is not economical, so the basic traffic-handling mechanism had to change for data.

PSTNs were also built on the premise of dumb voice telephones; therefore, they needed intelligent switches in the network to perform all the functions. Telephone company central offices house the intelligent switches that implement all the services, including call waiting, caller ID, call forwarding, conference calling, and so on.

Today, the "infrastructure of new" is being built around the world. It is aimed at transmitting data, and it consists of fiber optic links (glass fiber rather than copper wire) sending digital signals (ones and zeros instead of sine waves). It uses packet switching, where messages are divided into packets, each with an address header, and each packet is sent separately. No circuit is created; each packet may take a different path through the network. Packets from any number of senders and of any type, whether e-mails, music downloads, voice conversations, or video clips, can be intermixed on a network segment, making these next-generation networks able to handle much more traffic and a great variety of traffic. Packet nets can also handle voice. The analog voice signals are translated into ones and zeros, compressed, and packetized.

Unlike voice-centric networks, these new data-centric networks assume intelligent user devices that provide the addressing information; therefore, the network only needs store-and-forward routers to route the packets. This architecture allows new kinds of services to be deployed much more rapidly, notes PricewaterhouseCoopers, because the basic functions of the network need not be changed. Thus, for example, it was easy to add the World Wide Web as a kind of layer on the Internet infrastructure. Other such layers are e-mail, file transfer, and wireless Web pages. This infrastructure would not have been possible with PSTN. Witness the promise of videophone, which was announced at the 1939 World's Fair in New York. It still has not arrived, except over the Internet.

The Internet can handle new kinds of intelligent user devices, including smart phones, personal digital assistants (PDAs), and all manner of wireless devices. It can allow these devices to handle different kinds of services, such as voice, e-mail, graphics, gaming, and so forth. Thus, the global telecom infrastructure is changing from a focus on voice to a focus on data.

The Telecom Industry Is Being Transformed

The telecom infrastructure of old was originally provided by monopolies, such as AT&T in the United States and government-owned postal, telephone, and telegraph agencies (PTTs) in other countries, such as Nippon Telephone and Telegraph (NTT) in Japan, Telefonica de Espana in Spain, and so on. Gradually, the telecom industry has been deregulated, country-by-country, although in many countries the PTT has simply become the private monopoly. Even so, competition in the industry has increased.

The telecom industry is becoming like the computing industry says Rich Karlgaard, publisher of *Forbes* magazine,[2] in that each year brings predictable improvements. In fact, he believes the industry is now more competitive than the computer industry. Computer processing power has followed Moore's Law of doubling every 18 months since 1959; and it appears likely to continue at that rate for 10 more years, yielding processors with speeds of a trillion bits per second. Bandwidth on fiber, on the other hand, is now doubling capacity every four months.

The telecom industry basically has two kinds of carriers: long distance carriers, known as interexchange carriers (IXCs), and local exchange carriers (LECs). In the United States, the deregulation of AT&T in 1984 left AT&T in the IXC business and spun off seven LECs called Regional Bell Operating Companies (RBOCs): USWest, Bell South, Ameritech, Bell Atlantic, Northwest Bell, Southwestern Bell (now SBC), and Pacific Bell. Today, only four remain; they have bought up the others.

These RBOCs provided local access to the long distance carriers and had a monopoly on this "local loop." In short, they handled "the last mile": the connection between a subscriber and the telephone company's central office (neighborhood switch) where the network switching equipment resides. This last mile has proven to be the bottleneck in telecom.

Visualize the world's networks as huge fire hoses because they use fiber optic cables that can transmit at the whopping speed of a terabit (10^{12} bits per second). Then visualize the twisted pair phone line coming into your home or business as a straw, only operating at speeds of 56 kbps (10^4) for a modem or 1.2 mpbs (10^6 bits per second) for digital subscriber line (DSL). DSL runs over the same copper wire but has improved electronics that boost the speed, allows simultaneous voice and data, and is "always on," eliminating the need to dial in. The "last mile problem" means bridging this fire-hose-to-straw gap. See Figure 6-1.

FIGURE 6-1   Telecommunication Technologies and Their Speeds

Bits per second	Notation	Abbreviation	Amount	Term	Technologies
1,000,000,000,000	10^{12}	1 tbps	trillion	terabits	Optical fiber potential (and higher)
100,000,000,000	10^{11}	100 gbps			
10,000,000,000	10^{10}	10 gbps			Optical wireless local loop (20G), OC-768 (40G)
1,000,000,000	10^9	1 gbps	billion	gigabits	Microwave LANs (1.5G–2.0G), OC-48 (2.5G), ATM (2.5G), Gigabit Ethernet (1G)
100,000,000	10^8	100 mbps			OC-12 (622M), ATM (155M to 622M), T4 (274.176M), OC-3 (155.52M), Faster Ethernet (100M), infrared (100M)
10,000,000	10^7	10 mbps			T3 (44.736M), E3 (34.318M), frame relay (10M), Ethernet (10M), Wireless LANs (10M), cable modem (10M)
1,000,000	10^6	1 mbps	million	megabits	T2 (6.132M), infrared LAN (4M), stationary 3G wireless (2M), E1 (2.048M), DSL (1.544M to 7M), T1 (1.544M)
100,000	10^5	100 kbps			Wireless local loop (428K), mobile 3G Wireless (384K), ISDN (128K), 2G wireless (128K)
10,000	10^4	10 kbps			Modems (56K), 2.5G wireless (57K)
1,000	10^3	1 kbps	thousand	kilobits	2G wireless (9.6K to 14.4), infrared LAN (9.6K)
100	10^2	100 bps			
10	10^1	10 bps			

In the 1990s, the RBOCs began encountering competition for this last mile. So the jargon expanded. RBOCs became known as incumbent local exchange carriers (ILECs) and the new competitors became competitive LECs (CLECs). The importance of CLECs is the new kinds of connection options they have brought to businesses and homes, such as cable modems, optical fiber, wireless, satellite, and speeding up wire lines.

Some provide businesses with direct access to a fiber network. Dot-coms, ISPs, portals hosting their own Web sites, and others that handle huge amounts of traffic need such connections. These networks can handle 20 gbps (10^{10}). This type of service comes from CLECs that have built their own fiber optic rings around the largest business districts, and fiber backbones between these cities—a huge investment on their part. As PricewaterhouseCoopers point outs, 86 percent of total U.S. network growth is occurring in only 20 cities. These cities are obviously the ones being targeted by CLECs. In many cases, because it may be impossible to get the right of way to dig trenches for laying this cable, CLECs have teamed up with electric utilities, which already have the right of ways.

In response, incumbent local exchange carriers are bundling local phone access with Internet access, and Internet service providers (ISPs) are using their brand name recognition to expand into the local carrier market, becoming CLECs. You really need a scorecard to see who's who.

To illustrate these twists and turns in the telecom industry in the United States over the past 20 years, consider the following case of ICG,[3] whose history has mirrored these changes.

CASE EXAMPLE

ICG COMMUNICATIONS

ICG Communications is an infrastructure-based CLEC, providing voice and data services in the United States to ISPs and small and medium companies. It all began in the mid-1980s in Denver, Colorado. Teleport Denver, Ltd. (TDL), built a satellite teleport with eight earth stations so it could transmit voice around the world. It could reach five continents in a single satellite hop.

In 1984, when AT&T was forced to divest itself of its local telephone companies, TDL management looked into the possibilities of offering local telephone service to Denver. They originally planned to lease circuits from the local RBOC, but the costs were too high, so they decided to install their own private fiber optic links to connect to the international exchange carriers (IXCs) that carried long-distance voice calls.

Then, in the late 1980s, when the a new breed of telecom provider arose— the CLECs—TDL management again extended their view, this time to providing long-distance as well as private-line services to businesses.

Once the Denver network was in place in the early 1990s, its new parent,

(Case Continued)

IntelCom Group, expanded its geographic presence by buying other companies that provided fiber telecom services. In the mid-1990s, management signed fiber lease agreements with electric utilities—an innovative strategy at the time—that allowed them to more quickly and cost-effectively expand ICG's services.

Then ICG expanded its offerings beyond fiber-based transport—to offering switched services—by installing switches in its key markets. In 1995 ICG also formed a strategic alliance with Southern New England Telephone, through which it could offer an SS7 switched network across the United States.

The Telecom Act of 1996 allowed ICG to enter the local telephone market, so it began aggressively building staff and regional networks in California, Colorado, the Southeast United States, and the Ohio Valley. It also signed a 7-year agreement with Lucent Technologies to purchase switching systems and technical services. It entered the local telephone market in 1997, offering local, long-distance, and calling-card services to small and medium-sized businesses. By the end of the year, ICG was serving 141,000 lines in several markets.

In 1998 and 1999, ICG moved into the Internet services arena. It merged with Netcom On-Line Communications Services, a major ISP. Hence, it could also offer data services.

In 1999, it sold the Netcom U.S. consumer customer base to MindSpring, another major ISP, to focus on Netcom's backbone network, which has 227 points of presence serving some 700 U.S. cities. ICG also entered into an agreement with MindSpring whereby MindSpring would use ICG's data network and network management capabilities. This agreement moved ICG into becoming an "Internet enabler" for ISPs.

During the first half of 1999, ICG signed a number of multiyear agreements with ISPs to provide them with access, transport, and network management services. And in late 1999, it sold off its fiber optic division and its satellite division because management decided to focus on providing (1) access and transport to ISPs, (2) telecom services to businesses across the United States, and (3) direct connectivity to IXCs. ∎

As this case shows, ICG has moved from providing traditional voice telephone service via satellite to becoming an Internet infrastructure provider. It's an interesting story that shows that all roads are indeed leading to the Internet.

The Internet Is the Network of Choice

The biggest telecom news to most people is the Internet, the global packet-switching network that is the epitome of next-generation networks. What has surprised most people is the Internet's surprisingly fast uptake for business uses.

In the late 1990s, the Internet caught most IS departments by surprise, not to mention the hardware and software vendors who serve the corporate IS community.

The Internet actually began in the 1960s when it was funded by the U.S. Department of Defense's Advanced Research Projects Agency and called ARPANET. The network was intended for electronic shipment of large scientific and research files. And it was built as a distributed network, without a controlling node, so that it could continue to function if some of its nodes got knocked out in a nuclear war. But, much to the surprise of its creators, it was mainly used for electronic mail among government contractors, academics, researchers, and scientists.

In 1993 it was still mainly a worldwide network for researchers, scientists, and academics—and individuals who participated in news groups. It was only textual, no graphics. It had e-mail for sending messages, maintaining e-mail lists, and interacting with news groups. It had file transfer protocol (FTP) for sending files, Telnet for logging onto another computer, and Gopher for searching and downloading files from databases.

That all changed in 1994 when the World Wide Web was invented by Tim Berners-Lee at CERN in Geneva. This graphical "layer" of the Net made it much more user friendly. Web sites had addresses specified by their universal resource locator (URL). Its multimedia Web pages were formatted using hypertext markup language (HTML). All the Web sites could be accessed via an easy-to-use browser on a PC. Hyperlinks hidden behind highlighted words on a Web page, when clicked, would jump to the linked page. Following the links became known as "Web surfing." This graphical electronic world was first populated by homepages of computer geeks and "the younger generation." The Web's use by businesses began skyrocketing a few years later, in the late 1990s.

The Internet has done for telecom what the IBM PC did for computing: brought it "to the masses." In 1981, when the IBM PC was introduced, its architecture was open, all the design specifications were published. This openness led to thousands of peripheral manufacturers, component makers, and clone makers producing compatible products. An entire industry developed around this open architecture. The same is happening with the Internet because it provides the same kind of openness, this time, in the telecom arena. Vendors have a standard set of protocols to work with so that products can compatibly work with each other. And businesses do not need to commit to a proprietary architecture. Like the PC, this openness yields the most powerful solutions and the most competitive prices.

The Internet has three attributes that make it important to corporations: ubiquity, reliability, and scalability. It is global, thus it is ubiquitous. Enterprises, both large and small, potentially have global reach with a browser and global presence with a Web site. As noted earlier, the Internet was designed to survive computer crashes by allowing alternate routing. This capability makes it highly reliable. People might not be able to access a crashed server, but they can still access all other nodes that are operating. The Internet has also been able to sustain incredible growth since its beginning. Specific Web sites can handle tremendous amounts of traffic, in the tens of millions of hits a day, if they have been properly designed. That's scalability!

Today, the protocols underlying the Internet have become the protocols of choice in corporate networks, for internal communications as well as communications with the outside world. The norm is now end-to-end Internet protocol (IP) networks.

To illustrate how a company might build a corporate network from scratch utilizing the Internet, here is a fictitious example of XYZ Company.

CASE EXAMPLE

XYZ COMPANY

XYZ Company, which makes and sells widgets, is in the process of installing a corporate network. The chief technology officer (CTO) has a myriad of decisions to make. Of course he wants employees to be able to access each other, corporate data, and the Internet, so he will create an "IP network" using the Internet's standard protocol TCP/IP, which packages data into packets, each with a header that tells where it is to be delivered.

As part of management in an Internet Age company, the CTO sees the Internet as the heart of XYZ's corporate operation. Hence, he will create an *intranet* for use by employees, an *extranet* for use by suppliers and some large customers, and of course, the *Internet* as the all-important central public network.

The CTO has a basic way of thinking about all the computers in his company: he sees them as either clients or servers. Computers used by the employees are clients; they make requests of other computers. Computers that respond to these requests are servers. They can act as storage devices for shared files for teams or departments or even customers. They may house shared applications or shared peripherals, or they can connect groups of workstations to a network, including the Internet.

Serving Remote Users

Every PC will be outfitted with a Network Interface Card (NIC) that lets it talk to the network. XYZ has four choices of communication wiring: twisted pair (the standard telephone line), coaxial cable (like cable TV), fiber optic (glass fiber that carries signals via light pulses), and wireless. Fiber carries tremendous amounts of traffic, and they are expensive, so they are mainly used in "backbone" networks. Each NIC will support the medium the company will be using.

Each computer also needs a network operating system. These days, it is part of the computer's operating system. Furthermore, some of the machines need a modem, whose job is to convert (modulate) the digital signal from the computer to an analog signal for the telephone or cable system, and vice versa.

Modems will be used mainly by employees working from computers in their home. Most of the employees will use the standard telephone modems that communicate at 56 kbps (10^4 or about 7,000 characters a second). Digital subscriber line (DSL) modems, which communicate at 1.2 mbps (10^6), are 20 times faster, and allow simultaneous voice and data. It will be installed for some employees, such as IT staff, because they need high-speed access to the company's computers. Cable modems, a third option, communicate at a whopping 10 mbps (10^7 or 200 times faster than the telephone modem). Like DSL, however, cable modems are not available everywhere. Also like DSL, they are always on; no dial-up is needed. However, this convenience can present security problems because the session code does not change as it does with dial-up sessions.

(Case Continued)

A major decision the CTO needs to make is how to connect these remote users to the corporate network and provide the speed and security they need. The salespeople, for instance, no longer have company-supplied offices; their offices are in their homes. They have company-supplied laptops and PDAs; they dial in from hotels, client sites, or their homes, or use an always-on PCS for e-mail.

Serving Local Users

In the office, all the computers will be connected directly to an always-on local area network (LAN) via the NIC; they will not need modems.

The various LANs in XYZ's offices will use three types of computers to route traffic.

- *Hubs* are repeaters; they forward packets of data from one machine to another. When a number of computers share a hub, data sent from one goes to all the others. This configuration can get congested with many computers so hubs will only be used for work groups.
- *Switches* are smarter; they only forward packets to the port of the intended computer, using the addressing information in each packet's header. Switches will be used to connect work groups.
- *Routers* are smarter still; they use a routing table to pass along a packet to the next appropriate router on a network. Thus, they can direct packets via the most efficient route or relay packets around a failed network component. Routers also link network segments that use different

protocols, such as linking an Apple-Talk network with an Ethernet network. Routers also can connect to wide area networks (WANs). XYZ will use routers to connect its LANs to a WAN.

The CTO has a choice of protocols for his IP-based LANs. He could choose Ethernet, the most popular, which has a speed of 10 mpbs (10^7). Using Ethernet, when a computer has a message to send, it broadcasts the stream of packets and then listens for an acknowledgment of receipt. If it receives no reply within a specified time, it rebroadcasts, presuming the packets collided with packets from other computers and did not reach their destination.

A second option is token ring technology, which uses a ring network where a token passes around the ring asking each computer if it has a message to transmit. If so, it puts the data in the token, and when the token comes around again, releases it for others to use. Token ring runs at 4 to 16 mpbs.

To understand the magnitude of these speeds, a 10 mpbs LAN or cable modem is 200 times faster than a 56 kbps modem. Even so, due to his employees' demands for multimedia and video, these speeds will soon be too slow for XYZ, so the CTO is considering higher speed protocols, such as Fast Ethernet, which runs at 100 mpbs (10^8).

The LAN will give in-office employees always-on connection to the company's intranet, its employee-only Web site that is protected from the outside world by a firewall. The firewall is a server that lets in e-mail but not access to applications or executable code. The intranet will essentially be "the office" for XYZ

(Case Continued)

because it will house all their forms, processes, and documents. It will also be accessible by remote employees.

Communicating Between Offices

XYZ employees need to communicate between sites, so they need some sort of wide area network. As expected, the CTO has choices here as well. Asynchronous transfer mode (ATM) is high speed—up to 622 mpbs (10^8). ATM is used by telephone companies for their network backbones; they then offer ATM services to companies like XYZ for their WANs. ATM has the advantage of being suitable for transmitting time-sensitive voice and video traffic because ATM uses fixed-length packets and it establishes a connection with the receiving station that all the packets transverse and arrive in their transmitted order.

If the CTO chose ATM from a telecom company, he would get digital point-to-point connections between each XYZ office and the phone company's nearest central office. He would pay a fixed amount per month for unlimited use; the price per link would depend on the amount of bandwidth he orders, which, in turn, depends on the number of users at each office and the amount of traffic they generate. Engineers swapping widget computer-aided design (CAD) drawings between two sites would need a far larger "pipe" than office workers asking for sales spreadsheets or word-processing documents. However, due to the high cost of ATM long-distance bandwidth, the CTO might not be able to afford all his desires.

A fairly new option for XYZ to link several offices in a city, or link floors within a building, is Gigabit Ethernet, which operates at speeds of one gbps (10^9 bits per second). One hundred gigabit Ethernet (10^{10}) is on the horizon. In 1999, Gigabit Ethernet outsold ATM because it is a less costly technology, so it is an option the CTO needs to consider.

These issues then are some of the major considerations for the CTO. He is definitely going to base all his decisions on being Internet protocol centric. ■

Extranets.   Not long after creating intranets, businesses realized they could extend the intranet concept into an extranet—a special part of the intranet for use by trading partners, customers, and suppliers for electronic commerce. The notion caught on and extranets have become the primary approach for business-to-business e-commerce. The following case of National Semiconductor[4] illustrates the use of an extranet and shows how the company tackled the challenge of conducting e-commerce globally.

NATIONAL SEMICONDUCTOR

National Semiconductor, with headquarters in Santa Clara, California, designs and manufactures semiconductor products used in personal computers, consumer electronics products (cars, cameras, cell phones, and so on), and telecommunications systems. These days, National is focusing on its key competency—advanced analog and mixed analog/digital signal technologies—for use in the newest breed of electronic devices: "information appliances," which are low-cost, easy-to-use, wireless devices to interact with the Internet without the use of a PC. National has sales of $2 billion and employs some 11,000 people around the globe.

To gain market share, and move into new markets in Europe, South America, and Asia, National looked to the Web. It created an intranet that the salesforce could access to keep up-to-date on products and order products. And it created the "National Advisor," using Internet-based "push technology," to electronically send news, sales reports, and customer information to the salesforce and its management.

National also created an extranet for distributors and channel partners, and a Web site for design engineers who use its components in electronic and telecom products. This site contains descriptions of more than 30,000 products in the form of PDF databooks. Design engineers can view these databooks and order samples, either via the Web or through distributors.

To give far-flung engineers decent download times of these 10k-to-200k-size files, National initially installed mirrored servers in Germany and Hong Kong, and planned for eight more sites. But management discovered the logistics of maintaining 10 such sites would be a nightmare as well as cost prohibitive at approximately $4 million a year.

They thus turned to outsourcing with Digital Island, which has data centers around the globe and offers hosting and other Internet infrastructure services. Digital Island replicates Web sites on "edge servers," which are servers close to users (on the edge of the Internet) so that download speed is fast. Some servers even perform language translation. So when a request is made, the closest edge server detects the type of user device, type of network, and country (and its regulations), and adapts the content to those conditions.

The cost would be $400,000 a year, or one-tenth the in-house cost. More importantly, performance was so much better that National could reach markets in Asia, Eastern Europe, Indonesia, and Latin America where Internet service was generally slow. In addition, the company could distribute daily customer data and market information within 24 hours, which would speed product development and responses to design engineers' queries.

National's Web site now supports 1 million design engineers around the globe, who download more than 10,000 databooks a day, in about two seconds each. The company only needs to replicate its site once; Digital Island takes care of the global coverage. Finally, National receives reports on which pages are being accessed in each part of the world, which is important information to the sales and marketing staff. ■

Voice Over IP. More recently, enterprises have begun investigating use of the Internet not just for data but also for voice, to replace their telephone system. This new Internet use is called "voice over IP" (VoIP). It works in this manner, says James Cope:[5] A special IP phone, with an Ethernet jack in the back instead of the standard telephone jack, is attached to a company LAN, perhaps through a PC. Rather than the analog signals sent by traditional phones, the IP phone generates a digital signal. That signal is routed over the LAN just like any other data, in packets, either to (1) another IP phone on the LAN, (2) through the company's WAN to a distant IP phone on another of the company's LANs, or (3) through an IP voice gateway to the public switched telephone network to a standard telephone.

Few companies have yet given up their telephone networks for a VoIP network, but if the cost differential continues, more may switch. Like other devices on a network, IP phones have an IP address, so they can be easily moved to another location and can still be located.

Thus, the Internet and its protocols are taking over. To understand the complexity of telecommunications, we now look at the underlying framework for the Internet: the OSI Reference Model.

The OSI Reference Model Underlies Today's Networks

The worldwide telephone system has been so effective in connecting people because it has been based on common standards worldwide. Today's packet-switching networks are also following some standards in most cases. The underpinning of these standards is the OSI Reference Model.

Closed Versus Open Networks. The first concept that is important to understand is the difference between closed and open networks. A *closed network* is one that is offered by one supplier and to which only the products of that supplier can be attached. Mainframe and mini manufacturers used this approach for years to "lock in" their customers. Closed networks were originally adopted for the top three computing levels, described in Chapter 5: corporate, regional, and site. Companies generally used the proprietary network offered by their mini or mainframe manufacturer. In the Internet world, the first commercial offerings (CompuServe, Prodigy, America On-Line, and Microsoft Network) also used proprietary software initially. But as direct connection to the Internet spread, these firms all finally embraced the Internet's open system approach.

An *open network* is based on national or international standards so that the products of many manufacturers can be attached to it. Open networks have been favored by suppliers serving the lower three computing levels: departments, work groups, and individuals. Today, proprietary networks are out, open networks are in, because no company is large enough to serve all of a firm's telecom needs—to say nothing of connecting to other organizations and people.

We now live in an "open systems" world, and the most important architecture in this world is the open systems interconnection (OSI) model.

Why It Is Called a Reference Model. The International Standards Organization (ISO), CCITT, and other standards bodies have adopted the seven-level OSI Reference Model for guiding the development of international standards for networks of computers. It is called a "reference model" because it only recommends the functions to be performed in each of the seven layers; it does not specify detailed standards for each layer. Those details are left up to the standards bodies in the adopting countries. OSI is used by suppliers to make their products interconnectable. So, understanding the OSI reference model is a step toward understanding how telecom systems actually work.

An Analogy: Mailing a Letter.   In the model's layered architecture, control information is used to route messages to their destination. The following is a four-level analogy of an executive mailing a paper document to another executive (Figure 6-2). Although mailing letters is an old-fashioned way to communicate, this example makes the intricacies of message-passing understandable. Notice that control information—the

FIGURE 6-2 How Control Information Is Used to Route Messages

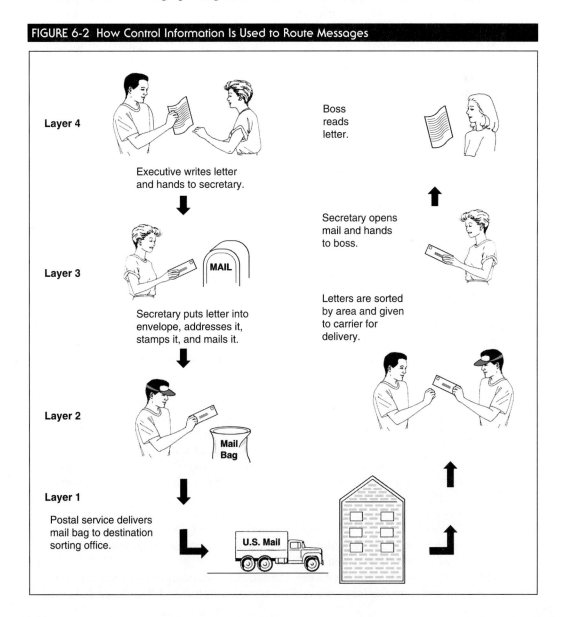

Layer 4

Executive writes letter and hands to secretary.

Boss reads letter.

Secretary opens mail and hands to boss.

Layer 3

MAIL

Secretary puts letter into envelope, addresses it, stamps it, and mails it.

Letters are sorted by area and given to carrier for delivery.

Layer 2

Mail Bag

Layer 1

Postal service delivers mail bag to destination sorting office.

U.S. Mail

address and type of delivery—is on the envelope or mailbag. This control information determines the services to be provided by the next lower layer, and it contains addressing information for the corresponding layer on the receiving end. It defines the interfaces between the layers as well as the dialog within a layer.

- At layer 4, the business executive writes a letter and gives it to a secretary.
- At layer 3, the secretary puts the letter into an envelope, addresses the envelope, puts the return address on the envelope, stamps it, and then mails it.
- At layer 2, the mail carrier takes the letter to the postal sorting office, where all mail for the same postal district is put into one bag with the destination postal office name on it. Mail of different types—Express Mail, first-class mail, third-class mail—have their own bags.
- At layer 1, the postal service delivers the mail bag to the destination sorting office.
- At layer 2, the sorting office checks that the bag has been delivered to the right office. Then the letters are sorted by area and passed on to the individual carriers, who deliver them.
- At layer 3, the recipient's secretary rejects any mail delivered to the wrong address, opens the letter, and passes it to the recipient, saying, "Here's a letter from . . ."
- At layer 4, the recipient takes the letter and reads it.

When a layer receives a "message" from the next higher layer, it performs the requested services and then "wraps" that message in its own layer of control information for use by the corresponding layer at the receiving end. It then passes this "bundle" to the layer directly below it. On the receiving end, a layer receiving a bundle from a lower layer unwraps the outermost layer of control information, interprets that information, and acts on it. Then it discards that layer of wrapping and passes the bundle to the next higher layer.

The Model's Seven Layers.   In a similar way, the OSI Reference Model describes the types of control data produced by each layer. See Figure 6-3.

Starting at the top of the model, or the layer closest to users, here are the layers and what they basically do.

- ***Layer 7 is the Application Layer.*** This layer contains the protocols embedded in the applications we use. One familiar protocol at this level is HTTP (hypertext transfer protocol), which anyone who had surfed the Web has used to locate a Web site. Other familiar TCP/IP protocols at this level are file transfer protocol (FTP), for transferring files on the Internet, and Telnet, for logging onto and using a remote computer on the net. OSI also has defined some somewhat-familiar protocols at this level that permit worldwide communication in various ways. For instance ISO's X.500 directory services protocol is for creating distinct Internet (or other) mailing addresses. OSI's X.400 mail handling service is for permitting dissimilar electronic mail systems to handle e-mail created and sent from dissimilar systems.
- ***Layer 6 is the Presentation Layer.*** The telecom protocols in this layer translate data to and from the language and format used in Layer 7. This layer does not

Layer	Name	Job	Protocol Examples
7	Application Layer	Interface to application	HTTP, X.500, X.400, ODA, Internet key exchange (IKE), Postscript
6	Presentation Layer	Translates data to and from language in Layer 7	NetBIOS
5	Session Layer	Controls dialog, acts as moderator for a session	Secure sockets layer (SSL)
4	Transport Layer	Controls flow, ensures reliable packet delivery	TCP
3	Network Layer	Addresses and routes packets	IP, X.25, Packet-level Protocol
2	Logical Link Layer	Makes sure no data are lost or garbled	Ethernet, Token Ring, FDDI, ISDN, ATM, Frame relay
1	Physical Layer	Defines physical connection to network	Ethernet 50 ohm coaxial cable, 10 Base-T, twisted pair, fiber optic cable

FIGURE 6-3   The OSI Reference Model

have many familiar protocols. For people in the IBM world, the protocol that might be familiar is NetBIOS, which is used to communicate among peripherals, such as the monitor, printer, and so on.

- *Layer 5 is the Session Layer.* Telecom protocols in this layer control the dialog for a session and act as moderator, seeing that messages are sent as directed and can be interrupted, if necessary. An important protocol in this layer is secure sockets layer (SSL), to provide Internet security. It uses a combination of public key and cryptography to provide confidentiality, data integrity, and authentication.
- *Layer 4 is the Transport Layer.* This layer ensures reliable packet delivery. Protocols in this layer handle flow control and ensure the integrity of each message, resequencing portions, if necessary. A main protocol at this level is transmission control protocol (TCP), which is the TCP found in TCP/IP. TCP manages the connections made by Internet protocol (IP) in the next lower layer, Layer 3.
- *Layer 3 is the Network Layer.* Protocols in this layer address and route packets to their destination. Here resides the all-important Internet protocol (IP) that allows packets to traverse an "internet"—that is, a network of networks.
- *Layer 2 is the Logical Link Layer.* Protocols at this layer mainly do error correction, making sure no data is lost or garbled. LAN protocols, such as Ethernet and Token Ring, work here.
- *Layer 1 is the Physical Layer.* Protocols at this level are responsible for defining the physical connection of devices to a network. This level is the most basic and actually defines the electrical and mechanical characteristics of connections. So, these protocols describe modem standards as well as the characteristics of transmission wires, such as Ethernet 50 ohm coaxial cable, 10 Base-T twisted pair wire, and so on.

These layers define the OSI model, which has provided the world with a map for implementing today's telecom architecture.

Wide Area Network Technology Has Changed

Companies used to lease lines from interexchange carriers to connect their offices. These dedicated private circuits were priced by bandwidth (capacity) and distance. With greater competition, pricing is changing. PricewaterhouseCoopers predicts that fixed monthly access fees, which started with the Internet, will spread to wireline and wireless services. Pricing will be based on bandwidth, traffic, and time, but not distance. Multiple quality of service (QoS) offerings—such as a committed data rate, guaranteed network latency (delay time), and bundles of services—will be developed.

In the early 1990s, companies began migrating to cheaper private switched digital services; the most popular was T1 links to the PSTN's central local office, running at 1.544 mpbs (10^6).

In the late 1990s, companies moved to packet-switching protocols, turning their data networks into IP networks, which are now the norm. Companies have relied chiefly on two packet technologies, frame relay and ATM.

Frame relay sends data in packets of different lengths. It is for bursty communication, which occurs between LANs, between corporate sites, and over the Internet. Frame relay wraps or encloses each packet in a frame that contains its destination information, hence its name, frame relay. Its advantage, notes PricewaterhouseCoopers, is that companies only pay for what they use, and they can have short bursts requiring lots of bandwidth once in a while without having to buy excess capacity. Users can also share bandwidth, lowering costs for each. Frame relay has become the predominant technology used in WANs and was used to establish the first IP virtual private networks (VPNs).

Use of frame relay for corporate WANs has had a major effect on network administration in corporations, says PricewaterhouseCoopers. It does not require on-site engineers because the intelligence is in the carrier network, not at the customer's location. So it offloads network management to the service providers. Furthermore, frame relay services are offered by international carriers who have partnered with other carriers giving customers a single point of contact and simplifying their global network management and billing.

Asynchronous transfer mode (ATM) is a second important high-speed packet protocol. As noted earlier, it transmits fixed-length packets with fixed intervals between packets. Thus, it produces natural-sounding speech and jerk-free video. If the packets arrived at varying intervals, voices could vacillate between sounding like Donald Duck to sounding like Goofy.

ATM has been used by carriers since its development in the 1980s. Like frame relay, it is used in WANs and campus backbones. ATM is widely used because it has built-in provisions for prioritizing traffic and reserving bandwidth, which means it can guarantee delivery and latency (delay time). This capability is important because companies want to be able to use one network for many tasks (from e-mail to video conferencing) but they want to be assured that time-sensitive live video conference signals will receive priority over non-time-sensitive e-mail traffic. Being able to provide such guarantees is called quality of service (QoS) and it is a major discussion point at telecommunication conferences today. Frame relay can give voice and video higher priority over data, but cannot guarantee quality of service. Thus, the preference is to run IP networks over ATM.

The Rate of Change Is Accelerating

Although no one seems to know for sure, many people speculate that data traffic surpassed voice traffic either in 1999 or 2000. And change seems to be coming thick and fast in computing and telecom, for good reason. Author George Gilder[6] explains why he believes the pace of IT change is increasing, and even more importantly, why it will increase ever faster from now on.

He notes that the technologies of sand (silicon chips), glass (fiber optics), and air (wireless telecom) are governed by exponential rules. Mead's law, named after Carver Mead of California Institute of Technology, says that N transistors on a sliver of silicon yield N^2 performance and value. It is the rule of semiconductors, which is why this technology has been so powerful. But now this law of semiconductors is joined by the law of the "telecosm"—networking N computers yields N^2 performance and value. Combining the two laws leads to the compounding force of exponentials that we see sweeping through the world economy today.

To get a sense of the power of exponents and why it is inexorable, consider the story of the emperor of China and the inventor of chess, says Gilder. The emperor was so exultant with the invention of chess that he told the inventor he could have anything he wanted in his kingdom. The inventor thought for a moment, and then said, "Just one grain of rice, your majesty, on the first square, two on the second, four grains of rice on the third, and so on through the 64 squares of the chess board."

Now, of the two possible outcomes to this story, one is that the emperor goes bankrupt, because at 10 grains per square inch, 2^{64} grains of rice would cover the entire surface of the earth with rice fields two times over, oceans included. The other possibility, which is even more alarming, is that the inventor loses his head. Confronted with exponential technologies, emperors often decapitate. So one rule of this story is "Keep an eye on the emperor," says Gilder, because they can suppress the spread of technology quite effectively. The governments of many countries have done just that in stifling IT through their PTTs.

It is also worth noticing, says Gilder, that after the first half of the chessboard (at 32 squares), the emperor only needs to give 2^{32} grains of rice (4 billion), which he could easily do from his rice fields. So nothing much happens during the first 32 squares. But after that, look out.

To relate this story to the present day, Gilder presented the following astounding facts: In 1995, exactly 32 doublings of computer power had occurred since the invention of the digital computer after World War II. So since 1995, we have been on "the second half of the chess board," and a stream of profound developments has taken place. E-mail outnumbered postal mail for the first time in 1995—95 billion external e-mails to 85 billion postal mails. The number of PC sales overtook the number of TV sales in late 1995. And on and on. Such changes will only accelerate, he predicts. For this reason, everyone in business must become comfortable with technology to cope with this brand new world of ever-increasing technological change.

The Optical Era Will Provide Bandwidth Abundance

Gilder also predicts an abundance of bandwidth around the world. He notes that an economic era is defined by the plummeting price of the key factor of production. During the industrial era, that key factor was horsepower, as defined in kilowatt hours, which dropped from many dollars to 7.5 cents. Since the 1960s, the driving force of economic growth has been the plummeting price of transistors, translated into MIPS and bits of semiconductor memory. The latter has fallen 68 percent a year, from $7 some 35 years ago to a millionth of a cent today.

We are now approaching yet another "historic cliff of cost" in a new factor of production: bandwidth. "If you thought the price of computing dropped rapidly in the last decade, just wait until you see what happens with communication bandwidth," said Gilder, referencing a remark by Andy Grove, CEO of Intel. Up to this point, we have used MIPS and bits to compensate for the limited availability of bandwidth, said Gilder, but now we are moving into an era of bandwidth abundance.

Fiber optic technology is just as important as microchip technology. Currently, some 40 million miles of fiber optic cable have already been laid around the world. And in the United States, it is being laid at the rate of 4,000 miles a day. But half of it is dark, that is, it is not used. And the other half is used to just one-millionth of its potential, because every 25 miles it must be converted to electronic pulses to amplify and regenerate the signal. The bandwidth of the optical fiber has been limited by the switching speed of transistors, 2.5 to 10 billion cycles per second.

But the intrinsic capacity of each thread is much greater. There is ten times more capacity in the frequencies used in the air for communication, from AM radio to KU band satellite. And the capacity of each thread is 1,000 times the switching speed of transistors—25 terahertz. As a result, using all-optical amplifiers (recently invented), we could send all the telephone calls in the United States on the peak moment of Mother's Day on one fiber thread. Putting thousands of fiber threads in a sheath creates an era of bandwidth abundance that will dwarf the era of MIPS and bits. Or to give a more personal example from *Business Week,*[7] downloading a digital movie, such as *The Matrix,* takes more than 7 hours using a cable modem and 1 hour over Ethernet; it would take four seconds on an optical connection.

Over the next decade, bandwidth will expand ten times as fast as computer power and completely transform the economy, predicts Gilder.

Wireless Is the Next Frontier

Wireless telecom is being promoted as "the next big thing," especially wireless access to the Internet because people want to stay connected even when they are traveling. The terms *mobile computing* and *wireless computing* are often used interchangeably. Generally, however, mobile computing means using a portable computer and communicating via landlines, such as a salesperson accessing the corporate intranet via a hotel telephone. It is "full-scale" touch-typing computing using a laptop computer—essentially, one's portable office. Wireless computing, on the other hand, generally means using a handheld device, such as a cell phone, smart phone, PDA, or information appliance, rather than a laptop computer, and communicating via a wireless service.

Wireless communications have been with us for some time, in the form of cell phones, very small aperture terminals (VSATs), pagers, building-to-building microwave links, infrared networks, and wireless LANs in warehouses. Tomorrow's uses span a vast spectrum. In this section, we discuss wireless for the following (Figure 6-4):

- Personal area networks (PANs): To connect a laptop computer to a cell phone, or to connect computers in a room creating an ad hoc LAN, or to create a PAN in one's office
- LANs: In an office building or warehouse as a wireless LAN
- Wireless local loop (WLL): To handle "the last mile"
- Long distance: To provide voice services to mobile people via their cell phones
- M-commerce: To transact business wirelessly via PDAs, smart phones, or other information appliances communicating through the Internet.

Wireless PANs. A personal area network is a short-distance network—about 30 feet (10 meters). This new kind of network could be used to synchronize a laptop and a PDA, to load cash onto a cash card from a banking machine, to dispense money to a toll booth, to link several laptops in a room, and so on. So it is not your typical LAN on a small scale; it allows distinctly new uses. The main technologies are infrared and Bluetooth, a standard developed by Ericsson and named after a warlord who unified a Scandinavian area. Bluetooth uses the same radio frequency as other wireless LAN technologies, so interference can be a concern if the PAN is used in an office near a LAN. But for other uses, such as with vending machines, this issue may not be critical.

Wireless LANs. Used within a building or among buildings on a campus, wireless LANs are generally not replacing existing wired LANs but extending them to portable

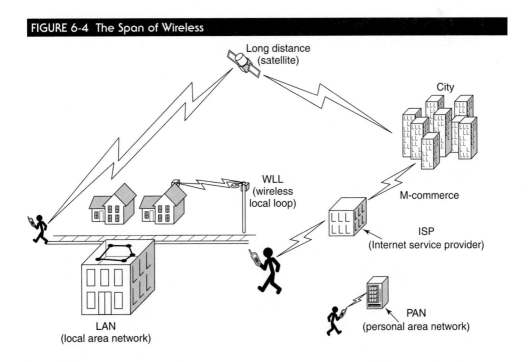

FIGURE 6-4 The Span of Wireless

devices. However, in some situations a wireless LAN might be a better choice than a wired LAN, notes the Wireless LAN Association.[8] Those situations include:

- In hospitals, so that doctors and nurses can use handheld or notebook computers to record patient data at the bedside, which is faster than using a wired computer.
- Teams that work at client sites, such as consulting and audit teams, which can more quickly set up a work group network using wireless LAN technology.
- Any group that needs to create a temporary LAN, whether for training, a trade show, emergency situation, or such, that can get up and running faster.
- A fixed setting where a wireless LAN can be configured more quickly, adding, moving, and changing participants.
- In older buildings where the wiring ducts are full.
- Backup for important applications that run over wired networks.
- Senior executives in a meeting who can draw on data, say, from the company intranet or other sources over a wireless LAN.

Wireless LANs use two technologies: infrared and microwave. Infrared is infrared light beams, such as used in TV remote control devices. Infrared transmits at frequencies just below red light, the lowest frequency in the light spectrum visible to humans. Like other forms of light, infrared cannot penetrate solids, such as walls, ceilings, dust, and rain. Therefore all the transmitters and receivers must be in line-of-sight with each other or be reflected off a surface. Infrared has the advantage of wide bandwidth, so it can transmit at high speeds, such as 100 mpbs, and it is not government controlled, so it can be used unlicensed anywhere.

Microwave and radio frequency (RF) are the most popular wireless LAN technologies, says author Cliff Roth,[9] because the signals can go through walls. A popular form uses spread spectrum technology in which the microwave frequency hops around, making the signal more secure because interceptors must continually change to the same frequency to capture the signal.

Wireless LANs use two topologies: peer to peer and client-server (Figure 6-5 on page 200). Peer to peer, where each unit communicates with every other unit, is the least expensive because the system has no central controlling unit. However, performance decreases as traffic increases because more and more collisions occur. In client-server topology, the server is the central coordinating node. It communicates with the clients wirelessly and links to a wired LAN on behalf of those clients.

Here's an example of a fairly typical use of a wireless LAN, in manufacturing. Several others are also cited on the Wireless LAN Association's Web page. The importance of this example is that the LAN is used to provide visibility into manufacturing operations, which is a crucial first step companies need to make internally to take advantage of e-commerce.

CASE EXAMPLE

BMW

Bavarian Motor Works (BMW) builds more than one million vehicles a year in Germany and the United States. It opened a facility in South Carolina and more than 30 suppliers have built facilities nearby to work with BMW. When this plant was slated to take on the manufacture of the company's sport utility vehicle, BMW wanted to implement the new assembly line quickly. It meant helping these suppliers scale up quickly as well.

Real-time delivery of data to the suppliers was one key for moving quickly. Suppliers especially needed accurate inventory data of the components they were supplying to BMW so they knew when to make just-in-time deliveries to the plant. BMW uses SAP's enterprise resource planning system to track parts inventory. To gather the inventory data that fed into SAP, BMW decided to place barcodes on parts. Those barcodes could then be scanned as parts moved through the assembly process so that BMW's planners, operations personnel, and suppliers knew the current status of all parts.

Originally BMW used Intermec barcode scanners attached to hardwired data terminals at different locations on the plant floor. But more recently they upgraded to Intermec's wireless scanning system. The scanner terminals transmit the data from the barcode readers to SAP via a wireless network that covers the entire 2-million-square-foot plant. The system uses RF technology.

The move to wireless allows BMW to more quickly reconfigure or expand the data collection system; they simply have to move the stations, not rewire them.

A number of BMW's suppliers have followed suit and implemented wireless data collection networks in their operations. As a result, the supply chain from supplier to supplier warehouse to BMW's production line to shipment to a dealer is supported by a flow of data that travels over interconnected wireless and wired networks. ■

Wireless Local Loops. With the goal of replacing the wireline link, wireless local loops use RF technology between a home or business and a telephone company's central office. This use of wireless technology is also called "fixed wireless" and is another approach to solving "the last mile" problem. Metricom offers such a service that it calls a radionet, using antennas on light posts to form a wireless mesh using spread spectrum technology; see Figure 6-4. Its Ricochet service operates at 428.8 kbps (10^5). Qualcomm and Hitachi are offering such a service to neighborhoods not served by DSL, with speeds up to 2.44 mpbs (10^6).

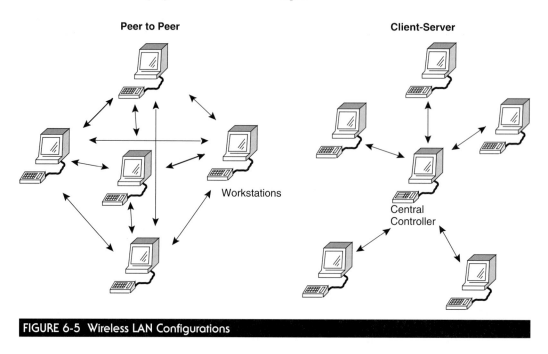

FIGURE 6-5 Wireless LAN Configurations

Laser beam local loops are being proposed, notes PricewaterhouseCoopers. These require line of sight, and they promise an awesome speed of 2.5 gbps (10^9) up to 1.2 miles (2 km). When multiplexed, they can get to 20 gbps (10^{10}) to 3 miles (5 km). It is being called the fiberless optical network.

Fixed wireless is being used in developing countries and remote locations in place of wireline because these networks are more rapidly deployed and less costly than buying cables. Some developing countries are bypassing wiring altogether.

Wireless Long Distance.   Whether the subject is wireless LANs or WANs, the only two wireless technologies are infrared light and radio airwaves (sine waves at specific frequencies) up into the microwave range. Figure 6-6 shows the bandwidth spectrum, which illustrates where the different technologies lie.

The most familiar wide area wireless technology is cell phones, where "cell" refers to a geographic area with a radio transmitter and receiver. The range of a cell explains why a cell phone used in a moving car fades in and out: as the call is passed from one cell to another it fades out of one and into another. In essence, the cell phone is like a miniature radio station, says Roth, broadcasting on a certain bandwidth. With the cellular structure, a phone only needs to compete for bandwidth with other phones in the cell. Cell phones operate in the upper radio waves—in the microwave frequency band of 2.4 GHz to 5 GHz.

The first cell phones used analog technology and circuit switching, now called first-generation (1G) wireless. Callers are charged for the amount of time they use the circuit, not for the amount of information transmitted. And, like a telephone or modem, users dial in.

FIGURE 6-6   The Electromagnetic Spectrum and Broadcast Frequencies

3000 EHz 300 EHz		Gamma rays	
30 EHz 3 EHz 300 PHz		X-rays	
30 PHz 3 PHz		Ultraviolet radiation	
		Visible light	
300 THz 30 THz 3 THz		Infrared radiation	
300 GHz	Extra high frequency	Microwave	Terrestrial microwave
30 GHz	Super high frequency		Satellites (.5-51.4GHz)
3 GHz	Ultra high frequency		Bluetooth/Wireless LANs (2.4-2.5 GHz) 3G wireless/PCS (1800-2200 Mhz) 1G cellular (800-900MHz) UHF TV (500-800 Mhz)
300 MHz	Very high frequency	Radio waves	VHF TV (175-216 MHz) FM radio (88-108 MHz)
30 MHz 3 MHz	High frequency		
	Medium frequency		Wireless local loop (1.25 MHz) AM radio (540-1800 KHz)
300 KHz 30 KHz	Low frequency		GSM 2G wireless (200 KHz)
3 KHz 300 HZ	Very low frequency		
30 HZ 7.5 HZ	Earth		

Cell phone technology was demonstrated by AT&T and Motorola in the late 1970s, notes PricewaterhouseCoopers, but the first commercial offerings were in Japan and Scandinavia, not the United States. In the early 1980s, Europe had nine cell phone standards, but seeing the need for one to allow continent-wide communication, they developed Global System for Mobile Communications (GSM), a digital standard. GSM operates at a slow 9.6 kbps, but it has encryption to prevent eavesdropping. In the main, GSM has become the mobile telephony standard for all but the Americas. Unlike the computing industry, a number of the leading global telecom manufacturers are outside the United States. NTT is in Japan, Ericsson and Nokia are in Scandinavia.

Although Europe and Asia had a single dominant standard, the United States did not. Two protocols vied for dominance. Time division multiple access (TDMA) divided the signals by time, while Code Division Multiple Access (CDMA) divided them by code. CDMA was developed in the late 1980s and uses spread spectrum technology. When a receiver knows a transmitter's code, it picks out only the signals with that code. 1G phones operate in the 800 MHz to 900 MHz range.

One 1G technology, cellular digital packet data (CDPD), uses existing cellular networks but transmits in packets. It does not connect to the telephone network but to the Internet or a private IP network. It is IP based, so each modem functions as an IP node and can be addressed. It works at a slow 19.3 kbps.

2G, which predominates today, uses digital technology, although it is still circuit switched. It aims at digital telephony, not data transmission, but 2G phones can carry data and messages using short messaging service (SMS). SMS is packet based and is used for paging and short messages, often from one cell phone to another. In GSM, SMS messages are limited to 160 characters; in CDMA, the limit is 256. Even with these limits, PricewaterhouseCoopers sees SMS being the largest driver of wireless data services. It has been hugely popular with Scandinavian teens who use it for instant messaging. And in Japan, NTT DoCoMo introduced i-mode phones for Internet services and e-mail in 1999. Within a year NTT had six million subscribers and some 12,000 i-mode sites, many for consumer uses, such as for banking, ticketing, weather reports, paying bills, and so on.

Upcoming is 2.5G, and then 3G. 2.5G got its name because it is meant to extend 2G digital technologies—GSM, CDMA, and TDMA—until 3G becomes available.

According to PricewaterhouseCoopers, a number of standards are vying for 3G. Global frequencies have been set aside and if a single global standard is not achieved, device makers plan to support dual-mode. The goals of 3G are to provide WANs for PCs and multimedia, allowing bandwidth on demand, having the flexibility to support multiple standards and be backward compatible; to allow roaming across disparate sets seamlessly; and to integrate fixed wireless access services, satellite services, and cellular at data rates of 384 kbps for mobile and 2 mbps fixed. These speeds are orders of magnitude greater than 2G wireless services. They could support multimedia and video, but might also have high subscription fees. So some people believe the low-bandwidth wireless services, such as the BlackBerry e-mail pager and SMS, are the true killer applications of m-commerce—that is, mobile commerce.

M-Commerce.   The intended uses of 2.5G and 3G are for personal communication services (PCSs) in the United States and personal communication networks (PCNs) in Europe—the foundation of what is being called mobile commerce (m-commerce). It is expected to change how we interact with the Internet. The vision is being able to conduct commerce digitally from wireless devices.

These wireless communication services use cellular radio technology but they use higher frequencies than cell phones, their transmitters and receivers have lower power, thus, their cells are smaller, says Roth. Radio network companies buy licenses from their government to use specific radio frequencies; they then lease these frequencies to companies that offer PCS services. But not all governments have utilized the same frequencies for the same purposes; hence incompatibilities exist around the world.

One way to send e-mail wirelessly is to connect a laptop's modem to a cell phone, dial an ISP, and transmit from the laptop. Faxes, too, can be sent wirelessly by dialing the appropriate fax number. As an example of use of both wireless and mobile computing, consider Country Company Insurance Group's business use of BellSouth's wireless network.

CASE EXAMPLE

COUNTRY COMPANY INSURANCE GROUP

Country Company Insurance Group, with headquarters in Bloomington, Illinois, now relies on wireless technology for its claims appraisers. Today, when a customer holds a company policy and has a claim, they call a toll-free number and give the information to an agent. The information is entered into the company's host computer and within 15 minutes, the appraisal is assigned to an appraiser and the information is transmitted over Bell South's wireless data network to that appraiser's laptop at 9.6 kbps. Each transmission takes up to 45 seconds. Not all appraisers are within range of the Bell South system, however, so those assignments must be done by land lines.

At night, the appraisers use a land line network to transmit their appraisals to the home office because the costs are less. To reduce transmission costs even more, each laptop contains static, or fairly static, information, such as automobile parts. The laptop database is a hefty 400 million bytes of data.

In addition, the laptops are equipped with a printer, so the customer receives a printout of the appraisal and a claim check on the spot.

The company uses the pro-Pen appraisal estimating package from ADP and the wireless communications use Smart IP software from Nettech. Smart IP uses the TCP/IP protocol yet reduces the number of packets by 80 percent and the amount of data by 60 percent. TCP/IP is not typically used for wireless because it requires too much data transmission, notes Matt Hamblen,[10] but Nettech's approach makes Country Company's wireless communications more affordable. ■

A second way to send e-mail wirelessly is to use a cell phone enabled with Wireless Application Protocol (WAP) from Phone.com. Phone.com sells the WAP browser, infrastructure software, and applications to telephone carriers who then have the browser installed in the phones they offer to their wireless service subscribers, notes David Lipschultz.[11] The carriers install the infrastructure software to handle the applications and they can either build their own applications or buy applications written by Phone.com. Phone.com has applications for telecom companies as well as for end users. WAP has caught on as a standard, even though it was originally intended to only access WAP-built Web sites. But enterprising third parties now create templates for existing sites that only pull off the appropriate content for Web-enabled phones.

WAP is actually fairly complex because unlike a PC, cell phones do not have a hard disk. Also the browser, unlike a PC's browser, knows where the user is located geographically. Thus, sophisticated smart applications can be developed to leverage this locational information.

The third way to send e-mail wirelessly is to use a handheld e-mail device and subscribe to a mobile radio service that uses packet-switching technology. Such services are accessed by a built-in card with an attached antenna. The most significant aspect of this mode of operation is that this connection is "always on," whereas cell phones require dialing in to establish a connection. And sometimes that connection is difficult to establish.

"Always on" is the communication mode of the New Economy because it allows instant notification. For example, a sales team may ask to receive news releases and intranet entries about their specific clients or their main competitors, so they are always up-to-date. If the team's devices allow them to have a team calendar, they might be able to schedule a quick telephone conference call if they receive important news, such as a competitor trying to snag an important customer or information about a market test. Or, they might just collaborate asynchronously via SMS. On-the-go multiparty collaboration is an important use of low-bandwidth wireless devices.

Or a collector might ask for instant notification when specific items, within specific price ranges, come up for auction. The service might give her one-click transaction capabilities so she can bid on an item once she receives notification.

These services are also cheaper than cell phones for sending brief messages, says Roth, and they provide e-mail accounts as part of their service, so consumers do not pay both a cell phone bill and an ISP bill.

Location-based services will also spring up. During slow periods near mealtime, for example, restaurants may send electronic discount coupons to people within a certain distance of their restaurant—redeemable within the next half hour.

Personalization is also an important part of this appliance-based wireless economy. In fact, wireless uses are apt to be quite different from wireline uses. Although people use PCs to surf the Web, wireless users are not likely to do that; it takes too long because the speeds are too slow and their window onto the Web is too small. In fact, 2.5G and 3G data services are likely to aim at specific applications, not Web browsing, surmises PricewaterhouseCoopers. For example, they will be important for logistics, due to the global positioning system (GPS) capabilities.

GPS brings up the subject of satellites. The problem with providing satellite-based PCS services, says PricewaterhouseCoopers, is that the handheld devices have small antennas and low power, so they cannot send signals to a satellite in the high geostationary orbit, some 22,000 miles above earth. Thus, companies have looked at using medium-earth-orbit and low-earth-orbit satellites, but both are not stationary about the earth so serving moving devices on earth from moving satellites in the sky is technically tricky. Thus, we have chosen not to talk about this possibility even though it could become a reality.

Turning back to "thinking in the small," handheld devices are also likely to be created for niche uses. Here is one from Simon Property Group.[12]

CASE EXAMPLE

SIMON PROPERTY GROUP

Simon Property Group owns more than 250 shopping malls in the United States; some 2.3 million shopping visits are made to these malls each year. Simon recently introduced a new way to shop in these malls that utilizes handheld infrared scanners and a Web site, FastFrog.com. To merge its brick-and-mortar operations (the malls) with the Internet (the Web site), Simon created a new subsidiary, clixnmortar.com.

To go shopping the new way, a mall shopper stops at a kiosk in the mall (the pond), registers using some form of identification, decides on a password, and checks out a cute palm-size green (like a frog) scanner called a ZapStick, made by Symbol Technologies.

The shopper, who could be a teenager whose birthday is coming up, takes the ZapStick shopping. When she sees something in a store that she would really like for her birthday, she points the ZapStick at the price ticket and pushes its button to scan the UPC bar code information into the scanner.

When she finishes shopping, she returns the frog to the kiosk, where the information is uploaded to the FastFrog Web site, which her parents and others can access to find out what she'd really like for her birthday.

This linking of retail stores and the Internet not only lets consumer create their own personal online gift wish lists, it also gives Simon Properties valuable information about what items consumers say they want. Simon can then sell this data to the store owners and chain owners in their malls. This information can tell the store owners what people are most likely to buy and perhaps also reduce the number of returned items.

Simon can also use the information themselves to understand changes in consumer buying habits, perhaps even spot consumer trends as they begin to develop, and maybe do targeted promotions—all from use of one type of wireless telecom technology. ∎

Is Wireless Safe? Although a lot of attention is focused on all the new wireless services, a troubling question has not yet been answered: Are these transmissions safe for humans? The higher frequency services, for LANs and PCSs, are in the microwave range. They use almost the same frequency as microwave ovens. Microwave frequencies are more dangerous than lower frequency radio waves because they cause molecules to vibrate faster, causing heat as the molecules rub against each other. This is how microwave ovens cook food. The power limits on cell phones, wireless modems, and wireless LANs (3 watts) aim to protect people from this short-term microwave heating phenomenon, says Roth. Microwaves operate at 500 watts. Long-term effects from low-level vibrations that do not raise body temperature are still possible. Some studies on rats showed damage to DNA that can cause disease, such as cancer.

Although such health concerns have been dismissed by many scientists and scientific studies, their confidence has not settled the issue. Many have long held a belief that electromagnetic radiation from power lines, electrical appliances, and computers can interfere with the body's bioelectromagnetic field, causing an imbalance.[13] These imbalances leave people feeling drained, fatigued, and stressed out. Although it is likely that our bodies can rebalance disruptions caused by occasional exposure to electromagnetic radiation (EMR), frequent bombardment has an effect. It is probably difficult to directly link exposure to disease; it is more likely that exposure will gradually lower a body's immunity.

Cell phone levels of radiation are limited by governments, but these limits are averages. Spikes are possible, which are known to kill cells; so holding a cell phone next to one's head for prolonged times is not wise. Voice use of cell phones by young people is especially disturbing. Thus, it is quite possible that before 2004 there could be a backlash against wireless devices, similar to protests against genetically modified organisms. Objective research is needed and protection could become a hot topic. Anyone care for metal-lined hats?

THE ROLE OF THE IS DEPARTMENT

This long discussion of telecom gives just a glimpse into its complexity as well as its increasing importance. Given this new central role for data networks in the New Economy, what is the IS department's role? We believe IS has three roles: create the telecom architecture for the enterprise, run it, and stay close to the forefront of the field.

A network architecture can contain a set of diagrams, as Zachman pointed out in Chapter 5, but it also needs a set of company policies and rules which, when followed, lead to the desired network environment.

The key challenge in network design is connectivity. Connectivity means allowing users to communicate up, down, across, and out of an organization. The goal is not a single, coherent network, but rather finding the means to interface many dissimilar networks. So one guiding principle is to build systems that are coherent at the interfaces so that users *think* they have one network.

The second key concept in architecture design is "interoperability," which means the capability for different computers, using different operating systems, on different networks to work together on tasks—exchanging information in standard ways without any changes in functionality and without physical intervention.

A truly interoperable network would allow PCs, laptops, and handheld devices to interoperate with servers running UNIX and Windows and mainframes running MVS and communicating over IP networks. This interoperability is the goal of architecture and is the main job of the IS department.

The second job of the IS department is to operate the network. This subject is discussed in Chapter 8, Operations; however, suffice it to say here that many companies are outsourcing this work to companies that specialize in this area because it is just too complex, with too few network specialists to go around and a costly infrastructure investment.

The third job of IS is to stay current with the technology. In this day and age, if an IS department is not already experimenting with how PDAs and other handheld devices can interact with their Web site, they are behind competitors who are. Keeping abreast of telecom requires continually peering into the future and testing out new ideas. It is a crucial job not enough IS departments are performing well enough.

CONCLUSION

The telecom world is big, and getting bigger by the day. It is complex, and getting more complex every day. Some see it as a global electronic highway system where the goal is to establish links and interoperability. Others see it as a cyberspace, where commerce is conducted and businesses operate.

The business world of old has depended on communications, of course, but not to the extent of the New Economy. The Internet has changed everything. First it unleashed e-mail, then Web sites for getting noticed globally, and now for transactions and business. Although worldwide communication over the Internet today allows global business, it also has the opposite effect: customized personal service to individuals anywhere, any time.

The first generation of the Internet economy has been wired. The second is unwired. This untethering will change how we think about computing. Today, telecom is all about connecting and the number of possible connections is about to explode worldwide.

QUESTIONS AND EXERCISES

Review Questions

1. What are the two ways to view telecom?
2. What is "the last mile," and why is it a problem?
3. What is a CLEC, what does it do, and why is it important?
4. What is the Internet, and what three attributes make it important to businesses?
5. Describe the functions of hubs, switches, and routers.
6. How does voice-over IP work?
7. Briefly describe each layer of the OSI Reference Model.
8. Give some examples of uses of wireless LANs.
9. How does a cell phone work?
10. Explain SMS.
11. What is m-commerce?
12. Why is "always on" important?
13. Why might wireless devices not be safe for humans?
14. What are the three roles of the IS department with respect to telecom?

Discussion Questions

1. The chapter implies that a company should stay at the forefront of telecommunications technology lest it fall seriously behind. On the other hand, it might be better to let others go first, and then learn from their mistakes. When is each approach most appropriate? Why?
2. None of us needs a phone at home and a phone at the office. All we need is one phone that we always carry around. Such a practice would relieve the pressures on the telephone system for so many additional phone numbers and area codes. Better yet, each phone should have an IP address. Discuss the pros and cons of these ideas.
3. Although having a wireless device is handy, it is also an intrusion. People need some privacy. They should not always be reachable. Discuss.

Exercises

1. Read five articles on telecom. What developments not discussed in this chapter do they see as important, and why? Present a short briefing on these issues to the class.
2. Contact the information systems manager at a company in your community. What is their telecommunications architecture? What telecommunications standards are they using? How are they using the Internet? What are their plans for wireless?
3. Find one article that discusses senior management's or line management's role in telecom, the use of the Internet, or m-commerce. What role do they play? Are they in partnership with IS? Briefly discuss in class.

REFERENCES

1. PricewaterhouseCoopers, *Technology Forecast: 2000; From Atoms to Systems: A Perspective on Technology,* PricewaterhouseCoopers Technology Center, 68 Willow Road, Menlo Park, CA 94025, www.pwc-global.com/tech-forecast, April 2000, pp. 774.

2. Kaarlgard, Rich, in a speech at Comdex, Fall 1999.

3. Bean, Bill, in a speech at Networld+ Interop, 2000.

4. National Semiconductor case is based on story found on Digital Island's Web site, www.digitalisland.com.

5. Cope, James, "Vendors Tout Voice Over IP," *Computerworld,* February 21, 2000, p. 64.

6. Gilder, George, *Telecosm: How Infinite Bandwidth Will Revolutionize Our World,* The Free Press, New York, 2000, and in a speech at the Aspen Institute on July 18, 1996, broadcast on C-SPAN.

7. Shinal, John and Timothy Mullaney, "At the Speed of Light," *Business Week,* October 9, 2000, p. 145–152.

8. Wireless Lan Association is at www.wlana.com.

9. Roth, Cliff, *Mobile Computing for Dummies,* IDG Books, Danville, CA, 1997.

10. Hamblen, Matt, "Wireless Rollout Eases Appraisers' Work," *Computerworld,* September 13, 1999, p. 78.

11. Lipschultz, David, "Internet World Interview with Alain Rossmann," *Internet World,* June 15, 2000, p. 63–68.

12. Simon Properties Group case is based on information from Symbol Technologies and from their Web site, www.symbol.com.

13. McNurlin, Barbara, "The Wireless Backlash," *Business Recreation AD 2000,* Gartner Executive Programs, Stamford, CT, January 2000.

7 | MANAGING INFORMATION RESOURCES

INTRODUCTION

"Managing information resources" used to mean "managing databases." Corporate databases were well structured, carefully defined, and generally under the jurisdiction of the IS department.

Now all of that is changed. The amount of internal and external data and information available to organizations is increasing by leaps and bounds. Internally, the intranet has caused a revolution, because it allows companies to bring internal data and information together from far-flung files and databases and make them available company-wide. It gives employees access to far more corporate data and information than they ever had before. The ability to handle and transmit multimedia—voice, video, and image—is increasing the variety of information formats and content as well. At the same time, the availability of external data, both hard facts and "soft" intelligence information, has exploded with the Internet.

In addition, the inherent structure of the information resources that need to be managed has broadened considerably. Consider:

- Corporate databases are still a major responsibility of the IS department, but increasingly they are distributed, remote, and exist in a variety of "models" such as hierarchical, relational, and object oriented. In addition to databases for transaction processing, data warehouses house large amounts of data to be analyzed with data mining techniques to support decision making for such applications as customer relationship management.
- Less structured, concept-based information is becoming dominant. Examples include electronic versions of all paper documents and multimedia digitized information such as video files, sound files, Web sites, photos, blueprints, and so on.
- Knowledge management is becoming a key to exploiting the "intellectual assets" of an organization. Included are the explicit captured and stored information (the know-what), as well as the tacit unwritten knowledge in people's heads and experience base (the know-how).

All of these forms of information resources need to be managed well, especially as information becomes an important strategic resource for most companies. In fact, information resources now include data, information, and knowledge. They can be defined as follows:

- *Data* consists of facts devoid of meaning or intent, where meaning and intent are supplied by a particular usage.
- *Information* is data in context, which means that the data has an explicit meaning within a specific context.
- *Knowledge* is information with direction, or intent, where intent is derived from strategies or objectives and is manifested in business rules.

Scope of Information

To characterize the full scope of information management, and to explore some of its ramifications, we consider four types of information. This framework or classification scheme is based on the intersection of two dimensions. The first is the source of the information—external or internal to the organization. The second dimension is based on the structure of the information—data record-based or document-based.

Data records contain primarily *facts* about entities, such as individual employees, customers, parts, or transactions. Well-structured data records are used to hold a set of attributes that describe each entity. In contrast, document-based information pertains primarily to *concepts*—ideas, thoughts, and opinions. Less well-structured documents or messages, with a wide variety of information forms, are used to describe this kind of information.

Figure 7-1 shows the differences in the structure of these two kinds of information. The item of interest in a data record is the entity, which is a part in an inventory system or an employee in a human resources system. Each attribute of interest is represented by a data item or field. The data record is the collection of the attributes necessary to describe the entity. Related records form a file, a group of files form a database, and a collection of databases can comprise an information system. Finally, a "data model" describes the relationships among the entities and attributes.

Trying to use this same structuring approach to organize concepts reveals the challenge of managing this growing information resource. We call this type of information document-based because it is generally packaged in multimedia documents. (We will define "document" more extensively in Chapter 14.) The item of interest is a concept or idea. The attributes that describe the concept are symbols such as words, diagrams, photos, sounds, and so on. Grouping all the symbols to adequately describe the concept might be called a logical paragraph, similar to the way high school English teachers recommend a new paragraph for each new idea. A group of related concepts could be packaged as a document, a set of related documents is stored in a file cabinet or file server, and a set of those make up a library. Models of document-based information might include classification systems, keywords, hypertext link networks, and so forth.

The challenge of managing this conceptual information resource derives from the ambiguity of language and the lack of a defined structure. In Chapter 14 we will discuss some of the enabling technologies for meeting this challenge. So the scope of information resource management can be represented by the matrix in Figure 7-2. In the next section, we discuss the upper left cell, managing internal record-based information. Then we explore some of the important aspects of the other three cells. The last section begins the discussion of knowledge management and includes use of information from all the cells.

MANAGING CORPORATE DATA RECORDS

In the midst of this growing richness of data and information, companies are still struggling to get their internal alphanumeric data under control. The installation of the companywide software packages such as SAP, enterprise data warehouses, and in-

---

FIGURE 7-1 Structure of Information

Structure of Information		
	Data Records	Documents
Item of interest	Entity	Concept or idea
Attribute of item	Field	Set of symbols
All attributes for item	Record	Logical paragraph
All related items	File	Document
A group of related files	Database	File cabinet
A collection of databases	Application system	Library, records center
Data "models"	Hierarchical	Keywords, hypertext
(representational approaches)	relational, etc.	

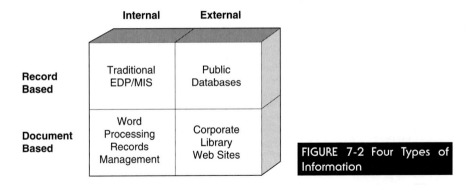

FIGURE 7-2 Four Types of Information

tranets has once again brought to the fore the problems of "dirty data," which is data from different databases that has different names, uses different time frames, or that otherwise does not match.

Attempts to get corporate data under control began way back in the late 1960s and early 1970s with the use of database management systems (DBMS). Not long after that, the "database administration" function appeared, to manage DBMSs and their use. Then, in the 1970s, the broader role of "data administration" was created to manage all the computerized data resources of an organization. Today, these two functions have become even more important as companies attempt to once again round up their data and make it consistent companywide.

The Problem: Inconsistent Data Definitions

In a nutshell, the problem has been incompatible data definitions from application to application, department to department, site to site, and division to division. How has this inconsistency happened? Blame expediency. To get application systems up and running quickly, system designers have sought the necessary data either from the cheapest source or a politically expedient source. Generally, it has meant using data from existing files and adding other new data. In effect, data has been "dribbled" from application to application. The result has been data showing up in different files, with different names for the same data, the same name for different data items, and the same data in different files with different update cycles.

The use of such data may be acceptable for routine information processing, but it is far from acceptable for management uses. Management cannot get consistent views across the enterprise under such conditions. Also, changes in data and programs are hard to make, because a change can affect files anywhere in the organization. Furthermore, such inconsistency makes it difficult to change the tracking and reporting of the organization's products, markets, control structure, and other elements needed, to meet changing business conditions.

If a major role of the IS department were *managing data,* rather than getting applications running as quickly as possible, then quite a different scenario would occur. All the types of data of interest would first be identified. Then the single source of each data type would be identified, along with the business function that creates that data. Finally, a transaction system would be built to collect and store that data, after which all authorized users and applications would have access to it.

This data-driven approach does not result in one huge database to serve the whole organization, but it does require administrative control over the data, as well as designing the databases to support users from the outset. It starts out by describing the data the enterprise needs. Then the approach is selected that provides the data that gives a good balance between short-term, application-oriented goals and long-term, data-oriented goals.

The Role of Data Administration

The use of DBMS reduced, to some extent, the problems of inconsistent and redundant data in organizations. It is clear, however, that merely installing a DBMS is not sufficient to manage data as a corporate resource. Therefore, two additional thrusts have moved organizations in this direction: broader definition of the data administration role and effective use of data dictionaries.

Database administration concentrates on administering databases and the software that manages them. Data administration is broader. One of its main purposes is determining what data is being used outside the organizational unit that creates it. Whenever data crosses organizational boundaries, its definition and format need to be standardized, under the data administration function.

The *data dictionary* is the main tool by which data administrators control standard data definitions. All definitions are entered into the dictionary, and data administrators monitor all new definitions and all requests for changes in definitions, to make sure that corporate policy is being followed.

To bring order to the data mess that *still* exists, data administration has four main functions:

- Clean up data definitions.
- Control shared data.
- Manage data distribution.
- Maintain data quality.

Clean Up Data Definitions. Data administration needs to have the responsibility and authority to ensure data compatibility throughout an organization by getting rid of redundancies and inconsistencies among definitions. For instance, two or more names should not exist for the same data item, nor should the same name be used for two or more different data items. In most companies, sorting out existing data synonyms and then reconciling them is a monumental job. More and more companies are finally tackling this job seriously, to support a data warehouse effort, to install a companywide ERP package such as SAP, or in some instances, to consolidate country-based corporate databases into an intranet where everyone in the company, worldwide, draws from the same data pool.

In this role of cleaning up data definitions, data administrators design standard data definitions, the data dictionary, and the databases to reconcile conflicting user needs. They also design the data integrity process to flag suspected data and guard against inaccurate, invalid, or missing data polluting the pool of correct data. Finally, they train users on the meanings and proper use of the data. Unless users understand the data definitions, the clean data will not stay that way for long.

Control Shared Data. Even though data used solely by one organizational unit might be considered "local" and under the control of that unit, data used by two or more units should be considered shared data. The data administration function must control the definitions, and some of the processing, of all shared data.

In a controversy in this area, one side says that essentially *all* the data in the organization should be under the control of data administration. Just because some data is currently not being used across organizational boundaries is no reason to suppose that it will not be in the future. The other view is that each organizational unit can do whatever it wishes with *its* data; only data that must flow to other units needs to be standardized. It is impractical to try to standardize everything, and it would impose unreasonable rigidities, say these people. Data administrators have to confront this issue and decide how broadly or narrowly to define "shared" data.

The data administration function must also analyze the impact of proposed changes to programs that use shared data. All programs that would require changes need to be identified before approving the change. A data dictionary is a tremendous help here, because it provides one place to look for all uses of the data. Finally, approval to proceed with the change might be held up until all affected programs have been changed in order to keep those applications from aborting. Changes also require informing users of changes in meanings of data, if it occurs. Otherwise, users may base decisions on incorrect assumptions about the data they are using.

Manage Data Distribution.   Shared data, as defined here, crosses organizational boundaries. Distributed data, on the other hand, is geographically dispersed data. Managing data in a distributed dimension, with probably several levels of detail, presents significant challenges to data administrators, challenges that have, to date, caused companies to stick with the single master file concept and only distribute copies that do not need to be kept in sync.

Maintain Data Quality.   Cleaning up data definitions, and the other important functions of data administration, can become useless unless policies and procedures are developed to maintain data quality. A dominant guideline has been to decentralize or distribute this function by putting the owners of the data in charge of editing and verifying the data accuracy and quality, but this practice requires resolving the question of who owns the data.

Maintaining data quality also requires putting processes in place that ensure that correct data is being input into databases. People do not enter incorrect data on purpose, but many times, the inputting process permits errors, rather than catching them at the source where they can easily be corrected. The two elements of maintaining quality are to clean up the current data in databases (the data pool) and then ensure that the data stream is not polluting that pool with bad data.

The Importance of Data Dictionaries

In the previous section, we referred to a data dictionary as the primary tool to manage data definitions. Data dictionaries are systems and procedures, either manual or automated, for storing and handling an organization's data definitions. Data definitions are often called *metadata* these days. A data dictionary does not, in itself, generally produce data for an organization. Instead, its purpose is to eliminate errors of understanding, ambiguities, and difficulties in interpreting data.

Ideally, a data dictionary should be considered at least as soon as a database management system is considered. An ideal sequence is to (1) set up the data administration function, (2) develop data standards, (3) purchase and install a DBMS, and (4) install a data dictionary as the first database application. Unfortunately, the most prevalent situation has been to bring in a data dictionary after the DBMS has been used as an access method rather than as a true DBMS. In this case, many database applications have been run with little integration among them and little or no documentation of data definitions, so they are redundant and inconsistent. This huge cleanup task faces many organizations head-on today.

To illustrate one company's success in getting its corporate data in shape, consider the work of Monsanto.[1]

CASE EXAMPLE

MONSANTO

Monsanto, based in St. Louis, Missouri, is a $9 billion provider of agricultural products, pharmaceuticals, food ingredients, and chemicals. It is heavily international, with some 50 percent of revenues outside the United States, and it has always had a tradition of being decentralized. The CEO's vision includes five global themes.

1. Being responsive and efficient in meeting customer needs
2. Thinking and acting from a global perspective
3. Taking some risks to enter new markets
4. Treating the earth as a closed system where consumption and contamination of finite resources cannot be sustained
5. Creating an environment of trust, honesty, openness, and initiative where people can thrive.

To accomplish these (and other) goals, Monsanto established three large enterprisewide IT projects. One is to redevelop operational and financial transaction systems using SAP. The second is to develop a knowledge-management architecture, including data warehousing. The third is to link transaction and decision support systems via common master data, known as enterprise reference data (ERD), as shown in Figure 7-3. Monsanto wants to be "small but connected," to benefit from both global integration and local flexibility. ERD is a key to achieving both simultaneously. The Center of Technical Expertise is implementing all three initiatives.

Transaction Systems. The worldwide operations and finance project is dominated by SAP software. SAP, a German firm, sells an integrated software product that covers all core business transactions, including finance, order processing, inventory management, product planning, and manufacturing resource planning. SAP is international and handles multiple languages and multiple currencies.

(Case Continued)

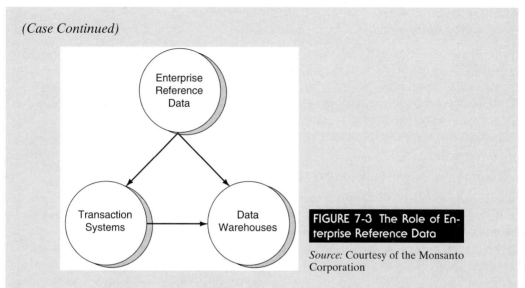

FIGURE 7-3 The Role of Enterprise Reference Data

Source: Courtesy of the Monsanto Corporation

Monsanto is too large and complex to operate SAP as a single installation. Hence, they have created a distributed SAP architecture, with separate instances of SAP for reference data, finance, and operations in each business unit. The master reference data integrates these distributed components.

Knowledge Management. To convert SAP data to knowledge, Monsanto uses data warehouses, which are targeted at mid- to upper-level management. These warehouses focus on the big picture of the company and contain data from internal and external sources that can be "sliced and diced" with drill-down capability from summary data to supporting details. Again, the reference data allows the warehouses to compare and leverage information across Monsanto.

Enterprise Reference Data. ERD, a separate use of SAP, is the repository for most master table information in the company. The information includes vendors, customers, suppliers, people, materials, finance, and control tables. Each table has

multiple views. For instance, materials has separate views for purchasing, engineering, accounting, safety, among others. The beauty of using a system such as SAP is that it can ensure referential integrity (adhering to complex relationship rules) of the data.

The sole source of master data is ERD, but the data can be distributed wherever it is needed in transactional SAP systems as well as in the data warehouses. However, as comprehensive as SAP is, it still does not contain all the reference data. Monsanto stores external data, such as crop statistics and economic trends, outside SAP.

The purpose of ERD is to enable integration. Vertical integration enables closer coordination with suppliers, which will reduce Monsanto's working capital and improve customer service. Horizontal integration across Monsanto's business units enables team marketing, leveraged purchasing, and interplant manufacturing. For example, common vendor and material tables enable Monsanto to leverage purchasing across the company. With

(Case Continued)

total purchases of about $5.5 billion a year, even a few percentage points of leverage can yield significant savings. Without ERD, Monsanto had to rely on limited polls of many purchasing functions—a process that could not be sustained.

Getting the Data in Shape

Turning data into a corporate resource is not an easy task for a large company with a history of decentralization. To accomplish its task, Monsanto has had to change its entire data management process. To start, it created a formal department known as ERD Stewardship. This department is independent of MIS or any other function and its job is to set data standards and enforce quality—hence its nickname, "the data police."

Another new function in ERD management is entity specialists. These key managers have the greatest stake in the quality of the data. For example, the specialist for vendor data is the vice president of purchasing. In cases of no obvious specialists, a steward has been appointed.

The third part of ERD management is the analysts who manage the data. In many cases, they are the same people who maintain systems, but they must now adhere to the new ERD rules. This require-

ment has led to a large cultural change, because these folks formerly only maintained local data. Now they maintain a global resource that the entire company uses. The idea of "tweaking" a system to fix a local discrepancy, which was formerly a common occurrence, can now cause a major disruption in operations or a bad decision based on faulty data.

Getting the data right in the first place is a large undertaking, one that can easily take several work-years per table to extract the data, put it in a common format, eliminate the duplicates, add missing data, and load into the ERD. Even with tools, it is a labor-intensive process. Where possible, Monsanto is using "standard" external codes, such as Dun & Bradstreet numbers, universal product codes, or European article numbers so that the company's trading partners can recognize the reference data for electronic commerce purposes. Unfortunately, none of these number schemes is truly universal, so the need to build, maintain, and cross-reference reference data appears to be unavoidable. Monsanto is working through this process, and is already reaping bottom-line benefits from better integration (horizontally and vertically) and greater flexibility. ■

MANAGING DATA

Database management systems are the main tool for managing computerized corporate data. They have been around since the 1960s and are based on two major principles: a three-level conceptual model and several alternative "data models" for organizing the data.

The Three-Level Database Model

One of the easiest-to-understand discussions of database technology is by James Bradley[2] in his description of the three-level database model, which was the result of work done by the Standards, Planning and Requirements Committee of the American National Standards Institute (ANSI/SPARC) in the mid-1970s. The concept is still an underpinning of the DBMS field. The following discussion is based on Bradley, Martin,[3] and Atre.[4] It begins with the level that the application developer sees.

- *Level 1* is called the external, conceptual, or local level. As Figure 7-4 illustrates, this level contains the various "user views" of the corporate data used by application programs—each has its own view. This level is not concerned with how the data will be physically stored or what data is used by other applications.

FIGURE 7-4 The Three-Level Database

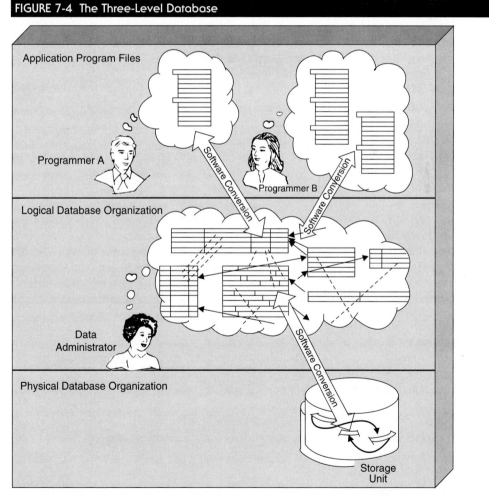

Source: James Martin, *Principles of Database Management* (Upper Saddle River, NJ: Prentice Hall, 1976).

- *Level 2* is called the logical or "enterprise data" level. It encompasses all an organization's relevant data under the control of the data administrators. Data and relationships are represented at this level by one or more DBMS. This level contains the same data as level 3, but with the implementation data removed.
- *Level 3* is called the physical or storage level. It specifies the way the data is physically stored. A data record consists of its data fields plus some implementation data, generally pointers and flag fields. The end user, of course, need not be concerned with these pointers and flags; they are for use by the DBMS only.

The advantage of this three-level model is that the logical data (the data administrators' view) can be separated from the physical storage method, so that different physical devices can be used without changing the application programs. The logical data relationships can also vary for different programs that use the data, without requiring data redundancy. In addition, applications can use a subset of the database and organize it, again without redundancy, in the best manner for the application.

Four Data Models

The second major concept in database management is alternate ways to define relationships among data. These so-called "data models" are methods by which data is structured to represent the real world and the way that data is accessed. Four main data models are in use today: hierarchical, network, relational, and object.

Hierarchical Model.   This model structures data so that each element is subordinate to another in a strict hierarchical manner, like the boxes in an organization chart. This model uses the terminology *parent* and *child* to represent these relationships. This approach, where a data item can have only one parent, is represented by IBM's IMS database management system.

Network Model.   With this model, each data item is allowed to have more than one parent. Assembly parts lists illustrate this structure, where the same part can be used in more than one assembly. This approach is represented by the Codasyl-type database management systems, such as Computer Associates' IDMS. In both the hierarchical and network models, the data relationships are stated explicitly, generally by pointers stored with the data. These pointers provide the means by which programs access the desired data records.

Relational Model.   Edgar F. Codd of IBM[5] proposed this model in 1970. In the relational model, the relationships among data items are not expressly stated by pointers. Instead, it is up to the DBMS to find the related items, based on the values of specified data fields. Thus, all employees of a certain department are found by searching for the department number in each employee record.

Relational databases store data in tables. Each row of the table, called a *tuple,* represents an individual entity (person, part, account). Each column represents an attribute of the entities. Eight relational operations can be performed on this data, as shown in Figure 7-5.

Relational systems are not as efficient as hierarchical or networked database systems, where the navigational maps through the data are predefined. But because relational systems allow people to create relationships among data on the fly, they are

FIGURE 7-5   Relational Operations

- SELECT chooses particular columns.
- PROJECT chooses particular rows.
- JOIN concatenates rows from two or more tables, matching column values.
- PRODUCT concatenates rows from two or more tables but does not match column values.
- INTERSECTION selects rows whose value(s) exist in both tables.
- DIFFERENCE selects rows whose value(s) exist in one table but not in the other.
- UNION merges two tables that have similar data, eliminating duplicates.
- DIVISION also merges two tables, but with more complicated selection capabilities. For a simple example, suppose a table contains all the products you buy and a table contains all your suppliers and the products they sell. Relational division can be used to find all suppliers that can supply all the products you buy.

much more flexible. Hence, they have become the database technology of choice in today's systems.

The relational model caught the attention of the industry because computer scientists see it as a good "theory" of data structure, while users find its tabular representation comfortable and familiar. Database management systems based on the relational model were first used primarily to handle end user queries; they are now widely used in high-volume transaction systems with huge files.

Much of the current interest in relational systems comes from their capability to enable on-the-spot concatenation of data from several sources. This capability is precisely what end users want, because they do not know the format of many of their ad hoc queries ahead of time. This capability also increases the flexibility of large mainline systems.

Object Model.   As the newest data model, the object-oriented approach expands the view of data by storing and managing "objects," each of which consists of the following:

1. A piece of data
2. "Methods," or procedures that can perform work on that data
3. Attributes describing the data
4. Relationships between this object and others.

Objects are important because they can be any type of data, whether a traditional name or address, an entire spreadsheet, a clip of video, a voice annotation, a photograph, or a segment of music. A collection of objects is called an *object base,* although such terms as *object database* or *object-oriented database* are also used.

Object data management techniques draw from the past. They retain traditional DBMS features, including end user tools, high-level query languages, concurrency control, recovery, and the ability to efficiently handle huge amounts of data. But they include two other major concepts as well. One is object management, which is the management of complex kinds of data, such as multimedia and procedures. The other concept is knowledge management, or the management of large numbers of complex rules for reasoning and maintaining integrity constraints between data.

Stonebraker and Kemnitz[6a] provide an example of an application that requires object management, as well as data management and knowledge management. It is a newspaper application that needs to store text and graphics, and be integrated with subscription and classified ad data. In this application, the customer billing requires traditional data management, while storage of text, pictures, and the newspaper's banner require object management. Finally, it needs the rules that control the newspapers layout. One rule might be, "Ads for competing department stores cannot be on facing pages."

Stonebraker and Kemnitz believe that *most* data management problems in the future will require all three dimensions: data, object, and rule (or knowledge) management.

A Look to the Future

Silberschatz, Stonebraker, and Ullman[6b] give seven examples of database applications that cannot be handled well, or at all, with today's database products or technologies.

1. NASA estimates that it needs to store 10^{16} bytes of satellite images from just a few years' worth of space exploration in the 1990s. How can it store and search such a massive database, which is enough to fill 10,000 optical disk jukeboxes?
2. CAD data for a skyscraper must maintain and integrate information from the viewpoints of hundreds of subcontractors. For example, when an electrician drills a hole in a beam to run an electrical wire, the system should, ideally, recalculate the stresses on the beam to ensure that its load-bearing capabilities have not been compromised.
3. The U.S. National Institutes of Health and the U.S. Department of Energy have a joint project for constructing the DNA sequence of the human genome, which is several billion elements long. Matching patients' medical problems to differences in genetic makeup is a staggering problem requiring new data representation and search technologies.
4. Large retail chains record every product code scanning action of every cashier in every store. Corporate buyers explore this data using ad hoc queries to uncover buying patterns. This procedure, called *data mining,* is growing, not only in retailing but in medicine, science, and many other fields.
5. Databases of insurance policies are going multimedia by storing photographs of damaged property, handwritten claim forms, audio transcripts of appraisals, images of insured objects, and even video walk-throughs of houses. Such image data is so large that these databases will be enormous. This application also pushes the limits of available technology.
6. A design database should notify designers when one of their system designs is affected by a modification made by another designer. These systems could encompass elaborate sets of triggers to track important actions. Separate rule-based systems, common today, probably are not efficient enough to handle these large complex situations.
7. We need new data models to handle spatial data, time, and uncertainty. Finding the closest neighbor to a data element in 3D space requires new multidimensional access methods. Exploring the state of a database at a point in time, or retrieving the time listing of a data value, are functions requested by engineers, retailers, and physicists. Unfortunately, time often is not supported in today's commercial databases.

Just as there is essentially one worldwide telephone system and one worldwide computer network, some believe we will eventually have a single worldwide file system.

To achieve this globalness requires collaboration among nations, which is actually happening in some areas. The human genome project is one example.

Defense contractors want a single project database that spans all subcontractors and all portions of a project. An auto company wants to give its suppliers access to new car designs, under certain circumstances. Both of these needs require intercompany databases. The challenge is making these databases behave as though they are part of a single database. This interoperability is the main challenge of distributed systems, as we noted in Chapter 5.

Yet another challenge is providing easy-to-use uniform browsing tools that work across heterogeneous databases. These query systems must be able to explain to a user where an inconsistency occurred, or where a database was missing; otherwise, these systems cannot be trusted to perform complete searches.

Finally, security is of major importance in today's DBMS, and distributed, heterogeneous Internet-linked databases exacerbate the problem. Companies may want to permit access to some portions of their databases while restricting other parts. This selective accessibility requires reliably authenticating inquirers. Unless security and integrity are strictly enforced, users will not be able to trust the systems.

To date, the database industry has shown remarkable success in transforming scientific ideas into products, say Silberschatz, Stonebraker, and Ullman.

Distributing Data

A major challenge in managing internal data records is distributed data. At the moment, difficulty with distributed data may sound a bit unusual, because everyone is placing so much emphasis on creating intranets that consolidate data. But, in truth, intranets and even e-commerce will foster more coordination among distributed data.

"True" Distributed Databases. Chris Date,[7] of Codd and Date Consulting Group, formulated 12 rules for a distributed database. These rules, listed in Figure 7-6, have become *the* fairly technical definition of a "true" distributed database. Although it is not stated, these operating principles depend on the underlying databases being relational.

A Standard Query Language. A myriad of technical challenges faces designers of distributed systems. Fortunately, a standard language for accessing relational databases is currently available: SQL. It is not a full application development language nor an end user query tool. Rather, it is an English-like language for manipulating data and performing queries against relational tables. It has three components.

1. A *data definition language* for creating relational tables, creating indexes to data, and defining fields of data
2. A *data manipulation language* for entering information into a database and accessing and formatting the data
3. A *data control language* for handling security functions

The use of SQL provides a number of benefits. It can be embedded in procedural languages, such as C or COBOL, and it can be incorporated in packages, such as spreadsheets, that run on PCs and workstations. It can act as an intermediary between production applications and databases, between client requests and server responses, and between browser-based applications and databases. It thus insulates applications from

FIGURE 7-6 Twelve Rules for Distributed Databases

1. *Local autonomy.* Local data are owned and managed locally, with local accountability and security. No site depends on another for successful functioning.

2. *No reliance on a central site.* All sites are equal, and none rely on a master site for processing or communications.

3. *Continuous operation.* Installations at one site do not affect operations at another. There should never be a need for a planned shutdown. Adding or deleting installations should not affect existing programs or activities. Likewise, portions of databases should be able to be created and destroyed without stopping any component.

4. *Location independence (transparency).* Users do not have to know where data are physically stored. They act as if all data are stored locally.

5. *Fragmentation independence (transparency).* Relations between data elements can be fragmented for physical storage, but users are able to act as if data were not fragmented.

6. *Replication independence.* Relations and fragments can be represented at the physical level by multiple, distinct, stored copies or replicas at distinct sites, transparent to the user.

7. *Distributed query processing.* Local computer and input-output activity occurs at multiple sites, with data communications between the sites. Both local and global optimization of query processing are supported. That is, the system finds the cheapest way to answer a query that involves accessing several databases.

8. *Distributed transaction management.* Single transactions are able to execute code at multiple sites, causing updates at multiple sites.

9. *Hardware independence.* Distributed database systems are able to run on different kinds of hardware with all machines participating as equal partners where appropriate.

10. *Operating system independence.* Distributed database systems are able to run under different operating systems.

11. *Network independence.* Distributed database systems are able to work with different communications networks.

12. *Database independence.* Distributed database systems are able to be built with different kinds of databases, provided they have the same interfaces.

Source: Chris Date, *An Introduction to Database Systems, Vols. I and II,* 4th ed. (Reading, MA: Addison-Wesley, 1987).

changes in physical and logical database structures. Furthermore, it provides the foundation for standard communications among heterogeneous databases, via application programming interfaces (APIs) for databases.

Alternatives to "True" Distributed Databases

Many databases do not have to be true distributed databases, as defined by Date. Many alternatives have sufficed quite well, including the following:

- Downloaded data files
- Copies of data stored at nodes
- Not fully synchronized databases
- Server-based databases
- Federated databases

Downloaded Data Files. Sending data from servers to PCs is common. In fact, it is the most popular method for distributing data. But most companies do not allow files to be updated on a PC and then uploaded directly to a production file for fear that the integrity of the data will be compromised. An intermediary verification process is involved. Many do not even allow direct downloading of data from production files to PCs. Instead, data is extracted from the production files and put into a data warehouse or Internet file.

Copies of Data Stored at Nodes.   A second approach to distributing data is to locate working copies of data at nodes such as a data warehouse or Internet file. These data files are accessible to remote users for query and sometimes to post updates and changes. This so-called "memo posting" provides fast answers to queries and helps process customer activity during the workday. The master files reside at one or more data centers, and the "official" updating of the files is done at these centers, usually at night. Then, during early morning hours, only the new and changed records are downloaded to the nodes for use during that workday.

Not Fully Synchronized Databases.   It may not always be necessary to have distributed databases that are synchronized at every point in time, as long as the errors can always be caught quickly and fixed easily. The distributed name service (DNS) on networks works in this manner. The service stores the names and addresses of files on the network. Each service node has one authoritative copy and one secondary copy of these names and addresses.

The secondary copy is kept in cache (fast memory), and is responsible for refreshing itself from the primary copy. But it does not worry about synchronization, because if it gives out a wrong address, the requesting message quickly discovers the error and returns and asks the primary copy for the correct address. Where this alternative is possible, it is a simple and robust solution.

Server-Based Databases.   Significant differences separate true distributed databases from server-based databases. The difference is in the concept of "location transparency." In a true distributed database, each node has a copy of the DBMS and the dictionary; therefore, the application need not know the location of the data because the node can determine the access strategy. In server-based systems, on the other hand, only a limited number of nodes run the DBMS, so the applications must know where the data is located. Therefore, they do not support location transparency. Nevertheless, they are appropriate for higher-performance transaction processing, he believes

Federated Databases.   Another alternative to fully distributed databases are "federated databases" rather than distributed databases. Therefore, the existing databases will retain their autonomy, their data will continue to be defined independently, and each local DBMS will essentially take care of itself, while retaining rules for others to access its data.

We have seen this approach work when incompatible databases, such as those that contain text, alphanumeric, and image, are needed in a single application. These databases are left intact on their own machine, and their data is pulled together at the workstation. The application software on the client machine calls on the various databases, and displays data from each one in a different window, in whatever format it has been programmed to use. For handling multidimensional data, companies typically take this approach. A good example is the Northwest Airline System, discussed in Chapter 5. This approach is also being used in intranet-based applications and data warehouse-based applications.

Data Warehousing

An important development in the use of internal record-based information is data warehousing. Briefly, a data warehouse is a database that contains data from many sources, including operational sources. It is updated periodically, and it comes with a repository of "metadata" that describes precisely what each type of data means in terms that marketing folks, the salesforce, management, and others can understand. A major driving force behind most data warehouses has been to more finely target marketing: the desire to gather customer data in one place, segment it into customer groups such as profitable and unprofitable customers, see the buying patterns in each customer group, and then develop new products and services targeted for each.

Typically, data is first extracted from mainframe and other databases. Prior to being placed in the data warehouse, the data is processed (i.e., "cleaned") to make it more usable for decision support. Many vendors provide software specifically for this purpose. The data is then maintained on a file server, and special-purpose software is used to support analysis activities.

Online analytical processing (OLAP) refers to managers and professionals doing decision support analyses without help from intermediaries or information systems professionals. The term contrasts with online transaction processing (OLTP). OLAP is driven by (1) the need for information; (2) the emergence of software that supports the building, maintenance, and use of data warehouses; and (3) more computer proficient users who are able and willing to do their own decision support.

Even though decision makers are better equipped to analyze the vast quantities of data stored by organizations, manual searching is inadequate because important developments may go undetected if no one is looking for them. In response to this problem, vendors now offer software agents, also known as intelligent agents, that continually send queries to databases to find exception conditions. When one is found, it is automatically sent to the appropriate person, often through e-mail. Software agents provide a "detect and alert" capability. They reflect an exciting integration of artificial intelligence and decision support. Because data warehousing and data mining are most relevant for decision support, and because they evolved primarily from work on the data component of decision support systems, we will treat the subject more fully in Chapter 12.

MANAGING INFORMATION

"Information is power." "We are in the Information Age." These and similar statements would lead you to believe that managing information is a key corporate activity. Indeed it is, and it is becoming increasingly so. In fact, some believe that information management, rather than technology management, is the main job of the IS department. We believe they are both important. The technology can be viewed as the infrastructure, the information as the asset that runs on that infrastructure. Yet, information is just an intermediary—an intermediary for action. In this important intermediary position, the management of information is important, and raises a number of management issues. We discuss several here, followed by four types of information.

Information Management Issues

If information is to be viewed as an asset, as many companies now do, it must be treated differently from the traditional assets of labor and capital, because it is different from them, says Thomas Davenport at Boston University. For one thing, it is not divisible. Nor is it scarce. In addition, ownership cannot be clearly defined. Davenport[8] discusses three categories of issues in managing information.

1. Value issues
2. Usage issues
3. Sharing issues

Value Issues.   Information's value depends on the recipient and the context; it is contextual. In fact, most people cannot put a value on a piece of information until they have seen it. Despite these drawbacks, people do, indeed, place values on information. Look at all the information services that people buy. Information marketplaces do exist, inside and outside companies. The only practical way to establish the value of information is to establish a price for it and see whether anyone buys. Pricing possibilities include charge for the information itself rather than for the technology or the provider, charging by the document rather than a smaller unit, charging by length or time or number of users, and charging by value rather than cost.

A number of tools are being used at companies to increase the value of information.

- *Information Maps.* These maps can be textual charts or perhaps even diagrammatic maps that point to the location of information, whether in written material, experts' minds, and so forth. IBM, for example, created a guide to market information, so that managers can find out where to get quick answers to their ad hoc questions. The result has been less money spent on duplicate information and increased understanding of the kinds of questions people typically ask.
- *Information Guides.* Guides are people who know where desired information can be found. Librarians have traditionally played this role. Hallmark Cards, for instance, created a guide job in its business units to help employees find computer-based information on available jobs. These guides have substantially reduced the time needed to find information.
- *Business Documents.* Business documents are yet another tool for sharing information. They provide organization and context. One fruitful way to embark on information management is to uncover what documents an organization needs. This process can be easier, and more useful, than defining common terms. Dean Witter, for instance, discovered that its brokers all used the same documents, over and over. Some 90 percent of these documents could be put on one CD-ROM, kept on local servers, and updated monthly, greatly facilitating information use.
- *Groupware.* Groupware is a tool for getting greater value out of less structured information. It allows people to share information across distances in a more structured manner than electronic mail. Lotus Notes is such a product. Groupware can ease discussions and aid distribution of information, but its success depends upon the culture. For one thing, better access to information increases

(not decreases) people's appetite for more information. However, employees using sophisticated groupware products need education to learn how the technology can be used to improve work habits and profits, neither of which flows naturally from the technology.

To have value, the databases need to be managed, even pruned and restructured. Knowledgeable people are needed to manage the information resource and its use. This need is true for intranet and Web sites as well.

Usage Issues. Information management is a management problem because it deals with how people use information, not how they use machines, says Davenport. Three points illustrate the importance and difficulty of managing information use.

One, information's complexity needs to be preserved. Information should not be simplified to be made to fit into a computer, because doing so truncates sharing and conversations. Information does not conform to common definitions. It is messy. It naturally has different perspectives, which are important and need to be preserved. A certain amount of tension between the desire for one common global meaning and numerous familiar local meanings is inevitable; therefore, companies that want to settle on common corporate terms must do so with line people, not technical people, because line people will use the end results. The IS organization can facilitate these discussions, but the business people should determine the meanings.

Two, people do not easily share information, even though its value grows as it is shared. Culture often blocks sharing, especially in highly competitive organizational cultures.

Three, technology does not change culture. Just building an information system does not mean that people will use it. It is a false assumption that too many IS people make. To change the information culture of a company requires changing basic behaviors, values, attitudes, and management expectations.

Sharing Issues. If information sharing is the goal, a number of contentious problems must first be resolved. Davenport explains that a sharing culture must be in place or the existing disincentives will thwart using a sharing system.

Technical solutions do not address the sharing issue. For example, much talk has touted "information architectures," where the definitions of stable types of corporate data, such as customers, products, and business transactions, can be specified ahead of time and used consistently across the firm. This approach has yet to fulfill its promise. The enterprise models are difficult to understand, they take years to populate, and they are probably outdated before they are usable. But even more importantly, information architectures have failed because they do not take into account how people use the information. Managers get two-thirds of their information from conversations, one-third from documents, and almost none directly from computer systems. So a common information architecture is not likely to solve the information management problem.

An issue in sharing is: Who determines who has legitimate need of the information? The "owning" department? Top management? And who identifies the owner? The development of the principles for managing information—how it is defined and distributed—is more important than the final principles, because the touchy subject of information sharing is brought out into the open. In short, working out information issues requires addressing entrenched attitudes about organizational control.

Is sharing good? Not in all cases. Forcing employees to share information with others above them can lead to intrusive management. Some executive support systems limit "drill down" for just this reason. Managers must think about these types of issues in information management.

Unlimited information sharing does not work. Limits are necessary. On the one hand, the sharing of corporate performance figures is beneficial, even when corporate performance is poor, because it usually increases morale; uninformed employees usually guess the worst. On the other hand, the sharing of rumors (noninformation) generally demoralizes people. Separating information from noninformation is an information management issue. Allowing employees to send messages to large distribution lists exacerbates the information management problem. Managements have awoken to the fact that they need to address this issue. Vendors are developing filters and "agents" to be used with electronic mail systems. These responses will only help resolve corporate information management issues if the correct underlying policies are put in place.

Even hiring practices play a role in information management. If promotions are based on circulation and publication of new ideas, a sharing environment exists. If these activities are not rewarded, sharing may be an anathema to the culture.

In all, getting value out of information requires more than technology. It is inherently hard to control. It is ever expanding and unpredictable. Only when executives view it in this light will they manage information for most effective use.

Four Types of Information

In Figure 7-2 we presented a 2 × 2 matrix to represent the full scope of information resources. Internal record-based information has been the focus of attention of information systems because it is the type of information computer-based application systems generate and manage easily. External record-based information can now be accessed over the Internet, or through other electronic means, via public databases. End users themselves have generally handled the procurement of this kind of data by subscribing to database services. Generally, IS executives have paid little attention to document-based information, either internal or external. Intranets have changed that. Documents are now an integral part of the kinds of information these sites house. Even in companies where the administrative vice president or the corporate library has felt this continues to be their realm, after a short time, they gladly turn responsibility for the technical issues over to IS. We now look at ways companies are managing and utilizing these four types of information.

Internal Record-Based Information.   Thus far, this chapter has dealt with the internal record-based cell of the matrix in Figure 7-2. As we have seen, the three-level database is the conceptual model for organizing internal record-based data. Database management systems manage data using data models that define the relationships among entities and attributes of the data. The four dominant data models are the hierarchical, network, relational, and object models.

Monsanto represents the recent resurgence of effort in getting record-based information into shape. They and others have discovered that it requires a two-pronged approach. One is to get the pool of data cleaned up. The second is to ensure that the data streams that feed that pool contribute clean data. Dealing with data inputting processes requires tracking those processes through the company to uncover any sources of errors, perhaps using a quality management approach. As Cornelia Varney noted, one company routed orders that contained errors into an "error bucket." The data quality group then followed these data errors "upstream" to find the root cause. From there, they and the users who input the data decided how to change the process to eliminate the errors. Oftentimes, all that was required was to explain the use of the data, something those users had never been told.

Internal Document-Based Information. The management of internal document-based information traditionally rested with the vice president of administration, who oversees records management (document records, not data records). However, document management is a crucial issue facing CIOs. For our purposes, a document is a semi-formal "package" of information, structured for human comprehension. It has organizational relevance, so it is stored, transmitted, and consequently maintained in that context.

Electronic document management, part of Chapter 14, includes a variety of technologies, such as document and image processing, text retrieval, hypertext and hypermedia, EDI, and desktop publishing. In addition, electronic document management includes the technologies that have been used for years in traditional records management areas: micrographics (film and fiche), computer output microfilm (COM), and automated records center applications. The documents handled by this enlarged set of technologies might be letters, blueprints, sales notes, voice mail messages, images, or multimedia documents. Increasingly, they include documents from external sources, such as news items, the Internet, government or industry reports, and even incoming correspondence.

We have identified data, information, and knowledge as the total information resource of the firm. Much of this resource exists in the form of documents. Despite more than 40 years of progress in computerizing information processes, many organizations still have a huge, crucial amount of "paperwork" required to do business. The amount of paper is not likely to decrease either, despite the use of the technologies already mentioned. Xplor International[9] estimates that the total number of electronic and paper documents will continue to soar from just over 2 trillion in 1998 to 20 trillion by 2005. See Figure 7-7.

The percentage of documents that will be printed will decline substantially from 90 percent today to 40 percent in 2005. However, the overall number of pages will offset the decline in percent printed, yielding an overall increase in the number of pages printed (from 1.8 trillion to 8 trillion). The remaining 60 percent of pages will be in the form of electronic documents existing in various repositories: the World Wide Web, corporate internal networks, government repositories, and so forth. *Conservatively, that's 60 percent of 20 trillion documents, or 12 trillion documents in electronic format.* A portion of the 40 percent printed will also reside in electronic format. These electronic documents will only be useful if they can be accessed, read, categorized, summarized, and shared.

Despite 15 to 20 years of developing management information systems, decision support systems, and executive information systems with data, we have just begun to include the valuable information contained in documents. So information management

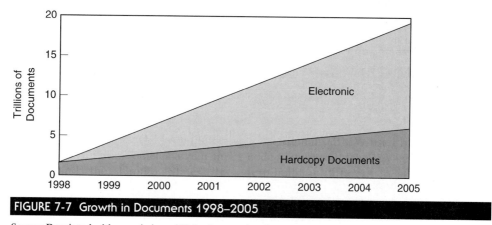

FIGURE 7-7   Growth in Documents 1998–2005

Source: Reprinted with permission of Xplor International at www.xplor.com.

needs to include managing the internal document-based information on which most organizations continue to depend.

External Record-Based Information.   It has generally been users, not the IS department, who have managed the acquisition of information from external databases. Strategic planning departments, financial planners, and other user departments have sought out services that provide this type of information. Yet, with the increasingly turbulent business environment, companies will want to coordinate their use of such external services, as well as combine internal and external information to better understand consumers. As an example of an external source of record-based information, consider Isuzu's use of geographic information system data.

CASE EXAMPLE

AMERICAN ISUZU MOTORS

American Isuzu Motors recently became a bigger user of external information, the director of strategic planning told a meeting of the Southern California Chapter of the Society for Information Management. At the time, Isuzu noted that a global shift was underway from mass marketing to one-to-one personal marketing. Furthermore, power was shifting from the manu-facturers to the retailers; Isuzu dealers controlled the shelf space, as they do today. With real-time point-of-sale data and credit card data, Isuzu and other companies could know what specific consumers liked. So the focus changed from completing transactions to building relationships.

Realizing that it costs five times more to get a new customer than to retain an existing one, Isuzu shifted its focus from share of the market to share of a customer's wallet. The goal was to integrate IT with marketing to bring customers in to find out where Isuzu could offer value.

Isuzu's Marketing Intelligence System allows it to get closer to its customers and get feedback directly from them. With current technology it is possible for Isuzu to house every customer record on one database. Furthermore, it is possible to amend these records with information gathered by conversations with customers who call on the toll-free number. To complete the customer profile, Isuzu is appending these records with information they buy from external sources. This external data comes in many forms, including lifestyle data, geographic data that pinpoints where consumers with each type of lifestyle live, automobile registration data, purchasing behavior data, economic data, and forecasting data. In many cases, Isuzu obtains this data over the Internet.

Isuzu's use of these external geographic information systems has changed how it does business. To be a better marketer, it has learned that it must know who its customers are and the message that entices them to buy Isuzu products. To meet this challenge, Isuzu initially hired an advertising agency to identify customers by lifestyle. It then created a profile of customers and ran these profiles through a geographic information system to find where consumers with those same profiles live. To validate these owner profiles, it has used several segmentation techniques such as cluster coding. In one case, cluster coding segments lifestyles into 48 different clusters, from most affluent to least affluent.

One of the most dramatic uses of this external data was to test the market launch of the *new* Isuzu Trooper four-wheel drive vehicle. Formerly, the Trooper had been boxy, practical, and cost $13,000. The new Trooper was luxurious, state-of-the-art, and cost $25,000. Via lifestyle clustering, Isuzu found that its Trooper buyers are generally established professional singles and young families. They often live in state capitols. They watch specific TV shows, and are often bowlers, avid book readers, and gourmet cooks. Income is the biggest differentiator (near $75,000), age is the next (the younger the better), and home ownership is the third.

To perform the market test, Isuzu used the Trooper owner lifestyle profile to find 600 prospects in a 32-square-mile test area in Washington state. Each was sent a video tape about the Trooper, invited to test drive it, and was also told that after the test drive they could be "product managers for a day" and critique the Trooper, telling Isuzu what they wanted in a $25,000 sport vehicle. For their effort, they would receive a gift.

Isuzu learned a lot from those consumers. They expected to love a $25,000 vehicle, not just like it. They wanted cup holders. They loved the sun roof. And on and on. Isuzu listened and made the changes. The results were dramatic. Sales of the Trooper in the two Isuzu dealerships in the test area increased by 300 percent and 450 percent respectively.

Since that time, Isuzu has tracked the profile of their Trooper buyers and has found that the profile has not changed. Isuzu continues to use cluster maps from external geographic information services to see where households with this profile live, to best target their advertising.

Isuzu now believes that to expand its relationships with its customers, it must have more knowledge, not just from internal systems but from external databases as well. It now sees the power of having this information. ∎

External Document-Based Information. Many IS executives consider external document-based information to be the least manageable form of information. It has been the responsibility of corporate librarians in most companies. Yet, as the amount of such external information grows, and as more and more of it becomes computerized, it will become increasingly important for inclusion in IS executives' jurisdiction. Just witness what is happening with the Web and its plethora of external documents.

One area is environmental scanning—searching the world of external information in areas relevant to an organization. Environmental scanning services have been available for many years. They review publications, clip out pertinent articles or create abstracts of these articles, and then pass them along to the client. A newer development is the delivery of this information to a company's internal computer, perhaps even a PC, where it can be searched, browsed, and interpreted by managers. Yet a newer development is the Web, with its plethora of information, search engines, and custom interest profiles.

The extremely rapid growth of computer-based document and reference services is not surprising. Jane Fedorowicz[10] describes this growth and the technology advances that have enabled it. She cites a study by Information Market Indicators, Inc., that shows U.S. businesses increased their online database expenditures by 117 percent in three years. Companies are retrieving more and more information from text databases, such as Dow Jones News Retrieval. The increased reliance on external market indicators and improved sources of information has dramatically boosted the demand for online text database services.

Typically, users of these systems are trained librarians who provide a service within their company, or PC users who access general-purpose databases. Most of the time, the results of the search are hard copy reports of bibliographic, financial, or other stored information; although, increasingly, they can be files downloaded from the Internet. Some decision support and executive information system products provide links to external databases and display the results of prespecified searches on the screen. The use of an online search service at California State University at Los Angeles illustrates the extent of external document based information.

CASE EXAMPLE

CALIFORNIA STATE UNIVERSITY AT LOS ANGELES

The librarian at Cal State L.A. trains the faculty and some 5,000 students each year how to use the Internet and online databases, such as Nexis Lexis. Students get eight hours of instruction in the class, and most of them can learn Nexis Lexis com-

mands in an hour, says the librarian. Then they can be considered power users.

Lexis contains 300 million legal citations, while Nexis contains 300 million business citations, from 1977 to present. They contain full text databases of biographical

(Case Continued)

reports of company, SEC filings, bankruptcy filings, and the like. Subdatabases contain financial information of companies worldwide. Online, the students can see the text of corporate filings 24 hours after they have been filed with SEC. Thus, market research people can find out what competition is doing, what companies say about themselves in a 10K filing, and so on.

Some 1,400 computers on campus can access Lexis Nexis. The freshmen love the news file, which contains the text of all major magazines and newspapers as well as transcripts of some evening news programs. They can search on a person's name and date, and get information that is up to 24 hours old. ■

In summary, IS executives need to take a broader view of information management if they plan to manage it as a corporate resource. As a way of representing the breadth of this topic, Figure 7-8 lists the four categories of information and shows the typical corporate authority, sources of information, and examples of technologies used in managing each.

TOWARD MANAGING KNOWLEDGE

The IS world seems to be moving from data management to information management to "knowledge management." This third arena, often referred to as *managing intellectual assets,* is just beginning to be explored.

FIGURE 7-8 The Scope of Information Management

	Typical Corporate Authority	Information Sources	Technologies Used
Internal record-based information	Information systems department	Transaction processing Organizational units	DBMS Data dictionaries Enterprise data analysis techniques
Internal document-based information	Administrative vice president Word processing center Records management	Corporate memos, letters reports, forms, email	Word processing Micrographics Reprographics Text retrieval products
External record-based information	End users Corporate planning Financial analysis Marketing	Public databases	Internet-based services Public networks Analysis packages
External document-based information	Corporate library	Public literature News services Catalogs and indexes Subscriptions Purchased reports	Bibliographic services Environmental scanning Public networks

Those who distinguish between information and knowledge appear to believe that knowledge is what is in someone's head, while information is in databases. Many feel that the term *knowledge management* creates the wrong impression. The term *management* often brings forth the "we can control it" mindset. Knowledge cannot be controlled or engineered, so the mechanical metaphor is wrong. It can only be leveraged through processes and culture. The biological or ecological metaphor is much better. The more people are connected, and the more they exchange ideas, the more their knowledge spreads and can thus be leveraged.

As an example of the people and process emphasis in managing knowledge, consider the definition used by the CEO of Xerox, a company that has promoted this topic for several years.

"Managing knowledge means creating a thriving work and learning environment that fosters the continuous creation, aggregation, use, and re-use of both organizational and personal knowledge in the pursuit of new business value."
—Paul Allaire, chairman and CEO, Xerox Corporation

The process is the key. An important concept is the difference between tacit knowledge (knowledge in someone's head that cannot easily be explained), explicit knowledge, and the process of transferring "tacit" knowledge to others. To emphasize this idea, several companies have stopped talking about knowledge management and use only the term *knowledge sharing*. In this regard, IT is seen as one enabler, but not the main enabler. The key seems to be getting people together face-to-face, to explain about how they do things. Once people sit down and talk about what they do and why, barriers fall, knowledge flows, and sharing increases. Unfortunately, people are not given the time nor the space these days for this kind of interaction; "free time" to share is not seen as important. Figure 7-9 further emphasizes these concepts by distinguishing between information management and knowledge management.

So, unlike information management, knowledge management is more akin to knowledge "gardening." It needs to be nurtured, the correct environment and sharing norms need to be in place, and only then will the sharing take place. To better understand the tack that can be taken to change processes and increase sharing, consider what one large pharmaceutical company is doing.

FIGURE 7-9 Information Management Is Different from Knowledge Management

Information Management	*Knowledge Management*
Emphasizes delivery and accessibility of content	Emphasizes adding value to content by filtering, synthesizing, interpreting, and adding context
Has heavy technology focus	Balances focus between technology and culture or work practice
Assumes information capture can be standardized and automated	Requires ongoing human inputs and links to communities

CASE EXAMPLE

A PHARMACEUTICAL COMPANY

A project at a major pharmaceutical company was aimed at improving the process of developing new drugs and getting them approved by the U.S. Food and Drug Administration (FDA), a process that takes 5–10 years, costs $250 million, and can yield revenues of $1 million a day per drug once it reaches the market.

This project, described at the Knowledge Imperative Conference,[11] revolved around creating a "knowledge infrastructure," one that manages information, enables understanding, and supports learning. The crux of the matter was to understand the customer's needs. In this case, the FDA is the primary customer; however, insurance companies, doctors, and consumers are also customers. The company sells all of them knowledge about disease, treatment, and how a drug will work in particular scenarios. When the employees understand the type of knowledge they need to create for these customers, and their role in its creation, then they figure out better ways to work.

The project began by studying and codifying 60,000 pages of documents filed with the FDA to discern how the teams developing drugs and filing their results were sharing knowledge. These regulatory files explain to the FDA what the company knows about a drug, how it learned those things, and what conclusions it has reached.

The knowledge infrastructure project team found the files lacking. Each should have four parts: purpose, content, logic, and context. Only one of the files had a statement of purpose, which stated the problem to be solved. A file without a statement of purpose shows that the author does not know the reason for the document. Many files had contradictions, which told the team that the authors had not talked to each other. For instance, they disagreed on whether the drug should be taken once or twice a day.

To rectify the situation, the study team created a generic knowledge tree of the questions the FDA asks when deciding whether to approve a drug. The top of the tree has their three main questions: Is it safe? Does it work? Does it have sufficient quality? The tree lays out the supporting questions for these three, in layers, which showed the teams which questions they needed to answer to the FDA's satisfaction. It also showed people why others needed specific information, thus giving them a context (beyond trust) for sharing.

In a pilot project, the knowledge infrastructure team also used a different process with one team: writing as a tool for thinking. They got the team to write up their 10-year drug study before they did it, so they were clear about the data they needed to gather and present to the FDA. Furthermore, they wrote this report template publicly as a team. To do it, they wrote critical points that had to be in the report on Post-It notes. Next, they prioritized them on huge sheets on the meeting room wall. Then they designed studies to prove the points that had to be proven. In creating this virtual prototype

(Case Continued)

of the knowledge to be presented to the FDA, publicly, on the wall, they could physically see what knowledge was needed. They created a common mental model of the results. It was a powerful technique.

They have seen tangible progress in filling in the report sections on content, logic, context, and purpose. In another case, where an existing drug was to be registered for use with a new disease, the team had not made much progress in two years time. After they were shown the knowledge tree over a two-day period, they were able to submit the file to the FDA in three months (they had previously estimated 18 months), and the FDA approved it in 18 months (the team had estimated three years). ■

CONCLUSION

As can be seen by the wide-ranging discussion in this chapter, the job of managing information resources is widening significantly. Not only must IS departments get corporate data in shape but they also need to create and build an infrastructure for managing the full range of information types. Finally, they play a role in helping their firm leverage the knowledge that its employees carry around in their heads. Companies that address all three areas, and start implementing IT-based programs in all three, will have a significant edge over their competitors because they will be able to leverage their "intellectual assets."

QUESTIONS AND EXERCISES

Review Questions

1. What is the difference between data, information, and knowledge?
2. What are the four kinds of information that define the scope of "information management"? Describe each briefly.
3. What is the main problem in managing data?
4. What are the four roles of data administrators?
5. What three ERD management components has Monsanto put in place?
6. Define the three-level database concept. What are its advantages?
7. What are four database "models"?
8. Give one example of an application that will require new DBMS capabilities in the future.
9. What are the 12 guiding principles that describe "true" distributed databases?
10. What are five alternatives to true distributed databases?
11. What are the purposes of data warehouses?
12. According to Davenport, what are three management issues in managing information? Briefly describe each.
13. How has American Isuzu Motors used external geographical information?
14. What is a better viewpoint than "knowledge management"?
15. How does knowledge management differ from information management?
16. What did the pharmaceutical company do to create a knowledge infrastructure?

Discussion Questions

1. In this chapter the assertion is made that IS departments should concentrate on getting data right rather than getting systems up and running quickly. Discuss the pros and cons of this argument.
2. Information is in databases; knowledge is in people's heads. Argue for or against whether we can store knowledge in computers.
3. Technology does not change culture. Agree or disagree? Explain your point of view.
4. An ethical question regarding electronic mail is whether the contents belong to the sender or the corporation. What is your opinion? Explain your reasoning.

Exercises

1. Find two articles on data management. Present any new ideas in these article to the class.
2. Find an example of each of the four kinds of information presented in Figure 7-2. They may be from company documents, the Web, or public publications. What new ideas on the (a) corporate authority, (b) technologies used, and (c) information sources did you gain from where you found these items? Did you find any evidence of a merging (or a diverging) of the management of these different types of information?
3. Find two articles on knowledge management. What new ideas did they contain? Present them to the class.
4. Visit a local company with a data administration function. Talk to the data administrator and find out:
   a. What kinds of data does the department control or not control?
   b. What types of data problems is the group trying to solve?
   c. What progress is the group having in bringing data under control?

5. Visit a local company and talk to either the corporate librarian or the manager of records management and find out:
   a. What information technologies are used to store, catalog, and retrieve documents, literature, and citations?
   b. What kinds of information sources are used?
   c. What various kinds of searching capabilities are available?
   d. What kinds of information technology are used to disseminate information?
6. Visit a local company and ask the CIO what kinds of projects have been conducted to nurture knowledge sharing.

REFERENCES

1. Varney, Cornelia, "Managing the Integrity of Distributed Systems," Wentworth Research Program (now part of Gartner Executive Programs, 56 Top Gallant, Stamford, CT), January 1996.
2. Bradley, James, "The Elusive Relation," *Computerworld,* March 8, 1982, In Depth 1–16. (This material was based largely on the author's book, *File and Data Base Techniques,* Holt, Rinehart & Winston, New York, 1982.)
3. Martin, James, *Principles of Data-Base Management,* Prentice Hall, Upper Saddle River, NJ, 1976.
4. Atre, Shaku, *Data Base: Structured Techniques for Design, Performance, and Management,* John Wiley & Sons, New York, 1980.
5. Codd, E. F., "Relational Database: A Practical Foundation for Productivity," *Communications of the ACM,* Association for Computing Machinery (1515 Broadway, New York, NY 10036), February 1982, 109–117.
6. "Special Sections: Next-Generation Database Systems," *Communications of the ACM,* October 1991; pp. 31–131.
   a. Stonebraker, M. and G. Kemnitz, "The Postgres Multi-Generation Database Management System," 78–92.
   b. Silberschatz, A., M. Stonebraker, and J. Ullman (editors), "Database Systems: Achievements and Opportunities," 110–120.
7. Date, Chris, *An Introduction to Database Systems, Vols. I and II,* 4th ed., Addison-Wesley, Reading, MA, 1987.
8. Davenport, Tom, "Saving IT's Soul: Human-Centered Information Management," *Harvard Business Review,* March/April 1994, 119–131.
9. Xplor International, 24238 Hawthorne Blvd., Torrance, CA 90505; www.xplor.com.
10. Fedorowicz, Jane, "A Technology Infrastructure for Document-Based Decision Support Systems," in Sprague, R., and H. Watson, *Decision Support Systems: Putting Theory into Practice,* 3rd ed., Prentice Hall, Upper Saddle River, NJ, 1993.
11. Seemann, Patricia, "Building Knowledge Infrastructure: Creating Change Capabilities," The Knowledge Imperative Symposium, Arthur Andersen and The American Productivity & Quality Center (123 North Post Oak Lane, Houston, TX 77024), September 1995.

CHAPTER

8 ‖ MANAGING OPERATIONS

INTRODUCTION

A discussion of managing the essential information technologies is not complete without describing operational issues facing information system executives. Due to mergers, corporate restructurings, the Internet, and e-commerce, the subject of computer opera-

240

tions is receiving a lot of attention. Systems operations are important because, if they are not professionally run, a company could suffer a computer or network crash that could shut down their business for some period of time. It is not a trivial area, especially as companies become increasingly reliant on networks and computers to run their business. Furthermore, poorly run IS shops cause IS executives to end up fighting fires instead of setting policy. Or they find themselves looking for a new job. Or their operations are outsourced. Actually, this last option is often seen as a welcome relief by many IS executives.

As shown in Figure 8-1, the main change in operations is the shift in viewpoint. Traditionally, managing operations has meant managing inward, that is, managing one's own operations staff, including those who work in the data center, data administration, network administration, and systems programming. Today, it is just as likely to mean managing outward, that is, managing the company's relationships with external IT service providers who have taken over the day-to-day operational work. That shift was noted in Chapter 2, in IS Lite, where the infrastructure support function is mainly outsourced.

We begin this chapter by presenting one former IS executive's views on the breadth of the operations job and how it needs to be managed. Then we discuss three major operational issues:

1. Outsourcing information systems functions
2. Security in the Internet age
3. Disaster recovery for distributed systems

WHAT ARE OPERATIONS?

In a lecture at the University of California at Los Angeles (UCLA), William Congleton described the important operational issues he faced in one IS department.

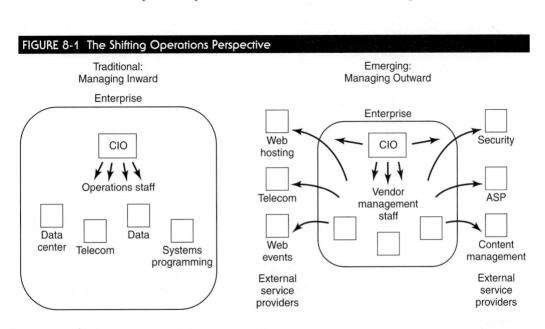

FIGURE 8-1 The Shifting Operations Perspective

Traditional:
Managing Inward

Enterprise

CIO

Operations staff

Data center   Telecom   Data   Systems programming

Emerging:
Managing Outward

Enterprise

Web hosting

Telecom

Web events

CIO

Security

Vendor management staff

ASP

Content management

External service providers

External service providers

Why Talk About Operations?

Keeping the shop running is getting increasingly difficult, he said. The reasons become apparent at budget time. His total annual IS department budget had the following split:

- 33 percent for systems and programming, of which 70 percent was for maintenance and 30 percent was for new development
- 10 percent for department administration and training
- 57 percent for operations.

So, one reason operations are important is because they involve more money than any other part of the department.

At his company, operations included computer hardware at 64 locations, including 12 seaports, 12 parts warehouses, and 12 sales offices. Hardware included computers, disk drives, tape drives, printers, and PCs. Operations also included communication lines and equipment, and software, such as operating systems, compilers, and networking software. In addition, the budget included data center personnel, such as systems consulting for developers, and operators who scheduled and ran production jobs, mounted tapes, delivered reports, and monitored the machines and network. And operations included disaster recovery planning and security.

"Putting all these things together sometimes gave me more excitement than I could stand," quipped Congleton, "plus they were more expensive than I wanted. Therefore, achieving a 10 percent reduction in operations had a far greater effect that a 10 percent reduction in any other area. That is why operations are important."

Solving Operational Problems

Systems operations problems are obvious to the entire company: Response times are slow, networks are down, data is not available, or data is wrong. What can be done to improve operations? Congleton describes three strategies. One is to buy more equipment. As equipment costs drop, this solution might appear the most cost-effective, unless you run out of room for the equipment. The second approach is to continuously fight fires and rearrange priorities, getting people to solve the problem at hand. This solution really only moves the problem of poor management from one hot spot to another. The third solution is to continually document and measure what you are doing, to find out the *real* problems, not just the apparent ones. Then set standards. It is the solution Congleton preferred. It is needed no matter who runs operations, the in-house staff or an outsourcer, and no matter whether the systems are long-time transaction systems or for Internet e-commerce.

Operational Measures

Operational measures are both external and internal. *External measures* are what customers see: system and network uptime (or downtime), response time, turnaround time, and program failures. These aspects directly relate to customer satisfaction. *Internal measures* are of interest to IS people: computer usage as a percentage of capacity, availability of mainline systems, disk storage utilized, job queue length, number of jobs run, number of jobs rerun due to problems, age of applications, and number of unresolved problems.

Problems reported by the external measures can generally be explained by deviations in the internal measures. To help uncover the problems related to equipment capacity, quality of applications, or improper use of systems by users, numerous venders sell monitoring software and devices. Other measurement systems log performance of the various kinds of computer and telecom equipment, said Congleton. Storage management systems manage space more efficiently. Schedulers schedule jobs. And library management systems keep track of versions and backups of files and programs. So plenty of tools are available to help IS departments measure how efficiently their equipment is being used.

The Importance of Good Management

Tools are useless, however, unless IS management has created a corporate culture that recognizes and values good operations, said Congleton. It is hard to find good computer operations managers because the absence of prestige (and sometimes pay) does not attract individuals with the proper combination of skills and training. This reality is unfortunate, he said, because in a good environment, an operations job can be particularly rewarding, both financially and professionally.

The skills required of an operations manager are similar to those needed in a factory or oil refinery. The factory manager must schedule work to meet promised delivery dates, monitor performance as work flows through the key pieces of equipment, and respond quickly to production breakdowns. In a well-run factory, the manager can usually recover from one or two individual problems. In a badly run factory, a manager faces many little problems and often does not know where to start to fix the problems. The same is true in computer and telecom centers where the "factory equipment" is the disk drives, database machines, host computers, servers, network gateways, routers, bridges, and the like.

In conclusion, CIOs need to be concerned about operations, said Congleton, by putting the proper operations environment in place. The key to managing operations is the same as in any management job: set standards and then manage to those standards by finding an outstanding operations manager.

What's New in Operations?

Since the last edition of this book, several changes have taken place in operations.

Companies Have "Cleaned Their Operational House." Y2K and the Internet have forced companies to "clean house" in their data and network center operations, says Rosemary LaChance of Farber/LaChance,[1] a company that provides consulting on automating data center operations.

In the late 1990s, companies were fearful their old computer applications could not handle processing in the year 2000 because many of the programs left out the digits "19" in, say, "1993." Once the millennium hit, these programs would think the year 2000 was the year 1900, yielding erroneous results.

Y2K forced companies to not only look at their existing software but also their computer operations, says LaChance, in particular, their standards and policies. Formerly, operations were managed reactively. They upgraded hardware but they rarely updated processes. Companies would not spend the money to improve procedures, thinking, "If it ain't broke, don't fix it."

Y2K, and then the Internet, required management to think about the processes that computer operations supported and ask, "How are we going to do what we say we will do? How will we be able to add services or outsource operations? Will we be able to support e-commerce?" The resulting changes have led to far better operational structure because management took the time to define the rules for operations and put better policies and procedures in place.

"Had they not gone through Y2K, most companies would not be operationally prepared for the Internet," says LaChance. Although automation provides discipline, the rules must be in place to automate. Y2K forced companies to define these rules, such as rules for gaining access to systems. They also got rid of such outdated procedures as transferring data via tapes (moving to more efficient and less costly online data transfers), and distributing reports on paper (moving to making them available via the company intranet).

In short, Y2K gave computer operations the attention it needed, but had not gotten. So companies are now in much better shape operationally. They have been forced to move from a survival mode ("Let's just get this job run") to a planning mode ("What do we need to support e-commerce?"). But challenges remain. Computer operators still cannot link identified problems with changes, so they do not have integration problem and change management. That piece of the operations structure is still missing.

Operations Managers are Beginning to Manage Outward. The picture Congleton paints is based on the traditional "managing inward" view where enterprises manage their own data centers. By and large, that view has been true and remains true. But as the next section on outsourcing points out, a growing number of companies are turning to a third party to run their data centers. Even more are contracting with a network provider to manage their networks. These changes do not mean CIOs can relinquish responsibility for operations. It just means they need to ensure that their people are properly managing the service providers.

Even for companies keeping their own data centers, an increasing number are taking advantage of operational services provided by third parties, especially for e-business operations. For example, some host their Web site at a company that specializes in Web hosting, such as Exodus Communications. Offloading Web operations allows enterprises to forego large equipment and brick-and-mortar investments, expensing operational costs instead. Furthermore, they offload the job of finding the needed talent to the specialist. Finding qualified employees is an acute problem in the IT field. It is easier to attract and retain IT talent when a company's core business is IT because staff can see a career path, the company is more likely to buy the latest tools and equipment, and the culture is more likely to be IT-friendly.

Operations are Being Simplified. Another trend is to simplify operations by centralizing applications in one place, rather than distribute them on PCs. Programs are then downloaded when requested. This practice is called "server-based computing," and was discussed in Chapter 5.

Certain Operations are Being Offloaded. Yet another trend in operations is to offload certain kinds of operations or certain aspects of computer and network operations. Often, these relate to the Internet. For example, a large growth area in Internet operations is "event management," which means hosting a real-time event over the Internet. When successful, such events, called *webcasts,* lead to a huge spike in Web site hits. To avoid being swamped and having the Web site crash, companies are offloading the operational aspects of these events to third parties that specialize in hosting such activities. Here is an example of such a webcast.

CASE EXAMPLE

MICROSOFT

When Microsoft officially announced its Windows 2000 operating system, it did so not only at a major launch event in San Francisco, California, but also via a public Internet broadcast, and a private webcast to 6,000 original equipment manufacturer (OEM) system builders in 83 countries.

This private, global webcast to OEMs was handled by Akamai. Akamai has more than 4,000 servers in 45 countries and specializes in hosting corporate Web sites "at the edge of the Internet," that is, close to end users. This approach gives users in far-flung locations fast downloads off these Web sites. Like the Internet, Akamai's global distributed system has no central control; therefore, if a server, or a data center, or even a major network link (a backbone) fails, data can be routed around these failures. Having no single point of failure makes the network fail-safe.

Akamai has also gotten into hosting the broadcast of live events via its customers' Web sites—webcasting—which requires high bandwidth capabilities to accommodate streaming media, that is, live audio and video. In addition, Akamai's Netpodium service allows such events to be interactive with the dispersed audiences.

The Microsoft webcast for the system builders was the largest online seminar Microsoft had held. It originated at Microsoft's headquarters in Redmond, Washington, and began with an introduction by Microsoft's OEM team. The webcast then joined the San Francisco event with an on-site commentator and special presenters.

At their sites, the system builders could use Netpodium to send messages to the presenters. They sent some 1,800 and received real-time responses. In addition, Netpodium was used by the presenters to poll the system builders at several points during the event.

Microsoft was well pleased with the private webcast because it set a record for attendance, global reach, and audience participation. ∎

In conclusion, the focus of CIOs in operations is changing. Their attention used to be focused on ensuring they had the in-house expertise to keep systems and networks up and running. Their attention now is toward determining where best to perform the various kinds of operations, in-house or with a third party. In an increasing number of cases, especially with respect to e-business, the choice is to use an outside specialist, which leads naturally to the next subject, outsourcing.

OUTSOURCING INFORMATION SYSTEMS FUNCTIONS

Outsourcing means turning over a firm's computer operations, network operations, or other IT function to a vendor for a specified time—generally, at least a few years, although that time frame is changing. In 1989, outsourcing became a legitimate management strategy by IS departments. Up until that time, the only companies that outsourced their IS departments were those that were poorly run. But in 1989, Kodak outsourced its well-run IS department to become a more competitive company. That surprising move caused top executives around the world to consider the use of outsourcers. Today, CIOs are expected to investigate outsourcing sufficiently to satisfy executive management that their IS operations are as efficient and effective in-house as they would be if they were outsourced.

The Driving Forces Behind Outsourcing

At a meeting of the Chicago Chapter of the Society for Information Management, Mel Bergstein of DiamondCluster Int'l.[2] gave an overview of outsourcing. His main message was that outsourcing is another step in the evolution of the information systems field.

Outsourcing descended on IS departments as a follow-on to the merger and acquisition activities in the 1980s, said Bergstein. In the 1960s, only 10 percent of the U.S. economy had global competition. In the 1970s, that rose to 70 percent. In response, companies had to *focus on core businesses* in the 1980s, which led to the huge amount of merger and acquisition activity. This activity was also driven by a new market for corporate control. High-yield bonds allowed a few people to buy a company and leverage it with debt. Companies were "priced" based on their *shareholder value,* that is, their discounted cash flow.

These two drivers—focus and value—are still leading companies to restructure and focus on core businesses by asking themselves, "Where do we really add value?" As examples, some apparel companies no longer cut, sew, manufacturer, or distribute goods because they see their core businesses as design and marketing. Likewise, some publishers no longer manufacture books. They manage and finance projects, and outsource everything else.

So outsourcing is part of the drive for focus and value, and it is not solely an information systems issue, said Bergstein; it is a business issue. Because top management must stress value, they must consider outsourcing in all their nonstrategic functions. In the age of e-business, they may even need to consider outsourcing their strategic functions to get a jump on the competition.

Changing Customer-Vendor Relationships

Outsourcers perform the same activities for a company that a IS department performs in-house. But, over time, the amount of work done by outsiders has increased, said Bergstein, as the following expansion in customer-vendor relationships illustrates.

Traditionally, IS departments have *bought professional services,* such as planning (or consulting), building or maintaining applications, building or maintaining networks, and training. They have also *bought products,* which may or may not include training. And they have *bought transactions,* such as payroll checks from a service bureau or credit reports from a credit rating service. This third type of relationship is good for buyers because their costs become variable, and hence more controllable. It is also good for the sellers because in taking on the risks, they can have higher margins.

With the increasing use of packages and the need to integrate components to create integrated systems, companies have contracted with *a systems integrator.* They generally handle the entire life cycle—planning, development, maintenance, and training—for major systems projects. Finally, the most bundled approach to contracting for IS services is *outsourcing,* where the outsourcer contracts to handle all or most of certain information system activities. The main difference between the latter two options is that system integration is project-based while outsourcing is time-based.

This five-option continuum, shown in Figure 8-2, demonstrates how the IT field has moved, said Bergstein. As you move from the more traditional professional services category (on the left) to outsourcing (on the right), four changes occur in the vendor-customer relationship:

1. Information systems management loses an increasing amount of control because more of the activities are turned over to outsiders.
2. Vendors take more risks as they offer options on the right.
3. Vendors' margins improve as they offer services on the right.
4. The importance of choosing the right vendor becomes more important to the right, because more is at risk in using an outside source.

FIGURE 8-2 Customer-Vendor Relationships

	Relationships				
Activities	Professional Services	Product	Transactions	Systems Integration	Outsourcing
• Planning/consulting	X				
• Building/maintaining applications	X				
• Building/maintaining networks	X				
• Training users/clients	X	X	X	X	X
• Operating platforms					
• Performing administrative functions					
• Building/using product					

Source: Mel Bergstein, DiamondCluster Int'l., Chicago, IL.

Outsourcing's History

In 1989, essentially only one kind of outsourcing was available: IT outsourcing. Since then, the field has expanded significantly, so here's a bit of history.

IT Outsourcing. IT outsourcing essentially began with "big bang" deals, or mega deals, which consisted of outsourcing all a company's data center operations for up to 10 years. These deals required selling existing equipment to the outsourcer, transferring all software licenses, moving significant numbers of IS personnel from the company payroll to the outsourcer's payroll, negotiating how the outsourcer would help in the transition and which party would carry which costs, establishing desired service levels and ways to measure performance, and specifying every single service to be provided—because if it wasn't in the contract, it would be an added cost.

In those early days, the goal of these large data center contracts was purely financial. Companies wanted to remove the huge hardware investments from their books. They wanted to shift fixed costs to variable costs, and they wanted to save money, generally about 15 percent. The deals were front-loaded, with the outsourcers losing money or breaking even the first year or two, but then becoming profitable after that, as the costs of technology dropped, as they leveraged licenses across clients, as they shared expertise across clients, and as they invested in productivity tools that made them more efficient.

Several problems occurred, however. An "us versus them" mindset often set in because neither the clients nor the outsourcers handled the transition well. A lot of finger pointing took place as outsourcers tried to charge for services clients thought were included in the contract. And service levels did not always live up to expectations, or interpretations of the contract language differed.

Furthermore, cultures clashed. Former employees might have kept their same desk, but once they became an employee of the outsourcer, they became a supplier and were treated differently. Users had higher expectations of outsourcers than of their IS departments. In short, companies learned that managing the relationship was really the tough job. Formerly, they had thought that negotiating the deal was the difficult part, so they had not carefully defined governance structures, that is, how the relationship would be managed.

Today, the industry has matured. Outsourcers have learned that heavy-handed treatment of clients can backfire. They are much more careful in transition planning. Clients' attorneys have learned what's important in a contract and where the pitfalls lie. Today, those initial contracts are being renegotiated, and although the clients may not change outsourcers, they have generally become more adept at renegotiating because they now know what they really need.

Of course, not all outsourcing deals were mega-deals. But even the small deals felt like a big bang to the employees who moved to the outsourcer.

Transitional Outsourcing. In the early 1990s, a new type of computing arose: client-server computing, as noted in Chapter 5. IT outsourcing had been around for a few years, so CIOs with their hands full supporting legacy systems looked into using outsourcing to transition to client-server computing. They chose one of two routes. Either they outsourced maintenance of their legacy systems, so their staff could concentrate on building new client-server systems, or they outsourced client-server development to specialists and kept maintenance in-house. In either case, once the new systems were brought in, the legacy systems they replaced were shut down.

Then, in the late 1990s, when the immense size of Y2K compliance surfaced—to retrofit old applications so they would work after the Year 2000—most companies outsourced as much of their Y2K work as they could. Because of the enormous volume of work, offshore outsourcing to India, Ireland, and other countries grew significantly. Unlike traditional IT outsourcing, however, contracts were generally shorter and did not include operations.

Best-of-Breed Outsourcing. All through the 1990s, IT departments outsourced different pieces of their work; mainly infrastructure support, as noted in Chapter 2 and IS Lite. However, CIOs learned that although selecting one outsourcer with broad capabilities might be easiest to manage, often no single company was "best in class" in all areas. Thus, selective outsourcing began, where one company handled desktop operations, another data center operations, and a third network management. Even though the concept was good for getting the best-of-breed providers, coordination among multiple providers became a nightmare.

A more recent trend has been what we call "collaborative outsourcing," where one company becomes the prime contractor for numerous facets of IS operations, but some of the work is provided by other external service providers (ESPs). Often an operations partner, a development partner, and a telecom partner collaborate to bid on the work, but one is the "prime." So teams of large ESPs now bid against other teams for contracts. In some cases, these contracts take on quite a bit more than simply operations; the work includes development of new systems as well. Best-of-breed outsourcing has perpetuated the tradition of long and complex outsourcing contracts.

Shared Services. When IT outsourcing began to gain credibility, executives wondered, "Can we get the same economies of scale by pulling disparate noncore functions together into one shared services group?" In many cases, they felt they could. So they "insourced" to themselves, creating an organizational unit for functions such as IT, legal, facilities management, real estate, mail room, finance, and on and on. The goal was to improve efficiencies and save money. Generally, companies created a center of expertise in each area, with all the centers reporting to one shared services vice president.

IT was not always included, but, as in the case of Mead Corporation, it was. Some executives believe having IT in shared services gives them the ability to leverage the IT underpinnings of the other services. Shared services also centralizes the management of outsourced functions because, in many cases, the functions are centralized and then outsourced. So shared services groups are becoming more adept at negotiating and managing contracts and supplier relationships because these tasks are a main part of their job.

Business Process Outsourcing. As the IT outsourcing field matured, data center outsourcing, desktop outsourcing, and other standard IT outsourcing areas became so well understood that they became like commodity services, hence profit margins dropped as the number of competitors rose. To move into higher-margin services, ESPs began specializing in specific functional areas, offering to handle specific business processes as well as their IT underpinnings. This business process outsourcing (BPO) is defined as outsourcing all or most of a reengineered process that has a large IT component.

Gaining the expertise of a provider, rather than cost cutting, has been the main goal in BPO. Improving a process by handing it over to experts has also been a goal. Generally, companies have been most willing to outsource their noncore functions. Thus, one oil company now outsources its accounting function to PricewaterhouseCoopers, moving 1,500 employees to PwC. Companies have long outsourced payroll processing. Now companies are outsourcing logistics, customer service, and many other essential, yet peripheral, functions to the experts.

Balboa Travel,[3a] a travel agency in San Diego, California, handed over its ticket accounting to Unisys. Each week, travel agencies must report the tickets they sold to the Airline Reporting Corporation. The process is important, yet burdensome, and the president of Balboa Travel did not want to hire a programmer to maintain such a reporting system, which is what he would have had to do if he had not outsourced the work. Unisys actually provides him a more sophisticated service than he could afford in-house. It lets him offer his clients—corporate travel departments—reports about their employees' travel habits via an extranet. Balboa is also able to do data mining on their ticket sales to uncover trends that will help them offer new and better services.

As is obvious, BPO moves IT-based outsourcing out beyond the IT department; it involves business units as well. BPO outsourcing is often quite a bit more complex than IT outsourcing because it requires clients to change their business processes to fit with the processes of the service provider. Furthermore, some clients want to retain parts of a process, so complex coordination may be necessary between the two firms as well.

BPO brought a mindset change to the field. Whereas IT outsourcing moved suppliers and customers closer to one another in terms of working together, a distance between the two came from not working from common goals. Clients want to save more money; outsourcers want to make more money.

In BPO, a number of the deals have tended to be more risk/reward, in that the parties enter a somewhat risky business venture together and if the business does well, both split the increased revenue.

Rita Terdiman,[4a] of Gartner, noted this phenomenon at a speech to the Sourcing Interests Group. As shown in Figure 8-3, BPO deals have aimed to be more like joint ventures and alliances, moving them to the right side of the chart where trust, joint financial investments, and "partnering" are part of the deal.

Even though BPO deals are difficult to structure and then manage, they are growing significantly, partly due to e-business.

E-business Outsourcing.   With the arrival of business use of the Internet, outsourcing has actually become the leading-edge way to run a company. In large companies, it started with marketing departments outsourcing the development of their corporate Web site. Once developed, IT took over operations. However, in dot-coms and Internet-based companies, outsourcing all or most of the IT function is the preferred mode of operation, for several reasons.

One, they need to move fast. They cannot spend a year developing a system; they need it up and running within months, or even weeks. Two, they want to remain flexible, which means staying small and focusing only on a few key functions. Generally, IT has not been seen as a core differentiating area because tailorable off-the-shelf products and services have rapidly become available. Three, they do not want to tie up their venture capital funds in computer and networking equipment, knowing it will become ob-

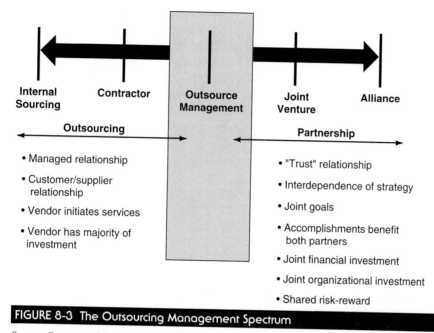

Internal Sourcing   **Contractor**   **Outsource Management**   **Joint Venture**   **Alliance**

← Outsourcing →   ← Partnership →

- Managed relationship
- Customer/supplier relationship
- Vendor initiates services
- Vendor has majority of investment

- "Trust" relationship
- Interdependence of strategy
- Joint goals
- Accomplishments benefit both partners
- Joint financial investment
- Joint organizational investment
- Shared risk-reward

FIGURE 8-3 The Outsourcing Management Spectrum

Source: Courtesy of Gartner, Stamford, CT, at www.gartner.com.

solete fairly soon. They would much rather rent than buy. And they want to draw on best-of-breed as well as be able to change course quickly if need be, swapping out one ESP and swapping in another, to keep pace with the market.

Major differences between e-business outsourcing and traditional IT outsourcing include: no need to buy machines from the client, no personnel to move, and no software licenses to take over. The outsourcing starts from scratch.

Few large companies have followed this route, mainly because they have invested in ERP and other large systems and have not wanted to throw these investments away. However, those that start Internet-based spin-offs have often followed the dot-coms and relied on ESPs for their IT needs.

Operating on the Web is coming to mean working closely with ESPs, of which there are now many kinds. Suppliers have jumped on the e-business bandwagon by providing their services over the Internet or via private IP networks. Besides being able to quickly draw on expertise via a net-based package or service, utilizing ESPs also reduces the burden of maintaining systems, which has accounted for up to 80 percent of IS departmental budgets. So the outsourcing model allows IT departments to move more at the speed of the business, which is an absolute necessity these days.

Application Service Providers (ASPs).   In 1999 a new term surfaced: application service provider, which is a company that rents software to others over the Internet. ASPs are not outsourcers in the traditional sense of the term because they do not take over a company's data center or manage its desktops. But, they are being seen as the next step in outsourcing nonetheless.

ASPs began offering software-for-rent over the Internet to smaller and medium-sized firms that did not want to invest in buying large systems. Large firms had the money to invest, so they kept the work in-house. ASPs charge a per-month, per-user rate to handle, say, benefits administration via their Web site. Now some external service providers sell specialized services only to ASPs, giving these ASPs broader service lines. The ASP business model has become so attractive that some ASPs are even offering ERP services over the net. Companies do not have to spend the millions (or tens of millions) of dollars to install ERP; they can rent the functions over the net.

The ASP model is expanding rapidly. One offshoot is corporate portals. Rather than house commonly used software on PCs, and have the headache of upgrading copies with fixes and new versions, employees can get their software off their corporate portal, which is hosted and supplied by an ASP. In short, ASPs are yet another step toward IS Lite.

Thus, in 10 years' time, IT outsourcing has changed significantly, from big-bang 10-year deals that took a year to negotiate to renting software over the net, by user and by the month.

Managing Outsourcing

Numerous aspects to managing outsourcing need to be taken into account to create a successful working relationship. Here are just four—organizational structure, governance, day-to-day working, and supplier development. All are based on research reports published by the Sourcing Interests Group, headed by Barry Wiegler.[3b, c]

Organizational Structure. Managing outsourcing is different from managing internal staff because, for one thing, it is a joint effort between parties that may not have the same goals, as noted earlier. Therefore, during contract negotiations, the two parties need to figure out and negotiate how they are going to jointly manage the contract they sign. In fact, governance needs to be explicitly addressed in the contract.

Typically, parties establish layers of joint teams. A top-level team of a couple executives from both companies has the final word on conflict resolution. An operational team, with members from both companies, oversees day-to-day functioning. They formally meet periodically, say, once a week to once a month, but they are generally in daily contact. Also, some joint special purpose teams may be created from time to time to deal with pressing issues. Some companies have ongoing standing committees, such as a pricing committee or a change management committee, to oversee the use of formal change management procedures.

Although joint committees are a common management structure, each side needs a single executive in charge of their side of the relationship. On the client side, these people are coming to be known as relationship managers. This job position has not been prevalent in IS departments, but we believe it is going to become the norm as companies move toward IS Lite. Needless to say, the skills of a relationship manager are far different from those of a data center manager. A relationship manager needs to be good at negotiating, cajoling, and being an effective liaison between end users and service providers. An operations manager needs to know how to hire the right people and keep the systems up and running—like a factory manager, as Congleton has pointed out.

To illustrate how one company has managed its outsourcing, we look at Eastman Kodak Company because it created a thoughtful and effective governance structure. The following description comes from the Sourcing Interests Group; it focuses on the alliance between Kodak and IBM Global Services, which provides outsourcing services.

CASE EXAMPLE

EASTMAN KODAK COMPANY

Eastman Kodak Company, with head-quarters in Rochester, New York, is an international manufacturer of imaging and chemical products. In 1989, the company rocked the information systems world by announcing strategic relationships with four suppliers to manage significant portions of its IS organization. Until that time, outsourcing had been viewed by those in the industry as a desperation move to improve poorly run IS departments. Because Kodak's unit was well run, and benchmarked accordingly, its pioneering stance caused many IS executives—and a few CEOs and CFOs as well—to seriously reconsider outsourcing.

Kodak announced that one would operate its data centers and networks, another would manage its telecommunications, a third would handle PC support, and a fourth would manage voice messaging. Initially the agreement with IBM to manage the data centers was U.S.-based; it was later expanded to include Canadian operations, other U.S. divisions, and eventually six international sites. Kodak encourages IBM to leverage its data center for both Kodak and other companies' work for improved efficiencies. Due to efforts on both sides, the Kodak-IBM relationship has worked well. They developed trust and good processes. As a result, few problems have developed, and when issues do arise, the relationship has effective processes to deal with them.

Outsourcing Management Structure

Kodak views its outsourcing management role as exercising leadership, staying in control, and managing the high value-added functions for flexibility. Kodak sets the tone for its key IT relationships. The key themes of that relationship have been collaborative (not adversarial), long-term mutual benefits (not short-term), and making systemic improvements on a global basis (not local). The management structure has six elements: a management board, an advisory council, a supplier and alliance management group, a relationship manager for each relationship, ad hoc working groups, and client surveys.

The Management Board. It meets twice a year, includes senior management from both companies. It focuses on strategic issues, in addition to any policies or practices on either side that are getting in the way of mutual success. It has dealt with international strategies, IT architecture, telecom directions, disaster recovery plans, and so forth.

The Advisory Council. It meets monthly and has 15 members, handles technical and operational issues by focusing on *what* Kodak wants, not *how* the services are or will be delivered. Gradually Kodak's trust in IBM has grown, so it leaves more of the *how* detail up to this service provider. The advisory council reviews service levels, usage measurements and forecasts, tactical plans, migration objectives, business recovery plans, and the like.

The Supplier and Alliance Management Group. It manages the longer-term outsourcing relationships as well as other contracts with large IT suppliers. It works

(Case Continued)

closely with IS management. This group of 10 people includes a manager, the relationship manager for each primary alliance, plus support staff and supplier management for other IT sourcing. Initially, this group managed only the alliances. Contracts with major vendors were handled in other groups. But eventually all these functions were brought together to increase their focus, leverage global agreements, and align the management of alliances and suppliers. About one-half these people have IS backgrounds; the other half come from purchasing.

The Relationship Manager. This manager is a key player in the success of a strategic relationship, Kodak believes, because this person is the focal point between itself and its service provider. The job of each of Kodak's four relationship managers is to ensure that Kodak receives more than just delivery on the contract. Thus they manage value creation, not just adherence to the contract. The relationship managers negotiate, coordinate, and manage agreements and ensure that the service level agreements (SLAs) are established. They also assist in pricing and billing strategies.

Working Groups. These groups were not part of Kodak's original outsourcing man-

agement structure, were added to deal with specific technology areas. They are chartered by the advisory council. Their goals are to facilitate changes in processes, promulgate standards, achieve business recovery in case of disruption, and promote effective use of IS services. They have proven to be effective vehicles for talking about important issues, such as agreeing on the timing and appropriateness of upgrading to new releases of software. The groups are represented mainly by operational people. For example, database administrators from the major sites are in one working group.

Client Surveys. These surveys are sent out twice a year to nearly 5,000 internal users of the services being provided. Feedback on quality, cycle time, and product and service leadership are assessed and shared with the service providers. Improvement plans are mutually developed to close any perceived gaps in performance.

Because Kodak's outsourcing has such a large scope, draws on four main suppliers, and covers a large geographic area, the company has discovered that it needs all these forms of coordination for effective supplier management. ∎

Governance. The foundations of governing an outsourcing relationship are laid out in the contract, which can be hundreds of pages long (with appendixes). A major governance item in the contract is the service level agreements (SLAs) because they are used to gauge supplier performance. For every contracted service, its SLA spells out responsibilities, performance requirements, penalties, bonuses, and so on. Completeness is an important attribute of good SLAs; generally everything should be detailed, perhaps even with times of deliveries, who will deliver what to whom, and so on.

Another important component of SLAs is metrics. An SLA needs to be measurable to be of use. Establishing metrics can be tricky because, in many cases, IS departments have not kept good measures of their own performance. Such measures are needed to establish benchmarks, against which vendors want to demonstrate improvements. Clients also need metrics to negotiate better deals. Clients who do not know their own performance levels negotiate from weakness; they know less than the vendor because they have not kept track of details, and vendors are not apt to correct mistaken impressions. Furthermore, they are likely to overlook important details, which will later cost them money.

In addition to SLAs, parties establish simple governance rules to be used when either party is making a decision, so that both are "singing from the same hymnal." Most parties in strong relationships say they put the contract in the drawer after it has been signed and work from trust and agreed-upon rules. It is only when trust in one another breaks down that they turn to the contract. Figure 8-4 lists some governance rules from a number of different enterprises.

Day-To-Day Working. The Sourcing Interests Group reports provide advice from outsourcing executives on how to manage the day-to-day interactions of the two parties. Here are a few of those recommendations.

Manage expectations, not staff. The outsourcer's staff is no longer under the purview of the client, so command-and-control is not a wise option—it only results in an acrimonious relationship. Facilitation becomes the mode of working. Rather than say "do this," the approach becomes "how can we solve this together?" Furthermore, the relationship managers have the important role of influencing the expectations of the users so that delivery meets business objectives.

Realize that informal ways of working may disappear. More formality is inevitable as outcomes are measured and more tightly controlled, especially if the relationship is handled strictly by the book, which happens in some cases. This change can be a real shock to people who are used to, say, getting a small job done by calling their friend "Joe" in the IS department. Once Joe works for the supplier, he may no longer be able to provide that service; he must follow the work authorization process defined in the

---

FIGURE 8-4 Examples of Outsourcing Governance Rules

- Service levels must stay in the top 25 percent, as benchmarked against the client's peers.
- Escalation of problems gets more painful as it goes higher, to encourage early resolution.
- The supplier is the grand project manager and is responsible for managing multiple vendors.
- Work style is based on respect and confidence; there should be no personalization of problems.
- Add significant value.
- Aim to operate in an "open book" manner, sharing key operating information with each other.
- New services can be put out for bid.
- No exclusive agreements.
- Meet our standards.
- Let us know about potential problems before they happen.
- Spend our money as if it were your own.

Source: Reprinted with permission of Sourcing Interests Group, Bell Canyon, CA, at www.sourcinginterests.org.

contract. This can cause unhappiness as users see providers as "them," making them the scapegoat. The two parties need to find ways to reduce this tendency.

Loss of informal ways of working can add rigor.   Rigor frequently improves work quality. Users may think twice before requesting changes, preparing better definitions of what they want. Furthermore, better processes can streamline work, improve effectiveness, and potentially cut out unnecessary work. Service providers do introduce new discipline; the client should prepare employees for this change and assist them in changing because it is generally best to take on the provider's processes. It is why transition planning is so important: To help the client move to new procedures with the least disruption and disgruntlement.

Integration of the two staffs requires explicit actions.   Some examples are to (1) grant outsourcing staff access to appropriate work areas, not unduly restrict them; (2) hold joint celebrations and social events; (3) invite each other to meetings; and (4) perhaps even have a client executive move on two-year loan to the provider in a management position to learn first-hand how they work internally. But integration generally can only go so far; the client still needs to remain in control and provide the guidance. Furthermore, the more side-by-side the parties work, the more likely they are to experience "scope creep" in which the provider takes on more work.

The best way to manage day-to-day is to communicate frequently.   One executive said he carried around a top-10 list in his shirt pocket, which he revised every week. They were the most important items he had to handle. They kept him on focus and turned out to be his best informal management technique.

Supplier Development.   A topic that is receiving increased attention in the production sourcing arena—that is, buying parts and services that go into one's own products and services—is supplier development. It means assisting one's suppliers to improve their products and services, generally by improving their processes. Although supplier development has not been prevalent in IT sourcing, we think it will be.

Here is an example from manufacturing from a Sourcing Interests Group research report.[3c]

CASE EXAMPLE

HONDA MOTOR COMPANY

Dave Nelson, now vice president of Worldwide Supply Management at Deere & Company, was formerly head of purchasing for Honda Motor Company, where he became widely known for his pioneering work in supplier development. To him it means being involved in improving suppliers' capabilities. The benefits include receiving higher quality goods, getting lower prices, tapping suppliers' expertise, and improving one's supply chain. In e-business, where alliances are so crucial, working together to improve processes will be of major importance.

(Case Continued)

In manufacturing, Nelson undertakes supplier development by sending two of his supply development engineers to a supplier, for free. They team up with two supplier engineers with the goal of cutting labor-hours and inventory of a single part bought by Nelson by 50 percent in 13 weeks' time. The team works under two main guidelines: No employees will be laid off. They will all have a job elsewhere in the company, perhaps teaching others how to improve their processes. Two, Nelson splits any savings 50/50 with the supplier.

The team of four starts by cleaning and painting the area where the part is produced. That single act gets everyone's attention. Then they ask for suggestions from the workers on how to improve the process. They map the existing process and try to implement (quickly and in any way possible) every suggestion so the workers can test it out. Generally, once the workers see they are being heard, the suggestions pour in.

The results can be dramatic. As one small example, one assembly line of 15 women on one shift and 10 on another made 1,500 air conditioning hoses a day using 15 machines. In total, the women walked 13 miles a day and hauled 3 tons of material. After redesign, only five women were needed on one shift to make 1,550 hoses, and they only needed to walk 50 yards and haul 100 pounds.

Nelson says it is like "walking around picking up money off the floor." So why isn't it more prevalent? He believes it is because manufacturing companies still maintain their internal focus. Although they now outsource most parts production—up to 70 percent at Honda—they have not shifted their resources to managing suppliers. They still treat suppliers as outsiders rather than departments in the company. Management has to be *sold* on the idea of investing in supplier *management*, and sold even more on supplier *development*. They need proof that supplier management will yield bottom-line benefits. ∎

In conclusion, outsourcing has become a crucial operational alternative for companies. With the pace of change so rapid in IT and e-business, the only hope of many enterprises is to tap the expertise of companies that are keeping pace with the change, rather than trying to do everything themselves. But outsourcing does not mean relinquishing responsibility. In fact, taken to its extreme, it can mean devoting resources to assist suppliers improve their processes. We believe it is a coming focus in the world of IS Lite.

SECURITY IN THE INTERNET AGE

Whereas security used to be an arcane, technical topic, today, even CEOs need to know about it, as they move their companies into e-commerce. Actually, all business executives now need to understand Internet-based threats and countermeasures, and continually fund security work to protect their businesses.

As one security officer told us, "If I were an e-tailer, I might not call the Internet a bad neighborhood, but I would certainly 'watch my back.' My equivalent brick-and-mortar store would have automatic locks on the doors, cameras watching every aisle, and only $20 in the safe, because I would never know what kinds of thieves might show up or what kinds of attack they might launch—from anywhere in the world. Furthermore, as an e-tailer, I would need more security than a brick-and-mortar store manager because customers can get a lot closer to the guts of my business."

The Threats

Since 1996, the Computer Security Institute and the San Francisco Federal Bureau of Investigation Computer Intrusion Squad[5] have conducted an annual survey of U.S. security managers to uncover the types of computer crimes committed. The 2000 survey, with responses from 643 managers in corporations and government, confirmed that (1) organizations are under cyberattack from inside and outside their electronic perimeters; (2) a wide range of attacks have been detected; (3) attacks can result in significant losses, and (4) defending against attacks requires more than the use of information security technologies.

Some 70 percent of the respondents noted in the 2000 survey that they had experienced a security breach within the past 12 months. Because most breaches go unnoticed, the percentage is likely to be quite a bit higher. However, Richard Power, editorial director of CSI, notes that the number answering "no" fell to just 16 percent in 2000, from 37 percent in 1996. He views this decrease as heartening because it means fewer are living in denial and are more closely scrutinizing their network activity. He believes the only honest answers to the question are "yes" and "don't know." No one can ensure that they have not had a breach.

Furthermore he notes that the conventional wisdom that most attacks come from within may no longer be true. The number of respondents stating that their Internet connections were a frequent point of attack has risen each year, from 37 percent in 1996 to 59 percent in 2000, while attacks through internal systems fell to 38 percent, from 53 percent in 1996. Figure 8-5 shows the kinds of attacks experienced, from highest number of attacks to lowest. Remote dial-in was the third attack approach; it accounted for 22 percent in 2000, versus 39 percent in 1996.

But number of attacks does not necessarily correlate with financial losses. Figure 8-6 shows the survey's estimate of losses in the same order as Figure 8-5. Note that theft of proprietary information has the largest lost, yet was reported by only 20 percent of the respondents. Second highest losses came from financial fraud, reported by only 11 percent. This discrepancy between number of attacks and loss indicates that companies need to think about where they are truly most vulnerable. The estimates are not conclusive, notes Power, because not every company reporting a theft quantifies it, and those who do generally can only estimate losses.

What about e-commerce? For the second year, the CSI/FBI survey asked about unauthorized access or misuse of Web sites. Some 93 percent of the respondents had Web sites and 43 percent of them conducted e-commerce over those sites. Some 19 percent reported unauthorized access or misuse; another 32 percent said they did not know. Some 64 percent of the attacks were vandalism, 60 percent were denial of service that blocked the site from use by legitimate Web site visitors, 8 percent reported theft of transaction information, and 3 percent reported financial fraud.

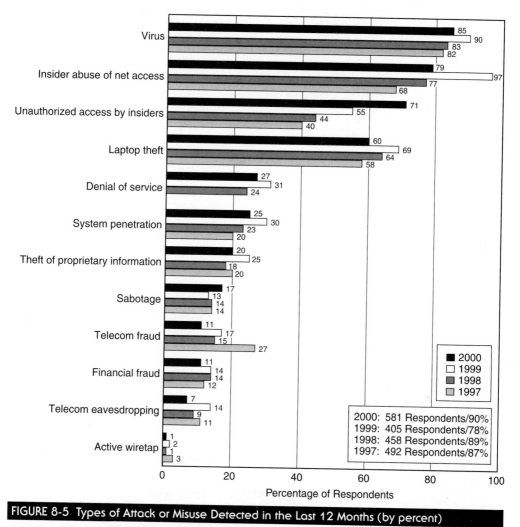

FIGURE 8-5 Types of Attack or Misuse Detected in the Last 12 Months (by percent)

Source: Reprinted with permission of Richard Power, "2000 CSI/FBI Computer Crime and Security Survey," Computer Security Institute, San Francisco, CA, www.gosci.com, Spring 2000.

The good news, says Power, is that financial fraud or theft of proprietary information via Web sites dropped from the previous year. Yet, the fact that some 30 percent did not know whether they have been attacked was unsettling. The report lists just a few cases of massive numbers of illegally accessed credit card numbers from Web sites in the first quarter of 2000 alone (25,000 in one case, 20,000 in another, 485,000 in another, for a total of 809,000). E-commerce crime is a reality, notes Power.

Information crimes are on the rise, says RSA Security Inc.,[6] a prominent long-time network security firm, for a number of reasons. One is the rise of distributed computing. RSA's analogy: It is easier to guard a bank vault than to guard every house in town. That's why many companies are outsourcing their data center operations to data center specialists with vault-like security.

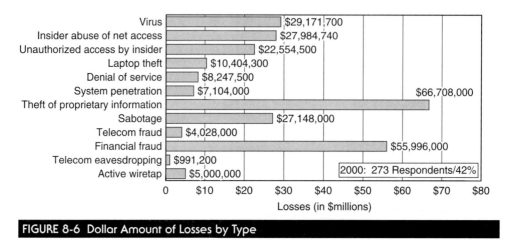

FIGURE 8-6 Dollar Amount of Losses by Type

Source: Reprinted with permission of Richard Power, "2000 CSI/FBI Computer Crime and Security Survey," Computer Security Institute, San Francisco, CA, www.gosci.com, Spring 2000.

Mobile computing and telecommuting also increase the possibility for crime because the greater number of network openings provides more opportunities for illegal entry. Needless to say, the rise of e-commerce and e-business put more communications online to the Internet, which is open to everyone, including hackers. And because the Internet does not have intrinsic security protocols, this public space is vulnerable.

In addition, the hacker community has become "a public club," says RSA, with hacker Web sites and newsgroups available to anyone who wants to learn hackers' tricks. Furthermore, hacker tools are becoming increasingly sophisticated and easier to use; and they are continually being revised to outsmart the countermeasures used by companies to protect themselves. It has become a cat-and-mouse game of a continual one-upmanship. So securing an e-business is not a one-shot deal; it requires constant vigilance.

RSA describes the following nine approaches hackers use:

1. *Cracking the password:* Guessing someone's password is easier than most people think, says RSA, because some people don't use passwords, others use the word "password," and still others use easy-to-remember words such as their child's name, a sports team, or a meaningful date. Hackers also use software that can test out all combinations, which is called "brute force" password detection.
2. *Tricking someone:* To get users to divulge their passwords, a "con artist" calls up an employee posing as a network administrator who needs the employee's password to solve an immediate (fictitious) network problem. It happens more than you think, says RSA.
3. *Network sniffing:* Hackers launch software that monitors all traffic looking for passwords or other valuable information. Because most network traffic is in "clear text" rather than encrypted (to appear as gibberish), sniffing can find information and write it to a file for later use.
4. *Misusing administrative tools:* Helpful tools can be turned against a network. For example, a well-known program written to uncover weak spots in a network, which is important for network administrators, has been used by hackers

to find weak spots in target companies' networks. Interestingly, that program's name is Satan.

5. *Playing middleman:* Placing oneself between two communicating parties and either substituting one's own information in place of one of the parties' information or denying one party access to a session, such as denying a competitor access to an important online auction is another common ploy.

6. *Denial of service:* This tactic floods a party, such as a Web site, with so much useless traffic that the site becomes overwhelmed and freezes. Legitimate messages are locked out, essentially shutting down the business for a period of time.

7. *Trojan horse:* A malicious program can be housed inside an innocent one or, better yet, one that appears to be helpful.

8. *Viruses:* These pieces of software run without permission. Their most common entry point has been as e-mail attachments. Once such an attachment is opened, the program is released and performs its task, such as destroying files (a worm) or replicating itself in e-mails sent to everyone in the e-mail directory. Internet-based viruses have attracted lots of attention, not just for PCs but for wireless devices as well.

9. *Spoofing:* By masquerading as a legitimate IP address, hackers can gain access to a site. Masquerading as a Web site and redirecting traffic to a fraudulent look-alike site which, for example, allows credit card information to be captured for later use.

The major problem these days, notes RSA, is that enterprises cannot have both access to information and airtight security at the same time. Due to e-commerce, companies want unimpeded information flow among a complex Web of alliance partners. Thus, it is no longer feasible to define "good" as "inside the network" and "bad" as "outside the network," as in the past. Today, companies must make tradeoffs between absolute information security and the efficient flow of information. And although they might think technology can solve security loopholes, the human dimension is equally important—making employees cognizant of security threats they may encounter and teaching them how to strengthen the company's security measures. Today, due to the importance of computers in company operations, security decisions are not just technical. They are being influenced by business managers, which affects the bottom line.

Because airtight security is not possible, companies need to prioritize their risks and work on safeguarding against the greatest threats. To give an example of one company's approach to overall network security, consider this case from a Gartner Executive Programs report.[4b]

CASE EXAMPLE

AN INTERNET SERVICES COMPANY

This firm provides services to Internet professionals and performs security assessments. The company, founded in 1994, has produced more than 400 digital business solutions.

Planning and Building for Security

When establishing network connections, the firm's starting point is to deny all access to and from the Internet. From there, it opens portals only where required and each opening has a firewall and only permits specific functions, such as FTP or e-mail.

In essence, the company has put a perimeter around itself. It determines the worth of the information inside the perimeter and spends the appropriate level of money to protect those assets. It can be hard to define the perimeter, though. For example, the company does work from client sites and that work needs to be protected as well.

It recognizes that it must also stay vigilant within the perimeter, to avoid having a "soft chewy center." It uses a layered approach, with numerous ways to protect each layer and some redundancy. For example, it worries about telephone hackers as well as computer hackers.

The IS organization is responsible for all in-house systems and all security. A central authority oversees all servers and workstations. In addition, all machines run the latest virus-detection software. When a system reboots, it accesses the central server where its virus definitions are checked. If they are not the latest ones, the newest version is downloaded.

Finally, the company has disaster recovery plans that include having servers geographically separated. It recommends that clients do the same so that e-business sites can remain operational, at least partially, if some of the servers are hit by an attack or become overloaded.

Monitoring

The company views security on the Internet as a war of escalation. Every few weeks someone finds a clever new way to penetrate software and a new type of attack is launched. Once the security team has closed one hole, attackers will find and attack another. The best the security team can hope to achieve is to deter attackers by closing more and more holes.

The security team therefore believes it needs constantly "to check the locks," which it does in the following ways:

- The team keeps track of the latest bugs found in systems. The company belongs to suppliers' bug alert communities. When it receives an alert, the team looks to see whether it applies to the company's systems. If so, the team assesses the vulnerability and takes any needed action.
- The team keeps up-to-date on the latest security attacks that have taken place around the world by subscribing to security organizations and constantly visiting their Web sites for the latest news.
- The team subscribes to hacker e-mail lists and bulletin boards to see what the bad guys are doing and

(Case Continued)

talking about. The security team believes it must think like the enemy.

- Team members personally explore some threats by setting up a test system and trying various attacks on it—attacks they have read about on the e-mail lists and bulletin boards. It's fun for the security staff, it provides a break from the normal work, and it presents a welcome technical challenge.
- The team logs and monitors all incoming and outgoing traffic. A dedicated team manages the firewalls.
- A senior security person scans the company's Web sites monthly from a remote site, comparing the services being run on the servers with the official inventory of services that should be running on the servers. Major surprises are investigated. He also checks to ensure that no servers are running known compromised software.

Education: The Key to Improving Security

The greatest security challenge is employee and customer apathy; they always say "This cannot happen to us." Hence the greatest security need is employee and customer education. The company tries to balance education with a taste of what "could happen," so that its security message is taken seriously but without employees and clients becoming so frightened that they think any

countermeasure is useless. Management has learned that fear-mongering becomes counterproductive if it is too scary or used too often.

Education is a two-way street, though. Business people need to determine the value of the assets but they also need input from IS on what is feasible technically to guard specific assets. For example, the company has alerted all its high-profile clients about the possibility of denial-of-service attacks. The bigger and more well-known the company and its Web site, the more it needs to be prepared for such attacks by having the technology and plans in place to identify and deal with any attacks when they occur. Management warns, "If you have a determined adversary, they are going to keep trying until they get you."

The company has found that business people do understand security when it is related to money. They understand that they, not the technicians, are the ones who need to justify security expenses because only they understand the worth of protecting different kinds of information. For example, they understand that protecting Web servers that contain public information requires keeping the servers from crashing. That type of protection costs less than safeguarding servers that house proprietary company or confidential client information, because those servers need to protect the data from prying eyes as well. ∎

Security's Five Pillars

Five pillars make up today's security techniques, says RSA:[6]

1. *Authentication:* verifying the authenticity of users
2. *Identification:* identifying users to grant them appropriate access
3. *Privacy:* protecting information from being seen
4. *Integrity:* keeping information in its original form
5. *Nonrepudiation:* preventing parties from denying actions they have taken.

Authentication. It means verifying someone's authenticity: They are who they say they are. People can authenticate themselves to a system in three basic ways, says RSA: by something they know, something they have, and something they are. "Something they know" really means "something only they know," generally a password or a mother's maiden name, for example. "Something they have" means "in your possession." In computer security, one possibility is a "token" that generates a code a user enters into the computer to gain access to, say, an e-mail system. Users just have to remember not to lose the token. Or they may have a digital certificate, discussed shortly. And "something they are" generally means a physical characteristic, such as a fingerprint, retinal scan, or voice print. These characteristics fall under the area called biometrics.

Each type of user authentication has its strengths and weaknesses, so RSA recommends choosing two of the three, called two-factor authentication.

Identification. It is the process of issuing and verifying access privileges. RSA says it is like being issued a driver's license. First, you must show proof of identity to get your driver's license. Once you receive your license, it becomes your proof of identity, but it also states your driving privileges (drive an automobile but not a truck or a bus). So identification is like being certified to be able to do certain things.

In the Internet world, identification is moving toward application-level security, says RSA, that is, authentication for each application. It requires users to sign on for each application, which many feel is a large burden. Single sign-on is an approach some companies are taking.

Data Privacy and Data Integrity. These mean keeping information from being seen (privacy) or changed (integrity). Both are especially important when information travels through the Internet because it is a public space where interception is more possible.

The most common method of protecting data is encryption. The most common is public key encryption.

Nonrepudiation. It means neither party in a sale or communication of sensitive information can later deny that the transaction or information exchange took place. Nonrepudiation services can prove that someone was the actual sender and the other the receiver; no imposter was involved on either side.

Countermeasures

The trend in computer security is toward defining security policies and then centrally managing and enforcing those policies via security management products and services, or policy-based management. Hence, for example, a user authenticates to a network once, and then a "rights based system" gives that user access only to the systems to which he has been given the rights. A finance employee might have the rights to company finance records but a manufacturing employee might not.

Figure 8-7, from the CSI/FBI survey, shows the types of security technologies used by the 643 security managers in the 2000 survey. All of them used antivirus software, 93 percent had access control, and 90 percent used physical security around data and network centers.

To explain a bit more about countermeasures, following are three techniques used by companies to protect themselves: firewalls, public key encryption, and virtual private networks.

Firewalls.   This hardware or software controls access between networks. It is widely used to create intranets and extranets, which only employees and authorized business partners can access. Typically implemented on a router, firewalls perform their job by (1) packet filtering to block "illegal" traffic, which is defined by the security policy, or (2) using a proxy server, which acts as an intermediary between, say, the Internet and the intranet. Proxy servers can look deeper into traffic than do packet filters, which just look at the header information on each packet. But proxy servers are slower. Some products do both. Without policy management, says RSA, firewalls may not be effective because they may just be treated as stand-alone devices. The most effective security programs create layers of security.

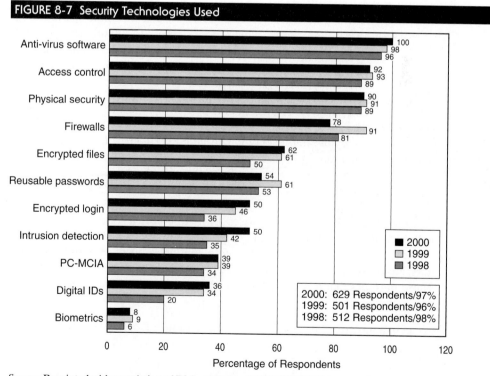

FIGURE 8-7 Security Technologies Used

Source: Reprinted with permission of Richard Power, "2000 CSI/FBI Computer Crime and Security Survey," Computer Security Institute, San Francisco, CA, www.gosci.com, Spring 2000.

Public Key Encryption. This technology is a powerful countermeasure for reaching all five goals of authentication, identification, privacy, integrity, and nonrepudiation, but it requires significant administration. The solution has been to subscribe to a public key management service. This third party issues two keys for a person and then manages the keys. One key is the private key; it is meant to be kept secret and is used by the person to both send encrypted messages and receive encrypted messages. The second key is the public key; it is made public and can thus be used by anyone to send an encrypted message to the person with the private key or to read messages from that person, and know that the sender is not an imposter.

Authentication is accomplished through a digital certificate, which is a type of online identity. As RSA explains, it is a special file issued by a public key system that attests to the authenticity of the bearer. Proof that it is legitimate occurs when that person's public key properly decodes a message sent from that person. An entire industry has grown up around public key technology.

Virtual Private Networks. Most offices now have a local ISP, so no matter where they are located in the world, the least costly way to create companywide networking is to utilize IP and the Internet. However, the Internet is not secure because, for one thing, none of the TCP/IP protocols authenticates the communicating parties.

One approach to security has been to obtain a virtual private network (VPN) from a CLEC or ISP. A VPN runs over a private IP network, so it is more affordable than leased lines, and it is secure. VPNs use "tunneling" technology and encryption to keep data secure as it is transmitted.

Tunneling creates a temporary connection between a remote computer and the CLEC's or ISP's local data center, which blocks access to anyone trying to intercept messages sent over that link. Encryption scrambles the message before it is sent, using an encryption algorithm, and then decodes it at the receiving end. While in transit, it cannot be read or changed; hence, it is protected.

VPNs can be used in three ways, according to PricewaterhouseCoopers.[7]

1. ***Remote access VPNs*** give remote employees a way to access an enterprise's intranet securely by dialing a specific ISP, generally a large one with local telephone numbers in many cities. The ISP establishes a secure tunnel through its network to the corporate network, where the user can access e-mail and the intranet. This option offloads network management to the ISP, something most IS executives want to do.
2. ***Remote office VPNs*** give enterprises a way to create a secure private network with remote offices. The ISP's VPN equipment encrypts all transmissions.
3. ***Extranet VPNs*** give enterprises a way to conduct e-business with trading partners, advisers (such as legal firms), suppliers, alliance partners, and customers. These partners dial a specific ISP, which then establishes a secure link to the extranet.

As an example of using a VPN, consider Plymouth Rock Assurance Corporation.[8]

CASE EXAMPLE

PLYMOUTH ROCK ASSURANCE CORPORATION

Plymouth Rock Assurance Corporation (PRAC), with headquarters in Boston, Massachusetts, sells personal automobile insurance through some 165 independent agents throughout the state. The company wanted to create an extranet, Agent Web, where an agent could transact business with PRAC: create an insurance policy, submit a claim against a policy, check on an existing policy and claims made against it, and so on.

The two main issues were to ensure that communications between the agents and the Web site were both secure and fast. Without secure links, the agents said they would not use Agent Web, and PRAC did not want agents to have to wait for page downloads.

PRAC considered using frame relay to get the speed, but that technology turned out to be more expensive than they wanted. So they looked into DSL, which would provide 20 times the speed of a regular dial-up modem. They also looked into creating a VPN from the local sites to the Agent Web site to ensure secure transmission of data back and forth.

They settled on using the services of HarvardNet, a local Massachusetts provider of Internet services, which offers a DSL-based VPN service. PRAC chose HarvardNet because its geographic "footprint" closely matched the geographic locations of the independent agents. Furthermore, the cost of connecting up these agents' offices with DSL was just one-third of the cost of frame relay. HarvardNet's RemoteConnect VPN service would also allow PRAC to extend its secure corporate network to all these remote independent agent sites. Creating the DSL-based VPN provides both the subsecond response time and the secure communication links PRAC wanted to provide to the agents to streamline claims processing and reduce paper.

In addition, PRAC decided to turn over all the operations of Agent Web to HarvardNet, so HarvardNet now hosts Agent Web and handles the VPN network management, so that PRAC's IT department only needs to focus on the applications on Agent Web. ∎

Gradually, information security has become an important management topic, and it has no clear-cut answers. It is too costly to provide all the security a company wants, and performing security checks on packets takes a lot of processor power, which can slow down performance. Even with world-class technical security, management needs to make sure all employees follow security policies because companies are only as safe as their weakest link. In fact, that weakest link could be a supplier or contractor who has secure access to a company's systems, yet has poor security of its own. The final thought: Security is as much a human problem as a technical problem.

DISASTER RECOVERY FOR DISTRIBUTED SYSTEMS

Although information systems are just one part of a company operation, they have become a crucial part. Thus, disaster recovery for information systems is imperative. Disaster recovery practitioners agree that (1) contingency planning needs to be an integral part of doing business, and (2) commitment of resources to a disaster recovery process must be based on an assessment by top management of cost versus risk. Companies essentially have two options for disaster recovery—use internal or external resources.

Using Internal Resources

Organizations that rely on internal resources for disaster recovery generally see this planning as a normal part of system planning and development. They cost-justify backup processing and telecom based on company needs during foreseeable emergencies. We found companies using the following approaches to backing up their computer systems, data, and communication links with company resources:

- Multiple data centers
- Distributed processing
- Backup telecom facilities
- Local area networks

Multiple Data Centers.   Organizations with large IT budgets have had multiple computer centers, although less so now with consolidation and outsourcing. These centers can provide at least some emergency backup for critical services. Organizations that do not have multiple data centers have backup telecom equipment and links to outside disaster recovery centers and service bureaus from their various operating sites.

For backing up data, companies create protected disk storage facilities, sometimes called direct access data storage, or "DASD farms." These farms are regularly refreshed with current operating data to speed recovery at an alternate data center. They are normally company-owned, unattended sites, and remote from the primary data center. They house disk controllers and disk drives that can be accessed either online or in batch mode.

Distributed Processing.   Other organizations use distributed processing to deal with disaster recovery. They perform critical processing locally rather than at a data center so that operations can continue uninterrupted when a disaster hits a data center. Companies that use this approach standardize hardware and applications at remote locations, so that each local processing site can provide backup for the others.

Distributed processing solutions to disaster recovery can be quite costly when data redundancy between the central and remote sites is required. Therefore, this alternative is most commonly used for applications that must continue to operate, such as order entry and financial transaction systems. Until true distributed database technology becomes available, files cannot be distributed cost effectively.

Backup Telecom Facilities.   Companies appear to be handling telecom backup in two ways: (1) by building duplicate communications facilities, and (2) by using alternate technologies that they redeploy in case of an emergency.

Depository Trust Company (DTC) of New York City is a cooperative owned by financial industry clients. It serves as a clearinghouse for the settlement of securities trades, and it provides services to the banking and brokerage industry. The company uses Sungard Disaster Recovery Services[9] facilities for processing backup. DTC operates a large telecom network, linking its users at remote sites to its data center in New York City through leased and dial-up lines. DTC is expanding its network with a complete duplicate backup communication center at an alternate location in New York City. This center includes duplicate lines, telecom switches, modems, and multiplexors that can be quickly linked to disaster recovery facilities at Sungard to keep the remote sites online if the corporate computer center becomes inoperable.

Other companies turn to alternate communication technology when their communication links fail, such as when the infamous Hinsdale fire destroyed the Hinsdale Illinois Bell Telephone Company central office switching station. The station handled 118,000 long distance lines, 30,000 data lines, and 35,000 local voice lines, reported Jeff Bozman.[10] It served as a hub for some 30 local exchanges in northeastern Illinois. The fire disrupted telephone service to the area for four weeks. Local companies used at least two alternative technologies to handle their telecommunications needs in this emergency.

Crockett[11] reported that MONY Financial Services in Syracuse, New York, switched a satellite link from its smaller San Juan, Puerto Rico, office to its large Hinsdale office by installing a very small aperture terminal (VSAT) dish on the roof. It was used to communicate via satellite to a communication hub in New York City, and from there via land lines to Syracuse. The San Juan office then instituted its own communication backup plan: using terrestrial lines to communicate to Syracuse.

Zurich Insurance Company, in Schaumburg, Illinois, used a different alternative, reported Crockett. They established a line-of-site microwave link between their headquarters office and an AT&T switching office located about two miles away. A number of companies turned to microwave to bypass the Hinsdale center. Crockett reports that 38 temporary microwave links were established either by AT&T or MCI in the Chicago area.

One way to avoid being dependent on one switching office is to have communication links to two local switching centers. This option appeared unnecessary and too expensive for many companies, until the Hinsdale fire. More recent outages, especially in New York City, have made most top executives aware of the danger of depending on one common carrier.

Local Area Networks.   Servers on one LAN can be used to backup servers for other networks. As with mainframe DASD farms, data servers used for such backup need to be refreshed on a regular basis to keep their data up-to-date. Keeping up-to-date is accomplished by linking the networks through shared cabling. Network master control programs permit designating alternate devices when primary ones fail.

Using External Resources

In many cases, a cost-versus-risk analysis may not justify committing permanent resources to contingencies; therefore, companies use the services of a disaster recovery firm. These services include:

- Integrated disaster recovery services
- Specialized disaster recovery services
- Online and off-line data storage facilities

Integrated Disaster Recovery Services. In North America, major suppliers of disaster recovery services offer multiple recovery sites interconnected by high-speed telecom lines. Services at these locations include fully operational processing facilities that are available on less-than-24-hours notice. These suppliers often have environmentally suitable storage facilities for housing special equipment for their clients.

Subscription fees for access to fully operational facilities are charged on a per-month basis. Actual use of the center is charged on a per-day basis. In addition, a fee is often charged each time a disaster is declared. Mobile facilities, with a mobile trailer containing computer equipment, can be moved to a client site and are available at costs similar to fully operational facilities. And empty warehouse space can be rented as well.

Recognizing the importance of telecom links, major disaster recovery suppliers have expanded their offerings to include smaller sites that contain specialized telecom equipment. These sites allow users to maintain telecom services when disaster recovery facilities are in use. They house control equipment and software needed to support communication lines connecting recovery sites with client sites.

Needless to say, companies now in the business of hosting corporate Web sites also handle disaster recovery for those sites.

Specialized Disaster Recovery Services. Some suppliers of backup services can accommodate mainframe clients who also need to back up midrange machines. In addition, a growing number of backup services are designed solely for midrange systems. Some will even deliver a trailer with compatible hardware and software to a client location.

Telecommunications backup has become an important consideration in many companies. In the United States, some of the regional Bell operating companies offer a type of recovery service, through network reconfiguration, where network administrators at user sites can reroute their circuits around lines with communication problems.

Other specialized telecom backup services are beginning to appear. For example, Hughes Network Systems, in Germantown, Maryland,[12] helped a company that had 49 of its pharmacies affected by the Hinsdale telephone switching station fire. Within 72 hours, Hughes installed a temporary network of VSATs at 12 sites. The 37 remaining sites had small satellite dishes installed within two weeks. Other firms offer data communications backup programs, where they will store specific data communications equipment for a customer and deliver that equipment by air to the customer's recovery site when needed.

Online and Off-Line Data Storage. Alternate locations for storage of tapes and other records have long been a part of disaster planning. Services generally consist of fire-resistant vaults with suitable temperature and humidity controls. Several suppliers offer "electronic vaulting" for organizations that need to have current data off-site at the time a disaster occurs. These suppliers use two methods to obtain current data from their clients. One method uses computer-to-computer transmission of data on a scheduled basis. The other uses dedicated equipment to capture and store data at a remote location as it is created on the client's computer. This latter method assures uninterrupted access to data from an operationally ready disaster recovery facility selected by the client.

In summary, when disaster recovery needs do not shape the architecture of an enterprise's computer systems, the cost of reconfiguring the systems to provide the needed redundancy and backup can be prohibitive. In these cases, external backup alternatives may be a more cost-effective form of "insurance." For e-business, however, mere backup capability does not suffice. Disaster recovery must be an integral part of the system design because companies need immediate roll-over to backup facilities when operations are interrupted.

To illustrate the use of disaster recovery facilities, consider the case of Household International.

CASE EXAMPLE

HOUSEHOLD INTERNATIONAL

Household International, with headquarters in Prospect Heights, Illinois, is a major provider of consumer lending, banking, insurance, and commercial financial services in the United States. The company also provides similar services in the United Kingdom, Canada, and Australia through subsidiaries.

The core of its consumer finance business is serviced by some 700 consumer lending branches and 60 bank branches throughout the United States. Household is also a large credit card issuer in the United States and operates a major credit card service center in Salinas, California. Household's major data center is in its corporate offices. The center is linked to the branch network via leased lines, with regional connections to more than 10,000 remote devices and terminals.

Typical of large financial services institutions, Household justified its disaster recovery planning based upon legal and regulatory requirements and the need to maintain uninterrupted customer service. The centralized design of its data network simplified recovery planning but made the headquarters data center critical to recovery.

The company established a full-time staff to prepare, maintain, and "exercise" (test out) disaster recovery plans. After exploring several alternatives, including adding reserve processing capacity to their network, Household decided to rely on Comdisco Disaster Recovery Services.[13] Comdisco is a major supplier of alternate site data processing services in North America.

Services provided by Comdisco include use of facilities at one or more of their several recovery centers throughout North America, and "hot site" equipment and software to provide immediate operational support on request. In addition, Comdisco provides technical assistance in disaster planning, testing, and the use

(Case Continued)

of recovery centers. Household viewed the monthly cost of these services as their most economical recovery alternative.

After six months, all critical banking applications had been tested at the alternate site and contingency procedures had been developed for the bank branches. Household had also begun developing contingency plans for the consumer lending operation and testing application programs at the alternate site. In addition, they had begun developing business recovery priorities and operating procedures for end users.

In the midst of this effort, nature intervened. At 9:00 A.M. on a Friday, after meeting with key personnel, Household declared a disaster. More than 9 inches of rain had fallen on the Chicago area in 12 hours. Widespread flooding had closed major highways, leaving thousands of homes and businesses without power or telephone service. A retention pond at corporate headquarters had overflowed, causing an overnight runoff into the basement of the headquarters building where the data center was located. By 10:30 A.M. the water had risen to 31 inches—9 inches above the 22-inch false floor—and it rose further before the disaster ended.

With telephone lines down in the area and the company PBX out-of-service, the recovery coordinator relied on plans made early in the year. Computer operations were transferred to the Comdisco alternate site in Wood Dale, Illinois, which was 20 miles away. Fortunately, he made his call to Comdisco early; other clients who called later were relocated to sites as far away as New Jersey—some 800 miles (1,300 kilometers) away. Because five Chicago area businesses declaring disasters, Comdisco's hot site resources in Illinois were quickly saturated.

At the backup site, work began on restoring vital bank and check processing systems. Critical processing for most bank branches resumed within 24 hours. Teller systems at branches used local computers, so they operated without interruption. However, online information on the current status of customer accounts was not available until the following Monday.

After pumping out the flooded data center, the data processing staff found extensive damage to disk drive motors and circuit boards below the high water mark. However, they were able to quickly restore the communication control units. They were then able to use these units as the links for all communications between the backup site computers and the remote terminals installed in the branches. Their local telephone company used a central switch to establish a link between the disaster recovery alternate site and the Household home office.

By the third day, all the important work that had been moved to key Household locations was up and running, and communication links among these locations were working. Communication links to all offices were available by the sixth day.

A few days after the disaster, more than 220 analysts and programmers were assigned to work at the alternate site on a 24-hour schedule. The disaster recovery coordinator arranged for special food service, dressing facilities, and rest areas at the alternate site. And workstations were created using rented furniture and equipment.

Special meetings were held with senior management to establish recovery priorities for the consumer lending operation. Daily meetings, chaired by the executive vice president of information

(Case Continued)

systems, were attended by nearly all managers and vendors affected by the disaster—some 40 to 50 people in all. These meetings became the day-to-day means for reporting status, handling special problems, and developing recovery schedules. The meetings turned out to be the best means for communicating quickly and making decisions using the existing organization. The meetings lasted several hours each day and covered a wide range of topics. Thus, no special organizational structure was used for managing the disaster, however the disaster recovery manager played a key role in coordinating the recovery.

The company left the backup site on the fifteenth day. Eighteen days after the disaster, normal operations had been fully restored.

Lessons Learned

Household learned six lessons from this disaster, which it offers as recommendations to others.

1. Consider the risks of a natural disaster in selecting a data center location. Areas with high exposure to flooding, heavy rainfall, fire hazards, or earthquakes will be more costly to protect against these risks.
2. Create a plan to return to the primary site after the disaster. This plan is just as important as a plan to move to an alternate site.
3. Do not expect damaged equipment, disks, and tapes to always be replaced in kind or restored to original condition. Therefore, make plans for new configurations, and regularly monitor sources of equipment

and supplies to assure early delivery of replacements.
4. Test hot-site resources under *full workload conditions* to ensure that sufficient computer capacity is available to meet high priority needs.
5. Plan for alternate telecommunications routing for multiple-site operations during a disaster. Household's original telecommunications disaster recovery plan called for key sites around the country to handle the headquarters processing load in case of a home office disaster. But the quick recovery of the communication control units at the headquarters data center allowed Household to use an alternate plan: to rely mainly on processing at the nearby disaster recovery site. Thus, for 16 days they operated with both the headquarters center and the disaster recovery center. The other key Household centers handled mainly their normal work, but their computers were available if needed.
6. Maintain critical data at the alternate site or at another nearby location for fast system recovery.

Household has used its experience to refine and complete the plans started before the rainstorm. In addition, Comdisco services have been extended to other subsidiaries under a corporatewide contract. In retrospect, key participants believe that the early restoration of the headquarters computer center, the existence of computer and telecommunications backup procedures, staff who were familiar with the backup plans, and use of normal management channels were all important in their rapid recovery. ∎

CONCLUSION

The subject of managing computer operations is, perhaps surprisingly, at an all-time high because of the emergence of e-business and its increasing use of outsourcing, and the news-grabbing viruses and attacks on major Web sites. Outsourcing, security, disaster recovery—all are important operational issues. As enterprises increasingly rely on computing and telecom for working closely with others, they open themselves up to more threats by electronic means. As we noted in the security section, one security manager would not call the Internet a bad neighborhood, but he would watch his back. That attitude increasingly means being vigilant to outside threats, just as outsourcing means learning to work with "outsiders." In short, the view of operations is shifting from managing inward to managing outward, on all fronts.

QUESTIONS AND EXERCISES

Review Questions

1. What is the main shift in the operations viewpoint?
2. What does the operations budget at Congleton's company include?
3. What are three solutions to operations problems, according to Congleton?
4. What have Y2K and the Internet done for computer operations?
5. How did Microsoft manage its special OEM webcast?
6. How thoroughly are CIOs expected to investigate outsourcing?
7. What are the driving forces of outsourcing, according to Bergstein?
8. What are the five customer-vendor relationships?
9. What are IT outsourcing, transitional outsourcing, best-of-breed outsourcing, shared services, business process outsourcing, e-business outsourcing, and application service providers?
10. What management elements has Kodak put in place to manage its outsourcing relationships?
11. What is supplier development?
12. According to RSA, what approaches do hackers use?
13. What ways does the Internet Services Company "check its locks"?
14. Describe the five pillars of information security.
15. According to PricewaterhouseCoopers, what are three uses of virtual private networks?
16. What internal disaster recovery alternatives are used by companies?
17. What external disaster recovery services are available to companies?
18. What lessons did Household International learn from its disaster?

Discussion Questions

1. Outsourcing offloads a burdensome technical responsibility and allows management to focus on its core business. Outsourcing strips a company of an important core competence—IT know-how. Which statement do you agree with? Why?
2. Security is such an important area that every employee should be required to carry around a security token that generates a new password every time they log on. Security threats are overblown; imposing on employees to carry a security token is too much to ask. Discuss both sides of this issue.
3. The Internet provides all the redundant routing and alternate sites an enterprise needs. It need not contract with a backup and recovery firm as Household International did. Present arguments against this belief.

Exercises

1. Read a few articles about outsourcing. What did you learn about outsourcing that is not mentioned in this chapter? Relay them to the class.
2. Read several articles on Internet security. Present new information to your class.
3. Visit a company in your local community. Learn about their disaster recovery plans. Which threats are they aimed at? Which threats are not dealt with? What are they doing about Internet security?

REFERENCES

1. Farber/Lachance Inc., www.farberlachance.com

2. Mel Bergstein, DiamondCluster Int'l., Chicago, IL.

3. Sourcing Interests Group, www.sourcinginterests.org.

   a. McNurlin, Barbara, *Business Process Outsourcing Research Report,* 1998.

   b. McNurlin, Barbara, *Managing Outsourcing Results Research Report,* 1997.

   c. McNurlin, Barbara, *Implementing and Managing High-Impact Strategic Sourcing,* 1999.

4. Gartner, 56 Top Gallant Road, Stamford, CT 06904; www.gartner.com.

   a. Terdiman, Rita, in speech to Sourcing Interests Group.

   b. Flint, David, *Security in an Online World,* Executive Programs (EXP) report, May 2000.

5. Power, Richard, "2000 CSI/FBI Computer Crime and Security Survey," Computer Security Institute, 600 Harrison St., San Francisco, CA 94107; www.gosci.com; Spring 2000.

6. "A Guide to Security Technologies," RSA Security Inc., Bedford, MA 01730, www.rsasecurity.com; 1999.

7. *Technology Forecast: 2000, From Atoms to Systems: A Perspective on Technology,* PricewaterhouseCoopers Technology Center, at www.pwc-global.com/tech-forecast, April 2000.

8. Washburn, Mark, CEO of HarvardNet, in a speech at Networld+Interop 2000.

9. Sungard, www.sungard.com.

10. Bozman, J. "Illinois Phone Effort Puts Data Links Last," *Computerworld,* May 23, 1988, pp. 101.

11. Crockett, B., "Users Turned to Satellite, Microwave Links After Fire," *Network World,* June 27, 1988, pp. 31–32.

12. Hughes Network Systems, www.hns.com.

13. Comdisco Disaster Recovery Services at www.comdisco.com.

PART

III

MANAGING TRADITIONAL SYSTEM DEVELOPMENT

Part III of this book consists of two chapters that deal with developing enterprise-based systems through traditional system development. As noted in the following figure, system development has traditionally been aimed at procedure-based work. Procedure-based activities are large-volume transactions where each transaction has a relatively low cost or value. The activities, which consist mainly of handling data, are well defined, and the principle measure for gauging their performance is efficiency. Information systems were, in most cases, first built to automate this kind of work, beginning initially with accounting, and then progressing into manufacturing, administration, sales and marketing, and so on. Development of these systems has been handled by IS professionals.

In Chapter 9 we describe the foundations of system development, which are the technologies and methodologies that have formed the basis of today's approaches. Then we discuss two areas of current importance: system integration and Internet-based systems. We conclude the chapter by discussing project management—the underpinning of successful large IT projects.

In Chapter 10 we discuss a number of management issues that surround traditional system development: IT staffing, managing the change that surrounds system implementation, what to do about legacy systems, and measuring the benefits of systems.

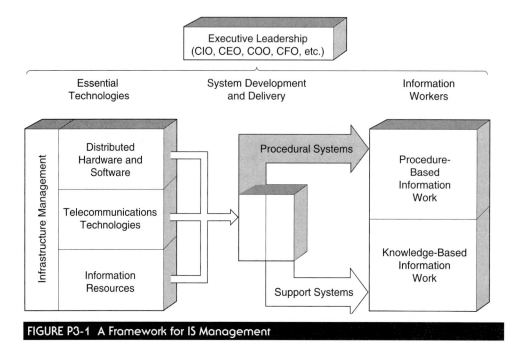

FIGURE P3-1 A Framework for IS Management

CHAPTER

9

TECHNOLOGIES FOR DEVELOPING SYSTEMS

INTRODUCTION

One of the toughest jobs in information systems management is developing new systems. It seems to be an area in which Murphy's Law—if anything can go wrong, it will—reigns supreme. In spite of the complexity of system development, the information

279

systems field has made significant progress in improving the process of building systems. The traditional approach, with variations, of course, appears in many textbooks and professional books. Two of the first books to describe a life cycle approach for developing systems were published in 1956 and 1957, both written by Richard Canning.[1]

During the 1970s, a relatively well-defined process, called the *system development life cycle,* emerged. This life cycle improved the development process significantly. However, continued backlogs, cost overruns, and performance shortfalls underscored the difficulty and complexity of the system development process.

The 1980s saw progress in more friendly languages and automation of portions of development, such as code generation. Yet, maintenance continued to eat up 70 to 80 percent of the system development resources in most companies. The 1990s began with the promise of significantly increasing developer productivity and reducing maintenance by relying more on packages, and by building systems by linking together components. The business process reengineering movement spawned the growth of integrated enterprise systems and the widespread adoption of enterprise resource planning (ERP) systems. Then, all of a sudden, in the late 1990s, e-business and Internet-based systems appeared.

The Internet brought the need for faster system development and integrated enterprise systems, that is, systems that pulled various aspects of the enterprise together. New tools for rapid development became available; they relied on reusable components and open systems architectures. As a result, application *development* projects became application *integration* projects, integrating prebuilt components. The late 1990s saw the beginning of a new industry, application service providers (ASPs), which represent the Internet version of outsourcing applications.

Technologies and tools have changed, but a great deal of systems work remains to be done, in-house or outsourced. And, as yet, no "silver bullets" have appeared on the horizon. In this chapter, we review the evolution of system development to provide an understanding of the underlying principles.

FOUNDATIONS OF SYSTEM DEVELOPMENT

In the early years, system development was considered a "craft," subject mostly to the whim and creativity of systems analysts. In the 1970s, structured system development emerged to make the process more standard and efficient. It was characterized by the following elements:

- Hand coding in a third-generation language (such as COBOL)
- A "structured programming" development methodology
- An automated project management system
- A database management system
- A mix of online and batch applications in the same system
- Development of mostly mainframe applications
- Programming by professional programmers only
- Various automated, but not well-integrated, software tools
- A well-defined sign-off process for system delivery
- User participation mainly in requirements definition and installation phases.

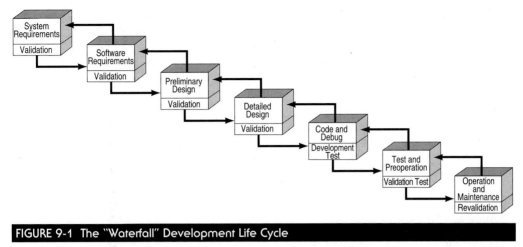

FIGURE 9-1 The "Waterfall" Development Life Cycle

Source: Barry Boehm, *Software Engineering Economics* (Upper Saddle River, NJ: Prentice Hall, 1981).

This development approach supposedly followed the famous "waterfall" approach, shown in Figure 9-1. However, says Bob Glass,[2] a well-known author in software development, this unidirectional waterfall was much touted but rarely used. Development did not proceed in a straight line from requirements through operation; a lot of backtracking and iteration occurred. Instead, says Glass, developers really always followed the spiral approach, also generally attributed to Barry Boehm and shown in Figure 9-2.

Structured Development

Structured development methodologies accompanied this system development life cycle and were meant to handle the complexities of system design and development by fostering more discipline, higher reliability and fewer errors, and more efficient use of the resources.

More Discipline.   By establishing standards for processes and documentation, the structured methodologies attempted to eliminate personal variations. At first they

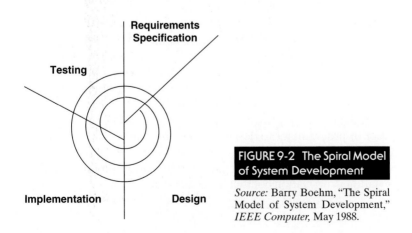

FIGURE 9-2 The Spiral Model of System Development

Source: Barry Boehm, "The Spiral Model of System Development," *IEEE Computer,* May 1988.

seemed to threaten programmers' creativity, but their discipline did increase productivity and permit developers to deal with greater complexity. The complexity was handled through successive decomposition of system components, coupled with preferred practices for conducting analysis, design, and construction. The result was a more disciplined system development process.

Higher Reliability and Fewer Errors.   The structured methodologies recognized that mistakes of both omission and commission were likely at all stages of system building. One of the main tools for coping with this tendency was (and still is) inspections, performed at every development stage and at every level of system decomposition. The goal has been to catch errors as early as possible. The methodologies also recognized that iteration would be required to redo parts of a system as mistakes were uncovered.

More Efficient Use of Resources.   The project management approaches usually included in the structured methodologies contributed to cost savings, increased productivity, and better allocation of human resources. By imposing a time and cost control system, the classic approach decreased (but did not eliminate) the tendency for system development efforts to incur cost and time overruns.

Fourth-Generation Languages

In the early 1980s, two major developments occurred. One was the availability of fourth-generation languages (4GLs). Previously, developers only had third-generation languages, such as COBOL and PL/1. The advent of 4GLs allowed end users to develop some programs, or allowed programmers to use a different development method: prototyping. Formerly, system requirements were fully defined before design and construction began. With prototyping, development was iterative: specify as much as possible, prototype it, try using the prototype, refine the prototype based on this experience, and so on until the specifications were fully defined via the prototype.

Both 4GLs and prototyping have proven to be important underpinnings for today's application development world.

Fourth-generation languages are really more than computer languages, they are programming environments. The major components or characteristics of 4GLs are listed in Figure 9-3.

The heart of a 4GL is its database management system (DBMS) for storing formatted data records as well as unformatted text, graphics, voice, and perhaps even video. Almost as important is the data dictionary, which stores the *definitions* of the various kinds of data. The language programmers and users use is nonprocedural, which means that the commands can occur in any order, rather than the sequence required by the computer. The commands can be used interactively to retrieve data from files or a database in an ad-hoc manner or to print a report (using a report generator). The screen painter allows a user or programmer to design a screen by simply typing in the various data input field names and the locations where they are to appear, or by choosing graphics off a menu. Some 4GLs include statistical packages for calculating time series, averages, standard deviations, correlation coefficients, and so on.

FIGURE 9-3 Features and Functions of Fourth-Generation Languages

- Database management system
- Data dictionary
- Nonprocedural language
- Interactive query facilities
- Report generator
- Selection and sorting
- Screen formatter
- Word processor and text editor
- Graphics
- Data analysis and modeling tools
- Library of macros
- Programming interface
- Reusable code
- Software development library
- Backup and recovery
- Security and privacy safeguards
- Links to other DBMS

Software Prototyping

According to *Webster's 20th Century Dictionary,* the term *prototype* has three possible meanings: (1) It is an original or model after which anything is formed, (2) it is the first thing or being of its kind, and (3) it is a pattern, an exemplar, or an archetype.

J. David Naumann and A. Milton Jenkins[3] believe the second definition best fits the prototypes used in software development because such prototypes are a first attempt at a design that generally is later extended and enhanced. Franz Edelman, a pioneer in the use of software prototyping, described the process of software prototyping as "a quick and inexpensive process of developing and testing a trial balloon."

A software prototype is a *live, working system:* it is not just an idea on paper. Therefore it can be evaluated by the designer and eventual users through its use in an operational mode. It performs actual work; it does not just simulate that work. *It may become the actual production system,* or it may be replaced by a conventionally coded production system. Its purpose is *to test out assumptions,* about users' requirements, about the design of the application, or perhaps even about the logic of a program.

A prototype is a software system that *is created quickly*—often within hours, days, or weeks—rather than months or years. With only conventional programming languages, such as COBOL, it was much too expensive to create both a prototype and a production version. So only production systems were developed. With end user tools, people can get prototypes up and running quickly. The prototype *is relatively inexpensive to build* because the language creates much of the code.

Prototyping *is an iterative process.* It begins with a simple prototype that performs only a few of the basic functions. Through use of the prototype, system designers or end users discover new requirements and refinements to incorporate in each succeeding version. Each version performs more of the desired functions and in an increasingly efficient manner.

To demonstrate a dramatic use of both a 4GL and prototyping, we describe work at Santa Fe Railroad in the early 1980s. Their use of a 4GL was unique because it took the opposite approach of just about everyone else. Most companies used 4GLs for management reports and end user applications, that is, as a sidelight for their operational systems. Santa Fe, on the other hand, used the 4GL for their operational system, and left the management reporting in COBOL. Their approach, using today's tools, would be just as unique. The reasons for their unusual decision are made clear in the case example.

CASE EXAMPLE

SANTA FE RAILROAD

The Atchison, Topeka and Santa Fe Railway Company, with headquarters in Topeka, Kansas, had 12,000 miles of railroad track, running from Chicago, Illinois, to California. They had 2,000 locomotives, 52,000 freight cars, and 9,000 truck trailers.

In the early 1980s, many of their trains were reaching their destinations without the accompanying paperwork, which was against Interstate Commerce Commission rules, and the railroad began receiving heavy fines for the missing paperwork. The railroad had to write a new waybill system in a hurry, but the systems department could not do the job using the traditional development methods. And no other railroad's application system was appropriate for Santa Fe, because much of their business was in "piggybacking"— loading two truck trailers on a flat car and shipping them to their destination. Then Santa Fe heard about Mapper, a fourth-generation language from Unisys. Because it appeared to be the only alternative, a freight scheduler and several clerical supervisors were taught Mapper and given the assignment of automating the paperwork for the huge Corwith piggybacking yard in Chicago.

In adopting Mapper, Santa Fe Railway made three significant programming decisions:

1. Create an operational system in a 4GL using prototyping.
2. Teach operational railroad employees to program, rather than teach programmers the intricacies of railroad operations.
3. Create generic databases that would remain stable and be used throughout the company.

The group started by creating the generic databases, with standard data definitions, formats, and functions. The basic

(Case Continued)

waybill system for the Corwith yard was created in several months' time, followed by a yard inventory system, and then a full-blown trailer-on-flat-car system. The complete operations expediter system (OX), which consisted of these three interrelated systems, was put into operation in 18 months. The system handled the day-to-day railroad operations and sent subsets of data to the corporate database for corporate marketing, accounting, and operating summary purposes. Later, as the system expanded—with the addition of more switching yards—new databases were created for each yard. Each database used the same generic data definitions, formats, and functions. The Mapper database grew large, but was composed of many small databases, identical for each yard. Mapper could handle this structure; in all it processed 1.7 million transactions daily.

With the adoption of Mapper, Santa Fe divided their information systems into two parts—the operational part and the corporate database part. The operational part was converted to Mapper, while the corporate database was kept in COBOL because the railroad had a large investment in IBM programs that they did not want to replace. Interestingly, the two parts had quite different characteristics. The IBM shop had 116 application programmers, 44 systems support people,

and 80 people in operations, for a total of 240. The Unisys center, which ran the railroad operations using Mapper, had only 35 application programmers, 11 systems support people, and 32 people in operations, for a total of 78.

Although the two shops performed an equivalent amount of work, the Unisys shop was more cost effective because it only needed one-third the people. The vice president of IS attributed the difference to Mapper. It required less support, but it required about twice as much hardware. In total, the overall costs for the use of Mapper were one-half that of COBOL applications.

Santa Fe IS management also believed the Mapper programmers were four to eight times more productive than the COBOL programmers. Furthermore, system problems could often be handled by operational people. They controlled the system, so essentially no operational complaints reached the IS department.

In retrospect, the vice president of IS believed a 4GL can have a *significant* impact on a company, but only if it was used to automate daily operations, not merely as a tool for generating reports. The operational world was the most volatile part of the railroad, so that was where Santa Fe wanted the fastest and most versatile programming. ■

Computer-Aided Software Engineering

Even though the structured programming and analysis techniques of the 1970s brought more discipline to the process of developing large and complex software applications, they required *tedious* attention to detail and lots of paperwork. Computer-aided software engineering (CASE) aimed to automate structured techniques and reduce this tediousness.

Definitions. At a CASE Symposium, sponsored by Digital Consulting, Inc., Carma McClure,[4] a CASE pioneer, defined CASE as any automated tool that assists in the creation, maintenance, or management of software systems. In general, a CASE environment includes:

- An information repository
- Front-end tools for planning through design
- Back-end tools for generating code
- A development workstation.

Often not included, *but implied and necessary,* are a software development methodology and a project management methodology.

An information repository. A repository forms the heart of a CASE system and is its most important element, said McClure. It stores and organizes all information needed to create, modify, and develop a software system. This information includes, for example, data structures, processing logic, business rules, source code, and project management data. Ideally, this information repository should also link to the active data dictionary used during execution so that changes in one are reflected in the other.

Front-end tools. These tools are used in the phases leading up to coding. One of the key requirements for these tools is good graphics for drawing diagrams of program structures, data entities and their relationships to each other, data flows, screen layouts, and so on. Rather than store pictorial representations, front-end tools generally store the meaning of items depicted in the diagrams. This type of storage allows a change made in one diagram to be reflected automatically in related diagrams. Another important aspect of front-end design tools is automatic design analysis, for checking the consistency and completeness of a design, often in accordance with a specific design technique.

Back-end tools. These tools generally mean code generators for automatically generating source code. A few CASE tools use a 4GL. Successful front-end CASE tools provide interfaces to not just one, but several, code generators.

Development workstation. The final component of a CASE system is a development workstation, and the more powerful the better to handle all the graphical manipulations needed in CASE-developed systems.

Timeboxing. One of the most intriguing CASE products and approaches in this timeframe is the "Timebox," which is a technique that uses CASE to guarantee delivery of a system within 120 days. Although CASE proponents would have argued that such an approach would not work with large, complex systems, which is where CASE proved to be the only alternative, IS departments now honor speed over complexity, which is why many are turning to a development technique known as rapid application development (RAD). This story illustrates a RAD technique, which is applicable today.

CASE EXAMPLE

DUPONT CABLE MANAGEMENT SERVICES

DuPont Cable Management Services was formed to manage the telephone and data wiring in DuPont's office buildings in Wilmington, Delaware. AT&T had owned and managed the wiring for DuPont's voice networks, but then responsibility passed to DuPont's corporate telecommunications group. At DuPont's Wilmington headquarters campus, cabling is complex and wiring changes are continual. The average telephone is moved one and one-half times a year. Much of the telephone moving cost is labor to find the correct cables and circuit paths.

When the cable management services group was formed, the manager realized he needed a system to maintain an inventory of every wire, telephone, modem, workstation, wiring closet connection, and other piece of telephone equipment. Technicians could then quickly locate the appropriate equipment and make the change. Although several cable management software packages were available, none could handle the scale or workload required by DuPont. The only option was to build a custom system.

The system had to be flexible because the company's telecommunications facilities would be expanding from voice to data and video. So it needed to handle new kinds of equipment. Furthermore, because cable management services was new and not unique to DuPont, the manager believed he could sell cable management services to other large companies. Therefore, the system needed to be tailorable.

Because the manager did not want to hire programmers, he decided to use DuPont Information Engineering Associates, another DuPont business service unit.

DuPont Information Engineering Associates (IEA)

IEA began selling system development services to others in the late 1980s. It had been spawned by some DuPont system developers who were using CASE. They believed they could significantly speed up development if they combined the code generator with software prototyping and project management. The resulting methodology, which was used by IEA, was called rapid iterative production prototyping, or RIPP.

Using RIPP, a development project could take as few as 120 days to complete; it had four phases.

- *Phase One: Go-Ahead.* Day One is the go-ahead day. IEA accepts a project, and the customer agrees to participate heavily in development.
- *Phase Two: System Definition.* Days 2 through 30 are spent defining the components of the system and its acceptance criteria. At the end of this phase, IEA presents the customer with a system definition and a fixed price for creating the application.
- *Phase Three: The Timebox.* The following 90 days are called a "Timebox," during which the IEA-customer

(Case Continued)

team creates design specifications, prototypes the system, and then refines the prototype and its specifications. The final prototype becomes the production system.

- *Phase 4: Installation.* On Day 120, the system is installed. The customer has three months to verify that the system does what it is supposed to do. If it doesn't, IEA will refund their money and remove the system.

Cable Management's Use of IEA

The cable management group contracted with IEA to develop the cable tracking system. After spending the first 30 days defining the scope of the project, IEA estimated that the system would require two Timeboxes to complete, or about 210 days.

During the first Timebox, IEA developed those portions that the cable management group could concisely define. During those 90 days, one cable management engineer worked full-time on the project, another worked part-time, and IEA had a project leader and two developers. The system they developed included display screens, the relational database, basic system processes, and reports.

At the end of the 90 days, IEA delivered a basic functional system, which DuPont began using. The second Timebox added features uncovered during this use. Both parties agreed this phase was ambiguous, which might affect the 90-day limitation. So they extended the project to 110 days. By that time, the development team had entered DuPont's complete wiring inventory, enhanced the basic system, and delivered a production version.

In all, the system took about nine months to develop. The department manager realized that was fast, but he did not realize how fast until he talked to other telecommunications executives who told him their firms had spent between two and three years developing cable management systems.

The cable management group was pleased with its system. It was initially used only to manage voice wiring, but has since been extended to handle data communications wiring. ∎

Client-Server Computing

In the 1990s, two developments became the major news: client-server systems and Web-based (or network-centric) development. Underlying these two trends, which continue today, is the increasing use of packages and system integration. As much as possible, companies prefer to buy a package rather than build the application in-house. To develop large applications, they "integrate" hardware and software components. For example, they buy a ready-made Web browser to become the standard access software for Web-based applications rather than write their own front-end client software. So, in both realms, the major construction method is system integration or component-based development.

Client-server systems generated a lot of excitement in the early 1990s because they promised far more flexibility than mainframe-based systems. The desktop and laptop client machines could handle graphics, animation, and video, while the servers could handle production updating. It was a clever way to meld the pizzazz of the PC world with the necessary back-end production strengths of the mainframe world, even though mainframes were not always in the picture. The following is a typical example of the allure of client-server, and how one company—MGM—developed its first client-server system.[5]

CASE EXAMPLE

MGM

Metro-Goldwyn-Mayer (MGM), the movie studio in Hollywood, has an extremely valuable asset: its library of TV shows and movies. The studio's first client-server application was built at the urging of end users to leverage this asset. The vice president of IS knew that the only way to meet the users' expectations for a multimedia, laptop-based system with a graphical interface was to employ client-server technology.

Previously, more than 26 disparate systems on PCs, minicomputers, and the corporate mainframe were used to maintain the rights to show MGM's films. As a result, it was not possible to get a consolidated, worldwide view of which films were being leased. The client-server system—the largest IS project in Hollywood at the time—collected and consolidated all data on the film library, so that MGM would know what films they have rights to license to whom.

Client-server technology was chosen because it could empower MGM's 20 worldwide film rights salespeople. They could visit the head of a cable TV network anywhere in the world with a SQL database on their laptop and built-in CD-ROM capabilities to play 20–30 second clips of their films. They could browse the laptop's inventory database to verify availability of films, and then print the licensing deal memo on the spot. Details of the deal could then be transmitted to headquarters when convenient. Only a client-server system would provide this flexibility.

The System's Three-Level Architecture

The system's architecture had three layers. At the core was an AS/400, which acted as the central processor for the database that contains descriptions of 1,700 TV shows and movies, an index, their availability in different regions, license time periods, status of bills, and so forth. MGM deliberately chose a tried and tested rights licensing software package to manage the database because it provided the needed processing, but it did not support graphical interfaces, laptops, or decision support. So MGM surrounded the package with the

(Case Continued)

most-tested technology possible for the client-server components. In fact, wherever possible, MGM minimized technical risk by using proven products.

The second layer was an HP 9000 server, which contained data and processing, but no presentation software. The Unix front-end was built using PowerBuilder. In one hour with PowerBuilder, developers could do eight to ten hours of COBOL-equivalent work.

The third layer was the client machines, either desktop or laptop. They contained local processing, local databases, and presentation software. The laptops also had a database for the salespeople. They would upload and download information from their laptops via dial-up lines.

The premier skill required in this environment was systems integration, where the developers needed both hardware and software expertise, encompassing Unix and NT, PowerBuilder and SQL Windows.

The Development Environment

Even though partnering was always possible in the mainframe era, it was mandatory with client-server computing. With tools like PowerBuilder, and a development life cycle that relied on prototyping, developers had to constantly interact with users. They could not seclude themselves for months. Moreover,

client-server teams had no boss. The users and developers were equal; neither told the other what to do.

So the role of IS at MGM changed from system development and delivery to one of cooperating and partnering. This change required a huge cultural shift in the roles and attitudes of the IS staff. Developers who formerly buried themselves in code had to conduct meetings and work side-by-side with users. In short, they had to learn people (interpersonal) skills and the business. Interestingly, the CIO felt that women had an edge because, generally speaking, they had better interpersonal skills.

With client-server systems, the hardware was cheaper than with mainframe systems, development was faster, and software support was cheaper—all by orders of magnitude. But operating costs were not as inexpensive as MGM had originally thought; they could even be more expensive than mainframe operational costs, but only by a small percentage. PCs were more expensive to operate when they were used to emulate terminals; and version control of client-server software was costly. Service and systems management were also causes for concern because they required more manual intervention. ■

These technologies—structured development, 4GLs, prototyping, CASE, and client-server systems—have all proven to be foundations of today's system development environment. So now we turn to that environment, beginning first by discussing the main method of building systems: system integration.

SYSTEM INTEGRATION

CIOs have long strived to integrate the information systems in their organizations because of the benefits of integration. However, integration is complex, expensive, and risky. Recently, competitive pressures have raised the importance of integrating business processes and, therefore, the underlying information systems. The trend away from in-house software development toward the use of off-the-shelf software has furthered the need for integration. And the growth of e-business has provided the means of integrating systems *across* organizations. Technology vendors have responded with a number of products to facilitate the integration of systems.

Three approaches to integration stand out:

1. Database management systems
2. Enterprise resource planning (ERP) systems
3. Middleware.

The database management systems approach takes a data-oriented view of integration. As discussed in Chapter 7, DBMSs allow applications to share data stored in a single or distributed database. The applications can come from a number of sources, but they employ a common DBMS.

The ERP approach, discussed in the next section, takes an application view of integration. All applications come from a single vendor and are specifically designed to communicate with each other.

The middleware approach takes a third-party approach; applications communicate with each other through third-party translation software.

Each of the three approaches has advantages and disadvantages, depending on the conditions in the enterprise. Typically, organizations use a combination of the three. Indeed, a quick look at the strategies of the vendors also reveals a mixture of the approaches. Oracle, firmly in the database management systems market, has moved toward offering enterprise applications. SAP, a major ERP vendor and long a competitor of Oracle, has modified its products to use standard DBMS, including that of Oracle. So the three approaches are not mutually exclusive.

Enterprisewide Resource Planning Systems

An enterprise resource planning (ERP) system attempts to integrate corporate systems by providing a single set of applications, from a single vendor, operating with a single database. The goal is to provide the means to integrate business departments and functions across an organization. ERP vendors offer a complete set of business applications, including order processing, human resource management, manufacturing, finance and accounting, and customer relationship management. By automating many of the tasks involved in business processes and standardizing the processes themselves, the ERP system can provide substantial payback to a company, if the system is installed properly.

Although the history of ERP implementation projects contains both successes and failures, the failures have been notable. Scott Buckhout and his colleagues[6] reported on a study of ERP implementations in companies with more than $500 million in revenues. The average cost overrun was 179 percent, and the average schedule overrun was 230 percent. Despite these overruns, the desired functionally was 59 percent below expectations, on average. Only 10 percent of the implementation projects actually finished on time and within budget; 35 percent of the projects were cancelled. Even IT companies have had problems. Dell Computer canceled its ERP project after two years and expenditures of more than $200 million.

Some of the failures can be attributed to factors common to other IS projects, such as the system's large size and complexity. But, ERP systems differ in a significant way, which is not always recognized. Because they are designed to integrate and streamline numerous business functions, ERP systems have significant implications for the way a firm organizes and operates. Many failures result from too much attention being given to the technical aspects of the ERP system and too little attention being given to the organizational impacts.

An ERP system contains a model of the business that reflects assumptions about the way the business operates. The vendor makes these assumptions and designs the ERP to reflect the vendor's understanding of business processes in general. As a result, the business model imbedded in the ERP system may be different from the way the customer actually operates. Even though the ERP system can be customized to some degree, configuring the system entails compromises. The company must balance the way it wants to operate with the way the system wants the company to operate.

In order to realize the benefits of an ERP system—integrated systems and integrated business processes—a company must therefore change their organizational structure and culture. From his extensive studies of ERP implementations, Thomas Davenport[7] stresses that companies that have derived the greatest benefits have been those that viewed the ERP system (he prefers the term *enterprise system, ES*) primarily in strategic and organizational terms, not in technical terms; they "stressed the enterprise not the system." He recommends therefore that before implementation decisions are made, managers need to ask the following questions: "How might an ES strengthen our competitive advantages? How might it erode them? What will be the system's effect on our organization and culture? Do we need to extend the system across all our functions, or should we implement only certain modules? What other alternatives, if any, for information management might suit us better than an ES?"

As an example of a successful implementation of ERP, consider Colgate-Palmolive.

CASE EXAMPLE

COLGATE-PALMOLIVE

Colgate-Palmolive Company is a 190-year-old consumer products leader. In the mid 1990s, they faced a competitive crisis. In North America, their sales of personal care products dropped 12 percent and their operating profits dropped 26 percent. They used a decentralized structure, with national or regional control in more than 200 counties. This structure produced independent operations that were expensive to coordinate, slow to respond to market changes, and a constraint on company growth. Management needed to develop new products, reduce product delivery cycles, and reduce the cost of operations.

Their vision was to abandon their decentralized structure and become a truly global company, with an integrated business environment and standardized business processes. Their first step toward this vision was to integrate their supply chain in 80 countries and distribution to 200 countries. The goal was to reduce the annual cost of the supply chain by $150 million and standardize business processes. But a key element to achieving this integration was a global ERP system.

After setting up a prototype environment in the United States, Colgate was convinced that the SAP R/3 modules for sales and distribution, materials management, finance, and human resources would provide the functionality and flexibility they needed worldwide. They also decided on Oracle's relational DBMS and a Sun hardware platform running the Solaris

operating system. The current network has 270 servers, 11 terabits of data storage, and can support 3,000 concurrent users accessing the network from PCs around the world. With installations in Latin America scheduled to be completed in 2001, the global ERP implementation will have taken five years and $430 million.

The company quickly met its goals, realizing savings of $50 million in 1997 and $100 million in 1998. These savings were invested into creating and marketing new products, including the successful Target toothpaste, which allowed Colgate to regain the number one market position for toothpaste in the United States that they had lost 34 years earlier. By 1999, the company had reduced the product delivery cycle by more than 60 percent. Integration allowed regional cooperation on purchasing, resulting in larger contracts to fewer suppliers, which saved the company $150 million between 1996 and 1998.

Colgate also accrued substantial savings in IT operations. The old highly complex, decentralized IT infrastructure, which had many data centers and local applications, was streamlined. Data centers around the world were closed, from 75 to 2. The complexity of its global data networks was also simplified. SAPs R/3 provides a standard for applications, although the core support for the applications remains with each division.

The success of Colgate's ERP project stems from senior management convincing

(Case Continued)

all the employees that the company faced a crisis that only a dramatic change in strategy and organization could solve. The need for global restructuring of strategies and operations drove the need for a global, integrated IT infrastructure. The initial focus on the supply chain led to immediate positive results, validating management's strategy and providing support for the organizational changes. Colgate was also under pressure to integrate its operations from their larger customers, who had already begun to integrate its own operations. The ERP project was actually part of a larger project to rethink and re-align Colgate's business strategies, structures, processes, and systems.

With the supply chain integrated and the IT infrastructure in place, Colgate is now moving ahead on several fronts. They are working on developing a global customer relationship management system. Management believes employees need an integrated view of customer information and activities, and that sales representatives need this information from anywhere around the world. In addition, management is working to integrate budgeting and financial planning and move Colgate into e-business. ■

Middleware

Most organizations have a wide range of applications, new and old, from a variety of vendors, running on numerous platforms. Replacing or rewriting these applications is not feasible. So one option is to employ a class of development products known as *middleware*. As its name implies, middleware is software that works between and connects applications, allowing them to share data. Without middleware, applications would have to be modified to communicate with each other, usually by adding code to each application—a risky endeavor. Middleware acts as a translator between the applications so they do not need to be changed.

As Woolfe[5] points out, middleware simplifies development by acting as the glue that binds the components together, allowing them to work together. A plethora of middleware is available, as Figure 9-4 illustrates. Some are for communicating among applications, others are for managing transactions across platforms, and still others provide general services, such as security, synchronizing timing, or software distribution.

A new type of middleware is gaining popularity among larger companies: Enterprise Application Integration (EAI) products. EAI tools typically use a message broker to transfer data between applications and add a new level of functionality that distinguishes it from other types of middleware. EAI tools allow users to define business processes and make data integration subject to rules that govern those processes. As an example, a rule might state that data moves automatically from the purchasing application to the accounts receivable application only after the appropriate person has signed off on the purchase.

FIGURE 9-4 Types of Middleware Used in Client-Server Applications

Inter-application communications facilities: Link components
- Application programming interfaces (APIs): provide a standard way of interfacing
- Remote procedure call (RPCs): enable a dialogue between two geographically dispersed applications
- Object request brokers (ORBs): allow applications or utilities to interwork in standard ways
- Message-oriented middleware (MOM): uses asynchronous message passing for interapplication communications

Transaction managers: Handle transactions across multiple platforms
- Standard query languages (SQLs): standardize the way in which databases are accessed
- TP monitors (CICS, for example): monitor online transaction processing with a database
- Two-phase commit: a protective mechanism for transactions that fail to complete successfully

Utilities: Provide general services
- Directory services: resource allocation
- Time services: timing
- Security services: encryption, and so on
- Software distribution: including configuration control

Source: Roger Woolfe, "Managing the Move to Client-Server," Wentworth Research Program (now part of Gartner Executive Programs, Stamford, CT), 1995.

Companies purchase a central module plus the interfaces needed to connect the applications. To handle unique integration needs, EAI vendors provide custom programming to modify the EAI modules to fit the company's requirements. Here's an example of a use of such middleware.

CASE EXAMPLE

A TELECOMMUNICATIONS FIRM

In the highly competitive telecommunications industry, a company must offer a wide range of products and services that must be rapidly modified to respond to market changes and new technologies. As a result, processing customer requests for new and updated services is a major source of company cost and customer dissatisfaction. It has been estimated that 65 percent of new and change orders in the telephone industry have errors that must be corrected after the fact. This situation leads to tens of millions of dollars in unnecessary direct costs and a 20 percent annual customer churn, due in large part to the order-processing errors. The result: significantly reduced profits.

(Case Continued)

To improve the process and retain customers, one telecom company acquired a high-end customer relationship management (CRM) system. But processing requests for new phone lines still remained quite tedious because each request required interaction with three back-office applications before the CRM system could respond to the customer. The connectivity with these systems was at the individual task level and required a number of manual steps, callbacks, and holds. Errors were still common and response to customers was still unacceptable because the flow from one step to the next could not be automated.

The company chose to address these issues by using enterprise application integration technologies. No new ordering process was required; the existing process was simply automated. The processing of an order request begins with a customer requesting service at the call center via the CRM. The customer's name and address is passed to the ERP system, which retrieves the necessary information for the provisioning application to validate the request and ensure that the new service is compatible with the existing services the customer is receiving. The telephone service is specified and, if appropriate, a new phone number is allocated. Next, pricing is retrieved from the packaged accounting system before all the information is returned to the call center for presentation to the customer through the CRM system.

The process is now entirely automated. What used to take days or weeks is now handled in minutes while the customer is on the line, tremendously improving customer responsiveness. Processing costs have been reduced, errors eliminated, and customer churn lowered. No new applications were required and the existing applications remained untouched. ■

INTERNET-BASED SYSTEMS

As discussed throughout the book, the Internet and e-business are changing the nature of information systems in organizations. Now that the Internet has gained wide acceptance as a medium for conducting business, companies must expand their Internet-based systems beyond simple Web pages. These Internet-based systems must be scalable, reliable, and integrated both internally and externally with the systems of customers and business partners. In developing such systems, companies have learned they must negotiate language differences. For example, a system may have to port old Cobol applications to Java, reconcile interface discrepancies, and interface with back-end legacy applications, often without documentation or past experience with those systems.

Many languages, tools, and frameworks are available for developing Internet-based systems. Currently, the application server framework appears to be the preferred method of users and vendors. Also, following the spirit of the Internet, customers are demanding open systems; they do not want to be tied to a single vendor's proprietary technology. One open system language standard, Java, has evolved from a proposed client-side programming standard to a server-side application development standard. We next look at the application server approach and the development of Java as a server-side platform.

Application Servers

Originally conceived as a piece of middleware to link a Web server to applications on other company systems, the application server has grown into a framework for developing Internet-based applications. Figure 9-5 illustrates the basic application server architecture. A set of application servers is connected to create a single virtual application server. This virtual server takes requests from clients and Web servers, runs the necessary business logic, and provides connectivity to the entire range of back-end systems.

In addition to the middleware and integration functions, application servers have become application development platforms, with a wide range of development and automatic code generation tools. Their functions can be divided into five categories, says Radding:[8] business logic processing, automation of low-level core processes, middleware, application development, and prebuilt components.

- *Business Logic Processing.* The application server stores and runs business logic components for applications. These components form basic, reusable building blocks for applications and might, for example, take the form of applets or JavaBeans. More recently, vendors are standardizing on Java 2 Enterprise Edition (see the following Standards section) to provide components.
- *Automation of Low-Level Core Processes.* The application server can generate networking and communication code, and code for a wide range of low-level functions. These functions can include security, session pooling, and database connectivity. This capability can drastically reduce the time needed to code an application, increasing programmer productivity by as much as 75 percent.

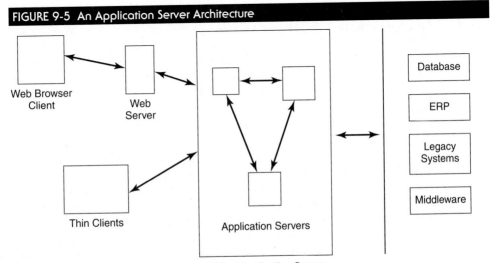

FIGURE 9-5 An Application Server Architecture

Web Browser Client

Web Server

Thin Clients

Application Servers

Virtual Application Server

Database

ERP

Legacy Systems

Middleware

- ***Middleware.*** As already mentioned, the application server becomes the back-end link to legacy systems. In addition, it becomes the link to systems of customers and business partners. Thus, the application server is the central point of integration for all Internet-based systems.
- ***Application Development.*** The application server is delivering many of the capabilities provided by integrated development environments (IDE). With the IDE an integral part of the application server, companies can build many of their client-server applications with the application server.
- ***Prebuilt Components.*** Recently, vendors of application servers have begun including prebuilt components, such as tag libraries, servlets, JavaBeans, or, in the Microsoft world, components based on the component object model. Again, the goal is to increase programmer productivity.

In addition to providing application development tools, the application server framework provides scalability. As demands on applications grow, a company can increase the power of its virtual application server by either installing more servers or replacing smaller servers with larger ones. In either case, the application server framework provides easy migration. The application server also provides automatic load balancing among the multiple servers and coordinates session information across multiple instances of an application.

In summary, the goal of the application server is to automate and manage many of the technical tasks in the development and running of Internet-based applications. In doing so, developers can focus more on the business issues, rather than the technical details.

Java Development Platform

If companies are to develop Internet-based systems quickly, as the e-business environment demands, they need component-based development tools. If, in addition, the systems being developed are to be portable and scalable, then the companies need to employ an open system architecture. For both component-based tools and open systems, industry standards are necessary. Currently, some of the most widely used standards for Internet-based systems development have evolved from Java.

Java was originally developed to provide applets that run on Web clients; however, it quickly evolved into a full programming language with the goal of providing a platform-independent language that could run on any system through a "Java virtual machine." This promised application portability was dubbed "write-once, run-anywhere." That promise has not been met, however. As a language for client applications, Java performed poorly relative to other languages, such as C++. So companies have not converted their client-based applications to Java. However, Java has evolved into a standard platform for developing server-side applications.

The two major components in the Java server-side platform are Enterprise Java-Beans (EJB) and the Java 2 Enterprise Edition (J2EE) software specification. EJBs emerged on the developer scene in 1998 when Sun Microsystems unveiled a specification for creating server-based applications using software components. These components, the EJBs, act as preconfigured pieces of code that IT staff no longer have to build from scratch. A component can be as simple as an order-entry form or as complicated as a virtual shopping cart that keeps track of where users have been and maintains their privacy. The use of these reusable components can greatly enhance programmer productivity.

In the Windows environment, and in direct competition with EJBs, Microsoft wants developers to build applications using the Component Object Model (COM) and Distributed Component Object Model (DCOM). Although COM components provide many of the same benefits of EJBs, they have some significant differences. COM server components can realistically be deployed only on Windows servers, and COM-based services are generally unavailable to non-Windows machines. On the other hand, EJBs supply data to Java-enabled Web browsers running on a wide variety of platforms. As a result, EJBs have emerged as the early preference for companies building Internet-related services.

The J2EE software specification defines a standard for developing Internet-based enterprise applications. It simplifies enterprise applications by basing them on standardized, modular components, by providing a set of services to those components, and handling many of the core functions for the applications. J2EE describes a collection of server-side application programming interfaces (APIs) that provide the functionality for server-side delivery of data and for thin-client software that interacts with users throughout the enterprise. Components of J2EE include an API for database access, security modules that protect data in the Internet environment, and modules supporting CORBA for interactions with existing enterprise applications. J2EE also provides full support of EJB components and Java servlets, as well as support for XML technology.

J2EE provides a standard, which vendors of application server products are quickly adopting. From the user perspective, J2EE and EJB provide an alternative to building e-business systems from scratch or buying packaged e-business systems. Having a multivendor platform with prebuilt, reusable components allows companies to reduce the development cost and the time-to-market for new enterprise applications or upgrades to existing enterprise applications.

Application Service Providers

A new alternative to system development exists that essentially outsources the entire process. As noted in Chapter 8, application service providers (ASPs) are companies that rent software applications over the Internet. Customers subscribing to an ASP use applications residing on the ASP's servers. Subscribing to an ASP allows companies to avoid purchasing, installing, supporting, and upgrading expensive software applications.

ASPs offer a wide range of applications and services, from Web hosting to ERP use, from database management systems to industry B2B e-commerce portals. If fully responsible for all application maintenance and upgrades, the ASP also manages the relationships with the vendors. The target markets for ASPs have been small companies that want minimally customized applications, large organizations in need of complex "niche" applications they cannot afford to develop themselves, and vertical industries that need B2B electronic commerce services or industry-specific software. Figure 9-6 shows one categorization of ASPs.

The key benefit of using an ASP is that a company can get an application up and running in a short time with little initial investment. The company can use the resources it saved on its core business activities. The downside, however, is that companies have reported problems with negotiating service level agreements and support during downtime. In addition, a company needs to consider the strategic implications of having applications running outside the direct control of the company.

The preceding sections have discussed the foundations of system development and the newer kinds of system development options. But, in the end, system development is

FIGURE 9-6	Types of ASPs
Type	**Capabilities**
Enterprise	Delivers a variety of high-end applications to enterprises and offers some degree of customization and availability guarantees.
General Business	Provides a variety of non- or minimally customizable applications to small and medium-sized businesses.
Specialist	Delivers only a particular type of application (i.e., ERP, customer resource management (CRM), human resources (HR), personal productivity, etc.).
Vertical	Provides packaged and/or specialized applications targeted at a particular vertical market segment.

Source: "The State of ASPs" (Robert Frances Group, 1999).

about projects. So a main tenet of good system development is good project management. Therefore we end the chapter by discussing this crucial piece of the development picture.

PROJECT MANAGEMENT

Project management is simply the management of a project, notes Michael Matthew of Matthew & Matthew consulting firm.[9] This definition may sound simple and self-evident but that does not make it easy. Many people get confused or concerned about IT project management because it involves the "T" word: technology. In reality, IT project management is not much different from other forms of project management, such as those used to construct an office tower or a bridge.

A project is a collection of related tasks and activities undertaken to achieve a specific goal. Thus, all projects (IT or otherwise) should:

- Have a clearly stated goal.
- Be "finite," that is, have a clearly defined beginning and end.

It has been said that IT project management is 10 percent technical and 90 percent common sense or good business practice. Indeed many of the best IT managers do not have a background in IT at all, but they possess the important skills of communication, organization, and motivation. Perhaps the most difficult component of IT project management is keeping in mind, and under control, all the interdependencies of the numerous tasks being undertaken.

Keys to Project Management Success

Numerous keys influence project management success. Here are some, writes Matthew:

Establish the Ground Rules.   Define the technical and architectural specifications for the systems following four guidelines:

- Adhere to industry standards.
- Use an open architecture.
- Web-enable the system.
- Power with subsystems.

These principles should help ensure no "nasty surprises" along the way, as well as provide the ready ability to update/switchover systems in the future. The basic tenet is that the systems should be as simple as possible while fulfilling all the (reasonable) user requirements.

Discipline, Planning, Documentation, and Management. In many respects, these elements are what project management is really all about. It does not matter how well the requirements have been specified or whether the "perfect" solution has been selected; if the process is not controlled properly, anything can happen or, more realistically, potentially "nothing" will happen.

A firm timeline for system rollout needs to be formally established and signed off. Once this task has been done, the project team needs to work backward from the critical dates and map out the timing for the intermediate steps, and include any "interdependencies." Teams actually should take the critical date and subtract some time, say one month, for unforeseen contingencies. The project must progress with the target critical date in mind, which requires strong discipline.

The project also needs to follow a sound methodology and have key points planned and documented (and reported on) using a product such as Microsoft Project. All members of the teams need to be aware of their responsibilities and timelines. Nothing should be left assumed. In addition, regular meetings and updates of this project plan are needed, along with proper documentation of the system development effort. Senior management needs to be able to see this documentation whenever they want. Management, key users, and even vendor personnel should be included on project steering groups, which should meet regularly to make sure the project continues on track and that all members are aware of their responsibilities. Such meetings also provide a venue for airing problems and raising issues that might affect others.

In addition it is desirable to have an overall IT project steering committee. Regular project manager meetings from the various projects are key to keeping each other informed of their progress and for raising issues that might affect other projects.

Obtain and Document (the "Final") User Requirements. Documenting user requirements is critical because it is the only way the team can evaluate its outcome. Scope creep (users asking for more and more functions) causes many system failures. Documenting requirements helps lock in the scope of the work, and helps reduce the possibility of costing problems and time overruns due to additional requests. Documenting user requirements can be done via a variety of methods, including facilitation sessions and one-on-one interviews.

A common mistake is to get too technical in writing user specs. Some IT consultants make this mistake in the interests of "maintaining the mystique." But the tendency can do harm. Similarly, IT project teams should not accept overly technical sign-off requests from software houses. They need to prove they can fulfill the users' requirements.

Obtain Tenders From All Appropriate Potential Vendors. Today, much software is bought rather than built in-house. And with the proliferation of e-commerce, a number of specialist software houses have appeared. This option needs to be considered when beginning a project, notes Matthew. In fact, companies that do not have expertise in the area under consideration might want to call in consultants to make a recommendation. Their extensive contacts in the IT community can significantly improve selection of the package or packages. Or they may simply help the IT project team create the selection criteria for evaluating the bids and selecting the winner.

Working with Suppliers.   If the development is to be handled by an outside firm, then a joint project team needs to be created. The supplier, or suppliers, will undoubtedly appoint their own project managers for their respective assignments. They need to be part of the governing team.

Convert Existing Data.   Data conversion needs to be properly planned to make sure the output data is complete and accurate. Although this task might appear quite simple, it is often the area that creates the biggest headaches. Here, perhaps the oldest maxim in the IT industry applies: garbage in, garbage out.

Moving Forward After Implementation.   Upon successful implementation of the various systems project managers need to cross their 't's and dot their 'i's in terms of documentation, future maintenance processes, and so on.

The bottom line is that IT project management is no different from any other form of project management. To be successful good planning is needed, along with good communication, and getting the active participation of all interested parties, says Matthew. These elements, along with some hard work, will better ensure a successful system.

Internet Project Management

The rules of project management do not change in the New Economy, says Matthew. The principles and practices of project management, such as the need to define the scope, set timelines, and monitor progress, still hold true. However, Internet projects do tend to be more collaborative and iterative than traditional projects. In reality user ownership and effective implementation are the goals of all IT development and project management. They have become a reality in Internet projects.

Web-Based Project Management Tools.   Even though the use of the term *Web-based* will hopefully shortly become largely meaningless—when all project management tools have a significant Web-based component—a number of excellent tools have emerged. These systems have been a boon to business but a "disaster" for airlines and the hotel industry, particularly in the United States where any of the "meetings" and much of the collaborations take place using these Web-based tools as opposed to people traveling to traditional face-to-face meetings. The features of such tools are shown in Figure 9-7.

Tips for Good Project Management

Most people would agree that a successful project has the following characteristics:

- It is "delivered" on time.
- It comes in on or under budget.
- It meets the original objectives.

And although all these elements are true, some people do not realize that a successful project is also one that meets the users' and organization's needs, which may have changed since the original objectives.

FIGURE 9-7 Features of Web-Based Collaboration Tools

- Discussion groups
- Links to e-mail
- Chat sessions
- Group setups
- Online conferencing and presentation capabilities
- Document sharing and organization
- Linking items (e-mails, documents, tasks, graphics) to each other and to people and groups
- Document searching and filtering facilities
- Event-driven notifications to individuals, groups, and project teams
- Decision support features such as voting and polling
- Workflow management

Source: Reprinted with permission of Michael Matthew, "IT Project Management: The Good, the Bad, and the Ugly," Matthew & Matthew, July 2000, at mandkmatthew@one.net.au.

Identifying the full user requirements as early as possible and meeting them is as critical to project success as the key components of planning, managing, monitoring and controlling the project. Projects that do not give the users what they want cannot be deemed a success. Assuming a project has been correctly defined and specified up front, the following items are necessary to ensure that a project is successful, notes Matthew.

Proper Planning.   Planning is the most powerful contributor to the success of a project for one simple reason: If done properly, it keeps the focus on the desired outcomes. Planning needs to address a number of questions to determine the project outcomes:

- What actions are required?
- When should those actions commence and finish?
- How long will they take?
- Who will do them?
- What equipment, tools, and materials will be needed?
- What interdependencies exist between the preceding issues?

These issues need to be controlled and monitored. To do so, the use of an appropriate software tool is recommended, if not mandatory. The best planning also includes anticipation of problems and potential courses of action if things go wrong, as they invariably do. Finally, whether it is called project planning or project organization, the essential steps in this area include generating the following:

- Project specifications
- Roles and responsibilities definitions
- Budget and accounting procedures
- Change control procedures

Above all, creating accurate estimates and budgets is vital to a project's success.

Appropriate User Involvement and Strong Visible Management Support.   This need might seem self-evident but its importance cannot be overstressed. Without these involvements, the project might as well be halted at the outset.

Project Manager(s) with Authority and Time. Although this point again may seem obvious, it is not always followed. Without the appropriate and supported authority, project managers, like other managers, will struggle to do their job.

More common and equally devastating is the part-time project manager who is expected to hold down a day job and at the same time run a project. No matter how good a person is, he or she cannot be the CFO and implement a new finance system nationwide at the same time.

The project manager is a key. Preferably, they need to have appropriate experience and be able to demonstrate a range of skills including leadership, communication, organization, motivation, and decision making.

Good Change Management. Project managers also need to have, or have access to, good change management skills. All projects have a target of creating change. The manner in which that change is managed makes a considerable difference to the project's success. Successful management of project change relies on:

- Commitment through involvement and explanation
- Allowing people to take responsibility for their own actions in the change process
- Giving people enough information and training to enable them to manage change effectively.

Working as a Team. Surprisingly, the creation of a team and the mechanics of how it operates are often overlooked or mishandled. The role of the team is vital to the success of a project. Members of project teams

- Have a shared purpose.
- Undertake cooperative action.
- Generate collective outcomes.
- Create defined, measurable team products or outcomes.

Team members should be chosen for their functional skills, their decision-making and problem-solving skills, and their skills in working with other team members. Put simply, projects rely on the creativity and skills of people to ensure their completion and success. To assist in this area, the project should have appropriate induction, team building, and counseling.

Proper Project Monitoring and Control. In addition to the normal management control and supervision needed, good project management also relies on formal project monitoring and provision of relevant information to management. Project monitoring is essential for providing key information of the project, such as performance, cost, time, and quality.

These items and other relevant information need to be reported and discussed at regular project meetings. In addition, such information should be available to management for all aspects of the project. The goal is to provide answers to such key management questions as:

- Will we finish on time?
- Will we achieve what we set out to do?
- Will we overspend the budget?

Proper Project Closure.   Project closure is as important as planning in contributing to project success. Effective and efficient closure is achieved by careful management of the project's people, its communications, its information, and its power structure.

Project postimplementation reviews, audits, and other appraisals should be conducted to evaluate the success of the project. These reviews should not only examine whether the actual benefits exceeded the plan but also record what lessons learned during the project could be useful for future projects. The best advice to project participants, notes Matthew is, "In all circumstances: Keep your focus on the end result."

CONCLUSION

The traditional approach to system development from the 1960s evolved to give the process more discipline, control, and efficiency. It was valuable in moving programming and system analysis from pure free-form "art" to a better defined "craft." Problems remained, however, with long development times, little user involvement, and lack of flexibility in the resulting systems. The tools and methods of the 1970s and 1980s— 4GLs, software prototyping, and CASE—permitted more rapid development and even experimental development; they were seen as revolutionary techniques to conventional developers.

The 1990s brought the need for integrated enterprise systems and Internet-based systems. Both required more flexibility and speedier development with a significant amount of integration, both internal and external to the company. With the integration efforts, companies realized the importance of focusing less on technical issues and more on the impacts of IT on business strategy and organization. Widely reported failures of large ERP projects reinforced this need to concentrate on the business.

The IT industry has responded with new tools and approaches. Application servers support integration across a wide range of new and legacy systems, as do component-based development tools. We have indeed entered a new era of application development where the focus is on application and business integration across organizational boundaries.

Finally, no discussion of system development is complete without noting project management. It is one of the main skills in high demand these days in IS departments. In fact, as more and more work in companies is performed by teams, the project management skills in IS departments are being requested by users for their own projects. It is becoming an increasingly crucial asset as IT becomes more critical to company success.

QUESTIONS AND EXERCISES

Review Questions

1. What are the goals of the traditional system development life cycle approach?
2. Refer to the list of features and functions of 4GLs in Figure 9-3. Briefly explain each.
3. What are the problems of "little databases" and "personal programs"? How do 4GLs help or hinder in dealing with these problems?
4. What are the main characteristics of the prototyping approach?
5. Describe the main points of Santa Fe Railroad's use of Mapper.
6. Define the components of a computer-aided software engineering system.
7. What is unique about DuPont Cable Management Service's use of CASE?
8. Describe the three main approaches to integrating the information systems within an organization.
9. What are the basic characteristics of an ERP system?
10. Why have so many ERP implementation projects failed?
11. Describe Colgate-Palmolive's approach to implementing their ERP.
12. Describe the five categories of functions for an application server.
13. What is the value of the Java 2 Enterprise Edition software specification?
14. Why would a company use an application service provider?
15. Give three keys to project management success.

Discussion Questions

1. IS departments will no longer need to develop a proprietary infrastructure, they can just rely on the Internet. Therefore, they will again focus mainly on developing applications. Discuss.
2. The field is moving too fast for companies to keep developers abreast of the state-of-the-art. To keep up, they should outsource application development. Discuss.
3. Changing an IS department's focus from application development to application integration can change the IS department's relationship with other departments in the company. Discuss how the relationship may change.

Exercises

1. Find a detailed description of an Internet-based application developed in a user company. What features does it have? What approach did the company choose to develop the application?
2. Visit a company in your community that has an information systems department with at least five professionals. Prepare a short case description to summarize the company's current approach to developing systems. Does it have one standard approach or a combination of several? Is it building client-server systems or Web-based systems? If so, describe one or two.
3. Visit the Web sites of three vendors of ERP systems. Summarize the similarities and differences among their products.
4. Present a scenario of what you think system development will be like in leading-edge firms in five years. What will change? What will not change?

REFERENCES

1. Canning, R. G., *Electronic Data Processing for Business and Industry,* 1956, and *Installing Electronic Data Processing Systems,* 1957, John Wiley & Sons, New York.

2. Glass, Robert, *Building Quality Software,* Prentice Hall, Upper Saddle River, NJ, 1992.

3. Naumann, J. D., and A. M. Jenkins "Prototyping: The New Paradigm for Systems Development," *MIS Quarterly,* September 1982, 29–44.

4. Carma McClure, Extended Intelligence, Inc., Chicago.

5. Woolfe, Roger, "Managing the Move to Client-Server," Wentworth Research Program (now part of Gartner Executive Programs), January 1995.

6. Buckhout, Scott, Edward Frey, and Joseph Nemec Jr., "Making ERP Succeed: Turning Fear into Promise," *Journal of Strategy & Business,* 15, Second Quarter 1999.

7. Davenport, Thomas, "Putting the Enterprise into the Enterprise System," *Harvard Business Review,* July/August 1998, 121–131.

8. Radding, Alan, "Application Servers Fuel E-Business," *Informationweek.com,* June 19, 2000, at www.information week.com.

9. Matthew, Michael "IT Project Management: The Good, the Bad, and the Ugly," Matthew & Matthew, July 2000, at mandkmatthew@one.net.au.

CHAPTER

10

MANAGEMENT ISSUES IN SYSTEM DEVELOPMENT

INTRODUCTION

Chapter 9 dealt with developing systems. This chapter looks at the issues surrounding system development. The context for this discussion is set by the ideas of John Hagel III and Marc Singer, both of McKinsey & Company.[1] They see companies being in three businesses:

1. Infrastructure management
2. Customer relationship
3. Product innovation

Traditionally, companies have bundled the three, which leads to compromises because the three have conflicting agendas. The Internet allows companies to unbundle them, say the authors, specializing in one to optimize it.

IS departments can be viewed as being in the same three businesses. Operations are infrastructure management. The help desk is the customer relationship business. And system development is product innovation. This division provides the context for this chapter, that is, seeing application development as being in the product innovation business. So let's briefly look at how Hagel and Singer believe each of the three should be viewed and managed.

Infrastructure Management. The goal of infrastructure management is reducing costs. Providing infrastructure, such as hospitals, roads, wireless networks, and so on, involves high fixed costs, so the battle is to build scale. High barriers to entry also mean that only the few largest players will dominate, which perhaps explains the huge battle now ensuing among telcos, portals, and others to become the largest wireless Internet provider. Management focuses on efficiency and standards, which is just what we have been seeing in network and computer operations. Companies outsource their network management and data centers to large ESPs, like IBM, CSC, and EDS. Their main goal in these areas is to lower costs.

Customer Relationship. The goal in the customer relationship business is service. Here the battle is for scope by having lots of custom offerings to increase the company's "wallet share" of each customer. In this business, the customer is king, and developing relationships with customers requires large investments. Here, again, Hagel and Singer see only a few large players dominating. In the IT arena, PC support and help desks are often outsourced to specialists to gain their expertise, especially in Europe where multilingual support is needed.

Product Innovation. The goal of product innovation is speed because it provides nimbleness. Low barriers of entry mean many small players. The key to success is talent. In IT, software companies follow these parameters. Their developers are king, so they give them the latest tools, allow them to work any hour of the day or night, permit their pets to work, always have a stash of free jolt cola on hand, and so on. These companies are always on the lookout for talent and they reward stars generously, which is one reason IS departments can have a hard time attracting the talent they need.

Thinking in these terms, the management issues surrounding system development begin with staffing, staffing, staffing—as well as speed and nimbleness. Thus, we begin this chapter by discussing managing IS staff. Then we move on to rethinking maintenance work, getting systems successfully implemented, improving legacy systems, and measuring the value of systems.

HOW SHOULD IS STAFF BE MANAGED?

Whereas managing operations was the task that took too much CIO time, cost too much money, and caused so much loss in credibility in the 1980s and 1990s, the issue that now garners this position is IS staffing. It is taking too much CIO time, costing too much money, and can lead to IS departments not being able to keep pace with their enterprise. The problem is not enough staff with the needed skills to go around. The situation was bad enough in the mid-1990s, but with the emergence of e-commerce and then e-everything, it has been exacerbated. In 2000, the ITAA[2] estimated a shortfall of 850,000 IT jobs in the United States alone.

Managing staff is complex. Scott Parry, of The Training House,[3] has been involved in consulting to HR departments for many years. He believes the job of managing staff encompasses eight areas, as shown in Figure 10-1. It begins with hiring, and goes through training and coaching to performance appraisal to assigning work to career planning to maintaining a skills inventory. As noted in the diagram, some of these functions are the responsibility of the HR department, others are shared, and others are the responsibility of one's manager. The goal is to align an individual's desires with the organization's needs.

Let's look at two of these areas: recruitment and assigning work.

Recruiting IS Staff

The major issue in recruiting is finding people with the right skills and then providing the work culture and incentives that suit them. It means knowing which skills are needed, that is, bridging the gap between in-house skills and desired skills. The charter for the NorthWest Center for Emerging Technologies[4] is to encourage IT education in the Northwestern United States. It has defined eight career clusters (groups of similar jobs) needed in IS departments, shown in Figure 10-2.

In general, skills are most lacking in the newest areas. We believe e-business is going to extend this list to include such jobs as designing architectures for e-business,

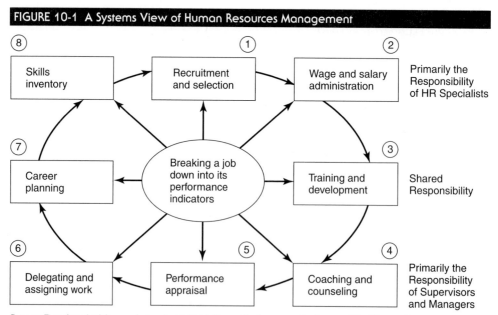

FIGURE 10-1 A Systems View of Human Resources Management

Source: Reprinted with permission from Scott Parry, *Performance Indicators: The Heart of Human Resources Management* (Princeton, NJ: The Training House).

FIGURE 10-2 Information Technology Career Clusters

- Database development and administration
- Digital media
- Enterprise systems analysis and integration
- Network design and administration
- Programming/software engineering
- Technical support
- Technical writing
- Web development and administration

Source: Reprinted with permission from *Building a Foundation for Tomorrow: Skill Standards for Information Technology, The Millenium Edition* (Bellevue, WA: Northwest Center for Emerging Technologies, 1999), www.nwcet.org.

managing vendors, managing electronic customer relationships, building wireless applications, and implementing supply chain management. That said, it is important to note that people with skills in older technologies are also in demand to maintain old systems. Unfortunately, they often do not want to do maintenance work; they much prefer working with new technologies. We address this maintenance conundrum shortly.

Due to the talent famine in IT, employers need to take new views in managing staff. One intriguing view, presented by Patricia Seemann of Zurich Group,[5] is that employees need to be seen as investors. They invest their time where they get the highest market value for their talent, which may not necessarily mean where they receive the highest salary. It might mean rather where they will receive the best training, or are given opportunities in their area, and so forth. Thus, it is up to firms to show they can provide this "highest return" to candidates. It means they need to know the talents they need, where they are most likely to exist, such as business schools or at competitors, and also how to develop that talent.

Peter Cappelli of the Wharton School[6] believes companies should no longer expect long-term employment by all employees. The market, not a company, determines the movement of employees. Attractive offers will pull people away. To deal with such a market, he offers several recommendations. One is to determine which jobs do not need the most sought-after talent and seek out underutilized sources. Or, if a steady supply of new recruits is available, such as from a local college, another possibility is to concentrate on hiring, not retention. A company can adapt to higher turnover by continually bringing in talent with the newer skills. One way to adapt to continual turnover is to focus on short-term projects; another is to cross-train staff so that a loss can be easily filled. A third suggestion from Cappelli is for management to decide which types of employees (or perhaps even which specific employees) they want or need to keep and focus retention efforts on them, and focus recruitment efforts on all the others. A fourth suggestion is to outsource the work that is difficult to perform in-house due to lack of talent. This route is one many IT departments have taken both in handling legacy system maintenance and in moving quickly into e-commerce.

As an example of how one company is addressing its IT staffing needs, consider Fidelity Investments, as described in a Gartner EXP report by Roger Woolfe.[7]

CASE EXAMPLE

FIDELITY INVESTMENTS

Fidelity Investments, a private company based in Boston, Massachusetts, manages $1 trillion of customers' financial assets in its numerous mutual funds (the best known of which is the Magellan Fund). About 10 percent of the trades on the New York Stock Exchange go through Fidelity and it is the number two online brokerage firm. Its Web site handles two million log-ins a day. One million of them are "Web call equivalents," which means they traditionally would have been handled by a call center employee. In fact, 80 percent of Fidelity's transactions now come through the Web, making it the largest distribution channel.

Some 25 percent of Fidelity's 30,000 employees are technologists focusing on system development, telecom, and computer operations. Because IT is crucial for the business, Fidelity does all IT work in-house; only training and development are outsourced. Recruiting and retaining IT staff are critical.

In late 1999, Fidelity brought together all its e-business components into a new company, Fidelity E-Business. This company has its own technical architecture and infrastructure, development teams, quality assurance, production, monitoring, online editing, and research and development.

Recruiting Staff

To show candidates that it is no longer "a suit-and-tie company," Fidelity made great efforts to create a "technology environment," featuring such things

as casual dress, flexible work schedules, telecommuting, a dot-com working environment, snacks and foosball. When recruiting, it emphasizes that it focuses on the Web and that new products are developed for the Web. Candidates like the security of Fidelity due to the turbulent times for dot-coms.

Fidelity makes it as easy as possible for job candidates to get in touch with the company. Thus, it uses Hire.com and its own Web site to establish an interactive relationship with candidates. On its site (www.oportunitiesatfidelity.com), potential candidates fill out only a profile; no résumé is necessary. Through Hire.com, Fidelity quickly tries to match a profile with job openings or potential job openings and to initiate an interactive dialogue with the candidate about all the possible options: jobs, locations, and so on. Its goals are to drive passive candidates to the Web site, treat candidates well, and shorten the time from "awareness of a candidate" to "talking with a hire," which is a key metric.

A major strategy at Fidelity is to fill jobs from within. Employees in non-IT jobs may have 80 percent of the qualifications for IT jobs. The company therefore encourages these employees to stay within Fidelity and move to IT. To date, 40 percent of Fidelity E-Business's staff has been recruited internally.

Bright young employees from customer service are a prime target for the IT group. These employees are trained, obtain their license, and then learn the

(Case Continued)

business. But after two years, they want to do something different. Rather than lose them and the business knowledge they have accumulated, the IT group is working with an external vendor that has a proven track record in training nontechnologists in basic IT skills.

The IT group's human resources strategy is to move seasoned mainframe employees to Web Technologies, rather than lose them, and then back-fill their jobs with the newly trained customer service employees. Later, they too will move into Web jobs.

Retaining Staff

The key to staff retention is to make managers accountable. Fidelity requires its IT managers to rank their subordinates each quarter as either a One, Two, or Three. "One" means the person is key to the business, may or may not have high potential, has important knowledge, is working on mission critical systems, and makes the company run; however, no correlation is made between "One" and performance ratings or bonuses. "Two" is not defined. "Three" describes someone who the manager would be sad to see leave, but who is not critical to the business. Managers can do this ranking quickly.

For each One (the target is 20 percent of all IT staff), managers are required to create a retention plan explaining what is needed to keep that person at Fidelity, and how the assignments, team experiences, training, conference attendance, and technology skills contribute to that goal. Part of each manager's bonus is tied to retaining his or her Ones. When a One leaves, a review takes place between the manager and the *company president*.

Fidelity has adopted quarterly compensation reviews, to stay in touch with the market. It subscribes to five compensation services to ensure that its people are paid ahead of the marketplace. Furthermore, it continually talks with recruiters to get a feel for changes in compensation, because the market for some jobs is changing faster than the surveys can keep up. The main benefit of these reviews is that they force managers to have a conversation with their employees about their work, issues in their lives, how things are going, and so on.

One of the subjects discussed in these conversations is how recognition can be personalized. Employees are asked, "If we wanted to say 'thank you' to you during the next year in a way other than a bonus or a t-shirt, what would be meaningful to you?" The thank you can be as small as a favorite candy bar or perhaps tickets to a favorite sporting event. The key is to recognize employees as individuals.

Rather than do an entire project, Fidelity E-Business acts as the general contractor. It knows the strategy and the business application. Then it contracts out the work to other areas of the company so that other IT staff is also involved in "cool Web work." This practice helps to leverage the intellectual capital that exists in mission critical areas. It also focuses a broader range of IT staff onto the Web, Fidelity's primary distribution channel.

These strategies have allowed the number of IT staff in Fidelity (including Fidelity E-Business) to grow by 45 percent in five months. The company believes that if it is aggressive on salaries and strives to keep people happy with good assignments, it can forestall employees from even taking recruitment phone calls. ■

Designing Motivating Work

Assigning the kind of work that motivates people may, in part, revolve around designing, or redesigning, jobs to fit the jobholders. Job design is one of the crucial elements in staffing. Cappelli gives an intriguing example of job redesign. Even though it does not apply to IT, it is illustrative of one way to rethink work. Here's the short case.

CASE EXAMPLE

UPS

United Parcel Service (UPS) is in the package delivery service and as such has been an important player in e-commerce. Dot-coms let it handle their logistics and shipping. An important jobholder at UPS is the delivery driver. Drivers have important skills, such as understanding city street numberings, commercial park layouts, and so on. Furthermore, they are in the crucial customer-contact role. Hiring a new driver is costly, and it can take a new driver months to learn the idiosyncrasies of a delivery route.

UPS wanted to reduce its turnover in this important job, so it studied why drivers left. Surprisingly, it discovered the task they disliked most was loading the packages into the delivery van each morning. The work was tedious and exhausting, so much so that it caused drivers to quit.

Therefore, UPS redesigned the drivers' job, offloading this work to a new group: loaders. Turnover on the loading job is tremendously high, 400 percent a year, Cappelli reports, but management can live with this high rate because loaders are easy to find. The job has high pay and requires low skills so there is a ready supply of students and other part-timers willing to do the work; and it is easy to train them.

Meanwhile, UPS has improved the job of the employees it really wants to keep: its drivers. ■

Job design is just as important in IS. As in the UPS case, doing a good job at design requires knowing what motivates IT staff. The best research in this area was performed by Professor J. Daniel Couger and his colleagues.[8] His research was prompted by problems encountered in managing IT staff. To better understand what motivated them, Couger drew on the Job Diagnostic Survey (JDS), developed by J. R. Hackman and G. R. Oldham. Hackman and Oldham established the validity and accuracy of their model of human motivation (Figure 10-3) by testing more than 6,000 people who were performing more than 500 different jobs at more than 50 organizations.

In short, the model says that motivated employees are those who experience meaningfulness in their work. Meaningfulness occurs when

---

FIGURE 10-3   A Model of Human Motivation Used by the Hackman-Oldham Job Diagnostic Survey (JDS)

Five Core Job Dimensions
1. Skill variety
2. Task identity
3. Task significance
4. Autonomy
5. Feedback from the job itself

Three Critical Psychological States
1. Experienced meaningfulness of work
2. Experienced responsibility for outcomes of the work
3. Knowledge of the actual results of the work activities

Leading to Personal and Work Outcomes
1. High internal work motivation
2. High-quality work performance
3. High satisfaction with the work
4. Low absenteeism and turnover

- A person needs to use a number of different skills and talents (skill variety).
- The work involves completing a "whole" and identifiable piece of work (task identity).
- The work has a substantial impact on the lives or work of other people (task significance).
- The person has freedom in accomplishing the tasks (autonomy).
- The job provides some built-in feedback or reward (feedback).

Their Job Diagnostic Survey consists of a series of questions that employees answer anonymously. Some questions are:

- How much independence and freedom do you have in the way your carry out your work assignments?
- How effective is your manager in providing feedback on how well you are performing your job?
- To what extent does your job require you to use a number of complex or high-level skills?

Employees answer each question by selecting a number from 1 (low) to 7 (high). Only the average scores of a group of people doing the same work are used; individual scores are not. Employees are likely to give their true feelings only when they believe the results will not be used against them personally, which argues for complete anonymity. The JDS is *not* to be used for placement purposes or in diagnosing jobs of individuals. The average values ("scores") on each question are then used to analyze employee perceptions about the job.

The JDS also includes questions about the employee to help match the person to a job type. From all the gathered data, the JDS computes several measures. Three are of importance here:

1. *Growth need strength* indicates a group's need for personal growth and development in the job. Groups with a high growth need strength become internally motivated if their jobs have a high motivating potential.

2. *Social need strength* measures a group's need to interact with others to feel it is doing a good job. A high group score indicates the people in the group have a strong desire to interact with others; a low score indicates they prefer to work alone.
3. *Motivating potential score* of a job is computed from the questions that measure the five core job dimensions: skill variety, task identity, task significance, autonomy, and feedback from the job itself.

Gauging IT Staff.   Couger's first survey (conducted with Robert Zawacki) included some 2,500 persons from 50 organizations. The database now contains information on more than 18,000 Americans and 19,500 people from other countries.

The U.S. data showed that programmers and analysts had the *highest* growth need strength of any job category that had been analyzed using the JDS. In a sense, this result is not surprising; IS executives have long known that systems professionals want to work on the latest technology, both hardware and software. However, their high growth need strength means that their managers must continually provide them with new challenges to keep them motivated.

In addition, the survey found that U.S. computer professionals had the *lowest* social need strength of any of the 500 occupations measured by the Job Diagnostic Survey. People with a high social need utilize meetings as a prime device for fulfilling their social need. "Programmers and analysts don't need meetings," noted Couger, "and users don't understand why systems personnel show frustration at lengthy or frequent meetings."

The same point applies to project or department meetings, stated Couger. "Programmers and analysts are not antisocial; they will participate actively in meetings that are meaningful to them. But their high growth need also causes intolerance for group activities that are not well organized and conducted efficiently."

In addition, noted Couger, system analysts who are expected to interact extensively with users probably should not be former developers because they will probably want as little interaction with users as possible, and tend to rush through whatever interactions they do have.

When he initiated his international studies, Couger hypothesized that the survey responses from people from different cultures would be different. His surveys covered such diverse cultures as Taiwan, Hong Kong, Singapore, Australia, Israel, Finland, South Africa, and Austria. The surprising result was that IT professionals in these countries also exhibit high growth need strength and low social need strength. The IT profession appears to attract people with similar characteristics, irrespective of their culture. So the approaches to improving motivation would be similar for all these employees.

Improving the Maintenance Job.   In many of the organizations surveyed, both nationally and internationally, low job satisfaction generally occurred in pockets—the developers in one unit or the analysts in another. To correct the problem, determine which of the five core job dimensions—skill variety, task identity, task significance, autonomy, or feedback from the job—is the problem, recommended Couger. Then use an approach to achieve a satisfactory match between growth need strength and motivating potential score. The following examples come from a study that concentrated on maintenance programmers, conducted by Couger and Mel Colter.[9]

Skill variety is the dimension that most often causes IT professionals to perceive maintenance work as less challenging, noted Couger and Colter. This job dimension contains two elements: (1) the variety of skills needed to carry out the tasks, and (2) the variety of tasks. When the variety of skills is constrained, such as confinement to maintaining a legacy application when the person has the skills to do Web work, task variety should be emphasized. An illustration is assigning two people to jointly maintain two systems, thereby increasing the *task variety* for both.

Task identity can be enhanced in a different manner. Lack of task identity can occur when an individual is working on a module with little awareness of how it relates to the whole system or to the company's work. Supervisors could place more emphasis on these relationships, thus enhancing task identity.

The other component of task identity is completing a whole and identifiable piece of work. An example is working with the user to define the needed changes, revising the program, testing, and then implementing the changes. If the maintenance developer can be given an entire job instead of only portions of this sequence, task identity increases.

In several of the surveyed organizations, maintenance programmers were quite removed from the users, so little interaction occurred between the two. In such situations, the importance of the work—*the task significance*—was not conveyed to the programmers. This interaction could be improved by asking users to make presentations to the programmers who are maintaining their systems, stressing the importance of their work, or by moving the maintenance people out to the user area.

Another job core dimension that is often rated low for maintenance work is *autonomy,* not because supervisors do not give programmers freedom to operate but because the procedures or policies provide little flexibility. The legacy systems provide the constraints. One way supervisors can enhance autonomy is by encouraging participative goal setting and then not supervising the programmers too closely in the activities required to attain these goals.

In the study, maintenance personnel saw "compliance with schedule" as the most important evaluation factor for their promotion. This factor also illustrates *feedback from the job.* Companies that provide good project management systems, where the information is primarily for the programmers and secondarily for the supervisors, enhance feedback from the job.

This discussion illustrates how the Job Diagnostic Survey can reveal the need to better match jobs with the types of people who fill them. By analyzing both activities and employees, individuals can be matched with tasks, according to their growth need. A proper matching leads to greater motivation, happier employees, higher productivity, and perhaps longer tenure.

Rethinking Maintenance Work

In most companies, maintenance of existing systems is at least 70 percent of the application development workload and budget; work on new systems accounts for only 30 percent. Even purchased packages require maintenance. Typically, 80 percent of the requests for maintenance are for enhancements, while 20 percent are to fix errors.

Maintenance programmers have been difficult to find and keep because most prefer to do exciting new development work, Couger found. A seemingly sensible route has thus been to outsource maintenance work, often to offshore programming houses that have a greater supply of people willing to do the work. But Dana Edberg, at the

University of Nevada, Reno,[10] brings a new perspective to this maintenance conundrum, causing us to question the wisdom of outsourcing maintenance.

For her dissertation, Edberg studied 15 groups in five companies that had worked with a computer application for at least six months and were requesting changes. Her goal was to find out why they were making these requests and how IS departments responded to the requests. She found that the IS departments regarded maintenance as negative because they believed that if they had built the system right in the first place, users would not ask for changes. So change requests were seen as making the system "wrong," thus their goal was to keep maintenance costs low by discouraging such requests. Furthermore, they saw most of the requests as unnecessary. However, they were willing to make changes that simply *exploited* the system, such as a new report. But they did their best to discourage requests that *explored* beyond the system and would reengineer a process. Exploitative learning involves refining current processes while people demonstrating exploratory learning seek completely new ways of getting work done. Both types of learning are required in a competitive setting.

The IS departments' attitude, of course, was clearly evident to the users. So they did not make as many requests for changes as they really wanted. Furthermore, when they did make a request, they felt it needed to be justified, so they trumped up their reasons, saying such things as "It's to meet a new regulation," or "The boss wants it." They did not dare give the real reason that it would improve a process, or save them time, or make their job easier, because they did not want the request to appear to be their "fault."

Edberg found that some 40 percent of the requests were actually based on individual learning. An employee heard of or thought of a better way to work and realized how a change in the software would support that work. (Of course, not all employees in a group always wanted to change the way they worked, so they too discouraged some changes.)

In short, IS's negative attitude toward maintenance only encouraged learning that exploited the current system. It did not encourage exploratory learning. Hence, only three of Edberg's 15 groups made exploratory-learning requests.

Edberg's further insight was that once a change was implemented, it led to organizational learning because others in the group used the change when they used the software. She therefore hypothesizes that perhaps a better view of maintenance is to see it as organizational learning.

Such a shift in thinking from maintenance-is-bad to maintenance-is-organizational-learning takes it out of IS's backwater and moves it to a much-needed value-added service. This change could significantly help companies keep better pace with their environment. As it is, systems become a brake on business because they cast business practices in "electronic concrete," not allowing new ways of working.

Edberg implies that taking this learning perspective requires job redesign. The programmers need close relationships with the users to encourage both exploratory as well as exploitative learning. Thus, it cannot be outsourced.

To return to Hagel and Singer's framework, it appears that IS departments have moved maintenance out of the product innovation business into the infrastructure business, because they aim to reduce costs rather than gain speed and nimbleness. In so doing, they do not reap the organizational learning value and flexibility it could provide. So maintenance work appears to be misplaced.

Managing staff is not the only system development issue that concerns CIOs. In fact, developing the system is only part of the work. The other part is getting it implemented, that is, successfully being used in the business units.

HOW CAN SYSTEMS BE IMPLEMENTED SUCCESSFULLY?

IS staff members are often so enthralled with the technical aspects of a new system that they presume a technically elegant system is a successful system. However, many technically sound systems have turned into implementation failures because the people side of the system was not handled correctly. Information technology is all about managing change. New systems require changing how work is done. Focusing only on the technical aspects is only half the job. The other job is *change management.*

Change management is the process of assisting people to make major changes in their working environment. In this case, the change is caused by the introduction of a new computer system. Management of change has not always been handled methodically, so choosing a change management methodology and using it is a step toward successfully introducing new computer systems.

Change disrupts peoples' frame of reference if it presents a future where past experiences do not hold true, says ODR, a change management firm in Atlanta, Georgia.[11] People resist change, especially technological change, when they view it as a crisis. They cope by trying to maintain control. In the case of an impending new computer system, which they do not understand fully or are not prepared to handle, they may react in several ways. They may deny the change; they may distort information they hear about it; or they may try to convince themselves, and others, that the new system really will not change the status quo. These reactions are forms of resistance.

ODR offers a methodology to help companies manage technological change. They use specific terms from the field of organizational development to describe the types of people involved in a change project.

- The *sponsor* is the person or group that legitimizes the change. In most cases, this group must contain someone in top management who is highly respected by the business unit because change must be driven from the business unit.
- The *change agent* is the person or group who causes the change to happen. Change agents are often the IS staff. They can introduce the change but they cannot enforce its use.
- The *target* is the person or group who is being expected to change, and at whom the change is aimed.

Using surveys completed by a project's sponsors, change agents, and targets, ODR aims to:

- Describe the scope of the change.
- Assess the sponsors' commitment to the project.
- Assess the change agents' skills.
- Evaluate the support or resistance of the targets.

The goal of these initial evaluations is to determine whether the change can be made successfully with the current scope, sponsors, change agents, and targets. By evaluating each area, the change agents can determine (1) whether the scope of the project is doable, or whether the organization is trying to change too much at one time, (2) whether the sponsors are committed enough to push the change through, or whether they are sitting back expecting the organization to change on its own, (3) whether the change agents have the skills to implement the change. or whether they are not adept at rallying support, and (4) which groups are receptive to the change and which are resistant. Once these assessments have been made, ODR assists IS project teams to understand the risks their project faces, and what they can do to mitigate those risks.

As an example of an organization that used this approach, and successfully implemented nine change management projects, consider BOC Group, as described by Neil Farmer.[12]

CASE EXAMPLE

THE BOC GROUP

The BOC Group is an industrial gas manufacturer with global headquarters in Windlesham, England, and U.S. headquarters in Murray Hill, New Jersey. The company operates in 60 countries and sells industrial gases such as oxygen for steel making, carbon dioxide for food freezing, and so on.

The industry is mature and highly competitive, so companies compete on price and service. To improve the company's competitive position, management committed $35 million to reengineer BOC's core processes. In all, nine reengineering projects were initiated. All succeeded over a two-and-one-half-year time frame—a significant achievement.

The company established nine full-time teams, each to improve a selected process. Following completion, all team members were guaranteed a return to their former (or equivalent) job. Each team was co-led by a business and information management (IM) process leader because IT was a major component of

most of the projects. Each team also sat together in a bullpen setting.

For the first six months, each team studied its chosen business process. The research was not parceled out among team members; every team member studied everything. So IM team members were like all the other members. They studied the existing processes, and then had a say in how implementation should be handled, they supplied input into the training plan, and they helped devise the customer communication plan. They were often significant influencers because the other team members respected their opinions and their technical knowledge.

Garnering True Executive Sponsorship

Although the president was the executive sponsor for all the teams, he was not intimately involved in each project. So the real executive sponsors were vice presidents and directors. Although they

(Case Continued)

understood the need for the changes and were committed to the "concepts" behind them, day-to-day operational pressures put a strain on true sponsorship. To address this problem, BOC called on ODR to teach sponsorship to the nine sponsors in a two-day event.

The sponsors were reticent to go off-site for two days to talk about managing change. They believed employees did what they were asked to do. The sponsors did not understand the full impact of the changes on employees nor how employees would be assimilating the changes. They also did not realize their sponsorship job included building sponsorship down through company levels.

During the two-day event, the ODR facilitator described the sponsorship job in basic here's-what-is-needed terms, and he challenged the nine sponsors to ask the important questions, such as: "What in our culture might make our project not work? What has failed in the past at BOC? Are we asking too much? Is this realistic?" The facilitator pressed the sponsors to question the company's capacity to assimilate change. He got them to be honest and identify obstacles. They were, indeed, challenged. Up to that point, they had not addressed these questions.

The workshop did the job. It opened their eyes to their sponsorship role, which turned out to be crucial to the success of all the projects. They had underestimated the involvement required from the total organization. They had been sitting back expecting their teams to make change happen. But the teams could only put the tools in place; the organization had to make change happen. The workshop taught the sponsors the difference. They

left understanding how they needed to drive change through the organization. The facilitator led them into planning their own strategies and examining possible consequences.

One Change Project

One of the reengineering projects changed the way BOC processed the paperwork for delivering gas products and invoicing customers. Previously, drivers received a batch of shipping tickets each morning from a clerk. These tickets described their route for the day. When they dropped off a cylinder of gas or picked up an empty one, they marked it on a full-size sheet of paper and handed it to the customer. They also returned handwritten notes to the clerk for entry into the system.

The solution was to replace the paper with a point-of-delivery handheld device (PODD). Schedules would be made at night and downloaded electronically to the PODDs. Loaders would use this information to load the trucks during the night. In the morning, the drivers would pick up their PODD, which contained their route for the day. When they delivered a cylinder, the PODD would accept the customer's signature and then print out a delivery document the size of a grocery store receipt. At the end of the day, the driver hung the PODD back on the rack and the billing data was automatically transmitted to headquarters.

To arrive at this solution, the team, as a whole, studied the process from order to delivery to billing. In working as a unified team, the IM folks began to act as business folks, and vice versa. At the end, the two were indistinguishable because they had absorbed each other's knowledge.

(Case Continued)

This interaction was a much-appreciated by-product of the process. Once the entire team devised the solution, the IM staff built the technical infrastructure.

Involving Middle Management. To engage middle managers in the nine reengineering projects, BOC established an advisory council for each one. Each advisory council's job was twofold, upward and downward. The upward job was to give feedback on recommended changes, pointing out implementation issues. The downward job was to describe the recommendations to employees and get their buy-in.

The PODD advisory council had 11 members, which included drivers, logistics, IM, field people, and managers. They met several times, and they had more influence than they realized. Their upward feedback significantly affected the PODD team's decisions and their downward communication gave the field people a way to be heard. Through all the advisory councils, BOC created a cascade of influencers, which was a key contributor to their success.

Training the Drivers. The PODD team developed a handheld device that was so logical and intuitive that little training was needed. However, to make the drivers comfortable and ensure success of the project, the team created a six-hour training program.

The training theme was "A day in a driver's life" and the purpose was to show the truck drivers how to use the PODD to do their job. The lead trainer (a former truck driver) first led the drivers through "A perfect day" scenario where nothing went wrong. With PODD in hand, each driver followed the lead trainer in going through an entire day's use of the PODD, from loading cylinders into the truck to dropping off the PODD at night. This rapid scenario gave them the overall feel of its use. The drivers made mistakes, but as they corrected their own mistakes, they became more and more comfortable with the PODD.

The drivers then worked at their own pace through three successively harder scenarios, following a laminated sheet of instructions that included cylinder bar codes, and other pertinent information. The drivers who got through all three had no problem with the PODD. Those who got through two might need a little support. Those who struggled would need a trainer to ride with them for a day or two.

To ensure the drivers were fully comfortable with the PODD, the PODD team offered to ride with *any* driver for a day. Many accepted, not just to build their confidence but because they enjoyed the company of another person. Whenever the driver raised a question during that day, the team member usually responded, "What do you think you should do?" Generally the driver's answer was right, which built up self-confidence.

Due to all the training, the PODD team encountered little resistance from the drivers. In fact, the drivers were so pleased the company was investing in them that they proudly showed their PODD to their customers; they were the only drivers in the industry to have them.

The project was successful because the PODD team had assessed its people aspects at the outset and mitigated the identified risks by holding the sponsorship event, involving middle management via the advisory council, and thoroughly training the truck drivers. ∎

Thus far, this chapter has dealt with the people issues of system development: managing staff and technology-based change. We now shift to a question that repeatedly comes around, "How can legacy systems be improved?"

HOW CAN LEGACY SYSTEMS BE IMPROVED?

Most information systems executives feel trapped by the past. They have thousands of old legacy programs and data files they would love to replace. The worst offenders were discarded because they were not Y2K compliant. But with the onslaught of e-commerce, CIOs may not have the resources to replace all the remaining legacy systems. Replacement is not the only option, however. In many cases, it may not even be the wisest option.

To Replace or Not to Replace?

To replace or not to replace? That is the question studied by the Boston Consulting Group (BCG)[13] in 18 manufacturing companies, service firms, and government organizations in North America, Europe, and Japan that had either just replaced or upgraded legacy systems or were in the process of replacing or upgrading. Of the 21 projects, 12 were successful in that they worked and had a bottom-line impact. But the other 9 were either unsuccessful or did not deliver the anticipated results.

From these findings, the BCG concluded that upgrading (rather than replacing) made more sense in most cases, even if it was difficult and not seen as exciting as a totally new system. They noted that people get seduced by a new technology and want to rush out and replace old systems with it. But BCG found that most of the replacement projects that failed could have been upgrade projects. In fact, in some cases, the company reverted to upgrading the old system anyway.

When a system's technology is so obsolete that it does not exist in many places, then replacement is probably the only choice. But otherwise, BCG recommends that companies perform three analyses. One, do a rigorous analysis of the costs and benefits of the new system. Most companies underestimate the cost of replacing a system and overestimate the achievable business value, even on the successful projects. Furthermore, they do not factor in the risk of failure. Two, determine how specialized the new system really is. Sometimes companies think they need a made-to-order system when a purchased solution would do just fine. Their requirements are not as unique as they think. And three, assess the IS staff's capabilities honestly. Several of the companies in the study failed to develop replacement systems because management had overrated the staff's skills. In conclusion, BCG recommends that the burden of proof lie with those who advocate replacement of a legacy system rather than with those who advocate an upgrade, especially for mission-critical systems.

Options for Improving a Legacy System

With this insightful study as a backdrop, let's discuss six choices companies have for dealing creatively with legacy systems, from (ideally) least to most amounts of change (Figure 10-4).

Any of these options can be performed in-house or sourced to an outside firm. In moving to a totally new platform, such as ERP, for example, companies take one of two strategies in using outsourcing firms. The first is to keep the legacy maintenance work

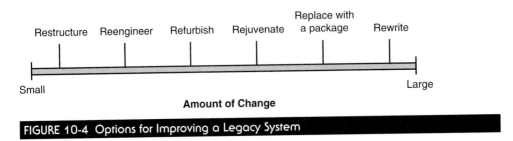

FIGURE 10-4 Options for Improving a Legacy System

in-house, hire a consulting firm to implement the new system, and then phase out the legacy maintenance work. Others have opted for the opposite. They outsource maintenance of the legacy systems so that the in-house staff can focus on developing the ERP system. As the new system comes online, the outsourcer turns off the legacy systems. Companies take this transitional outsourcing approach when they feel they have (or can get) the in-house expertise required by the new platform. As the Boston Consulting Group found in its survey, in-house skill levels can be the main determinant in deciding whether this second approach is even feasible.

Here then, is the spectrum of options for improving legacy systems.

Restructure the System. If an application program is basically doing its job but it runs inefficiently or is "fragile" or unmaintainable, then it may simply need to be *restructured*. For years, vendors have offered software products to aid in this process. The most popular ones use automated restructuring engines to turn "spaghetti code" into more structured code. The process involves the following seven steps.

1. Evaluate the amount of structure in the current system, including the number of layers of nesting, degree of complexity, and so forth. Use the tools to present a trace of the program's control logic. Subjectively evaluate the code to determine whether restructuring is warranted at all, or if more extensive change is required; this task can only be performed by people.
2. Compile the program to be sure it is in working order. A code restructuring tool will not make a nonoperative program run.
3. Clean up and restructure the code by running the program through a structuring engine. This automated process does not change the logic of the program; it simply replaces poor coding conventions with structured coding conventions, such as reducing the number of GOTOs, removing dead code and alter statements, highlighting looping conditions, and grouping and standardizing inputoutput statements. It uncovers the structure hidden inside the convoluted code.
4. Reformat the listing, making it easier to understand, by using a formatting package.
5. Ensure that the old and new versions produce the same output by using a fileto-file comparator.
6. Minimize overhead introduced by restructuring by using an optimizer package. After optimization, restructured programs generally require between 5 percent less and 10 percent more run time than the unstructured versions.
7. "Rationalize" the data by giving all uses of the same data one data name. This step is optional.

These seven steps can be used to restructure a functional system or to get it in shape to be reengineered.

Reengineer the System. A step beyond restructuring is reengineering, which means extracting the data elements from an existing file and the business logic from an existing program and moving them to new hardware platforms. This use of the term *reengineering* should not be confused with the term *business process reengineering,* which was used elsewhere. This term *system* or *application reengineering* is much narrower and refers only to software. The other term refers to redesigning business processes. Like code restructuring, reengineering requires automated tools because the process is too complex to be cost-justifiably done manually. Database reengineering tools began appearing on the market in the late 1980s.

According to Charles Bachman, a pioneer in the database field, the major problem in the computer field is that people consider existing systems as liabilities that must be maintained, which takes resources away from developing new and exciting applications. Instead, management needs to see existing systems as assets from which to move forward—a view similar to Edberg's.

If developers can "reverse engineer" a system, that is, extract the underlying business logic, they can "forward engineer" that business logic to a new system platform. With this approach, existing systems become assets. Developers can extract the intelligence in them, rather than start over from scratch.

Bachman believes a new system development life cycle can use automated products to help perform the reverse engineering. It encompasses all four basic development activities: maintenance, enhancement, new development, and migration. This life cycle is circular rather than linear, as shown in Figure 10-5.

- *Reverse engineering*—where existing programs, along with their file and database descriptions, are converted from their implementation level descriptions that include records, databases, code, and so on, into their equivalent design-level components of entities, attributes, processes, messages, and so on.
- *Forward engineering*—which goes the opposite direction, from requirements-level components to osperational systems. Design items created by reverse engineering are used to create new applications via forward engineering.

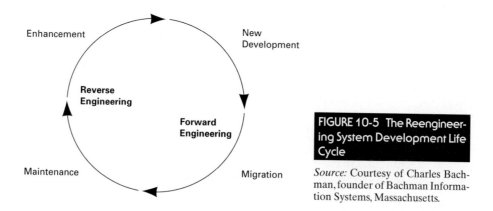

FIGURE 10-5 The Reengineering System Development Life Cycle

Source: Courtesy of Charles Bachman, founder of Bachman Information Systems, Massachusetts.

The cycle continues because as new applications go into operation, they become candidates for reverse engineering whenever they need to be changed. Neither people nor automated tools can use this new life cycle by themselves, noted Bachman, but together, it becomes feasible. GTE Directories is an example of a company that used such reengineering tools.

CASE EXAMPLE

GTE DIRECTORIES

GTE Directories produced, marketed, and distributed more than 1,500 different telephone directories in some 14 countries. To accelerate their response to changing markets, GTE Directories began automating their telephone directory publishing business.

The directory publishing system had four main databases. The largest supported all the administrative functions for creating and selling Yellow Page advertising, from sales to photo composition. The second was used by representatives to sell Yellow Page advertising for non-GTE directories. The third database handled billing. And the fourth database provided order entry for independent telephone companies, for whom GTE produced telephone books.

The databases were originally designed application-by-application. The result was records that contained data elements with no business relationship to each other, making them difficult to reuse, enhance, and change. The data administration group acquired reverse engineering tools to help them improve these databases.

To reverse engineer the database, a designer used a design administrator to display the existing database definitions graphically. The design was reversed engi-

neered, where the designer made changes by manipulating the graphical icons. The tool helped draw complete and consistent relationship diagrams because it had the intelligence to identify inconsistencies and incomplete structures.

Once the new database design had been created, the designer forward engineered the database design and ran the physical implementation design rules. When the design was satisfactory, the new database statements were automatically generated.

Such database reengineering was used on two projects.

The Blueprint Project

The largest database had not been properly designed, so the data administration group used the toolset to create a "blueprint" of what the database should look like. They reverse engineered the existing database from its physical to its data model from which they created a new, properly designed data model using entity-relationship modeling techniques. By experimenting with this model, they created a design that was more adaptable to change. It became their blueprint for the future and was used to guide maintenance work. As the database administra-

(Case Continued)

tors maintained the database, they made changes to align it more closely with this blueprint. Without the reengineering changes to align it more closely with this blueprint. Without the reengineering tools, they would not have even attempted this project, because they could not have done the "what if" modeling necessary to create the blueprint.

A Reuse Project

The database administrators reused some of the data elements in the largest database for a new production scheduling system. The company had scheduled production of their 1,500 directories among their three printing plants using a 15-year-old system. Some scheduling data was in the system, some was in the new administrative system.

The company created a new scheduling system, drawing some scheduling-related data from the administrative database. Again, they used reengineering tools to create the design models for the new scheduling databases. From these models, they used a tool to generate the necessary database statements. With the new system, salespeople no longer had to interrogate both the 15-year-old publishing system and the administrative system—which had different sets of data—to see directory publishing schedules.

Because maintenance was the bulk of the work of the database administration group, the tools became invaluable in helping them redesign old databases, design new databases using portions of existing ones, and create their blueprint for the future. ∎

Refurbish the System. If the old system is maintainable and is causing no major problems, it may be worthwhile adding some extensions. Potential extensions would supply input in a new manner, or make new uses of the output, or allow the programs to deal more comprehensively with data.

Refurbishment is actually occurring quite a bit these days because of the World Wide Web. Companies are leaving existing systems in place but adding a Web front end, along with accompanying query translation software so the system can be accessed directly by employees, suppliers, or even customers. Witness FedEx's Web site, which allows customers to directly access the company's tracking database. In such cases, companies generally follow a "surround" strategy, where they treat the old system as an untouchable "black box" and surround it with new facilities. This approach has been a popular way to upgrade legacy systems, even before the Web's appearance.

Rejuvenate the System. Rejuvenating an old system is a step beyond refurbishing the system because it adds enough new functions to a system to make it more valuable to the firm. The first step is to recognize a system's potential. The second is to clean up the system, perhaps using restructuring tools. The third step is to make the system more efficient, perhaps using the reengineering approach mentioned earlier, then port the system to a new operating environment and database structure. The fourth step is to give the system a more strategic role, such as allowing it to feed a data warehouse so that people in field offices can access data far more quickly. Another possibility is to give it a role in a company's electronic commerce strategy by using it as a back-end system accessible via the Web.

Replace With a Package or Service. Many old systems built in-house have been replaced by a package developed by a third party. In fact, these days, this alternative has become the norm. One reason for choosing this option is to replace numerous old and disjointed applications with one corporatewide system, such as SAP. The other popular option is to distribute an application's workload among a host computer, some servers, and many PCs and laptops. An increasing number of commercial packages permit such three-tiered processing. These packages not only support communication among the three types of machines but they also split the processing job and facilitate downloading and uploading of files.

Another reason to consider replacing an old system with a commercial package is that these products are becoming more versatile. Many offer selectable features that allow purchasers to tailor the package to their work style. The options can be turned on or off using control files, so no programming is necessary. Even end users can specify some of the operating instructions. Even so, replacing one or more applications with a package is not a trivial task. Just ask the people who have installed an ERP system.

The most recent option, and the one being touted as "the future," is replacing a system with a service delivered over the Internet. Now that software vendors have a ubiquitous delivery mechanism—the Internet—they can sell a per-seat, per-month service in place of leasing a package. Companies may reap several benefits from choosing this option. One, the software will be available quickly; speed is all-important these days. Two, the cost can be expensed rather than be a capital expenditure. Three, the software is run and maintained by the vendor. Four, it is centralized in that it is being handled by the vendor, but it is distributed in that it can be accessed from anywhere. Companies are even considering creating corporate portals where commonly used software is accessed via the Net, rather than housed on PCs. That software can be located anywhere.

Rewrite the System. In some cases, a legacy system is too far gone to rescue. If the code is convoluted and patched, if the technology is antiquated, and if the design is poor, it may be necessary to start from scratch. Today, few companies write new applications from scratch. It is just too time-consuming and too expensive. So rewriting a system now means system integration, that is, finding packages that do pieces of the work, then using middleware tools to link them together.

Whether a system is new or a replacement, or anything in between, the question that is always asked is, "What is this system worth to us?" It is a question all executives now need to be able to answer because investment in IT has become such a large part of corporate expenditures.

HOW CAN SYSTEMS BENEFITS BE MEASURED?

Measuring the value of information systems seems to be a continuing request. Never mind that the Internet has changed the world or that e-commerce and e-business are impossible without computers. Executives want specific links between new systems and corporate financial measures, such as an increase in earnings, stockholder value, or revenue. Achieving this link is devilishly difficult because IT is only one of the factors contributing to successful use of systems.

The value of decision support systems and data warehouses, for example, are difficult to measure because they are intended to change such unmeasurable actions as improved decisions, better identification of opportunities, more thorough analysis, and enhanced communication among people. E-commerce systems, which aim to improve a firm's competitive edge or protect its market share, also elude measurement. It makes no sense to determine their return on investment (ROI) in terms of hours saved when their intent is to increase revenue or help the firm enter a new market. Finally, infrastructure investments, upon which future applications will be built, cannot be justified on ROI because they have none. Only the subsequent applications will show a return on investment, which has caused the measurement conundrum.

In their research for *Uncovering the Information Technology Payoffs,*[14] Walter Carlson and Barbara McNurlin found the following three suggestions, as well as numerous others, on how to deal with these measurement dilemmas.

1. Distinguish between the different roles of systems.
2. Measure what is important to management.
3. Assess investments across organizational levels.

Distinguish Between the Different Roles of Systems

Paul Berger,[15] a management consultant, believes that companies can measure the value of IT investments by using many of the management measures now in place. Information systems can play three roles in a company, Berger told Carlson and McNurlin.

1. They can *help other departments do their job better.* Berger calls these "support systems." Their goal is to increase organizational efficiency.
2. Information systems can *carry out a business strategy.* Examples are CAD systems that customers and suppliers can use together to design custom products. Web-based systems and other such strategic systems need to be measured differently from support systems because they are used directly by customers, suppliers, and clients; support systems are not.
3. Systems can be sold as *a product or service or as the basis for a product or service.* Many Web-based information services fall into this category.

Measuring the benefits of these three kinds of systems differs.

Measuring Organizational Performance.   Organizational performance has to do with meeting deadlines and milestones, operating within budget, and doing quality work. Performance measures the *efficiency* of operations.

A number of years ago, Berger worked on developing a large human resources system with decision support capabilities, and then tracking its benefits. To measure the value of the system, the development team compared the productivity of people who used it to the productivity of people who did not. Data was collected on the cost of operating the system and the total costs of running the human resources departments.

Operating costs did not rise as fast in the human resources departments where the system was used, the team found. By the fifth year, the using department had a cost of $103 per work unit (up from $82) while the nonusing department's cost was $128 per work unit (also up from $82). During those five years, the unit costs in the department using the system rose about 25 percent; the nonusing department's costs rose more than 56 percent.

Measuring Business Value.   Measuring business unit *performance* deals with internal operational goals, whereas measuring business *value* deals with marketplace goals. Systems that are part of a business plan can be measured on their contribution to the success or failure of that plan. But, in order for systems to be measured on their business value, they must have a *direct* impact on the company's relationships with its customers, clients, or suppliers, says Berger.

Berger's HR system was measured on departmental performance. It could not be measured on business value because its effect on the corporate bottom line was indirect. No direct link to increased revenue could be identified. This distinction is important in measuring the value of IT investments.

In another firm, several information systems were developed to help marketing people analyze their customer base, both current and potential customers. The goal was to improve the quality of their customer base so that sales per customer would increase, while, at the same time, sales and promotion costs would decrease.

After implementing the systems, advertising and customer service costs decreased. The company also experienced higher customer retention and lower direct sales costs, compared to industry standards. By being able to equate the particular information system expenditures to marketing, they could identify a direct correlation between system costs and sales revenue. They could measure business value. The information systems affected their sales directly through the marketing decisions the system supported, so the value of the investment could be stated in business terms.

Measuring a Product or Service.   An information system can be offered as a product or service, or it can contribute to a product or service intended to produce revenue. In these cases, its value is measured as is any other business venture, by its performance in the market. The measures are typical business profitability measures, such as return on investment, return on assets, and return on equity.

Measure What Is Important to Management

Charles Gold,[16] an IT consultant, recommends measuring what management thinks is important. Information systems support can only be linked to corporate effectiveness by finding all the indicators they use, besides the traditional financial ones. Relating proposed benefits to these indicators can make it easier to "sell" a system, at both the individual and aggregate levels.

Gold suggests trying to assess benefits in terms of customer relations, employee morale, and cycle time, or how long it takes to accomplish a complete assignment. Each measure goes beyond monetary terms, which few executives deny are vital to a company's success. He gave Carlson and McNurlin two examples.

As a measure of customer satisfaction, one power company kept a log of how many complaint letters customers sent to the Public Utilities Commission each month; this commission regulates the utility companies within its state. The power company installed a computer system for its customer service representatives, giving them online access to the information they needed to answer customers' questions. When the system was in operation, the number of complaint letters decreased; when the system was down, the number of letters increased. So, one aspect of the effectiveness of this system was measurable in terms of public opinion.

A second possible measure is cycle time. Faster cycle times can mean much more than saving hours. It can mean higher-quality products, beating competitors to a market, winning a bid, and so on. The benefit may have nothing to do with *saving* money. Rather, it may focus on *making* money.

So, says Gold, concentrating only on cost and monetary measures may be short-sighted. Other measures can be even more important to management.

Assess Investments Across Organizational Levels

Kathleen Curley, now at Lotus Development Corporation, and John Henderson, Boston University,[17] recommended measuring IS benefits at several organizational levels. They developed the Value Assessment Framework to do just that.

The Value Assessment Framework.   Because the potential benefits of IT investments differ at various organizational levels, Curley and Henderson believe companies need a systematic way to separate these benefits by organizational level. They see three organizational levels, or *sources of value,* in particular, as receiving benefit from IT investment: the individual, the division, and the corporation.

Furthermore, the *impact focus* of an IT investment extends beyond business performance measures to encompass three dimensions:

1. *Economic performance payoffs* (market measures of performance)
2. *Organizational processes impacts* (measures of process change)
3. *Technology impacts* (impacts on key functionality)

Combining the two views creates a 3 × 3 matrix that can be used to systematically assess the impact of a potential IT investment in nine areas. This framework was used by a trucking company, and its use uncovered benefits that otherwise would have gone unrealized.

CASE EXAMPLE

A TRUCKING COMPANY

A small-to-medium-sized company in the refrigerated carrier business has been around since the 1920s. When the Motor Carrier Act deregulated trucking companies, competition increased. Small firms like this one were hit the hardest. Even though they had been one of the top five refrigeration trucking firms, their share of shipped tons fell to less than one-half

the former level because national and regional carriers took away their business. In response to the crisis, management made two decisions: First, they would manage the company by information, transforming company procedures and tracking success via a large suite of measures. Secondly, management would use information technology to differentiate

(Case Continued)

the firm from other refrigeration trucking firms, initially with a $10 million investment in a state-of-the-art satellite system and a computer in every truck cab, so that their drivers could be in constant voice and data communication with the company and customers.

The results were remarkable. Tons shipped increased from 300,000 tons to 1,100,000 tons and the trucker became an industry leader in the innovative manipulation of information. They introduced ground-breaking information services that provided superior levels of customer service.

Their Measurement Program

On the measurement front, the company developed world-class goals for each of their three mission statement objectives:

Our mission is to exceed the expectations of our customers, earn a return on investment that is the best in the industry, and provide our employees an opportunity to attain fulfillment through participation.

Overall performance was measured in these ways:

- Customer satisfaction—determined by "moment of truth" questionnaires filled out by customers to rate the company's service performance
- Return on investment—measured by an operating ratio
- Employee satisfaction—from questionnaires that captured employee sentiments and charted them on an index.

The company established interim performance improvement goals for the company and each department to be achieved by specific dates. These interim measures were to see how fast and how well they were progressing toward their world-class goals. As performance improved, the goals were raised so that performance improvement was built into their measurement system.

After studying their measurement and tracking processes, Curley said, "They have one of the most detailed sets of measures I have ever seen."

Measuring the Value of the Satellite System

Following IBM Consulting's recommendation, the trucker used the Curley and Henderson Value Management Framework to evaluate the satellite investment after-the-fact, with eye-opening results. They began by identifying the specific process improvements made possible by the system, entering them into the framework along with an outcome and outcome measure for each one. For example,

- At the individual level, they estimated that improved communications from the truck cab would increase driver production time by one-half hour a day. The result: a savings of $59.60 a month per driver.
- At the work group level, they estimated that improved load truck matching would save 1 percent deadhead time: a $49.68 savings per month per truck.
- At the business unit level, they estimated that improved customer service would increase market share, but they could not pin down a dollar amount for this increase.

(Case Continued)

Once these figures were calculated, a manager was assigned to assess the savings targets, allowing the company to evaluate whether they were realistically estimating the investment. They intended to manage the value they were receiving from their investment, not just make the investment and hope it paid off.

The most interesting piece of the Value Management Framework analysis, Curley said, was not the identifiable cost savings but the large, unexpected revenue benefits. Due to the analysis, management discovered that customers were willing to pay a premium price for the ability to call a truck driver directly from the customer's warehouse. Constant communication with drivers was worth a lot, a lot more than management thought. This discovery gave them even more confidence in their decision to bet on technology, and in their ability to sell information-based services. Due to their sophisticated and ingrained measurement system, they are even able to see the effect of their pricing on market share. So, indeed, they are managing by information. ■

CONCLUSION

As noted at the outset of this chapter, system development is in the innovation business, and in that business, developers are king. Therefore, staffing is a key management issue. Even with development moving to third-party firms, the programming mindset still pervades IS organizations. So CIOs need to understand the types of jobs and cultures that motivate IS professionals. Finding staff that enjoy doing maintenance work is particularly vexing. Perhaps the objective of maintenance needs rethinking, to change it from lowest cost to greatest added-value.

Managing development staff is only part of the people job in system development. The second is helping people adjust to the organizational changes that occur with a new system. The realm of change management and successfully implementing systems so they are actually used well involves ensuring that sponsors understand their role in enforcing change, giving change agents the tools and skills to foster the change, and assisting the targets in making the change, such as providing training.

Most software is devilishly difficult to keep up-to-date. As a result, at some point in time, management needs to decide what to do with aging software. Among the various options, the most common these days is to replace it with a package. A new alternative, however, is to "rent" the software off the Web, per-seat, per-month. Some contend this option is the wave of the future.

Finally, the question continually asked about applications is, "What is it worth to us?" Because it is not the only contributor to corporate operational improvements, a direct link can be difficult to establish. However, the process of justifying a new system can uncover what is important to management, and measuring benefits afterward can help companies spot benefits they had not originally planned.

QUESTIONS AND EXERCISES

Review Questions

1. What three businesses is the IS department in, using Hagel and Singer's framework?
2. Describe the product-innovation business.
3. What eight career clusters will be needed in IS departments, according to NWCET?
4. Explain Fidelity's One, Two, Three ranking scheme.
5. What are the five core job dimensions in the job diagnostic survey? What recommendations do Couger and Colter have for improving the job of the maintenance programmer?
6. How does Edberg suggest viewing maintenance work?
7. Describe ODR's three types of people involved in a change project.
8. How did BOC Group garner true executive sponsorship?
9. How did BOC Group involve middle management?
10. Which does the Boston Consulting Group recommend, replacing or upgrading a legacy system?
11. List the six ways to improve a legacy system.
12. Why did GTE Directories turn to reengineering?
13. What are the three roles of systems, according to Berger?
14. Explain the six elements of Curley and Henderson's Value Assessment Framework.
15. What benefits did the trucking company realize at the individual, group, and business levels?

Discussion Questions

1. IS staffing should become easier as more people gain experience in e-business or move from failed dot-coms. Agree or disagree? Discuss.
2. If companies are moving toward providing corporate portals where software is rented from a third party over the Internet, IS departments can get out of the application development business. Agree or disagree? Discuss.
3. The strategy of minimum maintenance until a system must be completely redone is still best for challenging and developing the programmer/analyst staff. The few people that like nitty-gritty maintenance activities can take care of the programs that need it, while the majority of the development staff can be challenged by the creativity of new development. The six options turn most developers into maintenance programmers. Agree or disagree? Discuss.
4. Management has no way to estimate the benefit of a system that is intended to generate new revenue, and so it must build the system on faith, not estimates. Agree or disagree? Discuss.

Exercises

1. Make a table showing the advantages and disadvantages of each of the six options for improving legacy systems. Derive from the table a list of characteristics of a legacy system that can serve as a management guideline for deciding which options are best in a given situation.
2. Find a company in your community that has more than 10 years' experience using computer systems. Develop a descriptive case study for that company showing how it deals with its legacy systems. Include an inventory of major systems and the company's strategies for maintenance and modernization. How does the company decide which applications to upgrade and which approaches to use? Explain how top

management and line management get involved in application portfolio decisions. If they don't, why not?

3. Read three articles or find five Web sites that discuss IS staffing issues. What new information did you learn? Present it to the class.

REFERENCES

1. Hagel, John, III and Marc Singer, "Unbundling the Corporation," *Harvard Business Review,* March/April 1999, 133–141, www.hbsp.harvard.edu.

2. *Bridging the Gap: Information Technology Skills for the New Millennium,* Information Technology Association of America, 1401 Wilson Blvd., Arlington, VA, www.itaa.org, 2000.

3. Parry, Scott, "Performance Indicators: The Heart of Human Resources Management," The Training House, Princeton, NJ.

4. *Building a Foundation for Tomorrow: Skill Standards for Information Technology: The Millennium Edition,* NorthWest Center for Emerging Technologies, Bellevue, WA, www.nwcet.org; 1999.

5. Patricia Seemann, Zurich Group, Switzerland, speaking at GIGA Information Group's Leveraging Knowledge Conference, March 1999.

6. Cappelli, Peter, "A Market-Driven Approach to Retaining Talent," *Harvard Business Review,* www.hbsp.harvard.edu, January/February 2000, 103–111.

7. Woolfe, Roger, "Evolving Competencies for IS Lite," Gartner Executive Programs, Stamford, CT, September 2000.

8. Cougar, J. Daniel, and Robert Zawacki, *Motivating and Managing Computer Personnel,* John Wiley and Sons, New York, 1980; Cougar, J. Daniel, and R. O'Callaghan, "Comparing the Motivation of Spanish and Finnish Computer Personnel with Those of the United States," *European Journal of Information Systems,* 3, no. 4, 1994, 285–291; Cougar, J. Daniel, "Comparisons of Motiva-

tion Norms for Programmer/Analysts in the Pacific Rim and the U.S.," *International Information Systems,* July 1992, 16–30.

9. Cougar, J. Daniel, and Mel Colter, *Maintenance Programming: Improved Productivity Through Motivation,* Prentice Hall, Upper Saddle River, NJ, 1985.

10. Edberg, Dana, and Lorne Olfman, "Organizational Learning Through the Process of Enhancing Information Systems," paper presented at Hawaii International Conference on System Sciences, January 2001.

11. From communications with ODR, 2900 Chamblee-Tucker Road, Building 16, Atlanta, GA 30341.

12. Farmer, Neil, "Changes in our Times," Wentworth Management Program (now part of Gartner Executive Programs), Stamford, CT, May 1999.

13. Kiely, Thomas, "Computer Legacy Systems: What Works When They Don't?" *Harvard Business Review,* July/August 1996, 10–12.

14. Carlson, Walter, and Barbara McNurlin, "Uncovering the Information Technology Payoffs," a special report, *I/S Analyzer,* Fall 1992.

15. From correspondence with Paul Berger of Paul Berger Consulting, Inc., Lawrenceville, NJ.

16. From correspondence with Charles Gold of West Cornwall, CT.

17. Curley, Kathleen and John Henderson, "Assessing the Value of a Corporate-wide Human Resource Information System: A Case Study," *Journal of Management Systems,* Special Issue, 1992.

IV

SYSTEMS FOR SUPPORTING KNOWLEDGE WORK

This part consists of four chapters that discuss supporting knowledge work. As shown in the book's framework diagram in the following figure, we distinguish between procedure-based and knowledge-based information-handling activities. The two previous chapters, in Part III, dealt mainly with building systems aimed at supporting procedure-based work. This part focuses on supporting knowledge-based activities: the *systems* that *support* people in performing information-handling activities to ascertain goals, pursue objectives, and solve problems.

Chapter 11 explores the expanding universe of computing. Although corporate computing initially aimed at automating office work, the world of computing has expanded to the point where corporations now need to support mobile consumers who carry around handhelds and expect to access corporate Web sites wirelessly.

Chapter 12 discusses decision support systems (DSS) and executive information systems (EIS), both of which are intended to provide people with the kinds of computer-based information that help them make better decisions.

Chapter 13 deals with group systems, which support the communication and interaction among people as they work in teams or groups.

Chapter 14 discusses leveraging the world of information by delving into document and knowledge management and their importance in today's e-world.

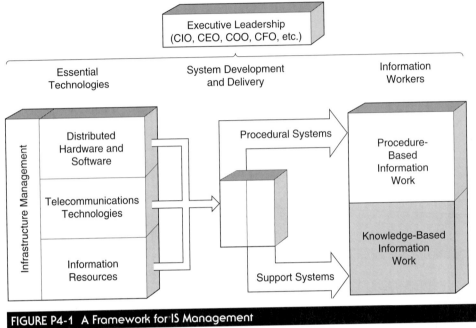

FIGURE P4-1 A Framework for IS Management

CHAPTER 11

THE EXPANDING UNIVERSE OF COMPUTING

INTRODUCTION

The use and impact of computers and information technology have been expanding since the beginning of this information age. Initially, use was limited to technical specialists who prepared the data, ran the programs, and distributed the output. The first major expansion was to nontechnical "end users" who were not computer specialists, and were sometimes barely computer literate but used the technology to accomplish their jobs in finance, accounting, sales, and so on.

IS departments established end user computing support groups, often called information centers, to support the use of PCs as well as fourth-generation languages on mainframes. The history of Mead Corporation's information resources department, presented in Chapter 1, is typical of this evolution: from developing applications in the 1970s, to encouraging end users to access computers directly on their own in the 1980s, to integrating end user computing into enterprisewide computing in the early 1990s.

In the 1990s, no widely accepted term described the use of computers by individuals to get their work done because this use was no longer just a small category of computer users; it had become the dominate category of computing. Computing does not emanate from a data center as it formerly did; now it is everywhere.

We see the universe of users of corporate computing also expanding. As shown in Figure 11-1, the users of corporate information services through the 1970s and mid-1980s were mainly employees, at their work site. In the mid-1980s, organizations opened up access to their computer systems to some supplier and customer organizations. In

FIGURE 11-1 The Expanding Universe of Users of Corporate Computing Services

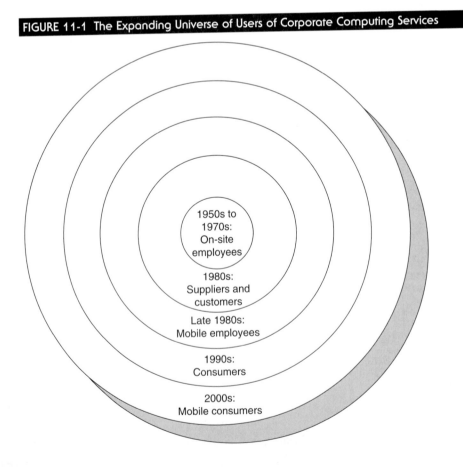

1950s to 1970s:
On-site employees

1980s:
Suppliers and customers

Late 1980s:
Mobile employees

1990s:
Consumers

2000s:
Mobile consumers

the late 1980s, with the advent of portable computers, IS departments began to support their mobile employees, giving them direct access to corporate computers wherever they were located. Then, with the explosion of the Internet, and especially the World Wide Web, this universe of "users" expanded further still, to consumers. Today, the expansion of the computing universe is to the mobile consumer. Serving them in the context of e-business is the "next frontier" for corporate IS departments.

The Internet has become the fundamental infrastructure for all computing, unifying all the audiences in Figure 11-1. Rather than technology serving a single category of user—employees (on-site and mobile), suppliers and partners, customers and consumers—all are served by the functions delivered through the Internet, intranet, and extranet. On-site and mobile employees are served by the intranet (B2E), suppliers and partners interact through shared Web sites and extranets (B2B), and customers (mobile and fixed) deal with the organization through B2C Web sites.

At the same time, the technology world seems to be growing by the minute, with more kinds of computing devices, new telecommunication options, and many new potential uses announced monthly. In traditional enterprise computing systems, applications were developed mainly by programmers using programming languages, databases, object libraries, middleware, and the like as discussed in the last two chapters. But end users use quite a different "toolset" to create their computer-based work environment. Three technologies underlie and enable this toolset.

1. *The Internet.* As we have often said thus far in the book, "The Internet changes everything." Global interconnected networks of computers called the Internet, and its "killer app," the World Wide Web, unify and expand the universe of computing in a stunning way.
2. *Mobile and Wireless Computing.* The explosion of devices to support mobile and wireless computing is leading to "anytime, anywhere" computing for work and play.
3. *Rich Media Content.* The digitization of information content, usually in multimedia form, transmitted over broadband telecommunication networks, provides a "window on the world" of information for computer users.

In this chapter, we first look at the attitudes of end users as they confront this expanding technology universe and the kinds of support they need to assimilate it. Then we look at the three underlying technologies already cited, which form the infrastructure for the new ways of working. We close the chapter with a discussion of the issues IS management faces in supporting this vastly expanded universe of computer users and computer technologies.

THE TECHNOLOGY CAMEL

Individuals, work groups, departments, even business units have different levels of eagerness concerning any new technology. Therefore, if the IS department is truly going to help them use a new technology, such as the Internet, it needs to understand user comfort levels. Elizabeth Ghaffari,[1] an IS consultant in Los Angeles, cites the Yankee Group and Find/SVP, two market research firms, who distinguish levels of comfort with technology by using five "clusters." The Yankee Group uses these clusters to describe the 100 million U.S. households and how they view contemporary technology:

- 1/2 million are innovators, constantly sniffing out new technologies.
- 5 million are early adopters of new technologies.
- 30–35 million are early majority households.
- 40–50 million are late majority households.
- 10–15 million are technically averse.

When graphed on a chart, these clusters look a lot like a two-humped camel, notes Ghaffari. It is lying on its stomach with its nose inside a tent, say, the Internet technology tent. The first cluster is his nose as he nudges the flaps of the tent. The second is his slowly rising neck. The third and fourth are his two big humps. And the fifth cluster is his rump. See Figure 11-2.

In marketing parlance, these five groups represent the spectrum from chomping-at-the-bit innovators (the camel's nose) to those who prefer to leave new technologies well enough alone (his rump). These concepts hold equally well for business users, departments, companies, and industries as they do for U.S. households.

For greatest success, IS departments would do well to first benchmark their customers, employees, and business units against these groupings, then introduce the new technology, such as wireless Internet access, in a manner that reflects each cluster's willingness and ability to assimilate this new technology. Here are the different possible strategies for assisting each group at its comfort level.

Eager Beavers: The Innovators and Pioneers

The smallest group is the noisiest: the zealots, proselytizers, salespeople, writers, and Internet server owners. Today, for example, they are ecstatic about the wireless Internet. Everything about it, by definition, is pretty wonderful.

FIGURE 11-2 The Technology Camel

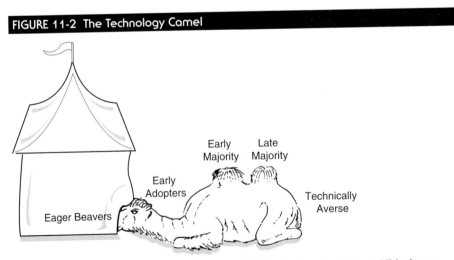

Source: Elizabeth Ghaffari and Barbara McNurlin, "The Technology Camel," unpublished paper.

Most of these people are in software and hardware companies, where their enthusiasm and vision might be an asset. Some large IS departments have an advanced technology group charged with tracking new technologies and determining when and how to begin testing and implementation. In the average corporation, however, eager beavers can be a money drain, if they are given the reins to lead the company into new technologies too early

The recommended IS approach to the eager beavers is to support them with some funding and to learn from them. Perhaps 1 to 3 percent of the IS budget is enough for R&D, provided some business objectives are being supported. But let the market shake out the hype before investing much more in their ideas. If, on the other hand, being at the bleeding edge of technology is a company's business, these folks need to be supported with more money. In other cases, companies take a big risk following these zealots.

Early Adopters: The First Consumers

In the early Internet days, companies could barely constrain early adopters of Internet technology. They were the disciples, not too far behind the innovators. They were pushing to get corporate data on the World Wide Web. They probably even had their own homepages. They also bought a lot of BetaMaxs, 8-track tapes, and CB radios. Today, they doubtlessly have innumerable handheld devices, most of which probably have mobile communication capabilities. They have a lot of discretionary income and tend to think their corporation does too.

Companies could miss a market by ignoring these folks. But they need to be managed. They need IS's help and encouragement, but they should not be allowed to overwhelm their department or the company. Use them to generate showpieces, a few early successes, but do not let them run the company's mobile Internet presence, because they will blow any budget and may not want to listen to the customer feedback that their success might generate. Monitor their performance like a hawk. And make sure they invest their own money in their experiments.

Early Majority: The First Big Wave

The first of the two big consumption waves includes the folks, departments, and companies that say they are willing to use new technologies, but they need some help to make it happen. They are not the self-sufficient pioneers nor the risk takers. In the Internet world, they are considering adding wireless capabilities to their Palm. They may be confused by the terminology, the proliferation of wireless products and services, and the multitude of options for accessing the Internet wirelessly. It may look like chaos to them, so they ask, "Is it worth my time, money, support costs to go this route?"

These early majority folks tend to be in relatively important positions in the organization, so they can make or break the introduction of a new technology, even more so than top management. The real business impact of a new technology depends on what these early majority folks do with that technology. So IS management needs to understand how they view the company, customers, and competition, then help them choose a strategy to expand their familiarity with, say, the wireless Internet at a self-paced rate that can be incorporated into the way their group does business. If wireless access to the Internet does not help them work better, it is not worth IS's time or money.

So IS management must become adept at creating options that can be tested for acceptance or rejection. At the same time, IS needs to provide some education and explanations to these folks on the options. What company Web pages do they want to access wirelessly? How global does their reach need to be? Are they interested in instant messaging? Do they want to do wireless e-mail? Investments with this group are well placed. But before approaching these folks, IS needs to understand the nontechnical products and services that consume these folks' time and attention. Learn about their business.

Late Majority: The Technology Skeptics

Late majority people, departments, and companies are not afraid of a technology, but they do have serious concerns about risks and costs. They are concerned about wasting time and money searching for information on the technologies and the kinds of investments needed to make solid, informed decisions about what it will do for them. Technology skeptics also ask questions about whether the company's clients really will benefit from the technology or whether early users are just a bunch of lookie-loos out for a free ride.

For these late majority folks, IS management needs to be as prepared to address risks and costs as they are to address technology opportunities. IS needs to show an appreciation of bottom-line concerns and answer security questions at the level that late majority people can appreciate. It is not necessary for corporations to allow their online store to be accessed wirelessly via the Web. IS can point to examples, such as Lands' End and Eddie Bauer, where online information is an adjunct to traditional information delivery methods. Or they can cite Home Depot, which only shows the items stocked in the consumer's chosen nearby store. Web sites can be a sales sampling resource, isolated and independent of the private, internal corporate network. Or it can be a complementary source of advertising or education, providing a richer customer experience for customers, without sacrificing the reputation and the relationship nearby brick-and-mortar stores already have with customers.

Technically Averse: "Not on My Time You Don't"

The people, departments, and companies who resist technology are not currently considering doing anything about the wireless Internet. In many cases, their concerns about loss of privacy, security, control, and possible exposure to competition override any perceivable benefits of this techology.

Two industries that have traditionally been technology averse are real estate and publishing. Real estate has a sunk cost and protected monopoly position over multiple listing books. Publishing has a sunk cost and a protected monopoly position over local media and advertisements. It is rare, but the breakthrough cases in these two industries generally come from companies capturing niches by going outside the system. In real estate, for instance, a few have set up Web pages that permit wireless access by realtors as they are driving potential home buyers around looking at homes. And while traditional publishing media have begun to offer digitized content that can be downloaded from the Net, they are not thinking about wireless access from handhelds. In general, they don't know how to take advantage of it.

To guide the technically averse, IS first needs to understand their concerns. They have justifiable business fears that need to be identified and addressed before any thought of using a new technology for business purposes can be entertained. The challenge here is education, not applications. These people need the greatest amount of time to assimilate all the change taking place in their lives. Only then can IS help them explore the potential.

The message, then, is for the IS department to recognize and acknowledge each cluster's concerns about new technology, and then develop a multitiered approach to respond to the diverse concerns.

SUPPORTING END USERS

End user computing (EUC) began as the way to introduce employees to computers in the 1970s and 1980s. During the 1980s, EUC gradually merged with mainline computing rather than being treated as a separate entity, as it originally started. The work of training end users, and then supporting their computing needs, became centralized in IS organizational units called information centers. Information centers were yesterday's response to the need to bring end user computing into firms, mainly via personal computers. The watchword of information centers was "support"—support and train every interested employee on every type of product. The centers focused on conducting training classes, staffing help desks, and troubleshooting and consulting. Their main goal was to help employees become self-sufficient in using computers and creating their own applications.

Supporting Today's End Users

Yesterday's information center performed its job by helping employees learn about computing, but that is not today's environment. So the information center solution, as originally conceived, is no longer the answer in most large firms, but the lessons are still valuable.

Today's end user computing environment differs markedly from the environment of the 1980s. Everyone who could be called a "power user"—someone who takes the initiative to learn how to use computer applications in their work—now has a computer, and a cell phone, a pager, perhaps a wireless e-mail device, or a Palm. And employees who use PCs generally know quite a bit about the computer products they use. Therefore, when they run into a problem, their requests and questions are complex, difficult, and time-consuming to answer. Furthermore, end user computing has evolved into a demand-pull environment, where users may want new products faster than the support staff can provide them.

As a result, today's response to end user support has become the help desk and its multiple tiers of assistance. The following case study of a computer company's response to this changing end user support environment is based on a presentation given at an Ernst & Young IS Leadership Forum.[2] It demonstrates how the company reduced its dependence on technical help line specialists, moved support into the business units, decreased support costs, and increased the computing knowledge level in the firm.

CASE EXAMPLE

A COMPUTER COMPANY

When the company first faced the computing industry's price wars, the IS department, like the other departments, had to cut back significantly. To handle the situation, the department created a war room to develop a plan and implement it within one month's time. The eight heads of IS from across the company met for two weeks to craft their plans and strategies. Every aspect of the department's work was challenged. The eight decided to reengineer IS based on four major objectives: (1) be a leader in supporting end users, (2) facilitate cross-functional decision making, (3) encourage the flow of information across the decentralized business units, and (4) target the bulk of all new investments to new applications thus minimizing investments in operations and support. Because new development was not to be cut, most of the cuts would come from support. Head count was to be cut by one-fourth.

Reengineering the Help Desk

One area that absorbed its share of cuts was help line support. Upon investigation, management found six specialized help centers, each focusing on particular applications. Furthermore, three tiers of support focused on the desktop (local assistance, help line, and on-site technicians); therefore, problems were not always solved quickly because of excessive infrastructure. Many of the experts who staffed the help desks sat waiting for the phone to ring, which did not add value.

The group was chartered to take a companywide view of employee support,

which consisted of three main support components: help line, product distribution and services, and repair/troubleshooting. The central support function was redesigned into a "virtual center" to be located in several places, to serve the entire company, and to provide training as well as support for the desktops, laptops, and handhelds. The main center was relocated to a less expensive region of the United States, and the company recruited local community college computer science majors as interns to staff the help lines. The students wanted to work part-time off-hours for as long as they were in school. The company had similar goals—a lower-cost, technical workforce willing to work off-hours.

In restructuring, head count dropped from 98 to 63. These 63 provided hardware and software upgrade support, help, tools training and desktop repair, and network repairs. Overseas hardware and network repair work was handled by other support people. The help line staff supported all 40 major applications—manufacturing, human resources, finance, sales, and so forth—for employees around the world.

The help staff also handled problem tracking, escalation, and resolution. The data showed that 85 percent of all calls were handled on the first phone call.

Getting Software Closer to Users

In addition, the company decided it was important to get the right software into the hands of the users. The company

(Case Continued)

does not dictate software standards, but it does recommend certain hardware and software products by supplying and supporting only those products.

To make supported technologies easy to obtain, the company expanded its program that delivers supported computing products—both hardware and software—once a week to 70 locations. Employees can therefore get supported products in about five minutes. Formerly, this program served only 20 percent of company locations. Following the reorganization, it was expanded to serve all sites. The center then distributed CDs containing site-licensed software to technical coordinators. More recently, software can be downloaded from the intranet. Given a choice, most employees opt to use a supported product rather than order a special, unsupported product, for two reasons. One, the supported product is available immediately, and two, the local technical coordinator will help install it or help with a problem. Some employees also prefer the hand-delivery mode over electronic download because they receive the user manual as well as the software, and they do not need to tie up their machine for the electronic download.

Increasing the Importance of Technical Coordinators

Concurrently, the company wanted to increase the number and role of its technical coordinators. These volunteer users spend 5 percent of their time making sure the workgroup near them has the latest software and a functioning network. They are considered part of the virtual support center and are the first line of support for all employees with computer problems.

Rather than add extra work for technical employees, the IS department consciously targeted administrative staff for this role, to elevate their skills. But technical coordinators do not become IS employees. They remain in their job function. Five people in the help center support the technical coordinator program, and the ratio is currently one technical coordinator to every 15 employees. Interestingly, the technical coordinators map to the worldwide population of the company.

The technical coordinator program grew by grassroots. Most often they were administrative staff, and they seem to be self-selecting highly motivated employees. They are trained and certified as system experts. They mainly use self-paced training, often during off hours. But, in addition, they attend brown bag lunches, billed as "a feast for your brain." At some, suppliers give training and product reviews. At others, they see video presentations. They also have an annual conference, funded by the IS department. It is both a reward and a training experience. One year it was held at Disney World. At this weeklong training, hundreds of workstations are networked to run simulated hardware and software problems. The technical coordinators receive hands-on training.

The technical coordinators are given a lot of recognition. They receive a banner in their cube with a designation of their skill level: Apprentice, Certified Technical Coordinator, or Champion. An Apprentice has not yet taken all the courses. A Certified Technical Coordinator has taken the minimum number of courses, used the self-paced learning, and passed a competency test. And an

(Case Continued)

Information Champion—a name they chose for themselves—has completed all the training and passed a competency test. The banner has been powerful; it is widely respected throughout the company.

Twice a year, the IS department meets with the managers of technical coordinators, encouraging them to recruit additional technical coordinators so that no one is overburdened. Managers now realize how productive their groups become with a technical coordinator in their midst. Most managers actively encourage people to volunteer.

In all, the technical coordinator program has saved the company large amounts of money in computer support, it has provided valuable services to work groups via local employees, and it has increased the level of computing know-how in the company.

The reorganization surpassed expectations. The virtual support center exceeded its workforce reduction goal and even delivered more with less. Call volume increased 300 percent yet due to a new call tracking system, wait time was reduced from 10 minutes to 30 seconds. The center receives about two kudos a day. Some employees even send flowers. It has received a great deal of positive reinforcement, especially from new managers who sincerely appreciate the staff's assistance in helping them do their job. So the center is seen as adding value and decreasing the amount of time needed to get systems up and working. ■

End User Training and Education Needs

In general, the emphasis with end users has been on training, as in learning skills and know-how, rather than on education, which deals with concepts and understanding. End user training has focused on how to use computers or applications directly. But with the advent of Web browsers, which have become the common way to access more and more applications, users—once they have learned to use the browser—have much of the basic training they need. Beyond that, to use a system competently, they need to understand the structure of the Web, information access and processing concepts, remote teamwork social protocols, and such, all of which are education, not training.

End users need five types of education and training:

1. Information systems concepts
2. Quick start
3. Refresher aids
4. Explanation of assumptions
5. Help in overcoming difficulties

Information Systems Concepts. Although training is skills oriented, some conceptual background is usually needed. A major focus of concepts training is literacy, or learning how things are done by computers. Examples include backing up data files, sending electronic messages from a remote site (such as a hotel room), transferring files over the Internet, adhering to the company's security procedures—all simple concepts that end users need to know. As noted earlier, people need to understand these mechanics, especially with regard to the Internet, so that they understand what is easy and what is hard for a computer, which is often not intuitively obvious. It helps greatly to have a mental picture of the way communication is handled on the Net, the role of servers, and the various uses of computers in accessing information, locating people, contacting people, joining communities, keeping up with events, and using the resources of another computer by logging onto it.

Quick Start.   End users need a way of quickly learning how to use a new machine, application, device, or service. As we noted earlier, the arrival of Web browsers has obviated some need for end user training because more applications use it as the access mode. Gloria Gery,[3] who has been in various aspects of the training field for more than 20 years, believes that an ideal quick start facility would first give users a mental picture of the organization of the entire system. Then it would present "global" procedures, which are the ones that can be used throughout the system in a consistent manner. Once the size and usefulness of the system are made apparent to users, they can choose what they want to learn. But without this global view, they will not understand the capabilities and limitations of the system.

Refresher Aids.   Because many end users do not perform the same tasks every day, they may forget how to perform some operations. For these circumstances, they need to refresh their memory, quickly and online. This facility should be easy to initiate and should allow users to choose the topics they want to review. Most software packages have embedded help, which can be retrieved by clicking on the icon that is not understood. Packages generally also come with tutorials or demo programs, which users can rerun to remember forgotten procedures.

Explanation of Assumptions.   People who create forecasts and projections using modeling packages must understand the assumptions underlying the models, or else they may use the packages incorrectly. Most computer-based training (CBT) products that deal with models present some basic concepts, but they may not explain under which circumstances the model could produce misleading information. Newer modeling packages often have a "parameter screen" or assumption list that acts as an assumption review, as well as a device for controlling the package.

Help in Overcoming Difficulties.   At times, all users run into a situation for which they cannot find an explanation. These days, with people working at all hours of the day or night, many companies have gone to round-the-clock help desks, staffed by people who rely on systems with answers to frequently asked questions (FAQs). And if help is needed to use the Web, numerous FAQ sites can be accessed for help.

THE INTERNET

We turn now to discussing the three underlying technologies that are creating the new work environment. First is the Internet, which has been already discussed from several viewpoints. Here, we take an end user view. Specifically, we deal with two aspects of the Internet. One is the mindset that exists on the Internet. The other is the important culture of communities on the Internet.

The Internet Mindset

Just as PCs turned the mainframe data processing mindset upside down, this new world of communications, with its multidimensions and interactivity, wreaks havoc with businesses unless they understand and embrace the mindset of the global online world. The four components of this mindset are described by Elizabeth Ghaffari.[4]

- Communication is personal, not mass market.
- Customer contact is interactive, not broadcast.
- The customer service time frame is theirs, not yours.
- The culture is bottom-up, not top-down.

Communication Is Personal, Not Mass Market. The World Wide Web makes a significant break with the past. Its communication is "up close and personal," not top-down mass marketing.

Personalized homepages have differed substantively from those of major corporations. Many are personal vanity plates, resembling family photo albums where individuals tell their life story. These pages are alive, interesting, entertaining, humorous, personalized, and constantly changing. Their message to traditional marketing departments is, "Your ad copy is boring, dead."

Other Web pages are owned by frustrated writers who publish their own electronic magazines, called "e-zines." Their message to the publishing industry is, "Your editorial filters are too tight. If you won't pay us to publish our work, we will publish it ourselves." The Web demands that customers be viewed outside the traditional publishing frame of reference. Who is the customer of a magazine, really? Is it the reader? Or might it be the writer? What are people willing to pay for?

Some corporate Web pages are stuck in the traditional advertising model, merely duplicating the printed page but in the new graphical, dynamic, and global medium. Large brand name companies have littered the online world with digital equivalents of paper-based coupons. They are using the wrong mindset: mass market rather than personal.

Some companies have gotten the message and given people a way to create MySite personalized pages. Yahoo! was probably the first, allowing people to create a My-Yahoo! homepage with whatever information they wanted to see: weather in a certain part of the country, sports, the stock market, just to name a few. Airlines, rental car companies, and stock brokerages now provide such personalized pages.

Customer Contact Is Interactive, Not Broadcast. The single most important point of view to take toward the Internet is to view it as interactive, not broadcast: incoming, not outgoing. It is a get-the-message, listen-to-the-customer, capture-the-feedback milieu. In essence, the Internet is a customer's window to companies. And it is substantially different from TV because customers can initiate communications with a firm rather than merely react to their ads. They can express satisfaction or dissatisfaction with products. They can suggest improvements for products or co-design products with the company. Today's consumers are self-sufficient and intelligent. They want to define what custom-made means to them.

An excellent example of online consumer-initiated communications is in the area of medical self-help information. Every major Internet service provider now has forums or conference areas where individuals can peruse medical information, outside the parameters of the AMA. Even though the medical establishment bemoans "snake oil salesmen," the Internet gives consumers a way to search for the information they want on their own terms. Departments or groups that use the Internet for such interactions will succeed because they tap this huge, latent reservoir of customer needs, current thinking, and goodwill.

Customer-initiated dialog supported by the Internet significantly challenges marketing departments, customer support groups, and fulfillment folks. The eight-week turnaround from postcards in once-a-month magazines, for example, pale in comparison with just-in-time delivery of information via the Web.

The Customer Service Time Frame Is Theirs, Not Yours. Through the Internet, customers are closer than most companies have ever experienced. In fact, they are closer than most companies can handle. For example, how can a company that serves its customers one at a time and answers its phones, "All our agents are busy . . . ," ever hope to handle tens of thousands of "hits" or customer inquiries from online requests for the latest product and pricing data?

Being put on hold will increasingly irk customers. Companies that stay with this level of disservice use the wrong mindset. Today's consumers are busy folks. They have little patience with waiting. In the Internet world, they can do two or more things at once, performing several tasks using multiple windows and fast comparison shopping. As with TV remote controls, customers who do not get immediate satisfaction will switch to the competition with a point and a click.

This more intimate customer environment means that companies can hear directly, "I couldn't find your product in three stores today. Where do I get it?" without the protective layers of "intermediaries" or other "buffers." Firms that have the organization in place to listen and respond to these closer voices of customers will hold on to those customers. If not, they could lose them.

Thus, before an IS department can assist other departments in exploiting the Internet world, it needs to assess its proposed Internet business solutions using a new metric: "Will our firm's Internet strategy truly help all our customers communicate with us?"

The Culture Is Bottom-Up, Not Top-Down. The Internet is not the expert's world, where the few impart their knowledge to the many. In this information-intense world, "netizens" know that "together, we know more than any one of us alone."

This lesson even holds true for government officials who think they know what's best for their constituents. In Spokane, for example, local officials tried to levy a 6 percent tax on Internet providers. Netizens revolted and inundated city leaders with e-mail and phone calls. So a Web site was established to gather their thoughts on the proposal.

The message is as clear for IS departments. IS cannot work in the top-down, broadcast mode, "I'm IS and I'm the expert, so here's your solution, customer." More than ever, IS must get input from its customers to determine the services they want, when they want them, and where they want them.

The traditional hierarchical expert model, where IS designed solutions followed by tests, migration, acceptance, and maintenance, no longer works as well. The customers of IS, too, can go elsewhere to find the expertise they need. They can "browse" the Internet to review lower-cost and lower-maintenance servers, view recommended best-business practices posted online, or download modeling software to compare alternative network costs in their market.

Furthermore, IS departments that are studying the feasibility of putting up an online parts catalog, or are talking to marketing about designing online ads, are using the outdated broadcast, top-down, mass market mindset. Departmental customers are one step ahead. They are sending e-mails asking when the latest releases of Java and Hot-Java will be available, because they want to develop applets so that suppliers can perform their own keyword searches on the parts inventory.

Rather than merely dump traditional corporate copy onto the Internet, the IS department needs to create channels for its departmental customers to continually communicate with other parts of the firm and alliance firms. Furthermore, it needs to help its company view customers through a finer, more timely, mesh.

To hear from customers directly, without intermediaries, is both a gold mine and a massive challenge to those with a broadcast mindset. To truly take advantage of this gold mine requires viewing the Internet as an interactive medium and redesigning the corporate listening mechanisms to hear and understanding all that feedback, straight from the customer.

Internet Communities

The Internet can be seen as a network that provides new kinds of "spaces": online communities, virtual chat rooms, 3-D virtual worlds. This cyberspace paradigm is markedly different from the highway one. In essence, it is a virtual universe that exists in parallel to our physical universe. People can join a deeply personal community (at 2 A.M., for instance) and talk about the things that really concern them, such as what it's like to live with a spouse with Alzheimer's disease. Or they can (if they wish) adopt many personae (creating avatars or virtual beings) that are far different from what they are in real life. They can have adventures unencumbered by physical laws and physical reality.

We believe that any talk of telecom needs to encompass both the highway view and the cyberspace view. The job of corporate executives, IS staff, and even company employees is to leverage both views for the good of the enterprise. Therefore, we now spend a bit of time talking about Internet communities.

In the *Harvard Business Review,* Arthur Armstrong and John Hagel III,[5] both of McKinsey & Company, point out that the notion of community has been at the heart of the Internet since its inception, with scientists and academics forming online research communities. More recently, online users have joined scores of different kinds of communities. And yet, say Armstrong and Hagel, commercial enterprises have been slow to understand the community-building capabilities of the Net, or make use of them. If they did, they could build customer loyalty that far surpasses what is possible off-line.

Electronic communities meet four needs, say Armstrong and Hagel:

1. ***Communities for transaction*** mainly facilitate buying and selling. These activities include auction sites, marketplaces, reverse auctions (bidding down prices), and other forms of online exchanges.
2. ***Communities of interest*** bring together people to talk about particular subjects: gardening, investments, wrestling, the Grateful Dead, and on and on. An interesting one has been the Motley Fool on AOL. David and Tom Gardner host this personal investment community where people comment on the Gardners' stock portfolio. The result is both information and entertainment, note Armstrong and Hagel.

3. ***Communities of relationship*** have developed around life experiences. They can be quite intense, because people may talk about troubling personal experiences, such as addictions, traumas, and life-threatening illnesses, as they are living through them. People can be unusually candid about their feelings, and as a result, people within these communities can form deep personal bonds. Some recent communities of relationship have dealt with sporting events, such as longer boating races, allowing the athletes to share their feelings during the experience.
4. ***Communities of fantasy*** are the fourth kind of online community and are where people take on different personae and act out all kinds of fantasies. Multiplayer Internet gaming is likely to increase the participation in this form of entertainment.

In conclusion, the kinds of "spaces" on the Internet are expanding to encompass not only one-to-one communication but one-to-many, many-to-one, and many-to-many communications. And the prospect is that these varied spaces will increase further with the advent of wireless computing.

MOBILE AND WIRELESS COMPUTING

No one can doubt that people are becoming increasingly mobile, not only in *where* they live and work but in *how* they live and work. Portability has become one of the strongest selling points in today's market, from travel-size cosmetics to pocket-size video games and CD players to pagers, cell phones, handheld devices, and laptop computers. Laptops are mobile, but often must be plugged into a telephone or other telecommunications link. The trend, however is to make these mobile devices also wireless.

Two of the driving forces behind mobile and wireless computing are the incredible shrinking computer and widespread use of electronic mail.

The Incredible, Shrinking Computer

Dick Tracy, here we come. The real world is driving toward the comic-book world at blinding speed, and providing more truly personal computing power than comic book artists dreamed possible. Massive computing power is being stuffed into smaller and smaller packages. We are in the age of the incredibly shrinking computer.

First came desktop computers. Then the "luggables," which felt like bowling balls, were followed by true portables: 7-pound PCs that fit inside a briefcase. Next came pen-based clipboard computers, which have had only limited acceptance, and handheld computers and personal digital assistants, electronic organizers and special-function PDAs (personal digital assistants) carried in a pocket.

Today we are witnessing the phenomenal growth of "pocket" devices that result from the convergence of cellular phones, handheld computers, and PDAs. Bill Joy, co-founder and chief scientist of Sun Microsystems, rates the pocket device as the next blockbuster product. He believes its scale of impact will exceed the PC. In a forecast included in the PricewaterhouseCoopers publication "Technology Forecast 2000[6]," Joy states that the production of these devices will exceed three billion units within a decade. When the worldwide, high-speed digital wireless network emerges, most people will have a PDA, a phone, and a pager that they will use for simple transactions much as we currently use cash, coins, and credit cards. These devices will swamp everything else. When you consider the number of pockets out there in the world, the PC market looks puny, says Joy.

Gartner[7] has coined the word *supranet* to describe the emerging ubiquitous network infrastructure that will link the "e-world" (the world of electronic devices such as computers, phones, and televisions) with the "p-world" (the physical world of paper, houses, people, vehicles, and other objects) in ways that are natural to humans. This supranet is enabled by the following phenomena:

- Computers embedded in everyday objects.
- Next-generation wireless networking, providing global indoor and outdoor connectivity to the Internet.
- Interfacing technologies that enable bidirectional communication between p-world and e-world components (such as bar code scanning, speech recognition, and electronic identification).
- Applications that satisfy user needs in natural ways, using combinations of media and devices.

One of Gartner's strategic planning assumptions is that by 2005, 25 percent of profitable Internet applications will be delivered via the supranet, integrating at least three types of communication media in each interaction. This assumption directly integrates the growth of mobile-wireless computing environments with e-business on the Internet.

The Widespread Use of Electronic Mail

Although electronic mail has been around since the first computer conferencing in the 1970s, it has only recently become an important element in the "corporate information technology infrastructure." In fact, it has become the corporate backbone for providing a host of enhanced communications services. Specifically, e-mail systems provide the platform for:

- Integrated voice mail, fax, and person-to-person messaging systems
- Work flow and work group applications
- People-to-application communications
- Continual communications among mobile employees and with their home office
- "Mail-enabled applications" via messaging application program interfaces (APIs)
- Intercompany transmissions via electronic data interchange (EDI)
- Worldwide people-to-people communication via the Internet.

Until recently, electronic mail networks were seen simply as the means to distribute text messages among users. Now, however, electronic mail is seen as a main infrastructure component, the piece by which people and computer applications can interact with each other, either through private networks or through the Internet. It has also become a major document delivery system through the use of attachments. Although the main use is still people-to-people communication, it can become the middleware for many people-to-application and application-to-application and machine-to-machine communications as well. The term *mail-enabled applications* refers to the use of application programming interfaces (APIs) for electronic mail systems. These interfaces allow applications to interact with each other using popular electronic mail systems as the go-between. The APIs provide standard interfaces between applications and mail systems.

In the 1980s, electronic mail was a primary feature of centralized office automation systems. These systems allowed internal electronic communications, but no links to the outside world. Today, LAN-based e-mail systems have replaced the proprietary ones, and they are used not only for person-to-person messaging but also for automated routing of work. Most recently, e-mail systems have been embedded in Web browsers, making them even more ubiquitous. In the future, they are likely to be used to allow machines, such as automobiles, refrigerators, elevators, tractors, and such, to communicate with maintenance services, ordering services, or alerting services.

Mobile Customers

The growth of mobile information technologies has thrown open the possibilities of who can use computers and when. Increasingly, the answer is anyone from anywhere at anytime. Companies are taking advantage of computing devices, e-mail, and wireless networks to serve customers in new and creative ways. Mobile computing is in full swing because companies can maintain the all-important link to their customers from wherever they are located—in their car, a customer's office, an airport, a hotel room, or at home.

To illustrate how companies are taking advantage of mobile wireless computing to serve customers better, consider Scandic Hotels.

CASE EXAMPLE

SCANDIC HOTELS

With more than 150 hotels in 10 countries, Scandic Hotels, based in Stockholm, Sweden, is the leading hotel company in the Nordic region. Being purely a hotel operator, Scandic's goal is to increase its market coverage in the Nordic region, around the Baltic, and in Northern Europe. Scandic was the first hotel chain in the world to offer its guests the flexibility of being able to make travel arrangements and hotel reservations via the mobile Internet, using a WAP-enabled cell phone by Nokia.

In October 1999, the company decided to offer 370,000 regular guests across Europe a package that contained both a WAP-enabled phone and a number of services. Scandic Hotels officially launched its mobile Internet service on January 21, 2000. Reservations, cancellations, changes, room availability, special offers, and news services are but a few of the services that currently make up Scandic Hotels' mobile Internet offering. Over time, the hotel plans to complement this suite with other services of interest to their customers.

(Case Continued)

An interesting feature of the system is the confirmation mechanism: The person reserving a hotel room receives confirmation via short messaging service, or SMS. Traditionally, guests making or changing a reservation via an ordinary telephone call often feel uncertain that all the details are correct. Through Scandic's WAP-enabled reservation, customers receive their confirmation "in black and white."

The automated reservation system also guarantees immediate assistance. Customers no longer have to wait on hold while the hospitality associate attends to other customers. Availability, 24/7 access, and independence of time and place are key benefits behind the implementation of the mobile Internet.

In addition to the reservation possibilities, a number of additional services relating to the operation of Scandic Hotels are included. For example, the hotel is able to reach customers through this completely new channel. Thus, they can proactively send information to customers rather than only receive inquiries from customers. Initially, the service has only provided information about offers and news, but the platform is open for other services that can make life easier for travelers. Scandic believes the mobile handset is becoming the hub for working while traveling, and that WAP technology simplifies much of the administration around reservations both for the customers and for the hotel. ∎

RICH MEDIA

Information delivery is becoming an important responsibility of IS departments. The goal is to present information in the most natural ways. Rich media (also called multimedia) plays a major role as a front-end to a growing number of systems, and it will be the technology of choice for public access systems.

What is rich media? A number of definitions are floating around the field. One, from Christine Hughes,[8] defines it as the combination of time-based media (voice, animation, and video) and space-based media (text, graphics, and images). Others believe that multimedia means full-motion video. This original definition has broadened, however. Most real-life business uses of rich media do not yet employ full-motion video because it is so expensive. In the long run, as the computing world becomes multimedia, perhaps Nick Arnett's[9] definition will have the most meaning. He says that rich media computing is not about combining media, it is about choosing the right medium for the message.

In the early 1990s, multimedia became *the* buzzword for selling PC products. The number of multimedia products ballooned, including video capture boards, multimedia authoring tools, CD-ROM products, audio and music production and editing packages, and multimedia clip art. Until that time, the multimedia folks had been in a world of their own, creating corporate presentations, movies, television, graphics art, and corporate training.

With the advent of the Web, the term morphed to *rich media* and took another step forward: Although video from the Web became splashy with the advent of streaming (presenting the video as it is downloading), slow modems make the experience less than enjoyable. As we approach the abundance of broadband communication channels such as DSL and cable modems, and media streaming software improves further, rich media usage will increase dramatically. Download and display time can be nearly instantaneous.

People used to ask how all the power in a PC would be used. The answer is now clear: to make the interface more natural and intuitive. Enhanced interfaces, in turn, cause people to want more kinds of information in electronic form.

Developers generally create a multimedia piece using an authoring tool to synchronize sound clips, graphics elements, and still images along a timeline, which is called a *score*. The fill-in-the-blank score has separate timelines for specifying tempo, color palette, transitions between elements, and graphics, image, sound, and video elements. For adding animation, the authoring tool provides special transition effects, each selectable by clicking on a menu item. It also has selectable options for animating graphics and words—such as bringing words on-screen from any position off-screen, fading in, and so forth—at any speed and following any path the developer wishes.

Using such a tool, a developer can specify a photograph or single frame of video as the background, and overlay it with a voice or music while animated graphics and words appear. So developing multimedia applications is more like making a movie than writing a software program. In fact, most multimedia developers use TV, film, and publishing terminology; multimedia is bringing about the convergence of the publishing, broadcasting, and computer fields.

The driving force behind the use of rich media, in proprietary systems as well as on the Web, is to make the use of computers more natural, by broadening the ways computers and people communicate with one another. Multimedia has significance in two areas:

- To help people cope with a more complex environment.
- To create more knowledgeable users.

Rich media will become increasingly important because it is a vastly better, that is, more understandable and more usable, way to present electronic information.

To Cope with Complexity

The business world is becoming more complex. Companies are analyzing more product characteristics in order to target their goods and services to more finely defined consumer groups. Businesses are accelerating their business processes. To become more dynamic, they are keeping track of more variables in a more timely manner. Firms are offering better and faster customer service by keeping more records at their representatives' fingertips. And companies are attracting employees by offering more flexible, and more complex, employment terms.

Two uses of multimedia have emerged to help people deal with such complexity. One area, the areas of interactive multimedia Web sites, helps people grasp complex information and concepts more easily. The second area of data visualization helps people cope with large amounts of data.

Interactive Web Sites.   Rich media are becoming the front end of choice on intranets, in the form of corporate Web pages to house all manner of corporate information in accessible, easy-to-use form. One example is corporate Web pages to help employees tailor the company's benefit plan to their needs. Flexible benefits plans have become complex because they offer a myriad of options in dental plans, vacation time, sick pay, stock purchases, charitable giving, and so forth. Because few human resources employees could possibly know the details of all the options, many companies are turning to multimedia Web pages to help their employees select the options that best fit their lifestyle. These systems can contain video clips of experts explaining the options in such areas as dental insurance, child care, health insurance, vacation time, and so forth. The various segments in the system can be controlled by an expert system, which answers an employee's question by showing the appropriate segment. The system is interactive in that it lets employees actually select the options they want online. Or they can send an e-mail message to the HR department if they have a question.

Information Visualization Systems.   The possibility of seeing the unseeable through computer simulation and visualization is becoming available to more and more potential users, as the price of computer power drops. For many years, the Xerox Palo Alto Research Center has done fundamental research on information visualization. As described by Rao and Sprague,[10] Xerox PARC uses 3-D graphics, animation, and the capabilities of human perception to create a spatial user interface called the hyperbolic tree that can be viewed on the Web at www.inxight.com.

The interface looks like a hierarchical web-like network of icons. Thus, a bookstore could present a site map of its Web site with categories (children's books, science fiction books, and so on) each in a small readable icon, from which sprouts a next lower level of linked icons (ages 3–5, ages 7–11, or American science fiction writers, European science fiction writers, and so on), and so on. This huge web can be dragged around using a mouse to pull an icon of interest to the fore, dragging all its sublinks along with it into readable view. Thus site visitors can quickly explore the categories on the site while maintaining their spatial context. This work is an exciting advancement in user interfaces because it builds on peoples' spatial capabilities and significantly improves their ability to navigate a huge number of linked items without getting lost.

Another research program began when Thomas DeFanti and Daniel Sandin established the Electronic Visualization Laboratory at the University of Illinois in Chicago in the late 1970s.[11] They, and their staff and students, initially concentrated on visualization in scientific computing, which is the interactive use of computer graphics animation to study scientific problems. At its best, it combines the number-crunching power of the computer with the pattern recognition capabilities of people, interactively.

More recently, the staff members turned their attention to the financial services industry. They held a weeklong workshop where seven financial experts each worked with a graduate student to see how interactive graphics could help them visualize financial data.

One of the two-person teams worked on a problem facing traveling salespeople—that is, finding the shortest route through a number of points scattered over a geographic area. The team found that by letting a person first create a rough path among the many points, and then giving that approximation to the computer to refine, that the problem got solved rapidly, in a few seconds' elapsed time. People are good at seeing large gaps among points and avoiding them. Had the computer been given this problem to do on its own, it would have taken hours, if not days, to solve. This example illustrates the power of a person and a computer working interactively on a problem using graphical data.

Another team wanted to see whether they could predict interest rate changes for the upcoming six months by matching the current partial patterns with past completed patterns. Once the user selected a section of the trend line, the computer searched the remaining data for a similar pattern, and highlighted the best matches found. Then the financial analysts studied those to find the best match.

Such visualization work in the business realm is new, but DeFanti, Sandin, and their staff believe that some of the lessons they are learning about scientific visualization can be applied to business problems as well.

A MacWorld conference was the site of an interesting demonstration along these same lines. The demonstration plotted automobile data, where each point represented one make of car in one year, with three variables: miles per gallon, weight, and price. The plot could be rotated to show the clusters of points from different angles. Groups of points could also be highlighted to compare U.S., Japanese, and European cars. For example, the points could even be animated to show changes in miles per gallon over time. The differences between car makes, and trends in their characteristics, became clear once shown in these various ways. This visualization technique is currently available for many complex data sets under the name Table Lens, from Inxight, a Xerox PARC spinoff. Several examples are shown in their Web site.

Those professionals who need to study reams of data to uncover patterns will find data visualization a boon to their work. They include market researchers studying buying trends, corporate executives determining locations for new plants and offices, and analysts studying trends in products.

For More Knowledgeable Users

Another great promise of rich media is training. Companies are in dire need of better and more cost-effective ways to train and educate their people, and perhaps even train consumers on the use of their products and services. Multimedia can address these needs.

On-Demand Training.   The main trend in this area is just-in-time training, sometimes called on-demand training, where people can access training whenever they need it via their PC. Systems with embedded training are being called "performance systems" because they contribute to increasing job performance. One example is an automobile diagnostic system, to help mechanics diagnose and repair today's increasingly electronics-laden cars. It contains an expert system that suggests tests the mechanic can run to isolate the problem. The context-sensitive help assists the mechanic in performing these tests, via graphics, schematics, and printed instructions. The system also helps the mechanic fix the problem.

Training Via Simulation.   In other cases, training is stand-alone, not embedded in an application. Using multimedia, simulation becomes feasible. The major difference from the past is that this computer-based training (CBT) is not meant to be an adjunct to traditional stand-up classroom instruction; it is meant to replace it. As an example of multimedia CBT, consider what the people at Codex have done.

CASE EXAMPLE

A TRAINING COURSE FROM CODEX

Codex, in Mansfield, Massachusetts, is an information networking company. They have an educational arm that provides CBT to their own people as well as to customers. Their courses can be obtained through Codex Express.[12]

Codex decided to experiment with multimedia training by creating a "Basics of Digital Voice Technology" course. The four-hour course demonstrated that using simulation to teach technical material cut training time in half, and the "students" had a lot of fun using it. The three developers at Codex gained so much experience through building the multimedia CBT course that they embarked on creating a second course, "Basics of Integrated Services Digital Network (ISDN)," without outside help.

This four-hour course is taken at a Macintosh or a PC. The first screen presents "your office." It shows a line drawing of the office of the communications manager of "Heart International," a fictitious global publishing company that has an advertising agency, lumber mill, lumber supply store, paper mill, printer, and direct mail house. Your task, as this manager, is to recommend to your boss which ISDN applications Heart should investigate, in some detail and with your reasons.

To begin the course, you can click on any item in your office: your inbox, telephone, diskette file, electronic mail, and so forth. It is recommended that you start with the memo from your boss, which explains your assignment. The final memo that you send to your boss to complete the course is a fill-in-the-blank form describing the ISDN applications you recommend. To gather the information to write this memo, you can talk to a colleague over lunch, visit a trade show, ask your mentor for guidance on where to find certain information, view a library of "videos," and attend a seminar in whichever order you choose, all simulated by the system.

The course contains animation so that when you click on the diskette file, it opens. When you talk to someone, you see a digitized image of that person talking. Codex created their own lip-sync program to make the mouths of these photographed people appear to speak as their voice is played. The course also contains humor; when you call on your communication analysts, they march across your screen, saying, "Hey, boss," and then provide you with information.

The people who have taken the digital voice technology and ISDN courses say the difference between these courses and traditional CBT is like night and day. CBT seems like electronic page turning, they say; multimedia training feels as if you are having an experience where you are in control of what you do.

Codex management says CBT is cost effective because training time is shorter (by at least one-half), it can be given when it is needed (reducing retraining), and it does not involve traveling to a training site. However, development is

(Case Continued)

more costly than classroom training due to the up-front design costs. The four-hour ISDN course took one work-year of effort, including the outside graphic art help and the instructional design and programming done in-house.

The Codex development manager's recommendations for companies embarking on writing multimedia training are threefold:

1. Use a knowledgeable consulting firm the first time, to learn the tricks of the trade.

2. Use an authoring language the first time, to obtain guidance.
3. Invest in quality graphics artists and designers.

People have high expectations of computers and multimedia based on their experiences with PCs and television. If you do not live up to these expectations, your credibility will be hurt. ∎

IMPLICATIONS FOR IS MANAGEMENT

What does this expanding world of handheld computers, wireless communications, rich media, and the Internet mean to IS executives? First, these new technological developments are causing computer use to take another great leap forward, as it did with the Internet. With the explosion of types of wireless devices, multimedia, and telecom options, computing is becoming a major tool in more people's lives. Information systems executives can take advantage of this more versatile computing environment in ways not envisioned before. Thus, we suggest forming teams to study ways to take advantage of wireless computing, instant messaging, rich media, and the wireless Internet. The more pilot projects initiated, the more technology transfer is likely to occur.

Second, use of these technologies should not go unguided. IS management needs to be out in front, not ignore or disregard these technologies. Otherwise, they will end up playing catch-up. In fact, some IS organizations may already be in this position. All these technologies that directly touch employees and customers should be viewed as new windows to organizational computing, windows that are sure to spur the new work environment and the new marketspace environment. IS managers should play a large role in creating these environments.

Third, these technologies can be used to record corporate memory. Laptops and handhelds, for instance, are not just smaller PCs, although they can be used that way. They have characteristics not associated with PCs. For instance, their portability makes them actually feel personal, convenient, and informal. They can be used on the spur of the moment, for a quick task, when on the move, something people do not do with a PC. Therefore, they lend themselves to people entering or retrieving small pieces of data and information. For example, if entering information is quick and easy and provides a benefit to the user, corporations will finally have a way to tap into the corporate knowledge that is going unrecorded. Coupled with wireless communication technology and the Net (and the sharing forums it encourages), these valuable entries by mobile employees can more easily be shared.

Finally, these technologies may need some new corporate guidelines. If handhelds and the Internet are to play a role in creating "corporate memory," some issues need to be resolved. Privacy is one. The reason many people prefer to tell others sensitive information, rather than record it, is to maintain some control over its dissemination. Once recorded, say, as a digitized voice note or e-mail, its privacy is essentially lost because it can be so easily rerouted to many people. Corporations need policies about which information should not be recorded and routed electronically. Searching electronic information is far easier than paper files, so the deterrent of effort is significantly reduced. Encryption may become an important weapon in safeguarding sensitive electronic information, but that has not happened yet.

CONCLUSION

In the first four editions of this book, excitement in computing first related to PCs and end user computing, and then most recently to the Internet. That excitement continues, unabated, but in the now-expanded universe of wireless Internet computing. The opportunities for IS departments to serve new audiences grows as computers shrink, as communications become untethered from wires and strands of glass, and as the Internet provides a whole new world of possibilities.

Support for end users in the 1980s centered around creating information centers and staffing them with people who liked to help people, rather than write computer programs. That approach was feasible when PCs were new. But now, IS departments must be more sophisticated. A promising approach is to help individuals, groups, departments, and even consumers use a new technology, such as the Internet, at their level of acceptance of technology, regardless of whether they fall in the eager beaver, late majority, or technology adverse category.

This chapter examines the exciting new technological developments that have expanded the computing horizons. The challenge then becomes putting these technologies to good use. In conclusion, supporting the expanded universe of computing involves assessing the proclivity of people to adopt a technology, assisting them at that level, and making computer use as natural as possible.

QUESTIONS AND EXERCISES

Review Questions

1. Describe how the universe of corporate computing has expanded.
2. What are the three technologies underlying the new work environment?
3. Briefly describe the five clusters that represent one's willingness to assimilate a new technology. How many U.S. households are approximately in each cluster, according to the Yankee Group?
4. What was an information center? What was the job of information centers in the 1980s?
5. At the computer company, who are the technical coordinators, what do they do, and how does the company recognize their importance?
6. What are the four mindsets of the Internet?
7. What are four types of Internet communities?
8. What are seven potential uses of electronic mail networks?
9. What are two uses of multimedia that help people deal with complexity? Give an example of each.
10. What are on-demand training and training by simulation?
11. What are four implications for IS management of this expanding world of computing?

Discussion Questions

1. IS departments should only address clusters of employees and customers who are receptive to new information technology. They should forget about the late majority and technology adverse, because it is not worth the effort. Agree or disagree? Discuss.
2. The original Internet culture, described by Ghaffari as four mindsets, is not going to last. It is going to revert to the mass communication mindset of TV and Madison Avenue. Agree or disagree? Discuss.
3. All that cyberspace stuff about Internet communities has nothing whatsoever to do with "real" business. We can ignore all that chatter. Discuss.
4. The only technology IS departments should promote in dealing with consumers is the Internet, specifically the Web. Agree or disagree? Discuss.

Exercises

1. Visit a local company and find out how the IS department is now handling end user computing. How has their approach changed from five years ago? What are their biggest concerns with supporting computing today? Do they have any multimedia applications? If so, briefly describe them. Do they have any computer systems used directly by consumers? If so, briefly describe them.
2. Visit a local information systems department and find out how they are using portable computers, electronic mail, multimedia, and the Internet. Summarize your visit for the class.
3. Experience an online community and report your impressions to the class.
4. Read several articles about, or several Web sites that deal with, data visualization. What sorts of data are being turned into graphs, animation, and so on? What are the most interesting aspects of this work, in your opinion? Present your findings and opinions to the class.

REFERENCES

1. Ghaffari, Elizabeth, and Barbara McNurlin, "The Technology Camel," unpublished paper. Contact author at http://techplace@earthlink.net.

2. Ernst & Young, IS Leadership Forum, Center for Business Innovation, Boston, MA, January 1993.

3. From correspondence with Gloria Gery of Gery Associates, East Otis, MA.

4. Ghaffari, Elizabeth, and Barbara McNurlin, "The Internet Mindset," unpublished paper.

5. Armstrong, Arthur and John Hagel III, "The Real Value of On-Line Communities," *Harvard Business Review,* May/June 1996, 134–141.

6. PricewaterhouseCoopers, "Technology Forecast 2000," at http://www.pricewaterhousecoopers.com.

7. Gartner, Stamford, CT, at http://www.gartner.com.

8. From communication with Christine Hughes of The Myriad Group, Coral Gables, FL.

9. From communication with Nick Arnett of Multimedia Computing Corporation, Santa Clara, CA.

10. Rao, Ramana, and Ralph Sprague, "Natural Technologies for Knowledge Work; Information Visualization and Knowledge Extraction," *Journal of Knowledge Management,* December 1998, 70–80.

11. For DeFanti's original, ground-breaking discussion, see "Visualization in Scientific Computing," a special issue of *Computer Graphics,* July 1987.

12. For more information about its training courses, contact Codex Express at 20 Cabot Boulevard, Mansfield, MA 02048.

12
DECISION SUPPORT SYSTEMS AND EXECUTIVE INFORMATION SYSTEMS

INTRODUCTION

Decision support systems (DSS) can be viewed as a third generation of computer-based applications. First, mainframe computers were used mostly for transactions processing. Then came a growing realization that computers and information technology could be used for purposes other than automating paperwork, for example, for management reporting, so the field of management information systems (MIS) took hold. Meanwhile, assistance for decision making was the domain of management scientists and operations researchers who created structured models, for which computers served primarily as computation engines. Now in the Internet age, a variety of decision support capabilities are available through a common browser interface.

During the 1970s and 1980s, the concept of DSS grew and evolved into a full field of research, development, and practice. DSS was both an evolution and a departure from previous types of computer support for decision making. Management information systems provided (1) scheduled reports for well-defined information needs, (2) demand reports for ad hoc information requests, and (3) the ability to query a database for specific data. Operations research/management science (OR/MS) employed mathematical models to better analyze and understand specific problems. But both MIS and OR/MS lacked some attributes needed to support decision making, such as focus, development methodology, handling of managerial data, use of analytic aids, and dialog between user and system.

Initially, various groups held different conceptualizations about what decision support systems were. Not only did academicians give different definitions, but vendors, quick to adopt anything to help sell their products, also applied the DSS label loosely. When the characteristics of DSS were described to vendors, they said, "That's it! That's the name we need for our new product." The term *decision support system* had such an instant intuitive appeal that it quickly became a buzzword.

DSS and Other Systems

As the DSS field evolved, continued questions surrounded how it related to, or differed from, MIS and management science. The structured-versus-unstructured decision making framework was helpful, but did not adequately explain the variety of activities that seemed to go beyond decision making. It became clear from conference discussions and academic papers that the focus of DSS should be higher than a single decision event. Decision making is a process that involves a variety of activities, most of which deal with the handling of information. And a wide variety of computer-based tools and approaches have evolved to support these decision making processes.

To illustrate these concepts consider a scenario of a problem-solving task and the technologies that might be used to assist decision makers in handling it.

PROBLEM-SOLVING SCENARIO

Using an executive information system (EIS) to compare budget to actual sales, the vice president of marketing discovers a sales shortfall in one region. Drilling down into the components of the summarized data, he searches for the apparent causes of the shortfall, but can find no answer. He must look further, so he sends an e-mail message to the district sales manager requesting an explanation. The sales manager's response and a follow-up phone call also reveal no obvious single cause, so they must look deeper.

The vice president investigates several possible causes:

- *Economic conditions.* Through the EIS and the Web, he accesses wire services, bank economic newsletters, current business and economic publications, and the company's internal economic report on the region in question. These sources, too, reveal no serious downturn in the economic conditions of the region.
- *Competitive analysis.* Through the same sources, he investigates whether competitors have introduced a new product, launched an effective ad campaign, or whether new competitors have entered the market.
- *Written sales reports.* He then browses the reports of sales representatives to detect possible problems. A "concept-based" text retrieval system allows him to quickly search topics, such as poor quality, inadequate product functionality, or obsolescence.
- *A data mining analysis.* He asks for an analysis of the sales data to reveal any previously unknown relationships buried in the customer database and relevant demographic data.

The vice president then accesses the marketing DSS, which includes a set of models to analyze sales patterns by product, sales representative, and major customer. Again, no clear problems are revealed.

He thus decides to hold a meeting with the regional sales managers and several of the key salespeople. They meet in an electronic meeting room supported by group DSS (GDSS) software such as GroupSystems by Ventana Corporation. During this meeting they examine the results of all the previous analyses using the information access and presentation technologies in the room, brainstorm to identify possible solutions, and then develop an action plan.

No discernible singular cause has led to the shortfall in sales, so the group decides that the best solution is to launch a new multimedia sales campaign that sales representatives can show on their laptop computer when they visit customers.

The vice president then enters a revised estimate of sales volume into the financial planning model, taking into account the new sales promotion plan, and distributes it to the salesforce in the region.

He holds a sales meeting in the GDSS room, and by video conference, launches the new campaign and trains sales personnel in the use of the multimedia presentation. ■

This scenario illustrates the wide variety of activities involved in problem solving. Where does the decision making start and stop? Which are the crucial decisions? It does not really matter because all the activities are part of the overall process of solving the problem. The scenario also illustrates the wide variety of technologies that can be used to assist decision makers and problem solvers. Which of the technology-based systems are DSS? In the broad sense, all of them are, because they all improve the effectiveness or efficiency of the decision making or problem-solving process.

The definition of DSS, which has evolved since the 1970s and prevails today, was articulated in *Building Effective Decision Support Systems,* by Ralph Sprague and Eric Carlson.[1] They define DSS as:

- Computer-based systems
- That help decision makers
- Confront ill-structured problems
- Through direct interaction
- With data and analysis models.

The last two items have become the basis of the architecture for DSS, which Sprague and Carlson call the DDM paradigm: dialog, data, and modeling. This conceptualization is based on *dialog* (D) between the user and the system, the *data* (D) that supports the system, and the *models* (M) that provide the analysis capabilities. Although the components differ somewhat from application to application, they always exist in some form. Sprague and Carlson make the point that a good DSS should have balance among the three capabilities. It should be *easy to use,* to support the interaction with nontechnical users; it should have access to a *wide variety of data;* and it should provide *analysis and modeling* in numerous ways. Many systems claim to be DSS when they are strong in only one area and weak in the others.

THE ARCHITECTURE FOR DSS

Figure 12-1 shows the relationships between the three components of the DDM model. The software system in the middle of the figure consists of the database management system (DBMS), the model base management system (MBMS), and the dialog generation and management system (DGMS).

The DDM model defines the architecture for DSS, and so it merits a closer look at each of the components.

The Dialog Component

The attributes of the dialog component can be called a "dialog style." For example, one dialog style requires users to keep a reference card and remember which commands to enter with a keyboard to obtain a printed report. Another dialog style uses a mouse to access pull-down menus and move icons on a color screen to get a graphical presentation of analysis results. The latter dialog style, popularized by the Apple Macintosh, revolutionized the dialog component in the 1980s. The explosive growth of Microsoft's Windows for the PC, and the Macintosh interface, popularized this dialog style. The current standard is the browser interface.

The DSS

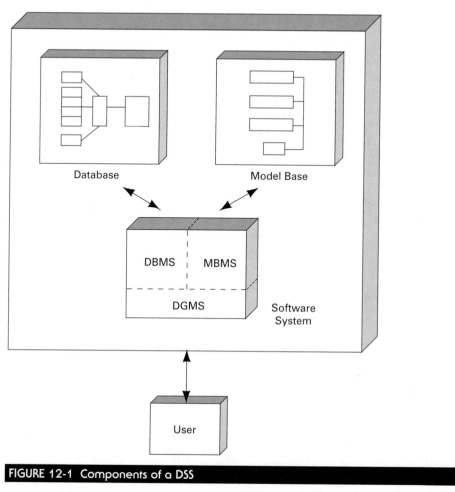

FIGURE 12-1 Components of a DSS

The Data Component

Data plays an important role in a DSS. Data is either accessed directly by the user or are an input to the models for processing.

Data Sources. As the importance of DSS has grown, it has become increasingly critical for the DSS to use all the important data sources within and outside the organization. Indeed, the concept of data sources must be expanded to *information sources*—moving beyond only accessing database records to accessing documents containing concepts, ideas, and opinions that are so important to decision making.

To characterize the full scope of information sources relevant to DSS, it is helpful to recall the four types of information discussed in Chapter 7. Figure 7-2 showed the four kinds of information that result from considering external and internal information that contains either (1) information based on data records such as found in data files, or (2) document-based information such as reports, opinions, memos, and estimates.

Few DSS need data at the transaction level. Summarized data is more typical and can be obtained in several ways. One way is to have the DBMS for the transaction processing system extract the transaction data, summarize it, and make it available to the DSS. Another option is to extract the data but have the processing done external to the DBMS. Although ideally the process is computerized, some DSS rely on manual processing. Manual processing may be appropriate when the processing requires little effort or when the DSS is needed quickly and a more "elegant" solution cannot be implemented in a timely manner.

Some organizations give end users access only to *extract files*. These files are maintained externally to the DBMS and are created specifically to meet the data needs of end users. Extract files are used for security, ease of access, and data integrity reasons. In organizations with extract files, the DSS obtains data from these files. This practice suggests that the database for a DSS may be separate from the transaction processing database, and, for several reasons, it indeed is the case in most organizations.

Data Warehousing and Data Mining.   Much of the work on the data component of DSS recently has taken the form of data warehousing and data mining. It has become such an important and complex activity that we devote a section to this topic later in this chapter.

The Model Component

Models provide the analysis capabilities for a DSS. Using a mathematical representation of the problem, algorithmic processes are employed to generate information to support decision making. The many different types of models can be categorized in various ways. The models in a DSS can be thought of as a *model base*. A variety of models can be included: strategic, tactical, and operational, as well as model-building blocks and subroutines. Each type of model has unique characteristics.

Problems with Traditional Modeling.   From an historical perspective, organizations' experiences with models are mixed. Although many successes have been noted, often organizations encounter failure. With hindsight, it is possible to identify the problems that lead to failure:

- Difficulties in obtaining input data for the models
- Difficulties in understanding how to apply the output from models
- Difficulties in keeping the models up-to-date
- Lack of confidence in the models by users, leading to a lack of trust
- Little integration among models
- Poor interaction between the models and users
- Difficulty for users to create their own models
- Too little explanation of the output

The DSS approach to modeling attempts to minimize the traditional modeling problems by emphasizing that a *system*—that is, dialog, data, and models working together—to support decision making is required. In other words, the models in a DSS are likely to be more useful because they are adequately supported by data and dialog components.

Summary

The dialog, data, and models paradigm provides a powerful conceptual model for understanding the components and relationships in a DSS. Each is critical if a DSS is to live up to its decision support potential. Let us now assess the current status of DSS and look at a few examples.

EXAMPLES OF DSS

It seems that new topics in information systems are introduced with grandiose promise, only to fall back to a limited and somewhat mundane role. Academics and visionaries develop a theoretical definition; practitioners understand only pragmatic solutions. If an idea survives the overpromise and underdelivery backlash, it can usually make a valuable contribution to the field.

Management information systems originally promised to be the "electronic nervous system" for organizations; they actually became well-structured reporting systems. Office automation promised the paperless office; it actually became first word processing, and later, personal computers. In a similar way, the promise of DSS was as already described. For a while, however, DSS to most practitioners meant a computer-based financial planning system. Fortunately, the promise of DSS is still understood and interest is still growing. Here are a few examples of DSS. Additional, more detailed examples are given by Sprague and Watson in *Decision Support for Management.*[2]

The size and complexity of DSS range from large complex systems that have many of the attributes of major applications down to simple ad hoc analyses that might be called end user computing tasks. We call these *institutional DSS* and *quick-hit DSS,* respectively.

Institutional DSS. Institutional DSS are generally systems built by professionals, often decision support groups. These systems are intended for organizational support on a continuing basis, and they are generally written using a decision support language. In the past, most have run on mainframes, but an increasing number are being designed to run on client-server systems and on company intranets. The following two case examples illustrate institutional DSS.

CASE EXAMPLE

ORE-IDA FOODS

Ore-Ida Foods, Inc., is the frozen food division of H. J. Heinz and has a 50 percent share of the retail frozen potato market. Marketing DSS must support three main tasks in the decision making process. The first is data retrieval, which helps managers find answers to the question, "What has happened?" The second is market analysis, which addresses the question, "Why did it happen?" The third is modeling, which helps managers get answers to, "What will happen if . . . ?"

(Case Continued)

For data retrieval, a large amount of internal and external market data is available at Ore-Ida. Much of the latter, such as economic indexes and forecasts, is purchased. However, the company makes limited use of simple data retrieval. Only about 15–30 pages of predefined reports are prepared each sales period.

Market analysis is the bulk (some 70 percent) of Ore-Ida's use of DSS, used for analyzing "Why did such and such happen?" Data from several sources are combined, and relationships are sought. The analysis addresses such questions as,

"What was the relationship between our prices and our share of the market, for this brand in these markets?"

Modeling, for projection purposes, offers the greatest potential value to marketing management. The company has found that, for successful use, line managers must take over the ownership of the models and be responsible for keeping them up-to-date. The models must also be frequently updated, as market conditions change and new relationships are perceived. ■

CASE EXAMPLE

SARA LEE

Sara Lee uses a DSS for sales forecasting. Formerly, when all sales forecasts came from the salesforce, the forecasts were too optimistic so inventories became excessive. When time-series analyses of historical data were used to give sales estimates, the analyses did not handle the impact of sales promotions well. So, the company began using multiple regression models to inject "explanatory variables" into the analyses. An explanatory variable is an additional variable, such as a sales promotion program or the consumer price index of food, that helps explain the performance of the main variable being forecasted. With some 200 stock-keeping units (such as flavors of a given product), it was hard to keep

these models up-to-date with all the product promotion plans and other such activities.

More recently, a policy decision (all products within a product line would have the same promotion plans) cut the number of models from 200 to 36. The Kitchens of Sara Lee uses the ADDATA sales forecasting system from Temple, Barker & Sloane. This method uses a bottom-up approach to performing time-series analyses of historical data at the SKU level. The trend line or pattern is then projected into the future to forecast the SKU sales for the next several periods. These SKU forecasts are then combined to forecast product sales, which in turn are summed to get product line sales and

(Case Continued)

so on. The percentage of sales per SKU to total product sales is developed.

Then a top-down approach is used. A multiple regression is used to analyze past total product sales, including one or more explanatory variables. The sales pattern is used to forecast total sales for a product. At this point, management reviews the model's total sales forecast and can override the model's figures to give the "final" forecast figures. These final total sales are then distributed back to the individual SKUs by way of the percentages that were developed. Forecast errors

in the order of 15 to 20 percent at the SKU level generally are reduced to 1 to 2 percent at the product level. Also, errors in weekly forecasts generally smooth out by the end of the forecast period.

Forecasts are prepared twice a month and transmitted to the company's mainframe for entry into the production planning process. This sales forecasting method has reduced inventories, while at the same time increasing the service level (sufficient stock in inventory to meet the demand) to greater than the industry average of 97 percent. ■

As these two case examples illustrate, institutional DSS tend to be fairly well defined, they are based on predefined data sources (heavily internal, perhaps with some external data), and they use well-established models in a prescheduled way. Variations and flexible testing of alternative what-if situations are available, but seldom done during interaction with the ultimate decision maker.

"Quick Hit" DSS.   The term *quick hit DSS* means a system that is quite limited in scope, is developed and put into use quickly, and helps a manager come to a decision, one that the manager might have to make on a recurring basis or one that is strictly one-time-only. The term *ad hoc* has also been used to distinguish from institutional DSS, although some quick hit systems become used regularly.

A quick hit DSS can be useful for (1) getting managers started in using DSS, (2) providing decision support for certain types of management decisions on either an ad hoc or a recurring basis, (3) providing a basis for deciding whether to build a full DSS, and (4) supporting decision situations where the executives cannot wait for a full DSS to be built. A quick hit DSS can be every bit as useful for small companies as for large ones. Three typical types of quick hit DSS include the following:

1. Reporting DSS
2. Short analysis programs
3. Programs built with a DSS generator

Reporting DSS.   These quick hit DSS are used to select, summarize, and list data from existing data files to meet managers' specific information needs. Other than summarizing the data, a few arithmetic operations may be performed. If computer graphics are used, trends, variances, and so on can also be shown. It is likely that reporting DSS is, and will continue to be, the most widely used form of computerized decision support.

In fact, reporting DSS were the forerunners to executive information systems, which emphasize reporting with fast response, flexibility, and high-quality presentation. EIS are discussed later in this chapter.

Short analysis programs. These programs analyze data as well as print or display the data; they can be surprisingly powerful. Managers can write these short programs themselves, and they generally use only a small amount of data, which may be entered manually.

A major services company with offices throughout the United States and Europe provides a good example.

CASE EXAMPLE

A MAJOR SERVICES COMPANY

The vice chairman of the board at a major services firm was considering a new employee benefit program: an employee stock ownership plan (ESOP). He wanted a study made to determine the possible impact of the ESOP on the company and to answer such questions as: How many shares of company stock will be needed in 10, 20, and 30 years to support the ESOP? What level of growth will be needed to meet these stock requirements?

He described what he wanted—the assumptions that should be used, and the rules that should be followed for issuing ESOP stock—to the manager of the information services department. The information systems manager herself then wrote a program of about 40 lines to perform the calculations the vice chairman wanted, then printed out the results.

These results showed the impact of the ESOP over a period of 30 years, and those results contained some surprises.

The vice chairman presented the results to the executive committee and, partially based on this information, the ESOP was adopted. Some of the other executives became excited about the results of this analysis and asked if the computer program could be used to project their individual employee stock holdings for 10, 20, and 30 years. The results of these calculations aroused even more attention. At this point, it was decided to implement the system in a more formal fashion. The company treasurer became so interested that he took "ownership" of the system and gradually expanded it to cover the planning, monitoring, and control of the various employee benefit programs. ■

This example shows that simple programs of 100 lines of code are indeed practical and can be used to support real-life decisions. In this case, a 40-line program was adequate for the initial evaluation of the ESOP. Eventually, of course, the programs for this system became much larger, but the 40-line program started everything. This example also illustrates the concept of iterative development (a form of prototyping), which is a key concept in DSS development.

Decision support system generators.   These products provide a third approach to developing quick, high-payoff DSS. Vendors sell products that are more than specific DSS packages or general DSS languages. These products include languages, interfaces, and other facilities for building a DSS. Sprague and Carlson point out that a DSS generator can be useful for building a number of DSS within a class of decision support applications. One component of a DSS generator that has proven valuable is computer graphics. As an example of a decision support system where graphics played an important role, consider the experience of Marine Terminals Corporation.

CASE EXAMPLE

MARINE TERMINALS CORPORATION

Marine Terminals Corporation operates marine terminals and provides stevedoring services at California and Alaska ports. Headquarters is in San Francisco, California, and the firm has a second major office in Long Beach. Marine Terminals used a DSS on a proposed project for building a new supply base terminal for the offshore oil industry near Santa Barbara, California.

The project made use of a PC to perform decision support analysis. By testing alternative ways to structure and finance the terminal, management and investors were better able to decide whether to go ahead with the project. Most of the decision support models were created by the vice president of marketing. He developed a financial projection model to show the financial effects of using different financing methods (borrowing, sale of stock, and so on) and following different operating policies.

One important aspect was the financial effects of different configurations of the terminal. A given number of ships could be loaded or unloaded using one number of berths and working only during daylight hours, or using a smaller number of berths and working around the clock, with consequent higher labor costs. Because each berth cost several million dollars each, this analysis was important to both management and potential investors.

The vice president made color slides of the numerous analyses, including net present value of fixed costs, income, operating costs, net income after taxes, and investment tax credits.

The proposed terminal was to be built at a scenic part of the California coast, so the effect on the environment was carefully studied. Different approaches for minimizing the visual and environmental impacts of the terminal were considered. The model showed the financial implications of each approach, with the results displayed in color graphics form. These graphics could be shown to small groups, such as a management meeting, directly on the computer display. Changes could

(Case Continued)

be suggested and entered, with the display changing immediately.

The terminal project was approved and the terminal was built. The vice president gives a lot of credit to this "corporate DSS on a PC," where graphics played an important part in the decision making and implementation. ■

DATA WAREHOUSING AND DATA MINING

The data component of the DSS architecture has always been a crucial part of the success of DSS. Recently, however, much of the advances in DSS have been in the area of data warehousing and data mining. Many key DSS academic visionaries are now working on this topic; one example is *Decision Support in the Data Warehouse* by Hugh Watson and Paul Gray.[3] One professional association that had emphasized EIS in the past has evolved into the Data Warehousing Institute.[4]

Within the past few years, several trends have converged to elevate data to a "strategic asset." First, the business world has moved from commodity marketing to niche marketing, or marketing to specific groups of valuable customers. For airlines, for example, one such set of customers is their platinum frequent flyer club members. Companies have come to realize the value of their data, especially their detailed customer data.

Second, software, storage, and processing capabilities have appeared that permit companies to store and massage huge amounts of data. As a result, data warehouses have come to be seen as strategic assets that can yield competitive advantage.

A data warehouse houses data used to make decisions. This data is generally obtained periodically from transaction databases—five times a day, once a week, or maybe just once a month. The warehouse thus presents a snapshot of a situation at a specific point in time.

Data warehouses differ from operational databases in that they do not house data used to process daily transactions. Operational databases are meant to be updated, to hold the latest data on, say, a customer's flight reservation, the amount of product in inventory, or the status of a customer's order. Data warehouses, on the other hand, are not intended to be updated as events occur, only at specific points in time. In addition, unlike transaction databases, data warehouses are used with tools for exploring the data. The simplest tools generate preformatted reports or permit ad hoc queries. Yet warehouses are reaching beyond reporting on internal data. They are being combined with purchased data, such as demographic data, late-breaking news, and even weather reports, to uncover trends or correlations that competitors might not spot.

The most common data being warehoused is customer data, used to discover how to more effectively market to current customers as well as noncustomers with the same characteristics. As a result, the marketing department has, in large part, been the driving force behind warehouses. They want to use customer data—from billing and invoicing systems, for example—to identify customer clusters and see the effect different marketing programs have on these clusters.

Due to the strategic nature of such uses of data, warehousing projects need sponsorship from top management, not only to provide funding and guide the project in truly strategic uses but also to ensure that departments cooperate and yield up their data for cross-correlations.

Key Concepts in Data Warehousing

As with all other areas of information technology, data warehousing has its own set of terms and concepts. Here are few of them.

Metadata: The Standardizing Element. One of the most important elements in a data warehouse is its metadata, that is, the part of the warehouse that defines the data. Metadata means "data about data." Metadata explains the meaning of each data element, how each element relates to other elements, who owns each element, the source of each element, who can access each element, and so on.

Metadata sets the standard. Without it, data from different legacy systems cannot be reconciled, so the data will not be "clean," that is, comparable. Without comparable data, the warehouse is not of much use. So an important aspect of data warehousing is creating and then enforcing common data definitions via metadata definitions.

Because the world continues to change, so too does the metadata. Thus, a metadata librarian is needed to keep it up-to-date, to enforce the standards, and even to educate users about metadata features of the warehouse. Metadata can be used not only to understand the data in the warehouse but also to navigate through the warehouse.

Quality Data: The Biggest Challenge. Once metadata definitions have been established, the largest job of data warehousing teams is to clean the data to adhere to those standards. This cleaning process is an onerous job, lament warehousing teams, because legacy data often has definitions that have changed over time, gaps in the data, missing fields, and so forth. Sometimes, the source data was not even validated properly, for instance, to ensure that the postal code field contained the right number and type of characters.

The older the data, the more suspect its quality. But because users want to track items over time, even with poor quality, data warehousing teams cannot discard the old, poor-quality data. They must find ways to align it with the more recent data, generally by estimating the data that should be in the missing fields, realigning figures based on the newer formulas, and so forth. This grueling manual task is one of the largest the warehousing team must perform.

Data Marts: Subsets of Data Warehouses. When data warehousing was first espoused in the early 1990s, the ideal was to build one huge, all-encompassing warehouse. But that goal has not always proved feasible or practical. For one thing, search times can be excruciatingly long in huge warehouses. For another, the cost may be too large.

More recently, the concept of data marts has become popular. A data mart is a subset of data pulled off the warehouse for a specific group of users. A data mart is less expensive to build, it is easier to search, and for this reason, some companies have even started their data warehouse work by first building data marts. Then they populate the data warehouse by drawing from these marts. This approach is the reverse of what was espoused just a few years ago when purists believed that data should go from a data warehouse to data marts.

The main challenge in following this mart-to-warehouse approach is that the company must have unifying metadata, so that the data in all the marts use the same definitions. Otherwise, the data cannot be meaningfully correlated in the warehouse.

To illustrate one firm's experience creating a data warehouse, consider the following insurance company.

CASE EXAMPLE

AN INSURANCE COMPANY

A few years ago, the chief financial officer, who headed up IS, saw a DSS as a way to differentiate his firm's health insurance from competitors. The DSS would give his customers—health care providers (doctors and hospitals)—a way to see and analyze their patients' medical and claims data. He initiated a small DSS project, which allowed some access. But, more importantly, it uncovered the significant problem of unmatched data between the company's financial and medical claims forms. A new CEO, when briefed on the matter, realized the company needed a data warehouse.

Rather than spend time analyzing the data being stored, the company opted for fast results. Using the work of the DSS group, they published a few core data warehouse tables in just three months' time. The main goal was to get the financial and medical people speaking the same language by giving them a common ground. To aid these discussions, the data warehouse team labeled each data item as either a financial definition or a medical economic definition.

This quick-and-dirty approach had two results. First, it uncovered bad data, which helped people see their past mistakes. But it also dashed expectations, which were initially too high. Everyone had expected the warehouse to lead to instant integration of the two sets of data. It did not. But it has gradually yielded more and more useful snapshots of data, which were not possible from the transaction systems.

Use of the warehouse started slowly because people wanted to continue using their old reports, and they did not want to hear that their numbers were wrong. It took nine months to go from 12 users to 30 users because users did not believe the data warehouse group, questioning everything they did. The sponsor was crucial in changing this mindset. He made the staff realize they needed to answer questions from hospitals quickly, and those answers had to be accurate. As he announced, "Hospitals and physicians cannot have better information than we have!"

Once the staff was comfortable with the warehouse, growth exploded. Use has even become central to many jobs, which has changed how the company hires analysts. New hires now need to know how to do data manipulation. Those employees who use the warehouse well move up quickly in the company because they have become valuable.

(Case Continued)

The data warehousing team assists users in as many ways as possible. They watch data warehouse usage and convert frequently asked questions into tables, almost like data marts. They issue definitions explaining what is in each table and suggest alternative ways to "slice and dice" the data, so that users can easily choose the method they want. This approach has significantly reduced processing time, serving 50 requests with one run rather than 50 runs. In addition, users get their answers quicker and make fewer query mistakes.

The company has created a three-tiered architecture. The Web, the top tier, captures the reporting parameters from the users. These reports are fed to SAS or SQL, which handle the database query. All the processing happens in the background, so that users can move on to doing other work while waiting for the answer to their request. When the answer is ready, an e-mail message is sent to the requester. Management sees this Web delivery as the way most reporting will be handled in the future, for one thing, because it has such a large geographic spread. The warehouse team also uses e-mail and the Web to announce changes to the warehouse and the team's upcoming chat time.

The warehouse cost $3.5 million in the first two years. The benefits have been responsiveness, accuracy, competitive survival, and quick assessment of options using realistic what-if analyses. The company attributes the success of the warehouse to several factors. The first is its design, which is modeled in a way that helps users and does not confuse them. A second success factor has been the firm's new hiring criteria, which brings in new employees who take more advantage of the warehouse. The third factor was the sponsor's guidance in getting the team to focus initially on the high payoff areas. ■

Data Mining

The most typical use of data warehouses has been users entering queries to obtain specific answers. But an even more promising use is to let the computer search for unknown correlations by looking for interesting patterns, anomalies, or clusters of data that people are unaware exist. Called data mining, its purpose is to give people new insights into data. For example, data mining might uncover unknown similarities within one customer group that differentiates them from other groups. Data mining is an advanced use of data warehouses and it requires huge amounts of detailed data. As an example of a leading-edge use, consider the following semiconductor manufacturer.

CASE EXAMPLE

A MANUFACTURING COMPANY

A U.S.-based semiconductor manufacturer has fabrication plants around the world; some operate efficiently, some do not. To increase overall efficiency of its manufacturing processes, worldwide, this company installed a data warehouse with state-of-the-art distributed analysis techniques, an automated data mining capability, and an automated alarm system.

Each manufacturing site generates thousands of measurements during the chip fabrication process. To improve processing steps, the company's engineers needed standard metrics among the different facilities, standard analysis tools, and standardized summarized yield data—how many units were tested and how many were good—for each process step. Before the data warehouse was built, the engineers wrote their own data analysis tools—that is, they did software development—rather than do the engineering work for which they were hired.

In the data warehouse project, an operational database was established at each of the more than 100 plants. These databases are equivalent to data marts because each one contains manufacturing measurement data specific to its plant. Each plant was also outfitted with an application server that provides all the tools the engineers would need to extract specific sets of data. This server also contains directories of the data in the databases and third-party tools for data analysis. A corporatewide data warehouse to store summarized yield data was also created.

Engineers can thus initiate a data acquisition tool from their application server to pull manufacturing measurement data from the operational database, request summarized data from the corporate warehouse, and then analyze the data with the resident tools.

Use of the data warehouse has several goals. One is to allow engineers to identify which early processing steps, and components of those steps, have the greatest effect on overall semiconductor yield. A second goal is to identify which steps can be omitted because they do not significantly change the performance of a chip product. Both of these goals are the responsibility of the engineers. The data warehouse was justified through yield improvements. A 2 to 3 percent yield improvement for two to three products would lead to an enormous payback, which would more than return the cost of the project.

A third goal is to spot trends and anomalies. This goal is handled by automated data mining. And a fourth goal is to catch process errors early to discard a poor lot before spending any more time and money on it. This goal is handled by a central alarm system.

The automated data mining system automatically monitors incoming data for anomalies. It compares new data to the distribution of historical data (such as the last 100 lots or last month's lots) looking for something unique. It looks for changes in spread of distribution, changes in trends, slow trends, peaks, valleys, and anomalies. Thus, it can spot a spike in sales, for instance.

To catch processing errors, twice a day, a central alarm server pulls data

(Case Continued)

going into the operational databases to see whether any of the data is unique. If so, it sends an e-mail to the people responsible for the product, saying something like, "Look at this production lot, it has a strange distribution for this particular parameter. Someone needs to investigate the root cause." The alarm system paid back handsomely in its first week of operation. It found a misprocessed lot and alerted someone to stop the processing, which saved the company $500,000 in scrap product. In addition, the alarm system is leading to greater yields, which impacts net income.

Interestingly, because the company had such a sophisticated distributed database system in its manufacturing plants, engineers and management had high expectations for the data warehouse when it was first implemented. Those expectations were hard to meet. For example, the first day of the data warehouse class, engineers saw how to do analyses in five minutes that formally took them two weeks. As a result, the warehouse team members were heroes that first day of class. But on the second day, the engineers returned asking for much more—more than the team could possibly handle—so the engineers were disappointed.

The initial training was effective, however. After just three-and-one-half days, the engineers made dramatic improvements in yield and performance because they could find new relationships and new associations much more quickly than in the past.

To handle all the requests, the company formed a steering committee. It reviews all the requests, prioritizes them each quarter, and publishes the list of approved projects for the upcoming quarter. Generally, the steering committee funds the highest payback projects. But if an engineer wants a specific project approved, the engineer is encouraged to lobby a steering committee member.

So IS took itself out of the prioritization business. It also took itself out of being responsible for cleaning the data. The engineering organization in each plant is responsible for ensuring that the data is clean before it is put into the data warehouse. Thus, they ensure that the right equipment is used and the right software is loaded to get the data to the data warehouse.

At the moment, the Web is used mostly for documentation, describing, for example, how data moves from a manufacturing area to the database. Eventually, however, the company hopes to make applications executable from a Web page.

The project manager gauges the success of the data warehouse and its subsidiary applications by the executive sponsor's reaction. He says, "When the executive sponsor tells others the system is working and it has paid back, and in six months we are going to have this or that additional feature, then you've got success. That's what our sponsor is doing." ∎

Steps in a Data Warehousing Project

A typical data warehousing project has five main steps. The first is to define the business uses of the data. Warehousing projects that are run solely by IT departments without a sponsoring user department are generally unsuccessful. The data need a business use to demonstrate payback.

The second step is to create the data model for the warehouse, which means defining the relationships between the data elements. This process can be quite a challenge, especially when commingling data from a number of systems.

The third step is the notorious cleanse-the-data step. This step requires moving the data out of the operational systems and then "transforming" it into the desired standardized format. Specific tools can help cleanse standard kinds of data, such as names and addresses, but defining the transformations is often manual, and filling in gaps is also manual.

The fourth step is to consider the users' point of view by selecting the tools they will use, and then training them on tool use.

The fifth step is to monitor usage and system performance. Warehouse teams need to be particularly alert to changes in use. In many cases, usage begins slowly. But when it catches on, performance can degrade seriously as the system and the team are swamped with requests. If, however, the team monitors use and creates standard queries that serve groups of users, rather than individuals, they can reduce their workload and speed up system response time as well.

Data warehouses are being seen as strategic assets that can yield new insights into customer behavior, internal operations, product mixes, and the like. But to gain the benefits, companies must take the often-delayed step of reconciling data from numerous legacy systems. At long last, the benefits appear to outweigh the costs, so companies are tackling this tremendous task. In fact, in some cases, the data warehouse is a survival issue for a company. In an award-winning article in the *MIS Quarterly,* Cooper and colleagues[5] describe the case of a bank for which the data warehousing project became the salvation for the company.

CASE EXAMPLE

FIRST AMERICAN CORPORATION

In 1990, First American Corporation (FAC) was suffering from rapid changes in the banking industry. They had lost $60 million and were operating under letters of agreement with regulators. By 1999, FAC was a profitable, innovative leader in the financial services industry. This change in fortune was the result of a set of decisions that formed an ambitious strategic vision coupled with a major investment in data warehousing that made the vision possible.

FAC's transformation was built around a customer relationship-oriented strategy

(Case Continued)

called Tailored Client Solutions (TCS), which positioned customers at the center of all aspects of the company's operations. Although many organizations espouse customer relationship management, FAC redesigned every aspect of its operations to meet its clients' needs as well as its own profitability goals. Underlying these efforts was the recognition that, to succeed with this strategy, it must know its customers exceptionally well and leverage that knowledge in product design, in decision making about distribution channels, and in every interaction with its clients.

The execution of this strategy was enabled by a data warehouse called Vision, which stored information about client behaviors (products used, transactions), client buying preferences (attitudes, expressed needs), and client value positions (profitability). To use Vision appropriately and implement TCS, FAC senior management realized they had to change the way employees thought about banking and about their jobs—shifting from "banking by intuition" to "banking by information and analysis." Once change was initiated, the information from Vision enabled the bank to:

- Identify the top 20 percent of its customers who provided virtually all of the consumer profits, and the 40 to 50 percent who were not profitable.
- Develop strategies to retain the top high-value customers.
- Develop strategies to move unprofitable customers to lower cost distribution channels, different products, or different pricing structures that boosted profitability, while still focusing on customer needs and preferences.
- Develop strategies to expand relationships with all customers.
- Redesign products and distribution channels to increase profitability and better meet customers' needs and preferences.
- Redesign information flows, work processes, and jobs to meet customers' needs and increase their use of profitable products.

All these combined actions moved FAC from losses of $60 million in 1990 to profits of more than $211 million in 1998. ■

EXECUTIVE INFORMATION SYSTEMS

Executive information systems—and a somewhat more general variant called "executive support systems"—appear to be experiencing renewed interest after a few years of quiet progress. Originally, some authors argued that CEOs would not use computers directly, and quoted CEOs who agreed with them. But the tone of such claims does not seem as confident now, because of the experiences of the past several years. In this section we discuss the nature of EIS, the critical factors that determine whether an EIS will be successful, what it should do, and what the future might hold.

EIS has been used by executives for the following purposes.

- *Company performance data:* sales, production, earnings, budgets, and forecasts
- *Internal communications:* personal correspondence, reports, and meetings
- *Environmental scanning:* for news on government regulations, competition, financial and economics developments, and scientific subjects

With this set of functions, these systems qualify for the broader term of *executive support systems* (ESS). The label EIS (executive *information* systems) is generally used to refer only to the set of functions involved with company performance data. In fact, using the DDM paradigm described earlier, EIS can be viewed as a DSS that (1) provides access to (mostly) summary performance data, (2) uses graphics to display and visualize the data in an easy-to-use fashion, and (3) has a minimum of analysis for modeling beyond the capability to "drill down" in summary data to examine components. ESS adds functions to support the other major responsibilities and activities of top executives: communications and environmental scanning and alerting.

The experience at Xerox is a good example of the successful development and use of ESS. Paul Allaire became the executive sponsor of Xerox's ESS project while he was corporate chief of staff. Although he felt that an ESS would be valuable to the executive team, he insisted that it earn its usefulness, not that it be "crammed down their throats." In fact, the system began small and evolved to the point where even skeptical users became avid supporters.

Improving communications and planning processes were clear objectives from the start. For example, Allaire describes the problem of getting briefing information to executives before regular executive meetings. Due to the time required to prepare the materials, and mailing delays to international offices, many executives ended up reading 100 pages or more the night before the meetings without access to related information or time for discussions with staff. When the materials were put on the ESS, the executives had enough information or preparation time to make the necessary decisions.

The other job that got executives involved in using the ESS was strategic planning. ESS helped make this crucial work more efficient, and resulted in better plans, especially across divisions. Instead of each division preparing plans that were simply combined, the ESS allowed the executives to explore interrelationships between plans and activities at several divisions. So the ESS played an important role at Xerox.

Stories such as this one appear frequently in the public and trade press. The implication is that computers are finally being used by executives to help them perform their management job better. The underlying message is that the use of computers for executive support is just a matter of using popular software packages, and that the only reason more executives are not using computers is their timidity.

The situation is not that simple. Successful support of executive work with computers is fraught with subtle pitfalls and problems. Consider the following description of a failure.

Doing It Wrong

Hugh Watson, a professor at the University of Georgia, has worked with many corporations in the development of EIS. Watson described a (hypothetical) company and its well-intentioned effort to develop and install an EIS. The IS director at Genericorp had heard of successful EIS experiences. He thought such a system would be valuable to his company, so he arranged for a presentation by a DSS vendor, which was well received by the executive team. After some discussion, they decided to purchase the product from the vendor and develop an EIS. The allocated budget was $250,000.

They assembled a qualified team of IS professionals, who interviewed executives concerning their information needs (whenever the executives could find the time), and developed an initial version of the system consisting of 50 screens to be used by five executives. The response from these executives was quite good, and in some cases enthusiastic. Several of them seemed proud to finally be able to use a computer, says Watson.

With the system delivered, the development team turned it over to a maintenance team and moved on to other new projects. The maintenance team was to add new screens and new users—in short, to evolve the system. Nine months later, little had happened, apparently because other systems maintenance projects had become more urgent. About this time, a downturn in revenue generated cost-cutting pressures on nonessential systems; the EIS was discontinued.

What went wrong? Watson identifies five problems that serve as a guide to the "hidden pitfalls" in developing a successful EIS.

1. *Lack of executive support.* Although it has been listed as a potential problem in system development for years, executive support is crucial for EIS for several reasons. Executives must provide the funding but they are also the principal users so they need to supply the necessary continuity.
2. *Undefined system objectives.* The technology, the convenience, and the power of EIS are impressive, maybe even seductive. But the underlying objectives and business values of an EIS must be carefully thought through.
3. *Poorly defined information requirements.* Once the objectives of the system are defined, the required information can be identified. This process is complicated because EIS typically needs nontraditional information sources, such as judgments, opinions, external text-based documents, in addition to traditional financial and operating data.
4. *Inadequate support staff.* The support staff must have technical competence, of course, but perhaps more importantly an understanding of the business and the ability to relate to the varied responsibilities and work patterns of executives. A permanent team must manage the evolution of the system.
5. *Poorly planned evolution.* Highly competent systems professionals using the wrong development process will fail with EIS. An EIS is not developed, delivered, and then maintained. It needs to evolve over time under the leadership of a team that includes the executive sponsor, the operating sponsor, executive users, the EIS support staff manager, and IS technical staff.

Although EIS development is difficult, many organizations report that it is worth the effort. Avoiding the pitfalls identified by Watson improves the probability of a successful EIS.

Many questions must be answered when considering an EIS. Some of the answers are specific to the organization—who it will serve, where and when it will be developed—so it would serve no purpose to discuss them. However, the other questions—why, what, and how—can have more general answers.

Why Install an EIS?

A range of possible reasons on the part of the project's executive sponsor motivates the installations of an EIS.

- *Attack a critical business need.* EIS can be viewed as an aid to dealing with important needs that involve the future health of the organization. In this situation, almost everyone in the organization can clearly see the reason for developing an EIS.
- *A strong personal desire by the executive.* The executive sponsoring the project may want to get information faster, or have quicker access to a broader range of information, or have the ability to select and display only desired information and to probe for supporting detail, or to see information presented in graphical form. A related motivation occurs within divisions, where corporate management is using an EIS and divisional management feels at a disadvantage without one.
- *"The thing to do."* An EIS, in this instance, is seen as something that today's management must have to be current in management practices. The rationale given is that the EIS will increase executive performance and reduce time wasted looking for information.

These motivations are listed in the sequence of strongest to weakest, as far as probable project success is concerned. A strong motivation, such as meeting a critical business need, is more likely to assure top management interest in, and support of, the project. At the other extreme, a weak motivation can lead to poor executive sponsorship of the project, which can result in trouble. Thus, motivation for the EIS is fundamental to its success, because it helps determine the degree of commitment by the senior executives.

What Should It Do?

What the EIS should do is second only to motivation as a critical success factor. It determines to what extent the executives will actually make hands-on use of the system.

In the following two views on what an EIS should do, each makes valid points. Perhaps these two views are more complementary than conflicting, but they are not synonymous. It is important that all the people associated with the project have the same understanding of just what the new system is expected to do, how it will provide executive support. These two viewpoints illustrate the types of points that should be settled at the outset of the project.

A Status Access System. At its heart, an EIS should filter, extract, and compress a broad range of up-to-date internal and external information. It should call attention to variances from plan and also monitor and highlight the critical success factors of the individual executive user.

This view sees an EIS as a structured reporting system for executive management, which provides executives with the data and information of their choice in the desired form. It is primarily a "status access" system for monitoring what is going on in the company and in the outside world. With this information at hand, executives can work to resolve any problems they uncover.

EIS can start small and quickly with this data-and-information approach, but still accomplish something useful. For example, EIS developers asked the company president of one large insurance company the 10 things he would look at first after returning from vacation. He gave them this list. Two weeks later, they gave him an EIS "system" with those 10 items listed on the main menu, as the first iteration of the EIS. The president was delighted, and was soon asking for more!

This data-and-information approach uses information the executives already get, or would like to get. But the EIS provides it faster, in more convenient form, pulling things together that previously had to be viewed separately, and using graphics to aid comprehension.

Human Communications Support. Much of the work of executives is based on person-to-person communications. The steps in getting results via such communications include:

1. Making a request and receiving a promise for action
2. Discussing and negotiating to clarify an assignment and the responsibility for results
3. Following up on progress toward, and barriers in the way of, obtaining the desired results
4. Redirecting the assignment when necessary and renewing commitments, or acknowledging failure of the assignment
5. Receiving (or delivering) results
6. Acknowledging completion of the assignment.

This viewpoint sees an EIS in terms of the human communications support that it provides. Data and information can help managers discover what is missing, but human communications are needed to bring the missing work into being. Managers make up their minds about some future action and then call on a "network of help." This network consists of personal relationships with peers, subordinates, clients, customers, suppliers, and others. The managers make requests, give instructions, and ask questions to selected members of this network to get people going on the desired action. Managers act through communications, and a critical role for many EIS is to support these communications.

Which Is More Important? Both viewpoints are valid, and they appear to be more complementary than conflicting. But the question remains: When initiating an EIS project, should it aim at performing mainly data and information handling or the communications needed for action? Some systems on the market accommodate both. Obviously, the choice will depend on the needs of an organization and its executives, but the choice should be made consciously. Ambiguity or, even worse, vacillation on purpose surely will lead to eventual lack of acceptance.

Which Data Sources?

Generally the EIS should *not* try to give executives direct access to production data, even through browser-based front-end software. Too much detailed knowledge is needed to access, interpret, and use such data. Instead, desired information should be extracted from the production databases, formatted, and put into the EIS database. In fact, data and information from many sources should be put into the EIS database. External information and predictive data generally are not found in production databases and will have to be supplied from other sources. The information should be organized in hierarchical fashion, so that highlights are in the top layer. The most important data must be the easiest to find. When an executive wants to see supporting detail, it should be available.

Many production data files carry mostly current information, with little historical detail. To spot trends, the EIS database needs to carry relevant historical data, such as time series data. Further, executives need to be able to track the external environment and to spot significant deviations from assumptions.

These criteria suggest that executives should not directly access the data warehouse either. As discussed earlier, the data warehouse is a source of data for analysis and data mining, usually based on large amounts of data and complex analysis routines. This analysis is most often done by specialists familiar with the complexity of the data and the techniques of analysis. Only the results of this analysis, not the data itself, should be placed in the EIS database.

In general, the information on which EIS would draw includes all four of the sources we identified in Chapter 7: data records and documents from both internal and external sources. Perhaps the fastest growing information sources, with the rapid growth of the Web and the development of text retrieval software and high-speed communication links, are from external document-based information. An EIS that taps this information source will give executives a greatly enhanced ability to assess environmental and competitive conditions.

But the widespread availability of information sources such as the Web has a downside. The information and data can be of questionable accuracy and reliability. And the data definitions, which are closely defined and controlled in an EIS, are not controllable. It often leads to confusion when the outside information is mixed with the well-defined EIS database.

DEVELOPMENTS AND TRENDS

Advances in recent years in several IT areas have combined to affect the growth and development of DSS. They include the following:

1. The PC revolution: the hardware, software, and emphasis on ease of use through common interfaces such as Windows, and common representations such as spreadsheets
2. The increasing capability and decreasing cost of telecommunications, both for wide area networks and local area networks
3. The Internet and its vast source of external data
4. The growth of artificial intelligence techniques such as expert systems and natural language processing
5. The rapid increase in end user computing as well as knowledge and computer literacy of end users
6. The increasing availability of large color screens and color graphic software
7. The increasing availability of mobile computing and communication

DSS Trends

Combining the continued progress in DSS and the technology trends cited here has resulted in some important developments in DSS. We have seen the following DSS trends:

1. Personal computer-based DSS have continued to grow. Spreadsheets took on more and more functions, eventually encompassing some of the functions previously performed by DSS generators. Newer packages for "creativity support" became more popular as extensions of analysis and decision making. These developments further strengthened the use of PCs for these applications, especially for personal support for independent thinking and decision making rather than for institutional DSS, such as budgeting and financial planning.

2. For the popular institutional DSS that support sequential, interdependent decision making, the trend is toward "distributed DSS" implemented in a client-server environment. Some vendors have developed a four-level architecture that includes a client, server, analytical engine, and database/data warehouse/data mart. See Mircrostrategy's Web site,[6] for example.

3. For interdependent decision support, "group DSS" has become much more prevalent in the past few years. The growing availability of local area networks and group communication services, such as electronic mail, chat rooms, instant messaging on the Internet, make this type of DSS increasingly available. We discuss these systems more fully in the next chapter.

4. Decision support system products are incorporating tools and techniques from artificial intelligence. The self-contained, stand-alone products in artificial intelligence have proven to be like the stand-alone statistical and management science models of a decade ago. They increasingly are embedded in DSS, which serve as a "delivery system" that facilitates their use. In the form of "agents," DSS are providing the mechanism for assimilating expert systems, knowledge representation, natural language query, voice and pattern recognition, and so on. The result is "intelligent DSS" that can suggest, learn, and understand in dealing with managerial tasks and problems.

5. Continued efforts to leverage the usefulness of DSS to gain benefit and value have resulted in versions targeted at specific sets of users and applications. The first strong thrust in this direction was EIS aimed at top managers. Another popular specialization of DSS is group DSS, to be discussed in the next chapter.

6. DSS development groups have become less like special project commando teams and more a part of the end user support team.

7. Cutting across all the preceding trends is the continued development of user-friendly capabilities. This feature, more than any other, is what enabled early DSS successes. Dialog support will be further advanced by speech recognition, handwriting recognition, and voice synthesis. Dialog support software, such as menus, windows, and help functions, continues to advance. The growth of Internet applications of all kinds is leading to the Web browser as the *de facto* standard interface for all applications, including DSS.

Future Challenges

As indicated in the discussion in Chapter 1 about the mission of information systems, the vision for DSS should be about applying a variety of technologies to improve the performance of information workers, especially where they deal with ill-structured problems. Goal-based information handling activities exist in a wide variety of forms, and systems to support them are equally varied.

Several challenges need to be met for this vision to be realized. One is connectivity: to link all the people who work together in decision making and problem solving. Another is richer data sources and more "intelligence" in the model bases to provide more contextual information in decision making.

Integrated Application Architecture. Information workers are becoming dependent on "windows" on the world of information through desktop workstations, handheld computers, and cell phones. A common dialog interface would allow people to access numerous information resources, even accessing previously separate systems run from this common interface. The graphic user interface represented by the Internet browser is becoming common enough to be the de facto standard for this purpose, but the applications and data must be compatible enough to be accessible from this window. The current product architecture for Comshare,[7] one of the long-term DSS software vendors, illustrates progress in this direction. The focus is business intelligence (BI), which includes applications for management, planning, and control, as well as custom BI applications, especially specific DSS, and a variety of database/data warehouse/data mart resources.

Connectivity. The "windows" of information workers will be connected whenever people must cooperate or communicate. Communication is recognized as an increasingly important function to be supported by technology, so it will be an integrated part of the information systems delivered through these windows. Connectivity means the ability to connect workstations through local area networks and among LANs through the Internet. It also means having a bandwidth or data transfer rate large enough to accommodate the interchange of large files, graphics and figures, digital images, photographs, and video. Rich communication in the process of decision making and problem solving will require rich media, and therefore high capacity communication channels.

Document Data. The well-structured data in databases has long been valuable for decision support. Even more important may be the concepts and ideas contained in less well-structured documents. Technologies are emerging that will allow access to, and management of, documents in addition to data records. This vastly increased set of information resources will have a major impact on the strength and effectiveness of DSS. These expanded information resources are made even more valuable with new search and structuring technologies such as concept retrieval, hypertext, and multimedia. Chapter 14 discusses the growing importance of document resources in DSS.

More Intelligence. As expert systems began to develop and be used, some thought they would replace DSS. DSS builders realized, however, that expert systems are enhanced forms of models, but if used only on a stand-alone basis, they suffer from the same limitations as stand-alone management science models. Thus, they were added to the model base and the DSS was used as a delivery system for the expert systems.

More recently, components of expert systems and other AI approaches have been integrated into DSS. The knowledge base becomes a form of combined data/model base. The inference engine can be viewed as a knowledge base management system similar to the database management system and dialog management system. The language system then is a part of the dialog. The future will bring much more integration and extension of the intelligence capability in DSS.

CONCLUSION

DSS have taken their place in the portfolio of applications and tools to support problem solving, decision making, and other goal-based information activities. The DSS label was first used to describe a large general class of applications, and the DSS movement defined the concepts, principles, and products to implement the systems. As the field grew, specialized views of DSS emerged for groups, for executives, and for office work. The DSS label now refers mostly to systems for analysis of complex situations, having absorbed most of the work of management science and operations research in business organizations.

The current status can be characterized by a predominance of institutional systems, increasing instances of personal DSS, and a growing interest in group DSS. Two other developments include the increased use of computer graphics and the popularity of spreadsheets. Businesses can expect continued growth of PC-based DSS, distributed DSS based on a multilevel client-server architecture, growing use of group DSS, and the addition of intelligent agents.

Of these trends, EIS was considered in some detail. Potentially, executive information systems that are within today's state-of-the-art can

1. Provide status information on how things are going both within and outside of the organization
2. Help executives communicate with others to identify and define needed actions
3. Help make those needed actions happen.

However, EIS cannot be imposed upon executives, they must individually be receptive to such a system. Furthermore, an EIS must present information in a manner desired by each individual executive, although some standards can be employed on designing the screen displays, including the use of colors, size and placement of text, and so on.

Success of an EIS depends on having a strong motivation for installing it in the first place, a committed and informed senior executive sponsor, an appropriate operating sponsor and project organization, a definition of what the EIS is expected to do (and not do) at the outset, and being easy to use, even for infrequent users.

QUESTIONS AND EXERCISES

Review Questions

1. What is the definition of a decision support system?
2. What is the DDM paradigm for DSS suggested by Sprague and Carlson? How is it useful? Summarize the most important attributes of each component.
3. What is an institutional DSS? Give an example.
4. What is a quick hit DSS? When is it useful? Define three types.
5. What are DSS generators?
6. Why have data warehouses become so popular?
7. What are the key concepts of data warehousing?
8. What is the definition of data mining? What does it accomplish?
9. What are the steps in a data warehousing project?
10. What is the difference between DSS and EIS?
11. What are the pitfalls in EIS development identified by Watson?
12. What is a strong reason for installing EIS? A weak reason?
13. Give two opinions on the main role of EIS?
14. What are the major trends in DSS?
15. What are the four future challenges for DSS?

Discussion Questions

1. Executives should be expected to draw on any information resources they can, and combine them with the EIS database and data warehouses to make their decisions. Agree or disagree?
2. From the case examples and discussions in the chapter, which of the attributes of a DSS or EIS do you think are most important? Why?

Exercises

1. If you have ever used a spreadsheet package, describe one of your uses and what decisions the package helped you make.
2. Find one or more current articles on DSS or EIS. What characteristics or attributes are described? How do they compare with the ones in the text?
3. Visit a local company and talk to a user or a developer of decision support systems. What types of DSS are being used or developed? What tools are being used? Briefly describe one or two applications.

REFERENCES

1. Sprague, Ralph H., and Eric Carlson, *Building Effective Decision Support Systems,* Prentice Hall, Upper Saddle River, NJ, 1982.

2. Sprague, Ralph H., and Hugh Watson, *Decision Support for Management,* Prentice Hall, Upper Saddle River, NJ, 1996.

3. Watson, Hugh, and Paul Gray, *Decision Support in the Data Warehouse,* Prentice Hall, Upper Saddle River, NJ, 1998.

4. The Data Warehousing Institute, Seattle, WA, at www.dw-institute.com/. *Journal of Data Warehousing* is at the same site.

5. Cooper, Brian, Hugh Watson, Barbara Wixom, and Dale Goodhue, "Data Warehousing Supports Corporate Strategy at First American Corporation," *MIS Quarterly,* December 2000.

6. Microstrategy is located at www.microstrategy.com.

7. Comshare is located at www.comshare.com.

CHAPTER

13 GROUP SUPPORT SYSTEMS

INTRODUCTION

In the previous chapter, we characterized group decision support systems (GDSS) as a special variety of DSS. GDSS are systems that support decision making by more than one person, working together to reach a decision. Group decision making may result from a sequential process in which one person makes a decision (or part of a decision) and passes it on to another person, called "sequential interdependent" decision making. Or several people may reach a decision jointly by working together simultaneously and interacting, which is called pooled interdependent decision making. The latter is the one usually supported by GDSS.

But, as illustrated in the problem-solving case example at the beginning of Chapter 12, it is increasingly difficult to tell when decision making starts and when ancillary activities such as data gathering, communicating, and interacting begin. For this reason, the "D" is disappearing from the GDSS label, as it has in the title of this chapter. So in this chapter, we focus on groups, rather than individuals, and the systems and technologies that support the communication and interaction among people as they work as groups. As in all the chapters in this "support systems" section of the book, we emphasize knowledge-based systems, which are systems that support work activities that do not follow the same or similar process every time and also deal with information and knowledge that cannot be easily encapsulated.

The difference between GDSS and GSS is more recognizable when the activities of groups are divided into two generic categories. One is *communication and interaction.* Communication is the transmission of information from one person to another or to several others; interaction is repetitive, usually back-and-forth, communication over time. The second major activity is *decision making or problem solving,* where members of a group reach a decision or form a consensus. It could be argued that communication is a necessary part of group decision making, so it is encompassed by the latter function. It seems, however, that communication is a valuable function in its own right, to aid in coordinating activities in an organization, whether or not a decision or consensus is reached.

Much of the current activity in group support systems has originated from one or the other of these two major functions. Office systems, and in particular electronic mail, are oriented toward supporting people-to-people communication. Researchers in the area of "computer supported cooperative work" generally emphasize technology to aid communication, such as enhanced computer conferencing and systems to assist two or more people to work on the same project.[1] On the other hand, group DSS work, evolving from the DSS community, focuses on reaching a conclusion, decision, or consensus, even though it includes technology to support communication.

Another way to organize the work of groups is the way Geraldine DeSantis, of Duke University, and Brent Gallupe, of the University of Minnesota,[2] did in one of the early frameworks. Their matrix, shown in Figure 13-1, has *proximity* of group members on one dimension (together/dispersed) and *duration* of interaction on the other (limited/ongoing). The figure gives one technology example per cell. Note that this matrix is relevant for both communication and decision making. For example, decision making has been the intent of decision rooms, while LANs are usually perceived mainly as communication support tools.

Yet a third way to organize the work of groups is to use a variation of the DeSantis-Gallupe matrix, by having *time* on one dimension (same time/different time) and *place* on the other (same place/different place). It appears that this third characterization has become dominant, so it is presented later in the chapter in the discussion of the different kinds of group support systems.

Characteristics of Groups

Not all groups are the same. Different types emerge for different tasks. Some of the characteristics that differentiate groups are the following.

Membership. Groups can be open, where almost anyone can join. Or they can be closed, where membership is restricted. Actually, a "gray scale" between open and closed indicates the degree of difficulty to gain membership.

Duration of Decision-Making Session

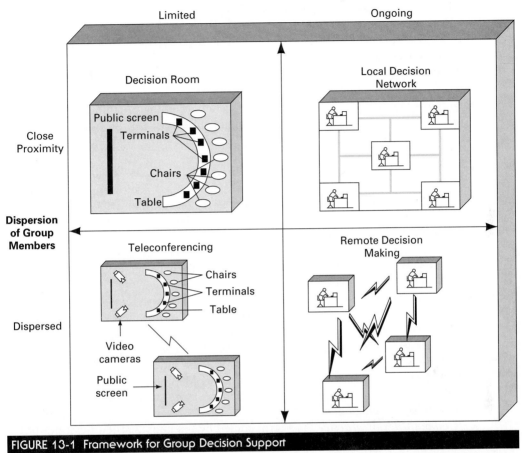

FIGURE 13-1 Framework for Group Decision Support

Source: G. DeSantis and B. Gallupe, "Group Decision Support Systems: A New Frontier," *Data Base,* Winter 1985.

Interaction.   The group can be loosely coupled, where the activity of each member is relatively independent of the other members. Salespeople who have their own sales territories often fall in this category. Or the group can be tightly coupled, such as a project team where the work of each member is tied closely to the work of the other members. As in the case of gaining group membership, group couplings range widely from loose to tight.

Hierarchy.   A group can be just one part of a "chain of command." Large public events, such at the Olympics or the Rose Parade, for instance, are planned and conducted by a hierarchy of committees. At the top is an ongoing committee that sets the general plans for years in advance and selects the site and the top people for putting on each event. The top committee then oversees the work of the various detail committees. In addition, each of the detail committees may have subcommittees working on specific portions of their responsibility.

We cite these characteristics to illustrate that providing computer-based support for groups is not straightforward because of the many variations. Initially, support was for intracompany groups, but the Internet has led to worldwide support. The main issues are what types of groups need support and why.

Types of Groups

Here is a list of just a few of the many, many kinds of groups.

- *Authority groups* involve formal authority (and often hierarchy), such as boss and subordinates, or team leader and team members. Membership is closed and coupling is tight. In matrix management, people may have two bosses, one technical and one administrative.
- *Intradepartmental groups* can have members all doing essentially the same work, often under the same boss. Membership is closed, seniority generally exists, and interaction can range from tight (only do one job, on their own) to loose coupling (work with their neighbor). LANs and departmental computers have been installed for these groups.
- *Project teams* generally have members who work full-time to accomplish a goal within a specific schedule. Generally, membership is closed, coupling is tight, and a hierarchy can exist.
- *Interdepartmental work groups* pass work from department to department (purchasing, receiving, accounts payable) in a chain, forming a super group. Membership is closed, coupling is tight, and hierarchy tends not to be present.
- *Committees and task forces* are formed to deal with a subject area or issue. Generally, neither requires full-time participation. Committees are usually ongoing; task forces just deal with the issue and disband. Membership may not be quite as closed as a project team, and interaction might not be as tightly coupled as among committee members.
- *"Communities of practice"* is a term coined by the people at the Institute for Research on Learning[3] to mean a group of people who work or play together for so long that they have developed an identifiable way of doing things. Such communities arise naturally at school, at work, in volunteer organizations, and in sports clubs.
- *Business relationship groups* are relationships with customers, groups of customers, suppliers, and so on. Membership often is closed, in that a new organization may have to "earn" real acceptance. Interaction is loosely coupled. A hierarchy is not too likely, but favored customers and suppliers can have dominating influences.
- *Peer groups* meet to exchange ideas and opinions. Examples are fraternal organizations, secretaries who call on each other for help, and prospects called together for a sales presentation. Membership can range from relatively open to closed and the interaction tends to be loosely coupled. Hierarchy usually is not much in evidence.
- *Networks* are groups of people who socialize, exchange information, and expand the number of their personal acquaintances.
- *Electronic groups* include chat rooms, multiuser domains, user groups, and virtual worlds, all forms of groups that have formed on the Internet to socialize, find information, entertain themselves, gain comfort, or just experiment with the

new online world. Membership is generally wide open, interaction is loosely coupled, and no hierarchy is generally present.

WHY ARE GROUP SYSTEMS IMPORTANT?

Why should information system executives be interested in supporting groups? Robert Johansen,[4] of the Institute for the Future and an author of two books on group working, notes that group support systems are important because most people spend 60 to 80 percent of their time working with others. Yet, from informal polls he has taken, people seem to feel they are most productive when they are working alone. Thus, they are not happy about how they work with others. This finding reveals a need for systems that support groups.

However, groupware—electronic tools that support teams of collaborators—represents a fundamental change in the way people think about using computers, says Johansen. The things people need to work with others are different from the things they need to work alone. So groupware is different from past software.

In the future, groupware that takes full advantage of information technology will be just another part of corporate information systems, says Johansen. The products most likely will be built on existing platforms—electronic mail systems, LANs, departmental systems, and public network services, such as the telephone or the Internet. Yet use of these technologies will advance beyond the "horseless carriage" stage and lead to new organizational structures, he believes.

Specifically, we see group computing being important for three reasons:

1. Teams may be the basis for future organizations.
2. Coordination theory may guide organizational design.
3. Companies want to "manage" knowledge.

These are now discussed in turn.

Teams: The Basis of Future Organizations?

In the *Harvard Business Review,* Peter Drucker's article, "The Coming of the New Organization," became the most reprinted *HBR* article in its first year.[5] Apparently it struck a responsive chord. In it, Drucker states that he believes organizations are becoming information-based, and that they will be organized not like today's manufacturing organizations but more like a symphony orchestra, a hospital, or a university. That is, organization will be composed mainly of specialists who direct their own performance through feedback from others—colleagues, customers, and headquarters.

This move is being driven by three factors, says Drucker. One, knowledge workers are becoming the dominant portion of labor, and they resist the command-and-control form of organization. Two, all companies, even the largest ones, need to find ways to be more innovative and entrepreneurial. And three, information technology is forcing a shift. Once companies use information technology to handle information and not data, their decision processes, management structure, and work patterns change.

For example, spreadsheets allow people to perform capital investment analysis in a few hours. The calculations are so complex that, before this technology was available, these investment analyses generally had to be based on opinion.

With computing, the calculations become manageable, and more importantly, the assumptions underlying the calculations can be given weights. In so doing, the investment analysis changes from being a budget question to being a policy question, says Drucker, because the assumptions supporting the business strategy can more easily be discussed.

Information technology also changes organizational structure when a firm shifts its focus from processing data to producing information, he says. Turning data into information requires knowledge, and knowledge is specialized. The information-based organization needs far more specialists than middle managers who relay information.

Thus, organizations are becoming flatter, with fewer headquarters staff and many specialists out in operating units. Even departments have different functions. They set standards, provide training, and assign specialists. Work is done mainly in task-focused teams, where specialists from various functions work together as a team for the duration of a project.

Team-based organizations work like hospitals or orchestras, says Drucker. Hospitals have specialty units, each with its own knowledge, training, and language. Most are headed by a working specialist, not a full-time manager. That specialist reports to the top of the hospital, resulting in the need for little middle management. Work in the units is done by ad hoc teams, assembled to address a patient's condition and diagnosis. Symphony orchestras are similar. They have one conductor, many high-grade specialists, and other support people.

Drucker believes we are at the beginning of the third evolution in the structure of organizations. The first, which took place around 1900, separated business ownership from management. The second, in the 1920s, created the command-and-control corporation. The third, happening now, is the organization of knowledge specialists.

Coordination Theory May Guide Organizational Design

Thomas Malone, of the Massachusetts Institute of Technology,[6] believes that lessons learned about how large groups coordinate their work can be applied to coordinating large groups of computing resources, or even hybrid groups that include both people and computers. Such an understanding is paramount in e-commerce.

Using ideas from economic theory, Malone and others at MIT have been studying how to allocate processing resources in a distributed computing environment using prices and competitive bidding. They have found that in networks of PCs, where the machines "contract" to process a task, several configurations are possible. These networks are analogous to human organizations, he says. For instance, the machines could coordinate their own work, as in a decentralized market. Or some machines could be brokers, as in a centralized market. Or these broker machines could be specialized—printer brokers, high-speed processing brokers, and such—as in a functional hierarchy. Or each processor might have its own peripherals, as in a product hierarchy.

These various forms of coordination all have associated costs. Yet, says Malone, it is likely that IT can be used to reduce these costs in human organizations. Look at what has happened as technology has been used to reduce transportation costs, says Malone: (1) people substituted train travel for horse-drawn carriage travel, which (2) increased the amount of traveling people did, because travel was cheaper and more convenient, which, in turn, (3) allowed people to move to suburbs and use shopping malls. These developments represent first, second, and third order effects of cheap, convenient transportation.

The use of IT to reduce costs of coordination could have similar effects: (1) IT replaces some forms of human coordination, such as middle management, which (2) may increase the overall amount of coordination, which (3) may encourage a shift toward more coordination-intensive organizational structures, such as highly networked, decentralized organizations. Uncovering desirable coordination structures and the effects they may have on organizations are two of the goals of Malone's coordination work.

Companies Want to "Manage" Knowledge

One of the hottest subjects in the IT field these days is *knowledge management.* Top corporate executives realize that their greatest corporate assets walk out the door every evening, taking with them another crucial asset, knowledge. Attempts to capture "knowledge" in computer systems continue. The next chapter discusses this subject. But for some experts and researchers in the field, knowledge is not something that can be captured in a machine; it only exists inside a person's head. Information can be captured in computers, knowledge cannot. This view, of course, is in hot debate, and it has raised the question, "If we cannot disembody knowledge, how do we better manage the knowledge within people to leverage this asset?"

Tony Brewer[7] researched this topic and noted that as we move from a service economy to a knowledge economy, companies move toward managing their "intellectual capital" in a more formal and deliberate way. In essence, knowledge exists in two states, tacit and explicit. Tacit knowledge exists within a person's mind and is private and unique to each person. Explicit knowledge has been articulated, codified, and made public. Western management practices have concentrated on managing explicit knowledge; but cultivating and leveraging tacit knowledge is just as important. Effective knowledge management requires transferring knowledge between these two states.

So how is that done? Well, says Brewer, because knowledge is not a physical asset, it is not effectively described in terms of manufacturing analogies, such as storing it in inventory. Rather it needs to be thought of in ecological terms, such as nurturing it, cultivating it, and harvesting it. Furthermore, ways to transfer knowledge back and forth between its tacit and explicit states are crucial, generally a result of encouraging the free flow of ideas and information, something that many of today's organizational norms, departmental boundaries, and national differences inhibit.

"The Rudy Problem." Just discovering who has what knowledge is a step in the right direction. Yet having knowledge is not always rewarded by management, as the following story illustrates.

At the Knowledge Imperative Symposium, Dr. Patricia Seemann,[8] who headed up a knowledge management project at a pharmaceutical company, told the story of Serge and Rudy (fictitious names but real people). Serge, she said, was a "real" manager. He had a three-window office, a big desk, and a title. And if you asked him what he did the past year, he would say, "I registered 600 products in 30 countries." Rudy, on the other hand, is a headache, his manager says, because he does not work. He just stands around and talks all day. Whenever you see him, he is talking to someone. And when you ask him what he did the past year, he says, "I sort of helped out."

The company downsized and guess who got laid off? Rudy. And then what happened? His department fell apart because there was no one to help, to provide guidance. When they fired Rudy, they fired their organizational memory, said Seemann. He was a crucial, yet unrecognized asset, because he was willing to share his knowledge.

While at this company, Seemann and her team created a yellow pages guide of company knowledge brokers. Guess who was in the book and who was not? Rudy, of course, was in the book. Serge was not, and neither was top management. How can companies fix what she calls "the Rudy problem"? One way is to create a technical career track and promote knowledge brokers. Giving Rudy a title would have made an enormous difference, Seemann said, because it would have sent a signal that knowledge sharing was recognized in the company. Companies cannot appoint knowledge brokers. They just emerge. And when they do emerge, they need support.

As another example of what a company can do to promote knowledge sharing (that is, group support), even on a global basis, consider the approach that Buckman Laboratories has taken. This description is based on Brewer's work.

CASE EXAMPLE

BUCKMAN LABORATORIES

Buckman Laboratories, an industrial chemical company based in Memphis, Tennessee, has more than 1,200 employees around the world. The concept of sharing knowledge and best practices has been around in Buckman for more than 10 years. In fact, the company's code of ethics reinforces the sharing culture. Buckman believes that successfully transferring knowledge depends 90 percent on having the right culture and 10 percent on technology.

To bring the knowledge of *all* Buckman's employees to bear on a customer problem anywhere in the world—whether in Europe, South Africa, Australia/New Zealand, or Japan—Buckman established a knowledge transfer system called K'Netix, the Buckman Knowledge Network. The goal of K'Netix was to get people who had not met each other, but

belonged to the same business, to communicate with each other and develop trust in each other: trust that one person was interested in the other's success, trust that what one person received from others was valid and sincere, and enough trust in the culture to help someone else.

Ten years ago sharing was accomplished mainly by people traveling all over the world to see each other, with lots of face-to-face conversations and meetings. Today, such meetings still occur, but the technology helps people stay in touch between these meetings, making communications more continuous.

When employees need information or help, they ask via forums, which are Buckman-only online forums over the Internet. In all, seven forums in TechForum are organized by industry and are open to all employees.

(Case Continued)

One particularly influential conversation, which set the tone for companywide sharing, took place over TechForum and concerned Buckman's global sales awards. A large cash award was split among the top three salespeople worldwide; the top 20 got plaques. It was based on a formula that took many factors into account. The salespeople, however, were unhappy with the formula. When this discussion appeared on the companywide forum, then-CEO Bob Buckman jumped into the fray and decided that the entire company should iron out the problems in front of all employees. Hundreds of messages were recorded, and the entire award structure was restructured online in front of everyone. It was a rare opportunity to allow everyone to share in an important, yet sensitive, company subject. Moreover, top management did not dictate the results. This conversation reinforced the sharing culture.

The conversations are the basis for transferring knowledge around the company. So the important ones are captured. Volunteer experts identify the ones that contain valuable information and, more importantly, valuable streams of reasoning. This information is then edited to remove extraneous material, given key words, and stored in the forum library. In essence, Buckman is capturing the artifacts of its virtual teams in action. In so doing, it is creating a self-building knowledge base, which can be used for what-if analyses and can be mined to create new knowledge.

The prime benefit is timely, high-quality responses to customer needs. For example, a new employee in Brazil was scheduled to visit a customer who had a particular problem. The salesperson posted both the problem and a suggested solution in a forum and sought advice from anyone with more experience. A response came quickly: "I've faced this problem and your pH is too high, it will cause odors and ruin the paper. Bring the pH down by two points. That won't hurt the process, and it will clear up the problem." As a result, this new employee, who had only modest experience, was able to present a proposal with the experience of a 25-year veteran, and make the sale. ■

TYPES OF GROUP SUPPORT SYSTEMS

As we noted earlier, Bob Johansen, of the Institute for the Future, is a leader in the field of groupware. He and his colleagues at IFTF extended the DeSantis/Gallupe matrix shown in Figure 13-1. Johansen's time/place framework, shown in Figure 13-2, appears to be dominant in discussions of where a particular groupware technology or product fits.

The two values, either same or different, on each dimension designate whether the group members are communicating and interacting over time and/or distance. The "same time/same place" cell in the upper right, for example, includes electronic meeting support systems. The "different time/different place" cell in the lower right incorporates the communication-oriented systems such as e-mail, computer conferencing, and use of Lotus Notes.

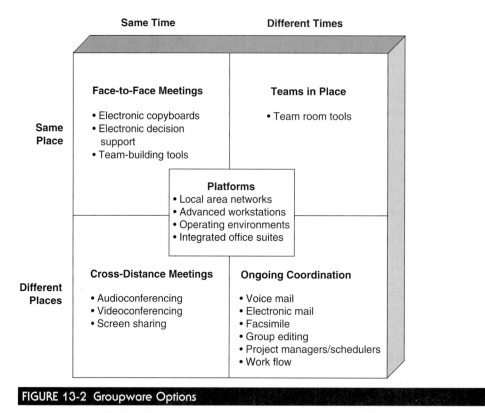

FIGURE 13-2 Groupware Options

Source: Courtesy of Robert Johansen of the Institute for the Future, Menlo Park, CA.

To date, the greatest amount of research and number of products have taken place in these two cells. Therefore, in the discussion that follows, we spend more time on them. Interestingly, little integration has taken place among the systems in these two cells, or with the other two cells, even though it is clear to researchers and developers that true group support systems must aim to support anytime, anyplace group working.

Now, on to discussing progress in the four cells, beginning with same time/same place.

Supporting Same Time/Same Place Groups

Supporting same time/same place groups has generally meant supporting meetings. And a lot of work has been focused in this area. Robert Half, the international recruiting firm, with headquarters in New York City, commissioned a study that found that the average executive in a U.S. company spends more than 800 hours a year in meetings. Not only does this figure represent a large portion of total work hours (on the order of 30 percent), but even worse, the executives reported that they considered about 240 of those hours to have been wasted in useless meetings.

The Problem with Meetings.   From the many meetings we have attended, many shortcomings have been evident. Meetings often have no agenda, or only a superficial one.

No problems are clearly spelled out in advance, and no specific action items are proposed to address the problems. If actions (or motions) are proposed, alternatives are not fully considered. If documentation about the issues has been provided before the meeting, some members choose not to study it; they expect to be "briefed" at the meeting. The chairperson may do little or no follow-up between meetings to see that the members carry out their assignments.

Some meetings are doomed from the start. Key people arrive late, or do not attend at all. Necessary information does not arrive. Some group members have forgotten to fulfill their assignments. Then the meeting chairperson may do a poor job of managing the meeting time. Discussion may be allowed to wander from the subject. Time may be spent on briefing attendees or on routine matters—reviewing and correcting minutes of prior meetings, getting committee progress reports, and so on. Such meetings tend to run over their allotted time, with important items receiving poor consideration. Often, too, a few people dominate the discussion; not infrequently, these people are repetitious, saying the same things over and over. Conversely, some people do not speak up and contribute their ideas. Finally, many meetings are wasteful from a cost standpoint. A meeting involving even a few managers and professionals costs hundreds of dollars per hour in salaries alone; large meetings can easily cost thousands of dollars per hour. If travel is required, costs are even higher. Add to these considerations the fact that the participants are unavailable for other activities while tied up in the meetings.

Information Technology Can Help. The goals of group support systems for improving meetings are to (1) eliminate some meetings, (2) encourage better planning and better preparation for those meetings that must be held, and (3) improve the effectiveness as they are held.

Eliminate some meetings. The most likely candidates for elimination are the meetings that do not call for a group decision or group action but are simply for group updating. Progress report meetings are an example, particularly if progress (actual progress versus planned progress) can be reported frequently by means of computerized information systems. Meetings where key people cannot attend, or where needed information is not yet available, can be canceled at the last moment. Electronic and voice mail systems allow the word to be spread rapidly. Intranets allow posting of progress and status reports in a form that is easily available to everyone. In short, some of the work done in meetings can be shifted from the "same time, same place" cell to the "different time, different place" cell in the time/place matrix.

Better preparation for meetings. Computer conferencing can play a significant role in improving preparation for meetings. A computer conferencing system is actually a form of enhanced electronic mail. Participants can log on at their convenience, read all entries made by others since they last logged on, and make their contributions. In the planning stage of a meeting, such a system can be used to obtain reactions to the proposed agenda, and those reactions might spur debate and alternatives. Furthermore, routine matters may be handled before the meeting, such as review and approval of minutes, receiving committee progress reports, voting on routine action items, and so on. Group members can give attention to these matters at their convenience, saving valuable synchronous meeting time for more important business. The chairperson can also use the conferencing system for follow-up activities. Finally, the system can provide a written record of pre- and postmeeting communications.

Improve the effectiveness and efficiency of meetings. One of the major benefits of meeting support systems is improved meeting efficiency and effectiveness. Meetings are more effective when the ideas generated by the group are more creative and group member commitment to the groups' activities is great. Meetings are more effective when group commitment happens more quickly. Following is a case in point.

CASE EXAMPLE

BURR-BROWN CORPORATION

Burr-Brown Corporation, with headquarters in Tucson, Arizona, manufactures and sells electronics parts to other electronic manufacturers. It has about 1,500 employees and $180 million in annual sales.

When the University of Arizona, also in Tucson, created a decision room in their IS department, the chief executive officer (CEO) of Burr-Brown decided to use it for management's three-day annual strategic planning meeting. He was so pleased with the results that the firm used it again the following year for the same purpose.

The Decision Room

The room has 24 workstations, arranged in a semi-circle on two tiers. Up to 48 people can use the room, two persons per workstation. In an adjacent control room is the file server, and at the front of the room is a facilitator's control station, as well as a rear projection screen for video, slides, and movies, and a white board. All the participants' workstations and the facilitator's workstation are connected by a local area network.

The University of Arizona has developed some 20 decision room software tools, and more than 100 groups have used their decision room. That software is now marketed under the name GroupSystems by GroupSystems.com.

The Electronic Brainstorming System is the most popular of the tools; it is used by more than 70 percent of the groups. Like most of the tools, it allows participants to simultaneously and anonymously key in ideas on a specific question. After an idea is entered and sent to the file server, the participant can see the ideas entered by others.

After the brainstorming portion of a meeting, many groups use the Issue Analyzer to organize the ideas. A voting tool ranks ideas and a topic commenter attaches comments to ideas already in the system. Finally, the groups can use the policy formation software to study alternatives. So most group "discussions" using these tools are done via keyboards rather than by talking. Some other tools do encourage face-to-face discussions.

Burr-Brown's Use of the Room

Burr-Brown's annual strategic planning meetings had always been held off-site, with some 9–10 executives attending. When they used the decision room, 31 executives attended. The IS department at the university provided a meeting facili-

(Case Continued)

tator to help plan the meeting and then facilitate it. During the meeting, the facilitator explained each tool before it was to be used. The facilitator also kept participants on track and was the neutral leader of the meeting so that Burr-Brown's CEO could attend as a participant. In addition, an assistant facilitator and three other assistants were present. They helped the participants use the hardware and software, made copies of the documents generated by the system, and so on.

Before the meeting, several planning meetings were held to settle on the meeting agenda. Each of the 11 divisions was asked to prepare a document to describe its one-year action plan and rolling five-year plan, including objectives and projected budgets. Participants received these plans before the meeting.

The agenda for the three-day meeting was:

- Day 1: Long-term strategy planning
- Day 2: Short-range action planning
- Day 3: Wrap-up in both areas

The meeting began with the group using the workstations to generate ideas about expected corporate performance in the coming years. They then organized these ideas to create the framework for discussing each division's plans.

For the next day and one-half, they entered comments on the five-year strategic plans and one-year action plans of each division, one division at a time.

They also spent some time brainstorming on ways to accomplish the year's objectives, and then ranking the ideas. The group settled on specific actions they would take on the top seven issues.

On the last afternoon, they divided into four groups to discuss important topics face-to-face. The planning meeting ended with the four groups presenting their recommendations.

Executives' Reactions

After the three-day session, the participants were asked to summarize their reactions to the room. They reported the following.

- *It increased involvement.* One senior vice president commented that the decision room allowed them to do in three days' time what would have taken months. The CEO noted that the past sessions could not be larger than 10 people to be manageable; and in those sessions, only two or three people really spoke up. With the decision room, 31 people were able to attend without hampering deliberations, and the group's comments were much more open than in the past.

  During one of the one-hour electronic brainstorming sessions, 404 comments were made, with the fewest number of comments from any of the 24 workstations, some of which had two users, being four and the highest being 27. Seven workstations contributed more than 20. So contributions were relatively evenly distributed across the group.

  The group had mixed reactions about the efficiency of the system. In a postsession questionnaire answered by 26 participants, 11 stated that it was more efficient than past meetings, nine said it was not, and six were neutral. However, the majority agreed that the facilitator was important in helping them use the room.

(Case Continued)

- **The planning process was more effective.** Several executives mentioned two aspects of the session that enhanced its effectiveness. The main one was anonymity. Due to anonymity, more people asked more questions and made more suggestions than they did in the former meeting format where all discussion was verbal, which identified the contributor.

Second, the planning process itself was extremely educational, said the CEO. "People walked in with narrow perceptions of the company and walked out with a CEO's perception. This is the view that is sought in strategic planning, but is usually not achieved," he commented three months after the session. This type of education had not happened at previous planning sessions.

One Year Later

One year later, 25 executives participated in a two-day session. About 16 of them had attended the year before. This year, the intent of the meeting was different. It was to critique plans, so that their impact on others and the support they needed from others were more explicit.

After the CEO described the firm's objectives and the economic climate, the planning session began with the group critiquing the previous year's results, companywide. The two-day session ended with each business unit manager commenting on the ideas received about his or her particular unit and how those ideas might affect the unit's action plan.

From the previous year's session, they learned that brainstorming is effective if the groups are structured properly. A large group can consider a few issues, such as corporate objectives, and present ideas on those topics. But a large group cannot "converse" because of the large number of ideas to consider.

For "dialogs," Burr-Brown found it is best to form several small groups, with each group addressing a few issues. One person puts in a statement, another person comments on it, then someone else comments, and so on. In the second year, they conducted small group dialogs and found them effective.

The company also learned that the room is not a substitute for a planning process. It is excellent for generating many ideas in a short time. But because face-to-face interaction is reduced, people are less likely to make commitments and agree on courses of action than in a face-to-face setting. So Burr-Brown does not use the room to reach consensus, but rather to critique plans.

The communications manager recommends that others who are planning to use such a room tell the participants about the room beforehand. Just send them a message that describes the room and includes a photograph, he suggested. Also, explain to participants how their comments will be used because the use probably will affect how they answer questions.

In all, Burr-Brown participants were pleased with the candor and objectivity the decision room elicited. They believe that its use has enhanced their annual planning meetings. ∎

Supporting Presentations and Discussions

Another popular same time/same place situation that can benefit from GSS is traditional presentation-discussion sessions found in classrooms, conference sessions, and business meetings. In an article in the *Communications of the ACM,* Robert Davison and Robert Briggs[9] explored the advantages of using GSS in a presentation-discussion session held in a workshop setting. The system they used was similar to the one used by Burr-Brown. Each member of the audience had a workstation, all interconnected by a LAN, with a public screen to show the interaction of the group. The presenter had a separate screen for audio-visuals to be used for the presentation.

To begin their exploration, Davison and Briggs identified the following potential advantages and disadvantages of allowing the workshop attendees to use a GSS.

More Opportunities for Discussion.   Using a GSS would eliminate the need to divide available airtime among potential speakers because participants could contribute simultaneously. The parallel, non-oral communication channels of the GSS would multiply the time available to the audience. And because they would be communicating online, the participants could even interact with each other during the actual presentation, which further multiplied available airtime.

More Equal Participation.   Because the GSS provides many parallel communication channels, loud or strong personalities probably would not dominate the discussion. Unlike oral discussions, the amount contributed by one person was expected to be independent of the amount contributed by others. This expectation was more likely to lead to a more equal distribution of discussion among the attendees.

Permanent Record of Discussion.   The GSS would capture a permanent electronic transcript of the online discussion. Thus, both participants and presenters could access the details long after the discussion was over.

Improved Feedback to Presenters.   With unrestricted airtime for audience members, and a permanent record of their discussion, presenters anticipated more comments as well as more detail in those comments. Furthermore, the anonymity allowed by the GSS would reduce some participants' concerns about negative repercussions if they contributed unpopular, critical, or new ideas. Thus, the presenters could receive more unfiltered critical analysis of their work using the GSS.

Improved Learning.   The GSS was also expected to reduce attention blocking, that is, the loss of attentiveness caused by people trying to remember what they want to say during the presentation. Working in parallel, participants could record their ideas when they occurred, then return their attention to the presentation. With more discussion time, reduced attention blocking, increased participation, improved feedback, and a permanent record, GSS users would retain more knowledge from a presentation than when using conventional methods.

Remote and Asynchronous Participation.   In addition, people who do not attend a presentation could still benefit by reading and contributing after the event. This opportunity does not mean replacing all face-to-face conferences and presentations with distributed online interaction. Many people find casual conversations in hallways and over meals to be as valuable as formal presentations.

Potential Negative Effects.   Despite such benefits, Davison and Briggs were concerned that online discussions during presentations might be a mixed blessing. Human attention is limited, so online discussions might distract participants to the point where they lose the thread of the presentation. Such distractions could outweigh other benefits. Furthermore, the online discussions could digress from the concepts in the presentation, or even devolve into flaming. And the anonymity of online discussion could hinder the evolution of a social community among the participants

To explore these hypotheses, Davison and Briggs conducted some experiments at a conference known for its interactive workshop-like sessions.

CASE EXAMPLE

HICSS

As part of the Hawaii International Conference on System Sciences (HICSS), 43 participants attended a three-hour tutorial on business process reengineering. The workshop had 24 laptops placed around two sets of tables, along with two large screens—one to show the PowerPoint slides for the presentation and the other to show the contents of the electronic discussion. To overcome concerns about politeness, the presenter encouraged the participants to use the equipment by saying that he considered typing while he was talking to be both polite and desirable. However, only eight comments were submitted during the three hours. Similarly low levels of participation occurred in two later nine-minute paper presentation sessions. Again, informal interviews revealed a widespread fear of rudeness.

Davison and Briggs hypothesized that because the attendees had not experienced using GSS during a presentation, they might not imagine how nonintrusive it could be. They also hypothesized that participants might not realize how easy the software was to use. Therefore, the

following day, they used the GSS for three 90-minute sessions. Each session had three paper presentations.

As each session began, the moderator asked participants to use the GSS to respond to the question, "What are the most pressing research issues facing the technology-supported learning research community?" Everyone contributed an idea, then responded online to an idea contributed by someone else.

The first presenter told the group that the oral discussion following the presentations would draw from the online discussion. Two subsequent speakers asked for online responses to specific questions. All others asked for critical feedback about their presentations. As soon as the first speaker began, members of the audience started typing. Participants contributed 275 comments during the three sessions, ranging from 20–54 per presentation. About 94 percent of comments were presentation-related, with no instances of flaming. Furthermore, during other sessions with no GSS, oral contributions to the post presentation discussions came from no more than four people. Observations in the GSS-supported sessions showed that contributions came from all over the audience.

During the following year, Davison and Briggs refined both their GSS methods and their questionnaire. They then conducted a more rigorous follow-on study at the next HICSS conference. The study addressed three primary research questions: What effect would GSS have on participation and perceived learning? Would the GSS be perceived as a detrimental distraction? What effect would GSS use have on the perceived value of the presentations and discussions?

At this conference, 34 laptops in a workshop setting let participants have a clearer view of the large public screen. All GSS-supported sessions began with a brief hands-on activity related to the session topic. A moderator invited online participation at the beginning of each presentation, and most presenters added their encouragement. Participants were urged to raise key issues from the online discussions during the postpresentation discussions. After the sessions, Davison and Briggs administered their survey questionnaire. They received data from 173 participants. Of those, 73 reported having used GSS, while 70 reported they did not

Participation and Learning

From the survey, Davison and Briggs learned that GSS users were significantly more willing to participate in the discussions than non-GSS users, and they reported doing so at significantly higher levels. The participants in both the GSS-supported and standard presentations had equal opportunity to contribute to oral discussion, and did so at approxi-

mately equal rates. However, the participants who used GSS also contributed hundreds of comments to the online discussions, so their overall participation was substantially higher. Furthermore, a much higher percentage of the audience got involved in the GSS discussion than in the oral discussion. Thus, it appears that the GSS may have accomplished its primary purpose: to increase participation and learning. But at what cost?

Distraction and Digression

Overall, participants were comfortable with the amount of distraction and digression in the sessions. Only three GSS users and four non-GSS users reported negative reactions—too few for meaningful statistical analysis. Thus, the GSS did not appear to create widespread perceptions of undue distraction or digression.

No online flaming occurred, and nearly all the online contributions were relevant to the presentations. Content analysis of the online transcripts suggested that participants grasped the key concepts of the presentations, which is further evidence the GSS did not distract them from the oral delivery of information.

Overall, the respondents also reported receiving positive value from the conference sessions and the GSS. This response suggests that the GSS enabled the groups to increase the quantity of something they valued—the discussions and feedback—without reducing its quality. Many participants chose to take electronic transcripts with them at the end of each session, while others downloaded transcripts from the Internet. Thus the value derived from the discussion was extended beyond the walls of the presentation hall. ■

Supporting Dispersed Groups

One of the most promising uses of groupware is for ongoing coordination by groups who work at different times and in different places. With the increasing marketplace emphasis on cycle time reduction, companies can use the globe and its three main regions (Europe, Asia, and the Americas) to extend their workday to round-the-clock, by passing work from groups in one region to the next at the end of each one's workday, as the following personal example attests.

> I had that experience for the first time a few years ago. On one of my first writing projects, the author of the report, who works in England, e-mailed me his thoughts and questions on the topic at the end of his workday. During my workday, while he was sleeping, I did some thinking and research on the topic, and then e-mailed my thoughts and findings back to him. And when I slept, he worked. He and I worked this way, swapped long e-mails, for about one week. But we got at least two week's worth of work done. It was tremendously exhilarating and productive without either of us having to work long hours.

One of the more exciting advances in group support is the development of virtual teams. These project teams usually disband after their project is complete. They tend to operate in three cells of Johansen's matrix.

- *Same time/same place:* Typically, the team meets face-to-face initially to develop the basic plan and objectives.
- *Different time/different place:* They then communicate by e-mail and do data gathering and analysis separately.
- *Same time/different place:* If their technology is strong enough, they may have audio or video conferences to discuss developments and progress toward goals.

Following is a case example of a successful virtual team, as described in the award-winning paper to the Society for Information Management by Carman, Lott, Malhotra, and Majchrzak.[11]

CASE EXAMPLE

BOEING-ROCKETDYNE

Boeing-Rocketdyne is the major manufacturer of liquid-fueled rocket engines in the United States. These engines are used to launch communication satellites. The company faced significant competition and price pressures from Eastern European companies, so it initiated a project called SLICE (Simple Low-Cost Innovative Engine). SLICE's business objectives were dramatic: To reduce the cost of the rocket engine to one-tenth, to get the engine to market 10 times faster than the

(Case Continued)

Space Shuttle's main engine, and to increase the useful life of the rocket engine by 300 percent. In short, it was a breakthrough project. It was so breakthrough, in fact, that none of the senior technical managers thought the goals were possible, and these managers, as a group, had hundreds of years of experience designing rocket engines. Only one advanced program manager was willing to give the project a try.

The team faced many challenges. The first was work style. To get the best people on the project, they needed to come from different disciplines and different organizations. Management would not allow them to be taken off their regular work, so they could not be collocated. They had to work virtually, without holding face-to-face meetings using electronic collaboration technology. Furthermore, the members had not worked together as a team, so they had different product experiences, and different design processes. Finally, they had to submit only one design, a design that Rocketdyne's conservative senior management would accept.

Despite these challenges, the project was a tremendous success. The project lasted 10 months, during which time the team held 89 online meetings using a collaborative technology called the Internet Notebook. They created and critiqued 20 designs and submitted more than 650 entries into the notebook. The seven senior technical managers who reviewed the project at its conclusion stated that it had successfully achieved its objectives. In fact, it surpassed them. The design was approved for the next phase: testing the assumptions about how the liquid would flow through the components.

The design accomplished the following:

- The engine's thrust changer had only six parts, down from more than 450.
- The manufacturing cost was estimated to be $1.5 million, down from $20 million.
- Quality was predicted to be nine sigma, up from industry-standard six sigma, which meant one failure in 10 billion.
- Development cost was $47,000, down from $4.5 million.

The team was awarded the Department of Defense's Advanced Research Program for "validating a process for virtual collocation teams."

In addition, no team member spent more than 15 percent of his or her time on the project, the team stayed within its budget even though the project took longer than expected, and total engineering hours were one-half normal using the collaborative technology.

Lessons Learned

Why was the team so successful? Carman and colleagues studied the life of this project and suggested the following success factors.

Prior agreement. Boeing-Rocketdyne anticipated the need for close cooperation on some significant projects well before the SLICE team was formed. Therefore, they began developing a partnership agreement to govern such teams before they were launched. It turns out that the legal aspects of intellectual property are complicated, so they need time to be defined. Because this agreement was in place when the SLICE team began its work, the team members could move ahead quickly without being concerned about who was able to know what.

(Case Continued)

Beyond communication to knowledge management. The team's collaborative technology—the Internet Notebook—was developed by a third party in response to a list of requirements drawn up by several of the team members. The technology allowed members to

- Access the notebook from anywhere.
- Create, comment on, reference-link, search, and sort entries that could consist of sketches, snapshots, hotlinks to desktop applications, texts, or templates.
- Use an electronic white board for near-instantaneous access to entries.

Thus, from the outset, the team had a technology suited to its needs, at least as the team initially defined them. The team focused its early discussions on creating a coordination protocol for facilitating its collaborative use. Figure 13-3 shows how the team members rated these features.

The team adapted ways of working that required it to change the fundamental way the members were used to collaborating: from face-to-face discussions to complete reliance on technology, from sharing information sparingly (only when someone needed to know the information) to sharing all information with everyone all the time, and from using personal collaborative tools (such as company-specific e-mail systems) to using a single system. So initially, the team believed that all information would be captured and shared among all members all the time. The result would be a much greater emphasis on knowledge management and retrieval, beyond just communication.

FIGURE 13-3 Ratings of Noteook Features for Information Retrieval

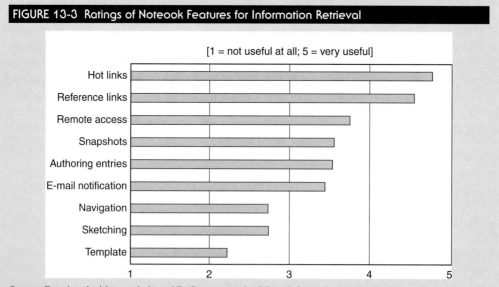

Source: Reprinted with permission of R. Carman et al., "Virtual Cross-Supply Chain Concept Development Collaborative Teams: Spurring Radical Innovations at Boeing-Rocketdyne," first place winner of 2000 paper competition of the Society for Information Management, www.simnet.org.

(Case Continued)

Meet Core Creative Requirements. The team learned that its ability to be creative required meeting three requirements:

1. Jointly understanding problems, possible solutions, analysis methods, and language
2. Interacting frequently as a team, with all members "present," to share work-in-progress, brainstorm ideas, and test out solutions
3. Being able to create new information quickly based on a particular

conversation or problem, and then equally quickly discard information that was no longer needed.

The team members discovered they needed to adapt the traditional work practices of a collocated team to function as a creative body. Figure 13-4 shows how the need to be creative is accommodated in collocated teams, and what the SLICE team members learned they would need to do to adapt these needs to their noncollocated situation.

FIGURE 13-4 Structuring Core Processes for Virtual Teams

Core Needs of Creative Teams	Practices of Collocated Teams	Practices Adapted by Virtual Teams
Development of shared understanding	• Lead engineer is "spoke-in-the-wheel" for coordinating information and consolidating ideas into new design proposals, which constitute the shared understandings of the team.	• From spoke-in-the-wheel coordination (with lead manager/engineer in center) to democratic coordination • Encourage development and use of common-language metaphors
Frequent opportunities for interaction with team members	• Collocation allows for frequent and spontaneous interaction.	• Coupling use of knowledge repository with frequent teleconferences • Allowing one-on-one discussions when need arises but documenting results for everyone
Rapid creation and sharing of context-specific transient information	• Most discussion is verbal and undocumented, and it is hard to capture the context.	• Promote only minimal cataloging of new information, even to the extent of restricting it to "touchstones" and "placeholders" • Timely and frequent discussions of new entries in knowledge repository to enable members to learn the context

Source: Reprinted with permission of Carman et al., "Virtual Cross-Supply Chain Concept Development Collaborative Teams: Spurring Radical Innovation at Boeing-Rocketdyne," first place winner of 2000 paper competition of the Society for Information Management, www.simnet.org.

(Case Continued)

Focus of Effort Changes. Over time, the team learned it had to shift its thinking among three components of the project, from thinking about strategy (how to fulfill the partnership agreement), to implementing a technology that would support collaboration of the dispersed team structure, to actual work practices that would take advantage of the technology. It learned that the strategy practices needed to be in place before the work or technology practices so that members did not have to be concerned with both doing the work and negotiating information-sharing arrangements at the same time.

Furthermore, the team discovered it needed the technology in place before it could think about work practices because the work style depended on the technology that would support it. Along the way, members also learned that the technology had to be flexible enough to be adapted to different ways of working because they discovered some of their initial work practices did not work as well as hoped. So, over the course of the project, they evolved their practices, and the tool had to support this evolution.

Figure 13-5 shows the allocation of effort over the course of the project among these three components of the project: strategy, technology, and work practices. As can be seen, the team needed to focus on both the technology and its own work practices over the entire span of the project. For example, a technology facilitator was required to attend all teleconferences so that problems could be fixed immediately. Members never knew when someone would not understand how to perform a particular operation, or a server would go down and communications would need to be rerouted. In addition, throughout the project, as the team found work practices not working as expected, members devoted some effort to decide on better ways of working. In the end, this attention paid off.

In summary, the SLICE team at Boeing-Rocketdyne was immensely successful, in large part due to the advanced group support technology used. As usual, however, the technology was necessary but not sufficient. The team also needed a carefully developed partnership agreement in place before work began, and work practices to leverage the technology, which it learned needed to evolve as it discovered their usefulness. ∎

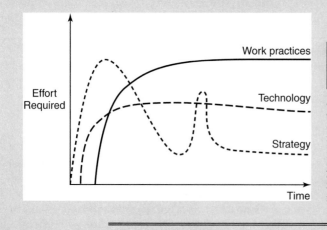

Effort Required

Work practices

Technology

Strategy

Time

FIGURE 13-5 Effort Distribution over the Team's Life Cycle

Source: Reprinted with permission of Carman et al., "Virtual Cross-Supply Chain Concept Development Collaborative Teams: Spurring Radical Innovations at Boeing-Rocketdyne," first place winner of 2000 paper competition of the Society for Information Management, www.simnet.org.

GROUPWARE ON THE INTERNET

Group support technology, like nearly all applications, is migrating to the Web. A Web environment naturally supports some aspects of group work such as e-mail, newsgroups, and other modes of communication. Until the Web, full group functionality, such as voting, structuring complex information, and brainstorming, have been available only in proprietary systems operating on a LAN.

The rapid growth of the Internet and the Web is changing the landscape of groupware and its usage. But how extensive is such support? What are the advantages and disadvantages of Web-based group systems versus proprietary systems?

Survey of Web-Based Groupware

To answer these questions, Brad Wheeler, Alan Dennis, and Larry Press conducted a survey of companies that were using groupware on the Web.[11] They received responses from 108 companies, 60 percent from the United States and 40 percent from other countries. Figure 13-6 shows the ways in which Web-based groupware was used in these companies. The three major categories of use were (1) to support project team activities, (2) to support education, and (3) to replace email listserv systems.

The most common application was support for project teams. Most of the teams used the groupware asynchronously, but 6 percent used it in networked decision support rooms at the same time and place. Most teams used the groupware to plan face-to-face nongroupware meetings or to begin the discussions that would be completed in those meetings.

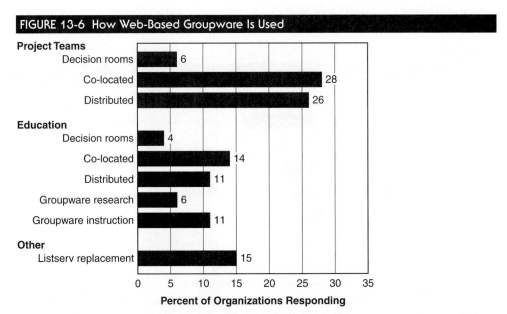

FIGURE 13-6 How Web-Based Groupware Is Used

Source: Reprinted with permission of Bradley Wheeler, Alan Dennis, and Laurence Press, "Groupware Comments to the Internet: Charting a New World," *Database,* Spring 2000.

A second major use was to demonstrate groupware or to supplement or replace face-to-face teaching or training. The third major use was to replace e-mail listservs, to support discussions of special interest groups.

The surveyed companies reported a number of advantages and disadvantages of Web-based groupware, as show in Figure 13-7.

The most often-mentioned advantages were technological: open network standards to permit anyplace, anytime interaction and open client standards (browsers) so that users did not need to install new software. Furthermore, people were familiar with browsers, so no training was needed. In fact, most of the software was free or relatively low cost, so setup costs were also low. A second set of advantages centered around specific functions that support group interactions, such as allowing "transformations" (structuring, sorting, and analyzing discussions) and functions of the software (anonymity, embedding HTML, and graphics).

Wheeler, Dennis, and Press grouped the disadvantages into three categories. The first pertained to the lack of features of today's tools, such as limited integration and no drag-and-drop interfaces. These facilities are available on PCs, which is why the users wanted them. Once they began to use Web groupware, they discovered the tools were limiting their PC-based work styles. The second group of disadvantages revolved around the network connection: slow, unrealiable, not secure, and sometimes not easily accessible.

The third set of disadvantages involved organizational changes required by the groupware that can inhibit its use. These changes include higher operating costs (from systems administration, training, and facilitation) and the need for group learning (in changing team skills and learning to take advantages of the new possibilities). Even though the use of browsers reduces the need for training, it does not reduce the need for teams to learn new processes. Wheeler, Dennis, and Press conclude that ongoing learning is a fundamental issue faced by all organizations that adopt Web groupware.

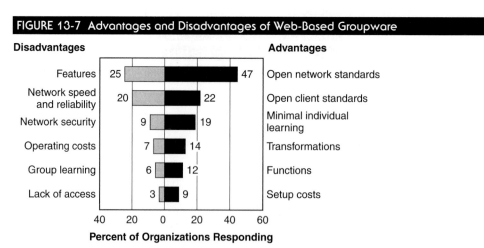

FIGURE 13-7 Advantages and Disadvantages of Web-Based Groupware

Disadvantages		Advantages
Features	25 — 47	Open network standards
Network speed and reliability	20 — 22	Open client standards
Network security	9 — 19	Minimal individual learning
Operating costs	7 — 14	Transformations
Group learning	6 — 12	Functions
Lack of access	3 — 9	Setup costs

Percent of Organizations Responding

Source: Reprinted with permission of Bradley Wheeler, Alan Dennis, and Laurence Press, "Groupware Comments to the Internet: Charting a New World," *Database,* Spring 2000.

THE FUTURE

Until the explosion of the Web, most groups depended on desktop software, access to file servers, and e-mail to collaborate electronically. Lotus Notes has been used, but not widely. So most teams have depended on tools that were not designed for easy sharing and collaboration. For instance, file servers do not help people find information. E-mail is for sharing, but mainly on a one-on-one basis, or groups of people whose interest in a subject is known to the e-mail sender. These messages miss others who might benefit or benefit the sender with their feedback. No central storage site is available. And these messages load up networks and hard drives because they send copies to each recipient. In essence, they follow the old print-, copy-, distribute paradigm. Companies that use groupware have also needed to deal with proprietary software, which has been expensive to buy and keep current.

The Web will move downward organizationally, due to the personal Web page authoring tools that make it as easy to publish information on an intranet as save it in a word-processing document. Each document can have access control and can be accessed by local or remote users, so it can be used by distributed work groups. By providing links to the new document, others can be made aware of its existence. The Web facilities of full-text searching and cataloging (to see documents by subject) are automatically available. Web authoring systems, such as Netscape's Communicator, will increasingly include software agents that monitor new documents added to the Web site. When one is added, it informs the catalog server so that the document can be cataloged.

In short, the Web will increasingly be used to support groups, teams, departments, and even interenterprise groups and communities.

QUESTIONS AND EXERCISES

Review Questions

1. What are the three ways to organize the work of groups?
2. What are the three characteristics of groups?
3. Name several types of groups and describe each briefly.
4. What are three reasons for the importance of group support systems?
5. According to Brewer, what are tacit knowledge and explicit knowledge?
6. What is "The Rudy problem," and how did Seemann attempt to deal with it?
7. Describe Buckman Laboratories' solution to sharing knowledge worldwide.
8. Describe the four cells of the time/place matrix, and give an example of a technology used in each.
9. What are some of the ways IT can help improve meetings?
10. What benefits did Burr-Brown get from its use of a group decision room?
11. List some of the ways GSS can improve the traditional presentation-discussion session? What are some potential negatives?
12. What were the secrets of success for the SLICE team at Boeing-Rocketdyne?
13. What were the three major uses of Web-based groupware in the Wheeler, Dennis, and Press survey?
14. What advantages and disadvantages of Web-based groupware were reported in the survey?

Discussion Questions

1. Support for communication and coordination is quite different from support for group decision making. The technologies should be different. Do you agree or disagree? Explain your reasoning.
2. Knowledge can be transferred onto computers. Agree or disagree? Explain your reasoning.
3. The Web is being touted as the solution to all computing needs, including group support. But it really will not truly help group work as much as full function LAN-based systems specifically designed as a groupware tool. Agree or disagree? Explain your reasoning.

Exercises

1. Find an article that describes a group support system of some kind. What is its major purpose? What technology is used?
2. Conduct a survey of products available in the marketplace for group support (by using a directory of software or contacting several vendors). What kind of support do the systems provide? How do they compare with the systems described in this chapter?
3. Visit a local company that is using technology to support group work. Map their activities onto the time/place matrix. What infrastructures have they developed?

REFERENCES

1. Computer Supported Cooperative Work is a series of bi-annual conferences sponsored by ACM, who publishes the *CSCW Proceedings.*

2. Desantis, G. and B. Gallupe, "Group Decision Support Systems: A New Frontier," *Data Base,* Winter 1985.

3. Institute for Research On Learning, Menlo Park, CA.

4. Johansen, Robert, Institute for the Future, Menlo Park, CA.

5. Drucker, P. F., "The Coming of the New Organization," *Harvard Business Review,* January-February 1988, 45–53.

6. Malone, T., and K. Cranston, "Toward an Interdisciplinary Theory of Coordination," CCS #120, MIT Sloan School of Industrial Management, April 1991.

7. Brewer, Tony, "Managing Knowledge," Wentworth Research Program (now part of Gartner Executive Programs, Stamford, CT), November 1995.

8. Seemann, Patricia, "Building Knowledge Infrastructure: Creating Change Capabilities," tape cassette #B13 at the Knowledge Imperative Symposium sponsored by Arthur Anderson and the American Center for Productivity and Quality, September 1995, AVW Audio Visual, 3620 Willowbend, Houston, TX 77010.

9. Davison, Robert, and Robert Briggs, "GSS for Presentation Support," *Communications of the ACM,* September 2000, 91–97.

10. Carman, Robert, Vern Lott, Arvind Malhotra, and Ann Majchrzak, "Virtual Cross-Supply Chain Concept Development Collaborative Teams: Spurring Radical Innovations at Boeing-Rocketdyne," first place winner of 2000 paper competition of the Society for Information Management, www.simnet.org.

11. Wheeler, Bradley, Alan Dennis, and Laurence Press, "Groupware Comes to the Internet: Charting a New World," *Database,* Spring 2000.

14 LEVERAGING THE WORLD OF INFORMATION

INTRODUCTION

As we have seen in previous chapters, the world of information is growing. Chapter 7 looked at the scope of information resources that must be managed, which has expanded to include external as well as internal sources, and documents as well as databases. The discussion in Chapter 11 focused on the growing universe of computing resources, including mobile computing, rich media, and Internet technologies. In this chapter we explore leveraging this expanded world of information to increase its business value. The themes of this chapter are:

- *Document management:* using new technologies to manage the information resources that do not fit easily into traditional databases
- *Knowledge management and knowledge sharing:* using new technologies to assist in capturing and sharing knowledge among people.

These two topics are closely related because they both require organizing and managing conceptual, descriptive, and ambiguous multimedia content, which is important in today's knowledge-intensive world.

Harnessing IT to manage documents is a major challenge facing IS managers because most of the valuable information in organizations is in the form of documents, such as business forms, reports, letters, memos, policy statements, contracts, agreements, and so on. Moreover, most of the important business processes in organizations are based on, or driven by, document flows.

Electronic document management (EDM) promises major productivity and performance increases by applying technology to documents and document processing. EDM is the application of technology to save paper, speed up communications, and increase the productivity of business processes. From a broader perspective, EDM expands the domain of information management, with a concomitant increase in the responsibilities of IS executives.[1] The pervasive importance of documents is not going to change anytime soon even though the form that documents take is changing radically.

Computer systems have mostly handled facts organized into data records. Far more valuable and important are the concepts and ideas contained in documents. Reports drawn from computerized databases fill important roles in status assessment and control. But frequently they must be accompanied by a memo or textual report that explains and interprets the computer report. Meetings, phone conversations, news items, written memos, and noncomputerized reports are usually rated more important by managers. Technology applied to handling documents promises to improve these forms of communication.

Until recently, technology for document processing has been limited mostly to better and faster ways to generate, print, and transport text documents. Now, several developments suggest that we are on the verge of a major advance in computer-based information management. These advances include digital image processing, large capacity storage, hypertext, multimedia documents, high bandwidth communication, electronic printing, electronic mail, facsimile, and improved techniques for retrieving concepts, information, and data. Many of these technologies are proving valuable for replacing paper, managing workflow, training and education, records management, and internal reporting.

In this chapter we first consider the definition and scope of EDM. Then we identify categories of applications that create business value from using document technologies. Those technologies can be summarized in a layered architecture. Then we consider what IS managers should do to prepare for document management. Finally, we present a conceptual model for the processes of knowledge management and sharing, and discuss the cultural challenges of knowledge management projects.

DOCUMENTS: DEFINITION AND SCOPE

A document can be described as a unit of "recorded information structured for human consumption."[2] It is recorded and stored; therefore, a speech or conversation for which no transcript is prepared is not a document. This definition accommodates "documents" dating back to cuneiform inscriptions on clay tablets. What has changed lately are the ways information is represented and the ways documents are processed. Information previously represented primarily by text is now also represented by graphical symbols, images, photographs, audio, video, and animation. Documents previously created and stored on paper are now digitally created, stored, transported, and displayed.

This definition also accommodates a wide variety of documents used in organizations. Examples include:

- Contracts and agreements
- Drawings, blueprints, and photographs
- Reports
- E-mail and voice mail messages
- Manuals and handbooks
- Video clips
- Business forms
- Scripts and visuals from presentations
- Correspondence
- Computer printouts
- Memos
- Transcripts from meetings
- News items and articles

Applying technology to process traditional documents makes a major change in what documents can accomplish in organizations. A definition more oriented to technology comes from *Byte* magazine.[3]

A document is a snapshot of some set of information that can

- incorporate many complex information types;
- exist in multiple places across a network;
- depend on other documents for information;
- change on the fly (as subordinate documents are updated);
- have an intricate structure, or complex data types such as full-motion video and voice annotations; and
- be accessed and modified by many people simultaneously (if they have permission to do so).

Another perspective suggests that a document is a "unit record" of conceptual information. A data record contains the attributes of an entity such as an employee in a personnel system or a part number in an inventory system; a document contains the information necessary to represent a concept or idea. Although most documents currently contain a set of these "concept nodes," future documents may be composed of a network or web of linked conceptual unit records. These "chunks" or "bundles" of information will have attributes that make them more useful and human than traditional data records. Context, tone, richness of representation media, and flexibility of structure will make the information in documents more consumable and accessible to humans. This perspective strengthens the understanding that document management is an expanded form of information management.

In spite of these broad definitions, the dominant connotation of a document is that it is relatively structured and formal information, primarily text, printed on paper. Therefore EDM must handle paper documents or their electronic equivalent. Older technologies for document handling include micrographics, computer output microfilm (COM), and automated records center applications. A newer technology is digital image processing, which represents a paper page as a digital image of that page.

Increasingly, EDM emphasizes *electronic documents* and their management. An electronic document uses a variety of symbols and media to represent ideas and concepts. In addition to traditional letters and numbers (text), an electronic document may contain graphical symbols, photographs and other images, voice, video clips, and animation. This clustered set of symbols can be stored, retrieved, and presented electronically as a "compound document." For example, an internal report on a product improvement may present, on a computer screen, the text explaining the feature, a photograph, an engineering diagram, a voice notation from the product designer, and a video clip of the product in use. Figure 14-1 shows the conceptual structure of such a compound document. A Web page is a popular example of a compound document. This is a richer, enhanced definition of what we have traditionally called a document, so EDM requires us to expand our connotation of this old and comfortable word.

The Roles Documents Play

It is hard to think of anything more pervasive and fundamental to an organization than documents. Figure 14-2 shows several examples of the roles documents play, with an example of each.

Taken together, these roles lead to the conclusion that documents are the stored memory for an organization, its groups, and its individuals, as well as being the primary mechanism for conducting business. In fact, we have identified four fundamental roles for documents in organizations.

1. As a product, or support for a product
2. As a fundamental mechanism for communication among people and groups within an organization and between organizations.
3. As the primary vehicle for business processes
4. As an important part of organizational memory

The impact of applying emerging technologies to document management is potentially significant. Because documents contain concepts and ideas, EDM promises to advance the management of conceptual information in organizations. And because most

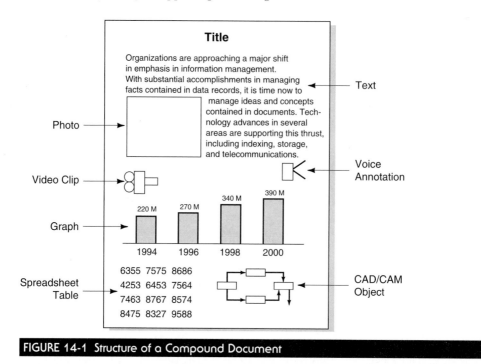

FIGURE 14-1 Structure of a Compound Document

of the work of information workers at managerial and professional levels deals with concepts and ideas, EDM promises improved levels of support and productivity. With documents as the primary vehicle for business processes, EDM promises to make a major contribution to business process redesign and quality improvement efforts.

ELECTRONIC DOCUMENT MANAGEMENT APPLICATIONS

This section describes some of the application areas that are particularly susceptible to EDM. They are generic functions in organizations that:

- Depend on documents as the primary mechanism for getting work done
- Are susceptible to emerging document technologies
- Have proven business value resulting from the use of EDM technologies and approaches.

As technologies and organizational processes evolve, EDM applications will be developed in several areas and for several purposes. To illustrate the areas in which EDM can be applied, consider the case of a medium-sized manufacturing firm that discovered several EDM applications evolving in separate areas. These application areas, and the departments in which they evolved, are summarized in Figure 14-3.

This case illustrates that EDM turns up in several application areas. Generally, the departments that install EDM are not aware of the developments in the other areas. These early EDM applications generate business value by improving customer service,

ROLES	*EXAMPLES*
To record or to "document" contracts and and agreements	Employment contracts, maintenance agreements, consulting contracts, purchase agreements, leases, mortgages, loans, etc.
To record policies, standards, and procedures	Procedure manuals, standards specifications, instruction handbooks, executive memos and letters that state corporate policy, etc.
To represent a view of reality at a point in time (reports and plans)	Status reports, problem analyses, operational reports, staff recommendations, budgets, strategic plans, etc.
To create an image or impression	Annual reports, marketing brochures, TV or radio commercials, etc.
To generate revenue as a product	A book for sale by a publisher, a report by a consulting firm to be sold to its client, a news item from a wire service, a reference from a bibliographic service, etc.
To support revenue by adding value to a product	A user's manual for a car or appliance or a software product, a warranty form, a catalog, a discount coupon for the next purchase, etc.
To act as a mechanism for communication	Memos, letters, presentations, e-mail, messages, and interaction among people and groups minutes of meetings, etc.
To act as a vehicle for organizational process	Orders, invoices, approval letters, most business forms, etc.
To provide a discipline for capture and articulation of concepts and ideas	Nearly all the kinds of documents that carry concepts and ideas

FIGURE 14-2 Roles Documents Play

simplifying business processes, accelerating the distribution of documents, reducing storage costs, or improving access to documents. They are different enough in structure, purpose, and users that they are separately developed, but they use similar technologies and approaches. Imaging, for example, is a technology used in several of the applications. A document server with multimedia storage and a strong search engine is needed for several. And the concept of just-in-time (printing, learning, forms processing) pervades the design philosophy in all areas. Without some planning in the development of these applications and their extensions, however, incompatibilities will limit the effectiveness of the applications in all areas.

EDM applications that generate value can be organized into the following seven generic categories:

1. To improve the publishing process
2. To support organizational processes
3. To support communication among people and groups
4. To improve access to external information
5. To create and maintain documentation
6. To maintain corporate records
7. To promote training and education

FIGURE 14-3 EDM Applications in a Medium-Sized Manufacturing Firm

Department	Application
Records Management	An imaging system for archival storage and access to legal and tax documents. Replaced an aging microfilm system. Implemented on a network to eliminate physical shipment of paper documents among several offices in different cities.
Manufacturing	An extended version of a CAD/CAM system to use imaging to manage the blueprints and engineering diagrams.
Human Resources Management	An imaging system to support the hiring process. Candidates' resumes are scanned into the system when they apply and then are circulated in image form among the many people involved in the hiring process.
Systems and Procedures	A plan to improve the process of printing and distributing the procedure manuals to secretaries and administrative assistants. Currently—manuals printed centrally and mailed to all users; revised yearly with interim modification sheets. Phase I—Print manuals over the network on high-speed remote printers at each major site (distributed printing). Phase II—Allow secretaries and administrative assistants to print sections of the manual on their local printer as needed (reprint on demand). Phase III—Add retrieval and reference capabilities so that users can access relevant parts of the manual online as needed.
Customer Service	A new system for publishing and distributing owner's manuals, repair manuals, product descriptions, and product specifications. In the past these have always been printed on paper and mailed to customers, distributors, and sales personnel. Recently they have begun to be distributed on CD-ROM.
Administrative Services	Development of work flow system utilizing electronic forms for such tasks as office supply orders from stores, check requisitions, internal office equipment orders, telephone change requests, etc. A new version of the system will include such features as authorization, encryption, and signature verification that will permit the use of electronic forms for larger and more important processes also.
Training and Education	A plan to evolve the process of teaching administrative assistants and secretaries. Currently—a classroom course, based heavily on the procedures manual, which uses multimedia presentation materials to explain the steps in these procedures and show the forms that must be used. Phase I—Convert the multimedia course to a computer-based training course for use on a workstation instead of in the classroom. Phase II—Structure the software so that each procedure module can be accessed as needed rather than as part of an entire course. Phase III—Use real forms instead of sample forms as part of the source material. These forms can be filled in on the workstation and sent over e-mail so that the system becomes a real work flow system that actually performs the tasks. Access to reference material and training/education are additional built-in features.

Before we look at the categories in greater detail, here is an example of a company with document systems in several of those categories. Through better forms management and electronic printing, they made major improvements in these applications, while enhancing the corporate image at the same time.

CASE EXAMPLE

TAPIOLA INSURANCE GROUP

Tapiola is a group of three insurance companies with headquarters in Espoo, Finland, a suburb of Helsinki. By Finnish law, an insurance company can sell only one type of insurance; therefore, each of the three companies in Tapiola sells either life, nonlife, or pension insurance. They call themselves "an insurance department store."

Some 90 percent of insurance in Finland is sold by five insurance "groups"; Tapiola is the fourth largest group. They have 14 percent of the market, with 1.5 million customers and 3 million policies. Each year their mail room sends out 4 million letters, so printing is an important and expensive part of their operation.

Formerly, the Tapiola group offered 150 kinds of insurance policies, and they had 300 different insurance policy forms— half in Swedish and half in Finnish— because both are official languages in Finland. The policy forms were all preprinted by an outside print shop, generally on sprocket-fed computer paper. Then the forms were filled in by printers connected to their IBM mainframes.

This mode of operation presented several problems. If a change was made to a form, the inventory of old forms had to be discarded. Reprinting new forms often took weeks. That time represented possible lost revenue. Also, the computer printers could print on only one side of each sheet of paper. Finally, for more complex policies, they had to use large-size computer paper that was often unwieldy to handle and mail.

Document Processing Goals

The production manager and the insurance applications development manager looked around for an alternate way to print policies and statements. They had several goals. One was, of course, to reduce costs. A second goal was to stop using preprinted forms. Their third goal was to give Tapiola marketing people new ways to advertise insurance products, by making computer-generated letters to customers more flexible. The fourth, and most important goal was to make Tapiola "the most personal insurance company in Finland." Thus, these two systems managers wanted their computer-generated correspondence to prospective and current policy holders to appear more "human," as if a Tapiola employee had used a typewriter to write a personal reply to an inquiry or request for information.

(Case Continued)

Centralized Solution

To overcome the computer-generated appearance of their output, they switched to plain paper printers from Rank Xerox, the European subsidiary of Xerox Corporation. Xerox is best known for their photocopiers, but they are increasingly creating products for electronic document processing, where a document can include text, data, image, and graphics. Conversion of the output equipment at Tapiola took 15 months, during which time they reduced their 300 pre-printed forms to four.

Four New "Forms"

Their four "forms" are actually four types of standard European A4 cut paper. (In the United States, the equivalent would be the 8 1/2 × 11 sheet of paper.) The first form is a plain white A4 sheet of paper. It is used for internal communications within Tapiola.

The second form is the same blank white paper with four holes punched along the left-hand side, to fit in the standard European four-ring binder. (In the United States, the standard is generally a three-ring binder.) This form is also mainly for internal use.

The third form has the Tapiola logo preprinted in green in the upper left-hand corner and both sides of the paper have the word "Tapiola" printed in *tiny,* faint green letters over most of the page. This form is their standard company stationery, and it has become one of their standard computer printout forms for communicating with the outside world.

The fourth form is the same as the third except that it has a 4 × 6 inch (10 × 15 cm) perforated area in the lower right-hand corner. This form is used for all

their insurance policy bills. The tear-off portion can be paid at any bank; the money and information about the payment go directly from the bank to Tapiola.

Programming and Conversion

Reprogramming the IBM applications was extremely easy, because only the output routines needed to be changed. That programming took two work-years of application programmer time. In addition, one systems programmer spent six months working with Xerox on the IBM-to-Xerox system software interfaces. One forms designer spent 15 months redesigning all 300 preprinted forms into 240 printing formats for the application programmers. About 60 forms disappeared altogether, because they were found to be unnecessary; the remaining 240 forms are not all different, because one-half of them are in Swedish and the other half are in Finnish.

The conversion was done in two stages. First, customer policy statements were printed in a form-like manner, on two sides of the new size paper. These looked somewhat like the old forms so that policy holders could understand the changeover. Then, the terse, table-like data was replaced with text, to make the statements look more like personal letters.

Envelope Stuffing

Interestingly, these redesigns of customer "documents" were the easy part of the conversion. The more difficult and sensitive part was making sure that each envelope contained the correct pieces of paper. Because Tapiola was now using smaller sheets of paper, they often needed to include several sheets in each envelope, and, of course, they did not

(Case Continued)

want to put a cover letter for one policy holder into the same envelope as a statement for another policy holder.

To solve this problem, they found an envelope insertion machine made by PMB Vector, in Stockholm, Sweden. This machine contains a microprocessor that can read an 8-dot code printed at the top of each sheet of paper. Thus, the Xerox printer not only prints the correspondence but, at the same time, it prints a code at the top of each sheet of paper—one code for all pages to go in one envelope. The Vector inserter machine makes sure that each envelope only contains pages with the same code.

Decentralized Expansion

This document processing conversion was just one part of their effort to improve and humanize their customer correspondence. In the midst of the document redesign, Tapiola also decided to move some printing of customer correspondence to their 62 branch offices.

To illustrate how a remote printer is used, consider the case of a female policy holder who has received medical care. She can mail the medical bills to Tapiola or visit her local office in person. If she visits them and presents her bills to a Tapiola employee, that employee uses an IBM terminal to access the policy holder's data from the central database. If she has brought all the proper documents needed for reimbursement, the employee can initiate a *direct electronic payment* from a Tapiola bank account to the policy

holder's personal bank account, no matter which bank they both use.

Once a day, Tapiola transmits all such electronic transactions to their bank and those transactions are cleared that same day. (The five major Finnish banks have collaborated and created a sophisticated and fast banking system. A large number of individuals and companies in Finland use debit cards and other forms of electronic banking rather than checks or cash.) The employee then gives the policy holder a letter verifying the transaction. That letter is generated by the central IBM computer but is printed on the local Xerox printer. If the policy holder is missing some information, the employee can create a personalized letter explaining what is missing, by assembling phrases stored in the central database, and then printing the letter on-site.

The people at Tapiola Data recommend that other information system departments become involved in electronic document management by first looking at the output their computers are generating. It was not difficult to mix traditional mainframe technology with document processing technology.

A recent poll of Finnish citizens showed that Tapiola is seen as a dynamic company, and they have the best reputation among young people of all the insurance groups. The people at Tapiola Data believe their use of document processing technology is helping to build and reinforce this image. ■

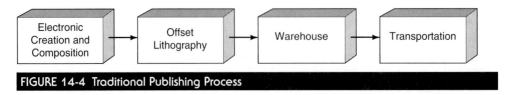

FIGURE 14-4 Traditional Publishing Process

As the Tapiola case illustrates, major benefits are available from developing EDM applications in several areas. Here is a short discussion on each of the seven areas listed earlier.

Improving the Publication Process

Technology enables a major restructuring of the process of publishing and distributing paper documents. For those organizations that produce documents as a product or as support for a product, this change is reengineering their document production processes. The stages of the traditional process, designed primarily for high-volume and high quality documents, is shown in Figure 14-4. The document is created, generally with the use of electronic tools, and a photographic plate is made for an offset printing press. The offset press requires long print runs to amortize the extensive setup costs. Thus, a large quantity of documents is produced and stored in a warehouse, then shipped to their destination when they are required.

This process has several inefficiencies. The offset presses are large, expensive, and use toxic chemicals. The infrequent long print runs require storing documents, which become obsolete between runs. And transportation is an inordinately large part of the total cost of the process. In fact, R.R. Donnelley & Sons Company, the country's largest publisher, estimates that 60 percent of the total cost of delivering these documents is in storage and transportation.

Figure 14-5 shows the steps in the revised publishing/distribution process using newer technologies. Documents are stored electronically, shipped over a network, and printed when and where they are needed. The major benefits result from reducing obsolescence (revisions are made frequently to the electronically stored version), eliminating warehouse costs, and reducing or eliminating delivery time.

Here is a case example that illustrates how traditional printing processes are being changed by emerging technologies.

FIGURE 14-5 Reengineered Publishing Process

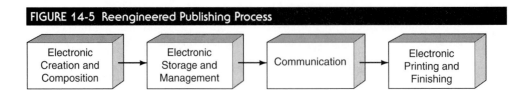

CASE EXAMPLE

HICSS PERSONAL PROCEEDINGS

The Hawaii International Conference on System Sciences has been held each January since 1967. It brings together academics and professionals to discuss research papers from a wide variety of computerrelated subjects.

The conference proceedings have made an important contribution to the literature for many years. But with more than 450 papers averaging 10 pages each in length, the proceedings have grown to 4,500 pages in nine volumes, weighing 25 pounds. As a result, the conference decided to produce a paper book of abstracts, with a CD-ROM of the full papers tucked in a sleeve inside the back cover. That reduced the paper problem, but many participants wanted to see the full papers at the conference during the presentations and discussions. They had been using the paper versions to take notes and to understand additional details of the presentation.

So the conference instituted personal proceedings. A month before the conference, participants can use a Web site to choose 20 papers they would like to have in their personal paper proceedings. The papers they choose are printed on a Xerox Docutech machine with their name on the cover, and delivered to them at the conference. Additional papers can be printed individually at the conference using the conference "print on demand" service, at a nominal cost. This new use of the print-on-demand technology has helped the conference cut costs, reduce paper, yet meet the participants' needs. ■

Supporting Organizational Processes

Documents are the vehicle for accomplishing most processes in organizations. Typical examples include processing a claim in an insurance company, hiring a new employee, or making a large expenditure. The documents are primarily forms that flow through the organization carrying information, accumulating input and approval from a sequence of people. These "workflow systems" are still heavily based on the physical circulation of paper forms in most organizations.

The use of technology to support these processes generates significant value in reducing physical space for handling forms, faster routing of forms (especially over geographical distances), and managing and tracking forms flow and workload. Two trends in organizations have increased the importance of workflow systems: quality improvement processes and business process reengineering. Both tend to depend heavily on documents.

In addition to transaction-oriented business processes, which can be improved with EDM, many organizations are finding that documents are important to the management processes of reporting, control, decision making, and problem solving. Several executive information systems now supply documents to supplement the more traditional data-based reports. Organizations with a custom-developed EIS are also adding so-called "soft" information, in the form of documents.[4]

Supporting Communication Among People and Groups

EDM can be used to facilitate communications among people and groups of people. In the broadest sense, all EDM applications support this function, but included here are specific systems to support transferring information across time and space. Communication *can* take place without documents, of course. A hall conversation, a phone call, a video conference, a presentation—all are communication events that do not require a document. However, if the concepts, ideas, and information are to be communicated over time, they must be captured in some sort of document. If they are to be communicated over distance, without voice or video connection, they must also be captured in a document. Even when communication takes place between people at the same time and in the same place, a document might be used to improve the articulation or formation of the concepts. The primary value of EDM applications in this category derives from the richer communication offered by multimedia or compound documents, and the reduced time needed to distribute documents electronically. An additional value comes from simultaneous sharing of documents among a group of people, coupled with the rapid feedback and interaction that ensue. The popularity of Lotus Notes and the Internet to support a variety of organizational communications illustrates these benefits.

Improving Access to External Information

EDM can provide better access to external information resources. Two general kinds of external resources are time-critical information (news) and reference material. The documents include news wire items, newspapers, periodicals, magazines, electronic bulletin board items, books, video tapes, research reports, proceedings of conferences, to name a few. Traditionally performed as library services, these applications are increasingly computer-based with online card catalogs, direct user access to online text databases (such as DIALOG, NEXUS, and the World Wide Web), circulation of full text research papers, and so on.

Creating and Maintaining Documentation

Another cluster of EDM applications involves creating, maintaining, and distributing documentation. The goal is to maintain policies, procedures, reference material, product descriptions, and such. They differ from records management, which captures and stores documents for archival purposes, and are infrequently accessed, and only on request. Documentation applications, on the other hand, maintain the "current version" of documents; therefore, they must be updated and accessed frequently by a wide variety of requesters. These documents tend to be reports, manuals, drawings, and reference material; they have been mostly text in the past, but are increasingly multimedia. Examples include:

- Internal standards and procedures manuals
- Engineering blueprints and diagrams, possibly created with a CAD/CAM system

- Systems documentation and operating manuals
- Product documentation manuals and other product information, both for internal users and external customers.

Access to documentation can be provided in several ways. For internal users, online access is most common, perhaps using the company's intranet. For external users, access to documentation improves customer service by providing answers to customer queries or solving problems with the right reference material.

The benefits of EDM for these applications are (1) quicker access to the documents, (2) a more efficient search process, (3) simultaneous access by several people to the most current version of the document, and (4) lower printing and distribution costs.

Maintaining Corporate Records

Organizations must maintain official documents and records concerning their obligations, agreements, and financial performance, primarily to satisfy legal requirements. Traditionally, the responsibility of the records management department, this application involves storage and retrieval of contracts, financial records, internal reports, and other important corporate documents. They are "documents" in the traditional sense, mostly text, mostly on paper. The role of EDM applications in this area is to manage this set of official corporate records by providing archival storage and occasional retrieval. The methodologies, approaches, and technologies have evolved from library traditions, from an earlier emphasis on automated records center applications, micrographics (film and fiche), and computer output microfilm (COM), to an emphasis today on digital image processing.

For large records management applications, the savings from image processing in storage space and ease of retrieval alone are impressive. Additional value comes from:

- Reduced misfiling of important documents
- Quicker and more accurate retrieval
- Better access and sharing over geographic distances
- Better version control
- Improved retention management.

Promoting Training and Education

EDM can be used to teach and train people. The documents are curricular training materials or reference materials, and multimedia documents, perhaps with hyperstructure. A primary characteristic of these applications is the continuous, sequential interaction over time between the user and the information through the learning process, rather than a specific search and retrieval event to obtain a document.

Training and education applications are good early examples of the use of multimedia documents and hypertext. Hypertext is the most promising approach to structuring conceptual information. The body of knowledge to be learned or understood consists of *concept nodes,* which are linked or cross-referenced to form a web of ideas and concepts.

Converging Application Areas

These categories of EDM applications illustrate the benefits and value of EDM. The good news is that many opportunities come from many different areas. But these applications use many common approaches and technologies, and, as the earlier case example illustrates, it will be desirable for them to converge eventually. If they have been developed separately, without a plan to integrate them, it will be difficult to reap the potential benefits.

DOCUMENT MINING

The applications just described are primarily based on document *processing* procedures. A potentially more important activity is evolving for *analysis* of documents: document mining. Document mining is the process of analyzing a semantically rich document or set of documents to understand the content and meaning of the information they contain.[5]

The value of document mining is fairly obvious. The amount of information to which document mining can be applied is staggering, and the growth rate is stunning. As information work becomes the true engine of economic wealth, the importance of applying technology to analyze complex information increases. Information overload has been a problem for several years. It now promises to overwhelm organizations that do not confront it, but it will strongly benefit those that mobilize technology to manage it.

Document Mining versus Data Mining

Data mining has proven extremely valuable to some industries. Chapter 12 discussed data mining in some detail. The process performs sophisticated analysis on large quantities of data records. The objective is to discover previously unknown relationships and patterns in the data. A major application has been the analysis of retailers' customer bases using large quantities of point-of-sale data. The term *document mining* benefits as an extension of the term *data mining*. Intuitively, the hope is to gain data-mining-type benefits from the much more voluminous and more important document information. More directly, data mining can be used to create the metadata records that represent a document.

The analogy between data and document mining also illustrates the potential value of document mining. In data mining, the first step is to capture or extract the data, and clean or "scrub" it by rationalizing coding conventions, and perhaps normalizing the data. The second step is aggregation, summarization, and visualization of the data and the various relationships. The third step uses sophisticated analysis techniques, such as regression, correlation, and cross-tabulation, to analyze the contents and relationships in the database.

By analogy, in document mining, the first step involves tagging, stemming, and index creation, while the second step includes summarization, visualization, clustering, and categorization. The third step is intensive analysis of the content of documents and document collections. The technologies and processes to perform this third step are just emerging.

The Value of Document Mining

Published case studies that demonstrate the value of document mining are limited because the technology is so new. Furthermore, companies are hesitant to talk about their activities because they consider them to yield competitive advantage. In a recent study, companies talked about the success of their projects and how these successes were leading to enhanced performance and larger projects, but they were reluctant to discuss the specifics of their work. Nevertheless, it is clear that document mining will be valuable in many areas. Here are a few examples:

- ***Supporting the Discovery Process in Litigation.*** The legal process of discovery requires examining large quantities of documents to find the occurrence of specific topics, concepts, and words relevant to a trial.
- ***Managing Intellectual Property.*** Document mining techniques can help analyze patent repositories. A display of the results graphically can highlight clusters of similar patents, or rank patents according to areas of interest. Such analyses support R&D planning, competitive intelligence, licensing management, and strategic market research.
- ***Managing Internal R&D.*** Document mining can be used to analyze internal research reports and lab reports to avoid previous pitfalls and blind alleys, and to exploit previous successes. The R&D director of a medium-sized engineering firm estimated saving $100,000 a year from such a system.
- ***Managing Knowledge.*** Hewlett-Packard has developed a productivity researcher for its professional services division. It is a repository of professional services documents, white papers, and presentations that can be analyzed to address clients' needs rapidly and efficiently.
- ***Business Intelligence.*** Eaton Corporation's markets span engines, transmissions, and a thousand other components in vehicle and power plants. They use document mining to monitor hundreds of markets for technology shifts, emerging competitors, and governmental regulations.
- ***Organizing Complex Information.*** Document mining can select relevant documents, cluster them into topics, and visualize the relationship among them. Many activities would benefit greatly from this capability. For instance, a university faculty member could use it to prepare a new course.
- ***Managing Customer Relationships.*** An electric utility in Europe uses document mining to analyze customer feedback, market data, media coverage, customer comments, and market strategy reports, to establish customer policies and procedures.

These examples present only a glimpse of the potential areas in which document mining will be valuable.

Functions and Technologies

Much of the current technology for document mining is based on the work of researchers at Xerox and IBM over the past decade. A partial list of the functionality that comprises document mining includes the following areas.

Enhanced Search and Retrieval. Search and retrieval based on keywords has been prevalent for more than 30 years. Lexical analysis technology, such as the LinguistX Platform (LXP) marketed by Inxight, however, improves the process greatly because it is based on the structure of language. Most of the popular search engines on the Web use LXP as the preprocessor for their search engines.

Summarization. A major contribution to the information overload problem is summarization, again based on lexical analysis. Several vendors offer summarizers for either "indicative summaries" (abstracts that indicate content) or "informative summaries" (summaries that contain enough content to replace the entire original document).

Visualization. This visualization capability is often called "InfoViz," as an analogy to data visualization or "dataviz," which has been so valuable in scientific fields. Xerox has a strong reputation in this area because of the long history of research work on this subject at PARC.

Categorization. The categorization function automatically assigns a document to one or more predetermined categories, again based on lexical analysis. The categories may be determined manually or by defining a sample document that represents the category.

Clustering. As a fully automatic process that groups documents based on their content, clustering provides an overview of the contents of a large document collection, identifies hidden similarities among documents, and accelerates the process of finding similar or related information in a document collection. The label for a cluster is comprised of the key terms occurring in the documents in the group.

Genre Identification. The genre identification process indicates the type (or genre) of documents based on the characteristics of the language, format, and content. It would, for example, separate news articles from research reports on the same topic, noting they are two different genres.

Metadata Extraction. The process of identifying key "features" of a document and extracting them to form a data record or an annotation of a document is called metadata extraction. Typical features include proper names (people, places, organizations), multiword terms, abbreviations, currency amounts, and such.

Language Identification. The ability to automatically recognize foreign languages and to estimate the percentage of each language in a multilingual document is called language identification. Because the underlying lexical analysis is based on the structure of languages, this capability also supports all of the preceding functions in several languages. LXP performs such multilingual functions and has shown good performance.

The Future of Document Mining

One way to ease the document mining challenge is to use a digital document format that incorporates structure, permitting it to be queried and mined in much the same way as databases. Perhaps the leading candidate to fill that role is the extensible markup language (XML), a specification for tagging text in Web-based documents. Although other tagging methods have been available for more than a decade, XML is gaining widespread interest because it is designed specifically for the Web, where structured documents are expected to have significant value.

XML is derived from the same standardized generalized markup language that underlies the current Web-standard format, hypertext markup language (HTML). But it is not a replacement for HTML. HTML defines how a document is displayed, and XML interprets the text.

Semantically rich information contained in documents will become increasingly important as the information age progresses. The phenomenal growth of the Internet and intranets guarantees it. Strong, sophisticated technology will be needed to manage, analyze, and understand these information resources. A plethora of products is appearing in the market to handle parts of this process. Simple file servers, office suites, browsers, search engines, and Web crawlers will soon become commodities. The value added in the next generation of products will be the integrated technologies that change how people master the information in their document collections.

TECHNOLOGIES FOR DOCUMENT MANAGEMENT

Underlying Infrastructure

The rapid developments in EDM are partly the result of advances in basic technology infrastructure. These underlying, enabling technologies improve handling information in any form, but several have attributes that support document processing and management. These enabling technologies can be organized in five major categories.

Stronger Desktop Workstations. Powerful desktop computers based on RISC technology are equipped with large, high-resolution color screens. These workstations permit the display of documents, a full page or two at a time, and delivery (and capture) of nontext media such as voice, video, and animation.

Storage Media. High-capacity storage media hold the large volume of bits required for rich media documents. The capacity of magnetic media (hard disks and diskettes) in workstations and file servers has been increasing rapidly, but is still barely adequate. Optical storage media such as CD-ROMs and laserdisks, perhaps in clusters called jukeboxes, provide orders of magnitude more storage capacity. Holographic storage devices increase the amount of readily available storage capacity by several more orders of magnitude

Networks. Networks will interconnect the workstations of most, if not all information workers, within and between organizations. These connections will have increasingly higher bandwidth to transmit the large volume of data contained in electronic documents and forms. Relevant technologies were discussed in Chapter 6.

User-Friendly Software. The continued growth of graphical user interfaces is enabling people who handle paper documents, many of whom are not yet computer literate, to deal more easily with documents on computers. Even for experienced computer users, however, interface software must continue to advance so that they can move beyond managing hundreds of files to managing thousands of documents on a desktop machine.

Operating Systems. Client-server operating systems and network management systems are increasingly document oriented. In fact, new operating systems shift focus from applications to documents. They are also object oriented. This approach is gaining popularity for improved software design and for the design of operating systems.

Document Processing Technologies

In addition to the underlying technology infrastructure, a set of technologies is aimed specifically at handling documents. Often called *document middleware,* these technologies provide the functionality for processing and managing documents, both electronic and paper. Document middleware actually has two sublayers: functions for document processing and functions for document management. Summarized in the following subsections is the set of document *processing* technologies (organized by the major steps in a document life cycle), and the document *management* functions; together they form the document technology infrastructure.

Capture and Creation. These technologies are used to digitize information. For documents already on paper, hardware and software digitizes an image of a page, and then electronically handles that image. Scanners capture the image while algorithms convert it to digital form, frequently with compression to save storage space. After a document page is scanned and digitized, it can be further analyzed to recognize the characters. Current software can capture full text in editable form in a variety of fonts, sizes, and formats. Extensions of these pattern recognition techniques can recognize voice, some images, and patterns in graphics, animation, and video.

Storage and Organization. Several technologies determine how documents are stored and organized. The primary developments are the compound document architecture, distributed storage management software, the integration of documents and databases, and hypertext.

Compound document architecture. Such an architecture is required for the different objects in a compound document to be handled together. In several implementations, the compound document consists of objects (such as a text object, a graphics object, a spreadsheet object, a digital photograph object) stored on different devices and brought together logically through the use of pointers.

Distributed storage. Documents are stored on local PC hard drives, servers (including large-capacity document servers), mainframes, and large repositories. A large percentage of the documents stored in a PC networked environment is stored on the local hard drives, not on the server. This practice underscores the importance of distributed document management software to provide organization and access to this valuable resource.

Integrating documents and databases. Making documents an integral part of the information resources of an organization requires integrating document collections and databases. So far, most approaches have extended databases to accommodate documents, or vice versa. However, organizing, cataloging, and retrieving concepts in documents is likely to require an entirely different architectural approach than those used for facts in data records.

Hypertext. Software that implements a hypertext structure enables nonlinear access to the logical structure of text within a document, and multiple cross-references between documents. *Hypermedia* technology provides the same functionality with multimedia and compound documents.

Retrieval and Synthesis. *Information retrieval* selects documents from a collection according to the presence or absence of keywords assigned by an indexer. *Text retrieval* uses algorithms that eliminate the need for an assigned index. All content-bearing words are indexed. A further enhancement, called *concept retrieval,* uses thesauri and word co-occurrence analysis to select documents that use similar, but different words to represent a concept.[6] Queries can result in a list of selected documents ranked in order of likely relevance. An extension of this approach allows automatic synthesis or summarization of documents.

Transmission and Routing.   E-mail systems are moving beyond simple text messaging to becoming the primary transport mechanism for electronic documents and forms. Object independence allows transmission of compound documents consisting of a variety of objects (text, graphic, image, audio, video). Other functionality required for business transport of electronic documents includes:

- *Authorization:* assuring that the correct user is accessing the workstation and documents
- *Authentication:* assuring that the "digital signature" of the user is valid
- *Encryption:* coding and decoding documents for security
- *Filtering:* automatically routing messages or documents according to their content

Print and Display.   Most documents will be printed at some time in their life cycle, so an important technology is the wide variety of digital printers and copiers on a network. These printers, along with text handling software, page layout languages, and WYSIWYG displays (what you see is what you get) put high-quality printed output within reach of nearly everyone. Laser printers significantly reduce the need for preprinted forms. Desktop printers permit distributed printing of richly formatted documents. Xerox's DocuTech production publisher operates on a network, accepts Postscript files, allows printed tab inserts, and offers a variety of covers and binding. The result is a new form of distributed printing and "print-on-demand" services that can print small or large runs of complex documents at remote sites under the direction of a workstation.

Document Management Functions

The second sublayer of the document technology infrastructure consists of document management functions that cut across the phases of document processing. This set of functions is what enables managing documents as an information resource rather than as a collection of files. These document management functions include:

- *Status reporting:* Who has a document? What is its recent activity?
- *Access control:* Who "owns" it? Who can read it? Change it?
- *Version control:* What is the current version? What previous versions are still needed?
- *Retention management:* What are the legal retention requirements? Corporate policy requirements? How do we destroy paper and electronic versions?
- *Disaster recovery:* How and where are backup copies kept? What are the recovery procedures?

This technology section can be summarized with the conceptual layered architectural diagram shown in Figure 14-6. The lower level is the basic infrastructure and the middle layer (with two sublayers) is the document infrastructure required for EDM. The top layer is the application layer, which shows four main areas of business value.

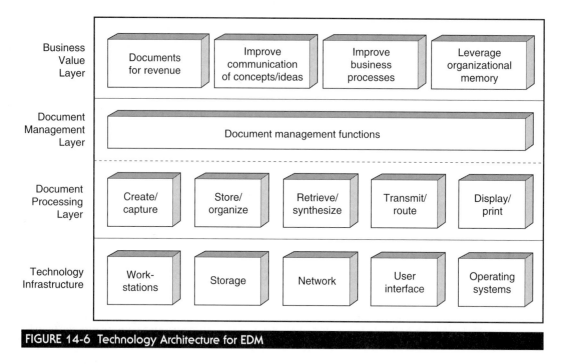

FIGURE 14-6 Technology Architecture for EDM

EDM GUIDELINES FOR IS EXECUTIVES

As usual, technology engineering is not as difficult or as important as "organizational engineering" in implementing EDM. IS executives face a number of challenges in developing EDM.

Roles and Responsibilities

One major management issue is structuring the roles and responsibilities of the departments and functions for which documents are strategic. Here are some of the organizational groups and departments that must play a major role in EDM.

- *The IS department:* The technology is now advanced enough and pervasive enough that the IS function will be responsible for evolving the technical infrastructure. However, the fundamental structure and processing of the conceptual information in documents is quite different from the facts in data records. Moreover, the principles and techniques of document storage, classification, indexing, retrieval, and retention are foreign to most IS professions.
- *Records management:* With its traditional role of managing corporate "records," and with its foundations in library science, the records management department has valuable experience in document management practices. But it tends to view technology in terms of its ability to meet specific short-term needs. The records management tradition also emphasizes paper documents and their electronic equivalent, the narrower view of EDM.

- *Office management:* Much office work has been computerized to some extent, but internal and external correspondence and reports still generate large amounts of redundant and hard-to-access paper files. In the future, these files will need to be cross-referenced among departments and linked with online databases.
- *Library:* External sources of information are increasingly available electronically, with search and retrieval capability from large document collections.
- *Print shop:* Computer-based technology is becoming dominant. The new DocuTech line of high-speed printers and copiers from Xerox are digital (not light-lens) and contain more computer power than many mainframes.
- *Training and education:* Increasingly based on multimedia technology and computer-based courseware, education and training can be delivered through EDM technologies and approaches.

Coordinating the roles and responsibilities of these and other departments is important because the applications and technologies required to realize the promise of EDM are evolving rapidly.

An Action Plan

The IS department has the opportunity to play a leadership role in coordinating the efforts of user departments and document support departments to evolve the infrastructure and applications needed to support EDM. Playing this role may be more difficult than it has been in the past. In this era of distributed systems and distributed responsibility for systems initiatives, IS executives need to educate user departments and document handling departments, convincing them to cooperate in developing an EDM strategy and technology infrastructure. Here are some steps IS executives can take to prepare for these developments.

Form a "Document Council." Form a council consisting of representatives from each document support department charged with managing some part of the document processing cycle. Their first assignment is to identify mission-critical documents and work back to applications and departments that depend on them. An initial set of applications will undoubtedly evolve from the members of the group. They have probably been responsible for producing and managing these documents in the past.

Also, important applications have already been developed directly by the user departments, so the group should find a way to uncover unknown important applications. Mechanisms for finding these existing applications include examining the areas and examples mentioned earlier in this article, finding examples in journals and trade publications, distributing surveys and questionnaires in the organization, and so on. The work of this group and the technology tracking group described next should proceed in parallel, with periodic joint meetings for coordination and status reporting.

Form a Document Technology Group. Assign the task of tracking and forecasting emerging document technologies to a small group with technical proficiency in several areas. If an advanced technology group already exists, this assignment would probably fit into their charter. The assignment should cover both infrastructure technologies and document technologies.

Prioritize Applications. The application group, perhaps in consultation with document users, should then prioritize applications by business value and technical feasibility. A difference in long- and short-range perspectives is inevitable, so both should be considered. Prioritization should also include consideration of fit or linkage between applications, especially when two or more applications can use the same technology or approach.

Develop an EDM Plan. As a result of regular joint meetings, the document council and the document technology group can jointly develop a plan for adding the necessary technology to the infrastructure and developing the applications. These applications might not be developed by the IS department, or even by the departments represented in the group, but their development and approximate time schedule should be included in the plan. As it is refined and developed over time, this plan becomes an integrated EDM architecture and a plan for implementing it.

Revise Responsibilities. By this time, it may become clear that some of the roles and responsibilities of some departments may need to be revised. The council can develop recommendations for these changes. By performing this step last, any shifts in responsibilities will result from discussions based on the evolution of the applications and technologies, measured by business value. This practice will reduce the probability of a "turf war" that could result from the changes in the way documents are managed.

The benefits of EDM will evolve as the technology and our ability to use it evolve over the next several years. It is not too early, however, for IS executives to begin planning to build an infrastructure for document management, and to harness new technologies to improve the performance of their organizations.

To give an example of how one organization improved a document management system, and in turn advanced the enterprise's management of its knowledge (the next subject in this chapter), consider the Tennessee Valley Authority.[7]

CASE EXAMPLE

TENNESSEE VALLEY AUTHORITY

The Tennessee Valley Authority (TVA) is the largest supplier of power in the United States, serving some 8 million customers in the eastern United States by generating energy using fossil, hydroelectric, and nuclear fuels. Not long ago, the nuclear division, which has three facilities, revamped its maintenance management system—a system that relies on documents, such as manuals from vendors, drawings, and work instructions, that are regulated by government.

TVA spends more than $48 million a year creating maintenance work orders and then planning and performing the work. One plant alone processes 14,000 work orders a year. Government regulations that oversee the documentation of this work contribute significantly to TVA's high maintenance costs.

(Case Continued)

The improvement project was handled by a team from various parts of the nuclear operation. They analyzed and charted the existing work processes, determined which improvements were most needed, and investigated how those improvements could be achieved. They spent 350 hours interviewing people and looked at 15 other utilities. One thing they discovered was that the work orders were inextricably linked to document workflow and the ways procedures were managed. Previously, the three areas—work order management, document workflow, and procedure management—had been viewed as separate, and thus managed separately. But, upon investigation, the team realized that every work order included accompanying diagrams, documentation, and procedure instructions. However, the three were not always in sync. For example, a work order might be planned several months in advance, but in the meantime, procedures might be changed, yet those changes were not noted when the work order was about to be performed.

The new process designed by TVA electronically combined maintenance orders in one system with procedural document management in another system, and eliminated a number of existing systems that did not talk to one another. Maintenance workers can now access documen-

tation on equipment, parts, and records as well as work instructions from desktop machines. Work orders are generated electronically and then routed for approval, with the most current drawings and procedures electronically attached. In addition, the documents are indexed by, say, piece of equipment, and the three plants now use the same systems. So, maintenance people can review past activity and better plan for the future.

The system has been successful, but the team underestimated the change management effort needed. They did not realize they had to bring many employees up-to-speed on using computers; some had not used keyboards. In addition, the team realized they should have set expectations differently. Rather than emphasize the benefits of the new systems to each employee (because sometimes the new systems required more work of some employees), the team should have emphasized the overall benefit of the system to TVA, which were significant. The average amount of human time spent processing a work order decreased by almost half, from 39 hours to 23 hours. So labor savings were large. But more importantly, maintenance workers now have captured data for improving processes. So the improved document management system is contributing to knowledge management. ∎

KNOWLEDGE MANAGEMENT AND SHARING

We have mentioned knowledge management numerous times throughout the book. In Chapter 7, we showed how information management has evolved toward knowledge management. In this chapter so far, we have discussed the organization and management of document-based information, which has a crucial role in knowledge management. In this section, we look at a model for knowledge management and knowledge sharing, and examine the functions, skills, and tools needed for this activity.

The model, published by the GIGA Information Group,[8] is circular. The four stages, shown in Figure 14-7, represent what people generally do with knowledge. First they create it, or capture it from a source. Next, they organize it and put it into categories for easy retrieval. Then they distribute it (push) or access it (pull). Finally, they absorb another's knowledge for their own use or to create more new knowledge. Thus, the cycle begins again.

The four stages create two kinds of "capital." Human capital, which consists of knowledge, skills, and innovativeness of employees as well as company values, culture, and philosophy, is created during the knowledge creation-capture and knowledge absorption-reuse stages because these two stages focus on getting people together to share knowledge. They deal with the people aspects of knowledge management. Their main question is, "How do we get people to have more knowledge in their heads?"

Structural capital, which is the capabilities embedded in hardware, software, databases, organizational structure, patents, and trademarks that support employees as well as relationships with customers, is formed in the knowledge organization-categorization and knowledge distribution-access stages because these stages focus on moving knowledge from people's heads to a tangible company asset. These stages deal with the technology issues surrounding knowledge management and sharing. Their main question is, "How do we get knowledge out of people's heads and into a computer, a process, a document, or another organizational asset?"

FIGURE 14-7 A Knowledge Management Framework

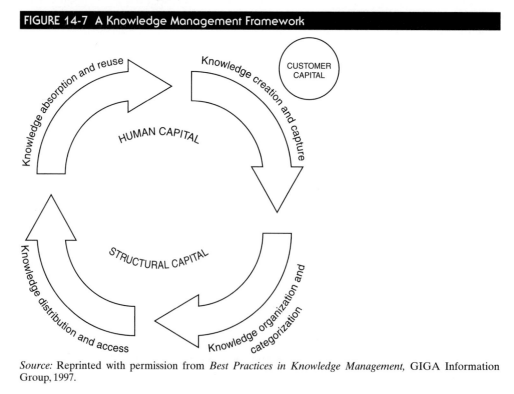

Source: Reprinted with permission from *Best Practices in Knowledge Management,* GIGA Information Group, 1997.

A third type of capital is customer capital. It is the strength of a company's franchise with its customers and is concerned with its relationships and networks of associates. Furthermore, when customers are familiar with a company's products or services, the company can call that familiarity customer capital. This form of capital may be either human (relationships with the company) or structural (products used from the company).

Based on a series of case studies, GIGA discovered that the human capital stages and the structural capital stages require different mindsets. Hence, companies have had to use different approaches to grow each one; and the techniques for one do not work for the other. The companies that focused on human capital used touchy-feely people-centric approaches. In some cases, no technology was used at all. The companies that focused on structural capital took a typical information systems approach: using technology to solve a problem. Little talk addressed individuals, communities, and work practices; talk mainly centered on yellow pages of experts, knowledge bases, and such. But to succeed in leveraging intellectual capital, companies need to do both.

The following paragraphs summarize the four stages of the model. Figure 14-8 shows the key activities in each stage, the form of capital, the skills required of people, and the tools and techniques that are proving valuable.

Knowledge creation and capture deal with generating knowledge, either by nurturing employees to create it or by acquiring it from outside. Hence, it deals with human capital and customer capital. As already noted, the cases that emphasize this phase of knowledge management use high-touch approaches, such as getting people to meet either in person or electronically, creating a sharing culture, and encouraging innovation.

Knowledge organization and categorization are often handled by creating best practices knowledge bases or metadata indexes for documents. It also involves measuring intellectual capital, an endeavor few companies have attempted. This second stage deals with creating structural capital, the "intellectual stuff" that stays with the company after employees have gone home at night. As noted, companies that emphasized this phase of knowledge management used high-tech approaches.

Knowledge distribution and access "push" knowledge out to users (distribution) and accommodate users who "pull" information to themselves (access). The GIGA cases that emphasized this phase also used high-tech approaches. They focused on implementing networks and networking tools to access human and structural capital. Intranets and groupware were important IT-based tools.

Knowledge absorption and reuse address the notion of getting knowledge into people's heads where it can be enhanced and reused. Some people believe that knowledge only exists in minds; it cannot exist in computers. Irrespective of a person's perception, the GIGA cases that emphasized this phase of knowledge management used high-touch approaches. They too focused on nurturing interactions among people, recognizing the knowledge brokers who exist in companies, and supporting communities of practice.

One of the most fascinating case studies in the GIGA report, all of which are anonymous, is the one about the vice president who came up with the notion of customer capital. Here is that story, based on that report.

FIGURE 14-8 Knowledge Management Stages			
Phase	*Emphasis*	*Skills/People*	*Tools/Techniques*
Creation and Capture Generate new knowledge Make tacit knowledge explicit Hire people with the right knowledge Create culture of sharing Encourage innovation Incentives for sharing	Human capital Customer capital	Knowledge harvesters Knowledge owners Mentoring/coaching Partner with universities Teamwork Business intelligence Top management	Easy-to-use capture tools E-mail Face-to-face meetings Knowledge tree Write-to-think Feedback
Organization and Categorization Package knowledge Add context to information Create categories of knowledge Create knowledge vocabulary Create metadata tags for documents Measure intellectual capital	Structural capital	Academics Knowledge editors Librarians Knowledge architect Authors Subject matter experts IS	Frameworks Cull knowledge from sources Best practices databases Knowledge bases Knowledge thesaurus Knowledge indexes Measurement tools
Distribution and Access Create links to knowledge Create networks of people Create electronic push and pull distribution mechanisms Knowledge sharing	Structural capital	Publishers Top management IS	HTML Groupware—Lotus Notes Networks, intranets Navigation aids Search tools
Absorption and Reuse Stimulate interaction among people The learning organization Informal networks	Human capital	Group facilitators OD Matchmakers Knowledge brokers	Team processes Electronic bulletin boards Communities of practice Yellow pages

Source: Reprinted with permission from *Best Practices in Knowledge Management,* GIGA Information Group, 1997.

CASE EXAMPLE

A NORTH AMERICAN BANK

After the U.S. savings and loan debacle and the devaluation of real estate in the 1980s, the vice president of organizational learning and leadership development at a North American Bank asked, "Why have banks become so exposed to risk in their lending practices?" The answer he arrived at was, "Because they do not understand the new information age and its underpinning collateral." At the time, and still today, banks lent money against hard assets, such as a shopping mall. But the value of such assets can dissipate almost overnight, making them risky collateral. "Perhaps there is less risk in lending against soft assets, such as a group's knowledge of a programming language or a patented process," he reasoned. Knowledge in a person's head does not disappear overnight. However, the vice president had no way of valuing such intangibles. Yet, he continued to work on the problem. Over time, his thinking changed the way the bank evaluated new hires and reshaped some of its operations.

To begin his quest on how to value knowledge, or intellectual capital, he drew on the ideas of human capital and structural capital, and then added his own: customer capital.

Human capital was the know-how to meet customer needs; he asked bank managers to measure it by assessing how fast their teams learned. To increase human capital, he shifted emphasis at the bank from training (pushing instruction to people) to learning (getting people to pull the instruction they needed to them)

because he believed the crux of increasing human capital was increasing the pace at which an organization learns. He believed people learned when they "owned" their learning and took responsibility for applying it to improve their performance. He developed a list of skills needed to serve customers and gave employees numerous ways to learn these skills, from reading specific books to choosing a mentor.

Structural capital was the organizational capabilities needed by the marketplace. The vice president measured them by uncovering the percentage of bank revenue that came from new services and similar metrics. He believed that although it takes human capital to build structural capital, the better the bank's structural capital, the higher its human capital. So, one feeds the other. Thus, he generated structural capital from human capital by creating a competitive intelligence "library" about the industry that the bank considers a valuable "intellectual capital repository." Rather than being a library of documents, however, it was a map that showed the kinds of knowledge the bank held and where it existed, whether in an employee's head or a database.

Customer capital was the intellectual assets in the minds of customers related to the bank. The vice president's team measured three aspects: depth of knowledge about the bank in a customer organization, breadth of knowledge by a customer, and loyalty to the bank. To strengthen these aspects, the vice president believed

(Case Continued)

the bank needed to assist its customers' employees in learning. Some of that learning pertained to learning more about the bank, which required making the bank's values and strategies congruent with those of its customers. The vice president therefore helped senior bank officials determine customer needs, establish a common language for communicating with customers, develop a sense of purpose for the relationship, and, most importantly, make learning within the customer organization an important part of the bank's services. The vice president believes that assisting customers will increase his bank's customer capital: depth, breadth, and loyalty. Thus, his knowledge management efforts focused outwardly as well as inwardly. ■

The Cultural Side of Knowledge Management

Success in knowledge management comes as much from changing organizational behavior as it does from implementing new technology, notes Cyril Brooks.[9] His company, Grapevine, offers an intriguing product for managing information and knowledge. But, he notes, besides the platitude of "create a culture that rewards sharing," few people recommend specifics on how to reduce the cultural roadblocks that can hinder knowledge management projects. He describes some cultural barriers, which he calls "red flags."

Cultural barriers can shut down knowledge management efforts because knowledge management is really about cooperation and sharing. To reach these lofty goals, the efforts need to turn the tacit knowledge in people's heads into explicit knowledge in a process, or a product, or other organizational artifact. Thus, knowledge management work must tap people's motivations to share and cooperate. Without the motivation, knowledge databases, for example, are not updated or errors are ignored. Or people avoid contributing to a knowledge-sharing network for fear they will give away their best ideas and lose their "competitive advantage" against their peers in the company. Such red flags are not blaring; they are often subtle, says Brooks, yet harmful.

Here are a few of his behavioral red flags that can derail a knowledge management effort:

- Being seen as a whistle-blower or messenger of bad news. Few people want to betray their boss, so they avoid presenting early warnings or disagreeing with internal documents. So in organizations where "messengers get shot," sharing good news is fine but sharing bad is not, which defeats the full value of sharing.
- Losing one's place as a knowledge gatekeeper. While knowledge brokers are important in organizations, their self-value comes from their controlling the knowledge they house and sharing it only with whom and when they choose. They may see a knowledge management system that encourages the free flow of ideas as decreasing their value, and therefore fight it.

- Knowledge sharing really does take time; therefore, experts may hide so that they are not bothered by requests from others. Others may not participate in, say, presenting their ideas, which may benefit the organization as a whole but have no personal reward, so they think.

These reactions are human; therefore, knowledge management efforts often need to build "cultural workarounds" so that these kinds of reactions do not block the work. Brooks offers some suggestions. For example, to reduce concerns about being a messenger, the system might allow only limited dissemination of some ideas, or give people the ability to rank feedback comments based on their significance. To counter concerns about losing personal advantage, contributions could require authorship, or comments might always be linked to the original items. And to reduce time consumption, the reward structure could reward contributions based on their value.

In addition to cultural red flags, management red flags are also a concern. Three red flags are (1) saying the project is not cost-justifiable because the benefits are intangible, (2) concern that too much participation will reduce employee productivity, and (3) concern that creating the taxonomy of knowledge categories will be just too expensive to undertake. Reducing these concerns is an important aspect of a knowledge management endeavor. Some examples for mitigating these management roadblocks, says Brooks, include illustrating the value of serendipity that has occurred due to sharing, as illustrated in vendor case studies; ensuring that the new system promotes feedback to contributors, which can increase productivity; and drawing on vendor expertise to create knowledge taxonomies rather than start from scratch.

So, as Brooks points out, organization culture is an important aspect of knowledge management efforts, and a key determinant of success.

CONCLUSION

Leveraging the world of information has been the subject of this chapter. We chose two aspects: electronic document management and knowledge management. Electronic document management is becoming prevalent because of a suite of new technologies that makes it possible to computerize the information contained in documents. These technologies include digital imaging processing; large capacity storage devices; high-bandwidth communication channels; multimedia devices for handling image, voice, video, and animation; hypertext and hypermedia; and improved methods for retrieval of information and text.

The impact of these developments is significant. Generally, EDM allows electronic handling of concepts and ideas in documents, as well as facts in data records. Because managers and executives deal heavily with concepts and ideas, EDM can improve the performance of these high-value employees. Furthermore, many important business processes depend on document-based information flows, and EDM will support the improvement of these processes.

A particularly important part of document management is document mining. Analogous to the importance of data mining, document mining moves beyond the *processing* of documents to the *analysis* of the content of documents and document collections.

The challenge for IS executives is to manage the evolution to EDM. New technologies should be adopted and used as they emerge because the benefits are substantial. But over time, they must be integrated to avoid separate, incompatible systems. This process will require a strategic plan for EDM that identifies what applications should be developed and in what order, what roles the many interested parties should play, and what technologies are required.

Organizing and analyzing document content also plays a strong role in advancing knowledge management and sharing. Two of the four phases of the knowledge management model depend heavily on the ability to structure, organize, and access conceptual information. But it is clear once again that in knowledge management, technology may be necessary, but it is not sufficient. The other two major phases of the knowledge management model depend much more heavily on human and behavioral issues than on technology. In summary, document management and mining, plus knowledge management and sharing, are important tools for leveraging information as organizations proceed into the increasingly knowledge-intensive world.

QUESTIONS AND EXERCISES

Review Questions

1. Give three definitions and several examples of a document.
2. What are the roles that documents play in organizations? Give an example of each.
3. What are the seven categories of EDM applications? Describe how each can improve an organization.
4. Give two of the major benefits realized by Tapiola Insurance from their EDM project.
5. What is the importance of the new publishing process enabled by new technologies?
6. What is the importance of document mining?
7. What are some valuable applications of document mining?
8. What are some of the functions of document mining?
9. What are the three layers of technology architecture for EDM? Identify the elements in each layer, including the two sublayers of the document management layer.
10. List the departments in an organization that would be involved in EDM.
11. What is the importance of an action plan for EDM? What are the steps?
12. What are the four phases of GIGA'S knowledge management model?
13. What is the difference between structural capital and human capital?
14. Give three cultural roadblocks to knowledge management projects, as noted by Brooks.

Discussion Questions

1. Do you agree that the IS department should take the lead in developing EDM? Why or why not?
2. If your answer to question 1 was yes, how can IS motivate the other departments? If no, who do you think should coordinate the development of the systems and how?
3. Should IS take the lead in the development of knowledge management and sharing? Why or why not?
4. Knowledge management is a misnomer because knowledge only exists in people's heads. So knowledge management is really just people management. Agree or disagree? Discuss.

Exercises

1. Consult the current literature to compile a list of technologies that are important for EDM. For each technology, describe it briefly, and indicate its role in EDM.
2. Visit a local organization that is developing applications in EDM or knowledge management. Who is leading the development efforts? What benefits are being realized? What are their plans for the future?

REFERENCES

1. Sprague, Ralph H., Jr. "Electronic Document Management: Challenges and Opportunities for Information Systems Managers," *MIS Quarterly,* March 1995, 29–49.
2. Levien, Roger E. *The Civilizing Currency: Documents and Their Revolutionary Tech-* *nologies,* Rochester, NY: Xerox Corporation, 1989.
3. Michalski, G. P. "The World of Documents," *Byte,* April 1991, 159–170.
4. Watson, Hugh, Candice Harp, Gigi Kelly, and Margaret O'Hara. "Including Soft

Information in EISs," *Information Systems Management,* Summer 1996, 66–77.

5. Sprague, Ralph H., Jr., "The Early Iterations of Document Mining: A Promise to Make Enterprise Knowledge Accessible," *Docuworld,* Fall 1999.

6. Chen, H., K. J. Lynch, K. Basu, and T. Ng, "Generation, Integration, and Activation of Thesauri for Concept-Based Document Retrieval," *IEEE Expert,* 1993.

7. Hildebrand, Carol, "Knowledge Fusion," June 1, 2000, www.cio.com.

8. *Best Practices in Knowledge Management,* GIGA Information Group, 1997.

9. Brooks, Cyril, "KM Red Flags: Overcoming Cultural Barriers to Effective Knowledge Management," unpublished manuscript, 2000.

PART

V

MOVING INTO THE
NEW ECONOMY

This part, which consists of just one chapter, lays out some potential operating principles for the New Economy. No one really knows the new rules of the e-economy game, but a number of perceptive people offer some intriguing possibilities. The purpose of this part is to stimulate thinking on such possibilities because the e-world does not obey the rules of the physical world.

The chapter then looks at some underpinnings of moving forward, such as how to choose which applications to implement, and why educating non-IT executives might be the most important job of CIOs.

In essence, this part is about leadership in the e-economy. So we end this book as we began it, highlighting the leadership box in our framework.

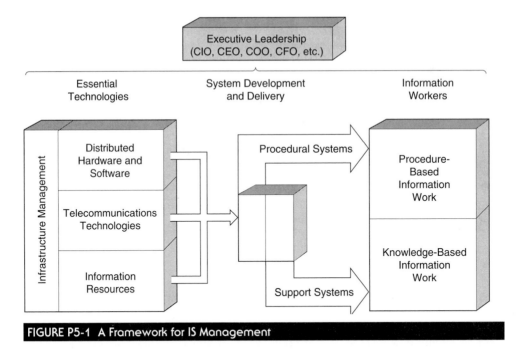

FIGURE P5-1 A Framework for IS Management

CHAPTER

15 | THE CHALLENGES AHEAD

INTRODUCTION

It is obvious to all of us that we are in the midst of a business revolution. The Internet has changed everything. As a result, enterprises around the world are in the throes of redefining their strategy, work environment, and skills—a tumultuous proposition. In this chapter we address the challenges facing IS departments worldwide by assembling a collage of opinions about the new work environment and the e-economy.

    The computer is an amazing machine because it leverages people's brain power, not just their muscle power. This capability is being used to process data, but more importantly, to communicate in new ways. This communication, in turn, allows companies to compete in new ways. As we noted in Chapter 1, we see four goals for thriving in the new work environment:

1. Leverage knowledge globally.
2. Organize for complexity.
3. Work electronically.
4. Handle continuous and discontinuous change.

Using these goals as a basis, we now explore some organizing principles being proposed for thriving in the Internet-based economy. Then we end the chapter by looking at ways to move forward.

ORGANIZING PRINCIPLES

This section is potentially the most exciting because we are in a time of such grand exploration—a new economy is being born. But it is equally the most frustrating because the tenets of this new economy are so different that the rules are just now being formulated. And, as the economy matures, some principles prove to be true and succeed while others fall by the wayside. The following are promising new thinking on organizing principles. They are the areas enterprises need to focus on to succeed in the e-economy.

Processes Rather Than Functions

In *Beyond Reengineering,* which is his follow-on book to *Reengineering the Corporation,* Michael Hammer[1] notes that the key point in the reengineering movement was not that changes needed to be dramatic (that is, in terms of orders-of-magnitude), but that they needed to be made from a process-centered viewpoint rather than a task-centered view. The industrial revolution deconstructed processes into specialized tasks, so the business world has focused on improving tasks. Tasks are about individuals; processes are about groups. We are now in a group economy.

Current organizational problems are process-based, he contends. They center around how specialized tasks fit together. Simple jobs require management and complex processes to get work done. When companies try to simplify these complex processes, they find it can only be done by creating complex jobs. A typical reengineering case in point is the move from a sequential workflow (where five people each perform just one or a few parts of a job) to a case management approach (where one person performs the entire workflow). The employees manage themselves, eliminating the need for a supervisor. Working and managing become part of everyone's job in a process-centered structure. Process-centered organizations can address today's organizational issues because solutions require shifting perspective from tasks to processes. A growing number of enterprises are taking the process-centered approach, Hammer notes, with an emphasis on teams.

The shift to processes has a number of ramifications. One is the need for a new position, such as process owners. In every process, virtually every department is involved. So one person needs to have end-to-end responsibility. Rather than managing the people, process owners provide the knowledge of the process. They own the design of the process. Furthermore, processes need to be designed from a customer's perspective. Process design and process improvement become the essence of management in a process-centered organization.

The move to a process-centered structure also requires measures of processes, which are different from measures of tasks. Measuring a process (how long it takes to complete, its accuracy rate, its cost, etc.) means measuring an outcome from the customer's point of view. A task metric would be measuring how many calls a customer service rep handles each hour. The process metric for the same job could be the percentage of problems (calls) handled completely on the first call, which is an outcome.

Yet another ramification of "process centering" is a sense of urgency and intensity. Teams are more intense, which allows less slack time. Work tends to be full-steam all day, all week, all year long, which wears down nerves and increases stress. Witness the burnout in software companies and dot-coms. This side effect is the dark side of this new economy.

Process centering also turns people into professionals rather than workers, says Hammer, if you define a professional as someone who is responsible for achieving results rather than performing a task. The professional is responsible to customers, solving their problem by producing results. To do so means doing what it takes to complete a process. A worker, on the other hand, aims to please the boss, keeping busy with lots of activity, to perform what he or she is told to do. Workers are told not to be concerned with the totality of the work. The shift to professional from worker is profound. It makes factory employees concerned with customer satisfaction rather than number of parts produced per hour. It requires greater knowledge and a more holistic view by all those involved.

Given this brief description of some of the principles underlying a process-centered organization, what would one look like? Following are two possibilities. The first example, NYNEX, is based on an article in *Communications of the ACM* by Patricia Sachs,[2] when she was technical director of the Works Systems Design group, and on work by Roger Woolfe.[3a] The second example, a football team, is from Michael Hammer.

CASE EXAMPLE

NYNEX

Due to the upheaval in the U.S. telecom industry, NYNEX, the New York-based telecommunications company, targeted 12 major processes for redesign in a company-wide business process redesign initiative. Eleven used the traditional Rummler-Brache approach: looking at lines and boxes "as is" and "should be" in a three-day off-site redesign effort.

The twelfth group used participative design and involved the Work Systems Design group, along with eight employees from across one provisioning process. The team spent one year from analysis to implementation, with everyone full-time. This project was the only one of the 12 implemented, and it yielded excellent results. (The other processes were addressed again in an intensive, large-scale process reengineering effort.)

The Work Systems Design group, whose charter was to create productive

(Case Continued)

workplaces, was an interdisciplinary group with expertise in computer science, telephony, anthropology, and graphic art. It took a sociotechnical view toward the analysis of work, which is fairly unusual in the industry. The quality movement in companies aims to correct processes to eliminate errors, whereas the sociotechnical view equips people to handle problems, believing that all errors cannot be eliminated. Rather than operate under the common assumption that work can be automated and thus people can be downskilled, the group wanted to upskill employees.

Work is accomplished by people in working communities who possess all kinds of expertise nurtured by that community. The Work Systems Design group therefore looked at "communities of practice" and their worlds of expertises. Redesigning processes required looking at an entire working community, its set of practices, its knowledge, and its expertise. To remain durable, such networks need to be nurtured, supported, and even made formal as teams or as communities of practice, a notion they got from working with the people at the Institute for Research on Learning in Menlo Park, California.

In the provisioning redesign project, the goal was to redesign how NYNEX provided one type of high-speed communication service to businesses. The team looked at how work was actually done, they created an implementable design, and then they disbanded. The operational members returned to their original provisioning work using the new process. That process was unique in NYNEX. Rather than pass a customer among specialized groups, all the people in the process worked together, in one area, as a multifunctional team. Thus, engineers worked alongside salespeople.

Because this multifunctional team structure was counter to NYNEX's culture and predominant work organization, it did cause problems. When new managers took over, they often did not understand this way of working. They wanted the group to return to the familiar "all the engineers in one group" structure. So the group's more productive structure weakened. A major difficulty with an innovative new process, NYNEX learned, was underrating how difficult it would be to keep it going when it is countercultural. ■

CASE EXAMPLE

A FOOTBALL TEAM

A football team is a good example of a process-centered organization, says Michael Hammer. It has two processes: offense and defense. It has process owners: offense coordinators and defense coordinators who select the players, train them, design plays, and script them. Their concern is the performance of the process.

The team also has "position coaches," such as the line coach, who train and develop the athletes for specific tasks, acting as counselors and mentors. Their concern is the performance of the performers.

Finally, the team has a head coach, the leader, who creates the organization, names the coordinators and coaches and then manages them, creates the team's culture and values, motivates the players to peak performance, and calls the plays during the game. But once on the field, the team is self-directed. It adapts to the unfolding play. ∎

Self-Organizing Rather Than Designed

Some of the most stimulating discussions about the form of future organizations are those centered around chaos theory, ecology, and biology, and that look at nature and how it organizes itself. Meg Wheatley's highly influential book, *Leadership and the New Science*[4] is one example. Two others are Kevin Kelly's mind-opening *Out of Control* and *New Rules for the New Economy.*[5] The basic tenet is that nature provides a good model for future organizations, that is, organizations that must deal with complexity, share information and knowledge, and cope with continuous and discontinuous change. In seeming chaos, we can get order for free, according to both authors. As with natural phenomena, enterprises will do much better if they are self-organizing or emergent rather than designed. Because it is easiest to illustrate these principles by example, we start there.

Examples of Self-Organization.   Wheatley, in both *Leadership* and her more recent book with Myron Kellner-Rogers, *A Simpler Way,*[6] describes the 1960s experiment by Stuart Kauffman, a theoretical biologist. He attached each of 200 light bulbs to two others and programmed them so that each one turned on or off depending on the behavior of the two partners. He was interested to see whether a pattern would emerge from the 10^{30} possible states. To his great surprise, a repeatable pattern emerged almost instantly, after 13 states. Even when he changed the connections, an organization (albeit a different one) emerged "instantly." His conclusion is that we get order for free, even without intelligence in the system.

Kevin Kelly, executive editor of *Wired* magazine, gives many, many examples in both his books. Here are just three. The first concerns the movie *Batman Returns,* in which computer-generated bats were to flock through Gotham City. One computer-generated bat was created and allowed to automatically flap its wings. Then it was replicated, by the dozens, until there was a mob. Each was instructed to move on its own following just three rules: don't bump into another bat, keep up with your neighbors, and don't stray too far away. When the computer simulation of the mob of bats was run, they flocked just like real bats! Craig Reynolds had discovered the flocking rules, writes Kelly, and they were simple. So even though the bats were seemingly out of anyone's control, they flocked. The same happened with the marching mob of penguins in the same movie, which also drew on a simple Reynolds algorithm. Kelly says this kind of behavior taught that order can be achieved from chaos in any distributed "vivisystem," organic or man-made.

In an equally striking example, Kelly describes how Loren Carpenter, a graphics wizard, demonstrated a similar kind of order-from-chaos in an auditorium with 5,000 computer graphics conferees. Each one had a cardboard wand, red on one side, green on the other. At the back of the auditorium a computer scanned the wands when they were held up high, picking up the color on each wand. At the front of the auditorium was a huge screen that displayed the sea of wands, like a candlelight parade. Attendees could find themselves in the sea, and change their color on the screen by flipping their wand.

Carpenter then projected the game Pong (like table tennis) on the screen, telling the audience that those on the left controlled the left paddle, those on the right the right paddle. Within moments, the 5,000 were playing a pretty good game of Pong, with the movement of the paddle being the average of the several thousand players' intentions. When Carpenter speeded up the game, the crowd adjusted, almost instantly.

When an airplane flight simulator was projected on the screen, Carpenter told the audience that the left side of the room controlled the roll and the right controlled pitch. In essence, the pilot became 5,000 novices. They became silent as they studied the controls in the cockpit, wrote Kelly. The plane was headed for a landing, yet it pitched left and right because the signal was latent and the crowd continually overcompensated. When it was obvious that they would arrive wing first on the landing strip, they somehow pulled the plane up and turned it around, even though no one gave a command. They acted as one mind, turned wide, and tried a second landing. But again, the plane was not straight, so in unison, and again without verbal communication, they pulled up. On the way up, the plane rolled a bit, then a bit more, and then, "at some magical moment" the same thought seemed to occur to everyone, "I wonder if we can do a 360?" In unison, without speaking, they rolled the jet, fairly gracefully, and then gave themselves a standing ovation. Kelly notes that the conferees did just what the birds did: they flocked.

Five years later Carpenter tried the same experiment at the same conference, states Kelly in *Ten Rules for the New Economy.* This time the game was more sophisticated (the controls had more choices) and the task more challenging (to steer a 3-D submarine in search of sea monster eggs). However, unlike previously, when the audience took control, nothing happened. The submarine did not move. So even after lots of fiddling with controls and shouting, still no movement took place. Finally, in exasperation, Carpenter said, "Why don't you go right?" Immediately, the submarine went right. He had unlocked the paralysis. The group needed leadership. It might only be a few words, but it was enough to initiate cohesion. From then on, the 5,000 copilots maneuvered the submarine deftly.

Finally, here is a business example from Kelly and *Business Week*[7] of a group acting as a self-organizing "swarm."

CASE EXAMPLE

CEMEX

Cemex (Cementos Mexicanos) delivers ready-mix cement in the state of Monterrey, Mexico. In the Guadalajara region of this state, delivering cement on time was extremely difficult, due to traffic jams, poor roads, and contractors not ready for their order. The situation was so bad that Cemex's on-time delivery rate was 35 percent. To improve, the company tried to enforce advanced reservations. But that actually made matters worse because when contractors changed their orders just hours before delivery, as happened half the time, Cemex could not reschedule the delivery for another week or so.

To deal with its biggest problem of unpredictability of orders, management then took the opposite tack: no reservations required and delivery faster than pizza. They turned their attention to managing information rather than managing assets. To do so, they installed a company-wide telecom system that included a global positioning satellite (GPS) system for the trucks and full information to all employees. And instead of dispatchers scheduling drivers, the drivers were to schedule themselves in real-time as calls came in.

To ensure fast delivery, the drivers stationed themselves throughout the city, forming a kind of web. The driver closest to a call delivered the cement. The dispatchers played the new role of checking on customers' creditworthiness and making sure no customer call was being overlooked. The result of this self-organization was 98 percent delivery rates, delivery times of 20 minutes (down from three hours), much less wasted (hardened) cement, 35 percent fewer trucks, lower fuel costs, and happier customers. ■

The Self-Organizing Point-of-View.   Wheatley and Kellner-Rogers believe that organizations, like the light bulbs and many natural phenomena, can be self-organizing. They believe self-organization requires taking the perspective of "organizing-as-a-process" rather than "organization-as-an-object." Processes can do their own work if supplied with what the processes need to begin: resources, information, and access to new people.

Self-organizing systems create their own structure, patterns of behavior, and processes to accomplish the work. People within a process "design" what is necessary to do the work and "agree on" the relationships that make sense to them. Systemwide stability depends on the ability of the members to change. Change occurs as conditions change. As a result, the members do not need to plans things into existence, they only need to work with the unknowns, and an "organization" will emerge. Systems are relationships that are seen as structures, but those relationships cannot be structured; they can only emerge. Webs develop as the individuals explore their needs, if they are free to create the relationships they need. Freedom and trust are paramount for self-organizing systems to thrive. And systems are healthiest when they are open to including diversity; it gives them strength and resiliency.

Kelly believes that the only way to create truly complex systems is to use biology's logic of self-governance, self-replication, partial learning, and some self-repair. He believes that the mechanical and biological worlds are merging, leading to bionic systems, which he calls *vivisystems*. On the one hand, a nation's flight control system needs mechanical clockwork systems. But when adaptability is needed, the best systems act as "swarms," like a hive of bees. Kelly notes that when bees swarm, that is, move en masse to a new hive, the process is not command-controlled. Instead, a few scouts check out possible new hive locations and report back to the swarm by dancing. The more theatrical a scout bee's dance, the better the bee liked the site. Deputy bees then check out one of the competing sites based on the dance that attracts them the most. If a scout concurs with the dancing bee's choice, the scout joins the dance. This activity induces others to check out the site and then join the dance if they concur. In this democracy, the favorite sites get more visitors, and, following the law of increasing returns, they get more dancing votes, and the others get fewer. In the end, one large snowballing dancing swarm dominates, and flies off to the new site, taking the queen bee with it.

Can an example of an organization with such a self-organizing principle be found? Consider Semco of Brazil.

CASE EXAMPLE

SEMCO S.A.

In his book, *Maverick: The Success Story Behind the World's Most Unusual Workplace,* Ricardo Semler,[8] CEO of Semco, describes how his company, a Brazilian manufacturer of industrial equipment, moved from fifty-sixth place to fourth place in its industry. To survive with Brazil's crippling inflation rate, Semler felt he had to "break all the rules" to gets costs down and productivity up.

As a result, factory workers at times set their own production quotas, help redesign products, formulate marketing plans, and even choose their own bosses. Bosses set their own salaries, yet everyone knows what they are, because workers have unlimited access to Semco's one set of books. And they have all been taught how to read balance sheets and cash flow statements. Finally, on the big decisions, such as relocating a factory, everyone decides. In one case, a factory was shut down for one day and buses took the employees to all three possible sites. Then the workers decided on a site that management would not have chosen.

(Case Continued)

Semco has no receptionists or secretaries, no perks, and Semler really does not know how many employees he has because some of his employees work part-time for him and part-time for competitors, others are contractors, and still others are vendor employees. When Semler took over the company after the death of his father, he threw out the rules, because they discouraged flexibility and comforted complacency. So for travel, for example, Semco sets no travel rules; employees are to spend whatever they think they should, as if it were their own money. The rationale: "If we're afraid to let people decide in which section of the plane to sit or how many stars their hotels should have, we shouldn't be sending them abroad to do business in our name, should we?" writes Semler. Employees are considered partners; they are self-managing and self-governing. They even vote on how the profit sharing pot will be split each year.

Things are rather messy around Semco, writes Semler. Machines are not in neat rows. They are set at odd angles, where the team that assembles a complete product puts them. Most workers do several jobs on a team, not just one, with the backing of the unions. And team members do not have to show up for work at the same time, but they do coordinate their schedules so as not to disrupt production. As the workers assumed more responsibility for their work, the number of supervisors decreased, as did corporate staff. Semco does not even have IS, training, or quality control departments. Three layers of management do the job that used to take 12, and those three are represented by three concentric circles.

Furthermore, departments can buy from whomever they choose. This competition keeps them on their toes. Management even encourages employees to start their own companies, even to the point of leasing Semco machinery to these start-ups at favorable rates. These companies sell to Semco and competitors. This strategy keeps Semco lean and agile.

The story goes on and on. The changes have been rough and not undertaken in an orderly or coherent fashion, as Semler recounts, but the radical changes to a far more democratic workplace allowed the company to grow 600 percent at the same time that the Brazilian economy was faltering. It is a dramatic story, and illustrative of the benefits of self-organization. ■

Communities Rather Than Groups

Another organizing principle for the New Economy is communities rather than groups. The distinction between the two is that communities form of their own volition. Groups are formed by design; their members are designated *a priori,* perhaps by a project manager, a select committee, or an executive.

"Communities of practice" are espoused by the Institute for Research on Learning in Menlo Park, California, a spin-off of Xerox PARC. As described by John Seely Brown, former director of Xerox PARC, and Estee Solomon Gray,[9] a founder of Congruity, a consulting firm, a community of practice is a small group of people (rarely more than

50) that has worked together for a period of time, but not necessarily in an organized fashion. They may perform the same job or collaborate on a shared task or a product. They have complementary talents and expertise; they are held together by a common purpose and a need to know what the others know. Most people belong to several communities of practice, and most important work in companies is done through them.

Communities are the critical building blocks of a knowledge-based company, state Brown and Solomon Gray, for three reasons. One, people, not processes, do the work. Big gaps separate official work processes and real-world practices (how things actually get done). The informal, perhaps impromptu, ways that people solve problems cannot be anticipated. And when companies compete on knowledge, the name of the game is improvisation. The challenge is to keep processes elegantly minimal, so that they give room for local interpretation and improvisation, that is, for grassroots practices.

The second reason communities of practice are important is that learning is about work, work is about learning, and both are social, say Brown and Solomon Gray. The crucial, unappreciated ingredient in companies is tacit knowledge—intuition, judgment, and common sense—which cannot be explained. Within groups, tacit knowledge exists in practices and relationships, based on people working together over time. When people recognize the importance of tacit and collective dimensions of work, they realize that learning has to do with being part of a community rather than absorbing information.

Third, communities of practice are important because organizations are webs of participation. When a pattern of participation changes, the organization changes. Participation is the core of the twenty-first-century company. Only people who make a commitment to their colleagues can create a winning company. Companies that realize the power of communities, and adopt minimal processes that allow them to emerge, are moving toward the twenty-first-century company.

CASE EXAMPLE

NATIONAL SEMICONDUCTOR

National Semiconductor has gone far in promoting communities of practice, according to Brown and Solomon Gray. The company began encouraging such communities after its business model that built low-margin commodity chips collapsed. The new CEO restructured and rationalized the company, then put it on a growth path and changed its business model. Part of the strategy was to build a core competence in "mixed signal technology," where chips function as the electronic interface between the "real world" of voice-video and the digital world of computing-communications.

Communities of practice are central to this plan. They energize and mobilize the firm's engineers. They even shape strategy, and then enact it. A community of practice on signal processing, for example, grew slowly over 18 months. It now includes engineers from numerous product lines and has been influential in strategy decisions.

(Case Continued)

Another community of practice has grown up around "phase lock loops" (PLL), a technology critical in some important company products. For 20 years, PLL designers swapped ideas, insights, and solutions to problems, even though they worked in different business units that did not work together. Within this loose community, some PLL engineers began reviewing new chip designs as a group. When product groups around National Semiconductor heard about these reviews, they informally brought their designs to the group for advice. The more reviews the group did, the more effective it became; it earned a reputation for excellence.

These engineers cannot publish their design criteria, teach others how to do design reviews, or create a library of design because their knowledge is embedded within their experience as a "community of practice." The only way someone can learn how to critique a design is to become part of that community and interact with it.

This PLL community of practice has now been formally recognized and has adopted a charter: to make its design know-how accessible, to make successes and failures known, and to continue to build the firm's PLL competence. This community does not report to anyone; it is "run" by its members. It provides a means of collaboration among National engineers concerning their PLL designs. It even received funding to develop two advanced PLL prototypes outside any National product line. And it has created a "PLL place," a lab that houses the equipment it buys.

National is extending communities of practice by formally recognizing them, offering funding for their projects, and handing out a toolkit to help people form their own communities of practice. And it encourages them to create homepages on the Web to communicate. ∎

Virtual Rather Than Physical

The virtual organization has come to be the popular description of a new organizational form. The underlying principle is that time and space are no longer the main organizing foundations. A virtual organization does not exist in one place or one time. It exists whenever and wherever the participants happen to be. As organizations expand globally but need to do so by adapting to local conditions, virtual organizations have emerged inside them, just as have communities of practice. As an example of a virtual organization within an existing company, consider Sun Microsystems as reported by Richard Rapaport.[10]

CASE EXAMPLE

SUN MICROSYSTEMS

John Gage, chief scientist of Sun Micro-systems, gives an intriguing description of virtual organizations within existing companies. He says that the network creates the company. "Your e-mail flow determines whether you're really part of the organization; the mailing lists you're on say a lot about the power you have." For example, he had been part of the Java group at Sun for four or five years when his name mistakenly was taken off. His flow of information stopped; he stopped being part of that organization. He got back on the list in a hurry, he says.

He notes that he uses Sun's alias file (the master list of its e-mail lists) to know what is going on in Sun. No one needs to tell him when a new project has started, he can see a new e-mail list. And when he sees a list balloon from, say, 35 to 200, he knows something important is happening.

People even create their own aliases, he says. His own alias list is his personal view of the company's power structure on a project, no matter where they work. The organization chart does not reflect the same list. These personal aliases have a secondary effect, too. They let others know whom you are keeping informed. In essence, each alias is a virtual organization. Web technology extends e-mail, says Gage, because it allows people to send "live" messages with embedded hyperlinks. So, rather than try to persuade people, you can just show them. ∎

The Learning Organization

Peter Senge, director of the Systems Thinking and Organizational Learning Program at MIT's Sloan School of Management, wrote the influential book, *The Fifth Discipline: The Art and Practice of the Learning Organization.*[11] No list of organizing principles for the new work environment would be complete without including his ideas.

Senge begins his book by noting that most organizations live only 40 years, which is only one-half the life of a person. The reason, he says, is because they have learning disabilities. In children, learning disabilities are tragic; in organizations, they are fatal. Therefore, he believes organizations will have to become learning organizations to survive.

Organizational learning disabilities are obvious, notes Senge. Here are just three. One, enterprises move forward by looking backward in that they rely on learning from experience. This approach means that companies end up solving the same problems over and over. Second, organizations fixate on events, such as budget cuts, monthly sales, competitors' new announcements. Yet the real threats come from gradual processes that move so slowly that no one notices them. Third, teamwork is not optimal, which is contrary to current belief. Team-based organizations operate below the lowest IQ on the team, leading to skilled incompetence.

Organizations that can learn faster than their competitors will survive. In fact, it is the only sustainable advantage. To become a learning organization, an enterprise must create new learning and thinking behaviors in its people. That is, the organization and its people must master the following five basic learning disciplines:

1. Personal mastery
2. Mental models
3. Shared vision
4. Team learning
5. Systems thinking

Personal Mastery.   People reach a special level of proficiency when they live creatively, striving for the results that matter most to them. In essence, their life turns into lifelong learning, in which they continually clarify and deepen their personal vision, and focus their energies. This personal mastery forms the spiritual foundation for the learning organization. Unfortunately, few enterprises foster such aspirations; they are not committed to the full development of their people. Therefore, they foster burnout rather than creativity.

Mental Models.   Peoples' mental models are the deeply ingrained assumptions, generalizations, and images that influence how they see the world and what actions they take. Senge notes that Royal Dutch/Shell was one of the first organizations to understand the importance of mental models, that is, how its managers viewed the world and the oil industry. Shell learned how to surface its managers' assumptions and challenge their inaccurate mental models. In so doing, Shell was able to accelerate its organizational learning process and spur the managers to investigate alternative futures by using scenarios. Then, when the 1974 oil crisis hit, its managers were able to react more appropriately than competitors, because they had already explored the possibility of such a crisis and the best steps to take if one did occur.

To change mental models, people must look inward, something few organizations encourage. But those that do realize that they have a powerful tool for fostering institutional learning.

Shared Vision.   A shared vision is an organization's view of its purpose, its calling. It provides the common identify by which its employees and others view it. Senge notes that Apple's shared vision has been to build computers for the rest of us. IBM's shared vision was exemplary service. A shared vision is vital to a learning organization because it provides the overarching goal as well as the rudder for the learning process. It becomes the force in people's hearts. It is the answer to: "What do we want to create?" Organizations with shared visions are powerful organizations.

Team Learning.   When teams learn, they produce extraordinary results. One of the major tools for team learning is "dialog," where people essentially think together. Senge distinguishes discussions from dialogs by saying that discussions occur when people try to convince others of their point of view. Dialogs, on the other hand, occur when people explore their own and others' ideas, without being defensive, in order to arrive at the best solution. Few teams dialog; most discuss, so they do not learn.

Team learning, rather than individual learning, is essential in the learning organization, says Senge, because teams are the fundamental unit of the modern organization. If teams do not learn, neither does the organization.

Systems Thinking. We live in a world of systems. To understand systems, people need to understand the underlying patterns. For example, people can only understand the "system" of a corporation by contemplating its whole, not its parts. Today's complex corporations are best understood by looking for patterns and viewing them as a whole entity. Systems thinking is a conceptual framework for making complete patterns clearer. Using and understanding systems thinking can help people see how to change the patterns effectively.

Of these five disciplines, Senge believes that systems thinking is the cornerstone. It is the fifth discipline. Until organizations look inwardly at the basic kinds of thinking and interacting they foster, they will not be able to learn faster than their competitors.

Embrace the Rules of Networks

The e-economy has three distinguishing characteristics, notes Kevin Kelly in *New Rules for the New Economy.*

1. It is global.
2. It favors soft things—intangibles, such as software, information, ideas, and most importantly relationships—over hard things, such as trucks, steel, and cement.
3. It is intensely interlinked.

Kelly believes hard things will increasingly follow the rules of soft things, with the soft creating the context within which the hard operates. Thus, for example, a farmer will still plow a field, but he will have a portable office in his tractor cab linked to a GPS system. The soil will have sensors that talk to his system. He will electronically receive weather data, scientific findings, and pricing information and use all these kinds of information to increase his yields, use fewer resources, and get higher prices for his crops. In short, he will try to replace the hard with the soft.

To understand how to win in this economy, you must understand the laws of networks, recommends Kelly. His book lays out ten such rules; here are three.

- Aim for relationship tech.
- Follow the free.
- Feed the web first.

Aim for Relationship Tech. Networks embody an amazing phenomenon: Connecting more devices to a network exponentially increases the value of the network for everyone on that network because so many new possible connections are created. So, a network of four people has 12 one-to-one connections. Increasing the network to five people leads to 20 connections.

The New Economy is all about networks, which means it is all about connecting. Whereas the industrial age was about increasing productivity, the network age is about amplifying relationships, that is, increasing the quantity and quality of economic relationships.

With unlimited connections and abundant information, the organization of choice is peer-to-peer rather than hierarchical. New peer-to-peer relationships are forming—

between customer and firm, between customer and customer—which question past ways of working. For example, when you pump your own gas, are you a customer or a nonpaid employee? Both, answers Kelly. Producers and consumers become one, and when consumers have a hand in cocreating, they are likely to be happier with the result. The amazing aspect is that as a customer and a company create together, on a peer-to-peer basis, they both get smarter together, and they develop a closer relationship. So the cost of switching to working with another company becomes high for a customer because the customer loses the time she has invested to teach the company her interests, and she loses what the company has learned about her. For example, if a florist sends a reminder of your Mom's birthday and says they will again send flowers to the same address and charge the same card as last year, how likely are you to call a different florist?

Technology that enhances such relationships is called *relationship tech,* says Kelly. These are the technologies companies should be investing in. One type is recommender systems, such as that used by Amazon.com. When you order a book from Amazon, it uses a recommender system to see what books other book buyers (who have bought that same book) have also bought, and then recommends those books to you. The power in this technology is that it can also be used to let people know of others who have similar interests, and thus spur new relationships.

It behooves companies to make their customers smarter, says Kelly, because the enterprise with the smartest customers wins. It is also wise to encourage customers to talk to each other, to even form affinity groups because that increases loyalty. The greatest expertise about a product does not reside in the company, it resides in its fanatical customers. Companies should encourage such groups and tap such knowledge. Instead, most sue the groups to take down their fan Web sites.

But having smarter customers requires more trust on both sides—the company trusting customers with information about product defects, for example, and customers trusting companies with information about themselves. At the heart of trust in the network economy is privacy. As a major issue privacy should not be viewed by companies as "an inconvenient obsession of customers" that needs to be circumvented, but rather as a way to build a genuine relationship with customers. The concern is that customers do not know what a company knows about them nor how this information is being used, which creates mistrust. Restoring trust means restoring symmetry, so that customers know who knows what about them (in detail), how that information was obtained, and who else has been given that information.

So Kelly believes the network economy is based on relationships, which means trust must be a basic tenet.

This "shop for relationship tech" rule has obvious implications for CIOs. The main one is to take this point of view, which may be quite a switch from the prevalent mindset that IT is for processing, not communications. Even if CIOs share this network economy belief, they might have to convince their peers of its value.

Follow the Free. One of the most fascinating aspects of the network economy can be seen today: The best gets better and cheaper at the same time. It was not too many years ago when to get something better you had to pay more. Today, if you just wait a few months, you will either get the same quality for a lower price or better quality at today's price. The industrial age brought automation and cheap energy, initiating this phenomenon. Computers have accelerated it. In fact, Kelly notes that a transportation specialist told him that almost nothing in the information industry is moved by ships, everything is flown, so that the price will not drop during shipment. The underlying principles are that the price drops from the volume. The more that is manufactured, the cheaper each unit. Furthermore, quality increases due to the learning curve.

The network economy is founded on this principle of decreasing price for increasing quality, so smart companies anticipate this cheapness and offer products for free. Paradoxically, those who do can make a fortune. It is a tenet of the network economy. Kelly recounts an interesting story to demonstrate his point. It involves Robert Noyce and Jerry Sanders, the founders of Fairchild Semiconductor. In the 1960s they were selling a transistor to the military that cost $100 to make. They wanted to sell the transistor to RCA for use in UHF tuners to replace the vacuum tubes RCA was using, which only cost them $1.05. Noyce and Sanders believed that learning and volume would decrease their production costs for transistors, so they boldly set their price at $1.05 from the start, even before they had built the factory or the manufacturing processes they would use. They anticipated the cheap and got 90 percent of the UHF market, and prospered. Within two years, they cut the price to 50 cents and still made a profit.

Any item, soft or hard, that can be copied adheres to this inverted pricing principle, says Kelly, so follow the free. Technology creates an opportunity for demand, and then fulfills it.

In the network economy, the most valuable goods and services are those that are most abundant, because they increase the value of every other one. If they become cheaper as they become more plentiful, then the most valuable items are ubiquitous and free, he reasons. The fastest way to make something ubiquitous is to make it free. This strategy of the network economy is well-tested, and it is the anathema of the strategy of the industrial age where scarcity was of the highest value. Netscape gave the browser away free and sold the servers. The strategy worked until Microsoft, with a larger network, did the same and took away market share.

So how do you make money in such a market? Kelly gives three answers. One, aim for "free" but only achieve "cheap." It will have the same effect. Two, give away the core product and sell the service. This strategy has happened with cell phones and satellite dishes. They give the phones and dishes away free and sell the service. Three, structure the business so that you will be profitable when your product is free.

The reverse tenet of following the free is to see what is free today that could have value, and thus a price, tomorrow. One early example on the Web was the early indexes, which were free and became ubiquitous. Their value came from helping people find sites that might interest them, via their categories. They drew people's attention, which is the scarce good in the network economy. Thus, they became valuable. Other free items that could have value in the future, surmises Kelly, are bots, remote cameras, catalogs, guides, distillations, and so forth. So offering a good free, and sharing with others, *can* lead to ubiquity, which, in turn, can lead to having a valuable item.

The founding norm of the Internet was its gift economy mentality. Lots of information and knowledge were exchanged, without money. In fact, software developers often asked for help by releasing their software as a "beta" version, to be tested and improved by others. The most popular operating system for Internet servers—Apache—was developed this way; it is free. And Linux, the freeware operating system, was too. It makes you wonder whether CIOs could tap this gift economy? Of course, they would need to allow their developers to assist others in exchange. It is an interesting thought.

Feed the Web First. In the industrial age, loyalty to one's enterprise was important. In the network age, it is more important to be on the right network or network platform. Kelly thus sees loyalty moving from enterprises to "platforms." As an example, he asks: "Are you a Mac or a Windows person?" Both are examples of competing platforms. Being on one means being out of the other. Thus, Mac users originally could not use the software provided for the PC, and vice versa. Similarly, in the network world, choosing the right platform makes an enterprise "in" or "out," so choice becomes important. In addition, once the choice is made, it is important for the company to "feed" that choice to ensure it grows so that they are on the right network, that is, the one that prospers. People who joined the Mac (closed, proprietary platform) network did not prosper; those who chose the PC (open, nonproprietary) did.

In the network economy, a company's success depends more than in the past on the standards it chooses. For example, many companies have chosen an ERP package. If they chose one selected by many other enterprises, then third-party providers see a larger market for their work so more of them write "bolt-ons" to add new functions. This tendency, in turn, expands the options for everyone in this "ERP network." Companies choosing a less-favored ERP package end up having fewer bolt-ons to choose from, fewer peers to learn from, fewer consultants with expertise in the package, and so on.

Kelly contends that the destiny of firms and their "web" (the platforms they choose) are intertwined so much so that a company's first duty is to "feed the web" because the firm's prosperity is linked to the prosperity of the network. A company cannot prosper unless its network prospers.

Here's an example in the software industry. Software companies, such as Microsoft, pay as much attention to their web as they do to their software. Thus, they hold conferences for developers who use their software. They provide tools for these developers. They copromote applications written using their software. They provide education for consultants to learn about their software. They give away software to schools to promote their name to future generations. In short, they feed the web (the ecosystem) that surrounds their product. The same is true in the video game industry, the music industry, and the movie industry. All three currently face challenges relating to providing their products over the Internet.

In the network economy, enterprises will shift their focus from maximizing their own value to maximizing the value of their network. Some networks will, of course, be more important than others. For example, choosing to support laser disk versus DVD platforms was obviously crucial to movie companies. It is too early to tell how important one wireless Internet access platform will be over another, and to whom the choice will have the greatest value. For example, if a company chose WAP as the platform to bet on, then they need to WAP-enable their Web site. But, more importantly, they will need to promote WAP devices with their customers. How will they do it? And if they are a company offering only Internet-based wireless services, their success could depend on their making the right choice in this crucial area.

A corollary is that standards thus become ever more important in the network economy. The prize is so large that many contend to become "the standard." That contest is now being waged in the wireless world. Which wireless protocol will win? It is still an open question. Companies that plan to offer services wirelessly must therefore decide before a clear winner is apparent. Then, they need to back it, promote it, and do all they can to ensure they have chosen the winner. The standard-making process becomes far more important in the network economy, so companies will devote much more time to it than in the past, says Kelly. In fact, technical standards will become as important as laws, he believes. Webs of relationships will be regulated by the technical standards upon which they are built. Eventually, the Internet will encompass everything; everything will be interconnected. Furthermore, commerce will migrate to the Internet. Perhaps not all transactions will occur there, but some parts of all transactions will involve the Internet. Thus, Kelly recommends siding with the Net: Invest in it, feed it, promote its use by everyone in your ecosystem because it will be the winner.

The important lesson for CIOs in this operating principle is that they need to inform their peers in top management of the importance of the IT platforms they choose, not just to run operations but also to offer to consumers and embed in their products and services. These choices are not IT decisions; they are business decisions.

Given these potential operating principles for today's e-world, we present a few ideas on how to move forward.

MOVING FORWARD

More than ever, IS and corporate management need to answer the age-old question: What sorts of applications should we deploy? In most cases, the answer has been left to line management, based on their needs. But as Bob Benson of Washington University in St. Louis and Marilyn Parker of IBM[12] pointed out years ago, a synergistic relationship forms between the business and IT. Their model was discussed in Chapter 4 and shown in Figure 4-4. Their model shows that the IT architecture needs to align with current strategy, and that IT opportunities influence or even change business strategy. Therefore, IS management has a responsibility to point out those opportunities to top management and line management to best help the enterprise. They cannot just sit and wait for users to figure out what they need.

Besides keeping alert to new opportunities, IS management also needs to take a portfolio view of applications and manage that portfolio to ensure that no serious gaps creep in. What sort of framework should management use to evaluate the application portfolio? Interestingly, we found an answer in two different places.

Take a Portfolio Approach

David Flint[3b] believes that applications must support all aspects of work, which means supporting three human activities: knowledge, transactions, and discussion. The interrelationship of these applications and activities is shown in Figure 15-1. Every job has aspects of all three components, although in different proportions. These three therefore form the portfolio framework for assessing future applications.

Traditionally, companies have *automated* mechanistic work via transaction processing systems, but they have not been so attentive to the other two aspects of work: intellectual work and interpersonal work. Effectively supporting intellectual work requires mastering the management of knowledge, notes Flint. And supporting interpersonal work requires mastering discussion management.

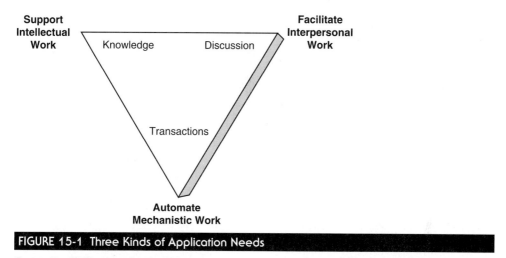

FIGURE 15-1 Three Kinds of Application Needs

Source: David Flint, "Applications Delivery in the 1990s," Wentworth Research Program (now part of Gartner Executive Programs), 1994.

Furthermore, all three need to be integrated at the desktop, creating a "user toolkit" as it were. So, a user screen might provide, for example, e-mail for discussing matters with others, an electronic catalog for purchasing supplies, and a library of job-related information. Providing this breadth requires developers who can concentrate on all three aspects of work, not just automate functions or processes, and developers who really understand the work being supported, so they can design the user interface properly. This understanding in turn, probably argues for prototyping, so that users are involved in the interface design and rapid application development.

In short, all three aspects of work need to be supported by the IS department, preferably in combination in many applications.

Follow Employees

In a stirring article in the September/October 2000 *Harvard Business Review,* Ricardo Semler of Semco[13] provides an update on his maverick company's progress in the digital economy. It is just as unconventional as in the Brazilian marketplace. He notes that his company has grown to $160 million in revenue, but he has resisted defining what businesses Semco is in because that would limit his employees' thinking. He much prefers for the employees to choose the work they want to do. This story illustrates the organic aspects of business described in the organizing principles in this chapter.

SEMCO S.A.

Since 1990, the company has quadrupled revenues and tripled employees, from 450 to 1,300. More importantly they have moved significantly beyond being a manufacturer. First they expanded into services, which have higher margins, and more recently into the marketspace of e-business services over the Internet.

In 1999, almost 75 percent of their revenues came from services. The shift from manufacturing to services was actually quite natural, states Semler; the employees led the march by listening to what customers wanted, not by directives from the top of the company. Semler believes that by giving his employees freedom, they will simultaneously act in their own best interest and the best interest of Semco, and lead to change naturally. On the other hand, when management defines the limits of the business, change becomes forced and frustrating.

As an example of natural change, Semler notes that they made cooling towers for commercial buildings in the early 1990s. Over time, however, the owners of these highrises complained to Semco salespeople about the hassles of maintaining these towers. So some of the salespeople proposed starting a service business to maintain these systems. They would charge the customers 20 percent of the savings they generated (thus letting the customers keep 80 percent), and they would give Semco 80 percent of that revenue and keep 20 percent as their pay, in the form of commissions. The business proved successful, saving customers money, re-ducing their hassles, and moving Semco into the service business.

In fact, the property owners were so pleased that they asked Semco to manage other parts of their buildings: their air conditioning compressors, cleaning, security, general maintenance, and so on. As the business grew, Semco teamed up with Cushman & Wakefield, major property managers, to launch 50–50 ventures in Brazil. Today they have a $30 million property management business.

In 2001, they expect 15 percent of their revenues to come from Internet-based services—another major shift that is occurring naturally at Semco. As Semler notes, most of the eight e-business initiatives to date have grown out of their expansion into services. For example, in a joint venture with Johnson Controls, they manage retail facilities. In making their rounds and talking to store managers, Semco's people noticed how much money retailers were losing from lost inventories. One employee even asked for a one-year paid sabbatical to study the possibilities of offering e-business services to these retailers. His sabbatical was approved and he later proposed a joint venture with the largest inventory tracking company, RGIS. Within two years, they had become the largest inventory managers in South America.

In addition, their property management work showed them the inefficiency of the construction industry, so they teamed up with Johnson Controls and Cushman & Wakefield to create an online

(Case Continued)

exchange for the commercial construction industry. Now, all the parties in a project, from architects and engineers to banks and project managers, can hold multiparty online real-time chats, issue proposals, send bids, share drawings and documents, and even hire people using this exchange.

Semco has taken it even further, teaming with a virtual trade show company to host virtual trade fairs associated with the exchange so that companies too small to exhibit their products in trade shows can exhibit them online. Semco and its partners held eight such shows last year.

All of this change has occurred by following the employees. When they have a good idea, Semco management is likely to provide the funding to test it out. They have had more winners than losers taking this portfolio approach, and it has led them naturally into marketspace. ∎

Educate Executives

Finally, we end this chapter, and this book, as we began it, on the subject of leadership. As we have noted, leadership of IT is no longer a technical challenge, it is a business challenge because the important aspect is the *use* of IT. Therefore, it needs to be led by all CXOs. However, due to their age and experience with industrial-age management (most are in their forties and fifties), they may not be as adept as leaders in today's e-economy as they could be. Thus, perhaps the most important action CIOs can take to move their enterprise forward in the e-world is to ensure that their fellow CXOs are educated on IT.

Chuck Gibson,[14] a long-time top-level consultant and now senior lecturer at the MIT Sloan School, points out that while these executives can be computer literate and somewhat familiar with desktop systems, few have the depth of background in IS that they have with other functions, such as marketing or finance. As a result, many may still not understand the issues that drive the IS function, such as the need to invest in infrastructure. This superficial awareness is exacerbated by the current hype, and potential, of the Internet and e-commerce. So organizations must be concerned with the potential for a gap between what executives *believe* is important about IT versus what they *really* need to know about for example, transforming to become an e-business.

Educate Executives for Their Leadership Roles.   Senior executives need education to carry out the following executive roles. Chuck Gibson contributes comments on why.

To set the tone of the organization toward technology.   One of the most important jobs of top management is to set the tone for the organization because they send a message through their actions. The importance of IT and information must be "modeled" by top executives through their personal use of the technology and their e-world knowledge. They may need education in performing this role well.

To use IT to promote business change. The emergence of e-business has exacerbated this leadership need. For one thing, change is occurring faster. The education needed here is that implementation of a powerful package, such as ERP, or the creation of a transactional Web site cannot bring about major business change on its own. But it can be a powerful catalyst and tool for top management.

To guide technology introductions. The IS department cannot be the driver of organizational change. Top management and line management must be. This issue goes back many years, says Gibson, yet it is still with us. Most executives are aware of the importance of the change process, so they are holding line management responsible for business change. If line management does not lead the change, it will not stick. Preparing them for change is a key educational challenge.

To envision how IT can serve business strategy. Top management must foresee how key business strategies can be enabled by IT. The educational component here is to sense technology trends and alternative scenarios of technological opportunities for business use. The goal is to achieve IT-business strategic *thinking* among all executives.

To align IT with business objectives. Without question, alignment is crucial to business success. Most executives now know just how crucial it is; e-commerce has made that abundantly clear. However, some still believe that the IS function is a machine room, the CIO is a technician, and the IS function can stay a step behind business planning. Where these attitudes persist, organizations encounter problems aligning IS projects with the business importance of IT and information. Education on the role of the CIO and how to effectively integrate planning are part of the remedy.

To assess costs and benefits. This subject continues to be relevant, because continuing tension characterizes the relationship between strategic objectives and the need to invest in IT infrastructure before people realize they need it. Companies must be ahead of requests for applications, and have data resources available for unanticipated user needs. Education in this area centers around the appropriate use of cost-benefit criteria, and the need to invest in IT infrastructure, which may have no easily measurable, near-term quantitative returns.

To use systems with comfort. Now, more than ever, executives need to be computer literate, which means being comfortable using a PC and the Web, perhaps even wirelessly. More than that, they need to be information literate. Jerry Kanter of Babson College distinguishes the two by saying that information literacy means being aware of the underlying issues in using information as a resource. Such issues include infrastructure and application development. Executives need to be comfortable discussing the technology at this level, not just at the PC use level.

Ways to Educate Executives. It has become clear that most companies can no longer afford to "stop the business" and send their senior executives away to an IT seminar for even a few days, says Gibson. But the necessity for education is greater, even while the audience is busier and more demanding of "learning relevance." Therefore, the rule these days is to present IT education integral to, or in conjunction with, discussions or meetings focusing on another topic, such as acquiring a business, strategic planning for participating in the e-economy, or forming an alliance or even a merger.

In such meetings, the business topic is in the foreground, discussions about technology or how IT fits into the business strategy are in the background. Half the discussion is about the business, half is about IT, but only the IT topics relevant to the business discussion. The outcome of such discussions is decisions on how IT affects the business issue, down to such specifics as desktops, integrated systems, packaged software, outsourcing, among others.

Such learning can also occur through a more direct executive exercise: the development of an IT strategy, says Gibson. Here, the business issue is *about* IT, its integration, position, and investments in the context of business strategy. Educational sessions on IT topics are easily viewed as relevant to this task.

The real challenge for CIOs and educators is that such focusing on relevance drives out discussions of broader IT issues and concepts. So learning important fundamentals about it may not occur. In short, says Gibson, the most effective executive education these days is "issues-based education," where the educators identify executives' current needs and design the education to address those needs.

Here are some options for educating executives.

Learn by doing.   A number of companies have followed the example of Charlie Feld when he was CIO at Frito Lay, notes Gibson. He knew he had to implement a large IT infrastructure in order to deliver an executive information system to the company. He also knew he had to do it in cost-justifiable pieces. Feld formed an alliance with the sales department to deliver handheld computers to route salespeople. This cost-justifiable project included a big part of building the data infrastructure. When it was ready to show to the executives, he was able to find an advocate for the EIS among the executive ranks. In his advocacy role, this executive became information literate. He learned by doing. It took a long time and it required a deeper understanding than most executives obtain, but it can be accomplished if the steps are each made to pay off and learning occurs in the doing.

Read publications.   In a similar vein, just reading can provide informal IT education. Publications aimed at executives are carrying more and more articles on IT. For years, *Business Week* has had a section on information processing. *Fortune, Forbes,* and *Newsweek* regularly have special advertising sections on various IT topics, with commentaries by leading consulting firms. *The Wall Street Journal* and *The New York Times* also have a growing number of articles on IT.

Through subordinates.   Subordinates can also educate their bosses. One highly progressive company regularly introduces new equipment and desktop products for use by staff and support personnel, knowing they will spread the word to their bosses and in some cases will try to sell them on acquiring the new products. In another company, where management is more conservative, the subordinates do not try to sell their bosses on a new system; they simply use it themselves to demonstrate the benefits.

Individual demonstrations.   CIOs can also keep top executives up-to-date by inviting them to see demonstrations of new systems and discussing possible uses and implications.

These informal approaches seem to work best in two types of companies: (1) highly progressive companies where the executives keep themselves abreast of new developments, and (2) companies where the executives are not yet ready for highly visible organizationwide information systems. These executives more readily accept implicit means of education than outright educational programs.

Executive briefings. A somewhat more formal approach is to hold short briefings, coordinated with management meetings, as Gibson has pointed out. In some cases, IS teams brief a high-level committee on a technology, such as the wireless Internet or remote diagnosis, before requesting project funding.

Brown bag theaters. A brown bag theater is where the training department presents a series of video tapes, outside speakers, or even company employees speaking about their work at lunch time. Attendance is voluntary, and the presentations generally have a wide audience appeal—not too technical, people-oriented, and entertaining. If a video is shown it may be followed by a company expert who answers questions.

Short seminars. More formal than the brown bag theater is the short seminar, which lasts one to three hours. Attendance is also voluntary. The seminar topic is chosen for a narrower audience. This approach is commonly used by vendors to introduce a new technology and their offerings.

Formal programs. These programs are designed to quickly introduce executives to new technology and the state of the art. They are therefore intensive, generally lasting one to three days, depending on the number of subjects covered. When custom-tailored and made relevant, they do play an important role in educating time-pressed managers.

Again, the issue in executive education is giving non-IT executives the educational foundation they need to lead their organization in the IT-based New Economy.

CONCLUSION

What stands out in the discussion of organizing principles at the beginning of the chapter and in the Semco case studies is the repeated emphasis on naturally forming relationships. Much more of the talk actually centers on people-to-people contact than on technology. Technology is the underpinning. The principles talk about natural phenomenon rather than human-made structures. They dwell on how to develop relationships that help people work effectively.

We are, indeed, in a business revolution. With it, the use of IT is changing in kind. It has shifted from amplifying thinking and processing to amplifying communicating and connecting. It is now about relationships more than transactions.

Information technology professionals have always been enamored with the technical aspects of computer systems; the human side has been of less interest. But it is people who make or break a system, through their use or disuse of it. So even though the e-economy relies heavily on IT, relationships and such mechanisms as communities of practice will play a major role. IT now allows such relationships to transcend time and space, and with the appearance of instant messaging, people can stay in contact easily. With cost-justifiable long-distance video, people will be able to communicate in richer ways across greater distances. In so doing, the foundations of past ways of working will change. That is the exciting exploration that is going on right now as people grapple with creating the new work environment and the challenges it presents.

QUESTIONS AND EXERCISES

Review Questions

1. According to Hammer, how does measurement of a task differ from measurement of a process?
2. What elements of a football team make it a process-centric organization?
3. What surprised Kauffmann in his lightbulb experiment?
4. According to Kelly, what were the three rules given to the computer-generated bats in *Batman Returns?* What was the effect of these rules?
5. What did the 5,000 copilots of the graphical submarine initially lack?
6. According to Kelly, what is the only way to create truly complex systems?
7. List some of the ways Semco operates differently from most companies.
8. According to Brown and Solomon Gray, why are communities the building blocks of knowledge-based companies?
9. What is a community of practice? And what has National Semiconductor done to encourage them?
10. According to Gage, how does he really know about the hot work being performed at Sun?
11. What are the three distinguishing characteristics of the e-economy, according to Kelly?
12. What does "invest in relationship tech" mean?
13. Why should companies invest in making their customers smart?
14. What two meanings does "follow the free" have?
15. What does "feed the web first" mean?
16. List the roles executives need to play in managing the use of IT.

Discussion Questions

1. Giving employees and small work groups the authority to make most of their own decisions seems to be of obvious benefit to companies. Why do you think this type of on-the-job self-management is not more prevalent? And what are the drawbacks?
2. Kelly, Wheatley, and Kellner-Rogers talk about self-organizing systems. These ideas will not work in organizations because they need defined structure, defined jobs, and limits. Agree or disagree? Describe your reasoning.
3. Executives over 50 really do not "get it." They just do not understand nor appreciate the Internet. They have the wrong mindset and they cannot be educated to have the right mindset. Companies need younger executives to provide the Internet-savvy leadership to thrive in the e-world. Present arguments for and against these ideas.

Exercises

1. Read several articles or scan several books on the New Economy. What management issues do these articles/books present with respect to work redesign? What potential roadblocks do they discuss?
2. Visit a local company and talk to an information systems executive about how the New Economy has changed the organization's work environment. Ask for one or two examples of new ways of working. Ask the CIO's opinions on Kelly's three rules for the New Economy.
3. Describe the work environment you would like to work in. Present it to the class. Describe how you might reach your goal.

REFERENCES

1. Hammer, Michael, *Beyond Reengineering: How the Process-Centered Organization is Changing Our Work and Our Lives,* Harper-Collins Publishers, New York, 1996.

2. Sachs, Patricia, "Transforming Work: Collaboration, Learning, and Design," *Communications of the ACM,* September 1995, 36–44.

3. Wentworth Research Program, now part of Gartner Executive Programs, Stamford, CT.
   a. Woolfe, Roger, "The Business of Innovation," May 1996.
   b. Flint, David, "Applications Delivery in the 1990s," March 1994.

4. Wheatley, Margaret, *Leadership and the New Science: Learning about Organizations from an Orderly Universe,* Berrett-Koehler Publishers, San Francisco, CA, 1994.

5. Kelly, Kevin, *Out of Control: The New Biology of Machines, Social Systems, and the Economic World,* Addison-Wesley Publishing, Reading, MA, 1994; *New Rules for the New Economy: Ten Radical Strategies for a Connected World,* Viking, New York, 1998.

6. Wheatley, Margaret and Myron Kellner-Rogers, *A Simpler Way,* Berrett-Koehler Publishers, San Francisco, CA, 1996.

7. Byrne, John, "The 21st Century Corporation: Management by Web," *Business Week,* August 28, 2000, 84–96, www.businessweek.com.

8. Semler, Ricardo, *Maverick: The Success Story Behind the World's Most Unusual Workplace,"* Warner Books, New York, 1993.

9. Brown, John Seely and Estee Solomon Gray, "The People Are the Company," *Fast Company,* Premier Issue, 1995.

10. Rapaport, Richard, "The Network is the Company: An Interview with John Gage," *Fast Company,* 1996.

11. Senge, Peter, *The Fifth Discipline: The Art and Practice of the Learning Organization,* Doubleday, New York, 1990.

12. Benson, Robert, and Marilyn Parker, "Information Economics: An Introduction," EWiM Working Paper, 1987, Center for the Study of Information Management, Washington University, St. Louis, MO.

13. Semler, Ricardo, "How We Went Digital Without a Strategy," *Harvard Business Review,* September/October 2000, www.hbr.org.

14. From communication with Chuck Gibson of Gibson and Associates, Concord, MA.

Glossary of Terms

Abend An abnormal ending of a software program, which is when it stops running because it encounters an error condition.

Advanced Technology Group A group within the IS department responsible for spotting and evaluating new technologies, often by conducting a pilot project.

Affinity Diagram Clustering "Post-It"–type notes of items (such as business activities) on a wall under headings (such as business processes) to show groupings.

Agent An electronic entity that performs tasks, either on its own or at the request of a person or a computer.

Analog Technology The method where signals are sent as sine waves rather than ones and zeros, as in digital technology.

Applets Small single-function applications, often written in Java, that are pulled from the Internet when needed.

Application Program Interface (API) An interface created for a software product that is like a standard because it allows programmers to write to that interface and thus link to and utilize that software product in their applications.

Application Service Provider (ASP) A company that rents out software over the Internet.

Architecture A blueprint that shows how the overall system, house, vehicle, or item will look and how the parts interrelate.

Authentication A method assuring that the digital signature of the user is valid.

Authorization Assuring that the correct user is accessing a network, application, or stored files or documents.

Avatar A virtual persona that is taken on by a person in a chat room or MUD on the Internet.

Backbone Systems Mainline corporate transaction processing systems.

Back-End Systems Computer systems that handle an enterprise's operational processing, as opposed to front-end systems that interact with customers.

Back-End Tools Tools, such as code generators, in computer-aided software engineering suites that automatically generate source code.

Best-of-Breed Outsourcing Outsourcing specific functions, each to the most appropriate provider, rather than outsourcing all functions to one provider who may not be the best for all the functions.

Brown Bag Theater Where the training department presents a series of video tapes, outside speakers, or even company employees speaking about their work during lunch time to educate IS staff on the business or new technologies.

Business Process Outsourcing (BPO) Outsourcing all or most of a reengineered process that has a large IT component.

Business Process Redesign/Reengineering (BPR) Significantly restructuring the operational business processes in a firm.

Cache Fast memory used for temporary storage.

Case Management A way to organize work where each person (or team) handles a customer (a case) or a set of customers from beginning to end rather than each doing a part of the work then passing it to others for further work.

Champion A person inside or outside IS who has a vision and gets it implemented by obtaining the funding, pushing the project over hurdles, putting his or her reputation on the line, and taking on the risk of the project.

Chaos Theory As applied to business, a theory that states that "order is free" when groups and organizations are allowed to be self-organizing because, as in scientific chaos theory, randomness (chaos) works within boundaries, which are called strange attractors. As a result, there is order in chaos.

Circuit Switching When a virtual (temporary) circuit is created between caller and receiver and that circuit is theirs alone to use; no other parties can share it during the duration of their telephone call. Most appropriate for voice calls.

Cleansed Data Data processed to make it usable for decision support; referred to in conjunction with data warehouses.

Cleartext Non-encrypted versions of passwords and messages.

Client-Server Splitting the computing workload between the "client," which is a computer used by the user and can sit on the desktop or be carried around, and the "server," which houses the sharable resources.

Closed Network A network that is offered by one supplier and to which only the products of that supplier can be attached.

Collaborative outsourcing Where one service provider becomes the prime contractor for numerous facets of an operation, but some of the work is provided by other external service providers (ESPs).

Communities of Practice Networks of people who work together in an unofficial way to get work accomplished using unofficial procedures that may be outside the company's formal corporate culture.

Competitive local exchange carriers (CLECs) Telecom carriers that compete with incumbent local exchange carriers (ILECs) and provide new kinds of connection options to businesses and homes, such as cable modems and optical fiber, wireless, satellite, and speeding up wire lines.

Concept Based A text retrieval system that allows searching on concepts—such as poor quality, inadequate product functionality, or obsolescence—rather than by text.

Connectivity Allowing users to communicate up, down, across, and out of an organization via a network.

Cookie A file in a Web user's computer that identifies the user to Web sites.

Cooperative Processing A computer system with various components cooperating with each other to perform a task, perhaps spanning several business functions within the organization or even linking to other organizations.

Corporate Memory The knowledge or information accumulated by a business, which is often stored in its software, databases, patents, and business processes.

Corporate Portal A Web site where employees, customers, and suppliers gain access to a company's information, applications, and processes. For instance, rather than have applications housed on PCs, they might be available via an application service provider accessed via the corporate portal.

Countermeasures Mechanisms used by people and enterprises to protect themselves from security breaches, such as stealing data or machines, destroying files, redirecting traffic, shutting down Web sites, and unleashing computer viruses.

Critical Success Factors (CSF) The few key areas of an executive's job where things must go right in order for the organization to flourish.

Cybermall A virtual mall on the World Wide Web; it exists in time but not in physical space.

Cyberspace A "space" on the Internet where people "exist" in a virtual world.

Cycle Time The amount of time it takes to accomplish a complete cycle, such as the time from getting an idea to turning it into a product or service.

Data Electronic information that is comprised of facts.

Data Dictionary The main tool by which data administrators control a company's standard data definitions to make sure that corporate policy is being followed.

Data Integrity Data that maintains its integrity because it cannot be modified in transit or in storage.

Data Mart A subset of a data warehouse created for a specific set of users, such as the marketing department.

Data Mining Exploring huge repositories of data to uncover patterns, trends, or anomalies.

Data Warehouse A huge repository of historical data used to answer queries and uncover trends; contains a snapshot of data at a point in time as opposed to operational databases that are updated with every new transaction.

Database Repository of data that is stored in a particular manner, such as in a hierarchy or tables.

Decentralization Moving the processing or storage of data out from a central site, often with little or no coordination with that central site.

Decision Support Systems (DSS) Computer applications used to support decision making.

Demand Chain The "chain" that runs from the customer back through the retailer to the raw-materials producer, which uses a demand-pull model where items are not made until they have been ordered by the customer; opposite of supply-push.

Denial of Service Attack Attack on a Web site from many coordinated computers that floods the site with so many empty messages that the site is overwhelmed and crashes and is therefore unable to process legitimate queries.

Desktop Clients Desktop machines used in a client/server system environment to make requests of a shared server.

Digital Subscriber Line (DSL) A telephone subscription service that provides speed up to 1.2 Mbps (10^6 bits per second) over copper wire, as compared to a modem's speed of 56 Kbps.

Dirty Data Data from different databases that does not match, has different names, uses different time frames, and so forth.

Distributed System A computer system that has components that are physically distributed around a company or among companies.

Document A unit of recorded information structured for human consumption.

Downsizing Reducing the size of a company workforce via layoffs.

Dribbling Data Obtaining data for a new application from data in an existing application.

Dumb Terminals Desktop machines without processing or storage capabilities.

Eavesdropping Intercepting messages on a computer network.

E-business Transacting business with other businesses over the Internet, often via the World Wide Web.

E-business outsourcing Outsourcing e-commerce and e-business aspects of one's company, such as Web site hosting, application hosting, telecom management, and so forth.

E-commerce Transacting business with consumers over the Internet, mainly via the World Wide Web.

E-procurement Buying items via the Web using company-tailored electronic catalogs of items for which the company has negotiated prices with the seller; e-procurement generally uses a third-party marketplace to handle the coordination between buyer and seller.

E-tailing Retailing over the Web.

Ecosystem A web of relationships surrounding one or a few companies.

Edge server A server that is at the "edge" of the Internet; that is, close to a user.

Electronic Data Interchange (EDI) Business transactions, such as orders, that cross company boundaries via a network using carefully defined protocols and data formats.

Electronic Marketplace A computerized marketplace with several buyers and several sellers where a third party generally acts as the marketplace intermediary.

Electronic Vaulting An off-site data storage facility used by organizations for backing up data against loss in case of a disaster.

Encapsulation Combining data and procedures in an object.

Encryption Coding and decoding documents for security.

Enterprise Resource Planning Systems Systems that aim to provide companies with a single source of data about their operations. The systems have financial, manufacturing, HR, and other modules.

Ethernet A network protocol used in many local area networks that broadcasts messages across the network and rebroadcasts if a collision of messages occurs.

Exchanges Business-to-business electronic marketplaces where many buyers purchase goods from many sellers. These are generally organized by industry or by specialties within an industry.

Executive Information System (EIS) A computer system specially built for executives to assist them in making decisions.

Expert Systems A computer system that houses experts' knowledge about a subject, such as how to make a batch of tomato soup.

Extended Enterprise Networks Interconnected single-organization networks that are not limited by industry and provide a type of electronic information consortium.

External Document-Based Information Electronic information that is available outside an organization and is text based, rather than numeric.

External Operational Measures Measures of computer operational performance that users can see, such as system and network uptime (or downtime), response time, turnaround time, and program failures. These directly relate to customer satisfaction.

External Record-Based Information Electronic information that is available outside an organization and is numeric, rather than text based.

External Service Provider A company that provides services to a firm, often acting as an outsourcer. There are numerous types of ESPs, such as those that provide Web site hosting, back-up and recovery, and application hosting.

Extract File A file extracted from a company's transaction database and placed in a decision support database or a data warehouse where it can be queried by end users.

Extranet A portion of an intranet that is made available to outsiders, often suppliers, customers, or subscribers.

Federated Databases A way of organizing databases where each retain its autonomy, where its data is defined independently of the other databases, and where its database management system takes care of itself while retaining rules for others to access its data.

Filtering Using a software program (a filter) to automatically route messages or documents according to their content.

Firewall Software on Internet servers to keep the public from accessing the company's intranet.

Fourth Generation Language A computer programming language used by end users, as opposed to COBOL (a third generation language), or Assembler (a second generation language), or programming via plug boards (first generation programming).

Frame Relay A fast communication protocol for data networks that uses variable-length packets rather than fixed-length packets (found in ATM protocol).

Freeware Software given away for free, generally via the Internet but also on CD-ROMs.

Front-End Tools Tools in a computer-aided software engineering suite that are used by analysts and designers to create the design of a computer system.

Gateway A data network connection that connects unlike networks.

Greenfield Approach A term used in reengineering to mean "starting from scratch."

Hacking The unauthorized access to a host computer. This access may be a direct intrusion or via a computer virus or Trojan horse.

Heuristics Rules that draw upon experience, common sense, ways of doing business, and even rules and regulations (p. 611).

Home Page A person's or organization's base page on the World Wide Web.

Hypertext A style of presenting text in computer systems or networks where the reader can click on a highlighted word and jump to a related thought or site. Hypermedia uses the same technique to link graphical items, as on the World Wide Web.

Incumbent Local Exchange Carriers (ILECs) Formerly called Regional Bell Operating Companies (RBOCs), these are telecom companies spun off from AT&T in 1994.

Information Data in context, where the meaning depends on the surrounding circumstances or usage.

Information Architecture A blueprint of stable definitions of corporate data—such as customers, products, and business transactions—can be specified ahead of time and used consistently across the firm.

Information Repository The heart of a computer-aided software engineering system that stores and organizes all information needed to create, modify, and develop a software system.

Information Resources The intangible information assets of a firm, including data, information, knowledge, processes, patents, and so on.

Infrastructure The physical manifestation of an architecture. An IS infrastructure includes the hardware, software, databases, networks, and system-wide rules that underlie a company's electronic means of working.

Insourcing Moving responsibility for specific services to a group within the company rather than to an external service provider. Commonly the insourcer is the shared services group.

Institutional DSS A decision support system built by DSS professionals using a DSS language that is intended to be used for the long term to support the organization's operations rather than to support an individual or small group for a short time.

Inter-Exchange Carriers (IXCs) Long distance telecom carriers (telephone companies).

Internal Document-Based Information Information that is available in-house and is text based, such as internal reports, memos, and so forth.

Internal Operational Measures Metrics of the performance of the computer operations group that are of interest to IS people, such as computer usage as a percentage of capacity, availability of mainline systems, disk storage utilized, job queue length, number of jobs run, number of jobs rerun due to problems, age of applications, and number of unresolved problems.

Internal Record-Based Information Information that is available in-house and is alphanumeric rather than textual.

Interoperate Different products working together, driven by the open systems movement.

Interorganizational Systems (IOS) Systems that require at least two parties with different objectives to collaborate on the development and operation of a joint computer-based system.

Intranet An internal company network that takes advantage of the Internet's infrastructure, telecommunication protocols, and browsers.

Issues-Based Education Where the educators identify executives' current needs and design the education to address those needs.

Knowledge Information with direction or intent; it facilitates a decision or an action.

Knowledge Management Managing the intellectual capital of an organization; some believe knowledge can reside in machines, others believe it only resides in people's heads.

Legacy Systems Mainframe computer applications that handle the day-to-day transactions of the company in a centralized, rather than distributed, manner. Alternatively, any system that does not use current technology.

Line Executive A business executive who manages a profit-oriented business unit, such as manufacturing, rather than a supporting staff unit, such as finance.

Linkage Analysis Planning A planning approach that studies the links between an organization and its suppliers and customers.

Local Area Network (LAN) A network that traverses a floor of a building, a work group, or a department, as opposed to a wide area network that crosses countries.

Local Exchange Carrier (LEC) Telecom companies that only handle local, not long distance, telephone calls.

Location Transparency A form of distributed databases where each node has a copy of the DBMS and the dictionary so that applications do not need to know the location of the data because each node can determine the appropriate access strategy for each database call.

Mail-Enabled Application The use of application programming interfaces (APIs) for electronic mail systems that allow applications to interact with each other using the mail systems as the communication link.

Mainframe A huge, very fast computer capable of handling all the computing for a large organization.

Marketspace A non-physical marketplace where information substitutes for physical products and physical location.

M-Commerce Conducting commerce via small wireless devices, such as buying an item from a vending machine using a cell phone or personal digital assistant (PDA) that contains digital money.

Meta Data Information about a data entity, such as its definition, how it was calculated, its source, when it is updated, who is responsible for it, and so forth.

Middleware Software that eases connection between clients and servers in a client/server system.

Mid-Tier Servers A network topology that has several tiers of servers, such as local work group servers, departmental servers, and an enterprise server (the corporate mainframe).

Moore's Law A "law" declaring computer processing power will double every 18 months. This law, stated by Gordon Moore, a founder of Intel, has proved true since 1959.

Mosaic Messages Electronic mail messages that contain former messages to show the flow of the discussion.

Multimedia The combination of text, graphics, sound, data, animation, and perhaps video in a message, a document, or at a Web site; alternatively called 'rich media.'

Netizens People who use the Internet and consider themselves citizens of the 'Net.

Network Computer (NC) Computers used much like telephones because they have no hard disk nor house applications, but rather just a browser, memory, keyboard, and a modem to pull applications off the Internet.

Non-repudiation Not allowing a party in an electronic transaction to repudiate, which means claiming that the transaction never took place; non-repudiation is an important cornerstone of electronic security.

Object In object-oriented programming, functions are packaged with data so that the two can be reused. These reusable components are called "classes," whereas at run time, each class can produce instances called "objects." Objects hold all the code and data in an object-oriented system.

Object-Oriented Programming A style of programming that encapsulates data and the operations that work on that data within an object, thus increasing the reusability of the code (as an object) and reducing the propagation of errors among objects.

Open Network or Open System A network (or system) based on national or international standards so that the products of many manufacturers work with each other.

Open source A source code that can be downloaded by anyone and can thus be modified.

Operating system The software in a computer or network that provides the basic functionality for the system. It is like the engine in a car—without it, nothing happens.

Optical Fiber Tiny glass fibers that use light to transmit voice or data signals.

Outsourcing Contracting with another firm to perform work that had previously been performed in-house, generally requiring a multi-year contract and generally for "non-core" work.

Packet Switching Method where messages are divided into packets, each with an address header, and each packet is sent separately. No circuit is created; each packet may take a different path through the network. Packets from any number of senders and of any type—be they e-mails, music downloads, voice conversations, or video clips—can be intermixed on a network segment.

Paradigm Shift A significant shift in viewpoint, such as shifting from seeing the mainframe as the center of computing to seeing the desktop or the Internet as the center of computing.

Partnering Allying with another organization that has different core competencies, often on a strategic alliance basis, for mutual benefit, such as when Visa partnered with United Airlines to offer the First Card credit card.

Password Sniffing Attempting to unveil passwords to gain access to a system.

Peer-Level Systems Systems that allow each unit to communicate directly with each other rather than go through a higher intermediary, such as a mainframe or a central server.

Peer-to-Peer Systems Distributed computers that accomplish a task without using a central coordinating computer.

Personal Area Network (PAN) An emerging type of network that allows computers in a "personal" area, such as a room, lobby, or building, to communicate wirelessly. An example is an airline's computer communicating with a passenger's handheld device once the passenger enters the airline's terminal, which provides flight confirmation and seat assignment.

Personal Digital Assistants (PDAs) Handheld computers that may or may not allow wireless connection to the Internet. They contain personal productivity tools such as calendaring, address book, and to-do lists, as well as games.

Piggybacking Loading two truck trailers on a railroad flat car and shipping them to their destination.

Power User Someone who takes the initiative to learn how to use computer applications in their work.

Privacy This includes the freedom from intrusion, the right to be left alone, the right to control information about oneself, and freedom from surveillance.

Private Programs Computer programs created and used by only one person.

Process Centering An approach to designing an organization where the business processes are the driving structures.

Process Owner A person in an organization responsible for an end-to-end process such as the ordering process or a research-and-development process.

Prototype A computer program that is used to test a new computing concept, such as distributed Java applets, for learning and experimentation purposes.

Public Key Encryption A methodology for encrypting and decrypting text to ensure identity of the parties. A message sender uses the assigned private key to encrypt the message and the recipient uses the sender's public key (known to anyone) to decrypt it, thus validating the sender's identity. The process also works in reverse, sending a message encrypted using a person's public key can only be decrypted and read by that person using their private key.

Quality of Service This refers to the ability of a network to provide a range of assured levels of performance.

Quality Systems Computer systems that do not break down, that do the work intended, and that are easy to maintain.

Quick-Hit DSS A system that is quite limited in scope, is developed and put into use quickly, and helps a manager come to a decision. The term *ad hoc* has also been used to distinguish from institutional DSS, although some quick-hit systems become regularly used.

Rationalized Data Using the same data name for all uses of the same data.

Reengineering Not to be confused with the term *business process reengineering,* this term, *system or application reengineering,* is much narrower and refers to rebuilding software for a new platform or new programming language.

Regional Bell Operating Company A regional telephone company formed by the 1984 deregulation of AT&T. Formerly, these companies were part of AT&T.

Relational Databases Databases that store data in tables.

Replication Software Software that duplicates (replicates) data, e-mail, or other items among databases, computers, or networks.

Repudiation Refusing a computer-based transaction, such as when one party reneges on an agreement after the fact, the other party may be left paying for the transaction processing unless it is repudiated.

Router A telecom server that routes messages in a network between networks using different protocols.

Rummler-Brache Approach An approach for deciding how to reengineer an organization.

Scenario A way to manage planning assumptions by creating a speculation of what the future will be like drawing on trends, events, environmental factors, and the relationships among them.

Secure Sockets Layer A protocol for providing security over the Internet.

Self-Managed Work Group Groups or teams that handle most supervisory tasks on their own, without a supervisor.

Self-Organizing Systems Entities, such as ecosystems, organisms, or organizations, that deal with their environment by responding to each stimuli in an appropriate manner, rather than in a pre-determined manner, so they self-organize when needed.

Sense-and-Respond Strategy Making A methodology for strategy making that keeps in close contact with the business world, continually sensing for important changes, and then responding quickly to changes by conducting experiments that test different possible futures—as opposed to betting on one strategy for the future.

Shared Services A department or division formed by consolidating and centralizing services formerly operated by business units. These services can include legal, travel, finance, IT, food service, fleet management, accounting, telecom, and others. It is a form of insourcing; business units draw on the expertise in shared services when needed.

Short Message Service An "always on" telecom service for communicating quickly and wirelessly using a small handheld device. The messages are typed using shorthand, code words, abbreviations, or short phrases.

Sniffing This is the interception and reading of electronic messages as they travel over the communication networks. Hacking is the unauthorized access to a host computer.

Soft Intelligence Information or knowledge that is not based on facts.

Spaghetti Code The way code in many legacy systems appears to a programmer because it has been patched so many times that the logic of the application weaves in and out like spaghetti on a plate.

Spiral Diagram A way of viewing the application development process as a spiral, as opposed to a waterfall.

Spoofing Masquerading as another party, such as a storefront to collect thousands (or millions) of credit card numbers and other information from naive consumers.

Status Access System A system for monitoring what is going on in the company and in the outside world.

Structured Query Language (SQL) A database language for asking queries of a database that has become the standard.

Supply Chain The "chain" that runs from the raw-materials producer through the retailer to supply goods to end customers. It uses a supply-push model where items are built to stock and the customer chooses from that stock; opposite is demand-pull.

Support Systems Systems that can help knowledge workers perform knowledge-based work.

System Development The process of building a system, originally by writing code to create an application and then linking together applications to form a system. A newer methodology is system integration.

System Integration The process of piecing together hardware components, software packages, database engines, and network products from numerous vendors into a single, cohesive system. Most often used to refer to the way client-server systems are built today.

System-Wide Rules An operating discipline for distributed systems that is enforced at all times and governs security, communication between nodes, data accessibility, program and file transfers, and common operating procedures.

Tacit Knowledge Knowledge "known" but not easily explained to others.

Technology Camel A way to distinguish levels of comfort with any technology using five clusters, which, when graphed on a chart, look a lot like a two-humped camel.

Telecommunications The electronically sending of information in any form from one place to another.

Thin Clients Network computers that are used much like telephones. They have no hard disk nor house applications, but rather just a browser, memory, keyboard, and a modem.

Third Generation Language A programming language, such as COBOL, used by a professional programmer.

Timebox A methodology for building a system in which the developers promise to deliver specific portions of the system within a specific timeframe (a timebox). The intent is to better control project delivery schedules.

Total Quality Management A management technique that focuses on managing the quality of a service or product, often through statistical quality control techniques, in order to achieve higher customer satisfaction and reduce costs as well.

Transitional Outsourcing The outsourcing of legacy systems for maintenance so that the in-house staff can focus on developing replacement client/server systems.

Tuple A row in a relational database model that represents an individual entity, such as a person, part, or account. Columns in the table represent attributes of the entities.

Value Chain A technique for describing a chain of business processes from product/service conception through cessation of the product/service, where each of the processes adds some kind of value.

Virtual Circuit A temporary circuit created between caller and receiver where that circuit is theirs alone to use; no other parties can share it during the duration of their telephone call.

Vision A statement of how someone wants the future to be or believes it will be. It is used to set direction for an organization.

Visual Programming A technique for programming, such as creating a graphical user interface, by pointing and clicking on generic items—menus, dialog boxes, radio buttons, and other components of graphical displays—and then arranging them to create a screen.

Waterfall Approach A way to view the system development process as a series of steps that, when diagrammed, appear as a waterfall.

Web Cast This is a broadcast of a live event over the World Wide Web.

Web Site This is a personal or organizational site on the World Wide Web.

Worknets Informal groups of people whose collective knowledge is used to accomplish a specific task.

Workscape The virtual workplace, which includes the Internet.

Workstation A high-powered desktop or portable computer.

Acronyms and Abbreviations

2D/3D Two dimensional, three dimensional.

4GLs Fourth Generation Languages

ACM Association for Computing Machinery

AI Artificial Intelligence

AIS Association for Information Systems

ALS Advanced Logistics Services

AM Amplitude Modulation

AMA American Medical Association

AmEx American Express

ANSI American National Standards Institute

AOL America Online

API Application Program Interface

ARPANET Advanced Research Projects Agency Network

AS/400 Advanced System/400 (An IBM midrange computer)

ASCII American Standard Code for Information Interchange

ASP Application Service Provider or Active Server Pages

AT&T American Telephone & Telegraph

ATM Asynchronous Transfer Mode

BPO Business Process Outsourcing

BPR Business Process Redesign/Reengineering

C/C++ Programming languages used with UNIX

CACM *Communications of the ACM* magazine

CAD/CAM Computer-Aided Design/Computer-Aided Manufacturing

CAI Computer-Assisted Instruction

CAL Computer-Assisted Learning

CALS Computer-Aided Acquisition and Logistic Support

CASE Computer-Aided Software Engineering

CBT Computer-Based Training

CCITT Consultive Committee for International Telegraphy and Telephony

CD-ROM Compact Disc—Read Only Memory

CEO Chief Executive Officer

CFO Chief Financial Officer

CGM Computer Graphics Metafile

CIO Chief Information Officer

CIR Corporate Information Resources

CIS Corporate Information Services

CISR Center for Information Systems Research

CLEC Competitive Local Exchange Carrier

CMI Computer-Managed Instruction

COBOL Common Business Oriented Language

COM Computer Output Microfilm or Component Object Model

COO Chief Operations Officer

CRM Customer Relationship Management

CSF Critical Success Factors

CTO Chief Technology Officer

CXO A Group of "Chiefs" (CEO, CFO, CIO, COO, etc.)

DARPA Defense Advanced Research Projects Agency

DASD Direct Access Data Storage

DB2 Database 2 (an IBM product)

DBMS Database Management System

DCOM Distributed Component Object Model

DDM Dialog, Data, and Modeling

DES Data Encryption Standard

DGMS Dialog Generation and Management System

DNS Distributed Name Service

DOS Disk Operating System

DPI Dots Per Inch

DSL Digital Subscriber Line

DSS Decision Support Systems

E-mail Electronic Mail

EDI Electronic Data Interchange

EDM Electronic Document Management

EDP Electronic Data Processing

EDS Electronic Data Systems

EIS Executive Information System

EIU Economist Intelligence Unit

EPRI Electric Power Research Institute

EPSS Electronic Performance Support System

ERD Enterprise Reference Data

ERP Enterprise Resource Planning

ESOP Employee Stock Ownership Plan

ESP External Service Provider

ESS Executive Support System

EUC End User Computing

E-zines Electronic magazines

FAQ Frequently Asked Question

Fax Facsimile

FDA U.S. Food and Drug Administration

FDDI Fiber Distributed Data Interface

FTC Federal Trade Commission

FTP File Transfer Protocol

GOSIP Government Standard Internet Protocol

GSM Global System for Mobile Communication

GSS Group Support Systems

GTE General Telephone Company

HBO Home Box Office

HDTV High Definition Television

HR Human Resources

HTML Hypertext Markup Language

HTTP Hypertext Transfer Protocol

IBM International Business Machines Corporation

IDC International Data Corporation

IDMS Integrated Data Management System

IDS Integrated Data Store

IFTF Institute for the Future

ILEC Incumbent Local Exchange Carrier

IMS Integrated Management System

IOS Interorganizational Systems

IP Internet Protocol

IPng Internet Protocol next generation

IPSS Integrated Performance Support Systems

ISDN Integrated Services Digital Network

ISO International Standards Organization

ISP Internet Service Provider

IT Information Technology

IXC Inter-exchange carrier

JAD Joint Application Design

JDS Job Diagnostic Survey

JIT Just in Time

Kbps Kilobytes per second

LAN Local Area Network

LEC Local Exchange Carrier

LN Local Network

LTL Less Than Truckload

MANs Metropolitan Area Networks

MBMS Model Base Management System

Mbps Megabytes Per Second

MGM Metro-Goldwyn-Mayer

MIDS Management Information and Decision Support System

MIPS Millions of Instructions Per Second

MIS Management Information Systems

MIT Massachusetts Institute of Technology

MOO MUD, Object Oriented

MU Multiple-User system

MUD Multi-User Dungeon

MVS Multiple Virtual System

NASA National Aeronautics and Space Administration

NC Network Computer
Net, The The Internet
NFS National Film Service
NGI Next Generation Internet
NLS On-Line System
NSF National Science Foundation
NT Network Technology
ODA Office Document Architecture
OLAP On-Line Analytical Processing
OLTP On-Line Transaction Processing
OR/MS Operations Research/Management Science
OSI Open System Interconnection
OX Operations Expediter System
PAN Personal Area Network
PARC Xerox's Palo Alto Research Center
PBX Private Branch Exchange
PC Personal Computer
PCS Personal Communication Service
PDA Personal Digital Assistant
PIN Personal Identification Number
PLL Phase Lock Loops
PODD Point of Delivery Device
POTS Plain Old Telephone Service
PRA Passenger Revenue Accounting
PSTN Public Switched Telephone Network
PTT Postal, Telephone, and Telegraph Authority
R&D Research and Development
RAD Rapid Application Development
RBOC Regional Bell Operating Company
RF Radio Frequency
RIPP Rapid Iterative Production Prototyping
RISC Reduced Instruction Set Computer
RN Remote Network

ROI Return On Investment
RPG Remote Programming Language
RU Remote Utility system
SEC U.S. Securities and Exchange Commission
SET Secure Electronic Transactions
SGML Standard Generalized Markup Language
SMS Short Message Service
SNA System Network Architecture
SQL Structured Query Language
SSL Secure Sockets Layer
STS Sociotechnical System
SU Single-User systems
SUMURU Single User, Multiple User, Remote Utility
TCP/IP Transmission Control Protocol/Internet Protocol
Telecom Telecommunications
UCAID University Consortium for Advanced Internet Development
UCLA University of California at Los Angeles
UNIX "Unics" operating system (an attempt at a pun)
UPS United Parcel Service
VAN Value-Added Network
VLSI Very Large System Integration
VPN Virtual Private Network
VSAT Very Small Aperture Terminal
WAN Wide Area Network
WAP Wireless Application Protocol
Web World Wide Web
WYSIWYG What You See Is What You Get
XML Extensible Markup Language
Y2K Year 2000

Index